MODERN CRIMINAL LAW

Fifth Edition

Cavendish
Publishing
Limited

London • Sydney • Portland, Oregon

MODERN CRIMINAL LAW

Fifth Edition

Professor Mike Molan, BA, LLM, ITLM, Barrister
Head of the Law Division, South Bank University

Professor Duncan Bloy, BA, LLM, PGCE
Academic Director, Forté-IRI, Singapore

Denis Lanser, LLB, Dip Crim
Lecturer in Law, Staffordshire University

Cavendish
Publishing
Limited

London • Sydney • Portland, Oregon

Fifth edition first published in Great Britain 2003 by
Cavendish Publishing Limited, The Glass House,
Wharton Street, London WC1X 9PX, United Kingdom
Telephone: + 44 (0)20 7278 8000   Facsimile: + 44 (0)20 7278 8080
Email: info@cavendishpublishing.com
Website: www.cavendishpublishing.com

Published in the United States by Cavendish Publishing
c/o International Specialized Book Services,
5824 NE Hassalo Street, Portland,
Oregon 97213-3644, USA

Published in Australia by Cavendish Publishing (Australia) Pty Ltd
45 Beach Street, Coogee, NSW 2034, Australia
Telephone: + 61 (2)9664 0909   Facsimile: + 61 (2)9664 5420
Email: info@cavendishpublishing.com.au
Website: www.cavendishpublishing.com.au

This title was previously printed in the Cavendish Principles series

British Library Cataloguing in Publication Data

Molan, Michael T
Modern criminal law – 5th ed
1 Criminal law – England 2 Criminal law – Wales
I Title II Lanser, Denis III Bloy, Duncan J
345.4'2

Library of Congress Cataloguing in Publication Data
Data available

ISBN 1-85941-807-4

1 3 5 7 9 10 8 6 4 2

Printed and bound in Great Britain

PREFACE

Building upon the work undertaken for the previous edition of this text, which appeared as part of the Principles of Law series, this new edition of *Modern Criminal Law* continues to reflect the rapid and dynamic development of criminal law in England and Wales. In addition to incorporating key recent developments, extensive revisions to the text have resulted in an improved and more reader-friendly arrangement of materials. As with previous editions, the text does not focus on the procedural or sentencing areas of the criminal law as these are rarely, if ever, dealt with in detail as part of a university level criminal law syllabus. What the authors have endeavoured to reflect are instances of significant recent judicial decision-making, such as the House of Lords' decisions in landmark cases such as *R v Hinks* (theft) and *R v Morgan Smith* (provocation) together with proposals for reform of the criminal law and legislative activity (notably the Sexual Offence Bill before Parliament at the time of going to print).

The authors would like to extend their thanks to the staff at Cavendish Publishing for their support and forbearance over the past year.

Mike Molan would like to thank Alison for continuing to take care of business so that the writing could be done and Denis would like to thank Melanie for all her support and assistance.

Duncan Bloy wishes to extend grateful thanks to his Personal Assistant, Rima Rachmawaty Pereira, who assumed an extra workload without complaint thus permitting the writing to be completed on schedule. Michael Yap, a lawyer in Singapore, has been a great friend and supporter and his contribution also deserves to be acknowledged.

We have stated the law as at 1 March 2003, but later changes in the law have been included where possible.

Mike Molan
Duncan Bloy
Denis Lanser
May 2003

CONTENTS

TABLE OF CASES

TABLE OF LEGISLATION

EU legislation

TABLE OF ABBREVIATIONS

AA	Abortion Act 1967
AAA	Accessories and Abettors Act 1861
AVTA	Aggravated Vehicle-Taking Act 1992
CA	Children Act 1989
CAtA	Criminal Attempts Act 1981
CDA	Criminal Damage Act 1971
CJA	Criminal Justice Act 1967/1972/1982/1988/1991/1993
CJPOA	Criminal Justice and Public Order Act 1994
CLA	Criminal Lunatics Act 1800
CLRC	Criminal Law Revision Committee
CLwA	Criminal Law Act 1967/1977
CMA	Computer Misuse Act 1990
CP(I)A	Criminal Procedure (Insanity) Act 1964
CP(IUP)A	Criminal Procedure (Insanity and Unfitness to Plead) Act 1991
CYPA	Children and Young Persons Act 1933
HA	Homicide Act 1957
HSWA	Health and Safety at Work, etc Act 1974
IA	Infanticide Act 1938
IL(P)A	Infant Life (Preservation) Act 1929
LA	Licensing Act 1872
MHA	Mental Health Act 1983
OAPA	Offences Against the Person Act 1861
PHA	Protection from Harassment Act 1997
PVS	persistent vegetative state
RTA	Road Traffic Act 1988/1991
SOA	Sexual Offences Act 1956/1967/1993
SO(A)A	Sexual Offences (Amendment) Act 1976/2000

TA	Theft Act 1968/1978
T(A)A	Theft (Amendment) Act 1996
WTA	Wireless and Telegraphy Act 1949

CHAPTER 1

AN INTRODUCTION TO
THE STUDY OF CRIMINAL LAW

1.1 COVERAGE OF THE BOOK

This book has been written specifically for students studying criminal law as part of their undergraduate or Common Professional Examination studies. It examines in depth the general principles of the subject and then applies them to a wide range of offences. The selection has been undertaken on the basis of those crimes that make the greatest impact on the life of the citizen and those which take up the majority of court time. No book of this type can offer a comprehensive review of the several thousand crimes that do not fall into either category but we believe that having studied the general principles of criminal liability, the student will be able to employ the same approach to those other crimes and be in a position to subject them to detailed analysis.

There are no chapters included on sentencing or criminal procedure. This is not because the subject matter is considered unimportant but for the functional reason that there is not enough time on most criminal law courses to deal with these matters. Those in any doubt about the significance of the latter need look no further than Auld LJ's *Review of the Criminal Courts of England and Wales*, 2001, London: HMSO. The document contains 328 recommendations which would tend to suggest that the comment in the last edition of this book to the effect that 'the implication is there for all to see that the current practice and procedures may not be delivering "justice fairly" and that public confidence in the rule of law is waning' may not have been too far wide of the mark.

Subjects such as evidence, sentencing and criminology are offered as options in many universities and therefore there would be a serious risk of diluting the content of a substantive criminal law course if such topics were to be included.

However, the subject cannot be properly understood without due regard to the context in which the rules originate and in which they are applied by the courts. The Human Rights Act (HRA) 1998, which came into force in October 2000, has been the catalyst from which numerous substantive law issues have become intertwined with procedural questions. For example, in *PG and JH v United Kingdom* [2002] Crim LR 308 on a charge of conspiracy to rob when the court had to decide whether the covert use of listening devices by the police at a person's home or at a police station contravened Art 8 of the European Convention on Human Rights (ECHR). Another recent example is the case of *Taylor* [2002] Crim LR 314 where the defendant who was charged with an offence under s 5 of the Misuse of Drugs Act 1971 was a Rastafarian and claimed that the possession of cannabis was 'part of my religion' and therefore his rights under Art 9 had been violated. The avid reader or, for that matter, the casual reader of the *Criminal Law Review* cannot help but be aware of the number of cases being reported where HRA issues are before the court. The Act imposes a mandatory requirement that all courts should '... act in conformity with Convention rights' (see Ashworth, 'Criminal proceedings after the Human Rights Act' [2001] Crim LR 855). One expects the trend to continue for some time to come.

1.2   A CRIMINAL LAW FOR THE NEW MILLENNIUM

What can reasonably be expected from the criminal law in the early years of a new millennium? The criminal justice system has been under the microscope since the Auld Committee began its investigations in December 1999 into the '… practices and procedures of, and the rules of evidence applied by, the criminal courts at every level …' There were those who believed that Auld LJ and his team had taken on an impossible task, but nevertheless the report was produced by 2001 and the government's response was available by mid-2002 (*Justice For All*, Cm 5563, 2002, London: HMSO).

The process has been severely criticised for a number of reasons. An editorial in the *Criminal Law Review* for April 2002 pulls no punches:

> It was perhaps inevitable that the government would cherry-pick amongst Auld's long list of 328 recommendations. Auld's remit was too vast, and too many of the subjects he had to deal with were too controversial, to expect him to 'do a Woolf' and produce a comprehensive reform plan which could be taken up and implemented as a whole. What is more surprising is how erratic government policy is turning out to be … It is surely time to stop this incessant vote-catching tinkering and for the government to give some much more serious and searching thought to the kind of criminal justice system that will produce better justice all round in the longer term [pp 247–48].

The government White Paper also includes responses to the *Halliday Report on Sentencing* (2002, London: HMSO) and gives prime importance to placing victims at the heart of the criminal justice system. The government at least seems clear that the present system is bringing too few criminals to justice, is too slow to bring offenders to trial and controversially 'too many guilty go unconvicted'. The government appears to be willing to embrace some fundamental changes including the Auld recommendation that a defendant may elect for trial by judge alone and the introduction of exceptions to the double jeopardy rule. This will mean an end to the principle that a person cannot be tried again for the same offence once there has been an acquittal. The Court of Appeal will be granted powers to quash an acquittal and order a re-trial. This power will, one assumes, be used sparingly and only where there is the introduction of significant new evidence that was not available at the time of the trial.

Another significant recommendation relates to the management of complex fraud cases. The proposal is that the judge should be able to direct, unilaterally, that the case will proceed without a jury. The obvious consequence is that the accused loses his right to trial by jury and with it the prospect of an acquittal, not necessarily based on the evidence but jury confusion, because of the complexity of the issues. This has of course been flagged on a number of occasions, for example, the Roskill Committee in 1986 and a Home Office consultation paper in 1998. (For an enlightening review of the proposals relating to fraud, see Corker, 'Trying fraud cases without juries' [2002] Crim LR 283.)

This book focuses on the substantive criminal law and is not primarily concerned with practice and procedure. However, if one were to take a snapshot of the criminal law at the beginning of 2003 one finds that there are significant areas of the law in need of urgent reform. One is entitled to assume that the principles of criminal law should be reasonably certain, consistent and, more than anything, accessible to everyone. One might refer to these as 'benchmark criteria'. Yet, note the comments of

Sir Henry Brooke, a former chairman of the Law Commission, who is on record as stating that the law in many areas 'is a disgrace, when judged in terms of simplicity, clarity and accessibility' ((1994) 158 JP 158). The meaning to be attributed to the critical *mens rea* word 'intention' has, thankfully, not been the subject of further House of Lords deliberation since the decision in *Woollin* [1998] 4 All ER 103.

In the last edition of this book we highlighted the controversy surrounding the defence of self-defence as a result of the *Martin* case where the defendant shot and killed an intruder at his remote farmhouse late at night. The defence remains in the spotlight for a number of reasons. The unique circumstances found in *Re A (Children)* [2000] 4 All ER 961 of conjoined twins, where the life of A could be saved by separation but only at the expense of the other twin's life, saw the defence finding some favour in the Court of Appeal. Ward LJ though referred to 'a plea of *quasi* self-defence, modified to meet the quite exceptional circumstances nature has inflicted on the twins'. B was kept alive only because of the oxygenated blood provided by A. If the operation to separate was not carried out, then both would die as A's body would not be able to withstand the strain imposed upon it by keeping her sister alive. B was therefore threatening A's life, albeit unintentionally and totally innocently. It was therefore not a criminal act to take B's 'life' to save A's. The relationship between self-defence and Art 2 of the HRA 1998 continues to be discussed. The key question is whether an honest, albeit unreasonable, mistake should be accepted as a basis for self-defence. The argument is that the 'mistake' has led to the death of an innocent person and therefore Art 2 of the ECHR which states that everyone's right to life shall be protected by law has been contravened. Article 2 goes on to say that no one shall be deprived of his life intentionally, save in the execution of a sentence of a court following conviction of a crime. Surely, goes the argument, that in order to comply with Art 2, the belief should at least be a reasonable one. In the absence of any definitive guidance from the House of Lords or parliament, the question remains a moot one as evidenced by the lively debate entered into by the late Professor Sir John Smith and Fiona Leverick in the *Criminal Law Review* in 2002 (see Leverick, 'Is English self-defence law compatible with Article 2 of the ECHR?' [2002] Crim LR 347; Smith, 'The use of force in public or private defence and Article 2' [2002] Crim LR 958; Leverick, 'The use of force in public or private defence and Article 2: a reply to Professor Sir John Smith' [2002] Crim LR 963).

The *Martin* ([2002] 2 WLR 1) case continues to pose questions that are wider than the law on self-defence. The Court of Appeal certified a point of law of general public importance namely:

Whether expert psychiatric evidence is admissible on the issue of a defendant's perception of the danger he faced (in a case where he relies on self-defence)?

There are numerous areas of the criminal law where the defendant's personal characteristics are relevant to a finding of guilt or innocence. There appears to be no 'golden thread' of consistency running through cases involving provocation, self-defence, necessity and duress. Here is an opportunity for the House of Lords to review the law generally rather than confining itself to the narrow area of private defence.

While the controversy surrounding the meaning of 'intention' in English criminal law has diminished the other major *mens rea* word, 'recklessness', has once again come under scrutiny. In *Gemmell and Richards* [2002] Crim LR 926, the Court of

Appeal certified a point of law but refused to give leave to appeal to the House of Lords, requesting an opinion on whether a defendant can properly be:

> ... convicted under section 1 of the Criminal Damage Act 1971 on the basis that he was reckless as to whether property was destroyed or damaged when he gave no thought to the risk, but, by reason of his age and or personal characteristics, the risk would not have been obvious to him, even if he had thought about it?

If the House of Lords grants leave, then it is likely the opportunity will be taken to undertake a reappraisal of the meaning of recklessness in the context of the Criminal Damage Act 1971. Professor John Smith offered the opinion that '... the law would be better without all the unnecessary complexity it [the decision in *Caldwell* [1982] AC 341] introduced' ([2002] Crim LR 928).

The case once again raised the thorny question of how courts should deal with children who have been 'responsible' for causing serious damage to property yet, nevertheless, claim they did not foresee the far-reaching consequences that actually occurred. The boys in question were aged 11 and 12. Early one morning they started a fire under a dustbin at the rear of a newsagent's shop and then left the scene. The ensuing fire caused £1 million worth of damage to the newsagent's and adjoining buildings. They claimed they had given no thought to the possibility that the fire could spread to the buildings. At their trial for causing criminal damage, being reckless as to whether such damage would be caused, the judge ruled that the *Caldwell* test should apply. He directed the jury that the 'ordinary reasonable bystander is an adult ... no allowance is made in law for the youth of these boys or their lack of maturity or their own inability ... to assess what was going on'. There can be no doubt that the boys deliberately set fire to the bin and are guilty of criminal damage, but assuming the jury found that they did not foresee the ultimate consequences, given the increasingly subjectivist approach to the criminal law, why should they be deemed reckless in respect of the final outcome of their behaviour? In these circumstances would an adult have foreseen the outcome? Age is a factor to consider when assessing whether a reasonable person with the attributes of the accused would have succumbed to provocative acts. Should age and the likelihood that a child's experiences are limited because of that factor count for nothing?

Uncertainty will always be a necessary element of the criminal law as circumstances and social mores change and the law strives to keep abreast of those changes. Some will regard uncertainty as a prerequisite to moving the law forward, and it is true that the frontiers of criminality are continually moving. However, it represents a significant departure from the view that the criminal law should be a pre-established and well known body of rules that governs our behaviour and which clearly tells us what we may or may not do. It transgresses one of the justifications for punishment, which is that, because ignorance of the law is no defence, the law should be accessible, certain and easily comprehendible.

Richard Buxton in his article 'The Human Rights Act and the substantive criminal law' [2000] Crim LR 331 believes that there are two reasons why certainty is desirable in the criminal law. First, the citizen is entitled to know what he can or cannot do and, as such, is entitled to be protected from the arbitrariness of state action that must 'attend punishment for breaches of a law that is erratic in its operation'. Secondly, uncertainty in, or difficulty in access to, the criminal law leads to unpredictability in the outcome of criminal trials, which in turn extends the length of trials and increases expense.

The answer, suggests Buxton, is a long overdue criminal code:

> [There is an] almost universal desire that the present jumble of ancient statutes, more modern accretions to them, and acres of judicial pronouncements, should be replaced by a criminal code that would set out the criminal law in rational, accessible and modern language.

It remains an ongoing conundrum as to why the nation that produced the Indian Penal Code that subsequently became the basis for Penal Codes in Malaya and Singapore steadfastly refuses to create such a document for its own people.

1.3   JUDICIAL LAW-MAKING

The late Professor Glanville Williams was of the opinion that judges are strongly influenced by their own ideas of what conduct should or should not be allowed and thus engage in extending and creating new law (*Textbook of Criminal Law*, 2nd edn, 1983, London: Stevens, p 14). In some ways, of course, this creative characteristic is inherent in the common law and can be a force for positive social change. Consider, for example, the decision in *R* [1991] 4 All ER 481, where the House of Lords changed the existing law and held for the first time that a husband was capable, in law, of raping his wife (see Chapter 7). Whilst this decision to overturn a rule of law dating back 300 years was accepted as being long overdue, only weeks before the House made its landmark ruling, the Law Commission was of the view that such a significant deviation from the current law should require legislative intervention (Law Commission, Working Paper 116, para 2.08).

A decade later the House of Lords has taken a similarly reformist approach to offences contained in the Sexual Offences Act 1956 in respect of whether a genuine belief that a female is over 16 years of age should provide a defence to, for example, a charge of indecent assault contrary to s 14 of the Act. Hidebound by the decision in *Prince* (1875) LR 2 CCR 154 courts have subsequently demanded that the belief be not only honest but also reasonable. However, in *B (A Minor) v DPP* [2000] 2 AC 428 and *K* [2001] 3 All ER 897 the House of Lords finally lost patience with the prospect of parliament making the change and decided that the requirement for reasonableness should no longer be part of the law. Lord Millet in the latter case put it this way:

> But the age of consent has long since ceased to reflect ordinary life, and in this respect Parliament has signally failed to discharge its responsibility for keeping the criminal law in touch with the needs of society. I am persuaded that the piecemeal introduction of the various elements of s 14, coupled with the persistent failure of Parliament to rationalise this branch of the law even to the extent of removing absurdities which the courts have identified, means that we ought not to strain after internal coherence even in a single offence. Injustice is too high a price to pay for consistency.

It should also be understood that much of this law-making is directed at people who would be regarded as seriously anti-social in any society, for example, people who devise new methods of stealing other people's money using new technology. Even so, in an attempt to develop the law senior judges, in particular, occasionally step beyond the traditionally accepted bounds of their law-making powers and consequently may introduce uncertainty in the law. Good examples over the last 20 years are *Metropolitan Police Commissioner v Caldwell* discussed in Chapter 3, *Shivpuri*

[1986] 2 All ER 334 and *Gomez* [1993] 1 All ER 1 in Chapter 8. It is also far from clear whether judges, as opposed to parliament or law reform agencies, are qualified or equipped to engage in law reform. They are not for most purposes accountable for the results of their decisions; they have little if any training in the social policy and economic implications of their decisions; and these issues will almost certainly not have been fully argued before the court prior to the decision. Contrast this style of law-making with that adopted by the Law Commission, where their carefully considered final report will usually have been preceded by a detailed consultation paper distributed to all parties with an interest in the criminal justice system. The comments received will inform the final report, which will then, if all goes well, be subjected to detailed parliamentary scrutiny.

But what of the rules of precedent and statutory interpretation – surely they prevent judicial law-making? In theory, this presumption may be correct but, in practice, they are only partly successful. In *C (A Minor) v DPP* [1995] 2 All ER 43, the Divisional Court had overturned an ancient rule of law to the effect that before a child aged between 10 and 14 years could be found guilty of committing a crime the prosecution had to prove that the child knew that the act was 'seriously wrong'. The court decided that this rule no longer applied since it had become outdated in the changed conditions of modern society. The House of Lords reversed this decision. Lord Lowry held that such an important change should only be made by parliament. He referred to five 'aids to navigation' for judges tempted to embark on the uncertain sea of judicial law-making. Judges should be cautious:

- where the solution is doubtful;
- where parliament has declined to legislate;
- where the matter is not purely legal but involves disputed social policy;
- where intervention involves setting aside fundamental doctrine; or
- where a change would not be sure to produce finality or certainty.

According to these criteria, much judicial law-making in recent years indicates that the judges were lacking in caution! Little wonder then that Lord Mackay of Clashfern, then Lord Chancellor, still felt the need publicly to caution judges against taking it on themselves to overcome defects in the law. His view is that the judge's duty is 'to apply the law as he finds it, not to seek to rectify perceived inadequacies by the use of creative interpretation ... when deficiencies in the law become apparent it is for Parliament to respond [(1997) *The Times*, 14 March] ...'

This essentially conservative approach was not reflected in the two recent cases referred to earlier in this section. The reasons for a more interventionist approach by the judiciary may vary. The judges may genuinely believe that the law is out of touch with modern societal views and that there is little prospect for parliamentary intervention. The consequences of a finding of guilt against a defendant have important ramifications, particularly for liberty and reputation, and therefore perceived injustices need to be remedied quickly. The 1966 Practice Direction does permit any uncertainty thus created to be remedied quickly (see *Shivpuri* overruling *Anderton v Ryan* [1985] AC 560). As Lord Bridge stated in *Shivpuri*:

> The 1966 Practice Statement is an effective abandonment of our pretention to infallibility. If a serious error embodied in a decision of this House has distorted the law, the sooner it is corrected the better.

Of course, judges often need to interpret the words of a statute because the words are ambiguous or unclear. Here, it is perfectly legitimate for the court to consider the legislative purpose, having regard to parliamentary materials, providing, according to the House of Lords case of *Pepper v Hart* [1993] 1 All ER 42, that:

(a) [the] legislation is ambiguous or obscure, or leads to an absurdity;

(b) the material relied upon consists of one or more statements by a minister or other promoter of the Bill, together if necessary with such other parliamentary material as is necessary to understand such statements, and their effect;

(c) the statements relied on are clear [p 43(e)].

Courts may, and frequently do, consult reports of the Law Commission, other law reform agencies and academic commentaries in order to discover the state of pre-existing law and the mischief that any particular statute was designed to remedy. The Law Commission has been as active as ever since the last edition of this book. Of particular note is its report on fraud (*Report on Fraud*, Law Com 276, 2002). Over two decades the Commission has generally opposed the creation of a new offence of fraud in favour of bolstering the existing plethora of offences, statutory and common law, substantive and inchoate, through amendment. In this report, the Commission abandons that approach and urges upon parliament a new general fraud offence comprising three types of conduct: misrepresentation, non-disclosure of information and 'abuse of position' from which gain may accrue.

Of course it remains to be seen whether parliament will find time to promote new legislation in this field but the document represents valuable research material for busy judges.

If this fails to resolve the doubt then the benefit of any significant ambiguity will be given to the defendant *(Attorney General's Reference (No 1 of 1988)* [1989] 2 All ER 1).

1.4   THE ROLE OF THE HOUSE OF LORDS AS THE FINAL APPELLATE COURT

The House of Lords is in a unique position to influence and shape the law because all the appeals before it must concern matters of general public importance (s 34 of the Criminal Appeal Act 1968) and the purpose of the appeal is not, therefore, confined to dispensing justice in the individual case. And yet one leading academic categorised the House as having 'a dismal record in criminal cases' (Smith [1981] Crim LR 392) and a second called for its criminal jurisdiction to be abolished (Williams [1981] Crim LR 580).

One of the primary aims of the House of Lords ought to be to produce certainty in the law. But can it do this when there might be up to five contradictory speeches? Look, for example, at their Lordships' decisions in the important cases of *Reid* [1992] 3 All ER 673 concerned with the meaning of 'recklessness'; and *Hyam v DPP* [1974] 2 All ER 41 concerned with the meaning of 'intention'. Try to ascertain the *ratio decidendi*. You will find this a formidable task as have many other students, lawyers, academics and, yes, judges. However, it would be wrong to suggest that the House is never unanimous in its decision-making. The specific intent rule in respect of the defence of drunkenness was upheld by seven judges in *DPP v Majewski* [1976] 2 All

ER 142, and the House in *Woollin* [1998] 4 All ER 103 was unanimous in allowing the defendant's appeal after a misdirection by the trial judge as to the meaning of 'intention' in the law of murder. The latter case is interesting because two of the five Law Lords, while agreeing that the appeal should be allowed, did not go so far as to endorse the sentiments of Lords Steyn and Hope who delivered the major speeches. This, though, should not be taken as a sign that the authority of the decision is in any way diminished.

Another problem facing the House of Lords is if counsel choose not to rely on or indeed argue a particular point of public importance because they believe their chance of success to be greater by relying upon another point. The result might be that a good opportunity to clarify the law on an important matter may be lost.

But the fundamental problem, according to Professor ATH Smith, 'is their failure to articulate goals for the criminal process [and] that their Lordships' collective ambivalence of purpose has frustrated a coherent treatment of the issues of general public importance' ((1984) 47 MLR 133). He contrasts their role with that of the American Law Institutes' Model Penal Code (1962, Art 11.02) which clearly states the objectives of criminal law in the US:

(a) to forbid and prevent conduct that unjustifiably and inexcusably inflicts or threatens substantial harm to individual or public interests;

(b) to subject to public control persons whose conduct indicates that they are disposed to commit crimes;

(c) to safeguard conduct that is without fault from condemnation as criminal;

(d) to give fair warning of the nature of the conduct declared to be an offence;

(e) to differentiate on reasonable grounds between serious and minor offences.

> By comparison with this, the response of the House of Lords has been one-dimensional. It tends to see itself as being above all the guardian of the public interest whose function is to prevent harm to the public. Where this purpose conflicts with others identified by the Model Penal Code, the interests of the defendant himself, or the demands of logic and principle, the House of Lords will act so as to protect its conception of social welfare [p 143].

The result is that the House of Lords has not managed to identify purposes other than the loosely defined 'protection of society'.

In 2000, the House of Lords delivered opinions in 11 criminal justice cases of which four dealt with substantive law issues. In nine cases the decisions were unanimous. The editorial to the January 2001 *Criminal Law Review* had this to say:

> It is clear already that the two cases decided by a bare majority – namely *Smith and Hinks* – are highly controversial and will continue to generate debate about the proper scope of the doctrine of provocation and the concept of appropriation in theft respectively.

However, the conclusion reached by the editor was:

> On balance the House of Lords probably comes out fairly well ... the majority of decisions in 2000 seem to command widespread assent as correct clarifications of difficult or disputed points. The quality of the judgments being handed down is generally high, with careful attention being paid to issues of principle and academic critique as well as to more technical analysis of the primary sources [pp 1–2].

1.5   THE PURPOSE OF THE CRIMINAL LAW

It may be easy to criticise senior judges but does society itself have a clear idea as to the aims or purpose of the criminal law, particularly in the area of morality? Two opposing views are traditionally argued. First, the 'libertarian' view which is that self-protection and to prevent harm to others is the only justification for interfering with the liberty of others (see Mills's essay 'On liberty' (1859), 1974, Harmondsworth: Penguin). Lord Wolfenden's *Report of the Committee on Homosexual Offences and Prostitution* (Cmnd 247, 1957) broadly agreed when it recommended that homosexual acts between consenting adults in private should no longer be a criminal offence. Wolfenden thought that the function of the law was to 'preserve public order and decency, to protect the citizen from that which is offensive or injurious and to provide sufficient safeguards against exploitation and the corruption of others, particularly those who are especially vulnerable' (para 13). The Committee's view was that there remains a realm of private morality and immorality with which the criminal law ought not to concern itself.

Contrast the libertarian approach with that of the 'authoritarian' view as represented by Lord Devlin, in *The Enforcement of Morals* (1967, Oxford: OUP). Lord Devlin felt that even apart from self-protection, 'there are acts so gross and outrageous that they must be prevented at any cost', and that 'the suppression of vice is as much the law's business as the suppression of subversive activities'. He was, in effect, criticising Wolfenden's conception of a private morality with which the criminal law ought not to be concerned.

Let us examine some of the cases where this problem has presented itself. In *Shaw v DPP* [1962] AC 220, the appellant published a booklet with the object of assisting prostitutes. It contained the names, addresses, phone numbers and description of various specialist perversions in which particular prostitutes were willing to engage. Mr Shaw had been found guilty at the Old Bailey of, *inter alia*, 'conspiracy to corrupt public morals'. He now appealed on the grounds that such a crime did not exist! In the result he was unsuccessful and his conviction was upheld. Lord Simonds, with whom the majority agreed, was:

> ... at a loss to understand how it can be said either that the law does not recognise a conspiracy to corrupt public morals or that, though there may not be an exact precedent for such a conspiracy as this case reveals, it does not fall fairly within the general words by which it is described. The fallacy in the argument that was addressed to us lay in the attempt to exclude from the scope of general words acts well calculated to corrupt public morals just because they had not been committed or had not been brought to the notice of the court before. It is not thus that the common law has developed. We are, perhaps, more accustomed to hear this matter discussed on the question whether such and such a transaction is contrary to public policy. At once the controversy arises. On the one hand, it is said that it is not possible in the 20th century for the court to create a new head of public policy, on the other, it is said that this is but a new example of a well-established head. In the sphere of criminal law, I entertain no doubt that there remains in the courts of law a residual power to enforce the supreme and fundamental purpose of the law, to conserve not only the safety and order but also the moral welfare of the state, and that it is their duty to guard it against attacks which may be the more insidious because they are novel and unprepared for. That is the broad head (call it public policy if you wish) within which the present indictment falls [p 452].

Lord Simonds was, in other words, reserving the right of the judges to expand the frontiers of criminality when, in their opinion, the circumstances so demanded.

Lord Reid, on the other hand, disagreed:

> Even if there is still a vestigial power of this kind, it ought not, in my view, to be used unless there appears to be general agreement that the offence to which it is applied ought to be criminal if committed by an individual. Notoriously there are wide differences of opinion today how far the law ought to punish immoral acts which are not done in the face of the public. Some think that the law already goes too far, some that it does not go far enough. Parliament is the proper place, and I am firmly of opinion the only proper place, to settle that. When there is sufficient support from public opinion, Parliament does not hesitate to intervene. Where Parliament fears to tread it is not for the courts to rush in.
>
> ... In my judgment, this House is in no way bound and ought not to sanction the extension of 'public mischief' to any new field, and certainly not if such extension would be in any way controversial. Public mischief is the criminal counterpart of public policy, and the criminal law ought to be even more hesitant than the civil law in founding on it in some new aspect [p 457].

He was, however, in a minority of one.

Since this case, the judges have denied themselves the power to create new offences. In *Knuller v DPP* [1972] 2 All ER 898, the House of Lords denied the existence of any residual power they may have had to create new offences – all they could do was recognise the applicability of established offences to new circumstances to which they were relevant (Lord Simon of Glaisdale, p 932). In addition the House of Lords has acknowledged its power to create new defences (see Lord Mustill's comments in *Kingston* [1994] 3 All ER 353). However, this is the formal position. In practice we have already seen that matters are not quite as clear as the above cases would have us believe. In the case of *R*, the House of Lords still felt able to declare that a man was capable in law of raping his wife – a classic example of judicial law-making.

1.6   A WAY FORWARD – CODIFICATION OF THE LAW?

Most other common law and civil jurisdictions have long accepted that the judicial process is unsuitable for major law reform and that many of the problems that we have examined would be most suitably remedied by the comprehensive codification of the criminal law. The Criminal Law Reform Committee was established in 1959 and the Law Commission in 1965 to keep the law under review and to suggest reform, but much of their work was piecemeal and failed to address the problem of judicial uncertainty. A major event in the history of English criminal law occurred, therefore, in 1985 when the Law Commission produced a first draft of a proposed codification of the law written by a team of academics headed by the late Professor JC Smith. It set out the aims of codification as being to improve the accessibility, comprehensibility, consistency and certainty of the criminal law (Vol 1, para 2.1). The (proposed) Code would do this by:

- bringing within one set of covers most of the important offences;
- establishing a dictionary of key fault terms (for example, 'intention', 'recklessness') which parliament henceforth would be presumed to have intended unless they indicated to the contrary;

- providing a draft Bill encompassing its recommendations;
- incorporating not only the existing law but also recommendations for reform made by law reform bodies.

The team attempted to draft the Code in such a way as to prevent the judiciary creating new offences or resurrecting old ones yet allowing them to extend the law providing the extension stayed within the boundaries of the proscriptive clause. In other words, it clearly indicated to the judiciary just how far they could go in defining the frontiers of criminality when dealing with novel forms of behaviour. The importance of the proposal is, therefore, that it:

> ... makes a symbolic statement about the constitutional relationship of Parliament and the courts, it requires a judicial deference to the legislative will greater than that which the courts have often shown to isolated and sporadic pieces of legislation [Vol 1, para 2.2].

The Law Commission took the view that it would not be unduly restrictive and hinder the development of the common law because evidence from other jurisdictions indicated that judges still retained a considerable amount of flexibility within the parameters of the Code's provisions.

A period of consultation followed the publication of the proposal which included the establishment of eight circuit scrutiny groups each headed by a circuit judge and whose membership included representatives of those who were likely to be professional users of a code. The weight of opinion was strongly in favour of codification. The eventual result of the consultation was the publication in 1989 of *A Criminal Code for England and Wales* in two volumes (Law Com 177). This was described by the editor of the *Criminal Law Review* as 'an impressive piece of work' ([1989] Crim LR 393). The proposals would, if implemented, cover about 90–95% of the work of the criminal courts.

The proposed Code was broadly welcomed by most of those involved in the criminal justice system although, as might be expected with such an ambitious exercise, criticisms have been made by a number of commentators. Much of it is to the effect that it goes further than merely codifying existing law and encompasses a substantial body of law reform. The Law Commission used as the basis for its proposals for reform its own previous reports, those of the Criminal Law Revision Committee and the Butler Committee on Mentally Abnormal Offenders (*Report of the Committee on Mentally Abnormal Offenders*, Cmnd 6244, 1975). It decided to incorporate reforms (Vol 1, para 3.30):

- when there was an inconsistency which represented a conflict of policies and where a choice had to be made to produce a coherent law;
- where otherwise it would be restating 'rules of an arbitrary nature fulfilling no rational purpose';
- where there had been a recent official report recommending reforms.

A second criticism is that the Code team may have maximised the certainty of language and minimised the inventiveness of judges (Wells, 'Restatement or reform' [1986] Crim LR 314).

So far as the future of the codification project is concerned, this will, inevitably depend upon the will of parliament to devote sufficient time to debating the proposals. It has shown a distinct unwillingness to do this. The Commission's response has been to produce 'mini-codifications' in relation to specific areas of criminal law in the hope that this will be more attractive to parliament. In the main, they have omitted some of the more controversial proposals. See, for example:

- *Legislating the Criminal Code: Offences Against the Person and General Principles*, Law Com 218, 1993;

- *Legislating the Criminal Code: Intoxication and Criminal Liability*, Law Com 229, 1995;

- *Legislating the Criminal Code: Involuntary Manslaughter*, Law Com 237, 1996.

This decision by the Law Commission has been described by Professor ATH Smith as 'a failure of nerve' ([1992] Crim LR 397) whilst Simon Gardner, writing in relation to the offences against the person proposals, has criticised them as involving 'a substantial but selective agenda of change in the law' ((1992) 55 MLR 839).

These developments highlight a fundamental problem with criminal law reform. Brooke LJ (as he now is) vividly described his experience upon assuming the chairmanship of the Law Commission:

> I must describe the scene that confronted me in January 1993. The Commission had an enviable reputation among the cognoscenti for the quality of its proposals, for eliminating unfairness and illogicalities in the law. Sometimes its reports involved policy proposals that were unacceptable to the government of the day, or were years ahead of their time. But much more often its reports – and those of the Criminal Law Revision Committee – were being shelved because there was no effective machinery for taking them forward, and because there was no general perception, particularly among non-lawyers, that there was anything much wrong with the criminal law that needed reform, let alone that large sums of money were being wasted, and countless unfairnesses perpetrated, because important parts of our basic criminal law were so difficult to access. There were a lot of powerful autonomous bodies each parading their own views, a general antipathy to intellectual solutions or to anything resembling a carefully co-ordinated approach to some fairly intractable problems, and above all, nobody seemed to be accepting personal responsibility for sorting out the muddle [[1995] Crim LR 913, p 915].

The House of Commons has no dedicated mechanism for examining proposals for criminal law reform on a routine basis. This is because it regards almost every such proposal as *prima facie* controversial. As the pressure on parliamentary time is so great, the result is that, as Brooke LJ put it, 'no government is ever likely to put aside much of this precious time for technical law reform Bills, however desperately they are needed by those who have to make the criminal law work, since they will win few votes and advance few ministers' reputations' ([1995] Crim LR 913, p 918). The Commission's own preference is for a type of 'fast track' procedure for dealing with its reports in the form of a joint committee of both Houses of Parliament. This would combine the legal expertise of the House of Lords with the political considerations present in the Commons. Until this occurs we can only agree with the comment:

> ... the Law Commission has produced a steady flow of Bills designed to bring order to the ragged edges of the legal system. Most deserve speedy implementation; all deserve scrutiny. The neglect of the Commission's labours does justice and the taxpayer a disservice [(1997) *The Times*, 14 March].

A clear example of the dilatoriness of government is to be found in respect of the Law Commission's 1996 report (*Legislating the Criminal Code: Involuntary Manslaughter*, Law Com 237). It is only recently that the government's response appeared in print. The Home Office consultation paper, *Reforming the Law on Involuntary Manslaughter: The Government's Proposals* (April 2000), invites views on a number of proposals emanating from the Law Commission report of 1996. What is somewhat galling is the fact that the government appears to accept the Law Commission's report in principle and agrees with the majority of the proposals. Why, therefore, take four years to publish a consultation paper? The editorial to the July 2000 issue of the *Criminal Law Review* comments:

> We trust that it will not take another four years for decisions to be made about matters which the Home Office paper seeks consultation.

It is sad to report that at the time of writing (March 2003) we are still awaiting legislation on involuntary manslaughter in general, and corporate manslaughter in particular. This is all the more surprising because the government accepted that the health and safety legislation 'provides insufficient incentive for corporate managements to address safety issues effectively' (Sullivan, 'Corporate killing – some government proposals' [2001] Crim LR 31).

The speed at which the Home Office worked on this area of law is in stark contrast to the Law Commission's response to the Home Office's request in April 1998 for it to examine the law on fraud and make recommendations for its improvement, while making it comprehensible to juries. The Commission produced a consultation paper, *Legislating the Criminal Code: Fraud and Deception* (Law Com 155, 1999) in spring 1999.

As we have seen, the Law Commission produced in autumn 2002 radical proposals for the reform of the law relating to fraud. The response of the government is awaited. It is salutary to reflect on the whole sorry story relating to fraud outside of the traditional ambit of the Theft Acts and conspiracy. The need for reform was apparent in the late 1970s at the time the Criminal Law Act came into force. Since then there has been no shortage of proposals and recommendations, for example, the Roskill Commission in 1986, but in 2003 we still do not have a comprehensive set of laws relating to theft, deception and fraud. We are, of course, close, with the publication of the Law Commission report in 2002 but the final step has to be taken by the government and its track record on developing the substantive criminal law leaves a lot to be desired. It is likely that government legislative time will be made available for further reform of the criminal justice system in light of Auld but what use is a reformed system if many of the laws that it administers are in need of urgent reform?

We are no nearer a criminal code in this country than we were at the time of writing the last edition of this book. Now, there are voices being raised advocating the need for a code of criminal procedure (see Spencer, 'The case for a code of criminal procedure' [2000] Crim LR 519). As Spencer says:

> In many respects, the case for a code of criminal procedure is the same as the case for a code of criminal law. Criminal procedure and substantive criminal law are in reality two sides of the same coin. Together, they contain the rules under which the State can strip the citizen of his reputation, his property, his liberty and – until recently – his life ... you would expect these two areas of law to be clearly formulated and made publicly accessible in codes.

One welcome innovation in this period has been the creation of the Criminal Cases Review Commission, set up in April 1997 with the remit to investigate alleged miscarriages of justice. There is evidence to suggest that the Commission has been 'widely accepted, in theory and in practice ... [and is] ... a great improvement on its predecessors, the C3 Department of the Home Office and an equivalent unit in the Northern Ireland Office' (James, Taylor and Walker, 'Criminal Cases Review Commission: economy, effectiveness and justice' [2000] Crim LR 140).

1.7   THE DECISION TO CRIMINALISE CONDUCT

This is a complex matter. Professor Andrew Ashworth's view is that 'political opportunism and power, both linked to the prevailing political culture of the country' is the main determinant (*Principles of Criminal Law*, 2nd edn, 1995, Oxford: Clarendon, p 55) but traditionally commentators have asked two questions:

- is the conduct *harmful* to individuals or to society?; and
- is the conduct *immoral*?

If the answer to both questions is 'yes' then the conduct is considered *prima facie* suitable for criminalisation. But this traditional view is too simplistic to be helpful to the student because some acts are both immoral and harmful and yet have not been criminalised (for example, adultery), whilst others are neither immoral nor harmful and yet are crimes (for example, failure to wear a seat belt and some other 'victimless' crimes).

The law does not criminalise all immoral acts because:

- there may be difficulties of proof (many such acts occur in private and in the absence of independent witnesses);
- there may be difficulties of definition (take the example of the husband whose wife deserted him many years ago and who has now found a new partner. If he engages in sexual intercourse, do we really wish to see him punished as an 'adulterer'?);
- rules of morality are sometimes difficult to enforce without infringing the individual's right to privacy;
- the civil law sometimes provides an adequate remedy to the parties affected by the conduct (for example, the deserted wife);
- in any event, how do we ascertain prevailing 'moral opinion' given the deep divisions within modern society?

Lord Devlin has argued that an act should be criminalised if it incurs 'the deep disgust' of the right-minded individual (*Enforcement of Morals*, 1967, Oxford: OUP) but as HLA Hart has pointed out: what if the right-minded man's opinion is based upon ignorance, superstition or misunderstanding? (*Law, Liberty and Morality*, 1972, Oxford: OUP.) It is arguable that if Lord Devlin's view prevailed law-making powers would, in effect, be delegated to the proprietors of popular tabloid newspapers – a horrible thought! On the other hand, if the law makers move too far away from the values of the 'right-minded man' we face the danger of a loss of respect for the rule of law itself amongst the general populace – an equally horrible thought!

Perhaps the most useful and practical contribution to the debate about what conduct ought to be criminalised has been made by the American academic Herbert Packer. He suggests the following criteria in addition to immorality and harm being caused to a person or property (*The Limits of the Criminal Sanction*, 1969, Stanford, CA: Stanford UP):

- most people view the conduct as socially threatening;
- the conduct is not condoned by a significant section of society;
- criminalisation is not inconsistent with the goals of punishment;
- suppressing the conduct will not inhibit socially desirable conduct;
- it may be dealt with through even-handed and non-discriminatory enforcement;
- controlling the behaviour will not expose the criminal justice system to severe qualitative or quantitive strains;
- there are no reasonable alternatives to the criminal sanction for dealing with it;
- the costs of enforcement are not prohibitive.

Look at the case of *Brown* [1993] Crim LR 961, in Chapter 7, where the House of Lords was called upon to decide whether men engaged in homosexual sado-masochistic acts could, by their consent, give each other a valid defence to charges of assault occasioning actual bodily harm contrary to s 47 of the Offences Against the Person Act 1861. In this case, consent was present, there was no permanent injury, no medical attention sought, no complaint to the police, the acts were carried out in private and there was no profit motive. Notice how the issue divided the House of Lords with three judges deciding that the consent given was no defence to such a charge but with two judges dissenting and regarding the acts as essentially a matter of private sexual relations for which a valid consent could be given (depending upon the degree of harm inflicted). Note that all five judges had little difficulty in thinking that professional boxers were capable of giving each other a valid consent to charges of assault even though the principal purpose of a boxing match is to render the opponent unconscious and/or inflict grievous bodily harm! A useful exercise is for the student to apply Packer's framework to the facts of *Brown* in order to determine whether the majority or minority view is to be preferred. We wonder whether the reader agrees with us that near the margins of human behaviour the decision to criminalise particular acts is random.

1.8   THE DEFINITION OF A CRIME

Professor Ashworth has written: 'The chief concern of the criminal law is seriously anti-social behaviour. But the notion that English criminal law is only concerned with serious anti-social acts must be abandoned as one considers the broader canvas of criminal liability. There are many offences for which any element of stigma is diluted almost to vanishing point' (*Principles of Criminal Law*, 3rd edn, 1999, Oxford: Clarendon, p 1). What, then, are the unique characteristics of a crime? How do we define a particular act as being criminal? Believe it or not this can be a very difficult question to answer. The act may or may not cause harm or be immoral. It is difficult to isolate unique characteristics other than procedural differences which exist between criminal and civil proceedings. For example, any citizen can, in general, bring a private criminal prosecution even though that particular citizen has not suffered personally as a result of the act whilst in civil cases usually only the 'victim' may sue. Professor Philip Kenny has, therefore, defined a crime as, 'an act capable of being followed by criminal proceedings having one of the types of outcome (punishment, and so on) known to follow these proceedings' (*Outlines of Criminal Law*, 15th edn, 1936, Cambridge: CUP, p 16). Kenny would urge us to look at the statute to try to identify a procedural issue indicating whether the proscribed act constituted a criminal or civil wrong. If, for example, the statute indicated that the matter was to be heard in the Crown Court or that the remedy was a fine or term of imprisonment then this would be a fair indication that it was a crime. The defendant would thus be entitled to the benefit of the rules of evidence, rules of procedure, public funding, rights of appeal, and so on, applicable to the criminal law.

Nicola Lacey and Celia Wells, in *Reconstructing the Criminal Law* (2nd edn, 1998, London: Butterworths), argue that the:

> ... intangible phenomenon of *'public opinion'* and, perhaps more importantly, perceptions of that phenomenon, are enormously influential. The politicians who are involved in the legislative process are ultimately accountable to the populace and are therefore liable to be influenced by what they think are prevailing opinions [p 63].

1.9   CLASSIFICATION OF OFFENCES: EXPLANATION OF TERMS

Throughout this book reference will be made to terms unique to the criminal law. It is important that the student understands them because that understanding will give an enhanced appreciation of the nature of the crime the defendant is facing and of the procedure which determines the court in which the case will be heard. This in turn will determine the appeal procedure. The majority of criminal law reports are reports of appeals.

Most crimes are, today, statutory offences although many of them have their origins in the common law. Surprisingly perhaps, some of the most serious crimes such as murder and manslaughter are still common law offences.

For procedural purposes crimes are classified, according to Sched 1 to the Interpretation Act 1978, as follows:

(a) 'indictable offence' means an offence which ... is triable on indictment;

(b) 'summary offence' means an offence which is triable only summarily;

(c) 'offence triable either way' means an offence which ... is triable either on indictment or summarily.

Generally, *summary offences* are the least serious and can only be heard in the local magistrates' court and without a jury. *Indictable* (pronounced inditeable) *offences* are the most serious and can only be heard before a judge and jury in the Crown Court. *Either way offences* are those which are capable of being tried either in the magistrates' court or Crown Court. They tend to be offences which encompass a very broad range of criminal behaviour. Take theft for example. At one end of the spectrum of seriousness, this includes the 12-year-old who steals a packet of sweets from a supermarket; at the other end, it could include a multi-million pound theft from a bank by a defendant with a lengthy criminal record. It would be incongruous if the proceedings which followed were the same in both cases. Hence theft is triable either way. The decision as to venue is made by the magistrates' court having regard to all the circumstances of the case and the wishes of the prosecution and the accused (s 17 of the Magistrates' Courts Act 1980). However, if the magistrates decide to retain jurisdiction over the case (and deny the accused the right to a trial by jury) the accused must consent. Thus, the accused can insist on a trial by jury. The Divisional Court has issued detailed guidelines setting out the factors which may make an either way offence more suitable for trial on indictment. They should usually be heard in the magistrates' court unless they contain various kinds of aggravating factors or the maximum sentence of the magistrates' court is insufficient. This is currently generally six months' imprisonment and/or £5,000 fine (see *Practice Direction (Criminal: Consolidated)* [2002] 1 WLR 2870, para 51, Mode of Trial).

A defendant charged with an either way offence may gain a substantial discount on sentence if there is a guilty plea on appearance before the magistrates' court (see s 17A of the Magistrates' Courts Act 1980). So in *Barber* [2001] Crim LR the defendant who had been convicted of possession of cannabis with intention to supply had one year of his three and half-year sentence deducted by the Court of Appeal in recognition of his early indication that he wished to plead guilty.

In May 1999, the Home Secretary announced that he intended to abolish the right of the defendant to elect jury trial for a number of 'either way' offences. Perhaps understandably, given the long standing nature of the right, the proposals have encountered significant opposition from lawyers and civil liberties groups. At the time of writing, the proposal has not become law and is unlikely to do so. Do note though the proposals from the *Criminal Courts Review Report* that recommends the abolition of jury trials in complex fraud cases.

Section 1 of the Criminal Justice Act (CJA) 1967 abolished the distinction between *felonies* (serious offences) and *misdemeanours* (less serious offences) and provided that both should be governed by the law previously applicable to misdemeanours. This is most significant in relation to secondary participation in crime, which will be dealt with in Chapter 4. The CJA 1967 introduced a new classification of arrestable and non-arrestable offences, that is, offences in relation to which a power of arrest exists without a warrant and those which do require a warrant. Section 2 has now been replaced by s 24 of the Police and Criminal Evidence Act 1984, which defines an arrestable offence as one for which the sentence is fixed by law (murder, treason, piracy) or for which a person can be sentenced to five years' imprisonment or more.

1.10   RIGHTS TO APPEAL

It is important to understand the appeal process because much of the criminal law has been established by the results of appeal decisions. Of particular importance are appeals from the Crown Court to the Court of Appeal where the grounds of the appeal may be that the trial judge failed accurately to explain the law to the jury in the summing-up (the 'direction' to the jury) at the end of the case.

The right to appeal and the grounds of appeal depend upon the trial venue.

1.10.1 Summary trials

The defendant or the prosecution can appeal *by way of case stated* to the Divisional Court of the Queen's Bench Division on the ground that the magistrates' court exceeded its jurisdiction or, more commonly, misunderstood or misapplied the law. The appeal will normally be heard by two or three Courts of Appeal or High Court judges. Either side may further appeal to the House of Lords if the Divisional Court certifies the point of law involved as being of general public importance and either the Divisional Court or the House of Lords grants leave to appeal. Cases in the House of Lords are normally decided by five Lords of Appeal in Ordinary (Law Lords).

A defendant may also appeal against conviction to the Crown Court which sits for these purposes with a single circuit judge assisted by (usually) two lay magistrates. There is no jury involved in the proceedings.

1.10.2 Trials on indictment

The defendant can appeal to the Court of Appeal (Criminal Division) only on the ground that the conviction was 'unsafe' (s 2(1) of the Criminal Appeal Act 1995) and only with the permission of the trial judge or leave of the Court of Appeal. The appeal may be heard by two or three judges of the Court of Appeal but currently is more likely to heard by one Court of Appeal judge together with one judge from the High Court and one senior circuit judge. If the defendant was acquitted at the original trial, the Attorney General may appeal to the Court of Appeal for a ruling on a point of law although the defendant's acquittal stands. This procedure accounts for the large number of important cases in this book with references such as *Attorney General's Reference (No 1 of 1992)* [1993] 2 All ER 190. The Attorney General may also appeal to the Court of Appeal if he considers that a sentence given at the Crown Court was unduly lenient and wrong in law. The court is then in a position to pronounce a 'guideline sentence' which trial judges thereafter are expected to follow (s 35 of the CJA 1988). It is also possible for a person convicted at the Crown Court to appeal against the sentence imposed. However, leave to appeal is required and the Court of Appeal may substitute any sentence that would have been available to the Crown Court.

Either side may further appeal to the House of Lords on a point of law if the Court of Appeal has certified the point as being of general public importance and either the Court of Appeal or the House of Lords has granted leave to appeal.

The Criminal Cases Review Commission was established under the Criminal Appeal Act 1995 and its role is to investigate cases involving an alleged miscarriage of justice and to refer the case, if appropriate, to the Court of Appeal. Please be aware that over the shelf life of this edition, and as a result of potential legislation emanating from the Auld Review of the criminal courts, changes are likely to be made to the basic workings of the criminal justice system that may include new or restricted rights of appeal for defendants.

1.11   BURDEN OF PROOF AND STANDARD OF PROOF

It is a fundamental principle of English law that a person is innocent of any criminal offence until proven guilty. The *burden of proving* the defendant's guilt falls upon the prosecution who must prove to the satisfaction of the jury (or magistrates) that the accused is guilty *beyond reasonable doubt* (this is referred to as the *standard of proof*). It is not for the accused person to prove his or her innocence and the accused is entitled to the benefit of any doubt as to his or her guilt. As Lord Sankey LC stated in the leading case of *Woolmington v DPP* [1935] AC 462:

> No matter what the charge or where the trial, the principle that the prosecution must prove the guilt of the prisoner is part of the common law of England and no attempt to whittle it down can be entertained [p 482].

Ashworth and Blake have argued that 'from time to time English judges have articulated fundamental principles which they believe to underlie criminal law and procedure' ([1996] Crim LR 306). These include the privilege against self-incrimination, the need for the prosecution to prove a guilty mind and, of course, the 'golden thread' acknowledged by Viscount Sankey that the prosecution must prove the prisoner's guilt. However, it should be noted that, in a parliamentary democracy, any of these fundamental rights can be withdrawn, and Ashworth and Blake consider that: 'Developments in recent years have cast grave doubt on the existence of these "fundamental principles".'

However, if the defendant raises a defence to the charge, for example, provocation, duress or self-defence, the law usually places an *evidential burden* on him to provide some credible evidence to substantiate the claim. At this point, the prosecution is then required to prove 'beyond reasonable doubt' that the defendant is not in fact entitled to the benefit of the defence. In a small number of exceptional cases (chiefly, insanity and diminished responsibility – see Chapters 10 and 6 respectively) the law places the burden of proof squarely on the shoulders of the defendant to prove that he or she was suffering from this affliction but the standard of proof here is that used in the civil courts, 'on a balance of probabilities' (*Carr-Briant* [1943] KB 607).

1.12   THE TRIAL AND THE ROLE OF THE JUDGE AND JURY

The trial commences with the prosecution presenting its evidence. This might be a combination of live witnesses, scientific evidence (for example, fingerprints) and documentary evidence (for example, a written statement made by the defendant to a police officer). At the conclusion of the prosecution's case, the defence is entitled to argue that it has 'no case to answer' because the prosecution has failed to make out even a *prima facie* case. If the judge (or magistrates) decide that a case has in fact been made out, the defence then presents its own evidence and again this might be a combination of witnesses and documentary evidence. At the conclusion of this part of the trial, the judge's task is then to 'sum up' for the jury. This involves summarising the evidence from both sides and highlighting those parts most relevant to the jury's task of deciding the guilt or innocence of the accused. This would include identifying weak or contradictory evidence which had been presented during the trial. The judge will then explain the relevant principles of law to the jury. For example, if the accused has admitted killing the victim but has raised the defence of provocation, the judge will explain the legal constituents of this defence. As Chapter 6 explains, this will involve outlining s 3 of the Homicide Act 1957 and several leading cases which have interpreted and clarified the meaning of this defence. The judge will then ask the jury to retire and reach a conclusion on the factual evidence they have heard and then to relate this to the legal issues that have been laid before it. If the jury finds the defendant guilty, it is discharged by the judge who then goes on to decide the appropriate sentence. The jury plays no part in the sentencing process.

1.13   APPROACHING THE STUDY OF CRIMINAL LAW

We suggest that the best method to analyse particular crimes and to answer problem questions is as follows:

- carefully examine the statutory definition of the offence;
- identify the different elements separating them into *actus reus* (see Chapter 2) and *mens rea* (see Chapter 3);
- identify any further explanatory provisions in the statute relating to each element (for example, the statute may define particular words);
- examine the leading case(s) in relation to both elements to ensure a sound understanding of how the law is currently defined and applied by the courts;
- consider whether any defence may be available to the defendant. This might be a general defence arguable in relation to all crimes, for example, insanity, or relevant only to a specific crime, for example, provocation can only be a defence to murder.

There are dangers if the student fails to adopt a structured approach to the study of criminal law. First, it is easy to fall into the trap of deciding upon the defendant's guilt or innocence in advance of the analysis, usually on the basis of 'instinct', revulsion or 'gut reaction'. This may, or may not, be in accordance with the law. Secondly, a failure to carry out this basic research may mean that the law is misunderstood, is out of date or that an important part of the problem is ignored, for example, the existence of a defence.

Take theft for example. The basic definition is found in s 1(1) of the Theft Act (TA) 1968: 'A person is guilty of theft if he dishonestly appropriates property belonging to another with the intention of permanently depriving the other of it ...' Consider the question: 'Is it possible in law to steal one's own property?' 'Instinct' and, on the face of it, s 1 would both indicate that the answer must be no. However, s 5(1) of the TA 1968 defines 'belonging to another' as follows: 'Property shall be regarded as belonging to any person having possession or control of it, or having in it any proprietary right or interest ...'

The answer to the question is clearly not as simple as might have first been thought. Further research will reveal the Court of Appeal decision of *Turner (No 2)* [1971] 1 WLR 901. In this case, the appellant had taken his car to a garage for repairs. The repairs were completed and the car left outside the garage overnight awaiting collection by the owner. Unknown to the garage proprietor, Mr Brown, the appellant had a spare set of keys which he used to remove his car from the garage without Mr Brown's consent and having omitted to pay for the repairs which had been carried out. He was found guilty of theft by a jury and the Court of Appeal dismissed his appeal. This conclusion was only possible because the words of s 1 of the TA 1968 were qualified by s 5 of the TA 1968.

How does one identify the different elements of the crime and divide them into the *actus reus* and *mens rea*? A full analysis of these terms will be found in Chapters 2 and 3 respectively. In outline, however, the *actus reus* consists of those aspects of the definition of the crime which relate to the defendant's conduct or the consequences or circumstances of the defendant's act. *Mens rea* refers directly or indirectly to the mental element which the prosecution must usually prove in relation to the defendant in order to secure a conviction. In relation to the basic definition of 'theft' contained in s 1 of the TA 1968:

Actus reus words are:

- appropriates; and
- property belonging to another.

Mens rea words are:

- dishonestly; and
- intention of permanently depriving the other of it.

Once you have sub-divided the conduct into the basic *actus reus* and *mens rea* elements you will have to give further consideration to the meaning of the words and phrases that constitute the definition of the offence. If one issue centres on whether the defendant has in law appropriated property belonging to another then your research needs to be at three levels. The first is to identify any assistance the statute may provide. In this case you will discover a definition at s 3 of the TA 1968. Secondly, you will need to identify case law relevant to the issue of appropriation and through this determine what are the legal issues centred around the concept of appropriation. Thirdly, you will need to identify any relevant academic writings that will assist you in understanding the problem(s) with the case law or legislation. See, for example, the article by Stephen Shute, 'Appropriation and the law of theft' ([2002] Crim LR 445) prompted by the House of Lords' decision in *Hinks* [2000] 4 All ER 833. As the author admits, the decision 'has provoked extreme hostility from academic criminal lawyers'. He, however, seeks to show that much of the criticism is misplaced. This is valuable material for the law student.

Also, do not forget to consider the possibility of a defence being available. The defendant may admit to having 'stolen' sweets from a local shop but what if he was intoxicated at the time he took the sweets? What if he was 11 years of age? What of the student in halls of residence who enters his best friend's room in order to borrow some sugar only to find the friend absent but the sugar bowl on the desk. If the student removes the sugar, is he guilty of theft or could he rely on s 2(1)(b) of the TA 1968 and claim that he appropriated the sugar, '... in the belief that he would have the [owner's] consent if the [owner] knew of the appropriation and the circumstances in which it had taken place'? (See Chapter 8 for the answer.)

The message is clear: there is no substitute for a structured and methodical approach to the study of the criminal law. It is not enough merely to rely on a textbook.

1.14   KEEPING UP TO DATE WITH THE LAW

Most students find criminal law to be an exciting and challenging subject but it can also be frustrating at times as a result of its tendency to change very quickly as a consequence of new statutes and appellate decisions. The Law Commission has produced a large body of work in recent years and most commentators agree that its reports and consultation papers are of an excellent standard. They often provide a thorough and critical review of the law in a particular area, sometimes compare English law with that of other jurisdictions, and propose reforms. For the serious student or the practitioner who seeks a detailed appreciation of the criminal law, their reports and papers are essential reading. Throughout this book you will be referred to the work of the Law Commission. It is vital to keep abreast of current developments and the best method of doing this is by regularly perusing the *Criminal Law Review* published monthly and available in every university law library. It contains helpful case notes which not only analyse the decision in the case but often, in addition, compare and contrast the decision with the previous law and with the recommendations of law reform bodies such as the Law Commission. It also contains articles on current issues affecting the criminal law and the criminal justice system. The *Criminal Law Review* also appeals to judges, practising lawyers and other professionals with a serious interest in the criminal law.

There are often themes running through the pages of the *Criminal Law Review*. One that you should pay particular attention to is the impact on the criminal law of the Human Rights Act 1998, which came into force on 2 October 2000. The potential impact of the Act on the substantive criminal has already been much discussed by contributors to the *Review*, but ultimately it is the judges and politicians that will decide whether Arden J's provocative title to her article in the June 1999 issue proves to be prophetic ('Criminal law at the crossroads' [1999] Crim LR 439). Her view is that codification of the substantive criminal law offers the best way of ensuring compliance with the HRA 1998. She states:

> The criminal law faces a choice. The choice is between having a strategy and an overall vision of a well considered, consistent, coherent and modern criminal law on the one hand, and on the other hand patching up an area of law which is already seriously defective and out of date under a policy of mend and make do. The right choice is obvious. But it needs courage and political will. It needs the support of the judiciary and the profession. It will also take time and effort, but ... it is the only course that will lead to the real improvement in the criminal law that we would all like to see.

A new code for a new millennium?

We wait in eager anticipation.

SUMMARY OF CHAPTER 1

AN INTRODUCTION TO
THE STUDY OF CRIMINAL LAW

CRIMINAL LAW: THE LOST DECADE

Criminal law should be certain, consistent and accessible. There is now widespread concern that the law satisfies none of these criteria. This is due in large measure to judicial law-making, a lack of general agreement as to the purpose of criminal law and inadequate machinery for law reform. Codification of the law would largely meet these problems and the Law Commission published a proposed codification in 1989. The proposal had been preceded by widespread consultation with all those professionally involved in the criminal law. However, parliament has failed to allocate time in order to consider codification and as a result the Law Commission has published a series of 'mini-Codes' in the belief that they will be more appealing to politicians. Unfortunately, this tactic has also failed and proposals for law reform were largely ignored during the 1990s.

DEFINING CONDUCT AS CRIMINAL

The decision to criminalise conduct is traditionally taken when a particular activity is both immoral and harmful to people or property. However, there are many exceptions and acts can be identified which meet both criteria and yet which are not classified as criminal. Conversely, other acts do not meet either criteria and yet are classed as criminal. It is in fact difficult to define unique characteristics of a 'crime' other than by reference to the nature of the proceedings which follow the commission of the act.

CLASSIFICATION OF OFFENCES

The great majority of crimes are statutory offences and they are classified as being either indictable, summary or either way offences. This classification determines the court in which the case will be heard (and whether or not a jury will be involved) and any rights to appeal which may exist.

BURDEN OF PROOF

It is important to understand what is meant by the burden of proof and the standard of proof and upon whom the burden is placed. This is particularly relevant when the defendant wishes to argue that he or she is entitled to the benefit of a defence. Similarly, it is important to understand the roles of the judge and jury in a trial and the terms used throughout this book to describe their role such as 'model direction' or the judge's 'summing up'.

STUDYING CRIMINAL LAW

A structured approach is provided for the study of this complex, fascinating but rapidly changing subject. This will lead the student away from the trap of deciding problem questions on the basis of 'instinct' and will ensure that the correct law is fully understood and applied to legal problems. In order to keep up to date students are urged to regularly consult the *Criminal Law Review* and the reports and consultation papers published by the Law Commission.

CHAPTER 2

ACTUS REUS

2.1   INTRODUCTION

The prosecution's task is to demonstrate to the jury (or magistrates) beyond reasonable doubt:

- that the defendant brought about the prohibited act, omission or state of affairs. This is called the *actus reus*;
- that the defendant did this with the state of mind prescribed by the definition of the crime. This is called the *mens rea*; and
- that the defendant is not entitled to the benefit of any defence which may have been argued on his or her behalf.

Traditionally, this is encapsulated in the Latin maxim, *actus non facit reum, nisi mens sit rea*, which means that an act does not make a person guilty of committing an offence unless the mind is legally blameworthy. The use of this expression has been criticised as likely to mislead those involved in the study and operation of the criminal law, not least by Lord Diplock in his speech in *Miller* [1983] 1 All ER 978. He pointed out that as long ago as 1889 the eminent criminal lawyer, Stephen J, in *Tolson* (1886–90) 23 QBD 168; [1886–90] All ER Rep 26 'condemned the phrase as likely to mislead'. Lord Diplock considered that 'it naturally suggests that, apart from all particular definitions of crimes, such a thing exists as a *"mens rea"*, or "guilty mind", which is always expressly or by implication involved in every definition. This is obviously not the case, for the mental elements of different crimes differ widely'. While acknowledging that Stephen J was criticising the phrase *mens rea*, he believed that *actus reus* is equally liable to mislead since 'it suggests that some positive act on the part of the accused is needed to make him guilty of a crime and that a failure or omission to act is insufficient to give rise to criminal liability unless some express provision in the statute that creates the offence so provides' (p 979).

Lord Diplock thought it preferable to think and speak about the prohibited *conduct* of the defendant and his state of mind at the time of the conduct instead of speaking of *actus reus* and *mens rea*. However, these two expressions are now firmly established and commonly used by those professionally involved in the criminal law and they are a convenient way of referring to the differing requirements of the definitions of particular crimes. The Law Commission, in its (proposed) draft Criminal Code (*Criminal Law: A Criminal Code for England and Wales*, Law Com 177, 1989), preferred the expressions *external elements*, in place of *actus reus*, and *fault elements*, in place of *mens rea*, and used them throughout the work. Whichever terms are preferred, it is important to note that they are merely convenient tools of analysis for the lawyer. At the conclusion of the trial, what matters is that the prosecution has established that all the ingredients contained within the definition of the crime have been satisfied; it matters not whether the ingredients are categorised as *actus reus/external elements*, *mens rea/fault elements* or in any other way.

2.2   CIRCUMSTANCES REQUIRED BY THE DEFINITION OF THE CRIME

The prosecution must always prove the 'external elements' if they are to succeed in their task. These elements might include:

- positive acts on the part of the defendant; or
- (in some circumstances) *omitting to act*; or
- (very rarely) being involved in a *state of affairs*.

It is, therefore, incorrect to state that the *actus reus* refers merely to 'the guilty *act*'.

The importance of proving the *actus reus* is illustrated by the case of *Deller* (1952) 36 Cr App R 184. The defendant was convicted of obtaining a car by false pretences (now s 15 of the Theft Act (TA) 1968). When obtaining some property, he had made statements which he thought were untrue. It turned out that in fact the statements were true. Despite his best efforts Mr Deller had in fact spoken the truth! Whilst he certainly possessed the *mens rea*, the *actus reus* (that he made false pretences) was missing and he was, therefore, entitled to be acquitted (today he would almost certainly be guilty of attempting to obtain property by deception contrary to the Criminal Attempts Act 1981 – see Chapter 5).

Any analysis of the *actus reus* must, therefore, take account of the fact that particular conduct may only be forbidden in the particular *circumstances* required by the definition of the crime. With theft, for example, the prosecution must prove that the property belonged to another; with rape that the victim did not consent to sexual intercourse with the defendant; with handling stolen goods that the goods are indeed stolen. The case of *Haughton v Smith* [1973] 3 All ER 1109 graphically illustrates this point. Police stopped a van on a motorway and found it contained stolen goods. The officers took control of the vehicle and decided that it should continue on its progress towards London where other members of the criminal gang were planning to meet the lorry in order to unload it. The defendant was one of those awaiting the goods and when the lorry arrived he was arrested and charged with attempting to handle stolen goods. His appeal against his resulting conviction was allowed by the House of Lords on the basis that at the time he had attempted to handle the goods they were no longer stolen because they had been restored to law custody (ie, the custody of the police officers who had taken control of the lorry).

2.2.1   Result and conduct crimes

A further dimension of the analysis of the *actus reus* is the distinction often drawn between result crimes and conduct crimes. It is important, therefore, when considering a particular crime, to consider not only the circumstances required by the definition, but also whether it is a result or conduct crime. In *Miller*, Lord Diplock referred to *arson* contrary to s 1(3) of the Criminal Damage Act (CDA) 1971 as an example of a result crime. This he defined as a crime which is not complete unless and until the conduct of the accused has *caused* property belonging to another to be destroyed or damaged. He went on to emphasise that with all result crimes the 'conduct of the accused that is *causative* to the result may consist not only of his doing physical acts ... but also of ... failing to take measures' (p 980).

An example of a *conduct* crime is the offence of dangerous driving contrary to s 2 of the Road Traffic Act (RTA) 1988 (as substituted by the RTA 1991). It is clear from the wording of the offence that the *actus reus* of dangerous driving is driving a mechanically propelled vehicle on a road or other place. Nothing more needs to be established and there is certainly no need to show that any dire consequence ensued. However, for the crime to be completed reference needs to be made to the circumstances. The driving must be *dangerous* and s 2A(1) and (2) make it clear that what is deemed to be *dangerous* is to be largely assessed by using the objective standard of the 'competent and careful driver'. Obviously, to drive a car is not a crime but to do so in such a way that the conduct is dangerous inevitably establishes the offence.

2.2.2 Justification

Sometimes the law allows some form of justification for the act which the defendant committed, for example, the use of force in self-defence renders the accused's conduct lawful (see below, 10.10, for further details). Justification is not, as such, an aspect of *actus reus* or *mens rea* – it is a 'true' defence – as it effectively renders the defendant's actions lawful, but it begs the question as to whether a defendant's conduct is still to be regarded as justified in law where he is unaware of the facts giving rise to the justification. In *Dadson* (1850) 4 Cox CC 358, the defendant was a police officer who shot a man escaping from a wood from where he had stolen timber. At that time, it was lawful to shoot an escaping felon. The victim was in fact a felon because he had several previous convictions for theft but this was unknown to the policeman. He was convicted of unlawfully wounding the felon with intent to commit grievous bodily harm. Dadson pleaded justification, that is, what he had done was justified in law; the law allowed escaping felons to be shot and this was all he had done. His appeal was dismissed because the court for Crown Cases Reserved held that his act could only be justified if he was aware of the facts which gave rise to the defence and here he was not.

The Law Commission's view is to be found in cl 27 of *Legislating the Criminal Code: Draft Criminal Law Bill* (Law Com 218, 1993) which adopts the *Dadson* principle. The Law Commission originally intended in its 1989 (proposed) codification of the criminal law to engage in law reform and reverse the *Dadson* principle but eventually concluded that:

> Although opinion was not unanimous on consultation, we think it right to maintain this long-standing common law rule. Citizens who react unreasonably to circumstances should not be exculpated by the accident of facts of which they were unaware [para 39.11].

2.2.3 The *actus reus* must always be voluntary

In *Bratty v Attorney General for Northern Ireland* [1963] AC 3862, Lord Denning stated that: '... the requirement that it should be a voluntary act is essential ... in every criminal case.' This requirement applies to all crimes including those classed as *strict liability* offences where the prosecution does not have to prove *mens rea* in relation to one or more aspects of the *actus reus* (see Chapter 3). A car driver would not, therefore, be guilty of a driving offence if he suffered a heart attack or was attacked by a swarm of bees, as a result of which he crashed into a second vehicle, because his actions would have been involuntary and an essential element of *actus reus* of such offences would be missing. However, the courts are concerned to ensure that involuntary conduct is kept within narrow boundaries and emphasise the importance of the absence of fault on the part of the defendant. For example, if the car driver was prone to heart attacks and had experienced heart tremors shortly before the accident, but had continued driving, it is unlikely he would be able successfully to demonstrate the absence of *actus reus*. In these circumstances, he should have immediately stopped the car and sought help (see below, 2.3.1).

2.2.4   State of affairs cases

Despite the fact that the term *actus reus* is suggestive of some positive action by D, it is clear that proof of *actus reus* can be satisfied by evidence that a particular state of affairs existed at the relevant time. Simple examples include offences such as sexual intercourse with a girl under the age of 16 contrary to s 6 of the Sexual Offences Act 1956 – the conduct element of the *actus reus* is the sexual intercourse, but the gender of the complainant and her age are circumstances that the prosecution must establish. Where the *actus reus* of an offence is entirely based on proof of circumstances or state of affairs, the possibility arises that D may be convicted even though he did not act voluntarily to bring those circumstances about. Consider the two leading cases of *Larsonneur* (1933) 24 Cr App R 74 and *Winzar v Chief Constable of Kent* (1983) *The Times*, 28 March. In the former case, Ms Larsonneur, a French citizen, was granted leave to enter the UK on 14 March 1933. On 22 March, the permission was varied and she was required to leave the UK by the end of that day. The appellant *chose* to travel to Eire. Whilst there she was deported by the Irish police and taken by them, and against her will, back to the UK where she was immediately detained by police officers at the port of entry. She was convicted under the Aliens Order 1920 in that, she, 'being an alien to whom leave to land in the UK had been refused, was found in the UK'. Her appeal was unsuccessful despite her claim that she lacked both the *mens rea* and the *actus reus*! Lord Hewart CJ held during the course of a short and terse judgment that the manner of her return to the UK was 'perfectly immaterial'. All that mattered was that 'she was found here' and 'was in the class of person whose landing had been prohibited ... by reason of the fact that she had violated the condition on her passport' (pp 78–79).

Not every commentator has chosen to criticise the judgment, however. David Lanham, for example, concluded that Ms Larsonneur was, to a significant extent, the author of her own misfortune and that whilst:

> ... no one could claim that *Larsonneur* stood as a shining example of English jurisprudence ..., it can hardly be regarded as the last word in judicial depravity. If Ms Larsonneur had been dragged kicking and screaming from France into the UK by kidnappers and the same judgment had been given by the Court of Criminal Appeal, the defence of unforeseeable compulsion would truly have been excluded and the case would be the worst blot on the pages of the modern criminal law. But she wasn't, it wasn't and it isn't [[1976] Crim LR 276].

Winzar v Chief Constable of Kent is a similar case. Here, the appellant had been convicted of having been found drunk in the highway and fined £15. Winzar had been taken to hospital on a stretcher but was there diagnosed as being merely drunk and told to leave. This he declined to do and was found slumped in a corridor. The police were summoned and they carried him to a police car parked on the road outside the hospital. His appeal to the Divisional Court was on the grounds:

- he was not 'found on the highway' as he had been carried to the police car;
- his presence on 'the highway' was momentary;
- he was not there of his own volition.

Robert Goff LJ upheld the conviction because in his judgment all that mattered was that:

- a person is in a public place or highway;
- he is drunk;
- he is perceived to be there and to be drunk.

Here, Winzar was found guilty of an offence which was in fact procured by the police! It can be argued of course that if a drunken man refuses to leave a hospital after repeated requests to do so, it is inevitable that the police will be called and that if their requests to him to leave are declined they will remove him by force. Perhaps Winzar, as with Ms Larsonneur, was at least partly the author of his own misfortune.

2.3   NON-INSANE AUTOMATISM

A further qualification must be introduced into any discussion of the importance of the voluntary nature of the *actus reus* and this concerns 'non-insane automatism'. This has been described as 'a modern catchphrase [to describe] an involuntary movement of the body or limbs of a person' (*Watmore v Jenkins* [1962] 2 QB 572). Imagine that a dental patient kicks out whilst recovering from an anaesthetic and injures the dentist. This *prima facie* is the *actus reus* of one of the charges contained within the Offences Against the Person Act 1861. The charge could be defeated on the ground not only that the prosecution would be unable to prove the *mens rea* requirement of the offence but also on the ground that as the act was involuntary the defendant had not committed the *actus reus* – it took place whilst the defendant was in a state of automatism.

Of course, it might be thought that so long as the defendant escapes conviction it does not matter whether this is because the prosecution is unable to prove the existence of either the *mens rea* or *actus reus*. In fact, it does matter because, as will be seen in Chapter 3, many criminal offences are categorised as offences of *strict liability*. This means that the prosecution does not have to prove *mens rea* in relation to one or more aspects of the *actus reus*. If automatism was considered to be a part of the *mens rea*, it follows that in crimes such as these the defendant might not escape conviction.

The basic principles were outlined by Lord Denning in *Bratty*, drawing support from Lord Sankey LC in *Woolmington v DPP* [1935] AC 462, where he said:

> ... when dealing with a murder case the Crown must prove (a) death as the result of a voluntary act of the accused and (b) the malice of the accused.

Lord Denning continued:

> No act is punishable if it is done involuntarily: and an involuntary act in this context – some people nowadays prefer to speak of it as 'automatism' – means an act which is

done by the muscles without any control by the mind such as a spasm, a reflex action or a convulsion; or an act done by a person who is not conscious of what he is doing such as an act done while suffering from concussion or whilst sleepwalking.

In practice, automatism is closely related to the defence of insanity and works within a narrow sphere because any *automatic* behaviour which results from a *disease of the mind* results in the actor being found 'not guilty by reason of insanity' (as a result of the *M'Naghten* Rules of 1843 – see Chapter 10). The law distinguishes between 'external factors' responsible for the automatic behaviour and 'internal factors', the former potentially leading to an acquittal, whilst the latter is liable to result in detention in a secure hospital. Insanity and non-insane automatism are thus mutually exclusive defences. As Nicola Padfield has noted, 'the legal definition of both automatism and insanity bear little relationship to their medical counterparts. Indeed, insanity is not a medical concept and automatism only exists in medical texts in relation to some forms of epilepsy' ([1989] CLJ 354). Little wonder that Lawton LJ has described the whole area as a 'quagmire seldom entered nowadays save by those in desperate need of some sort of defence' (*Quick* [1973] QB 910).

The distinction between external and internal factors is supposed to distinguish between those who suffer from 'one-off' problems and who pose no future threat to society and those who, due to a continuing medical condition, are likely to experience the problem again and reoffend. Unsurprisingly, defendants often go to great lengths to avoid pleading the insanity defence and risking committal to a secure hospital. The distinction can and does lead to injustice. In *Quick*, the defendant was a diabetic charged with causing actual bodily harm whilst in a hypoglycaemic state (low blood sugar) brought on by taking his insulin and failing to eat properly. His defence was that of automatism but the trial judge ruled that the evidence amounted to a defence of insanity. The defendant at this point changed his plea to guilty and was then sentenced. He now appealed on the ground that the judge's ruling was wrong and that a diabetic in a temporary condition of hypoglycaemia was not, whilst in that condition, suffering from any defect of reason from disease of the mind. The Court of Appeal quashed his conviction on the ground that an external factor was in fact responsible for his act, that is, the taking of the insulin. It held that a malfunctioning of the mind does not occur if it is caused 'by the application to the body of some external factor such as violence, drugs including anaesthetics, alcohol and hypnotic influences'. The court drew a distinction between a person suffering from a hypoglycaemia condition, such as Mr Quick, and a person suffering from a hyperglycaemia condition (excessive blood sugar). The court held that the former case was caused by the external factor of taking insulin whilst the latter was caused by an internal defect (and the fact that it was treated and controlled by insulin was deemed to be irrelevant!) Padfield has posed the obvious question, 'why should [a] failure to eat be less likely to recur than [a] failure to take ... insulin?' ([1989] CLJ 354, p 356).

Sleepwalking is also now regarded as an internal factor (despite Lord Denning's opinion in *Bratty*). In *Burgess* [1991] 2 All ER 769, the defendant and his female friend both fell asleep while watching television in her flat. She awoke to find Burgess attacking her. She screamed and as a result, 'he seemed to come to his senses' and showed great remorse. He was charged with wounding with intent and he raised the defence of lack of *mens rea* because, he said, at the time of the act he was sleepwalking and this constituted non-insane automatism. The trial judge ruled that this amounted to a plea of 'not guilty by reason of insanity' and ordered him to be detained in a secure hospital. He appealed on the basis that the judge's ruling was incorrect. The Court of Appeal dismissed the appeal, Lord Lane CJ stating:

> One can perhaps narrow the field of inquiry still further by eliminating what are sometimes called the 'external factors' such as concussion caused by a blow on the head. There were no such factors here. Whatever the cause may have been, it was an 'internal' cause. The possible disappointment or frustration caused by unrequited love is not to be equated with something such as concussion. On this aspect of the case, we respectfully adopt what was said by Martin JA giving the judgment of the court in the Ontario Court of Appeal in *R v Rabey* (1977) which was approved by a majority in the Supreme Court of Canada (see [1980] 2 SCR 513, p 519) (where the facts bore a similarity to those in the instant case, although the diagnosis was different):
>
> > Any malfunctioning of the mind, or mental disorder having its source primarily in some subjective condition or weakness internal to the accused (whether fully understood or not), may be a 'disease of the mind' if it prevents the accused from knowing what he is doing, but transient disturbances of consciousness due to certain specific external factors do not fall within the concept of disease of the mind ... In my view, the ordinary stresses and disappointments of life which are the common lot of mankind do not constitute an external cause constituting an explanation for a malfunctioning of the mind which takes it out of the category of a 'disease of the mind'. To hold otherwise would deprive the concept of an external factor of any real meaning.

Epilepsy is also classed as an internal factor. The House of Lords dealt with this condition in *Sullivan* [1983] 2 All ER 673. Mr Sullivan suffered from epilepsy. There had been a period in his life when he was subject to major seizures but medication had lessened their intensity and at the time of the relevant conduct he was proved to suffer minor seizures known as *petit mal*, perhaps once or twice each week. On the day in question, he was chatting to elderly neighbours when he was suddenly overcome by a seizure. One of the neighbours, a Mr Payne, aged 80, was kicked by the appellant and required hospital treatment. The prosecution accepted that he had no recollection of the events but the trial judge ruled that his defence was one of insanity and not automatism which Sullivan's counsel had wished to establish. As a consequence of that ruling, the defendant pleaded guilty to assault occasioning actual bodily harm. He appealed against the judge's ruling. Lord Diplock, in giving the decision of the House of Lords, considered the law relating to insanity and held that the word 'mind' in the *M'Naghten* Rules 'is used in the ordinary sense of the mental faculties of reason, memory and understanding'. Therefore:

> If the effect of a disease is to impair these faculties so severely as to have either of the consequences referred to in the latter part of the Rules, it matters not whether the aetiology of the impairment is organic, as in epilepsy, or functional, or whether the impairment itself is permanent or transient and intermittent, provided that it subsisted at the time of the commission of the act.

Lord Diplock ended his speech by saying, 'sympathise though I do with the appellant, I see no other course open to your Lordships than to dismiss this appeal' (p 677).

In *Bratty*, Lord Denning emphasised that an act is not to be regarded as involuntary if the person was conscious but nevertheless could not control his actions (irresistible impulse) or could not remember after the event exactly what had taken place. There must be a total destruction of voluntary control. In *Attorney General's Reference (No 2 of 1992)* [1994] QB 91, it was alleged that the defendant, a lorry driver, had fallen asleep at the wheel of his lorry and had collided with a stationary vehicle on the hard shoulder of a motorway which resulted in two people losing their lives. He had been driving for some 350 miles and had been at the wheel for approximately six out of the preceding 12 hours. He had taken the regulation meal and rest breaks. His defence was that he had no awareness of what was taking place until the very last moment due to being in a trance-like state induced by driving for long distances on 'straight, flat, featureless motorways'. Expert medical evidence supported the contention. The defence claim was that he was in a state of automatism. The trial judge left the defence to the jury, which acquitted. The Attorney General referred to the Court of Appeal the question whether the defence was open to the respondent. The court held that the condition known as 'driving without awareness' could not support the defence of automatism. Lord Taylor CJ stated:

> In our judgment, the 'proper evidential foundation' was not laid in this case by ... [the] evidence of driving without awareness ... The defence of automatism requires that there was a total destruction of voluntary control on the defendant's part. Impaired, reduced or partial control is not enough. [Expert evidence] suggested that he would be able to steer the vehicle and usually to react and return to full awareness when confronted by significant stimuli.

The court relied upon the decisions in *Watmore v Jenkins* and *Robert v Ramsbottom* [1980] 1 WLR 823. In the former case, Winn J referred to the need for 'such a complete destruction of voluntary control as could constitute in law automatism', and in the latter case, the court accepted the proposition that 'one cannot accept as exculpation anything less than total loss of consciousness'.

In *Broome v Perkins* [1987] Crim LR 271, the defendant had been charged with driving without due care and attention. He had driven his vehicle erratically for some six miles. His conviction was upheld even though there was evidence to establish that he was suffering from hypoglycaemia (low blood sugar); he must have been exercising conscious control of the vehicle, albeit imperfectly, in order to have manoeuvred the vehicle reasonably successfully over such a distance. This case had been criticised by the Law Commission (Law Com 177, 1989, Vol 2, para 11.4) and was distinguished in *T* [1990] Crim LR 256). In this case, T, a young French woman, stabbed another woman in the course of a robbery. It was later established that she was suffering from post-traumatic stress as a result of having been raped three days prior to her arrest. The Crown argued that she must have had some control over her actions to be able to open the blade of the knife prior to the stabbing. It was held that the case could be distinguished on the basis that T had been in a 'dream', whereas in *Broome v Perkins* there had been partial control. It is perhaps reassuring that the court thought that the categories of automatism are not closed, although there are no real signs of them being widened.

2.3.1 Self-induced automatism

The position in relation to self-induced automatism was originally established in *Quick*. The Court of Appeal held, in the case of a diabetic who had failed to eat properly and who had consumed too much alcohol after taking his insulin, that:

> a self-induced incapacity will not excuse ... nor will one which could have been reasonably foreseen as a result of either doing or omitting to do something, as, for example, taking alcohol against medical advice after using ... prescribed drugs or failing to have regular meals while taking insulin.

The conviction in that case was reversed on the ground that the defence of automatism ought to have been left to the jury to decide at the trial. As a result of *Bailey* [1983] 2 All ER 503, operation of the 'prior fault' doctrine in automatism is dependent upon whether the crime the defendant is alleged to have committed is classed by the courts as one of *specific intent* or *basic intent*. As will be seen in Chapter 3, the former is one where the prosecution must establish that the defendant *intended* to bring about the prohibited result; whereas the latter may be committed *recklessly*, that is, the defendant has knowingly engaged in risk-taking activity (with the exception of s 1 of the CDA 1971, where recklessness has an alternative, objective meaning). A defendant cannot be guilty of a crime requiring specific intent if he or she was suffering from automatism, even if it was self-induced. Where the crime is one of basic intent, however, and the automatism was induced by the voluntary consumption of drink or drugs or was otherwise self-induced, then the defendant has no defence, even if the effect of the intoxication was to deprive him of *mens rea*. This is because subjective awareness on the part of the defendant that, for example, consuming drugs or failing to eat properly may render him uncontrolled, aggressive or unpredictable, amounts to recklessness on his part and thus he is liable for crimes of basic intent where recklessness suffices for the *mens rea*. Griffiths LJ in *Bailey* stated the law as follows:

> The question in each case will be whether the prosecution have proved the necessary element of recklessness ... if the accused knows that his actions or inactions are likely to make him aggressive ... with the result that he may cause some injury ... and he persists in the action or takes no remedial action ... it will be open to the jury to find that he was reckless [p 765].

It follows that if the defendant was taking medically prescribed drugs and was *unaware* that they would make him or her aggressive, then he may be able successfully to plead automatism. In *Hardie* [1984] 3 All ER 848, the defendant consumed several Valium tablets which belonged to his former girlfriend. He was unaware of the effect of this drug. He started a fire in his friend's flat and was convicted of damaging property with intent to endanger life contrary to s 1(2) of the CDA 1971. His appeal was allowed. Parker LJ stated:

> In the present instance, the defence was that the Valium was taken for the purpose of calming the nerves only, that it was old stock and that the appellant was told it would do him no harm. There was no evidence that it was known to the appellant or even generally known that the taking of Valium in the quantity taken would be liable to render a person aggressive or incapable of appreciating risks to others or have other side effects such that its self-administration would itself have an element of recklessness. It is true that Valium is a drug and it is true that it was taken deliberately and not taken on medical prescription, but the drug is, in our view, wholly different in kind from drugs which are liable to cause unpredictability or aggressiveness. It may well be that the taking of a sedative or soporific drug will, in certain circumstances, be no answer, for example in a case of reckless driving, but if the effect of a drug is merely soporific or sedative the taking of it, even in some excessive quantity, cannot in the ordinary way raise a *conclusive* presumption against the admission of proof of intoxication for the purpose of disproving *mens rea* in ordinary crimes, such as would be the case with alcoholic intoxication or incapacity or automatism resulting from the self-administration of dangerous drugs.

2.3.2 Reform of automatism as a defence

The law is clearly in need of reform in this area. The Butler Committee on Mentally Abnormal Offenders (*Report of the Committee on Mentally Abnormal Offenders*, Cmnd 6244, 1975) recommended radical reforms and most of its proposals have been adopted by the Law Commission in its proposed Criminal Code. The Commission's proposals would, if enacted, effectively abolish the distinction between internal and external factors.

Clause 33(1) proposes that:

A person is not guilty of an offence if:

(a) he acts in a state of automatism, that is, his act:

    (i) is a spasm or convulsion; or

    (ii) occurs while he is in a condition (whether of sleep, unconsciousness, impaired consciousness or otherwise) depriving him of effective control of the act; and

(b) the act or condition is the result neither of anything done or omitted with the fault required for the offence nor of voluntary intoxication.

However, to deal with the defendant who still poses a continuing 'threat' to others, cl 34 provides that a defendant acquitted under cl 33 would be the subject of a 'mental disorder' verdict and the court would still have wide and flexible sentencing powers (which would include the power to compel the individual to receive in-hospital medical treatment). If parliament adopted these proposals, many of the problems experienced by those suffering from some kind of mental disorder, short of insanity, would be alleviated and the defence would cease to be the 'quagmire of law' identified by Lawton LJ in *Quick* as long ago as 1973 (for a detailed analysis of the Law Commission's proposals, see Pt 2 of the proposed Criminal Code (Law Com 177, 1989)).

2.4 CAUSATION

Establishing causation is not a science. Many find causation a complex issue because, as has been outlined, it is often difficult to identify strict principles of law. In determining whether or not causation has been established, judges often seem to be strongly influenced by policy considerations.

The authors of the leading work explain the problem as follows:

For writers of the first school 'policy' is just a name for an immense variety of considerations which do weigh and should weigh with courts considering the question of the existence or extent of responsibility. No exhaustive enumeration can be given of such factors and no general principles can be laid down as to how a balance should be struck between them. Policy, on this interpretation, is atomised: the courts must focus attention on the precise way in which harm has eventuated in a particular case, and then ask and answer, in a more or less intuitive fashion, whether or not on these particular facts a defendant should be held responsible. The court's function is to pass judgments acceptable to society for their time and place on these matters, and general policies can never take the place of judgment [Hart and Honoré, *Causation in the Law*, 2nd edn, 1985, Oxford: OUP, p 103].

The issue of causation is best understood as a two-stage process. The first involves proof that the defendant, as a matter of fact, caused the prohibited result. The second stage involves proof that the defendant was the cause in law of the prohibited result.

Causation in fact is normally established by resort to the so-called 'but for' test – 'but for the defendant's actions would the victim have died?' If the answer is 'no', causation in fact is established. If the answer is 'yes', it in effect means that the victim would have died anyway – hence the defendant's act cannot be seen as causative. For example, D is involved in a fight with P and as a consequence D strikes P a blow which renders him unconscious. An ambulance is called, and as it speeds P to hospital it is involved in a traffic accident which results in the death of the driver and patient. For the sake of simplicity, let us assume that the ambulance driver bears no responsibility for the accident, it having being caused solely by the fact that the front tyres blew out as a result of a defect in the manufacturing process. Is D responsible for P's death? One fact is clear: P would still be alive but for his involvement in the fight and if he had not been hit by D. *White* [1910] 2 KB 124 is authority on this point. D put poison in his mother's drink intending to kill her. She consumed the drink but died shortly afterwards of natural causes. Clearly, D had intended to kill his mother but he was not a cause in fact of her death. In such cases, the prosecution would now obviously proceed with a charge of attempt contrary to the Criminal Attempts Act 1981.

Assuming causation, in fact, can be established beyond all reasonable doubt by the prosecution, causation in law will have to be established. Although, as will be seen, there have been a number of notable cases where difficult issues of causation have had to be determined by the courts, it should be recognised that these are very much the exception. In simple cases, it may prove that no direction to the jury is needed at all – indeed the defence will not contest the facts relating to causation. Where some direction is felt necessary, the most simple approach is to direct the jury in terms of reasonable foreseeability. Was the causing of the prohibited result the reasonably forseeable consequence of the defendant's act? The test is objective. At this stage of the inquiry, the law is not concerned with what the defendant might or might not have foreseen. Where the defendant is tried on indictment, therefore, it is essentially an issue for the jury to determine. Such additional guidance as the trial judge might consider necessary might emphasise the following:

- in cases of homicide, it is rarely necessary to give the jury any direction on causation as such;

- how a victim comes by his death is not usually in dispute: it is usually other matters which are in dispute, for example, did the accused have the necessary intent?;

- the established principle to put to the jury is that, in law, 'the accused's act need not be the sole cause or even the main cause of the victim's death, it being enough that his act contributed significantly to that result', and that the actions of the defendant were an 'operative, proximate or substantial cause of the *actus reus*'. As Widgery LJ observed in *Cato* [1976] 1 All ER 260:

  ... it was not necessary for the prosecution to prove that the heroin was the only cause of the death. As a matter of law, it was sufficient if the prosecution could establish that it was a cause, provided it was a cause outside the *de minimis* range, and effectively bearing on the acceleration of the moment of the victim's death ...

- it is possible for there to be more than one cause of a result and two or more people can be independently liable in respect of the same harm.

What argument can a defendant raise in order to refute the prosecution assertion that he has caused the prohibited consequence as a matter of law? Provided the facts supply some evidential basis for doing so, he can assert that the prohibited consequence, for example the death of the victim where the charge involves homicide, was caused not by his act, but results from a *novus actus interveniens* – literally a new intervening act. Given that, if successful, such an argument will absolve a defendant from liability for the completed offence the courts have, perhaps understandably, been reluctant to recognise many instances where such a break in the chain of causation can be said to have arisen.

Broadly, the issue of *novus actus* can be divided into those instances where the assertion is that the victim of the offence, through his own action or inaction, broke the chain of causation in law, and those where the assertion is that the acts or omissions of a third party constitute the *novus actus*.

A defence argument that blames and identifies the victim as the author of his own misfortune is never going to be particularly attractive in a criminal case. Early cases, such as *Holland* (1841) 2 Mood & R 351, show that the courts would not regard the refusal of medical treatment by the victim of an assault as a factor that could absolve the assailant of liability where the victim subsequently died from his injuries. The deeper rationale here is clearly that if the defendant had not carried out the original assault, the victim's refusal of medical treatment would not have become a factor. The modern authority on this point is to be found in the Court of Appeal's decision in *Blaue* [1975] 3 All ER 446, which confirmed the applicability of the civil law principle that 'one takes one's victim as one finds him' to the criminal law of causation (this is often referred to as the 'thin skull rule'). If there is something unusual about the physical, mental or emotional make-up of the victim so that the consequence is much more serious than the defendant foresaw, or could have foreseen, then this is irrelevant so far as the *actus reus* is concerned and the defendant is considered to have caused the consequence. In *Blaue*, the deceased had been stabbed and required a blood transfusion if her life was to be saved. The woman was a Jehovah's Witness and refused to contemplate a blood transfusion and died a few hours later. Counsel argued that if her decision not to have a blood transfusion was unreasonable then it should be held that the chain of causation had been broken. But, pondered Lawton LJ, reasonable by whose standards?

> Those of the Jehovah's Witnesses? Humanists? Roman Catholics? Protestants of Anglo-Saxon descent? The man on the Clapham omnibus? ... It has long been the policy of the law that those who use violence on other people must take their victims as they find them. This in our judgment means the whole man, not just the physical man. It does not lie in the mouth of the assailant to say that the victim's religious beliefs which inhibited him from accepting certain kinds of treatment were unreasonable. The question for decision is what caused her death. The answer is the stab wound. The fact that the victim refused to stop this end coming about did not break the causal connection between the act and the death [p 1415].

Both *Blaue* and *Holland* are cases of omission, in the sense that in both cases the victims chose not to avail themselves of the help available. Can the principle that the defendant takes his victim as he finds him be extended to positive acts on the part of the victim that exacerbate harm caused by the defendant? *Dear* [1996] Crim LR 595 appears to support the view that it can. Following allegations by the appellant's 12-year-old daughter that the deceased had sexually assaulted her, the appellant badly injured the deceased with the result that he was hospitalised. He died two days later and there was some evidence to suggest that he had committed suicide, presumably because of his shame and remorse. In particular the evidence suggested that the deceased had either picked at the wounds inflicted by the appellant, thus causing them to become infected, or that they had re-opened naturally and the deceased had failed to secure medical treatment to prevent infection. The appellant argued that the suicide therefore acted as a *novus actus interveniens* and that his conviction for murder should be overturned. The Court of Appeal dismissed his appeal on the basis that the question which had been left to the jury, simply whether the injuries inflicted by the appellant were an 'operating and substantial' cause of the death, was correct and that the jury had been perfectly entitled to answer that question in the affirmative.

The defendant may well, by his actions, endanger or threaten a victim with the result that the victim feels compelled to attempt some sort of escape from the danger. Such perilous situations raise the possibility that the victim may be injured in the course of effecting such an escape. When, if ever, can a defendant cite the victim's actions as a *novus actus* absolving him from responsibility for the injuries caused in any such escape?

In *Roberts* (1971) 56 Cr App R 95, the victim jumped from the defendant's car in order to escape from his sexual advances. The car was travelling between 20 and 40 mph and she sustained injuries. The defendant was convicted of assault occasioning actual bodily harm and he appealed on the basis that there was a lack of causation. His appeal was dismissed because the victim's actions were a natural consequence of the attack and a likely reaction in the circumstances she found herself in. Significantly, however, Stephenson LJ went on to observe, albeit *obiter*, that the chain of causation in law could be broken if the victim undertook an escape that was so foolhardy as to be 'daft' or so 'unexpected ... that ... no reasonable man could be expected to foresee it ...'

The potential for conflict with *Blaue* is apparent. The defendant must take his vicitim as he finds him – the whole person, not just their physical idiosyncracies – but the chain of causation is broken if the victim acts foolishly. Would not the refusal of medical treatment on unacceptable grounds break the chain of causation? Suppose the victim refuses to receive a blood transfusion unless it can be guaranteed that the donor was of the same ethnic origin as the victim and the victim dies before such supplies can be arranged. Is such a refusal 'daft' or should the court proceed on the basis that, notwithstanding the refusal, the harm inflicted by the defendant is to be regarded as the operating and substantial cause of death? What of the rape victim who subsequently commits suicide? Could the rapist also be convicted of her murder? There has never been a successful prosecution in England and the problems of proof for the prosecution would be formidable (it would have to be proved, for example, that the victim would not have killed herself but for the rape). However, it is submitted that the case law would support such a conviction. This could be either on the *Blaue* principle that a defendant takes his victim as he finds her, or on the basis of the foreseeability test.

Where the court is dealing specifically with an 'escape' scenario, where the victim has acted on the spur of the moment, perhaps in a panic and without the opportunity for mature reflection, in response to real or imagined circumstances which the victim would prefer to avoid, it will endeavour to find a middle way between these two positions. This is evidenced by the analysis of the problem offered by the Court of Appeal in *Williams* [1992] 2 All ER 183. The deceased had been hitchhiking to a festival in Glastonbury and was offered a lift in a car driven by Williams and containing two friends. Five miles later the deceased jumped from the car and died from head injuries sustained by falling onto the road. The car was travelling at about 30 mph. Evidence was adduced to establish that as he jumped from the moving car an object, thought to be his wallet, flew into the air. The Crown's case was that the occupants of the car had made to rob the deceased and he had sought to take avoiding action. The Court of Appeal was of the opinion that the deceased's conduct had to be proportionate to the gravity of the threat, otherwise the deceased's conduct would amount to a voluntary act, a *novus actus interveniens*, which would break the chain of causation. Stuart-Smith LJ expressed the test to be:

> ... the nature of the threat is of importance considering both the foreseeability of harm to the victim from the threat and the question of whether the deceased's conduct was proportionate to the threat; that is to say that it was within the ambit of reasonableness and not so daft as to make his own voluntary act one which amounted to a *novus actus interveniens* and consequently broke the chain of causation.

He emphasised, however, that it had to borne in mind that a victim '... may in the agony of the moment do the wrong thing ... and the fact that in the agony of the moment he may act without thought and deliberation ...' (p 191).

In the result, the failure of the trial judge to give any direction to the jury on the matter of causation was held by the Court of Appeal to amount to a misdirection and the conviction was quashed.

It is, therefore, incumbent upon trial judges to give a direction on causation, in such circumstances, which should be in these terms:

- was it reasonably foreseeable that some harm, albeit not serious harm, was likely to result from the defendant's threat?

- in addition, was the reaction one which might have been expected from someone in that situation, taking account of any particular characteristic and the fact that one might act instinctively in the circumstances?

- there is no need to establish that the accused foresaw the victim's actions, although the objective test of reasonable foresight is based on what a reasonable person in the accused's situation (excluding his personal characteristics) would have foreseen (see *Majoram* [2000] Crim LR 372).

At some point, however, the line has to be drawn between those actions of the victim that are linked by a chain of causation to those of the defendant and those that are not. If D supplies P with a loaded gun and P, being a sane adult with full knowledge that the gun is loaded, places the barrel of the gun in his own mouth and pulls the trigger, it would be very hard to say that D was the cause in law of P's death. The case would be treated as one of suicide. At most, D might be charged with aiding and abetting the suicide if there was any evidence to suggest this. The rule in *Blaue* would cease to apply because P would not be a 'victim' of D's actions. P's death is brought about by his own independent positive and sentient act. As Professor Glanville Williams contended in his *Textbook of Criminal Law* (2nd edn, 1983, London: Sweet & Maxwell):

> What a person does if he has reached adult years, is of sound mind and is not acting under mistake, intimidation or other similar pressure, is his own responsibility and is not regarded as having been caused by other people [p 39].

Prosecutions of defendants supplying drugs to those users who subsequently overdose have raised similar causational problems. It was decided in *Dalby* [1982] 1 All ER 916 that the accused's supply of the drug Diconal to the deceased, albeit an unlawful act, was not a cause of his death. The act of supply had not caused immediate injury and it could not be maintained that the supply was a substantial cause of death. The deceased had injected himself with the drug and this action, and not the supply, was the cause of his death. This approach was followed in *Dias* [2002] Crim LR 490, where D was convicted of manslaughter having purchased heroin with P, and having prepared the syringe containing a heroin mixture that P then injected himself with. Although the possession of heroin by D was an unlawful act, that unlawful act did not cause P's death. Regarding the extent to which P's actions could be said to have amounted to a *novus actus*, Keene LJ observed that P was an adult able to decide for himself whether or not to inject the heroin. He added:

> His own action in injecting himself might well have been seen as an intervening act between the supply of the drug by the appellant and the death of [the deceased]. The chain of causation was probably broken by that intervening act ... Assistance and encouragement is not to be automatically equated with causation. Causation raises questions of fact and degree. The recipient does not have to inject the drug which he is encouraged and assisted to take. He has a choice. It may be that in some circumstances the causative chain will still remain. That is a matter for the jury to decide.

Regarding the actions of third parties, there is evidence to suggest that these will not break the chain of causation provided they are a reasonably foreseeable consequence of the defendant's actions. In *Pagett* (1983) 76 CR App R 279, for example, the defendant shot at armed police whilst using his pregnant girlfriend as a shield. The girl was killed by shots fired at the defendant by the police. He was acquitted of the murder of the girl but convicted of her manslaughter. He appealed on the ground, *inter alia*, that on the question of causation the trial judge erred in directing the jury that it was for him to decide as a matter of law and not for the jury whether the defendant's act caused or was a cause of the girl's death. The Court of Appeal rejected his appeal and held that the act of the police officer was 'a reasonable act performed for the purpose of self-defence'. As it had been caused by the defendant's own acts, it did not operate as a *novus actus interveniens* and thus he was liable for the death of the victim.

Poor medical treatment after the defendant's initial unlawful act is often alleged to be a *novus actus interveniens*. In *Jordan* (1956) 40 Cr App R 152, the appellant stabbed the victim in a cafe and the victim died eight days later in hospital. The defendant sought to introduce further medical evidence to demonstrate that the wound was not the cause of death. The court found that the stab wound had penetrated the victim's intestine in two places but that it had mainly healed at the time of death. To prevent infection he was given an antibiotic but he soon displayed signs of intolerance to the drug and it was withdrawn. Unfortunately, the next day a different doctor ordered that the treatment be resumed and as a result the victim died from broncho-pneumonia. The court held that death resulting from any normal treatment employed to deal with the after-effects of an unlawful assault would normally be regarded as having been caused by the injury. In this case the treatment was not normal, hence the conviction was quashed.

Not surprisingly, the decision in *Jordan* led to concern within the medical profession that this was placing too much emphasis on the treatment given by medical staff and diverting attention away from the wrongdoer whose actions had led to the need for medical attention in the first place. Whilst never having been expressly overruled, it has been described as 'a very peculiar case' (*Blaue*) and is therefore best considered to be an unusual case and to be confined to its facts.

Much more representative of the law today is *Smith* [1959] 2 All ER 193 where the Courts Martial Appeal Court distinguished *Jordan* and upheld the defendant's conviction for murder. Here, an army doctor failed to diagnose the victim's pierced lung which resulted from a fight between two soldiers. The evidence suggested that the treatment given to the soldier was 'thoroughly bad and might well have affected his chances of recovery'. Nevertheless, the court dismissed his appeal. Lord Parker CJ stating that:

> ... if at the time of death the original wound is still an operating cause and a substantial cause, then the death can properly be said to be the result of the wound, albeit that some other cause of death is also operating. Only if it can be said that the original wound is merely the setting in which another cause operates can it be said that the death does not result from the wound. Putting it another way, only if the second cause is so overwhelming as to make the original wound merely part of the history can it be said that death does not flow from the wound ... [p 198].

In *Malcherek and Steel* [1981] 2 All ER 422, two appeals giving rise to very similar points of law, both defendants were convicted of murder. They appealed on the basis that the doctors, by switching off life support equipment as a result of their belief that the victims were brain dead, had caused the deaths. The court dismissed their appeals, Lord Lane CJ making it clear that:

> ... if treatment is given *bona fide* by competent and careful medical practitioners, then evidence will not be admissible to show that the treatment would not have been administered in the same way by other medical practitioners ... The fact that the victim has died despite or because of medical treatment for the initial injury given by careful and skilled medical practitioners will not exonerate the original assailant from responsibility for the death.

Thus, the fact that medical treatment was inadequate or even negligent will not necessarily relieve the accused of liability for his or her actions. In *Cheshire* [1991] 3 All ER 670, Beldam LJ referred to the Australian case of *Evans and Gardiner (No 2)* (1976) VR 523 as an illustration of how difficult it can be to shift the burden of responsibility onto medical practitioners. In that case, the appellants had stabbed the victim but death had not occurred for nearly a year, during which time he had 'resumed an apparently healthy life'. The cause of death was a stricture of the small bowel which is a not uncommon occurrence after surgery carried out to repair stab wounds. Should the doctors have diagnosed the problem and taken remedial action? Was their failure tantamount to negligence? The Supreme Court of Victoria applied the accepted English test by posing the question whether the original act was still an 'operating and substantial cause of death' – taken from the *dictum* of Parker CJ in *Smith* – and concluded that it was.

In *Cheshire*, the appellant shot his victim in the thigh and stomach. Whilst being treated in hospital, the victim developed respiratory problems and was given a tracheotomy. At his trial a medical witness suggested that the original wounds were no longer life-threatening and that his chances of survival were good. Indeed, it was suggested that medical negligence had caused the victim's death. The court dismissed the appeal, Beldam LJ stating:

> Even though the negligence of the treatment ... was the immediate cause of his death, the jury should not regard it as excluding the responsibility of the accused unless the negligent treatment was so independent of his acts, and in itself so potent in causing death, that they regard the contribution made by his acts as insignificant ... it is not the function of the jury to evaluate competing causes so as to choose which is dominant provided they are satisfied that the accused's acts can fairly be said to have made a significant contribution to the victim's death.

A new dimension to the medical treatment cases arose in *McKechnie* [1992] Crim LR 194 where the wound prevented medical treatment for an independent condition which would have saved the victim's life. The accused had attacked the victim causing severe brain damage. Soon after his admission to hospital it was discovered that he had a duodenal ulcer but the medical opinion was that because of his injuries no attempt should be made to operate on the ulcer. Five weeks later the ulcer burst and as a result the victim died. The trial judge had directed the jury that they must be convinced that the injuries to the head had significantly contributed to his death. He also stressed that they must be satisfied that the medical decision not to operate was reasonable. The Court of Appeal found nothing wrong with this direction and in light of the strong wording in *Cheshire* this must be regarded as correct. Presumably, there was nothing 'extraordinary and unusual' in the decision not to operate, nor in the medical treatment that ensued following his admission to hospital. The beating the victim received at McKechnie's hands put him in a position where he was unable to receive the necessary treatment and, in principle, there seems to be no difference between this and the case where the defendant's act results in the victim receiving medical treatment from which he dies.

2.4.1 Reform

This area has not been subjected to comprehensive law reform consideration either by the Law Commission or the Criminal Law Revision Committee. The Commission's (proposed) codification of the criminal law (Law Com 177, 1989) sought in these circumstances simply to restate the existing common law principles. Clause 17 provides:

(1) A person causes a result which is an element of an offence when:

    (a) he does an act which makes a more than negligible contribution to its occurrence; or

    (b) he omits to do an act which might prevent its occurrence and which he is under a duty to do according to the law relating to the offence.

(2) A person does not cause a result where, after he does such an act or makes such an omission, an act or event occurs:

    (a) which is the immediate and sufficient cause of the result;

    (b) which he did not foresee; and

    (c) which could not in the circumstances reasonably have been foreseen.

The codification team debated whether the code should contain a provision on causation at all, because two types of objection had been received as a result of the consultation exercise held between 1985 and 1989. These were, first, that such a provision was unnecessary because causation is a matter of fact for the jury to decide; and, secondly, that such a definition would provoke unproductive argument among the jury (Vol 2, para 7.20). The Commission decided in the event to include cl 17 because it felt that a failure to include it would necessitate trial judges going back to the common law principles and thus one of the principal aims of codification – to state the known law clearly – would be defeated (para 7.21). They felt that judges would be well able to explain the meaning of the clause in language suitable to the jury's needs and that this would not produce any more confusion than exists at the present time. For a detailed and well-argued critique of cl 17, see Professor Glanville Williams' article, *'Finus* for *novus actus'* ([1989] CLJ 391).

English law is similar to American law so far as causation is concerned. The American Law Institute's Model Penal Code (1962) provides:

Section 2.03

(1) Conduct is the cause of a result when:

    (a) it is an antecedent but for which the result in question would not have occurred; and

    (b) the relationship between the conduct and the result satisfies any additional causal requirements imposed by the Code or by the law defining the offence.

(2) When purposely or knowingly causing a particular result is an element of an offence, the element is not established if the actual result is not within the purpose or the contemplation of the actor unless:

    ...

    (b) the actual result involves the same kind of injury or harm as that designed or contemplated and is not too remote or accidental in its occurrence to have a just bearing on the actor's liability or on the gravity of his offence.

Issues of disputed causation are, therefore, left to the jury's sense of 'justice'.

Since 1989, the Law Commission has given further consideration to aspects of causation in its report on *Legislating the Criminal Code: Involuntary Manslaughter* (Law Com 237, 1996) where it recommended a new offence of corporate killing based upon management failure by a corporate body. It recommended that corporate liability should arise if the failure was the cause or one of the causes of a person's death. The Commission took the view that the ordinary rules of causation would be inadequate to link the decision-making processes of corporate bodies with the ultimate consequence of death. The risk would be that the management failure would simply be regarded as a 'stage already set' and thus the corporation itself would avoid liability. The Commission is adamant that even though the management failure is not the immediate cause of death, liability ought not to be avoided unless a jury accepts that the intervening act or omission of an *individual* is a complete *novus actus interveniens* (see Chapter 6 for a more detailed discussion of the report).

2.5   OMISSIONS

The general rule is that there is no liability for omissions unless either the statute creating the offence has been interpreted by the courts as creating such liability or the omission comes within one of the common law exceptions to the rule. As Stephen J stated in 1887:

> A sees B drowning and is able to save him by holding out his hand. A abstains from doing so in order that B may be drowned. A has committed no offence! [*Digest of the Criminal Law*].

The court will look at a particular statutory word or phrase and decide whether it is capable of creating liability for omitting to act. Parliament has established many positive duties to act and they usually present few problems. Examples of such crimes are:

- failing to report a road traffic accident (s 170 of the RTA 1988);
- failure to provide a police officer with a specimen of breath (s 6 of the RTA 1988);
- failure to provide for a child in one's care in terms of food, clothing and medical care (s 1(2) of the Children and Young Persons Act 1933).

These are all examples of crimes where parliament's wishes are perfectly clear. But this is often not the case. In *Shama* [1990] 2 All ER 602, for example, the defendant was convicted under s 17(1)(a) of the TA 1968 for falsifying a document when he had *omitted* to fill in a form which it was his statutory duty to complete. Section 17(1)(a) provides that a defendant is liable if he 'destroys, defaces, conceals or *falsifies* any ... document made or required for any accountancy purpose' (emphasis added). In *Firth* (1990) 92 Cr App R 217, a doctor was convicted of deceiving a hospital contrary to s 2 of the TA 1978, when he failed to inform the hospital authority that some of his patients were being treated privately and were not NHS patients. Section 2 makes it an offence, *inter alia*, 'to dishonestly *secure* the remission of ... any existing liability to make a payment, whether his own liability or another's' (emphasis added). Words such as 'obstructing a highway' (*Gully v Smith* (1883) 12 QBD 121) and 'misconduct' are other examples which the courts have held capable of creating liability for omission. 'Causing' (*Price v Cromack* [1975] 2 All ER 113), 'harbouring' (*Darch v Weight* [1984] 1 WLR 659) and 'assisting the doing' (*Brown* [1970] 1 QB 105), on the other hand, have been held to exclude liability. Other words, such as 'act', have been held to be capable of both interpretations. Compare *Yuthiwattana* (1984) 80 Cr App R 55 with *Ahmad* (1986) 84 Cr App R 64. Both are concerned with the meaning of 'act' as found in s 1(3) of the Protection from Eviction Act 1977. The former case held that the offence was capable of creating liability for omission, whilst the latter adopted a more strict approach to statutory interpretation and decided the opposite. The result is a degree of uncertainty in this area of the law.

The common law contains a number of important exceptions to the general rule. Whilst they are best approached as separate instances of areas in which the courts have established a positive duty to act, they tend to share a common theme – the defendant has assumed a responsibility, creating an expectation in the minds of others that he will act.

2.5.1 The common law duty to act: a relationship of reliance

Problems can arise in the situation where a person voluntarily assumes a responsibility towards another person and then fails to act in accordance with that duty. This is a particularly challenging problem in an era of a rapidly ageing population where the relatives of elderly people increasingly feel obliged to provide a degree of help and support. The question arises as to the standard of care such carers are obliged to provide and the consequences of failing to meet that standard if the elderly person – who may be very frail, ill and confused – dies. Is the carer (who may have been reluctant to assume any responsibility both before and during the assumption of responsibility) guilty of manslaughter?

Early cases such as *Instan* [1893] 1 QB 450 indicated that the moral duty to care for one's blood relatives – especially where the arrangement was that one member of the family (D) had agreed to live with and sustain another member of the family (P) – would be reflected in a common law duty resting upon D to maintain P. If D failed to discharge this duty, D could be held liable for the consequences:

> It would not be correct to say that every moral obligation involves a legal duty; but every legal duty is founded on a moral obligation. A legal duty is nothing else than the enforcing by law of that which is a moral obligation without legal enforcement.

Today there would be no need for the courts to identify a blood relationship between D and P. The key to whether or not a common law duty can be imposed is the issue of reliance. The leading authority is the Court of Appeal's decision in *Stone and Dobinson* [1977] 2 All ER 341. Stone, a 67-year-old, cohabited with Dobinson, aged 43. The latter was described as 'ineffectual and inadequate'. Mr Stone was partially deaf, nearly blind and of low intelligence. They both looked after Stone's mentally subnormal son. Stone's 61-year-old sister, Fanny, came to live with them. Fanny suffered from anorexia nervosa and had very little to do with the rest of the family. She spent most of her time alone in her room, although she sometimes cooked herself some food when Stone and Dobinson visited the pub. In the spring of 1975, the defendants unsuccessfully attempted to contact Fanny's doctor but they walked to the wrong village. In July, Fanny fell ill and was confined to bed. Both defendants were incapable of using telephones and a neighbour was unsuccessful in getting a local doctor to visit Fanny. The sister died in August and a pathologist's report indicated she must have been in serious need of medical attention. The defendants were both convicted of manslaughter and appealed on the basis that they had not assumed a duty of care in relation to her. They argued the point on the basis that Fanny had come to the house as a lodger and that, due to her own eccentricity, she became infirm and immobile and unable to look after herself. The court dismissed their appeal, Geoffrey Lane LJ commenting that:

> ... whether Fanny was a lodger or not she was a blood relative of the appellant; she was occupying a room in his house; Dobinson had undertaken the duty of trying to wash her; of taking such food to her as she required ... This was not a situation analogous to the drowning stranger. They did make efforts to care ... The jury was entitled to find a duty had been assumed.

But this analysis presupposes that the carer *freely chooses* to assume a duty of care and then neglects to discharge it adequately. What if the carer felt he or she had little real choice because the elderly and infirm relative had nowhere else to go, or, simply refused to go elsewhere? What if the carer provides a room on the clear understanding that the 'lodger' is to be solely responsible for his or her own health and welfare? What if the carer is himself old, infirm, sick and barely able to cope with his own problems, never mind anybody else's? How can the carer *give up* a duty once assumed? Inform the Social Services Department? What if Social Services have run out of money and are unable to provide the sick person with alternative accommodation? As Professor Hogan commented:

> What is disturbing about *Stone* is that the evidence hardly supported the inference that these two elderly [one was 43!] incompetents had taken it upon themselves to discharge the onerous task of looking after the sister. Did they really kill the sister? ['Omissions and a duty myth', in Smith (ed), *Criminal Law: Essays in Honour of JC Smith*, 1987, London: Butterworths].

A second point arising from the case law is that, as we have seen, it takes very little for the law to place this duty of care on the carer's shoulders. Simply providing a room might be enough, particularly if the person involved is a relative. The more one does for somebody in Fanny's position the more likely it is that a voluntary duty will have been assumed. Conversely, the more harsh and uncaring a person is the less likely he is to assume such a duty!

Even if a relationship develops where D owes a duty of care to P, it may nevertheless be possible for P to relieve D of that duty, as the first instance ruling in *Smith* [1979] Crim LR 251 suggests. In this case, Mrs Smith was very suspicious of doctors and asked her husband not to seek medical assistance for her after she had experienced a stillbirth at home. Mr Smith complied with her request but her condition deteriorated and she died. He was charged with manslaughter (although acquitted as the jury were unable to reach a verdict). In his summing up to the jury, the judge placed considerable emphasis on the ability of the wife to engage in rational decision-making. If 'not too ill it may be reasonable to abide by her wishes. On the other hand, if she appeared desperately ill, then whatever she may say it might be right to override'.

2.5.2 The common law duty to act: creating a dangerous situation

The common law is reactive rather than dynamic. This means that new rules are 'discovered' when and if litigation throws up an opportunity for the courts to advance the law in any given area. Thus, the common law provides only a patchwork of rules on when liability for failing to act can arise. This creates the possibility that a situation may come before the courts where there does not appear to be any legal duty upon D to act, but the courts feel that there ought to be one. The facts giving rise to the appeal in *Miller* illustrate this problem only too well. The appellant was a squatter who lay on a mattress in a house and fell asleep with a lighted cigarette in his hand. He awoke to find the mattress on fire and he responded by simply going to the next room and resuming his slumbers. The house caught fire and was damaged. He was charged with arson contrary to s 1(3) of the CDA 1971 ('damaged by fire a house ... intending to do damage to such property or reckless as to whether such property would be damaged'). Consider the problems for the prosecution in this case. The appellant committed a positive act in lighting the cigarette but this was not an offence – the cigarette was his property. The burning of the mattress did involve damage to property belonging to another, but the appellant lacked *mens rea* at that point – he was asleep (effectively a defence of automatism).

Once he awoke the mattress was on fire and he did nothing to stop the fire spreading – hence his liability has to be based on his failure to act. The problem for the prosecution is that the common law duties applicable at the time related to circumstances of reliance, as outlined above. These were clearly inapplicable on the facts. As a matter of public policy Lord Diplock was of the view that those who accidentally caused harm and realised that they had done so should be under a legal duty to limit the harmful potential of their accidental or unconscious acts. As he observed:

> I see no rational ground for excluding from conduct capable of giving rise to criminal liability, conduct which consists of failing to take measures that lie within one's power to counteract a danger that one has oneself created ... provided that, at the moment of awareness, it lies within his power to take steps, either himself or by calling for the assistance of the fire brigade if this be necessary, to prevent or minimise the damage to the property at risk ....

Note the interplay here between *actus reus* and *mens rea*. The common law duty to act only arises if D is aware that his accidental or unconscious actions will cause harm. If D is blithely unaware that he has caused such harm, no legal duty to act arises. Lord Diplock was understandably reluctant to enlarge upon what D is required to do once he discovers that his accidental or unconscious act is causing harm. The test appears to suggest a subjective approach which, it is submitted, must be right. D should do the best that *he* can to limit the effect of the harm. It would be pointless to require D to take steps he could never be capable of taking. Hence, what is required may vary according to the age, knowledge, experience and skills of D. It begs the question as to what would be expected of D who knocks over a paraffin lamp, starting a fire, but who fails to take basic steps to limit the harm because he has recently consumed LSD.

2.5.3   The duty to act arising from contract or office

Where a contract of employment can be identified, the courts may be willing to hold that the employee is under a duty to act to prevent harm to members of the public. For example, it will be an implied if not express term of the contract of employment entered into by a lifeguard at a swimming pool that he should go to the aid of any swimmer in difficulties. The duty inures to the benefit of the swimmer, notwithstanding that the parties to the contract are the employer and employee. Authority for this proposition is to be found in *Pittwood* (1902) 19 TLR 37. The defendant was employed as a gatekeeper responsible for closing the gates of a level crossing when a train was due. On this occasion he failed to shut the gate and a hay cart crossing the line was involved in a collision with a train. A man was killed as a result. The defendant was convicted of manslaughter. See also *Benge* (1865) 4 F & F 594.

The holding of a public office can also give rise to a positive duty to act. In *Dytham* [1979] 3 All ER 641, the appellant was a police officer who had been on duty outside a nightclub at 1 am and witnessed a security guard employed at the club carrying out a violent assault on the victim. The victim subsequently died from his injuries. The appellant was convicted of the common law offence of misconducting himself whilst acting as an officer of justice (that is, being present and a witness to a criminal offence and wilfully failing to carry out his duty as a police constable by omitting to take any steps to preserve the Queen's peace). Note that the offence charged related to the breach of duty itself and not to the consequence of the breach of duty – the death of the victim. A manslaughter charge against the appellant may have been viable but causation would have posed some difficulties. Could it be proved beyond all reasonable doubt that but for the appellant's failure to intervene the victim would not have died?

2.5.4 The duties of medical practitioners

The extent to which medical practitioners are under a positive legal duty to act to preserve the lives of patients has been subjected to judicial scrutiny, particularly by the House of Lords in *Airedale NHS Trust v Bland* [1993] 1 All ER 821. In this civil law case, the judges had to decide whether a young man, who had suffered 'catastrophic and irreversible' brain damage in the Hillsborough football stadium disaster and who was being fed artificially via a nasogastric tube, should cease to have this life-sustaining treatment with the inevitable result that death would occur a few days later. He had been in this persistent vegetative state (PVS) for some three years and it was agreed that there was no hope of improvement or recovery. He displayed no cognitive functions, sight, hearing, capacity to feel pain, and could not move his limbs or communicate in any way. On the one hand, it was submitted that by starting and continuing to feed and treat Anthony Bland, the doctors had undertaken a duty to provide medical treatment for an indefinite period. If this was so, then to withdraw artificial feeding, which would be treated as an omission rather than a positive act, would constitute murder. On the other hand, it was argued that when treatment started it was possible that recovery might occur and therefore it was in the patient's best interests that it should continue. However, when all hope of recovery had been abandoned it was not in his best interests to be kept alive. The result was that the justification for what was a non-consensual regime of treatment had disappeared and the doctors were not under a duty to provide nourishment. It followed that failure to do so did not amount to a breach of any duty and so could not be a criminal offence. This latter argument was accepted by the House of Lords. As Lord Mustill put it:

> Absent the duty, the omission to perform what had previously been a duty will no longer be a breach of the criminal law.

The House of Lords held that:

- there was no absolute rule that a patient's life had to be prolonged regardless of circumstances and that respect for human dignity had to be considered;
- the wishes of the patient must be considered. Where the patient is incapable of giving an informed consent, treatment may be provided if it is in the patient's best interests;
- if the treatment is futile there is no duty on the doctor to continue it if it is not in the patient's best interests.

The House of Lords held unanimously that medical staff could discontinue the treatment except for the purpose of enabling Mr Bland to die with maximum dignity and with the least distress.

It should also be noted that doctors are expected to act in accordance with any relevant professional guidelines and to seek the opinion of the Family Division of the High Court before discontinuing the treatment (see *Official Solicitor's Practice Note* [1994] 2 All ER 413). Lord Mustill acknowledged that the law was unclear on when a duty should be held to exist and went on to comment that the current state of the law was unsatisfactory, both morally and intellectually.

In *Re A (Children)* [2000] 4 All ER 961, the Court of Appeal was asked to rule on the legality of an operation to separate conjoined twins, M and J. The evidence was clear that if no operation was carried out, both M and J would die. If the twins were separated, J stood a good chance of survival but M was certain to die as she lacked her own vital organs. Ward LJ expressed the view that if the parents failed to arrange medical treatment to separate J from M, it could be argued that they themselves could incur criminal liability on the basis that they had failed to act in the best interests of J when under a legal duty to do so. Equally, he felt that the doctors could be guilty of murder for failing to carry out the separation. As he put it:

> I am bound to ask why the law will not hold that the doctors ... have come under a duty to [J]. If the operation is in her interests the parents must consent for their duty is to act consistent with her best interests ... The sole purpose of the enquiry is to establish whether either or both parents and doctors have come under a legal duty to [J], as I conclude they each have, to procure and to carry out the operation which will save her life. If so then performance of their duty to [J] is irreconcilable with the performance of their duty to [M]. Certainly it seems to me that if this court were to give permission for the operation to take place, then a legal duty would be imposed on the doctors to treat their patient in her best interests, ie, to operate upon her. Failure to do so is a breach of their duty. To omit to act when under a duty to do so may be a culpable omission.

The court proceeded to hold that doctors acting to separate the twins would be causing the death of M with intent to kill, but would either be excused from liability on the ground of necessity of circumstances, or on the basis that their actions were justifiable as reasonable force to protect J (see further Chapter 10).

2.6 THE CONTINUOUS ACT THEORY

Finally, reference has been made in this chapter to the importance of the *Miller* decision. This case decides that if the accused has done something which creates a dangerous situation then he is under a duty to prevent a particular result from occurring.

The House of Lords considered liability in the context of the continuous act and duty theories. The former is based upon the assumption that a crime is complete once the *mens rea* supervenes upon the continuing act. So, in *Fagan v Metropolitan Police Commissioner* [1968] All ER 442, the *actus reus* commenced when the car was driven onto the policeman's foot and continued until the car was removed. If during that period the defendant intended to allow it to remain there or was reckless as to whether or not it remained there, then the crime would be complete. The Court of Appeal favoured this approach in *Miller*. The mattress smouldered for a considerable period before setting alight. The defendant then became aware of the situation and chose to do nothing. At that moment the *mens rea* coincided with the *actus reus* and the crime was then complete. However, the House of Lords preferred the duty theory to found liability. Miller had created the danger, albeit inadvertently. Once he became aware of the situation he was under a duty to limit the damage as far as reasonably possible. His failure to react in a positive way was evidence of the breach of duty. (Note that Lord Diplock preferred the word 'responsibility' rather than the breach of duty.) This approach has the advantage of avoiding a decision on whether certain conduct is deemed 'continuing' for the purpose of the *actus reus* element of a crime. In *Kaitamaki* [1985] AC 147 and *Cooper v Schaub* [1994] Crim LR 531, it was held for the purposes of the law of rape that penetration was a continuing act. Therefore, if a man continues to penetrate a woman after she has withdrawn consent, then he commits rape, always assuming the other elements of the definition of the crime are present.

Miller did not deliberately set the mattress alight. A charitable interpretation is that it was merely an accident and therefore no fault element was present. The duty theory identifies the fault via the breach of duty rather than any fault at the outset of the escapade. The disadvantage of the breach of duty theory, however, is that, as has been pointed out by Professor Hogan ('Omissions and a duty myth', in Smith (ed), *Criminal Law: Essays in Honour of JC Smith*, 1987, London: Butterworths):

> it is likely to mislead a jury into thinking of duties in other than legal terms; into a consideration of the immorality of particular conduct; into convicting the defendant merely for his callousness ... To introduce an imprecise, ill defined concept of 'duty' into the equation only serves to confuse the issue.

He would prefer a judicial approach based upon causation and which simply examines all the conduct of the defendant and asks the question, did the defendant *cause* the *actus reus* and do so with the relevant *mens rea*?

2.7 REFORM

In the first draft of its proposed codification of the criminal law (*Criminal Law: Codification of the Criminal Law: A Report to the Law Commission*, Law Com 143, 1985), the Law Commission proposed to confine omissions to the more serious crimes involving offences against the person. However, as a result of the consultation exercise which followed, the Law Commission decided not to engage in elaborate law reform because it was too fraught with legal technical difficulties (their deliberations were informed by Professor Glanville Williams, 'What should the Code do about omissions?' ([1987] LS 92)). Hence, 'we have found ourselves unable to include a provision relating to omissions in our draft Bill' (Vol 2, para 7.9). The result is cl 16, which merely restates existing law ('references in this Act to an "act" shall, where the context permits, be read as including references to the omission, state of affairs or occurrence ...').

English law is similar to that prevailing in the US (American Law Institute, Model Penal Code, 1962, s 2.01(3)).

The problems involved with reforming this area of the law are:

- It is often difficult to distinguish between an act and an omission. For example, if a doctor withdraws life-saving medication from a newly-born and profoundly-handicapped baby who then dies, is this an act on the doctor's part or an omission?

- A general duty to act might impose liability on a large number of people and over-extend the frontiers of criminality. For example, if a large crowd of spectators at a football match observe a fight taking place and fail to take any action to stop it, are they *all* to be guilty of an offence? In *Stone and Dobinson*, ought the neighbour who helped wash Fanny also be liable for manslaughter?

- A general duty to act might cause people to over-interfere in their neighbour's business. For example if you passed the authors' houses and heard young children crying and in distress (a not uncommon occurrence!) should you notify the police? If you fail to do so and a child subsequently suffers injury at the hands of one of the authors, ought you to be a party to our crime?

- A general duty to act might give rise to problems with causation. Take the man identified by Stephen J who observes another man drowning and who could save him merely by holding out his hand but declines to do so. It is difficult to say the man died *but for* the defendant's failure to save him. The real reason he died was because he fell into the water or was carried away by the current – neither of which is in any way the fault of the defendant. More important in practice, however, are cases involving a failure to provide medical help. It might be very difficult for the prosecution to prove, beyond reasonable doubt, that the consequence, for example, death, would not have occurred at that particular time and in that particular manner, had medical help been sought.

SUMMARY OF CHAPTER 2

ACTUS REUS

THE REQUIREMENT FOR THE PROSECUTION TO PROVE THE EXTERNAL ELEMENTS OF THE ACT AND THAT IT WAS COMMITTED VOLUNTARILY

Actus reus refers to the external elements of an act (or in some cases an omission) together with circumstances and consequences required to establish the prohibited conduct elements of an offence. The prosecution must always prove these external elements if it is to succeed in its task. This applies even in the case of crimes classified as offences of strict liability.

The *actus reus* must be a voluntary act on the part of the defendant. In most cases this presents few problems. However, an exception concerns what is known as non-insane automatism. This consists of an involuntary movement of a person's body or limbs. The law attempts to identify the reason for the involuntary behaviour. If it is due to an 'external' factor, the actor's behaviour is excused because of its involuntary nature. But if the reason for the act relates to an 'internal factor' caused by a 'disease of the mind', the actor will be found to be not guilty by reason of insanity and might well face detention in a secure hospital. This can lead to injustice – particularly in the case of those suffering from epilepsy or diabetes. The Law Commission has published proposals designed both to alleviate this injustice and to protect society from people who pose a potential future threat. Parliament has yet to consider them.

CAUSATION

Causation can sometimes pose particular problems for students. It consists of a requirement that the prosecutor demonstrate that the defendant's conduct *caused* the prohibited result, that is, it would not have occurred 'but for' the defendant's conduct. Sometimes the defence claims that an intervening act occurred at some point between the commission of the initial act and the prohibited result; for example, the defendant might admit stabbing the victim but claim that the cause of the victim's death was the negligence of medical staff in the hospital where the victim was taken for treatment. The law is very reluctant to admit such claims. It is enough to ensure conviction if the defendant's acts were a significant cause of the prohibited result. They do not have to be the sole cause or even the main cause provided that they are not now 'merely part of the history'.

LIABILITY FOR OMISSIONS

The general rule is that there is no liability for omissions but there are many common law and statutory exceptions to this rule. Liability for omissions can cause particular problems for those who voluntarily assume the care of another (for example, elderly relatives) and for medical personnel who wish to discontinue life-preserving treatment for patients. The law is in urgent need of reform but the Law Commission has decided not to engage in reform at the present time because the area is too fraught with legal difficulties.

CHAPTER 3

THE MENTAL ELEMENT – *MENS REA*

3.1 INTRODUCTION

We saw in Chapter 2 that the prosecution must prove that the defendant brought about the prohibited act (or in some cases an omission or state of affairs). The prosecution's next task is to prove that the defendant did this with the state of mind prescribed by the definition of the crime. This is usually referred to as the *mens rea*, but is sometimes also described as the 'fault element' or 'mental element'. However, some caution is necessary here because 'fault' may be defined more broadly than *mens rea* or 'mental element'. So, there is no doubt that negligence is 'fault' but, traditionally, it is not included within the definition of *mens rea*. At common law, *mens rea* usually means intention or recklessness. If the prosecution merely has to prove negligence to establish the further element for liability, then the offence is one which requires proof of fault but not of *mens rea*. Yet, such distinctions cannot be made with absolute conviction, since the courts have recognised a concept of 'objective' recklessness which very closely resembles negligence. As Nicola Lacey observed in her article, 'A clear concept of intention: elusive or illusory?' ((1993) 56 MLR 621):

> *Mens rea* is the (not entirely happy) umbrella term used by most criminal law scholars to refer to a range of practical attitudes or states of mind on the defendant's part, which form part of the definition of many offences'.

There is a large number of offences in which the prosecution does not have to prove any fault element at all, neither *mens rea* nor even negligence. These are known as offences of *strict liability* (though, confusingly, judges sometimes refer to *absolute liability* which, as explained below at 3.8, is an even harsher form of liability).

The focus of this chapter will be:

- intention;
- recklessness;
- offences of strict liability.

Negligence will be considered in Chapter 6 in the context of involuntary manslaughter.

Difficulties of definition arise. Lord Simon referred to these in *DPP for Northern Ireland v Lynch* [1975] AC 653:

> A principal difficulty in this branch of the law is the chaotic terminology, whether in judgments, academic writings or statutes ... 'will, ... motive, purpose ... specific intention' ... such terms which do indeed overlap in certain contexts, seem frequently to be used interchangeably, without definition, and regardless that in some cases the legal usage is a term of art differing from the popular usage [p 688].

It is suggested that there are two principal reasons for the constantly changing meanings of such key words and expressions:

(a) If the courts adopted the standard dictionary definition of these terms, that would have the effect of excluding from criminal liability a number of defendants whom the judiciary believe ought not to be excluded.

(b) There is a lack of confidence amongst a number of senior judges in the ability of juries to understand complex evidence and to be able to discern truth from falsehood in some cases. The result is that some defendants are acquitted whom judges believe ought not to have been.

3.2   MOTIVE

Before analysing *mens rea* words it is vital to understand the role of motive in proving *mens rea*. A common mistake is to confuse these two, separate matters. Motive, be it good or bad, is generally said to be irrelevant. Take a so-called 'mercy killer' who the jury believe acted from what he understood to be the highest motives when he gave his terminally ill wife, at her own request, a fatal dose of drugs intending that her horrific suffering might cease and that she die quickly and with dignity. If he killed and intended to kill her, why he did so – his motive – is irrelevant to the issue of guilt. This man is guilty in law of murder. In *Chandler v DPP* [1964] AC 763 Campaign for Nuclear Disarmament activists planned a 'sit-in' at a military airfield in order to prevent aircraft movements. They were convicted under s 1 of the Official Secrets Act 1911 which makes it an offence, 'If any person for any purpose prejudicial to the safety or interests of the state: (a) approaches ... any prohibited place ...'. The airfield was a prohibited place. They appealed to the House of Lords on the ground that their campaign and their actions were in fact in the interests of the state and of the entire UK population and that they consequently had no guilty motive. The House of Lords dismissed their appeal on the ground that their motives were irrelevant and did not alter the nature or content of the offence; all that mattered was that they had planned to enter and obstruct the operational use of the airfield.

Conversely, bad motives do not of themselves affect the *mens rea*. In *Cunningham* [1957] 2 QB 396, the defendant wrenched a gas meter from the gas pipes in a cellar in order to steal the money contained within. Unknown to the defendant, his actions fractured the gas pipe and gas escaped and entered the bedroom of a house on the adjoining side of the wall. The result was that the occupant inhaled gas and suffered injury. Cunningham was convicted of s 23 of the Offences Against the Person Act (OAPA) 1861: '... unlawfully and *maliciously* causing to be administered ... any ... poison or noxious thing ... so as to endanger life ... or to inflict grievous bodily harm.' The trial judge had directed the jury that 'malicious' meant 'wicked'. The jury convicted him presumably on the basis that he had acted wickedly. The Court of Criminal Appeal quashed his conviction, holding that 'malicious' is not the same as 'wicked'. 'Malicious' required that the defendant either *intended* to administer the noxious substance (which he clearly did not) or, without intending to do this he nevertheless foresaw that by fracturing the pipe the prohibited consequences might occur (and again he may not have foreseen this result).

On the other hand, as Viscount Radcliffe conceded in *Chandler v DPP*:

> All controversies about motives or intentions or purposes are apt to become involved through confusion of the meaning of the different terms and it is perhaps not difficult to show by analysis that the ideas conveyed by these respective words merge into each other without a clear line of differentiation [p 794].

The case of *Steane* [1947] 1 All ER 813 is sometimes mentioned as an example where the facts and circumstances of the case were so unusual that they led the court to confuse intention with motive. Steane was a British actor working in Germany at the outbreak of the Second World War. His wife and two sons lived in Germany. He was arrested, threatened and beaten by the Gestapo who wished him to broadcast radio propaganda on the German Broadcasting System and to produce films. He was told that if he failed to comply he and his family would be placed in a concentration camp. He eventually acceded to the demand solely because he wished to save his wife and sons. After the war, he was convicted, under reg 2A of the Defence (General) Regulations 1939, 'of doing acts likely to assist the enemy with intent to assist the enemy'. Were his actions consistent with those of a man intending to aid the German war effort? He could only save his family by broadcasting and thereby assisting the enemy. Lord Goddard CJ compared his case to British prisoners of war in the power of the Japanese who helped build the Burma military railway during the War: 'It would be unnecessary surely in their case to consider any of the niceties of the law relating to duress because no jury would find that merely by doing this work they were intending to assist the enemy' (p 817). The court allowed his appeal and quashed his conviction despite the fact that he possessed what is called 'oblique' intention (see below, 3.3.2). Lord Goddard would have been able to achieve the same result if he had found that Steane had in fact intended to assist the enemy but that the defence of duress was available to him (see Chapter 10).

In reality, motive is only irrelevant to criminal liability if we define motive in a very narrow way and ignore the fact that the law adopts a variety of devices to attribute significance to all kinds of reasons for which defendants act. In effect, the law has pre-selected some reasons or 'motives', and has excluded all others:

- An offence may actually require proof of a particular motive as part of the elements of the offence. For example, the Crime and Disorder Act 1998 contains provisions which turn the commission of various non-fatal offences, harassment, criminal damage and some public order offences into separate and more serious offences where they are *racially or religiously aggravated*. For these purposes, s 28 states that an offence is racially or religiously aggravated if immediately before, or during, or immediately after the commission of the offence, the offender demonstrates hostility towards the victim based on the victim's membership (actual or presumed by the offender) of a racial or religious group, *or if the offence is motivated wholly or partly by hostility towards members of a racial or religious group based on their membership of that group.*

- An offence may include an element in its definition which permits an enquiry into the defendant's reasons for his acts which cannot be contained within notions of intention or recklessness. Examples are 'dishonesty' in theft and related offences and the requirement of an 'unwarranted' demand with menaces in blackmail.

- Specific or general defences may be available which enable the defendant to justify or excuse his acts and the harm caused. The law considers his reasons for his acts to be sufficiently acceptable. Examples are to be found in 'lawful excuse' for criminal damage, the abortion of a foetus by a doctor because it was necessary to do so to prevent grave permanent injury to the physical or mental health of the mother, and acts in self-defence or under duress or duress of circumstances.

Apart from its relevance in this way, motive may be very important:

- as evidence at trial tending to demonstrate the accused's guilt;
- at the sentencing stage.

3.3   INTENTION

Parliament has not defined this term and yet many of the most serious crimes carry the requirement that the prosecution should prove beyond all reasonable doubt that the accused intended a particular consequence. The definition of murder demands that the accused must have intended to kill or intended to cause grievous bodily harm. Theft requires, in addition to dishonesty, that the defendant *intended* permanently to deprive the owner of his property. One who attempts to commit a crime is guilty under s 1 of the Criminal Attempts Act 1981 only if 'with *intent* to commit an offence ... he does something more than merely preparatory to the commission of the offence'. The person who enters a building as a trespasser commits the offence of burglary (s 9(1)(a) of the TA 1968) only if he has the *intent* to commit theft, rape, criminal damage or grievous bodily harm.

The *Oxford English Dictionary* defines intention in this way: '... that which is intended or purposed; a purpose or design; ultimate purpose; the aim of an action ...' How is intention defined by the courts? There are two aspects to this question.

3.3.1   Where a consequence is wanted for its own sake

This is often called *direct intention* and is relatively easy to define. If a particular consequence is wanted for its own sake then clearly the consequence is intended by the actor. If the actor is fighting an opponent and is trying his best seriously to injure that person then he clearly *intends* serious injury. He may still intend serious injury if he realises that his chances of success are less than 100%. In fact, it is not simply that a belief in a 100% chance of success is not required. It will make sense to say that he intends as long as he thinks that there is *some* chance of success, however small. For example, if he appreciates that his opponent is a much more skilled fighter than himself but nevertheless he keeps on trying to knock the opponent unconscious, he still *intends* serious injury to the victim.

3.3.2   Consequences foreseen but not wanted

Problems arise however where the actor does not have an aim, purpose, goal or desire to cause a prohibited consequence, but he realises that he will cause it, or is almost certain to cause it, if he goes ahead and engages in his planned conduct and pursues his true aim or purpose. Examples discussed below include *Hyam v DPP* [1974] 2 All ER 41, *Hancock and Shankland* [1986] AC 455, *Nedrick* [1986] 3 All ER 1, *Moloney* [1985] AC 905 and *Woollin* [1998] 4 All ER 103.

There is no doubt that this is a different state of mind from that of an actor who aims to cause a prohibited consequence, but, viewed as a matter of the actor's blameworthiness for causing the prohibited consequence, it is strongly arguable that there is no great difference between the two states of mind. Consequently, foresight of this kind without aim or purpose is often included within the definition of intention by calling it *oblique intention*. Take the example of a defendant who insures a package scheduled to travel on a transatlantic plane and who conceals a bomb in the package timed to explode in mid-flight. He does this in order to be able to claim on the insurance policy. The defendant bears no personal animosity towards the passengers and crew. Indeed, he has no idea whatsoever as to their identity and might actually prefer that they did not die. However, he realises that in order to achieve his goal of collecting the insurance money it is inevitable that the passengers and crew will die when the bomb explodes. Does the defendant *intend* to kill them? The dictionary definition of intention confines its meaning to what is called *direct intention*, that is, where a consequence is wanted for its own sake. If the law confined its definition in this way, the defendant, who does not seek the fatalities for their own sake, would not be guilty of murder. This would strike most of us as wholly unreasonable and likely to lead to a loss of respect for the rule of law. Thus, the meaning of the word has been 'stretched' by the judges to encompass this kind of behaviour. However, defining the precise limits of *oblique intent* has caused the judiciary considerable problems.

An analysis of 'intention' can best be achieved by focusing on six cases which, if analysed chronologically, help to illustrate the difficulty which has faced the judiciary over the last 40 years. The cases are: *DPP v Smith* [1961] AC 290; *Hyam v DPP*; *Moloney*; *Hancock and Shankland*; *Nedrick* and *Woollin* [1999] 1 AC 82.

DPP v Smith and the objective approach

DPP v Smith was authority for the proposition that intention should be assessed *objectively*, that is, by reference to the *foresight* of the reasonable man and not by proof that the defendant actually foresaw the particular consequence of his actions. Smith was the driver of a car which contained stolen goods. He was ordered by a police officer to leave his vehicle. Smith panicked and accelerated away with the police officer still holding onto the car. At a speed thought to be in the region of 60 mph the officer was thrown from the car and fell under the wheels of an oncoming vehicle causing his death. The House of Lords concluded that a person could be taken to have foreseen the nature and probable consequences to flow from his actions (or presumably inaction). If the jury concluded that a reasonable man would foresee the consequence then, despite any protestations to the contrary, the defendant could be said to have intended that consequence. Viscount Kilmuir said:

> The only test available ... is what the ordinary responsible man would, in all the circumstances of the case, have contemplated as the natural and probable result ... [p 327].

This case was authority therefore for the view that the intent required for the crime of murder (an intention to cause death or serious bodily harm) was purely objective. It mattered not that the defendant did not foresee the prohibited consequence of his act. The decision was subjected to enormous criticism and many judges were seriously concerned at the width of the judgment. The matter was referred to the Law Commission who reported in 1967 (*Imputed Criminal Intent: DPP v Smith*, Law Com 10). The Commission recommended the adoption of a subjective test with the jury free to infer intent from the totality of the evidence they had heard. This led to parliament eventually, but arguably unsuccessfully, seeking to prevent a person being convicted of a crime requiring intent even though he did not in reality foresee the outcome of his conduct. Section 8 of the Criminal Justice Act (CJA) 1967, provides that:

A court or jury, in determining whether a person has committed an offence:

(a) shall not be bound in law to infer that he intended or foresaw a result of his actions by reason only of its being a natural and probable consequence of those actions; but

(b) shall decide whether he did intend or foresee that result by reference to all the evidence, drawing such inferences from the evidence as appear proper in the circumstances.

Section 8 has since been confirmed as an evidential provision only and not one which amended the substantive law. It can be argued that the section did not reverse the decision in *Smith* although plainly that is what parliament thought it was doing, as was confirmed by subsequent judicial pronouncement (see *Wallett* [1968] 2 All ER 296 and Lord Hailsham in *Hyam v DPP* [1975] AC 55). It is of interest to note that, in *Frankland v R* [1987] 2 WLR 1251, the Privy Council (composed of five Law Lords) declared *Smith* to have been wrongly decided. However, decisions of the Council cannot overrule decisions of the House of Lords.

Hyam v DPP and foresight of high probability

In *Hyam v DPP*, a strong House of Lords (Lords Hailsham LC, Dilhorne, Diplock, Cross, Kilbrandon) engaged in detailed analysis of the *mens rea* for murder and, in particular, of the degree of foresight of the prohibited consequence it was necessary for the defendant to possess in order to incur liability:

• ought he to be *virtually certain* that the consequence would occur; or

• would an appreciation that the consequence would be *highly likely* to occur be enough; or

• would mere *likelihood* or ordinary *probability* be enough?

In this case, the appellant had been a man's mistress for some time but the relationship had largely ceased. The man commenced a relationship with another woman, Mrs Booth, and the appellant became jealous. Eventually she drove to her rival's house and set fire to it at 2.30 am by pouring petrol through the letterbox and setting it alight. She then drove home. She did not warn the occupants of the house or call the emergency services. As a result two of her rival's daughters were killed. She admitted to the police that she knew what she had done was very dangerous but said that she did not intend to cause death or serious harm to any person; she wished only to frighten or scare Mrs Booth into leaving the district in order that she could herself recommence her relationship with her former lover. She was convicted of murder. The House held (Lords Diplock and Kilbrandon dissenting) that a person murdered another if he knowingly committed an act:

• which was aimed at someone; and

• was committed with the intention of causing death or serious bodily injury.

However, Lord Hailsham stated that intention can also exist:

... where the defendant knows that there is a serious risk that death or serious bodily harm will ensue from his acts and he commits those acts deliberately and without lawful excuse with the intention to expose a potential victim to that risk as the result of those acts. It does not matter in such circumstances whether the defendant desires those consequences to ensue or not [p 79].

Lord Hailsham was of the view that only evidence that the accused foresaw the consequence as a 'moral certainty' would be sufficient evidence from which to conclude that she intended that consequence. Viscount Dilhorne said:

A man may do an act with a number of intentions. If he does it deliberately and intentionally, knowing when he does it that it is *highly probable* that grievous bodily harm will result, I think most people would say and be justified in saying that whatever other intentions he may have had as well, he at least intended grievous bodily harm [emphasis added] [p 82].

Lord Diplock took the 'uncomplicated view':

... that ... no distinction is to be drawn ... between the state of mind of one who does an act because he desires it to produce a particular evil consequence and the state of mind of one who does the act knowing full well that it is likely to produce that consequence although it may not be the object he was seeking to achieve by doing the act [p 86].

The following passages taken from the judgment of James LJ in *Mohan* [1975] 2 All ER 193 illustrate the deep division of opinion held by the judiciary at this time as to how the word intention should be defined. Judges in the Court of Appeal rejected the view that the *Hyam* meaning of intention was applicable throughout the criminal law. Having reviewed the speeches in *Hyam* James LJ went on to comment:

We do not find in the speeches of their Lordships in *Hyam* anything which binds us to hold that *mens rea* in the offence of *attempt* is proved by establishing beyond reasonable doubt that the accused knew or correctly foresaw that the consequences of his act unless interrupted would 'as a high degree of probability', or would be 'likely' to, be the commission of the complete offence ...

He went on to state:

... evidence of knowledge of likely consequences, or from which knowledge of likely consequences can be inferred, is evidence by which intent may be established but it is not, in relation to the offence of attempt, to be equated with intent. If the jury find such knowledge established they may and using common sense, they probably will find intent proved, but it is not the case that they must do so [p 200].

Similarly, in *Belfon* [1976] 3 All ER 46, Wien J stated that:

... we do not find ... in any of the speeches of their Lordships in *Hyam's* case anything which obliges us to hold that the 'intent' in wounding with intent is proved by foresight that serious injury is *likely* to result from a deliberate act [emphasis added] [p 53].

Moloney, Hancock and Shankland, Nedrick – foresight as evidence of intention

Clearly, the judges in *Mohan* and *Belfon* saw foresight not as *intent*, but merely *evidence* from which a jury might, or might not, infer intent. Such disarray amongst the judiciary was evident throughout the 1970s, and an attempt was made to introduce clarity to the debate in two significant House of Lords cases in the mid-1980s. In both *Moloney* and *Hancock and Shankland*, the House of Lords considered the relationship between foresight of consequence and proof of intention. In the former case, the defendant tragically killed his stepfather with whom he had 'enjoyed a happy and loving relationship'. Death occurred as a result of a contest between the two men to see who was the faster at loading a shotgun. Moloney was then challenged by his stepfather to fire the gun which he did, killing him instantly. Both men had been drinking. The House of Lords in allowing his appeal against a murder conviction was of the opinion that knowledge of foresight of consequences was at best 'material from which the jury, properly directed, may infer intention when considering a crime of ... intent'. It was clearly stated that the trial judge should seek to avoid any 'elaboration or paraphrase of what is meant by intent ... and should leave to the jury's good sense the question as to whether the accused acted with the necessary intent'. Lord Bridge, who gave the leading speech, with which his brethren concurred, laid down guidelines for juries in the few cases where it is necessary to direct a jury by reference to foresight of consequences. These cases would be those where the defendant's purpose was something other than causing death or serious bodily harm but where one of these results was inevitable or probable. In such a case the jury should, according to Lord Bridge's guidelines, be invited to consider:

- whether the consequence which has to be proved was the 'natural consequence' of the accused's act; and

- whether the accused foresaw that it was a natural consequence of his act.

If positive answers to both these issues were agreed by the jury then it would be 'proper' for them to *draw the inference* if they so wished that the accused intended that consequence. It is advisable to note that, in Lord Bridge's view, in such circumstances juries *may* rather than *must* reach the conclusion that intention is proved, because foresight of consequences is no more than evidence of the existence of the intent.

The significance of *Moloney* was that it marked a shift away from attempts to define intention for juries to a recognition that intention was a matter for the 'good sense' of the jury. At Cardiff Crown Court in May 1985, Mann J used the *Moloney* guidelines in his summing up to the jury in the case of *Hancock and Shankland*. The defendants, striking miners, were accused of murdering a taxi driver who had been driving a miner to work during a bitter industrial dispute. A concrete block weighing 46 lbs and measuring 18 x 9 x 5 inches was dropped by them over the parapet of a bridge in an endeavour, it was claimed, to block the road and thus prevent the man from getting to work. Sadly, it hit the taxi, with fatal consequences for the driver. They pleaded guilty to manslaughter but the Crown was not prepared to proceed on that basis. The jury convicted them of murder but, in a decision subsequently upheld in the House of Lords, the Court of Appeal substituted convictions of manslaughter on the grounds that the *Moloney* guidelines, as they stood, were unsafe and misleading because they contained no definition of what was meant by 'natural consequence'. If one accepts that the intention was to block the road and frighten the occupants of the taxi, then the defendants' desire or purpose was not to cause grievous bodily harm or death. Therefore, foresight became a vital factor in the equation. Lord Scarman, commenting on the *Moloney* guidelines, felt that the jury may not have gained much assistance because of the absence of any guidance 'as to the relevance or weight of the probability factor in determining whether they should, or could properly, infer from foresight of a consequence ... the intent to bring about that consequence' ([1986] 1 AC 455 at 471). The *Moloney* guidelines referred only to *natural* consequences flowing from the act and ignored the matter of probability.

The House of Lords considered that it was possible that a jury might understand *natural consequence* as indicating something which followed in an unbroken causal chain from the initial event whether it was highly likely or not. The guidelines did not refer to probability and Lord Scarman concluded that they were therefore defective 'and should not be used as they stand without further guidance'.

The following points need to be noted about the *Moloney/Hancock and Shankland* approach:

- The mental element in murder is a specific intent, that is, to kill or cause serious bodily harm.

- 'Foresight of consequence is no more than evidence of the existence of intent; it must be considered, and its weight assessed, together with all the evidence in the case. Foresight does not necessarily imply the existence of intention, though it may be a fact from which ... a jury may think it right to infer the necessary intent' ([1986] 1 AC 455, p 471).

- The probability of the result of an act is a matter for the jury to consider in seeking to determine whether or not the result was intended. Thus '... the degree of probability of death or serious injury resulting from the act done may be critically important. ... the greater the probability of a consequence the more likely it is that the consequence was foreseen and that if the consequence was foreseen the greater the probability is that the consequence was also intended' ([1986] 1 AC 455, p 473).

This issue of the degree of foresight required by the defendant was pursued further by Lord Lane CJ in *Nedrick*. The facts were essentially the same as those in *Hyam*. The Court of Appeal had the benefit of Lord Scarman's speech in *Hancock and Shankland* and Lord Lane asserted that a jury should be directed to consider:

- how probable was the consequence which resulted from the defendant's act; and

- whether he foresaw that consequence.

From this, it follows that if the defendant does not appreciate that the consequence (death or serious bodily harm in this case) is *likely* to result from his act, he cannot have intended to bring it about. If, however, he believed there was a risk of the consequence occurring, the jury would have to consider the probability of that consequence occurring and his foresight of it. No degree of probability is specified but it would be unlikely that a jury would infer intention except on proof of foresight of a very high degree, perhaps of virtual certainty. However, Lord Lane did not leave it at that. He concluded his judgment ([1986] 3 All ER 1) by stating:

> Where the charge is murder ... the jury should be directed that they are *not entitled* to infer the necessary intention, unless they feel sure that death or serious bodily harm was a virtual certainty (barring some unforeseen intervention) as a result of the defendant's actions and that the defendant appreciated that such was the case [emphasis added] [p 4].

Of course, this *does* specify a minimum degree of probability which must exist and which the defendant must foresee before the jury is *entitled* to infer intention. It means that, though the jury has not lost its discretion on whether or not to draw the inference that the defendant intended death or grievous bodily harm, it can only do so if first satisfied that the defendant had foreseen that result as a virtual certainty. This approach has the merit that it draws as sharp a line as possible between intention and recklessness, insisting that foresight of nothing less than overwhelming probability (virtual certainty) will permit intention to be inferred. Risk taking involving foresight of lesser degrees of probability is the province of recklessness.

Even so, just as different juries may in practice interpret a term such as virtual certainty in different ways, so judges in this area cannot be relied upon to maintain consistency of language in directing juries. Thus, in *Walker and Hayles* [1990] Crim LR 443 the trial judge used the words 'very high degree of probability' on at least three occasions when responding to a jury question as to what would amount to an intent to kill. The Court of Appeal held that there was little if any difference between what was highly probable and virtually certain to occur, and therefore the use of the words 'a very high degree of probability' did not amount to a misdirection. The process of erosion seemed to have gathered pace when the Court of Appeal in *Woollin* refused to reject the trial judge's direction to the jury that an inference of intention could be drawn from proof of foresight of a *substantial risk*, a term redolent of recklessness if ever there was one.

To summarise the position before the decision of the House of Lords in *Woollin*:

- Neither parliament nor the courts had supplied any clear definition of intention. An aim or purpose to bring about a desired result amounted to an intention to bring it about, but it was not necessary to prove desire. Where the actor had an aim or purpose, he was only required to foresee some chance of success. He did not need to foresee any high degree of probability of success.

- In the absence of aim or purpose to cause the result, the actor's foresight that he would or might cause the result was not *in itself* an intention to cause the result. So, to call foresight of virtual certainty (or any lesser degree of probability) oblique *intention* was misleading. As *Moloney, Hancock and Shankland, Nedrick* all loudly proclaimed, foresight of a consequence did not equate to intending it.

- In those cases where there was foresight of a consequence without aim or purpose to cause that consequence, a jury was *entitled* but not *bound* to infer intention from proof of such foresight. The House of Lords in *Moloney* and *Hancock* had not specified foresight of a minimum degree of probability, but the Court of Appeal in *Nedrick* asserted that the jury must be satisfied that the defendant foresaw the consequence as *virtually certain*. However, in *Walker and Hayles*, the Court of Appeal reluctantly accepted the formula *'very highly probable'* as an alternative expression for virtual certainty, and, before being overruled by the House of Lords, the Court of Appeal in *Woollin* was prepared to countenance *'substantial risk'*. Wherever the line was drawn, any lesser degree of probability was neither intention nor evidence from which intention could be inferred.

- It was unnecessary to give the jury anything other than simple guidance in straightforward intention cases. More complicated guidance should be given only in cases raising difficult issues of foresight.

Criticisms of the Moloney, Hancock and Shankland and Nedrick approach

The lack of any clear definition of intention did not cause problems where the defendant had an aim or purpose to cause the consequence, but it created a good deal of confusion in the problematic 'foresight' cases. Juries were being invited to infer one state of mind (intention) from another state of mind (foresight of virtual certainty) without being told what intention was. Moreover, since intention probably meant aim or purpose, it was difficult to understand how such a state of mind could be inferred from foresight in those cases where the jury had probably ruled out aim or purpose in the first place. In this context, it is as well to remember that the foresight cases were those in which the defendant did not appear to have an aim or purpose to cause the consequence. As Lord Lane said in his judgment in *Nedrick*:

> ... if the jury are satisfied that at the material time the defendant recognised that death or serious harm would be virtually certain ... then that is a fact from which they may find it easy to infer that he intended to kill or do serious bodily harm, *even though he may not have had any desire to achieve that result* [p 3].

Small wonder, perhaps, that Lord Lane stated in an extra-judicial capacity to the House of Lords Select Committee on Murder in 1989 that '*Nedrick* was not as clear as it should have been'.

The process of inferring intention was subjected to very strong academic criticism. The gist of this criticism was that, since foresight of virtual certainty should be regarded as included within intention (in other words, it *is* intention, albeit oblique), there is no further state of mind to be inferred. Thus, Professor Glanville Williams ((1989) 105 LQR 387) asserted:

> The proper view is that intention includes not only desire of consequence (purpose) but also foresight of certainty of the consequence, *as a matter of legal definition*. What the jury infer from the facts is the defendant's direct intention or foresight of a consequence as certain; there is no additional element to be 'inferred'.

Similarly, Professor Andrew Ashworth (*Principles of Criminal Law*, 1991, Oxford: Clarendon) explained:

> What the courts probably meant to say is that intention includes both purpose and foresight with regard to a particular consequence occurring in the ordinary course of events ... the evidential process of drawing inferences – which is basic to every case where the defendant does not confess, since one cannot see into another person's mind – should not be confused with the legal definition of intention [pp 150–51].

A perhaps less important, but nonetheless puzzling, aspect of Lord Lane's judgment in *Nedrick* was his assertion that, before the jury could infer intention from foresight of virtual certainty, they had to be satisfied not only that the defendant foresaw such virtual certainty, but also that the consequence actually was virtually certain to occur. Whilst *foresight* of virtual certainty would generally imply that a consequence *was* virtually certain, it is the defendant's state of mind which is in issue. If he went ahead with an action in the belief that a consequence was virtually certain to result, the fact that it was not (for reasons perhaps unknown to him) would make no difference to the degree of blameworthiness which he bore.

Woollin and foresight of virtual certainty as intention

In *Woollin*, the defendant had been left with the task of feeding his three-month-old baby son. He admitted that he had 'lost his cool' when the baby started to choke on his food. He had shaken him and then, in a fit of rage or frustration, had thrown him in the direction of his pram which was standing against the wall some three or four feet away. He knew that the baby's head had hit something hard (the wall or, possibly, the floor) but denied intending to throw him against the wall or wanting him to die or suffer serious injury. The trial judge directed the jury that they might infer intention to cause serious bodily harm if they were satisfied that when he threw the baby, the defendant appreciated that there was a *'substantial risk'* of causing serious bodily harm. The Court of Appeal rejected the defendant's contention that 'substantial risk' was merely a test of recklessness and that the judge should have used the phrase 'virtual certainty'. The question put to their Lordships on a further appeal to the House of Lords was whether in murder, where there is no direct evidence that the defendant's purpose was to kill or inflict serious injury on the victim, it is necessary to direct the jury that they may only infer an intent to do serious injury if they are satisfied: (a) that serious bodily harm was a virtually certain consequence of the defendant's voluntary act; and (b) that the defendant appreciated that fact. In other words, was the *Nedrick* direction correct?

Their Lordships were unanimous in quashing the conviction for murder and substituting a conviction for manslaughter. Lord Steyn delivered the principal speech. He rejected the trial judge's use of the phrase 'substantial risk' since it blurred the line between intention and recklessness. He upheld the validity of the *Nedrick* direction but made modifications to it. First, the jury should not be asked to consider the two questions which Lord Lane derived from Lord Scarman's speech in *Hancock and Shankland*, namely, how probable was the consequence which resulted from the defendant's act, and, did the accused foresee that consequence (see the discussion of *Nedrick,* above)? Secondly, instead of being invited to *'infer'* intention from proof of foresight of virtual certainty, the jury should be invited to *'find'* it from such proof. Thirdly, he stated that Lord Lane's suggestion that there may be an irresistible inference that a man intends a result which he knows for all practical purposes to be an inevitable consequence of his actions was not part of the direction. Consequently, the amended direction now reads:

> Where the charge is murder and in the rare cases where the simple direction is not enough, the jury should be directed that they are not entitled to find the necessary intention, unless they feel sure that death or serious bodily harm was a virtual certainty (barring some unforeseen intervention) as a result of the defendant's actions and that the defendant appreciated that such was the case. The decision is one for the jury to be reached on a consideration of all the evidence [[1999] 1 AC 82, p 96].

The elimination of the first two questions removes the logical inconsistency evident in Lord Lane's judgment in *Nedrick* between allowing the jury to deliberate on the whole range of probability and requiring them to be satisfied that the defendant foresaw nothing less than virtual certainty. It is important to note that, in making the second modification, replacing *infer* by *find*, Lord Steyn specifically referred to and accepted the criticisms of the *'infer'* formula expressed by commentators such as Professor Glanville Williams and Professor Ashworth (see above). The clear message of this modification, therefore, seems to be that Lord Steyn accepted that foresight of virtual certainty is intention, not merely evidence of intention. This message is reinforced by other comments made by Lord Steyn. For instance, he said of the original *Nedrick* direction: 'The effect ... is that a result foreseen as virtually certain is an intended result' ([1999] 1 AC 82, p 93). Similarly, he pointed out (p 91) that in *Moloney* Lord Bridge said that if a person foresees the probability of a consequence as little short of overwhelming, this "will suffice to *establish* the necessary intent"' (Lord Steyn's emphasis).

A definition of intention or merely a rule of evidence?

It is clear that intention in English law comprises both direct and oblique intention. That the latter is part of the law follows from the fact that the jury is free to find that the defendant intended to produce a result in circumstances where there is no evidence that that result was the defendant's purpose, aim or desire. They can do so where they are satisfied that the defendant realised that that result was virtually certain. Nevertheless, the correct interpretation of the decision in *Woollin* remains in one sense in doubt. Did it give us a definition of intention or did it continue the *Nedrick* approach of merely stating, for the assistance of the jury, a rule of evidence?

On both interpretations the jury are to ask themselves whether they are sure that death or grievous bodily harm was a virtual certainty (barring some unforeseen intervention) as a result of the defendant's action and that the defendant appreciated that such was the case. On both interpretations, if the answer is in the negative, the jury are bound to conclude that the necessary intention is not proved. The difference arises where the jury are satisfied that death or grievous bodily harm was a virtual certainty and that the defendant realised that fact.

On one interpretation, such a finding is conclusive and amounts to a finding that the defendant had the necessary intention. On this interpretation, the jury has no choice but to find that the necessary intention has been established. In this case, foresight of virtual certainty is intention, not merely evidence of intention. If this is correct, Lord Steyn has converted what in *Nedrick* was a rule of evidence into a definition of intention.

The other interpretation is that a finding that the defendant realised death or grievous bodily harm was a virtual certainty is merely a gateway. Once through the gateway, the jury may or may not find the necessary intention proved. It allows, but does not require, the jury to find that the defendant intended to cause death or grievous bodily harm. It is thus not a definition of intention. On this interpretation, the decision of the House of Lords in *Woollin* has merely confirmed the law as stated in *Nedrick* and in the process tidied it up somewhat. That this is the correct interpretation is now established as far as the Court of Appeal. In *Matthews and Alleyne* [2003] EWCA Crim 192, the Court of Appeal held that the direction laid down in *Nedrick* and modified in *Woollin* was a rule of evidence. The victim, a young man who could not swim, was thrown from a bridge into a river and drowned as a result. The two defendants were charged with his murder. The Court of Appeal held that the trial judge had been in error in directing the jury that the prosecution 'will succeed' in proving the intention to kill if it is shown that death was a virtual certainty and that the defendant realised that fact. Such a direction wrongly elevated a rule of evidence into a rule of law. The jury should have been directed, in relation to each defendant, that they were entitled to, not that they must, find the necessary intention if they were satisfied that the defendant realised death was a virtual certainty.

Other doubts about the effect of *Woollin* arise, first, because Lords Browne-Wilkinson and Hoffmann did not express any support for Lord Steyn's reasoning and, secondly, because Lord Steyn himself was clear that he was discussing intention only in relation to the offence of murder: '... it does not follow that "intent" necessarily has precisely the same meaning in every context in the criminal law.' It should also be noted that, in approving the rest of the *Nedrick* direction, Lord Steyn appears to perpetuate the difficulties arising out of Lord Lane's suggestion that death or serious bodily harm must actually *be* a virtual certainty rather than merely be *foreseen* by the defendant to be such.

3.3.3   Reform

The struggle of the courts over the last 40 years to devise a coherent approach to the meaning of intention, and the fact that, even after *Woollin*, it is impossible to be confident about accurately interpreting that approach, suggest that a statutory definition of intention is desirable. Attempts to provide such a definition have now been made on a number of occasions. In its 1989 draft Criminal Code (*Criminal Law: A Criminal Code for England and Wales*, Law Com 177, cl 18(b)), the Law Commission offered the following definition:

> ... a person acts intentionally with respect to a ... result when he acts either in order to bring it about or being aware that it will occur in the ordinary course of events.

This definition was criticised on the grounds both that it was under-inclusive and over-inclusive. It did not catch the terrorist bomber who knew that he would cause death if the bomb went off but who also knew that the bomb had only a 50% chance of exploding, because he was not 'aware that it will occur in the ordinary course of events'. Conversely, it allegedly did catch the person who acted from the best of motives but who knew that death would occur in the ordinary course of events, such as a father who throws his young son off the top of a blazing block of flats in a vain attempt to save his life.

In response, the Law Commission produced a revised definition in its report, *Offences Against the Person and General Principles* (Law Com 218, 1993). According to this definition, a person acts intentionally with respect to a result when:

(a) it is his purpose to cause it; or

(b) although it is not his purpose to cause it, he knows that it would occur in the ordinary course of events if he were to succeed in his purpose of causing some other result.

This definition was substantially reproduced in the Home Office consultation paper of 1998 (*Violence: Reforming the Offences Against the Person Act 1861*) dealing with proposed reform of the law on offences against the person. The second limb includes the bomber and excludes the desperate father. Yet, Professor JC Smith considered that even this improved version was defective. Considering the facts of *Woollin*, Professor Smith argued ([1998] Crim LR 317, p 318, [1998] Crim LR 317, p 318) that, even if it could be proved that the father foresaw the virtual certainty of the baby's death or serious injury, he would not have intended it on this definition because he did not have a purpose to cause it and did not have any other purpose sufficient to fall within the second limb of the definition (he argued that the defendant in *Woollin* was merely venting his anger, which is not a purpose to cause a result). In consequence, Professor Smith suggested that the second limb should be amended to read, 'he knows that it *will occur in the ordinary course of events*, or that it would do so if he were to succeed in his purpose of causing some other result'. This amendment would certainly deal with the *Woollin* issue but surely at the cost of once again endangering the desperate father.

Of course, if *Woollin* is interpreted as ruling that foresight of virtual certainty is intention, then it can be argued that the courts have already succeeded in defining intention in much the same way as in this proposed statutory definition. This depends in part on whether *foresight of virtual certainty* can be equated with *knowledge that a result will occur in the ordinary course of events*. In his speech in *Woollin*, Lord Steyn certainly considered that the two were 'very similar'.

In his article, 'After *Woollin*' ([1999] Crim LR 532), Professor Alan Norrie has suggested that a clear definition of intention which includes foresight of virtual certainty (either derived from *Woollin* or from a statutory provision) will raise further problems. He argues that it will be too narrow to include cases which should be included, such as *Hyam v DPP*, and yet may be too broad in including cases which should not be included, such as *Steane*, or cases in which doctors act out of medical necessity. In putting this argument, he takes the view that there is a moral dimension in judgments about liability for an offence such as murder which depends on good and bad motives and which cannot be captured in the language of intention and foresight. As long as the jury are given the discretion whether or not to infer intention, they can reflect society's moral perceptions in the exercise of that discretion. This remains the case if Lord Steyn's reformulation of the *Nedrick* direction has not removed that discretion. It now appears from *Matthews and Alleyne* that it has not done so. If it had done so, or if a statutory definition were to do so, then some other way would have to be found to reflect moral perceptions, so as at the least to absolve those with sufficiently good motives. Professor Norrie is not even convinced that *Woollin* has put an end to the possibility that liability in murder may yet be founded on foresight of high probability rather than of virtual certainty:

> Another case with different moral facts, reflecting a more manifest malice, could well let the *Hyam* genie out of the bottle. Indeed, the broader spirit of *Hyam* has always lurked within the indirect intention cases even when they have denied it, and this is as true of *Woollin* as the others.

3.3.4   Specific, basic and ulterior intent

Such is the commitment to establishing intention as a key determiner of fault that certain crimes are designated as *specific intent* offences. The term was recognised at the highest level in *DPP v Beard* [1920] AC 479, where Lord Birkenhead dealing with the relevance of a plea of intoxication in respect of a brutal killing said: '... that where a specific intent is an essential element in the offence ... drunkenness ... should be taken into consideration ... [p 499]'

Lord Birkenhead later referred to specific intent as meaning simply the intent required to constitute the particular crime. However, though Lord Simon attempted, in *DPP v Majewski* [1976] 2 All ER 142, to provide a more detailed exposition of what is meant by *specific intent*, it cannot be said that he was successful or that his approach has been adopted. He tried to argue that specific intent required an element of *purpose*, but this is at odds with the actual requirements of crimes considered to be specific intent offences. In truth, no clear meaning of the term has emerged and no principle seems to underlie the designation of crimes as requiring proof of specific intent.

In practice, *specific intent* crimes need to be distinguished from *basic intent* crimes mainly because intoxication is, as we shall see in Chapter 10, normally a defence for crimes of *specific* intent but not for those of *basic* intent. Lord Simon in *DPP v Morgan* [1975] 2 All ER 347 stated that basic intent crimes are those where the *mens rea* does not 'go beyond the *actus reus*'. He cites assault as an example where the consequence is 'very closely connected with the act'. The *actus reus* is 'an act which causes another person to apprehend immediate and unlawful violence. The *mens rea* corresponds exactly'. The problem with Lord Simon's view, however, is that his exposition does not always neatly fit in with the decided cases. Take, for example, murder where the *mens rea* is an intention to kill or commit grievous bodily harm. This is universally agreed by the case law to be a crime of *specific* intent. However, with this crime the *mens rea* not only fails to extend beyond the *actus reus* but actually falls short of it in the case of a defendant who intended only to commit grievous bodily harm to the victim! The position is similar in relation to the crime of causing grievous bodily harm with intent to cause grievous bodily harm, contrary to s 18 of the OAPA 1861. This is categorised as a crime of *specific* intent despite the fact that this is not a crime where the *mens rea* extends beyond the *actus reus*. When attempting to identify a crime of *specific intent*, best practice is to refer to the leading case(s) to see how the crime has been categorised by the courts.

Thus murder, causing grievous bodily harm with intent, theft and attempts are *specific intent* crimes; manslaughter, rape, criminal damage and ss 20 and 47 of the OAPA 1861 are crimes of basic intent. As a rule of thumb, those crimes requiring intent to be proved in relation to one element of the *actus reus* fit into the former category whilst those having either intent or recklessness as part of the definition fit into the latter. This means that in the case of a crime of *basic intent* the prosecution need not prove intention. Proof that the defendant acted recklessly will be enough.

A further term, *ulterior intent*, is evident in some case reports. This is taken to refer to definitions of crime where the *mens rea* goes beyond an element of the *actus reus*, that is, the *mens rea* of the crime requires the prosecution to prove that the defendant intended to produce a consequence beyond the *actus reus* of the crime. Burglary will serve as an example where the *actus reus* is complete once a person enters a building or part thereof as a trespasser. However, there is a further requirement ulterior to the *actus reus* which demands an *intent* to commit one of four crimes (theft, grievous bodily harm, rape, unlawful damage). It is this element to which the label ulterior intent is attached. *Specific intent* crimes may, of course, incorporate *ulterior intent*, as with burglary which does not include recklessness as part of the required *mens rea*.

3.4   RECKLESSNESS

Recklessness suffices for most crimes where the prosecution needs to prove *mens rea* in relation to at least one element of the *actus reus*. As with intention parliament has yet to define this key fault term and so the task has been left to the courts. The *Concise Oxford Dictionary* defines the word 'reckless' as 'lacking caution, regardless of consequences, rash, heedless of danger'.

Traditionally, in law the term has been taken to mean the deliberate and conscious taking of an unreasonable risk by the defendant. The defendant realises that if he carries out a particular act or fails to do so he is taking a risk that a particular consequence or result will occur. It does not matter that he has no particular wish or desire that it will occur; all that matters is that the defendant realises that he is engaging in risky activity.

The risk must not be one which he would be justified in taking and the courts judge this objectively on the basis of the social utility of the act. For example, a surgeon developing a new form of surgical procedure for seriously ill patients may take a large risk when performing an operation but if the operation goes badly and the patient dies the courts would be unlikely to find that he acted recklessly, at least if there was no safer alternative procedure available. The court would balance the very high social utility value of his acts (assessed objectively) against the risk he took. They would almost certainly conclude that the former outweighed the latter and that he had not, therefore, acted recklessly. Contrast the surgeon with the armed political terrorist who robs a bank in an effort to secure funds for his organisation. In order only to attract the attention of staff and customers, he fires his pistol into the ceiling, but unfortunately the bullet ricochets from the ceiling and wounds a customer. Let us suppose that expert evidence presented at the subsequent trial suggests that the statistical chance of this happening was very small indeed. Was the terrorist reckless? Provided he realised when he fired that there was a risk of the bullet hitting someone, the answer is 'Yes', because here the court would judge the social utility value of his act as nil and therefore *any* risk of injury associated with the act would constitute recklessness on his part. He would, therefore, be guilty of an offence under the OAPA 1861 for which recklessness sufficed for the *mens rea*.

But what of the person who simply gave no thought to the consequences of his action and therefore did not appreciate that he was taking a risk? Is this person reckless? This has been a major dilemma for the judges since the early 1980s. It had been assumed prior to the decision in *Metropolitan Police Commissioner v Caldwell* [1981] 1 All ER 961 that the approach to the assessment of recklessness should be a subjective one. The decision of the Court of Criminal Appeal in *Cunningham* is the major authority for this assertion. The court was concerned with the meaning of 'maliciously' in the OAPA 1861. Modern statutes tend to use the word 'recklessly' instead of 'maliciously'. The court adopted the principle contained in Professor Kenny's *Outlines of Criminal Law* (16th edn, 1952, Cambridge: CUP, p 186) that malice was not synonymous with wickedness but required either intention or 'recklessness as to whether such harm should occur or not (that is, the *accused had foreseen* that the particular kind of harm might be done and had yet gone on to take the risk of it)'. Thus, the foundation was laid for the proposition that recklessness should be assessed subjectively. This was confirmed more than 20 years later by the Court of Appeal in *Stephenson* [1979] 2 All ER 1198 the facts of which invite us to examine our own views on whether or not a person who is schizophrenic should be facing criminal charges. The appellant had crept into a hollow in the side of a large haystack to sleep, but feeling cold he had lit a fire of twigs and straw inside the hollow. Needless to say the stack caught alight and damage amounting to £3,000 was caused. It is obvious that the ordinary person would be likely to have foreseen the immediate consequence of such an action and presumably if he or she had not desisted then one would have no difficulty establishing culpability. Section 1 of the Criminal Damage Act (CDA) 1971 requires evidence that property belonging to another was damaged or destroyed by the accused either intentionally or being 'reckless as to whether any such property would be destroyed or damaged'. The judge directed the jury that the defendant could be found guilty if 'he closed his mind to the *obvious* fact of risk from his act'. They convicted. The Court of Appeal, in allowing the appeal against conviction, confirmed that the correct test of recklessness (at least for the purposes s 1 of the CDA 1971) was *subjective* in the sense that the *accused* must be proved to have foreseen the risk of damage from his act. If such knowledge or foresight was present, then liability would not be avoided simply by suppressing or closing one's mind to the risk. If the accused was suffering from a mental abnormality which affected his ability to foresee the risk, then this was an issue for the jury to consider in deciding whether or not the risk had been appreciated. *Cunningham* was applied by the Court of Appeal and this unequivocal statement appears in the judgment of Geoffrey Lane LJ ([1979] 2 All ER 1198):

> We wish to make it clear that the test remains subjective, that the knowledge or appreciation of risk of some damage must have entered the defendant's mind even though he may have suppressed it or driven it out [p 1204].

It is difficult to imagine a clearer statement of principle. This approach endorsed the Law Commission's view expressed in its 1970 working paper, *General Principles: The Mental Element in Crime* (Law Com 30), and little evidence exists to show that the test did not work well or that it was a particular cause of concern for those professionally involved in the criminal law.

However, *Stephenson* was overruled when the House of Lords decided to depart from the subjective approach in the leading cases of *Metropolitan Police Commissioner v Caldwell* [1982] AC 341 and *Lawrence* [1982] AC 510, two controversial decisions. The judgments were delivered by separate divisions of the House of Lords on the same day. In *Caldwell*, the defendant had a grievance against the owner of a hotel and he set fire to the hotel. The fire was discovered before serious damage occurred. He was convicted of arson under s 1(1) and (2) of the CDA 1971. At his trial, he had pleaded guilty to the s 1(1) charge of intentionally or recklessly damaging the property of another, but not guilty to the more serious charge of damaging property with intent to endanger life or being reckless whether life would be endangered. His defence was that he was so drunk at the time of the act that the thought that he might be endangering the lives of the guests had never crossed his mind. He successfully appealed to the Court of Appeal but the prosecution appealed to the House of Lords on the basis that intoxication was no defence to a charge under s 1(2). This led the House of Lords to consider the meaning of recklessness in detail because (as will be seen below, 10.3) intoxication is usually a defence for crimes where the *mens rea* requirement is intention but not where recklessness suffices for the *mens rea*. The House of Lords was divided. Lords Keith and Roskill agreed with Lord Diplock ([1982] AC 341) that:

> ... recklessness covers a whole range of states of mind from failing to give any thought at all to whether or not there is any risk of those harmful consequences, to recognising the existence of the risk and nevertheless deciding to ignore it ... Neither state of mind seems to me to be less blameworthy than the other; but if the difference between the two constitutes the difference between what does and what does not ... amount to a guilty state of mind for the purposes of [the Act] it would not be a practical distinction for use in trial by jury. The only person who knows what the accused's mental processes were is the accused himself ... If [he] gives evidence that because of his ... drunkenness the risk of particular harmful consequences of his acts simply did not occur to him, a jury would find it hard to be satisfied beyond reasonable doubt that his true mental process was not that, but was the slightly different mental process required [by] *Cunningham* ... *mens rea* is by definition, a state of mind of the accused himself ... it cannot be the mental state of some non-existent, hypothetical person [p 351].

> ... a person is reckless [for the purposes of s 1(1) of the CDA 1971] if (1) he does an act which in fact creates an obvious risk that property will be destroyed or damaged, and (2) when he does that act he either has not given any thought to the possibility of there

being any such risk or has recognised that there was some risk involved and has nonetheless gone on to do it. That would be a proper direction to the jury.

It is interesting to examine the views of his two dissenting colleagues. Lord Edmund-Davies (with whom Lord Wilberforce concurred) expressed the opinion that:

... I have to say that I am in respectful but profound disagreement ... [[1982] AC 357]

and that:

... unlike negligence which has to be judged objectively, recklessness involves foresight of consequences, combined with an objective judgment of the reasonableness of the risk taken [p 358].

Lawrence was an equally significant judgment and this time the House of Lords was united in its decision. The *Caldwell* definition of recklessness was applied to the *actus reus* of the offence of causing death by reckless driving (this offence has been superseded by s 1 of the Road Traffic Act (RTA) 1988 which created the offence of causing death by dangerous driving). In *Lawrence* the House of Lords held that, before a jury can convict a defendant of driving recklessly, the jury must be satisfied (a) that the defendant was in fact driving in such a manner as to create an obvious and serious risk of causing physical injury to some other person or of causing substantial damage to property and (b) that in driving in that manner the defendant did so without having given any thought to the possibility of there being any such risk or, having recognised that there was some risk involved, he had nevertheless gone on to take it.

However, there still remains the issue of a defendant who fails to give *any* thought to either the circumstances or likely consequences of his actions. A person may decide to ride his motor cycle at 60 mph but give no thought whatsoever to the possibility that injury to health or damage to property may result from his decision to drive at high speed. Such a person may well be found to have been driving recklessly. One basis on which a defendant can, on the *Caldwell/Lawrence* test, be found to have been reckless is that he failed to give any thought to an obvious and serious risk. A risk is obvious if it would have been obvious to the ordinary prudent person. It is irrelevant that it was not obvious to the defendant, what matters is that the risk would be obvious to the ordinary prudent person, not the accused. Support for this conclusion comes from Lord Diplock's speech where he refers to the ordinary prudent person on two occasions ([1982] AC 510):

Recklessness on the part of the doer of an act presupposes that there is something in the circumstances that would have drawn the attention of an ordinary prudent individual to the possibility that his act was capable of causing ... serious harmful consequences ... and that the risk of those harmful consequences occurring was not so slight that an ordinary prudent individual would feel justified in treating them as negligible [p 526].

So in answer to the question 'obvious to whom?' the answer is the reasonable or ordinary person – not the accused. In the result, Lawrence's appeal was dismissed. Lord Diplock was concerned with the position of the person who failed to give thought to an obvious risk and, if there was an *obvious* risk, the defendant was guilty. It makes no difference whether he realised there was a risk or not. 'Not giving thought' is classed as a state of mind. Professors JC Smith and Brian Hogan point out:

Once the obvious (and serious) risk is proved, there seems to be only one way out for the defendant. He can escape liability only if he considered the matter and decided that there was no risk, or a 'negligible' risk [*Criminal Law*, 10th edn, 2002, London: Butterworths, p 82].

The impact of the decisions was immediate, harsh and confusing. Peter Glazebrook ([1984] CLJ 5) commented:

The present generation of Law Lords is unlikely to admit that a great mistake has been made. But it seems probable that their successors, fortified perhaps by amending legislation, will look back on these cases ... and condemn them ... as a disaster.

Professor JC Smith described the two cases as 'pathetically inadequate' ([1984] Crim LR 393) and Professor Glanville Williams described them as 'slap happy and profoundly regrettable' ([1981] Crim LR 581). These are strong words but justified, because the decisions created considerable uncertainty as to the meaning of one of the key fault terms in the criminal law. Professor Smith wrote ([1992] Crim LR 821) that 'many judges have reported that, when they give the *Caldwell/Lawrence* direction the jurors' eyes glaze'. Lord Browne-Wilkinson in *Reid* [1992] 3 All ER 673 observed: 'Although after long and careful analysis of Lord Diplock's direction with the help of very skilled counsel I have, *I think*, understood it, and find it legally correct, I cannot believe that a direction in that abstract conceptual form is very helpful to a jury' (emphasis added). As Smith observed, 'if that is the reaction of so eminent a judge, what hope has the average juror?' ([1992] Crim LR 821).

Much of this uncertainty has been as a result of the Court of Appeal feeling obliged progressively to depart from Lord Diplock's direction in relation to specific crimes. In *Pigg* [1982] 2 All ER 591, Lord Lane CJ purported to apply *Caldwell* on a charge of attempted rape. The issue of recklessness arose as a result of s 1 of the Sexual Offences (Amendment) Act (SO(A)A) 1976 which required that a person must either intend to have intercourse without consent or be 'reckless as to whether that person consents to it'. In delivering the judgment of the court, the Lord Chief Justice, Lord Lane, said:

... so far as rape is concerned, a man is reckless if either he was indifferent and gave no thought to the possibility that the woman might not be consenting in circumstances where if any thought had been given to the matter it would have been obvious that there was a risk she was not, or he was aware of the possibility that she might not be consenting but nevertheless persisted regardless of whether she consented or not [p 599].

The difficulty with this statement is that it expects the prosecution to prove that the defendant is both indifferent *and* fails to give thought to the issue of consent. As has already been asked, how can a person be indifferent to something he has not considered?

The whole issue of recklessness in rape has developed since *Pigg* on the basis that *Caldwell* recklessness is inappropriate to the offence despite, of course, the definition of rape being found in a modern criminal statute to which, according to Lord Diplock, the new definition ought to apply. In S (*Satnam*) (1983) 78 Cr App R 149, the Court of Appeal accepted that there was ambiguity in the *Pigg* direction and was of the opinion that the use of the word 'obvious' might mislead juries into believing that an objective test should be used when considering recklessness in the context of rape. The law on rape had been clearly stated in the case of *DPP v Morgan* and the

SO(A)A 1976 was deemed to be declaratory of the existing law as determined in *Morgan*. The case confirmed that if the accused in fact honestly believed that the woman consented, irrespective of whether or not that belief was based upon reasonable grounds, then the essential element of *mens rea* would be absent and he could not be convicted of the offence. Thus *Cunningham* recklessness applies to the law of rape and a defendant is guilty only if he was subjectively aware of the possibility that the victim might not be consenting and yet nevertheless proceeded to engage in sexual intercourse. It therefore follows that the 'failure to give thought' element contained in *Caldwell* has no relevance to this offence (see Chapter 7). A similar approach was adopted with regard to the offence of indecent assault in *Kimber* [1983] 3 All ER 316 with Lawton LJ urging acceptance of the proposition that the 'state of mind' aptly described in the colloquial expression, 'couldn't care less', amounted to recklessness in law.

It has been steadfastly maintained that *Caldwell* and *Lawrence* have no application to offences requiring malice, and *Cunningham* recklessness will apply to s 20 of the OAPA 1861. In *W (A Minor) v Dolbey* (1983) 88 Cr App R 515, the defendant, a 15-year-old, possessed an air gun and pointed it at a friend telling him 'there is nothing in the gun; I have got no pellets'. He fired and his friend was wounded. He was charged with unlawful and malicious wounding contrary to s 20. It was found as fact that he believed the gun to have been unloaded because he thought he had used his last pellet while shooting at bottles earlier in the day; that he had not opened the gun; and that he had ignored the risk that the gun might be loaded. It was concluded by the justices that he had been reckless and they convicted. His appeal was allowed on the basis that *Cunningham* was still the authority to be applied and this approach has been confirmed by the subsequent House of Lords' decision in *Savage; Parmenter* [1991] 4 All ER 698. Therefore, in order to obtain a conviction, it would have to be shown that on the facts known to the defendant at the time, he actually foresaw that a particular kind of harm might be done to his victim. If the defendant honestly believes that a gun is not loaded, then he could not have foreseen the consequences and the defendant could not be found to have acted maliciously. However, if he had pointed his gun at his friend's property, discharged it and caused criminal damage (within the meaning of the CDA 1971), say to a window, then *Caldwell* would apply if he had failed to give thought to the possible consequences of his actions, providing the ordinary person would have given thought and the risk of damage to property was obvious. Recklessness, therefore, has a variable meaning depending upon the offence in question. This was confirmed in the House of Lords' decision of *Reid* despite Lord Roskill's view in *Seymour* [1983] 2 All ER 1058 that the *Caldwell/Lawrence* meaning should be used throughout the criminal law, 'unless Parliament has otherwise ordained'.

The potential harshness of the *Caldwell* decision is illustrated by the case of *Elliott v C* [1983] 1 WLR 939, where a 14-year-old girl who was a member of the remedial class at her school set fire to a carpet in a garden shed after staying out all night without sleep. The fire flared up out of control and destroyed the shed. It was accepted that, because of her age and general understanding, and in view of her physical condition on the night, she had not appreciated the risk of burning down the shed by dropping lighted matches onto white spirit which she had poured onto the carpet. In the magistrates' court, the argument was accepted that Lord Diplock in *Caldwell* had been referring to a risk which would have been obvious to the particular defendant if she had given any thought to the matter, and she was found not guilty. Goff LJ, in allowing the prosecutor's appeal, reluctantly followed the reasoning that the arbiter of risk in circumstances where thought had not been given was *not* the defendant but the ordinary prudent person. The harshness, acknowledged by the court, is in finding someone with limited mental capacity guilty of a crime which requires blameworthy conduct, that is, *mens rea* in its fullest sense. As Goff LJ ([1983] 1 WLR 939) said:

> I agree with the conclusion reached by Glidewell J, but I do so simply because I believe myself constrained to do so by authority ... I would be lacking in candour if I were to conceal my unhappiness about the conclusion which I feel compelled to reach [p 947].

Presumably, Goff LJ, like the present writers, was questioning the purpose of labelling this particular girl a 'criminal'.

Nor is the ordinary prudent person to be bestowed with any of the characteristics of the accused (*R (Stephen Malcolm)* (1984) 79 Cr App R 334). This is in direct contradiction to the development of the law on provocation which, since *Camplin* [1978] AC 705, has allowed juries to take account of age, sex and any other relevant characteristics of the accused in deciding whether or not a reasonable person would have lost his or her self-control (see Chapter 6). Similarly, the ordinary prudent individual possesses no particular expertise. As Tucker J stated in *Sangha* [1988] 2 All ER 385:

> Is it proved that an ordinary, prudent individual would have perceived an obvious risk that property would be damaged ...? The ordinary prudent bystander is not deemed to be invested with expert knowledge relating to the construction of the property nor to have the benefit of hindsight [p 390].

On the other hand, if the defendant holds himself out as possessing specialist knowledge, for example, a surgeon, then in terms of appreciation of the risk he will be compared to a 'reasonable' member of his peer group and not the ordinary prudent individual (*P & O European Ferries (Dover) Ltd* (1990) 93 Cr App R 72). If the defendant's failure to appreciate an obvious risk was due to intoxication as a result of consuming drugs not generally thought to be dangerous, for example, Valium, then he will not be considered to have acted recklessly (*Hardie* [1984] 3 All ER 848; see above, 2.3.1).

Gemmell and Richards [2003] 1 Cr App Rep 343 is the latest in the line of cases where the Court of Appeal has loyally applied the *Caldwell* ruling on recklessness. In that case two boys, aged 11 and 13, were charged with criminal damage. The boys said that it never occurred to them that the damage would occur. The judge gave a *Caldwell* direction, namely that the test of recklessness was whether the risk of property being damaged would have been obvious to an ordinary reasonable bystander; that the ordinary reasonable bystander was an adult; and that no allowance was to be made for the youth of the defendants or their inability to assess what was going on. The boys were convicted. In the Court of Appeal they used Art 6 of the European Convention on Human Rights to attack the law established in *Caldwell*. Article 6 establishes the right to a fair trial. The Court of Appeal, dismissing their appeal, rejected their argument. It held, in line with other cases on the Convention, that Art 6 deals only with procedural unfairness and is not concerned with unfairness of the substantive provisions of criminal law. It is clear that only the House of Lords can now review the *Caldwell* ruling. In *Gemmell and Richards*, the

Court of Appeal has, as is now usual in criminal damage cases where the appellant wishes to challenge the law established in *Caldwell*, refused leave to appeal to the House of Lords. When eventually the House of Lords is prepared to reconsider the matter, it will be up to the House itself to give leave to appeal.

3.4.1 Ruling out the risk

In *W (A Minor) v Dolbey*, the defendant had adverted to the possibility that the gun was loaded and concluded, albeit without checking, that it was not. This situation, where thought is given to the potential risk, but after due consideration the defendant proceeds having dismissed the possibility of an unwanted consequence arising as non-existent, became known as the 'lacuna'. It does not fit into either strand of *Caldwell* recklessness. With subjective recklessness, the actor contemplates the risk and then goes ahead, having recognised that a risk exists; in the case of objective recklessness the person has to be proved to have given no thought to the possibility of risk. While the lacuna has been acknowledged by academics, the judiciary is far from positive in its attitude towards recognition. In *Chief Constable of Avon and Somerset Constabulary v Shimmen* [1986] Crim LR 800, the respondent was charged with destroying a shop window contrary to s 1(1) of the CDA 1971. He had proceeded to demonstrate to friends a particular form of Korean martial arts in which he was trained and qualified. Despite warnings that he might cause damage, he made as if to kick the window. He claimed to have 'weighed up the odds and thought he had eliminated as much risk as possible by missing the window by two inches instead of two millimetres'. The magistrates dismissed the charge and the prosecution appealed by way of case stated. The Queen's Bench Divisional Court concluded that the respondent had been reckless in that he had created an obvious risk that the property would be damaged, recognised the risk and went on to take it. The appeal was allowed and the case remitted back to the magistrates' court with a direction to convict. It was clear that Shimmen had recognised there was a risk, but had failed to take adequate precautions to eliminate it. Professor Glanville Williams ('The unresolved problem of recklessness' (1988) 8 LS 74) made the pertinent comment that:

> This was a case where the defendant needed to be cross-examined. 'Would you have kicked with such force towards ... your baby's head relying on your ability to stop within an inch of it? No? Then you knew that there was *some* risk of your boot travelling further than you intended.' A person may be convinced of his own skill and yet know that on rare ... occasions it may fail him [p 75].

If, however, D believes that he has eliminated all risk by some, in fact inadequate, precaution he cannot be held reckless. In fact, the Court of Appeal showed no inclination to accept this argument in *Merrick* [1995] Crim LR 802. The defendant had removed old cable television cabling with the consent of the owner of the property and in so doing had exposed live wiring for a period of some six minutes. He admitted that he was aware this was dangerous but believed there would be no actual risk and would not have undertaken the work if he had not been competent to do so. He was convicted of damaging property, being reckless as to whether life was endangered contrary to s 1(2) of the CDA 1971. On appeal, it was maintained that his situation did not fall within the ambit of the *Caldwell* definition of recklessness. He had considered the risk and had gone ahead believing there to be no danger in what

he was doing. The Court of Appeal drew a clear distinction between avoiding a risk
and taking steps to remedy a risk which had already been created. Any steps which
are taken must be aimed at preventing the risk, rather than remedying it once it had
arisen. In his commentary on the case, Professor JC Smith found the distinction
drawn by the Court of Appeal to be 'unsound' ([1995] Crim LR 802, p 805). If one
draws a parallel with *Miller* ([1983] 1 All ER 978; see above, para 2.6) the defendant
having created the danger is under a duty to remedy it. If he palpably fails to take
adequate steps to rectify the problem, then given that he is aware of the danger he
could be said to be reckless to the extent that he is failing to comply with his 'duty'
or 'responsibility'. It is arguable that the courts are seeking to establish a policy
designed to deter individuals from creating dangerous situations in the first place
and thereby absolving them of the responsibility to assess risk after the event. The
actions perpetrated by the defendants in *Shimmen* and in *Merrick* really have little or
no utility value at all and certainly no benefit was likely to accrue to the shopkeeper
in the former case nor the property owner in the latter.

Shimmen is not a lacuna case simply because the defendant realised there was a
risk, whereas the true lacuna operates where the defendant considers the situation
and concludes there is no risk if the conduct is undertaken. Professor Smith in his
commentary on *Merrick* concluded: 'There is no doubt that the so called lacuna exists
in the propositions stated by Lord Diplock in *Caldwell* ... and the decision of the
House of Lords in *Reid* [1992] 3 All ER 673.' In *Reid*, Lord Goff asked, in the context
of the old offence of causing death by reckless driving, what of the case of a
defendant who considers the possibility of risk but concludes that there is none? This
might happen where the driver is genuinely mistaken in respect of some crucial
information, for example, he believes he is driving in a two-way street when in fact it
is one way. The act is objectively dangerous, but is it reckless? The driver does not
consider there to be a risk because he is labouring under a genuine mistake of fact.
Lord Goff goes on to say:

> If that was indeed the case, his driving might well not be described as reckless, though
> such cases are likely to be rare. It has been suggested that there is therefore a
> 'loophole' or 'lacuna' in Lord Diplock's definition of recklessness. I feel bound to say
> that I ... regard these expressions as misleading ... it is not in every case where the
> defendant is in fact driving dangerously that he should be held to be driving
> recklessly [p 690(h)].

The lacuna may well exist, as suggested by the decision in *Reid*, but as yet there has
been no unequivocal endorsement by the courts.

3.4.2   The future of recklessness

What of the future of recklessness? The House of Lords considered the matter in
Reid. In this case, the appellant was convicted of causing death by reckless driving,
with the judge giving a *Lawrence* direction to the jury on the meaning of driving
recklessly. The House of Lords refused to take the opportunity to overrule *Lawrence*,
because as Lord Keith of Kinkel opined:

> Those who fail to display the requisite degree of self-discipline through failing to give
> any thought to the possibility of the serious risks they are creating may reasonably be
> regarded as no less blameworthy than those who consciously appreciate a risk but
> nevertheless go on to take it. The word 'reckless' in its ordinary meaning is apt to

embrace the former category no less than the latter, and I feel no doubt that Parliament by its use intended to cover both of them.

However, the *Lawrence* direction was modified by Lord Goff, supported by Lord Browne-Wilkinson, to the extent that the driving should be in such a manner as to create a *serious* risk of causing physical injury or damage to property. Lord Goff expressed the view that, 'the requirement that the risk be obvious ... cannot be relevant where the defendant is in fact aware that there is some kind of relevant risk' (p 691). This must, of course, be correct if the accused recognised that there was some risk of the type mentioned and nevertheless went on to take it. In this situation there is simply no need to invoke the foresight of the ordinary prudent person because the accused has acknowledged the existence of a serious risk of harmful consequences. On the other hand, it is still vital to refer to the risk being obvious if the accused failed to address his mind to the possibility of risk. In *P & O European Ferries (Dover) Ltd*, the judge held there was no evidence of recklessness because of the absence of evidence of an 'obvious' risk that dire consequences would ensue if the ferry sailed with its bow doors open. Thus, a defendant is culpable as a result of failing to appreciate what ordinary people would foresee as obvious. A direction to the jury on a criminal damage charge should now be phrased, according to Smith and Hogan (*Criminal Law*, 10th edn, 2002, London: Butterworths, p 80), in the following terms:

The jury must be sure that:

(i) D did an act which created a serious risk that property would be destroyed or damaged; and

(ii) either (a) he recognised that there was some risk of that kind involved but nevertheless went on to take it; or (b) that, despite the fact that he was acting in such a manner, he did not even address his mind to the possibility of there being any such risk, and the risk was in fact obvious.

Rather more intriguing is the suggestion by Lord Keith that 'inadvertence to risk is no less a subjective state of mind than is disregard of a recognised risk'. He justified this statement by arguing that 'if there is nothing to go upon apart from what actually happened', then it would be impossible for a jury to decide which state of mind was present. The defendant's chance of acquittal is possible only if he did give thought to the possibility of risk and concluded there was none, that is, the lacuna argument. To recognise the existence of the risk and go ahead will lead to *mens rea* being established as will failure to give thought providing a *serious* risk has been created and it would have been *obvious* to the ordinary prudent person.

There are also some suggestions in *Reid* that some of the harshness created by *Caldwell/Lawrence* might be alleviated if the defendant failed to recognise an obvious and serious risk because he or she lacked the capacity to recognise it due, for example, to illness, shock, mental incapacity (see in particular the speeches of Lord Keith, p 675, and Lord Goff, p 690). However, this possible means of avoiding some of the harshness of objective recklessness appears to be limited. In *Coles* [1995] 1 Cr App R 157, the Court of Appeal affirmed the decision of the trial judge not to admit evidence of a young person's low average mental capacity. This is likely to mean that pre-existing incapacity such as that in *Elliott v C* will not be affected and that this particular form of injustice will continue. It might be possible to argue, however, that an incapacity which was not in existence prior to the *actus reus* could be introduced and the defendant's foresight compared not with that of the ordinary prudent individual but with a person of his or her own capacity and capability (see further Field and Lynn, 'Capacity, recklessness and the House of Lords' [1993] Crim LR 127).

Reid applies the *Lawrence* test. *Caldwell* and *Lawrence* are virtually indistinguishable in terms of principle and therefore it is arguable that *Reid* should be equally applicable to the offence of criminal damage. *Seymour* had considered the *Caldwell/Lawrence* definitions and applied them to the offence of manslaughter on the basis that the legal ingredients of the common law offence of manslaughter (when caused by poor driving) and the statutory offence of causing death by reckless driving were the same. It is, however, no longer necessary to consider whether *Reid* should apply to the common law offence. The House of Lords overruled the *Seymour* decision in *Adomako* [1994] 3 All ER 79 on the basis that the underlying statutory provisions pertinent to the decision have now been repealed. While *Reid* is an important decision, it does highlight many of the difficulties experienced with the concept of recklessness since *Caldwell* in 1981. Lords Keith and Ackner appear to support the *Lawrence* direction without modification, whereas Lords Browne-Wilkinson and Goff favoured omitting the word 'obvious'. The *ratio* on this point at least remains obscure. However three Law Lords agreed that the meaning of *reckless* could well vary by reference to the particular statutory context. The result is that the *Caldwell/Lawrence* meaning of recklessness is confined for most practical purposes to offences under the CDA 1971.

3.4.3   Reform

The Law Commission in its 1993 report (Law Com 218, para 10.1), was of the view that 'much of the debate in both *Caldwell* and in *Reid* was occasioned by the fact that neither in the CDA 1971 nor in the RTA 1988 was the term "reckless" defined. Both courts were, therefore, led to speculate on the normal, usual or natural meaning of that word'. The Commission is clearly of the view that it is imperative that a statutory definition of recklessness be established. Paragraph 10.2 puts it this way:

> Indeed, the history of attempts to expound an undefined 'recklessness' ... reinforces our view, which was also that of the CLRC [Criminal Law Revision Committee] that statutory definition of the term is essential. As the CLRC put it, discussing both intention and recklessness: 'If the law is to be consistently applied, [these terms] cannot be left to a jury or magistrates as "ordinary words of the English language".' That is particularly so of the word reckless, which in its undefined form has a wide and far from generally agreed range of meanings. Possible dictionary synonyms include 'careless, regardless or heedless of the possible consequences of one's act'; 'heedlessness of risk (non-advertence)'; but also simply negligent or inattentive. Left to its own devices, therefore, a jury asked to think in terms of undefined recklessness might well apply nothing more than the civil, tortious, standard of liability.

The Law Commission, therefore, proposed the following definition of 'recklessly':

> A person acts recklessly with respect to:
>
> (i)   a circumstance, when he is aware of a risk that it exists or will exist; and
>
> (ii) a result, when he is aware of a risk that it will occur, and it is unreasonable, having regard to the circumstances known to him, to take that risk [cl 1].

This proposed definition is exactly the same as that contained in the proposed 1989 draft Criminal Code (Law Com 177, cl 18(c)) (apart from a minor textual readjustment).

We make one final point before leaving recklessness. It is important to understand that fault terms such as intention and recklessness do not exist independently of the specific crime of which they form a part. There is no crime called 'intention' or 'recklessness'. But there are specific crimes where the prosecution are required to prove that the defendant possessed the *mens rea* required by the offence.

3.5 OTHER KEY WORDS

We have analysed the meaning of intention and recklessness but how have the courts interpreted other words commonly found in statutory offences?

3.5.1 Wilfully

This word is frequently found in statutes but unfortunately the courts have not been entirely consistent in their interpretation. The leading case is *Sheppard* [1980] 3 All ER 899 where the House of Lords was called upon to interpret s 1(1) of the Children and Young Persons Act 1933, which provides that: 'If any person who has ... authority, charge or care of any child or young person ... *wilfully* assaults, ill-treats, neglects, abandons, or exposes him ... in a manner likely to cause him unnecessary suffering or injury to health ... that person shall be guilty ...' This case involved a failure to provide medical aid to a child. Lord Diplock suggested that in such a case the following direction should be given to the jury:

> ... the prosecution must prove (1) that the child did in fact need medical aid at the time at which the parent is charged with failing to provide it [the *actus reus*] and (2) either that the parent was aware at that time that the child's health might be at risk if it were not provided with medical aid, or that the parent's unawareness of this fact was due to his not caring whether his child's health were at risk or not [the *mens rea*] [p 903].

'Wilfully' is therefore a *mens rea* word and covers both intention and recklessness. However, in a number of cases the courts have limited this requirement to merely one part of the *actus reus* and not to the other. In *Maidstone BC v Mortimer* [1980] 2 All ER 502, the defendant was convicted of *wilfully* destroying a tree in contravention of a preservation order. The Divisional Court held that 'wilfulness' only applied to the destruction of the tree; it was irrelevant to his conviction that he had in fact no knowledge that a preservation order was in existence.

3.5.2 Knowingly

'Knowingly' is a *mens rea* word and includes a defendant who:

- Knows something is true or is virtually certain that it is true (as with intention it is irrelevant that it is not the defendant's aim, wish, purpose or desire that the prohibited act occur or circumstance exist).

- Is wilfully blind to the truth. Lord Bridge defined wilful blindness in *Westminster CC v Croyalgrange Ltd* [1986] 2 All ER 353 as, 'the defendant ... deliberately shut his eyes to the obvious or refrained from enquiring because he suspected the truth but did not want to have his suspicions confirmed' (p 359).

When 'knowingly' is found in a statute it normally applies to each element of the *actus reus* of the offence.

3.5.3   Permits

This word has been the subject of considerable judicial uncertainty. Its meaning is different in different statutory offences. Sometimes it imports a requirement of full *mens rea*; sometimes it does not. In *James & Son Ltd v Smee* [1955] 1 QB 78, a case concerned with *permitting* a person to use a vehicle with defective brakes, the Divisional Court held that the word 'permit' imported a requirement for *mens rea* to be proved. A defendant could not be guilty of permitting use of a vehicle with defective brakes unless he either knew that the brakes were defective or at least was reckless in the sense that he was wilfully blind, deliberately shutting his eyes to the possibility that they might be defective. On the other hand, the same court held in *DPP v Fisher* [1992] RTR 787, in relation to the offence of driving without insurance, that the only *mens rea* the prosecution need prove was that the owner permitted some other person to drive his vehicle. It was unnecessary to prove knowledge that the driver permitted to drive was uninsured.

In *Vehicle Inspectorate v Nuttall* [1999] 1 WLR 629, the charge, against the owner of a coach business, was that he had permitted drivers of his coaches to contravene the requirements of Community rules restricting driving hours. The defendant had failed over a period of more than two months to check the drivers' tachograph charts. The House of Lords held that: 'Depending on the context the word 'permit' is capable of bearing, on the one hand a narrow meaning of assenting to or agreeing to, or on the other hand, a wider meaning of not taking reasonable steps to prevent, something in one's power' (Lord Steyn at p 635). In the words of Lord Nicholls of Birkenhead:

> The former meaning ('allowed' or 'authorised') will usually import knowledge, in the sense of knowledge of what was being allowed or authorised. In the normal way, a person cannot be said to allow a particular activity, still less authorise it, unless he is aware of the activity being carried on or expected to be carried on. The latter meaning, however, directs attention in a different direction. Under the latter meaning the offence consists of an omission ('failed to take reasonable steps to prevent'). Thus ... failure to take reasonable steps to prevent a contravention by the driver is prescribing a standard of conduct an employer is required to attain. The effect is to impose on the employer a duty. The prescribed standard is the objective standard of a responsible employer [p 631].

Their Lordships unanimously held that in the offence with which they were dealing the word had the latter, wider meaning, since it was clear from the rules that the operator was obliged to perform periodic checks of the tachographs. In other cases, the result may not be so obvious. Nor did their Lordships completely turn their back on there being a requirement of *mens rea* in the offence with which they were dealing. Lord Steyn, with whom the majority agreed, held that there was also a requirement of recklessness, at least in the sense of the defendant 'not caring whether a contravention of the provisions of the regulations took place'. He held that the defendant's failure over a significant period to examine the tachograph records was *prima facie* evidence of such recklessness. So apparently, in this offence, the word 'permit' does not import a requirement of full knowledge of the drivers driving more hours than the rules allow but it does require: (a) a failure to take reasonable steps to prevent a contravention; and (b) a mental state of not caring whether a contravention takes place.

3.6   TRANSFERRED MALICE

The *mens rea* of an offence must of necessity relate to the *actus reus* in order for liability to follow. What is the position where the defendant has produced the *actus reus* of one crime but had the intention (or *mens rea*) to produce a different one? Suppose D shot at A intending to kill him but missed and killed B. B may in fact be a person against whom he had no animosity whatsoever. Nevertheless, a human being has lost his life and it must be determined if D is legally to be held responsible. Examples abound to illustrate the principle of transferred malice which is the idea that the intent held by D against A can be transferred to B in order to sustain a conviction against D. In *Mitchell* [1983] 2 All ER 427, Staughton J reinforced the point:

> We can see no reason of policy for holding that an act calculated to harm A cannot be manslaughter if it in fact kills B. The criminality of the doer of the act is precisely the same whether it is A or B who dies. A person who throws a stone at A is just as guilty if, instead of hitting and killing A, it hits and kills B [p 431].

In this case, the defendant had intentionally assaulted a man in a post office queue which caused the man to stumble against a frail 89-year-old woman who fell and later died following an operation to treat the injuries she sustained. The Court of Appeal upheld Mitchell's conviction for manslaughter.

Precise liability will inevitably depend on the *mens rea* of the defendant. Two leading 19th century authorities support the principle of transferred malice. In *Latimer* (1886) 17 QBD 359, the defendant hit out at another man (C) with his belt, which glanced off him and struck and wounded R who was standing nearby. Even though the jury found that R was hit accidentally, the *mens rea* held by Latimer towards C was held to be capable of being transferred and he was found guilty of malicious wounding contrary to s 20 of the OAPA 1861. Here the two crimes involved were the same and the principle will only apply in such circumstances. This means that the prosecution cannot join the *mens rea* of one type of offence with the *actus reus* of a different type of offence. The principle applies only when the *actus reus* and *mens rea* of the same crime are present. This point is well illustrated by the second of the cases, *Pembliton* (1874) LR 2 CCR 119. P, who was involved in an altercation outside a public house, threw a stone at the persons with whom he had been fighting. It missed them and broke a window. Undoubtedly, whilst he did intend an offence of violence, he did not intend to break the window and his conviction for malicious damage was quashed because there was no evidence that he possessed the *mens rea* in relation to the *actus reus* he had caused. Putting this case into a modern context would result in a charge of criminal damage and if in the circumstances P was found to have acted recklessly in relation to the criminal damage then a conviction could be achieved, as it apparently could have been under the Malicious Damage Act 1861 if there had been evidence from which it could have been proved that D was reckless.

Transferred malice has caused a number of problems in relation to the defendant who intentionally causes serious injury to a pregnant woman, who subsequently gives birth to a child who later dies as a result of the initial injury to the mother. This was the scenario which the House of Lords had to consider in *Attorney General's Reference (No 3 of 1994)* [1997] 3 All ER 936. The established facts of the case included the following. The defendant had stabbed a woman who was 26 weeks pregnant with intent to cause her grievous bodily harm. The woman later died of those wounds. The accused pleaded guilty to, and was convicted of, two offences in relation to the woman: (a) causing grievous bodily harm with intent to cause grievous bodily harm; and (b) manslaughter. The child which the mother was carrying was born alive and later died. The accused was charged with murder of the child. He was acquitted on the trial judge's ruling that no offence of homicide was disclosed. Thus, the charge of murder of the child never went to trial. It was, therefore, never conclusively established that the accused's attack on the mother was a cause of the child's subsequent death. The Attorney General referred the matter to the Court of Appeal and it was then referred to the House of Lords. The judgment of the House of Lords was reached on the basis of assumed facts which included the following: the accused had no intent to kill or to injure the child; he had no intent to kill the mother; he did have intent to cause grievous bodily harm to the mother; the injuries inflicted by the accused were a significant cause of the child's death. On those assumed facts, their Lordships held that the accused could not be convicted of murder of the child. Their Lordships accepted the existence of the rule that, in murder, an intent to cause grievous bodily harm is sufficient *mens rea*. They also accepted the existence of the doctrine of transferred malice whereby an intent to cause a particular kind of harm to one person can be used to justify a conviction of causing that same kind of harm to another person, for example where one aims at one person but misses and accidentally hits another. Thus, an intention to cause grievous bodily harm to one person can be used to justify a conviction of intentionally causing grievous bodily harm to another person. Equally, an intention to kill one person can be used to justify a conviction of murder of another. Their Lordships, however, placed a limitation on this transfer of *mens rea*. They held that for the transfer to be possible, there must be 'compatibility' between the harm intended to the first person and the harm which actually resulted to the other person. Thus, it is possible to justify, and the law allows:

- conviction for the murder of Y where the accused intended to cause grievous bodily harm to Y;

- conviction for intentionally causing grievous bodily harm to X where the accused intended to cause grievous bodily harm to Y;

- conviction for the murder of X on the basis that the accused had intended to kill Y.

It is not possible to justify, and the law does not allow:

- conviction for the murder of X on the basis that the accused intended to cause grievous bodily harm to Y.

After the decision in *Attorney General's Reference (No 3 of 1994)*, the decisions in *Latimer* and *Pembliton* remain good law but there is now a significant limitation on any further development of the doctrine of transferred malice, namely the requirement of compatibility.

As regards manslaughter, their Lordships were of the opinion that on the assumed facts the accused was guilty of manslaughter of the child. That decision did not, however, require any reliance upon the doctrine of transferred malice. It was on the basis that the death of the child was caused by an unlawful and dangerous act (the stabbing of the mother). That version of manslaughter (constructive or unlawful act manslaughter) did not require any *mens rea* other than: (a) an intention to commit the unlawful act; and (b) an objective assessment that it was dangerous, involving the risk of some harm to some person.

3.6.1   Reform

The Law Commission considered both transferred malice and transferred defences in its proposed 1989 draft Criminal Code (Law Com 177) and decided in favour of a general provision in relation to transferred fault (cl 24). Its recommendations have since been slightly modified to take account of developments in the law of recklessness and now appear in cl 32 of its 1993 Report (Law Com 218):

(1)   In determining whether a person is guilty of an offence, his intention to cause, or his awareness of a risk that he will cause, a result in relation to a person or thing capable of being the victim or subject-matter of the offence shall be treated as an intention to cause or, as the case may be, an awareness of the risk that he will cause, that result in relation to any other person or thing affected by his conduct.

(2)   Any defence on which a person might have relied on a charge of an offence in relation to a person or thing within his contemplation is open to him on a charge of the same offence in relation to a person or thing not within his contemplation.

The Commission considered such a provision necessary because, as they explained in para 42.1 of the report:

Where a person intends to affect one person or thing (X) and actually affects another (Y), he may be charged with an offence of attempt in relation to X; or it may be possible to satisfy a court or jury that he was reckless with respect to Y. But an attempt charge may be impossible (where it is not known until trial that the defendant claims to have had X and not Y in contemplation); or inappropriate (as not describing the harm done adequately for labelling or sentencing purposes). Moreover, recklessness with respect to Y may be insufficient to establish the offence or incapable of being proved. The rule stated by [cl 32] overcomes these difficulties.

3.7   COINCIDENCE OF *ACTUS REUS* AND *MENS REA*

In the overwhelming majority of cases the *mens rea* and the *actus reus* will coincide in the sense that at the time the consequence occurred the accused possessed the requisite mental element.

Reference has already been made to the continuous act theory (see above, 2.6) and in these circumstances the crime is deemed to be complete once the *mens rea* is evident at any time whilst the act continues. For example, the Judicial Committee of the Privy Council decided in *Kaitamaki v R* [1985] AC 147 that in the context of the law of rape, sexual intercourse is a continuing act starting at the moment sexual intercourse commences and finishing when it stops and that, if penetration continues when the consent has been withdrawn part way through the act, then the crime is complete. The assumption in this type of case is that the intercourse is consensual at the outset, but consent, for whatever reason, is then revoked. The celebrated case of *Fagan v Metropolitan Police Commissioner* [1968] All ER 442 also illustrates the general point.

Fagan had been told by a police officer to park his car against the kerb. In attempting this manoeuvre, Fagan drove the car onto the policeman's foot. Despite several requests to remove it the appellant left it there, until finally reversing off the constable's foot. He was charged with assaulting a police officer in the execution of his duty. Fagan claimed that the act was unintentional and that, of course, may have been true. What is also beyond doubt is that he realised the car was on the officer's foot and he deliberately chose to leave it there, telling the constable in no uncertain terms that he would have to be patient. The Court of Appeal was of the opinion that it was unnecessary for the *mens rea* to be present at the inception of the *actus reus*, taking the view that it 'can be superimposed on an existing act'. The court sought to draw a distinction between a completed act where any later *mens rea* will not complete a crime and a continuing act where subsequent *mens rea* arising at any point during the act's continuation will result in a crime being committed. In this case, the car was driven onto the foot and the appellant knew what had happened before turning off the ignition. The act could, therefore, be said to have continued certainly until the engine was cut, during which period the evidence of his intention to leave it there was clearly articulated. (This case must now be read together with the *Miller* decision (see above, 2.6).)

Other circumstances may arise where one is dealing with more than one act, usually where the defendant(s) are carrying out a preconceived plan. In *Thabo Meli* [1954] 1 All ER 373, the appellants acting in concert lured a man into a hut and attacked him. Believing him to be dead they took his body and rolled it over a cliff hoping to make it appear that he had died accidentally. It transpired that at the time he was pushed over the cliff he was still alive and died from exposure while lying unconscious at the foot of the cliff. It was argued for the appellants that two acts had been carried out, the attack in the hut when there was clear intent to kill and the second in pushing the victim over the cliff when there was no intent to kill as they believed him already to be dead. It was maintained that the first act did not cause death and that the second, which did, was not accompanied by the *mens rea* of murder although they could be guilty of manslaughter. The Privy Council upheld the conviction for murder because it was:

> ... impossible to divide up what was really one series of acts in this way. There is no doubt that the accused set out to do all these acts in order to achieve their plan, and as parts of their plan; and it is much too refined a ground of judgement to say that, because they were under a misapprehension at one stage and thought that their guilty purpose had been achieved before, in fact, it was achieved, therefore they are to escape the penalties of the law [p 374].

Similar reasoning was applied in *Church* [1966] 2 All ER 72, although in that case there was no antecedent plan. The appellant had taken a woman to his van where sexual relations were attempted. He was unable to satisfy her and she slapped his face as a result of which a fight ensued and he rendered her unconscious. He attempted to revive her for approximately 30 minutes but failed. He then panicked and threw her body into a nearby river. She died by drowning. The Court of Criminal Appeal applying the reasoning in *Thabo Meli* thought there to be a series of acts which culminated in death. However, it cannot be said that *at the outset* he intended to kill or cause grievous bodily harm otherwise the conviction would have been for murder. It is thus difficult to isolate the series of acts which culminated in death. The only act which brought about death was the disposal of the body into the river, there being no evidence whatsoever of any prior thought that this chain of events would unfold. He went to the van with Mrs Nott for sexual pleasure, she taunted him and struck him first and to say that any of his actions were designed to cause death is hardly an accurate reflection of what took place. This is a case which is better examined in light of the *Miller* decision, that is, having created a dangerous situation he failed in his duty to render assistance. A manslaughter conviction is certainly sustainable.

However, all this should now be read in light of the Court of Appeal decision in *Le Brun* [1991] 4 All ER 673, where *Church* was applied to convict a husband of the manslaughter of his wife. The couple had been arguing as they walked home early one morning. He struck her, knocking her down unconscious. He then attempted to lift or drag the body away from the scene but she slipped from his grasp, hit her head on the pavement and subsequently died from a fractured skull. The trial judge directed the jury that they could convict of either murder or manslaughter (depending on his *mens rea* at the time of the initial assault) if Le Brun had accidentally dropped her while attempting to take her home against her wishes or whilst attempting to dispose of her body, or whilst covering up the initial assault in some other way. The court was of the opinion that if the act of unlawful force and the eventual act causing death were part of the 'same sequence of events', then the initial *mens rea* was sufficient to sustain the verdict of unlawful killing because the act which caused death and the necessary mental state did *not* have to coincide in point of time. Two separate points arise as a result of this decision.

The first is that this type of case can be analysed in the context of the principles of causation. As Lord Lane CJ put it:

> The original unlawful blow to the chin was a *causa sine qua non* of the later *actus reus*. It was the opening event in a series which was to culminate in death: the first link in the chain of causation, to use another metaphor. It cannot be said that the actions of the appellant in dragging the victim away with the intention of evading liability broke the chain which linked the initial blow to the death [p 678].

Do note that this suggests that the principle applies where the accused is seeking to 'evade liability' but not where he is acting in an attempt to redeem something from the situation, for example, trying to place the victim in a comfortable position or moving her inside a house in order to render assistance. However, given that there is only one question as far as causation is concerned: whether the act was a significant and operating cause of death, then whatever follows should not break the chain, unless it is a new cause wholly unrelated to the initial act.

The second point confirms that the 'transaction' or 'series of events' approach remains good law. Lord Lane explains it in this way:

> ... where the unlawful application of force and the eventual act causing death are part of the same sequence of events, the same transaction, the fact that there is an

appreciable interval of time between the two does not serve to exonerate the defendant from liability. That is certainly so where the appellant's subsequent actions which caused death, after the initial unlawful blow, are designed to conceal his commission of the original unlawful assault ... in short, in circumstances such as the present ... the act which causes death and the necessary mental state to constitute manslaughter need not coincide in point of time.

This judgment is particularly interesting for two reasons. First, it confirms that the whole transaction or series of events cannot be split up and that together they constitute the *actus reus*. This approach admits that the *actus reus* and *mens rea* do not have to start or finish together but leaves intact the requirement that there must be a time (however fleeting) that the two coincide. Secondly, it suggests that the defendant must have been engaged upon a further unlawful activity. If he was acting for humanitarian purposes the outcome might well have been different.

3.8   STRICT LIABILITY

For the majority of this chapter, it has been asserted that *mens rea*, usually intention or recklessness, must be proved in order to obtain a conviction. From this it may be assumed that the overwhelming majority of crimes are *mens rea* offences, and this is true in respect of the major offences. However, there are many minor regulatory offences, usually statutory, which do not require intention or recklessness or even negligence to be proved in respect of at least one element of the *actus reus*. These are known as *strict liability* offences. It is estimated that nearly half of the approximately 7,500 statutory crimes come within this description. Contrast strict liability with *absolute liability* offences. Here the prosecution is relieved of the duty of proving *mens rea* in relation to any element of the *actus reus* and it may be that access to general defences is denied. Additionally, it may not be necessary to prove that the *actus reus* was committed voluntarily. Such absolute offences are rare (for two examples, see above, 2.2.4). The modern approach to offences of strict liability was enunciated by Lord Reid in *Sweet v Parsley* [1970] AC 132 at 148 who spoke of the firmly established view that:

> Our first duty is to consider the words of the Act: if they show a clear intention to create an absolute offence that is the end of the matter. But such cases are very rare. Sometimes the words of the section which creates the particular offence make it clear that *mens rea* is required in one form or another. Such cases are quite frequent. But in a very large number of cases there is no clear indication either way.
>
> In such cases, there has for centuries been a presumption that Parliament did not intend to make criminals of persons who were in no way blameworthy in what they did. That means that whenever a section is silent as to *mens rea* there is a presumption that, in order to give effect to the will of Parliament, we must read in words appropriate to require *mens rea* ... In the absence of a clear indication in the Act that an offence is intended to be an absolute offence, it is necessary to go outside the Act and examine all relevant circumstances in order to establish that this must have been the intention of Parliament. I say 'must have been' because it is a universal principle that if a penal provision is reasonably capable of two interpretations, that interpretation which is most favourable to the accused must be adopted.

Lord Scarman provides a valuable analysis of the modern approach to strict liability offences in the Privy Council case of *Gammon (Hong Kong) Ltd v Attorney General for Hong Kong* [1984] 2 All ER 503, p 508:

(1) there is a presumption of law that *mens rea* is required before a person can be guilty of a criminal offence;

(2) the presumption is particularly strong where the offence is 'truly criminal' in character;

(3) the presumption applies to statutory offences, and can be displaced only if this is clearly or by necessary implication the effect of the statute;

(4) the only situation in which the presumption can be displaced is where the statute is concerned with an issue of social concern; public safety is such an issue;

(5) even where the statute is concerned with such an issue, the presumption of *mens rea* stands unless it can be shown that the creation of strict liability will be effective to promote the objects of the statute by encouraging greater vigilance to prevent the commission of the prohibited act.

In *B (A Minor) v DPP* [2000] 1 All ER 833, the most recent case in which the House of Lords has considered the issue of strict liability, their Lordships relied in particular upon the approach in *Sweet v Parsley* and also on that in *Gammon (Hong Kong)*.

It must not be assumed that strict liability can only be found in the context of statutory offences. There is limited recognition in certain areas of the common law. In one area, that of criminal contempt of court, the strict liability rule which applied to the common law was put onto a statutory basis by s 1 of the Contempt of Court Act 1981. This section provides that someone may be guilty of contempt *regardless of intent* where the publication in question creates a substantial risk of serious prejudice or impediment to particular proceedings *and* those proceedings are active. Public nuisance and criminal libel are two crimes which are exceptions to the common law rule in favour of *mens rea*. However neither of these offences would appear to be of relevance in modern law. Blasphemous libel is a common law offence which was resurrected in 1979 when the editor and publishers of *Gay News* were prosecuted. It was held by the House of Lords in *Whitehouse v Lemon and Gay News Ltd* [1979] 1 All ER 898 that to obtain a conviction it was sufficient for the prosecution to prove *mens rea* only so far as the intention to publish the materials was concerned. It was not necessary to prove that the defendants intended to blaspheme. It was denied by the majority that they were creating a strict liability offence although the minority were convinced that the opposite was true. Blasphemous libel occurs when material is published which outrages and insults a Christian's religious feelings. If, as the majority decided, the only *mens rea* relates to the intent to publish and not to whether it will outrage Christians then a strict liability offence would appear to have been created.

The courts appear to have blown hot and cold as regards the recognition of offences as being strict liability. *Sheppard* and *Gammon (Hong Kong)* seemed to herald a growing reticence towards the expansion of strict liability with Lord Diplock in the former case stating:

The climate of both parliamentary and judicial opinion has been growing less favourable to the recognition of absolute offences over the last few decades, a trend to which s 1 of the Homicide Act 1957 and s 8 of the CJA 1967 bear witness in the case of

Parliament, and in the case of the judiciary is illustrated by the speeches in this House in *Sweet v Parsley* (1969) ... [p 906].

On the other hand, in *Champ* [1982] 73 Cr App R 367, for example, the Court of Appeal held that the crime of cultivating cannabis was a strict liability offence despite the fact that it is punishable by up to 14 years' imprisonment. Indeed, in *Gammon (Hong Kong)*, a case concerned with Hong Kong's Building Regulations, the offence was punishable by up to three years' imprisonment. Many people would view both crimes as 'truly criminal in character' but this did not prevent the courts classifying them as strict liability offences. Contrast this situation with s 6.02(4) of the US Model Penal Code, which proposes that the availability of imprisonment should be a conclusive reason against a finding of strict liability.

The House had no difficulty in *Pharmaceutical Society v Storkwain Ltd* [1986] 2 All ER 635 in concluding that s 58(2)(a) of the Medicines Act 1968 created an offence of strict liability particularly as other sections in the Act expressly required *mens rea* to be proved. Thus, 'by omitting s 58 from those sections [of the Act] ... Parliament intended that there should be no implication of a requirement of *mens rea* in s 58(2)(a)'. The outcome was that a pharmacist who supplied prescription only drugs as a result of being given a false prescription was guilty of the offence albeit he was not at fault. Section 58(2)(a) provides:

(a) no person shall sell by retail, or supply in circumstances corresponding to retail sale, a medicinal product of a description, or falling within a class, specified in an order under this section except in accordance with a prescription given by an appropriate practitioner ...

Another example of the courts' willingness to recognise strict liability is to be found in *Kirkland v Robinson* [1987] Crim LR 463. In this case, the appellant was convicted of possessing live wild birds contrary to s 1(2)(a) of the Wildlife and Countryside Act 1981 on the basis that as s 1(1) includes the word 'intentionally' but s 1(2) does not, parliament must have intended it to be an offence of strict liability. Therefore the court held that his claim that he did not know that the bird in his possession was wild did not provide him with a defence. The Divisional Court thought the Wildlife and Countryside Act 1981 had been designed to help protect the environment which was viewed as 'an objective of outstanding social importance'.

How important is this point that parliament by using a *mens rea* word in one section but omitting to use it in another can be taken by the courts as an indication that *mens rea* is not required in the latter section? It should be possible to provide a simple answer but in this area, as with so many aspects of strict liability the position is unclear as a result of inconsistencies between the cases. We saw above in the *Pharmaceutical Society* and *Kirkland* cases that it can be very important. Both cases followed the old Divisional Court case of *Cundy v Le Cocq* (1884) 13 QBD 207. Whilst it is an important factor, it cannot on its own justify a conclusion in favour of strict liability. As Lord Reid commented in *Sweet v Parsley* [1970] AC 132:

It is also firmly established that the fact that other sections of the Act expressly require *mens rea*, for example, because they contain the word 'knowingly', is not itself sufficient to justify a decision that a section which is silent as to *mens rea* creates an absolute offence [p 149].

Strict liability is by no means a relatively recent judicial creation. Its roots were firmly established in the 19th century and in a series of cases from 1846 onwards judges showed little reluctance towards the creation of strict liability offences. In the *Cundy v Le Cocq* case, C, a publican, sold alcohol to a drunken person, an action which contravened s 13 of the Licensing Act (LA) 1872. C claimed that he had no knowledge that the customer was drunk. The Divisional Court upheld his conviction and declared s 13 to be one of strict liability. Stephen J thought the words of the section amounted to 'an absolute prohibition' and that however genuine the publican's mistake regarding his customer's state of intoxication this would not provide him with a defence. As we have seen, the court was influenced by the fact that, whereas other sections of the LA 1872 contained the *mens rea* word 'knowingly', this word was absent in s 13.

In *Callow v Tillstone* (1900) 83 LT 411, a negligent examination of a carcass by a veterinary surgeon had resulted in a butcher selling meat which was unfit for human consumption. He, of course, had relied upon the veterinary surgeon's certificate that the meat was sound and would have no reason to assume that he was breaching the law. The butcher was convicted on the basis that the offence was one of strict liability. He had in fact sold meat which was unfit for human consumption. Just to compound his misery, the veterinary surgeon who was charged with aiding and abetting the offence had his conviction quashed on the basis that aiding and abetting required knowledge of the facts and an intention to encourage. Although he had been negligent in his examination of the animal, it could not be proved that *he knew* the meat was unsound.

Perhaps the best known example of the judiciary's approach to strict liability in the 19th century is *Prince* (1875) LR 2 CCR 154. The accused had been charged with s 55 of the OAPA 1861 (now, s 20 of the Sexual Offences Act (SOA) 1956). The offence provided:

> Whosoever shall unlawfully take or cause to be taken any unmarried girl, being under the age of 16 years, out of the possession and against the will of her father or mother or of any other person having the lawful care or charge of her, shall be guilty of a misdemeanour ...

It will be noted that the section does not contain any of the conventional *mens rea* words – intention, recklessly, maliciously, knowingly, and so on. The accused had enticed a girl aged 13 away from her parents. The girl looked much older than her years and she had informed the defendant that she was in fact aged 18. It was accepted by the court that he believed her story *and* that it was not unreasonable for him to hold such a belief. In holding that the intention of the legislature was to create a strict liability offence, Blackburn J commented:

> ... the question, therefore, is reduced to whether the words of s 55 of the OAPA 1861, that whosoever shall unlawfully take 'any unmarried girl being under the age of 16, out of the possession of her father' are to be read as if they were 'being under the age of 16, and he *knowing* she was under that age'. No such words are contained in the statute, nor is there the word 'maliciously', 'knowingly', or any other words used that can be said to involve a similar meaning [p 170].

The defendant was accordingly convicted. *Prince* is a good illustration of a point previously made that strict liability simply means that the prosecution is relieved from the task of proving *mens rea* in relation to one or more elements of the *actus reus*.

Mens rea may still need to be proved in respect of the other elements. In this case Prince possessed *mens rea* in relation to every element of the offence save that she was under 16 years of age.

The decision in *Prince* has now been overturned by the House of Lords in *B (A Minor) v DPP*, where their Lordships held that a requirement as to age is no different from any other ingredient of an offence and is thus subject to the presumption in favour of a *mens rea* requirement that the accused was aware of the victim's lack of age. In *B (A Minor) v DPP*, the victim, a girl aged 13, and the defendant, a 15-year-old boy, were travelling on the same bus. The defendant sat next to the victim and asked her several times to perform oral sex with him. She repeatedly refused. He was charged with inciting a girl under 14 to commit an act of gross indecency contrary to s 1(1) of the Indecency with Children Act 1960. The primary facts were admitted at the trial, as was his honest belief that the victim was over 14 years of age. The defendant argued that he must be acquitted on the facts as admitted, but the prosecution submitted that the offence was one of strict liability. The justices ruled that the defendant's state of mind could not constitute a defence to the charge and he changed his plea to guilty. When the case found its way to the House of Lords, their Lordships were unanimous in quashing the defendant's conviction. They considered that the *actus reus* element as to age was no different from any other *actus reus* element and was subject to a presumption in favour of a requirement for *mens rea*. This presumption was an expression of the principle of legality and could only be negatived by a compellingly clear implication, to be found in the language used, the nature of the offence, the mischief sought to be prevented and any other relevant circumstances. In this context, there were two very important factors in favour of the presumption and against strict liability:

- the offence is a serious offence with a severe punishment (10 years' maximum imprisonment) and correspondingly high stigma for conviction;

- the offence is drawn broadly ('an act of gross indecency'), embracing conduct ranging from 'predatory approaches by a much older paedophile' to 'consensual sexual experimentation between precocious teenagers of whom the accused may be the younger of the two'. Thus, the conduct might be 'depraved by any acceptable standard', or 'relatively innocuous behaviour in private between two young people'.

They further considered that neither the aim of protecting young children, nor the alleged difficulty in proving knowledge of age if *mens rea* were required, were strong arguments against the presumption. Nor, in their view, did the statutory context compel the rejection of a requirement for *mens rea* because 'the motley collection of offences, of diverse origins, gathered into the SOA 1956 displays no satisfactorily clear or coherent pattern', and so could give no compelling guidance. Their Lordships also rejected the option of requiring that the defendant's mistaken belief that the girl was aged 14 or over must be a reasonable belief.

The decision and reasoning in *B (A Minor) v DPP* is perhaps rather surprising for its rejection of strict liability and welcome for its approach to the issue of mistake in criminal law. However, it is doubtful whether it will have any major impact on the general approach to the imposition of strict liability. For example, we have already seen that the fact that a sentence of imprisonment is available for an offence is no guarantee that it will not be considered to impose strict liability. Is the strong reliance placed upon the availability of a maximum sentence of 10 years' imprisonment by their Lordships in *B (A Minor) v DPP* likely to change this position? Probably not in view of Lord Steyn's assertion in that very same case that the offence under s 5 of the SOA 1956 (sexual intercourse with a girl under the age of 13) 'plainly creates an offence of strict liability', despite the fact that the offence carries a maximum sentence of life imprisonment and looks like a 'truly criminal' offence if ever there was one! It is true that his Lordship was considering s 5 along with s 6 (the offence of sexual intercourse with a girl under the age of 16), and derived his conclusion from his belief that they must be viewed as a pair, but this is unlikely to obscure the main message that a sentence of imprisonment, even one of life imprisonment, is not necessarily protection against imposition of strict liability.

The decision in *B (A Minor) v DPP* left a question mark over the correct interpretation of a number of sexual offences where age is an element of the offence. Some of these doubts were removed by the later House of Lords' decision in *K* [2001] 3 WLR 471. In that case the accused, aged 26, was charged with an indecent assault on a girl under the age of 16, contrary to s 14 of the SOA 1956. The law was, and is, that the girl's consent is a defence if she is aged over 16 but not if she is under the age of 16. His defence was that: (a) she had consented; and (b) he had believed her to be over 16. Their Lordships followed *B (A Minor) v DPP* and applied the presumption in favour of a requirement of *mens rea*. Thus, they held that where a defendant is charged under s 14 of the Sexual Offences Act with indecently assaulting a girl under the age of 16 who consented, the prosecution has to prove an absence of belief on the part of the defendant that she was over 16 years of age. If the accused believed, however unreasonably, that she was over 16, he is not guilty. Their Lordships also removed the doubts over two other offences contained in the Sexual Offences Act 1956: s 5 (unlawful sexual intercourse with a girl under 13 years of age) and s 6 (unlawful sexual intercourse with a girl under 16 years of age). They made it clear that in those offences the presumption in favour of a requirement for *mens rea* does *not* apply. This was because parliament had made its intention clear in these offences. In relation to s 6, s 6(3) provides a defence for a man aged under 24 who has never previously been charged with a like offence and who believes, and has reasonable cause to believe, the girl is 16 or over. Clearly parliament intended that a mistake as to the girl's age is to be no defence to a charge under s 5 or, apart from where this young man's defence applies, under s 6.

It will be apparent that it is not just minor regulatory crimes to which strict liability will apply, although it has been consistently stressed by the judiciary that the more serious the crime the less likely that the presumption in favour of *mens rea* will be displaced. This presumption was recognised in the 19th century and specifically alluded to in *Sherras v De Rutzen* [1895] 1 QB 918 by Wright J. The following words have been quoted and accepted as correct by the higher courts on numerous occasions (for example, see *Lim Chin Aik v R* [1963] AC 160 and *Sweet v Parsley*):

> There is a presumption that *mens rea* is an essential ingredient in every offence; but that presumption is liable to be displaced either by the words of the statute creating the offence or by the subject matter with which it deals, and both must be considered [p 921].

In this case, a publican had been convicted of an offence contrary to s 16(2) of the LA 1872 in that he unlawfully supplied liquor to a police constable on duty. He had reasonably believed the constable to be off duty. The Divisional Court in quashing his conviction believed that a strict approach to the construction of the section would place publicans in an invidious position because 'no care on the part of the publican could save him from a conviction' if it was unnecessary to prove knowledge as to whether a constable was or was not on duty.

Whilst it may be true that most of the regulatory offences will be viewed by the majority of people as minor this is by no means always the case. We have already seen in *Champ* and *Gammon (Hong Kong) v Attorney General of Hong Kong* that the possibility of substantial terms of imprisonment for those who transgressed the legislation did not deter the judiciary from classifying it as strict liability.

Where there is an obvious danger to the community as a result of engaging in a particular activity, the courts are more likely to deny that the presumption in favour of *mens rea* should apply. In *Howells* [1977] 3 All ER 417, the appellant had in his possession a firearm which he believed to be an antique, and he therefore concluded that he did not require a firearms certificate for the gun. In fact, the gun was a modern reproduction and did require a certificate. He was found guilty of contravening s 1(1)(a) of the Firearms Act 1968 which makes it an offence for a person:

(a) to have in his possession, or to purchase or acquire, a firearm ... without holding a firearm certificate in force at that time ...

Howells argued that s 1 should not be construed so as to make it a strict liability offence and that an honest and mistaken belief should be recognised as a defence. The Court of Appeal had no doubts that the section should be construed strictly for the following reasons:

- the wording of the section would appear to indicate such a conclusion;

- the danger to the community from those possessing unlicensed firearms is so great as to warrant an absolute prohibition against their possession without proper authority;

- to allow a defence based upon an honest and reasonable belief that the firearm was antique and therefore didn't need a certificate would defeat 'the clear intention of the Act'.

In *Blake* [1977] 1 All ER 963, the defendant was found guilty of an offence under s 1(1) of the Wireless Telegraphy Act 1949 of 'using any apparatus for wireless telegraphy without a licence'. Investigation officers were concerned that 'pirate' broadcasts were frequently interfering with emergency service radio communications. They raided the premises of Ragga FM and discovered DJ Casanova playing music. The Court of Appeal considered *Gammon (Hong Kong)* and concluded that the fact that offenders were potentially subject to imprisonment must indicate that parliament viewed such broadcasts to be a matter of serious social concern which it wished to prevent in the interests of public safety. They concluded, therefore, that the offence was one of strict liability.

These cases would seem to emphasise the sort of public policy considerations which the judiciary take into account when construing legislation which lacks an obvious reference to *mens rea*.

It is possible to categorise strict liability offences by reference to the social context in which they operate although this is subject to the obvious comment that the cases display marked inconsistencies. For example, the courts have frequently construed legislation dealing with drugs and their misuse on a strict liability basis although there is a lack of clarity in at least one notable case. The House of Lords was given opportunity in *Warner v Metropolitan Police Commissioner* [1968] 2 All ER 356 to consider whether s 1(1) of the Drugs (Prevention of Misuse) Act 1964 should be construed strictly. Warner had been found in possession of two boxes. One contained scent and the other 20,000 tablets of amphetamine sulphate. He was charged with possession of a prohibited drug contrary to s 1(1) of the Act. He claimed that while he was aware that he had the boxes in his possession he assumed they both contained scent. The House of Lords by a 4:1 majority dismissed his appeal. The dilemma facing the House was whether a person who possessed a package was deemed also to be in possession of its contents, even if he were to be mistaken as to their nature. Views ranged from possession of a package meant possession of its contents to the possibility of rebutting the presumption if the contents were of a wholly different nature from what it was thought the box contained, for example scent and dangerous drugs. One of the Law Lords thought that the 'innocent' possessor should not be guilty if, for example, someone without the knowledge of the owner slipped prohibited drugs into her bag. Thankfully the subsequent Misuse of Drugs Act 1971 included a section which provided a defence if the accused could prove that he neither believed nor suspected nor had reason to suspect that the substance or product in question was a controlled drug (s 28(3)(b)).

In *McNamara* [1988] Crim LR 440, the Court of Appeal thought that the burden was on the prosecution to establish that the defendant 'had, and knew that he had, the box in his control *and* also that the box contained something'. This will be sufficient to establish possession (it is assumed that the prosecution proved that the package contained the particular drug alleged in the indictment). After that, the provisions of s 28(3)(b) come into play and the defendant is entitled to be acquitted if he can demonstrate that he 'neither believed nor suspected'. As will have been noted, this statutory defence, in line with many others, firmly places the burden of proof on the defendant.

Sweet v Parsley can be contrasted with *Warner* and reflects a more enlightened approach to strict liability. In *Sweet v Parsley,* Miss Sweet was charged with contravening s 5(b) of the Dangerous Drugs Act 1965 in that she was 'concerned in the management of premises' which were used for the purpose of smoking cannabis. She was a sub-tenant of a farm who let rooms to students. She did not live on the premises but kept a room for her occasional use. It was discovered that cannabis had been smoked at the farmhouse, although she had no idea that this had occurred. Her conviction was quashed on the basis that the offence required that the presumption in favour of *mens rea* should apply. Their Lordships emphasised the importance of the effect of the strict liability in achieving some desirable purpose. Lord Reid observed:

> If this section means what the Divisional Court have held that it means, then hundreds of thousands of people who sublet part of the premises or take in lodgers or are concerned in the management of residential premises or institutions are daily incurring a risk of being convicted of a serious offence in circumstances where they are in no way to blame. For the greatest vigilance cannot prevent tenants, lodgers or

inmates or guests whom they bring in from smoking cannabis cigarettes in their own rooms. It was suggested in argument that this appellant brought this conviction on herself because it is found as a fact that when the police searched the premises there were people there of the 'beatnik fraternity'. But surely it would be going a very long way to say that persons managing premises of any kind ought to safeguard themselves by refusing accommodation to all who are of slovenly or exotic appearance, or who bring in guests of that kind. And unfortunately drug taking is by no means confined to those of unusual appearance [p 150].

This point had been earlier addressed by the Privy Council in *Lim Chin Aik v R* where the defendant had entered Singapore in contravention of an order the existence of which he was unaware. His appeal against conviction was allowed. Lord Evershed expressed the opinion that:

It is not enough ... merely to label the statute as one dealing with a grave social evil and from that to infer that strict liability was intended. It is pertinent also to inquire whether putting the defendant under strict liability will assist in the enforcement of the regulations. That means that there must be something he can do, directly or indirectly, by supervision or inspection, by improvement of his business methods or by exhorting those whom he may be expected to influence or control, which will promote the observance of the regulations. Unless this is so, there is no reason in penalising him, and it cannot be inferred that the legislature imposed strict liability merely in order to find a luckless victim ... Where it can be shown that the imposition of strict liability would result in the prosecution and conviction of a class of persons whose conduct could not in any way affect the observance of the law, their Lordships consider that, even where the statute is dealing with a grave social evil, strict liability is not likely to be intended [p 174].

Sweet v Parsley was welcomed because it avoided the great injustice that could result to all those who manage hotels, guest houses and lettings. Although it is true that they can choose their tenants, it is unrealistic to assert that they can control what they do once they are behind the door of their hotel room. Hotels would attract few guests if they were to install spy cameras in each room in order that the management could observe whether or not anything illicit was taking place!

3.8.1 The justification for strict liability

Legal scholars are generally critical of the concept of strict liability. Arguments against its imposition include:

- that it is *unjust* to impose criminal liability upon a person who is not at fault. For example, what purpose is served by criminalising the acts of a butcher who unknowingly sells contaminated meat (with resulting damage to his reputation and livelihood) when he purchased the meat from a reputable supplier at market value and who had no reason to suspect that the quality of the meat was anything less than first class? The fact that the sentence imposed by the court is likely to be modest is irrelevant in this context;

- that it is unnecessary and does not lead to higher standards of protection for the public.

The arguments in favour of strict liability include:

- that it helps to prevent prohibited acts because it keeps people such as butchers 'on their toes' and in this way ensures higher standards than would otherwise prevail;

- that without it many of those charged with such offences would plead not guilty and the prosecuting authorities have neither the time or the personnel to litigate each case through the courts in the face of a large number of such pleas. This would lead to additional costs to the state and increased delays in the criminal justice system;

- those responsible for enforcement usually exercise their discretion and rarely prosecute in the complete absence of fault;

- the existence of specific statutory defences in some cases helps to alleviate possible injustice.

But does the certainty of conviction ensure higher standards for the public? No one would doubt that this is a laudable aim but whether imposing strict liability over a range of offences achieves these results is open to doubt. In *Alphacell Ltd v Woodward* [1972] 2 All ER 475, the view was taken that contraventions of the Rivers (Prevention of Pollution) Act 1951 were 'not criminal in any real sense but acts which in the public interest were prohibited under a penalty'. Lord Salmon was of the opinion that to enforce strict liability would deter potential polluters. They would, he thought, 'not only ... take reasonable steps to prevent pollution but [would] do everything possible to ensure that they do not cause it'. That expectation was certainly not at the forefront of the defendant's mind in *FJH Wrothwell Ltd v Yorkshire Water Authority* [1984] Crim LR 43, when a director of the company deliberately poured 12 gallons of a poisonous herbicide into its drains. He assumed that the liquid would remain in a public sewer until it reached a public sewage works. Unfortunately, the drains from the company premises led into a nearby stream and enormous damage was caused to the stream and its fish population. The charge under s 2 of the Rivers (Prevention of Pollution) Act 1951 was that the company did cause to enter a stream 'poisonous noxious or polluting matter ...'. The magistrates, following *Alphacell v Woodward*, took the view that the offence was absolute and convicted. The company appealed. They did not seek to deny that the offence could be established without proof of *mens rea*, but rather that the company director's state of mind should have been taken into account particularly as he had no idea whatsoever that the actual consequence would flow from his actions. The Divisional Court dismissed the appeal on the basis that 'cause' was a simple English word which should be given its 'ordinary common sense' meaning. There was only one *cause* of the consequence that being the director's action in pouring the herbicide down the drain. The word *cause* does not appear to suggest that a mental element needs to be established and therefore the company had little chance of succeeding with its argument.

But what is it reasonable to expect from someone in the company director's position to do before he undertakes such an action? Must he check first with the water company, insist upon seeing the plans of the local sewage system or invest large amounts of money in order to ascertain the correct position if the other two courses of action are unproductive? Or take the risk? One suspects that many will adopt a standard of care which essentially balances the costs of prevention against the predicted likelihood of detection, conviction and the size of the penalty. Many companies will run the risk of being fined for their activities rather than invest time, effort and money in ensuring they stay within the law.

One suggestion is that liability should depend upon proof of negligence and that this would be a suitable compromise between the need to establish *mens rea* and strict liability. Would it not be preferable to impose penalties only on those who did not act reasonably? Someone who has no reason to suspect that his actions may breach the criminal law and who has acted reasonably in coming to that conclusion surely does not deserve to find himself in the same position as someone who deliberately flouts the law.

Genevra Richardson has conducted research into those responsible for enforcing strict liability offences and the enforcement practices of the agencies they work for. She found that many enforcement personnel share the belief that many such offences are not 'real crimes' and see their primary duty as being not to enforce the law strictly but to ensure standards as high as possible. She found that they often viewed the sanctions imposed by the courts as derisory and were aware that in many cases their agencies' funds and resources were inadequate to enforce the law strictly. Despite this, however, she found many of the enforcers favoured the retention of strict liability because it made their job of routinely enforcing the law against the background of the criminal law and the implied threat of its invocation markedly easier (see 'Regulatory crime: the empirical research' [1987] Crim LR 295).

This does not of course mean that one has to agree with the views of the enforcement officials. Many people would consider it wrong that the determination of blame and the decision to prosecute is made by administrative bodies and their employees, in private, and with potential defendants denied the procedural safeguards normally available to those who face being charged with criminal offences.

3.8.2   Proposals for reform

The Law Commission's proposals are contained within the proposed codification of the criminal law (Law Com 177, 1989) and involve the provision of a standard definition of such key fault terms as 'intention', 'knowledge' and 'recklessness' (see cl 18). Clause 20(1) provides:

(1) Every offence requires a fault element of recklessness [that is, *Cunningham* style recklessness] with respect to each of its elements other than fault elements unless otherwise provided.

(2) [This] does not apply to pre-code offences ...

The Commission expressed the justification for such a clause to be:

An enactment creating an offence should ordinarily provide that the offence is one of strict liability in respect of one or more identified elements. It is necessary, however, to have a general rule for the interpretation of any offence the definition of which does not state, in respect of one or more elements, whether fault is required or what degree of fault is required. The absence of a consistent rule of interpretation has been a regrettable source of uncertainty in English law. Clause 20 provides such a rule ... The proposal to include this provision was well supported on consultation [para 8.25].

It is important to note that the proposal is expressed to apply in respect of *future* statutes only and that it would not, of course, fetter parliament's right to pass future statutes imposing strict liability or liability for negligence. However, in order to do this, parliament would have to make this clear in the legislation.

SUMMARY OF CHAPTER 3

THE MENTAL ELEMENT – *MENS REA*

The prosecution must prove that the defendant brought about the *actus reus* with the state of mind prescribed by the definition of the particular crime. This state of mind is usually referred to as the *mens rea*.

DIRECT AND OBLIQUE INTENTION

Some crimes require proof that the defendant acted *intentionally*. Intention is not the same thing as motive. Where the prohibited consequence is wanted for its own sake this is referred to as *direct intention*. Where the defendant does not have an aim or purpose to cause a prohibited result but knows that his conduct is certain or almost certain to cause it, this is said to be *oblique intention*. This is true whether or not the defendant has some other aim or purpose in engaging in the conduct. Parliament has failed to define intention and the courts have experienced considerable difficulties in attempting to define the term. The jury is not entitled to find an intention to kill or cause grievous bodily harm unless satisfied that the defendant appreciated that this result was virtually certain.

RECKLESSNESS

Defining *recklessness* has also proved problematic for the courts during recent years. Originally, it meant that the defendant undertook a deliberate and *conscious* unreasonable risk but in two landmark cases in 1981 the House of Lords added to this subjective test an objective element. These decisions are viewed by many legal scholars as flawed and wrong in principle because they lead not only to injustice in some cases but also because they have created serious uncertainty in the criminal law. Despite a ruling by the House in 1983 that the new definition applied throughout the law, subsequent decisions have shown that the new objective element does not apply to particular offences. Indeed, currently the objective element now only applies, for most practical purposes, to offences under the CDA 1971.

TRANSFERRED MALICE

The doctrine of *transferred malice* is that the malice a defendant bears towards his intended victim may, in certain circumstances, be transferred to the actual victim. For example, if A intends to shoot B but misses and kills C, A's malice may be transferred from B to C and A can be convicted of murder. It cannot be transferred, however, if there is no compatibility between the harm intended (or foreseen) and the harm actually inflicted.

COINCIDENCE OF *ACTUS REUS* AND *MENS REA*

The *actus reus* and *mens rea* must normally coincide in point of time. However, in some cases the courts have held the *actus reus* to be a continuing act and liability can be established if the defendant can be proven to have possessed *mens rea* at any point during the continuance of the act. Other cases have established that it is enough if the *mens rea* and *actus reus* can be said to have existed during a sequence of events.

STRICT LIABILITY OFFENCES

Many crimes do not require the prosecution to prove that the defendant acted either intentionally or recklessly or even negligently with respect to at least one element of the *actus reus*. These offences are usually, although not always, of a minor regulatory nature and are referred to as crimes of *strict liability*. Whether a particular crime will be found by the courts to require *mens rea* or to be a *strict liability* offence depends upon a variety of factors. The case law is inconsistent on this important point despite numerous attempts to clarify the matter. Whilst there are arguments both for and against strict liability legal scholars are, in general, hostile. Many would prefer an approach based upon negligence. The Law Commission favours a minimum liability threshold of (subjective) recklessness unless parliament provides to the contrary.

CHAPTER 4

PARTICIPATION IN CRIME

4.1   INTRODUCTION

In this chapter, we consider the basis of liability for those who engage in criminal activity but who are not directly or immediately responsible for causing the *actus reus* of the particular crime. In broad terms the law distinguishes between principal (or joint principal) offenders and secondary parties who, to use the terminology of the relevant legislation, aid, abet, counsel or procure the commission of the offence. It may be that assistance has been given to a bank robber prior to his attempt to relieve the bank of £100,000. This assistance may take many forms. The bank manager, A, may have been involved to the extent of supplying the principal offender, D, with information about how to avoid the security systems installed at the premises. The bank manager may be out of the country on holiday with his family when the crime takes place. Nevertheless, it cannot and should not be denied that he has made an important contribution towards the perpetration of the offence. Another person, B, may have supplied the weapon used by the principal offender when the crime is attempted. Again, it follows that the individual who is associated with the offence by prior involvement should bear some responsibility for the consequences which eventually ensue. A third person, C, may be waiting a couple of streets away ready to drive the principal offender from the scene of the crime. All these people are participating in the illegal enterprise and, providing they do so with the requisite knowledge and, of course, voluntarily, there is every reason why the law should seek to ensure that criminal liability should follow.

The subject and the issues which arise can present difficulties because it is not just a matter of assessing the defendant's actions but also linking the actions with those of others. There must, of necessity, be an assessment of the *mens rea* not only of the perpetrator of the full offence but also those charged with aiding or encouraging the offence. For liability to result, should those assisting or encouraging have to foresee the consequences of their involvement with the projected offence? Suppose that the robbery were to go wrong and a bank security guard is killed as he tries to prevent the principal offender from escaping. The bank manager, A, who supplied the information in return for cash may never have given a moment's thought to the prospect of someone being killed as a result of the attempt to carry out the crime. He may have had no idea that D would carry a weapon. However, B who has supplied the weapon may know that D wishes to have a weapon with him yet seeks to distance himself from a murder charge on the basis that D assured him that it would be used only to frighten anyone who tried to hinder his progress. He may be willing to admit his participation in the robbery but not murder as he 'never thought it would come to that'. It will be evident that the *mens rea* for participation will be an important element in the analysis of the principles relating to 'secondary' party activity. Yet should the fact that those who encourage an offence or give assistance at an early stage are not involved in carrying out the crime, make them less culpable than the principal offender? The relevant legislative provision clearly suggests not. Section 8 of the Accessories and Abettors Act (AAA) 1861, as amended by the Criminal Law Act (CLwA) 1967, states:

> Whosoever shall aid, abet, counsel or procure the commission of any indictable offence whether the same be an offence at common law or by virtue of any act passed or to be passed, shall be liable to be tried, indicted and punished as a principal offender.

It follows that the liability of a secondary party flows from the prosecution establishing at least that the *actus reus* of a crime has been committed by the principal offender (see *Millward* [1994] Crim LR 527; see below, 4.5). Section 1 of the CLwA 1967 abolished the distinction between felonies and misdemeanours and therefore the s 8 of the AAA 1861 provision applies to all offences. Similar principles are applied to summary offences as a result of s 44 of the Magistrates' Courts Act 1980. As Lord Widgery CJ said in *Attorney General's Reference (No 1 of 1975)* [1975] 2 All ER 684:

> Thus in the past, when the distinction was still drawn between felony and misdemeanour, it was sufficient to make a person guilty of a misdemeanour if he aided, abetted, counselled or procured the offence of another. When the difference between felonies and misdemeanours was abolished in 1967, s 1 of the Criminal Law Act in effect provided that the same test should apply to make a secondary party guilty either of treason or felony.

Therefore, both principal and accessory face the same consequence if convicted. It is reasonable to assume that parliament when choosing to use four words to describe the spheres of influence relating to an accessory meant those words to convey different meanings. As Lord Widgery CJ observed in *Attorney General's Reference (No 1 of 1975)*, if four words are employed:

> ... the probability is that there is a difference between each of those four words, and the other three, because, if there were no such difference, then Parliament would be wasting time in using four words where two or three would do, we approach the section on the footing that each word must be given its ordinary meaning.

To give the four words their 'ordinary meaning' as proposed by Lord Widgery does present some problems. For example, the word 'abet' is one which by no stretch of the imagination is to be found in everyday use. The House of Lords in *Lynch v DPP for Northern Ireland* [1975] 1 All ER 914 suggested that the words 'aid and abet' are really a single concept in which 'aid' represents the *actus reus* and 'abet' the *mens rea* of the prohibited activity. However, as the Law Commission in its consultation paper, *Assisting and Encouraging Crime* (Law Com 131, 1993, para 2.12), points out 'it is difficult or impossible to lay hands on authority for that analysis nor is it clear to what legal results the analysis would lead'.

4.2   PROCURE

The term 'procure' essentially means 'to cause'. Lord Widgery in *Attorney General's Reference (No 1 of 1975)* expressed this in terms to the effect that 'procure' 'means to produce by endeavour'. One procures a consequence by 'setting out to see that it happens and taking the appropriate steps to produce that happening'. It must be emphasised that there need not be a conspiracy between the principal and secondary party. The principal offender may be acting in all innocence, even though the act of the procurer results in the principal offender committing the prohibited conduct. As the facts that gave rise to *Attorney General's Reference (No 1 of 1975)* indicate, however, there must be a causal connection in fact between the act of the alleged procurer and the commission of the offence. The accused in that case had surreptitiously laced his friend's drink with alcohol. The friend (that is, the principal offender) had then driven his car whilst over the legal limit contravening s 6(1) of the Road Traffic Act 1972. It was held that the accused was in fact guilty of procuring the absolute offence under s 6(1). It had to be shown that the person lacing the drink knew the other was going to drive and knew that the ordinary and natural result of lacing the drink would be to bring his blood alcohol concentration above the legal limit.

Note that the court also addressed the legal position of the 'generous host' who with their consent keeps topping up the glasses of his guests with alcoholic drinks. If he knows that some or all of his guests are likely to drive home at the end of the dinner party, does this mean that his generosity will result in a conviction for procuring a 'drink-drive' offence if any of his guests contravene the relevant laws as a result of his actions? The court thought not. The first point to note is that his actions are not surreptitious. Secondly, there is dialogue between the parties. The host may well have enquired whether his guests wished to have more alcohol. Thirdly, it is the guests who will make the decision whether or not to drive having knowledge of all the circumstances. On balance the blame or fault rests with the drivers not the host. It could also be argued that the freely-willed decision of the guest to consume the alcohol and drive effectively breaks the chain of causation between the act of the host and the commission of the offence. The generous host is supplying the means by which an offence could be committed, but it would be difficult to prove that it was his intention that any of his guests contravened the drink-drive laws.

4.3 COUNSEL

Counselling implies suggesting or advising on the commission of the offence, although in reality the term is wider, encompassing situations where the accomplice instructs, orders, or threatens the principal offender into committing an offence. It usually occurs prior to the commission of the offence but need not necessarily do so. The actions of a person at the scene of the crime giving the principal offender advice on how to bypass a bank security system may amount to both counselling and abetting. If that same person were 100 miles away and communicating with the burglar by mobile phone, giving instructions on how to enter the building without raising the alarm, that would be an act of counselling. The action of counselling in this example is concurrent with the attempt by the principal to enter the building. It should not matter how the advice is given or from where it comes. The key question is whether there is something that amounts to assistance or encouragement and that it is done with the required *mens rea*.

A good example of counselling is where the accomplice hires the principal offender to commit an offence. In *Calhaem* [1985] 2 All ER 266, the appellant had hired a man, Zajac, to carry out a contract killing. Having been paid some money in advance, Zajac intended to act out a charade that involved attacking the victim to make it look as though he had tried to kill her. In fact, he had no intention of actually committing murder. When Zajac attacked the victim she screamed and he panicked. During the struggle that ensued he stabbed the victim causing her death. Calhaem contended that, on Zajac's own evidence, he had not killed the victim because he was carrying out her instructions but because he lost control of the situation and panicked. Dismissing her appeal Parker LJ emphasised that the offence was made out provided the principal, in committing the offence counselled, was acting within the scope of the accomplice's authority. It was not necessary for the counselling to be the cause of the offence. Providing the principal offence is 'committed by the one counselled and providing the one counselled is acting within the scope of his authority' then the offence is made out. Whilst counselling will, therefore, normally involve some agreement or consensus between the parties, there is no necessity for a causal connection between the act of counselling and the offence.

4.4   AID AND ABET

Aiding, taking its ordinary dictionary definition, means to give help, assistance or support; and to abet means 'instigation, aid or encouragement' (*Compact Oxford English Dictionary*). 'Aiding and abetting' is, therefore, synonymous with the concepts of giving assistance and encouragement to the principal offender. This may take many forms, as we have seen above, such as supplying weapons or driving a getaway car.

In practice, aiding and abetting is generally treated as a single concept. Lord Widgery CJ in *Attorney General's Reference (No 1 of 1975)* thought that aiding and abetting:

> almost invariably involves a situation in which the secondary party and the main offender are together at some stage discussing the plans which they may be making in respect of the alleged offence, and are in contact so that each knows what is passing through the mind of the other.

In other words, there will usually be some consensus and a causative link between the aiding and abetting and the commission of the completed crime by the principal offender. As was suggested by Devlin J in *National Coal Board v Gamble* [1959] 1 QB 11:

> If voluntary presence is *prima facie* evidence of encouragement and therefore aiding and abetting, the intentional supply of an essential article must be *prima facie* evidence of aiding and abetting.

It would be wrong, however, to presume that causation or agreement is a prerequisite of this type of accessorial liability. For example, A might happen upon P attacking a third party, V. If A then prevents passers-by or police from helping V because he desires V to be seriously injured by P, it is clearly the case that A is giving aid to P even though A and P have never met or discussed the matter. On these facts A should be found guilty of aiding and abetting the offence committed by P.

As indicated above, presence at the scene of the crime may be suggestive of aiding and abetting but more evidence will be needed to secure a conviction. There must, according to *Clarkson* [1971] 3 All ER 344, 'be an intention to encourage; and there must also be encouragement in fact' (*per* Megaw LJ). In that case, a group of soldiers had stood by and watched while a woman was raped. They gave neither physical or verbal encouragement to the principals. Their appeals against conviction were allowed on the basis that the court martial was not given the opportunity to consider whether the intention to encourage and actual encouragement were present. Similarly, in *Coney* (1882) 8 QBD 534, the defendant's presence at a prize fight was not conclusive evidence of actual encouragement, although it would seem to indicate an intention to encourage the fighters to continue trading blows. Without the presence of the spectators, the fight would be without purpose. Thus, *Coney* is authority for the proposition that voluntary presence at the scene of a crime may amount to encouragement but it is not conclusive.

The case of *Bland* [1988] Crim LR 41 has confirmed these principles and made it absolutely clear that those who share premises with others, being aware they are engaged in criminal activities, will not simply by their voluntary presence at the scene, be accessories to any offences. Bland lived with Ratcliff who was engaged in drug-dealing from the premises. There was sufficient evidence from which a jury could have inferred knowledge on Bland's part that Ratcliff was dealing but no more. The court held that assistance, though passive, required more than simply knowledge. There should be evidence of encouragement or at least the right to control the person which had been 'entirely lacking' in this case. This is not meant to suggest that the *actus reus* is proved only if assistance and encouragement are proved. Evidence of either will be enough to establish the *actus reus*.

Presence by an accomplice at the scene of a crime may be categorised as encouragement in circumstances where the parties have agreed that a crime be committed, even though the accomplice does nothing by way of a positive act. In *Smith v Reynolds and Others* [1986] Crim LR 559, R and three others had been charged with wilfully obstructing a police constable in the execution of his duty. R was present in a van which was part of a 'peace convoy' seeking to get to Stonehenge. The driver of the vehicle drove it directly at a police constable. R's submission was that he was not assisting or encouraging the driver to steer at the police officer. He was clearly at the scene of the crime but claimed he was not giving assistance to the principal offender. The Divisional Court held that R could be guilty of aiding and abetting. He was part of a group of people who were prepared to confront the police in their endeavours to reach Stonehenge. There was clearly an agreement that they should act in this way. Therefore, there was no need to show any express words were spoken by way of encouragement to the driver. The mere fact they remained in the van was evidence enough that R and his colleagues were aiding and abetting the driver to commit the offence. The onus will be on the prosecution to prove that there was evidence of encouragement based upon mere presence, together with an intention to encourage the principal offender.

If there is a duty to control the principal offender and that duty is relinquished, then in such circumstances, providing the requisite intention is present, the failure to control can amount to assistance or encouragement, by way of endorsement, of the principal's activities. In *Tuck v Robson* [1970] 1 All ER 1171, customers at a public house were found to be drinking after hours because the licensee failed to comply with his statutory duty to ensure all drinks were consumed by his customers within 10 minutes of closing time. It was held that simply by standing by and watching his customers continue to consume alcohol was evidence that he had encouraged them to breach the law. Here was a case of deliberate refraining from exercising the power and control that he undoubtedly possessed by virtue of being the licensee. Interestingly, the court was of the opinion that even if the publican had gone as far as to call 'time' or switch off the lights, this still may not be enough to prevent a jury concluding that he had encouraged his patrons to continue drinking. This would appear to suggest that in such 'control' cases the licensee or agent may have to demonstrate positive action in order to show that the patrons' licence to drink had been revoked. This places an onerous duty on licensees to the extent that they may have to remove their customers' glasses at the appointed moment or at least show they have done everything reasonably possible to persuade their customers to comply with the law. Similar principles apply to those car owners who allow others to drive their vehicles and fail to prevent the drivers from breaching the speed limit or driving in a dangerous manner. In *Rubie v Faulkner* [1940] 1 KB 571, a learner driver was convicted of driving without due care and attention through overtaking on a dangerous bend. The defendant, who was a licence holder and whose job it was to supervise him, was convicted of aiding and abetting by failing to exercise control over his pupil.

It follows that a parent who, whilst present at the scene, fails to take action to prevent ill treatment of his or her child may also be an accomplice to the harm caused by the principal offender. In these circumstances, there is no right to control the principal offender, but there is the duty to act in the best interests of the child. Failure to seek assistance or intervene on the child's behalf could be perceived by the principal as an encouragement to continue to ill-treat the child providing always, of course, that there was evidence of an intention to aid the principal offender. It is worth noting Slade J's comments in *National Coal Board v Gamble*:

> Mere passive assistance is sufficient only, I think, where the alleged aider and abettor has the power to control the offender and is actually present when the offence is committed.

This view is further supported by *JF Alford Transport Ltd; Alford; Payne* [1997] 2 Cr App R 1, where the Court of Appeal held that a company and its managers could be guilty of aiding and abetting employees in the act of making false entries on tachograph records contrary to s 99(5) of the Transport Act 1968, provided there was evidence that they had known what the drivers were doing, they had had the right to intervene to prevent it, and that they had taken no steps to prevent the misconduct. The presence or absence of the defendants at the time of the misconduct was not seen as being critical.

4.5   VARIATIONS BETWEEN THE LIABILITY OF THE PRINCIPAL OFFENDER AND THE ACCOMPLICE

It is often said that accessorial liability in English criminal law is derivative, in the sense that the liability of the accomplice is derived from that of the principal offender. As a consequence, difficulties can arise where the principal offender escapes liability, has less *mens rea* than the accomplice, or perhaps has a defence not available to the accomplice.

The derivative nature of accessorial liability is most clearly illustrated by *Thornton v Mitchell* [1940] 1 All ER 33, where a bus driver, acting on instructions from his conductor, reversed his bus and in so doing injured two pedestrians. The driver was charged with careless driving and the conductor, who was offering assistance to the driver, with aiding and abetting this offence. On the facts, the driver was found not to have been careless and therefore had not committed the *actus reus* of the offence. That being so, the Divisional Court quashed the conductor's conviction for aiding and abetting for the obvious reason that 'a person cannot aid another in doing something which that other has not done'. In short, there was no *actus reus* for the conductor to be an accomplice to. On this basis, suppose A encourages P to have sexual intercourse with V, A believing that V will not be consenting. When P encounters V she in fact proceeds to have consensual intercourse with P. A is unaware that the sexual intercourse is consensual. Clearly, P has committed no offence. Presumably, neither has A, even though he was 'willing' for an offence to be committed. Why should he escape accessorial liability due to a change in circumstances outside his control? The only alternative in such cases is to charge A and P with conspiracy to commit rape, assuming that evidence can be obtained to substantiate this.

The situation will be different where the principal offender does commit the *actus reus* of the offence but escapes liability due to a lack of *mens rea*. This situation is sometimes referred to as innocent agency. For example, A might ask P to place a tablet in V's drink. A tells P that it is a vitamin tablet. A knows that, in fact, it is a deadly poison. Quite clearly, if P acts as A requires and V dies, P does not possess the *mens rea* for murder having no intent to kill or cause grievous bodily harm. In this example, the *actus reus* of homicide is present with the *mens rea* for the offence being possessed by the person procuring the offence – that is, A.

The problem is illustrated by *Cogan and Leak* [1975] 2 All ER 1059, where Leak was charged with aiding and abetting Cogan to commit rape on his (Leak's) wife. They were both found guilty at the Crown Court and sentenced to two years (Cogan) and seven years (Leak). Cogan's conviction was quashed on appeal in light of the House of Lords' decision in *DPP v Morgan* [1975] 2 All ER 347, which determined that a defendant to a rape charge should be acquitted if he was found to have an honest belief that the woman was consenting. In this case, it was clear that Leak had intended throughout that his wife should submit to intercourse with Cogan, irrespective of whether she wished to permit the act. His role in the whole sequence of events is reflected in the heavy sentence he received as compared to that initially given to Cogan. Leak's conviction was, however, confirmed on the basis that he had procured the offence. The Court of Appeal had no doubt that the *actus reus* of rape was present and that *per* Lawton LJ:

> ... [the *actus reus*] ... had been procured by Leak who had the appropriate *mens rea*, namely his intention that Cogan should have sexual intercourse with [Mrs Leak] without her consent. Leak was using him as a means to procure a criminal purpose.

The tentative conclusion to emerge from this decision is that an accessory may be found guilty as a result of conduct that encourages the *actus reus* in circumstances where the principal offender is not liable.

There are, however, problematic aspects to the decision in *Cogan and Leak*. For example, Lawton LJ believed that Leak could have been indicted for raping his wife as a principal offender via the doctrine of innocent agency (that is, acting through Cogan as an innocent agent). The problem was that in 1975 the common law provided that a man could not be convicted of raping his own wife during cohabitation because 'the law presumes consent from the marriage ceremony' (*per* Lawton LJ, p 1062). Rather weakly, it is submitted, Lawton LJ reasons this objection away by asserting that the presumption did not to apply 'when a man procures a drunken friend to do the physical act for him'.

On this basis it becomes possible for a female accomplice to be convicted of rape where she persuades the male principal offender to have sexual intercourse with V, on the basis that V is consenting where A knows this not to be the case. In *DPP v K and C* [1997] Crim LR 121, two girls aged 14 and 11 ordered another girl, W, to remove her clothes and have sexual intercourse with a boy.

The court stated:

> It would be singularly unattractive to find that because of the absence of a mental element on the part of the principal, the procurers could thereby escape conviction when they were found to have the requisite *mens rea* – the desire that rape should take place and the procuring of it.

Where the principal commits the *actus reus* of a completed crime and both accomplice and principal have *mens rea* it may be possible for the prosecution to charge each with different offences reflecting the varying degrees of fault. For example, suppose A hires P to attack V in order to cause V grievous bodily harm. P agrees to this but attacks V intending only to cause actual bodily harm. In attacking V, P accidentally goes beyond what he intended to do and causes V grievous bodily harm. On these facts, P could be charged with maliciously inflicting grievous bodily harm contrary to s 20 of the Offences Against the Person Act 1861 (an offence carrying a maximum penalty of five years' imprisonment) and A could be charged with counselling, causing grievous bodily harm with intent, contrary to s 18 of the 1861 Act (an offence carrying a maximum penalty of life imprisonment); see *Burke and Clarkson* [1987] 1 All ER 771 where Lord Mackay observed that:

> ... I would affirm ... that where a person has been killed and that result is the result intended by another participant, the mere fact that the actual killer may be convicted only of the reduced charge of manslaughter for some reason special to himself does not, in my opinion in any way, result in a compulsory reduction for the other participant ...

Hence, as Lord Mackay went on to explain, if A hands a gun to P informing P that it is loaded with blank ammunition only and telling P to scare V by discharging it, and in fact the ammunition is live (as A knows) and V is killed, P will be convicted of manslaughter, but A will be convicted for murder. P is not an innocent agent because he knows he is committing an offence, but he lacks the knowledge that would inform him as to how dangerous his actions really are. The term coined to describe such a person is 'semi-innocent agent'. Earlier cases such as *Richards* [1974] QB 776 which suggest that A's liability could be no greater than P's should be regarded as having been incorrectly decided. For details of offences against the person, see further Chapter 7.

If the principal offender commits the *actus reus* of an offence with the requisite *mens rea* but has a defence that reduces his liability or indeed absolves him from liability, it by no means follows that the defence operates to reduce or abrogate the liability of the accomplice. This conclusion is supported by decisions such as *Bourne* (1952) 36 Cr App R 125. Bourne's conviction for aiding and abetting buggery, where he had forced his wife to have sexual connection with a dog, was upheld on the basis that the *actus reus* was present. It had been assumed by the court that if the wife had been charged she would have had a good defence based upon duress (coercion). The only difficulty with this is acceptance by the court that duress works on a confession and avoidance basis. As Lord Goddard CJ put it:

> Assuming that she could have set up duress, what does that mean? It means that she admits that she has committed the crime but prays to be excused from punishment for the consequences of the crime by reason of the duress.

Thus, in effect, admitting that the *mens rea* was present. However, it could be argued that her husband participated in her *mens rea* and therefore he has procured an offence or conversely could be the principal offender by merging his *mens rea* with the *actus reus* of his wife. It is less than satisfactory to convict people of offences that they cannot commit as principals in their own right. The 'device' of procuring an *actus reus* would seem better in principle, although as we have said, at present it is to be confined within very narrow limits.

4.6   *MENS REA*

Generally, an accomplice must be shown to have intended to do the acts that constitute the participation in the offence and to have at least contemplated the type of offence committed by the principal offender. In many cases the accomplice will have foreseen the principal committing the offences in question. Indeed, it may have been the accomplice's purpose that the principal offender should so act, but establishing this may be difficult. If P asks A to lend him a knife because P has someone he wants to 'sort out', what *mens rea* does A have? Suppose P uses the knife to stab his wife to death. Is it sufficient that A suspected P would use the knife to wound someone, or must A's *mens rea* be more specific?

4.6.1   Contemplation

As a general principle, an accomplice will have sufficient *mens rea* if he is shown to have contemplated the type of crime committed by the principal offender. In *Bainbridge* [1960] 1 QB 129, the Midland Bank at Stoke Newington had been broken into and access had been gained to the strongroom through the use of oxygen cutting equipment. £18,000 had been stolen. The defendant did not dispute that he had purchased the equipment using false names and addresses but said that whilst aware that it would be used for a criminal purpose, he had 'no knowledge that the equipment was going to be used for any such purpose as that for which it was used'. It was held that providing he knew the particular type of crime for which the equipment would be used, then that was sufficient, but simply to have knowledge that it would be used for a criminal purpose was not. As Lord Parker CJ put it:

> The court fully appreciates that it is not enough that it should be shown that a person knew that some illegal venture was intended. To take this case, it would not be enough if the appellant knew – he says he only suspected – that the equipment was going to be used to dispose of stolen property. That would not be enough. Equally, this court is quite satisfied that it is unnecessary that knowledge of the intention to commit the particular crime which was in fact committed should be shown, and by 'particular crime' I am using the words in the same way as that in which counsel for the appellant used them, namely, on a particular date and particular premises.

The jury obviously disbelieved him and the Court of Criminal Appeal upheld his conviction. On this occasion, the equipment had been left behind in the bank but if we assume that the miscreants had taken it away and used it in raids on other banks would Bainbridge have been a secondary party to all activities of a similar type? Logically, the answer must be yes.

Neither will an accomplice escape liability by claiming that he contemplated a principal committing any one of a large number of possible offences rather than a specific type of offence. In *Maxwell v DPP for Northern Ireland* (1979) 68 Cr App R 128, the secondary party guided terrorists to a remote country public house unsure of the nature of the 'attack' to be carried out. He knew that violence was to be perpetrated and that premises could be damaged with life being endangered. The House of Lords held that a person could be convicted of aiding and abetting without proof of prior knowledge of the actual crime, provided he contemplated the commission of one of a limited number of crimes by the principal and intentionally lent his assistance to the commission of such a crime. In this case, as he was a member of an illegal organisation (the Ulster Volunteer Force), he must have realised a bomb attack was an 'obvious possibility' among the offences likely to be committed. *Bainbridge* was approved and Lord Hailsham accepted that mere suspicion was not the test but knowledge of the type of crime. This approach does raise the question of which crimes fall within the definition of 'type of crime'. If A thinks that D is to enter a building in order to steal (burglary) by using a crowbar supplied by A for the purpose of gaining entry to X's house, will A still be an accomplice if the crowbar is actually used to commit criminal damage on a motor vehicle in order to steal its stereo cassette recorder? What if the burglary took place but the principal offender was disturbed and used the crowbar to attack the occupier? Certainly, in this latter case, one could not imagine that he would be an accessory to grievous bodily harm, unless of course this course of action was initially within the contemplation of the parties.

4.6.2   Recklessness

Is 'contemplation' to be equated with recklessness? In *Blakely, Sutton v DPP* [1991] Crim LR 763, the Queen's Bench Divisional Court considered a charge of procuring the commission by another of a drink-drive offence and concluded that that *Caldwell* recklessness was not enough. The facts were similar to those in *Attorney General's Reference (No 1 of 1975)*, except that the driver's drink was laced, not in order that he might commit the offence, but in order to prevent him from taking to the road. He was in the habit of occasionally staying the night with his mistress but on other evenings would return to his wife. On the evening in question, he had declared his intention to return home. He was careful never to consume more than two pints of beer if he was driving. Knowing this, and in the hope of keeping him from returning home, his mistress and a friend laced his tonic water with vodka. They intended to tell him later in the evening that it was unwise to drive. Unfortunately, he left before they had a chance to tell him the truth. He was arrested and charged with a drink-drive offence. The others were charged with aiding and abetting the offence by procuring. It is clear that they did not intend the offence to be committed but were they reckless in the circumstances as to whether it would be committed? Relying on Lord Widgery's definition of procuring in *Attonrey General's Reference (No 1 of 1975)* of producing by endeavour the court stated:

> You procure a thing by setting out to see that it happens and to take the appropriate steps to produce that happening. That strongly suggested that the procurer must be

shown to have intended to bring about the commission of the principal offence, and that mere awareness that it might result would not suffice. There was no hint that recklessness, let alone inadvertent recklessness, might suffice to convict the procurer.

The court held that the word 'recklessness' was best avoided when considering the *mens rea* of a person accused of procuring the commission of a substantive offence. In this case, the intention was to create the circumstances which would prevent him from driving. The conviction was quashed on the basis that the magistrates had applied the *Caldwell* test of recklessness in respect of whether he would drive or not, that is, she had given no thought to the obvious and serious risk that he would drive. Despite the strong opposition to the use of the word 'reckless' there is just a suggestion that if the magistrates had applied the test of advertent recklessness the conviction may have been upheld.

Some support for this latter view can be found in *Carter v Richardson* [1974] RTR 314. In this case, a learner driver was convicted of driving with excess alcohol. His supervisor was convicted of abetting. The supervisor quite clearly was aware that his pupil was over the limit and, therefore, there was sufficient evidence to conclude that he intended to encourage the offence. However, the court thought that it would have been sufficient if the supervisor had known that his pupil was 'probably' over the limit, that is, advertent recklessness.

4.6.3   Indifference

What if A supplies the knife, suspecting that P will use it to cause unlawful injury but is indifferent to whether or not P does so, being interested only in the money P will pay A for supplying the knife? Devlin J in *National Coal Board v Gamble* thought that in such circumstances the supplier would still be an aider and abettor. That case decided that there had to be an intention to assist with knowledge of the relevant circumstances. An employee of the National Coal Board (NCB) allowed an overloaded coal lorry operated by a private company to leave a colliery, even though he was aware that it was overloaded and if driven on the highway would contravene the Motor Vehicles (Construction and Use) Regulations 1955 (SI 1955/482). Although the driver was made aware of the overloading he said he would 'risk it' and the NCB employee thereupon issued the necessary document which allowed the lorry to leave the colliery. The NCB was charged with and convicted of aiding, abetting, counselling and procuring the carrier to commit the offence. It is clear that the employee had knowledge of the circumstances and then provided the document to the driver, which in turn facilitated the crime. There was a clear intention to aid the commission of the crime, although one does not doubt that the employee was totally indifferent as to whether or not the driver actually drove his lorry on the road.

The focus on intention to do the act of assistance as opposed to intending the consequence of the principal's conduct is reinforced in *Gillick v West Norfolk and Wisbech AHA* [1985] 3 All ER 402. Lord Scarman, when considering any possible criminal liability for doctors supplying contraceptives to girls under 16 years of age knowing that the girls may engage in unlawful sexual intercourse, said:

> Clearly a doctor who gives a girl contraceptive advice or treatment not because in his clinical judgment the treatment is medically indicated for the maintenance or restoration of her health but with the intention of facilitating her having unlawful

sexual intercourse may well be guilty of a criminal offence. It would depend ... on the doctor's intention.

4.6.4   Legal obligation to supply

Problems can arise in circumstances where the accessory is under a legal obligation to return property to the principal offender that he knows is going to be used to commit a crime. It would appear harsh to convict in such circumstances, it is argued, because the secondary party is legally obliged to return the property. Against this view, one can hardly envisage that he could be successfully sued for its return if the true purpose for which the item is to be used is known to a court. The distinction is untenable and it is suggested that, irrespective of the legal position vis à vis ownership, a conviction could follow if in returning, say, a gun, there clearly is an intention to aid with knowledge of the circumstances. *Lomas* (1913) 9 Cr App R 220 is authority for the proposition that if, when returning property, there is simply an intention to comply with one's civil duty, this cannot amount to aiding and abetting. This would appear to be correct as there would be no intention to aid the commission of a crime. But, if the person returning the item is aware of the purpose to which it will be put, then he should not be allowed to hide behind his civil law obligations and therefore avoid criminal liability. Support for this comes from the decision of the Court of Appeal in *Garrett v Arthur Churchill (Glass) Ltd* [1970] 1 QB 92. In this case, the court held that any duty to hand over goods to the owner takes second place to the public interest in preventing an unlawful act being perpetrated with the items.

4.7   JOINT ENTERPRISES

The discussion above has proceeded on the basis that there is a clear delineation between the principal and secondary party, in the sense that it has been implicit that for the most part the secondary party has played a supportive role. There may be situations where the principal and accomplice embark upon a joint unlawful enterprise, the essence of which is a common design. As was said in *Petters and Parfitt* [1995] Crim LR 501, for a joint enterprise there has to be evidence of a common purpose and an understanding between the principal and accomplices that they are acting in concert. At common law the significance of joint enterprise has been the rule that if several persons act together with common intent, every act in furtherance of such intent by any one of them is, in law, an act done by all (see *Macklin* (1838) 2 Lew CC 225). As the Law Commission's 1993 consultation paper (Law Com 131) observed (at para 1.13), the doctrine of joint enterprise, in its modern form, has become a means of imposing liability on an accomplice, A, where A and the principal, P, embark on a joint enterprise during the course of which P commits a 'collateral' crime. To this extent, the doctrine of joint enterprise normally distinguishes between those cases where P accidentally commits a collateral crime whilst carrying out the joint enterprise, and those where the collateral crime is the result of P deliberately departing from the scope of the joint enterprise. If the collateral crime is an accidental consequence of the joint enterprise, A will be a party to that collateral crime. Where the collateral crime results from a deliberate departure from the joint enterprise by P, A will have no accessorial liability as regards the collateral crime. Hence, if A and P agree to burgle V's house and P enters V's bedroom, whereupon V dies of shock, P may incur liability for manslaughter and A can be an accomplice to manslaughter. By contrast if, on those facts, P had entered V's bedroom and stabbed V to death, A not being aware that P was armed, P would have exceeded the joint enterprise and he alone would incur liability for the death of V.

It follows therefore that should any one or more parties to the agreement break ranks and go beyond the agreed joint enterprise then the others should not be liable for those consequences. This rule was established in *Davies v DPP* [1954] AC 378, where Lord Simonds LC said:

> I can see no reason why, if half a dozen boys fight another crowd and one of them produces a knife and stabs one of the opponents to death, all the rest of his group should be treated as accomplices in the use of a knife and the infliction of mortal injury by that means, unless there is evidence that there is intended or concerted or at least contemplated an attack with a knife by one of their number, as opposed to a common assault. If all that was designed or envisaged was in fact a common assault, and there was no evidence that (L), a party to that common assault, knew that any of his companions had a knife, then (L) was not an accomplice in the crime consisting in its felonious use.

The leading authority on joint enterprise is now the House of Lords' decision in *Powell and Daniels; English* [1997] 4 All ER 545. The appeals arose out of two unrelated incidents but they were heard together because of the related points of law arising. In relation to both appeals, their Lordships had to consider the extent to which the definition of the *mens rea* for murder applicable to a principal offender applied in the case of an accomplice charged with murder. Previous cases, such as *Hyde* [1991] 1 QB 134 and *Chan Wing Sui v R* [1985] AC 168, had held that it was sufficient for the accomplice to have foreseen the possibility of death or grievous bodily harm as a possible incident of the joint enterprise. The question certified for consideration by the House of Lords, therefore, was as follows:

> Is it sufficient to found a conviction for murder for a secondary party to a killing to have realised that the primary party might kill with intent to do so or must the secondary party have held such intention himself?

The House of Lords, confirming that it would suffice that the accomplice had foreseen that death or grievous bodily harm was something that might have occurred, sought to rationalise the decision by way of reference to the dictates of public policy. Lord Hutton acknowledged that the disparity between the fault that had to be proved in respect of the principal charged with murder as compared with the accomplice was anomalous but went on to assert that:

> ... the rules of the common law are not based solely on logic but relate to practical concerns and, in relation to crimes committed in the course of joint enterprises, to the need to give effective protection to the public against criminals operating in gangs ... unlike the principal party who carries out the killing with a deadly weapon, the secondary party will not be placed in the situation in which he suddenly has to decide whether to shoot or stab the third person with intent to kill or cause really serious harm. There is, in my opinion, an argument of considerable force that the secondary party who takes part in a criminal enterprise (for example, the robbery of a bank), with foresight that a deadly weapon may be used, should not escape liability for murder because he, unlike the principal party, is not suddenly confronted by the security officer so that he has to decide whether to use the gun or knife or have the enterprise thwarted and face arrest ...

Lord Steyn acknowledged that application of the rule could result in a defendant being convicted of murder when, in truth, he could not have been said to have intended to kill or do grievous bodily harm, but he sought to refute the predictable criticism that the rule amounted to the imposition of constructive liability on accomplices. As he observed:

> ... liability is imposed because the secondary party is assisting in and encouraging a criminal enterprise which he is aware might result in the commission of a greater offence. The liability of an accessory is predicated on his culpability in respect of the greater offence as defined in law. It is undoubtedly a lesser form of *mens rea*. But it is unrealistic to say that the accessory principle as such imposes constructive criminal liability.

Lord Steyn went on to acknowledge that, if the prosecution had to prove that an accomplice to murder had foreseen the death of the victim, or at least the causing of grievous bodily harm, as virtually certain, there would be very few convictions for participation in murder. An accomplice would nearly always be able to provide evidence that his foresight fell short of this test, not least because the test would not be what he foresaw as the consequence of his actions, but what he foresaw as the consequence of the actions of another (the principal offender) – an altogether more difficult issue.

As Lord Steyn explained:

> ... it would in practice almost invariably be impossible for a jury to say that the secondary party wanted death to be caused or that he regarded it as virtually certain. In the real world, proof of an intention sufficient for murder would be well nigh impossible in the vast majority of joint enterprise cases.

This aspect of the decision has survived subsequent challenge on the basis that it might be contrary to the European Convention on Human Rights (see *Concannon* [2002] Crim LR 213). Rejecting the appellant's contention that the disparity in *mens rea* required between a defendant charged with murder as a principal offender and one charged with murder as an accomplice in cases of joint enterprise was inconsistent with the requirements of Art 6 of the Convention, the court confirmed that, whilst it was open to parliament to amend the law relating to joint enterprise if it saw fit to do so, the substantive content of the law was a matter for individual signatory states.

The House of Lords in *Powell and Daniels; English* was willing to accept that an accomplice might escape liability where he genuinely foresaw the risk of the principal killing or causing grievous bodily harm as merely negligible. However, an accomplice would not escape liability where he had proceeded with the joint enterprise foreseeing the possibility of death or grievous bodily harm, but nevertheless maintaining a 'pious hope' that neither eventuality would transpire.

In *English,* a further certified question arose regarding the extent to which an accomplice would be held to be a party to the actions of the principal offender that deliberately exceed the scope of the agreed joint enterprise. E had agreed with W that they would attack police officers with a fencing post. During the course of the resultant disturbances, W pulled out a knife and stabbed a police officer to death. E had no knowledge that W had the knife.

The House of Lords considered the following certified question:

> Is it sufficient for murder that the secondary party intends or foresees that the primary party would or may act with intent to cause grievous bodily harm if the lethal act

carried out by the primary party is fundamentally different from the acts foreseen or intended by the secondary party?

In broad terms, the House of Lords held that an accomplice would escape liability where the principal deliberately exceeded the scope of the joint enterprise, but, as will be seen below, such a summary barely does justice to the nuances of the ruling.

Suppose an accomplice, A, agrees to act as a look out whilst the principal offender, P, attacks V. Assume that A foresees that P might cause grievous bodily harm to V in the course of carrying out this attack. If V dies and P is proved to have intended death or grievous bodily harm P will be convicted of murder. Given the answer to the first certified question in *Powell and Daniels; English*, A can be convicted of murder as an accomplice. As indicated above, however, if the agreement was that P would not use any weapon on V, but unknown to A, P arms himself with a knife that he uses to kill V, A should escape liability for murder.

The House of Lords in *Powell and Daniels; English*, following previous authorities, such as *Davies v DPP* and *Anderson and Morris* [1966] 2 QB 110, held that, even though, in the given example, A would have sufficient *mens rea* (because he foresaw that P might cause grievous bodily harm), he would not be an accomplice to the murder because of P's deliberate action in exceeding the scope of the joint enterprise. By choosing to use a weapon, P was acting on his own. A had ceased to be an accomplice to his actions. The only rider one might add to this, in the light of observations made subsequently by the Court of Appeal in *Uddin* [1998] 2 All ER 744, is, if P, having agreed not to use a weapon in an attack on V, suddenly produces a weapon. If A, knowing that P is now thus armed, continues to participate in the attack on V, it could be argued that A has tacitly agreed to an altered common design and will incur liability for the consequences flowing from the use of the weapon.

In *English*, the accomplice had contemplated the use of a weapon by the principal offender, but the principal had deliberately and independently opted to use a more deadly weapon. The House of Lords held that this too amounted to a deliberate departure from the common design, thus relieving the accomplice of liability for the murder. This raises the difficult issue of how the courts determine that one type of weapon is more deadly than another. A fencing post is qualitatively different to a knife, but what is the difference between a broken bottle and a knife? The point was subsequently considered by Beldam LJ in *Uddin*, where he observed that:

> If the character of the weapon, for example, its propensity to cause death is different from any weapon used or contemplated by the others and if it is used with specific intent to kill, the others are not responsible for the death unless it is proved that they knew or foresaw the likelihood of the use of such a weapon.

In *Greatrex* (1998) *The Times*, 2 April, the Court of Appeal appeared willing to accept that, if the common design envisaged P hitting V with an iron bar, there would be no deliberate departure from that plan by P if he opted to kick V with a shod foot instead.

It follows, therefore, that, if A contemplates the use of a deadly weapon by P to kill or do grievous bodily harm to V, and P kills V using a different, but equally deadly, weapon, A should be convicted as an accessory to murder. As Lord Hutton observed in *Powell and Daniels; English*:

> ... if the weapon used by the primary party is different to, but as dangerous as, the weapon which the secondary party contemplated he might use, the secondary party

should not escape liability for murder because of the difference in the weapon, for example, if he foresaw that the primary party might use a gun to kill and the latter used a knife to kill, or vice versa.

This will normally be the result, but care is still required as the courts might be prepared to distinguish between the way in which A contemplated the weapon would be used to cause grievous bodily harm, and the way in which P actually used a deadly weapon to kill. The case of *Gamble* illustrates the point well. G agreed to be an accomplice to what he thought would be the 'kneecapping' of V. The *modus operandi* contemplated was that the principal offender would use a gun to shoot the victim through the back of the knee. G, therefore, contemplated that V would suffer grievous bodily harm, caused by the use of a gun. Had V died from these wounds, G could clearly have been charged as an accomplice to the murder of V. He contemplated grievous bodily harm and the weapon used. Instead of 'kneecapping' V as expected, however, the principal offender slit V's throat with a knife, killing him. The court held that this act of the principal amounted to a deliberate departure from the common design that relieved G of liability as an accomplice. Contentious as the decision may seem, it was expressly approved by the House of Lords in *Powell and Daniels; English*. Hence, the principal offender, using the weapon contemplated by the accomplice, or an equally deadly weapon, but in a different way, can amount to a departure from the common design.

Note that, in the examples above, where P deliberately exceeds the scope of the common design, A escapes liability completely in relation to the death of V. There is no residual liability for manslaughter because, by the time the killing is carried out, P is effectively acting independently. A has ceased to be an accomplice. In what circumstances, therefore, might P be convicted of murder, and A convicted of manslaughter?

Suppose that A and P agree that they will burgle a house and during the course of the burglary P attacks and kills V, the householder. How is A's liability, if any, for the killing to be assessed? A is part of a joint enterprise and if A and P had not been inside the house V would still be alive. A will be guilty of burglary, but should he be liable for the homicide? The cases discussed above would suggest that an assessment should be made as to the purpose of the joint enterprise and what was within the contemplation of the parties at the time of the agreement. If A was aware that P was of violent disposition and thus contemplated death or grievous bodily harm (perhaps on the basis that he knew that P carried a weapon and was prepared to use it), then he, along with P, could well be found guilty of murder. If, however, A merely suspected that P might use it to threaten anyone who disturbed them, it would appear that A ought to be liable for manslaughter as opposed to murder. He would not have contemplated the possibility of death or grievous bodily harm occurring but would, on the basis of the *Newbury and Jones* [1976] 2 All ER 365 test have foreseen some harm, albeit not serious harm.

Stewart and Schofield [1995] 3 All ER 159 appears to confirm this result. The Court of Appeal held that a person who was a party to a joint enterprise which resulted in another's death could be guilty of manslaughter on the basis that the actions of the principal offender causing death were within the contemplation of the accomplice, even though the accomplice had not foreseen death or grievous bodily harm. Hobhouse LJ put it this way:

... where the allegation is joint enterprise, the allegation is that one defendant participated in the criminal act of another even though several defendants may, as a result of having engaged in a joint enterprise, be each criminally responsible for the criminal act of one of those defendants done in the course of carrying out the joint enterprise, their individual criminal responsibility will, in such a case, depend upon what individual state of mind or intention has been proved against them. Thus, each may be a party to an unlawful act which caused the victim's death. But one may have had the intent to kill him or to cause him serious harm and be guilty of murder, whereas another may not have had that intent and may be guilty only of manslaughter [p 165g].

The decision leaves open the question of whether a principal offender actually exceeds the scope of the common design where he acts in the way contemplated by the accomplice, but opts to do so with more *mens rea*. There are *dicta* in *Anderson and Morris* suggesting that an accomplice should cease to be regarded as a party to the principal's actions in such cases. To the extent that there is a conflict between the decision in *Anderson and Morris* and that in *Stewart and Schofield*, there is support for the former decision in *Lovesey and Peterson* (1969) 53 Cr App R 461 and *Wan and Chan* [1995] Crim LR 296. Support for the *Stewart* line of reasoning comes from *Smith* [1963] Crim LR 63, *Betty* (1963) 48 Cr App R 6, *Reid* (1975) 62 Cr App R 109 and *Gilmour* (2000) *The Times*, 21 June. In the latter case, G assisted in the petrol-bombing of a house. He foresaw damage being caused by fire. The principal offender had thrown the petrol bomb at the house intending to kill. The ensuing fire caused the death of three young boys who had been asleep in the house. The Court of Appeal of Northern Ireland held that G could be guilty of manslaughter because the principal had committed the very act contemplated by G, albeit with more *mens rea*.

As the late Professor John Smith states in his commentary to the *Wan and Chan* case:

... it [is] clear that there is a conflict in the case law which should be resolved by the House of Lords as soon as possible [p 301].

The Law Commission in its 1993 consultation paper (Law Com 131) has gone as far as contemplating the abolition of aiding, abetting, counselling and procuring in favour of retaining the law of common design or joint enterprise. Professor Smith regards this last suggestion as heretical. The doctrine of joint enterprise, he believes, is not something distinct from the ordinary law of secondary participation but simply an aspect of it ([1995] Crim LR 298; see also Smith, 'Secondary participation in crime: can we do without it?' (1994) 144 NLJ 679, p 680). The law is clearly in urgent need of clarification.

4.8   WITHDRAWAL FROM A JOINT ENTERPRISE

Where one party is actually aiding the other or has counselled the offence, it is clear that certain other offences will already be complete irrespective of whether the accomplice seeks at a later stage to withdraw from the course of conduct which will eventually lead to the completed offence. If there is an agreement between the parties that satisfies the definition of conspiracy in s 1 of the CLwA 1977, then that crime is already complete. The mere suggestion that the crime be committed might result in an offence of incitement (see further Chapter 5). For an attempt, it must be shown that the principal offender has done an act which is more than merely preparatory to the completed offence (see s 1 of the Criminal Attempts Act (CAtA) 1981).

This section therefore addresses the question of whether or not the law will allow a party to resile from the criminal enterprise, thereby indicating that any further action by other parties is done without the assistance or encouragement of the person intent upon withdrawal. In principle, the law should, and in practice does, encourage a party to withdraw providing certain criteria are fulfilled. What is sought is clear evidence of a change of heart, that there is no wish to give assistance and certainly no intent so to do. The law's demands differ according to whether the act is one of counselling or aiding. In the former case, if D is simply advising A on how the crime may be committed then all that is required is for D to make it absolutely clear that he is withdrawing co-operation, will no longer give further information and that any action taken subsequently by A is without his approval. For example, in *Grundy* [1977] Crim LR 543, the accused had, some six weeks before a burglary, given information to the burglars relating to premises which were to be entered and the movements of the owners. Two weeks prior to the burglary he had been trying to stop them breaking in. It is to be noted that he directed his attempts at the others and did not take action to inform the police or warn those likely to have their premises invaded, which arguably would have been the most effective way of dissuading the other participants from embarking upon their criminal enterprise. It was held that he was entitled to have his defence of withdrawal left to the jury. The principle therefore appears to be that one can repent providing it is soon enough and the decision is communicated. In *Whitefield* [1984] Crim LR 9, D admitted to police that he had told two men who had broken into an adjoining flat that it was unoccupied and agreed they could break in by way of his own flat. However, he said that subsequently he decided not to take part and informed the others before the burglary took place. The trial judge withdrew his defence from the jury and he changed his plea to guilty. In allowing his appeal the Court of Appeal said that:

> ... it would have been sufficient for the appellant to communicate his withdrawal from the common enterprise by indicating that if the other person proceeded it would be without his aid and assistance.

Some would argue that this is unduly favourable to the accessory because the information given by both *Grundy* and *Whitefield* is of lasting use to the burglars. Perhaps withdrawal in such cases should only be recognised if the police have been informed or the owners of the premises warned. This of course is not always practicable or feasible and it is submitted that it be for the jury to decide, on a case-by-case basis, whether there is sufficient evidence to indicate that he has done everything possible in the circumstances to withdraw and make it clear that he is no longer giving assistance or encouragement to the principal(s).

The Law Commission makes the point that once an accessory has encouraged or helped the principal then no change of mind will affect liability. Nevertheless, it acknowledges that social policy considerations have lent credence to the counter-argument that if an accessory counters his assistance with equally obstructive measures, he should be acquitted because of his efforts to right the wrong. For that reason, the law has for centuries recognised that an accomplice, in at least some circumstances, may escape liability for the final offence by withdrawal before the crime is committed. It goes on to point out that repentance without action is insufficient (Law Com 131, 1993, paras 2.96 and 2.97).

In *Baker* [1994] Crim LR 444, the appellant together with another man attacked S with knives. B inflicted three stab wounds on S and then stated 'I'm not doing it'. He did not touch S again although the attack was continued by others. B moved a short distance away and turned his back. S died as a result of receiving a total of 48 stab wounds. B accepted that at the outset he was part of a joint enterprise to cause serious harm to S. The Court of Appeal found no evidence from which to conclude that B had indeed withdrawn from the joint enterprise. The report puts it this way:

> The court was far from confident that B by his words and actions had effectively put an end to the joint enterprise so that he had no criminal responsibility for what happened after the three stab wounds which he inflicted. The words 'I'm not doing it' and the turning around and moving a few feet away were far from unequivocal notice that B was wholly disassociating himself from the entire enterprise. The words were quite capable of meaning no more than I will not myself strike any more blows. They were not an unequivocal indication that he did not intend to take any further part in any further assault on S and indeed he did no more than withdraw by a few feet [p 445].

Where the issue is one of aiding the principal offender, for example, being at the scene of the crime, then simply to change one's mind once the situation has taken a turn for the worse will not absolve the defendant from liability. In *Becerra* (1975) 62 Cr App R 212, the accused set out to commit burglary. B had given C a knife to use against anyone who might interrupt them. Once inside the property they heard someone approaching whereupon B said, 'Come on, let's go'. C stayed behind, stabbed and killed the approaching person. In B's defence to a murder charge, it was argued that he had withdrawn from the common design. The Court of Appeal in upholding his conviction concluded there was no evidence of an effective withdrawal. Something vastly different and more effective was required. The court contemplated the possibility that the only effective withdrawal in these circumstances would have been physical intervention so as to prevent use of the knife.

There is evidence that a less rigorous test is applied where violence erupts spontaneously and a participant seeks to indicate that he wants to disassociate himself from it. In *Mitchell* [1999] Crim LR 496, the Court of Appeal indicated that in such a case the defendant's act of distancing himself physically from the action might be enough. Only where violence was pre-planned did the court think there was a need for the accomplice to communicate his intention not to assist the enterprise any further.

In conclusion, it is probably true to say that an operative withdrawal can be more easily achieved at a preparatory stage than at the scene of the crime. The Law Commission's provisional conclusion is that for withdrawal to be effective the accessory should either:

- countermand his encouragement with a view to preventing the commission of the principal offence; or
- take all reasonable steps with a view to preventing its commission.

4.9   REFORM OF ACCESSORIAL LIABILITY

Although the issue of accessorial liability was addressed in Pt 9 of the commentary on the draft Criminal Code Bill (see cll 25–29), it is the Law Commission's 1993 consultation paper (Law Com 131) that provides the most recent review of this area of liability and proposals for reform.

In its review of the existing law, the paper:

(a) observes that it is difficult to attribute discrete meanings to aid, abet, counsel and procure;

(b) rejects any notion that presence is necessary for any of the four modes of participation;

(c) observes that normal rules on causation cannot apply because what has to be caused by the accomplice is another's voluntary action. Normally the voluntary action of another will actually break the chain of causation;

(d) identifies problems with consensus – none is needed for procuring or aiding.

The Commission's report, endorsing the opinion of Professor Sandford Kadish, supports the view that English criminal law should move away from the derivative approach to accessorial liability.

In a bold departure from the existing law, therefore, the Commission expresses support, at least provisionally, for the abandonment of the modes of participation, as they currently exist at common law. The reform proposals envisage the creation of separate offences of first, assisting crime and secondly, encouraging crime, with the assisting offence operating as an inchoate offence.

As the consultation paper explains:

4.14 The separate consideration of assisting crime on the one hand and encouraging crime on the other enables us to isolate, and to confine to their proper sphere, some of the most pressing policy issues ... That is because two of the most important issues arise in connection with assisting, rather than with encouraging, crime. First, the question of whether assisting should become an inchoate offence, in the sense that the assister may be guilty even if the principal crime is not in the event committed. Second, the question of whether the mental state of an assister necessary for conviction should be expressed in terms of purpose that the principal crime be committed; or, as in the present law of aiding and abetting, merely in terms that the accessory is liable when he does an act of assistance and is aware that the principal may be going to act with the fault required for the principal offence.

4.15 These are not live issues in respect of encouraging crime. The terms of the proposed offence of encouraging crime that we submit for consideration are broadly the same as the rules of the present offence of incitement. An inciter or encourager's *mens rea*, in terms of purpose that the principal offence should be committed, follows naturally and inevitably from the nature of his conduct. The very description of that conduct as having encouraged, provoked, incited, stirred up or cheered on the commission of a crime presupposes a desire on the encourager's part that that crime should be committed. Nor has there ever been thought to be difficulty about incitement as an inchoate offence. If D positively encourages P to commit a crime, it has never been questioned that D should be guilty of the offence of incitement even if, for whatever reason, P did not in the event commit the offence incited. It has long been accepted that positively to encourage another to commit a crime is a sufficiently undesirable act to be punishable by the law whether or not the crime encouraged is in fact committed.

The inchoate nature of the proposed assisting offence would mean that the same rules would apply to a defendant who helped in some way whether or not the principal crime was actually committed. The offence would cover the whole of the law of assisting, rather than being a special offence used only when the principal crime was not committed. As to the *mens rea* for such an offence, the consultation paper envisages that the accessory must be shown to have known or believed that the principal was acting to cause the commission of an offence. Mere suspicion, or the presence of suspicious circumstances, would not suffice to establish the existence of belief.

The suggested formulation of the new offence is to be found in para 4.99 of the consultation paper:

(1) A person commits the offence of assisting crime if he

   (a) knows or believes that another ('the principal') is doing or causing to be done, or will do or cause to be done, acts that do or will involve the commission of an offence by the principal; and

   (b) knows or believes that the principal, in so acting, does or will do so with the fault required for the offence in question; and

   (c) does any act ... that he knows or believes assists or will assist the principal in committing that offence.

(2) Assistance includes giving the principal advice as to how to commit the offence, or as to how to avoid detection or apprehension before or during the commission of the offence.

(3) A person does not assist the commission of an offence for the purposes of this section if all that he does is to fail to prevent or impede the commission of that offence.

(4) 'Offence' in sub-paragraphs (a)–(c) of sub-section (1) above means the breach of a specified prohibition laid down by statute or the common law; but, provided the defendant knows or believes sufficient facts to show that such a breach is taking place or will take place, he need not know the time, place or other details of the offence.

(5) A person also commits an offence under this section if he knows or believes that the principal intends to commit one of a number of offences and does any act that he knows or believes will assist the principal in committing whichever of those offences the principal in fact intends.

The second proposed offence, that of encouraging crime, would replace counselling and the common law offence of incitement. As with incitement at present the offence would be inchoate – there would be no need to prove that the crime encouraged was actually committed. The *mens rea* required would be intention that the completed crime be committed, a matter that would normally be self-evident from the fact of encouragement.

The suggested formulation of the new offence of encouraging crime is to be found in para 4.163 of the consultation paper:

(1) A person commits the offence of encouraging crime if he

   (a) solicits, commands or encourages another ('the principal') to do or cause to be done an act or acts which, if done, will involve the commission of an offence by the principal; and

(b) intends that that act or those acts should be done by the principal; and

(c) knows or believes that the principal, in so acting, will do so with the fault required for the offence in question.

(2) The solicitation, command or encouragement must be brought to the attention of the principal, but it is irrelevant to the person's guilt whether or not the principal reacts to or is influenced by the solicitation, command or encouragement.

(3) The defendant need not know the identity of the principal, nor have any particular principal or group of principals in mind, provided that he intends his communication to be acted on by any person to whose attention it comes.

(4) 'Offence' in sub-paragraphs (a)–(c) of sub-section (1) above means the breach of a specified prohibition laid down by statute or the common law; but for the purposes of this section the defendant may solicit, command or encourage the commission of such an offence without intending that it should be committed at a specific time or place.

4.10   VICARIOUS LIABILITY

The law of torts recognises the principle that an employer may be liable for the tortious acts of his employee provided the employee is acting in the course of his employment. In *Pearks, Gunston and Tee v Ward* [1902] 2 KB 1, Channell J said:

> By the general principles of the criminal law, if a matter is made a criminal offence, it is essential that there should be something in the nature of *mens rea*, and, therefore, in ordinary cases a corporation cannot be guilty of a criminal offence, nor can a master be liable criminally for an offence committed by his servant. But there are exceptions to this rule.

Viscount Reading CJ in *Mousell Bros Ltd v London and North-Western Rly Co* [1917] 2 KB 836 confirmed the general principle but added:

> It may be the intention of the legislature, in order to guard against the happening of the forbidden thing, to impose a liability upon a principal even though he does not know of, and is not party to, the forbidden act done by his servant. Many statutes are passed with this object.

Atkin J in the same case commented:

> The legislature may prohibit an act or enforce a duty in such words as to make the prohibition or the duty absolute; in which case the principal is liable if the act is in fact done by his servants. To ascertain whether a particular Act of Parliament has that effect or not, regard must be had to the object of the statute, the words used, the nature of the duty laid down, the person upon whom it is imposed, the person by whom it would in ordinary circumstances be performed, and the person upon whom the penalty is imposed.

Judicial interpretation will be the determiner of whether a statute is deemed to impose vicarious liability as it is with strict liability offences. The offences in question are likely to be regulatory in nature as, for example, those imposing duties on licensees. It would be unreasonable to expect the licensee of a public house to carry out all the duties assigned to him under the terms of his licence. In practice, he will delegate the majority of functions to his employees but this would not absolve him of responsibility should there be a breach of the law. The onus remains on the landlord to ensure that there is compliance with the duty. The delegation principle therefore imputes the *mens rea* of the employee upon whom the responsibility for complying with the duty has been delegated, to the employer making him liable for the breach of duty. In simple terms, the delegator will, through his employee, have brought about the *actus reus* with the requisite *mens rea*. This will only apply where the offence is one which requires *mens rea*. If it is an absolute liability offence then *mens rea* will be irrelevant and the delegation principle will be redundant. If it is a strict liability offence where *mens rea* to one or more aspects of the offence need be established, then providing the employee possesses the necessary guilty mind, liability will rest with the delegator.

In *Somerset v Hart* (1884) 12 QBD 360, Lord Coleridge CJ said that a man may put another in his position so as to represent him for the purpose of knowledge. This statement was cited with approval by Lord Hewart CJ in *Allen v Whitehead* [1930] 1 KB 211, where the licensee of a refreshment house was charged with an offence of allowing prostitutes to congregate on the premises. He had been warned by the police that it was an offence to harbour prostitutes at the said premises. The licensee had issued instructions to his manager not to allow women to enter the premises after midnight and had posted notices to this effect. He visited the property two or three times a week but there was no evidence of misconduct nor did he have any knowledge that his instructions were being ignored by his manager. Lord Hewart was of the opinion that the provision in the statute would be rendered nugatory if the licensee's contention that he had no knowledge of the events were allowed to prevail:

> This seems to me to be a case where the proprietor, the keeper of the house, had delegated his duty to a manager, so far as the conduct of the house was concerned. He had transferred to the manager the exercise of discretion in the conduct of the business, and it seems to me that the only reasonable conclusion is, regard being had to the purposes of this Act [s 44 of the Metropolitan Police Act 1839] that the knowledge of the manager was the knowledge of the keeper of the house.

The key question, then, is what in law amounts to delegation? *Vane v Yiannopoullos* [1965] AC 486 determines that there must be a complete delegation of the licensee's duties and responsibilities and accordingly the licensee of a restaurant was not guilty of knowingly selling alcohol to those not partaking of a meal contrary to s 22(1)(a) of the Licensing Act 1961. He had informed the waitress not to serve alcohol to those not having a meal and then left the premises. She disobeyed his instructions. It is clear that he had in no way handed over the running of the restaurant to her and therefore her knowledge could not be imputed to him. The House of Lords indicated some unease with the delegation principle but nevertheless felt it to be too well-established to overturn. To convict a person who has no *mens rea* of an offence requiring knowledge is unfair and if parliament wishes to impose liability, it ought to draft legislation making it clear how this is to be achieved without recourse to what is in essence a legal fiction. This view is supported by the Law Commission in its draft Criminal Code (Law Com 177, 1989):

> ... [the] delegation principle was regarded as anomalous by members of the House of Lords in *Vane v Yiannopoullos* and our Working Party proposed its abolition. Parliament will have to provide clearly for the attribution to one person of the fault of another if it wishes this to occur [cl 29].

4.10.1 Defences

The statutes which are construed to create vicarious liability will occasionally make available defences to those who may be caught by the vicarious liability principle. For example, see s 24 of the Trade Descriptions Act 1968. A rather harsh ruling in *Tesco Stores Ltd v Brent LBC* [1993] 2 All ER 718 prevented the store from relying on the statutory defence created by s 11(2)(b) of the Video Recordings Act 1984. A cashier at one of the company's stores had sold an '18' classification film to a 14-year-old boy. It was accepted that she had reasonable grounds for believing the boy to be under 18 years of age. The company was convicted of the offence, one assumes on the basis of the construction of the statute rather than an application of the delegation principle, as the management of the premises was certainly not delegated to the cashier. It is a defence if the defendant neither knows nor has reasonable grounds to believe that the person concerned has not reached the relevant age. The company clearly did not have this knowledge. Nevertheless, the Divisional Court drew no distinction between the company and the person supplying the video, that is, the cashier. The knowledge of the cashier was imputed to the company which in consequence lost its defence. The defence is rendered otiose by this decision in all cases where the employee has reasonable grounds for believing the purchaser to be under the relevant age. If the cashier has no grounds for believing the person is underage, then the company's defence will succeed. If the delegation principle were to apply then the defence would also be rendered redundant as the knowledge would establish the offence and not assist the defence.

4.10.2 Corporate liability

In Chapter 6, the Law Commission's recommendations and those of the government are examined in the context of the review of the law on involuntary manslaughter regarding potential criminal liability of corporations for causing death. The Law Commission recommends the creation of a new offence of corporate killing. This section will therefore concentrate on possible corporate liability for offences other than those causing death.

Salomon v Salomon [1897] AC 22 confirms a corporation is a separate legal person although it has no physical existence. As such it can only act through those who are employed by the company or acting as agents of the corporation. Criminal liability may therefore arise through the operation of the vicarious liability principle, as we saw in the *Tesco* case above, or the so-called identification principle. This latter principle seeks to identify those who control the corporation and bestow upon them the privilege of being the embodiment of the corporation for the purposes of criminal liability. To put it simply, the acts and states of mind of these people are in law those of the corporation. Without either of these two principles applying, it follows that a corporation may not be guilty of a criminal offence. As Lord Hoffmann said in *Meridian Global Funds Management Asia Ltd v The Securities Commission* [1995] 2 AC 500:

> To say that a company cannot do something means only that there is no one whose doing of that act would, under the rules of attribution, count as an act of the company [pp 506H–07A].

Examples of how the vicarious liability principle worked are *Director General of Fair Trading v Pioneer Concrete (UK) Ltd* [1994] 3 WLR 1249 and *British Steel plc* [1995] Crim LR 654. In the latter case, the company was prosecuted under s 3(1) of the Health and Safety at Work, etc Act (HSWA) 1974. The company had employed subcontractors whose actions had resulted in two workers losing their lives. In upholding the conviction the Court of Appeal held that there was no due diligence defence in the HSWA 1974. Section 3 was deemed to create an absolute prohibition subject only to the words 'reasonably practicable' in the section. The section reads:

> (1) It shall be the duty of every employer to conduct his undertaking in such a way as to ensure, so far as is reasonably practicable, that persons not in his employment who may be affected thereby are not thereby exposed to risks to their health or safety.

As the court stated:

> It would drive a juggernaut through the legislative scheme if corporate employers could avoid criminal liability where the potentially harmful event is committed by someone who is not the directing mind of the company. Although there may be circumstances in which it might be regarded as absurd that an employer should even be technically guilty of a criminal offence, such cases are unlikely to be the subject of prosecution.

In the former case, the Director General had obtained an injunction restraining the company from acting in ways which breached the Restrictive Trade Practices Act 1976. The company gave explicit instructions to its staff, making it absolutely clear that the injunction was to be obeyed. Unknown to the management, a number of employees broke the terms of the injunction. The Director General succeeded in sequestrating the company's property on the basis that the company was liable for the acts of its employees carried out during the course of their employment. Lord Nolan explained that liability could only be avoided if the company had put into place completely foolproof preventive measures. See further on this point *Gateway Foodmarkets Ltd* [1997] 3 All ER 78.

4.10.3 The principle of identification

The genesis of this rule dates back to 1944 and three cases decided that year, viz, *DPP v Kent and Sussex Contractors Ltd* [1944] KB 146, *ICR Haulage Ltd* [1944] KB 551 and *Moore v Bresler Ltd* [1994] 2 All ER 515.

The principle is relatively straightforward. One seeks to identify those who manage or control the affairs of the company. These people are regarded as embodying the company itself (*Legislating the Criminal Code: Involuntary Manslaughter*, Law Com 237, 1996, para 6.27). The result is that a corporation may face criminal liability for virtually any offence as the *mens rea* of those embodying the company will be determined by reference to the states of mind of these individuals. Lord Steyn in *Deutsche Genossenschaftsbank v Burnhope* [1995] 4 All ER 717 put it this way:

> A company can be indicted for an offence of which *mens rea* is an ingredient. Indeed it is common ground that a company can be guilty of theft of property. If that is so, there can be no reason in principle why a company cannot be guilty of burglary. After all, the essence of burglary is simply theft while trespassing on the property of another. Thus, if the chairman of a company dishonestly instructs an innocent employee to

enter the assured's warehouse and remove a bag containing valuables the company may be guilty of burglary [pp 724j–25a].

And in the same case Lord Keith of Kinkel said that in the circumstances the reason why the company was guilty of theft was that its directing mind and will, Mr Smith, was himself guilty of theft.

Explaining the ambit of the identification principle, Denning LJ in *HL Bolton (Engineering) Co Ltd v TJ Graham & Sons Ltd* [1957] 1 QB 159, observed:

> A company in many ways may be likened to a human body. It has a brain and a nerve centre which controls what it does. It also has hands which hold the tools and act in accordance with directions from the centre. Some of the people in the company are mere servants and agents who are nothing more than hands to do the work and cannot be said to represent the mind or will. Others are directors and managers who represent the directing mind and will of the company, and control what it does. The state of mind of these managers is the state of mind of the company and is treated by the law as such.

The leading authority on the identification principle is *Tesco Supermarkets Ltd v Nattrass* [1972] AC 153. Washing powder advertised for sale at a reduced price in one of the company's stores was in fact sold at a higher price. Due to an oversight by an employee, the manager of the store was not informed that special packs of the product had all been sold leaving only the normal priced commodity. The company successfully pleaded the due diligence defence found at s 24(1) of the Trade Descriptions Act 1968. The fault was borne by the branch manager who had failed to supervise the assistant who had actually committed the offence. The act was, therefore, due to another person, as specified in s 24(1). The branch manager was not part of the company.

It may not be absolutely clear who are the controlling officers of a company particularly if the company is large. Lord Reid in the *Tesco* case thought that a company could be criminally liable for the acts of its board of directors, the managing director and other superior officers who carry out the functions of management and speak and act as the company. Viscount Dilhorne thought that a company must identify the person or persons who are in actual control of the operations and who are not responsible to someone else in the company as to the manner in which those duties are carried out. Another way to identify the key people in the organisation is to look at the memorandum and articles of association and discover who is entrusted with the exercise of the powers of the company. The various ways of approaching the task may lead to slightly different results but what is clear is that there must be an attempt to discover who is the directing mind and will of the company and that is a matter of law not fact.

As discussed in Chapter 6, the Court of Appeal in *Attorney General's Reference (No 2 of 1999)* [2000] 3 All ER 187 has reaffirmed the adherence of the courts to the identification principle as regards corporate liability, notwithstanding the fact that the aggregation of the fault of various persons, each of whom could be regarded as the controlling minds of the company, could have made it easier to impose corporate liability for manslaughter arising out of the Southall train crash in 1997.

4.10.4 Distinction between vicarious liability and the identification principle

Although the eventual outcome may be the same, the process of establishing the necessary nexus between the company and the consequence is different. It is probably best summed up by the statement of Bingham LJ in *HM Coroner for East Kent ex p Spooner* (1989) 88 Cr App R 10:

> It is important to bear in mind an important distinction. A company may be vicariously liable for the negligent acts and omissions of its servants and agents, but for a company to be criminally liable for manslaughter it is required that *mens rea* and *actus reus* should be established not against those who acted for or in the name of the company but against those who were to be identified as the embodiment of the company itself.

4.10.5 Conclusion

The larger the organisation, the more difficult it is to identify one or a small number of persons who are in reality the embodiment of the company, making it easier for large organisations to escape criminal liability. It has been argued that the principle of aggregation should be used in this case where the *mens rea* of a number of people are aggregated to establish the required degree of fault necessary to achieve a conviction. For further discussion of this point in the context of corporate manslaughter, see Chapter 6.

SUMMARY OF CHAPTER 4

PARTICIPATION IN CRIME

GENERAL PRINCIPLES

The law distinguishes between the contribution to a criminal enterprise by the principal offender(s) and any secondary parties. The liability for the completed offence remains the same, albeit their respective contributions to the offence varies from participant to participant.

Section 8 of the AAA 1861, as amended by the CLwA 1977, states:

Whosoever shall aid, abet, counsel or procure the commission of any indictable offence whether the same be an offence at common law or by virtue of any act passed or to be passed, shall be liable to be tried, indicted and punished as a principal offender.

The words used in the AAA 1861 are an attempt to reflect the different modes of participation, either at the scene of the crime or beforehand. It must be remembered that secondary liability requires both an *actus reus* and a *mens rea* to be proved. The *actus reus* is established by proving that an act of assistance or encouragement has taken place. The *mens rea* is proved by establishing an intention to aid with knowledge of the circumstances. In the cases of aiding and abetting and counselling the law requires a consensus between the parties as well as a causal connection between the encouragement and the consequence. However, procuring has been deemed to be a unilateral act, therefore requiring no consensus between the parties. Nevertheless, there will still need to be a causative element in respect of the act and the consequence. Those who assist the principal offender prior to the offence taking place do not need to know precise information about the crime to be attempted. The House of Lords and Court of Appeal have determined that knowledge of the type of crime to be carried out is all that is needed. So in *Bainbridge*, the fact that the defendant knew the oxy-acetylene equipment was to be used for a bank robbery was sufficient to establish the *mens rea* for aiding and abetting robbery.

JOINT ENTERPRISES

When parties act out their roles as a result of a common design, the law refers to them being engaged in a joint enterprise. The general principle is that all parties to a joint enterprise will be liable for the consequences which ensue from the joint enterprise being carried out as agreed, irrespective of whether or not they are foreseen. Parties may be classed as joint principals in a situation were both or all have caused the *actus reus*. For example, A and B both stab C causing his death. In other cases, although there are two or more people engaged in carrying out the common design only one may cause the *actus reus* of the completed offence. In this case the other parties will have their liability determined by reference to the established principles of secondary participation. Where there is an intention to aid, but one party states that he never believed for one moment that the principal offender would act as he did, then liability will be determined by reference to the foresight of the secondary party. Thus, if D goes beyond the scope of the enterprise and kills someone, the secondary party may be guilty of murder if he realised that death or grievous bodily harm was a possible outcome. This will be proved by reference to all the evidence. So, if he knew that his fellow activist was carrying a gun or a knife, then it will be difficult to convince a jury that he did not realise that the weapon might be used to cause serious harm.

It is possible to extricate oneself from a joint enterprise but, as the case law illustrates, there has to be evidence of an effective withdrawal. This may mean doing everything possible to prevent the crime taking place or continuing. So, if A and B having broken into a warehouse are approached by the night watchman and A pulls a knife, it will not avail B if he simply tells A not to use it. If he tried to intervene and disarm A, that might well lead to a different outcome even though he did not succeed and the watchman was killed.

Do not assume that the secondary party will always have played a minor role relative to that undertaken by the principal offender. Thus, it will be recalled in *Cogan and Leak* the husband, although a secondary party, was deemed the more culpable, having sought someone to have intercourse with his wife.

VICARIOUS LIABILITY

Judicial interpretation will determine whether or not a statute imposes vicarious liability. There are two recognised methods of determining vicarious liability:

- the delegation principle;
- the extended construction approach.

CORPORATE LIABILITY

This may be imposed through the use of the identification principle or through being vicariously responsible via the legal mechanisms outlined above. See Chapter 6 for discussion of the principles in the context of the law on involuntary manslaughter.

CHAPTER 5

PRELIMINARY OR INCHOATE OFFENCES

This chapter considers the three inchoate or preliminary offences recognised by the criminal law: incitement, conspiracy and attempt. All three were originally common law offences but conspiracy, in part, and attempt have been put on to a statutory footing. Incitement and the rest of the law on conspiracy are still subject to the common law. The conduct covered by these offences is necessarily preliminary to the completed crime and liability is not dependent upon whether or not the crime in question is actually committed. In broad terms, incitement relates to the activity whereby someone seeks to encourage another to commit an offence. Conspiracy has at its heart the striking of an agreement between two or more parties to commit a crime and an attempt is established, if with the requisite *mens rea* the party or parties have done something more than merely preparatory to the completed offence. In many cases, of course, the parties will go on to complete the offence and in practice any charges will relate to it, but it does not preclude the prosecution from deciding to proceed with the inchoate offence particularly if there is only circumstantial evidence to connect the accused with the completed offence.

It would be a mistake to treat these offences as being in some way inconsequential in comparison to the completed offences. The law seeks to discourage this type of conduct and severe penalties can follow conviction for any of these offences.

5.1   INCITEMENT

The cases of *DPP v Armstrong* [2000] Crim LR 379 and *Goldman* [2001] Crim LR 894 have confirmed the judiciary's approval of incitement contained in the draft Criminal Code (*Criminal Law: A Criminal Code for England and Wales*, Law Com 177, 1989) at cl 47 viz:

> (1) A person is guilty of incitement to commit an offence or offences if –
>
> (a) he incites another to do or cause to be done an act or acts which, if done, will involve the commission of the offence or offences by the other; and
>
> (b) he intends or believes that the other, if he acts as incited, shall, or will do so with the fault required for the offence or offences.

In *Armstrong* the appellant was charged with inciting another person to commit an offence contrary to the Protection of Children Act 1978 in that he telephoned the other person requesting pornography. The Divisional Court applied the above definition and held there was no need for parity of *mens rea* between the inciter and the person incited. A similar view was expressed in *Goldman*, although it should be noted that was a charge of attempt and not incitement.

In *Whitehouse* [1977] 3 All ER 737, Scarman LJ referred to the case of *Higgins* (1801) 2 East 5 which stated that incitement at common law consists of inciting another person to commit a crime. He also referred to the passage from *S v Nkosiyana* (1966) 4 SA 655 *per* Holmes J (cited in Smith and Hogan, *Criminal Law*, 10th edn, 2002, London: Butterworths, p 290) to the effect that an inciter 'is one who reaches and seeks to influence the mind of another to the commission of a crime'. There are many differing opinions as to whether or not incitement should be regarded as an activity which should attract criminal liability. Wayne LaFave and Austin Scott (*Criminal Law*, 2nd edn, 1980, Belmont, CA: Wadsworth) consider that 'mere solicitation ... not accompanied by agreement or action by the person solicited, presents no significant social danger'. The opposing view is that this kind of activity is even more dangerous than a direct attempt at bringing about the crime because 'it may give rise to that cooperation among criminals which is a special hazard'.

5.1.1 Suggestion or encouragement

The *actus reus* can be anything from suggestion to actual encouragement of someone to commit a crime. In *Hendrickson and Tickner* [1977] Crim LR 356, the accused had admitted 'mentioning' to another (M) that a robbery was to take place and he had 'approached' M with a view to him taking part. Their appeal against conviction was dismissed on the basis that the jury had been entitled to draw the inference that there had been the necessary element of persuasion and encouragement. It is also instructive to consider the words of Lord Denning MR in *Race Relations Board v Applin* [1973] QB 815 to the same effect, which emphasise the elements of encouragement or persuasion, but also includes inciting by 'threatening or by pressure, as well as by persuasion'.

5.1.2 General or particular

The incitement can be general or particular and need not be aimed at any particular person. Thus, one might commit the *actus reus* by advertising to the world at large in a newspaper or on television. A person seeking to incite may not wish to do so in a particularly overt way and, according to *Invicta Plastics Ltd v Clare* [1976] Crim LR 131, incitement may even be implied from the circumstances. In the event that the person solicited does not comprehend what is being communicated or the message fails to reach him, then the law admits of the possibility of a charge of attempted incitement providing something more than merely preparatory has been done (in order to comply with the requirements of the Criminal Attempts Act (CAtA) 1981 (see below, 5.9)). The old case of *Ransford* (1874) 13 Cox CC 9 is authority for this proposition. A letter sent to a boy at school inviting him to commit gross indecency was intercepted and handed over to the school authorities. It was cited with approval in *Rowley* [1991] 4 All ER 649 as an example of attempted incitement. In *Rowley*, the accused had left notes in public places offering money and presents to boys. There was nothing lewd, obscene or disgusting in the notes but the Crown claimed that they were designed to lure boys for immoral purposes. A conviction for attempted incitement was quashed on appeal simply because the notes went 'no further than to seek to engineer a preliminary meeting'. At the most he was 'preparing the ground for an attempt', but had not done anything which was more than mere preparation.

The Law Commission in its consultation paper, *Assisting and Encouraging Crime* (Law Com 131, 1993), identifies as a main characteristic of incitement, as with conspiracy, the fact that a person may be guilty of the offence even when the offence incited is not in fact committed.

5.1.3   The act must amount to a crime

A further important point to note is that if the person incited commits the act, it must be proved that it amounts to a crime. In *Whitehouse*, a man was charged with inciting his 15-year-old daughter to aid and abet him to commit incest with her. He had invited her to have sexual intercourse with him but she had refused. Under s 11 of the Sexual Offences Act (SOA) 1956, a girl under 16 years of age could not be found guilty of incest as the law is designed to offer her protection from exploitation from those such as the defendant. Therefore, she could not be guilty of aiding and abetting a man to commit incest with her. The indictment did not disclose an offence known to the law as it charged the accused with inciting his daughter to commit a crime which in law she was incapable of committing. While this decision may seem harsh in that it allowed the defendant to escape liability, it is submitted that it is entirely logical and the court is to be congratulated for not ignoring logic and reason in order to support a conviction simply because of the defendant's reprehensible conduct. Parliament, however, has created an offence under s 54 of the Criminal Law Act (CLwA) 1977, which makes it unlawful for a man to incite a girl under 16 years of age whom he knows to be his daughter, granddaughter, or sister, to have sexual intercourse with him. The result is that an accused would be charged as a principal offender to the statutory offence which avoids all complications with the inchoate offence of incitement. The principle is that a victim by reason of that status cannot be an accessory to an offence and cannot incite the offence.

5.1.4   Inciting incitement

There is also authority to support the proposition that one can incite incitement as where X persuades Y to encourage Z to take part in a crime. In *Sirat* [1986] Crim LR 245, the appellant was convicted of incitement to cause grievous bodily harm, by inciting B to cause grievous bodily harm to the appellant's wife. The prosecution's case was that S would have been content if he could have persuaded B to commit the offence or to have found someone else to do it for him. The case appears to decide that the common law offence of incitement to incite still exists. However, if A incites B to enter into an agreement with C to commit an offence, this would amount to inciting a conspiracy as agreement between B and C would be a necessary precondition to the final act. Section 5(7) of the CLwA 1977 abolished the offence of incitement to commit conspiracy. The crucial distinction is whether A is inviting B to conspire with C or whether he is asking him to persuade C to commit the offence. This latter situation can arise without there being any agreement between B and C and A may simply require B to give information to C in the hope that C will respond on his own initiative to bring about the result A desires. Support for this proposition is to be found in *Evans* [1986] Crim LR 118 where the charge was incitement to solicit to murder. The particulars of the offence were that the appellant unlawfully incited B to solicit, encourage, persuade, endeavour to persuade and propose to a person or persons unknown to murder E. The Court of Appeal found that what she had done was not the equivalent of incitement to conspire because she had not wished B to enter into an agreement with a third party. B was 'being urged to procure an assassin and was not being urged to enter into a conspiracy with anyone'.

5.1.5 *Mens rea*

It is clear that in order to establish the *mens rea* for the offence, the prosecution must prove that the accused intended the offence which was incited to be committed and intended any consequences inherent in the *actus reus* of the crime. Additionally, there must be knowledge of or at least wilful blindness to the circumstances. In respect of the former point, incitement is similar to the crime of attempt in that the accused must intend the actual consequence. Thus, if the incitement or attempt relates to causing serious harm and not to killing the victim, then if the incitee does in fact kill, he will be liable for murder but the incitement or attempt will not relate to murder only grievous bodily harm. In *Curr* [1968] 2 QB 944, the Court of Appeal thought that the incitee should possess the *mens rea* for the offence incited, and as she did not the accused had his conviction quashed. This decision is surprising simply because with the law relating to preliminary offences, liability should not depend on the knowledge the person holds in relation to the final offence. The focus should be on the knowledge of the accused. Did he believe that the woman incited had the guilty knowledge? If so, then he should have been found guilty. This principle should apply even if they actually did have the requisite knowledge and the accused honestly believed they did not.

The argument that, as a general principle, there need be parity of *mens rea* between inciter and incitee was rejected by the Divisional Court in *DPP v Armstrong*. The accused had been put in touch with J on the basis that J would supply him with some child pornography. The accused spoke to J on the telephone and outlined what sort of material he wanted J to supply. Unknown to the accused, J was in fact an undercover police officer. When charged with incitement contrary to common law, the accused successfully argued that he could not be convicted because J had no intention of supplying the material. On appeal by way of case stated, the Divisional Court accepted the prosecution's argument that the offence of incitement was made out if, had the incitee done what was asked, he would have committed a criminal offence. *Curr* was distinguished on the basis that the offence under consideration in that case required proof that the women collecting the welfare benefits payments knew that they were not entitled to do so.

In *Invicta Plastics Ltd v Clare*, the company had produced a device called 'Radatec' and advertised it in motoring magazines, inviting readers to send for further information. One implication to be drawn from the advertisement was that use of the device would ensure that drivers need never be caught out by police radar traps. The company was convicted of incitement to commit an offence contrary to the Wireless Telegraphy Act (WTA) 1949, that is, to operate the device without the appropriate licence. The company argued that there had to be evidence of an incitement to use the device and as this was not evident from the wording of the advertisement they should be found not guilty. Presumably, the company's purpose was to maximise its income from sales of the device. It was from the company's viewpoint irrelevant whether anyone would use the machine. Nevertheless, the company was found guilty on the basis that the word 'incite' was wide enough to encompass advertising in this particular way. But would any potential purchasers know or even suspect that they were in contravention of the WTA 1949 by using the device? In light of the decision in *Curr*, the assumption must be that the justices believed purchasers were intent upon committing the offence, although very few if any would have been aware of which piece of legislation they were likely to contravene. Surely, the better approach is to convict on the basis that the company intended purchasers to breach the WTA 1949. If they clearly did not produce the devices for this purpose, then it should be found not guilty. A better way to prevent proliferation of such devices is to enact legislation designed to ensure that the end users become principal offenders based upon their usage of such devices and publicise this fact as widely as possible. In *James and Ashford* (1985) 82 Cr App R 226, the appellants had bought battery chargers for adaption to use in causing false readings on electricity meters, intending to sell them to another person, that is, a 'middleman' who presumably would seek to sell them, at a profit, to members of the public. These machines had one use only and therefore it was clear why they would be purchased. Nevertheless, there was no certainty that people would actually use them. The court quashed convictions for conspiracy to incite others to contravene s 13 of the Theft Act (TA) 1968 based upon s 1 of the CLwA 1977 (see below for discussion of statutory as opposed to common law conspiracy). However, the court was of the opinion that a common law conspiracy to incite might succeed in these circumstances. *Invicta Plastics* may be distinguished on the basis that supply to a wholesaler or 'middleman' would not constitute incitement as there would be no 'advertisement or open persuasion to others to use these devices' (that is, the general public). In the *James and Ashford* situation, there is a conspiracy between the accused to incite the 'middleman' to purchase the machines but this does not prove that they sought to incite the end user to breach the law. In the *Invicta Plastics* case, the advertisements were designed to persuade the public to purchase and there could only be one purpose in mind, to avoid the police radar traps, given the thrust of the advertising.

In *Shaw* [1994] Crim LR 365, the defendant claimed he had only persuaded a fellow employee to accept false invoices and thus receive company cheques in order to expose the weaknesses inherent in the company's security system. His appeal was allowed but it is difficult to support the decision. It would appear that the court was not convinced that he had the *mens rea* for the completed offence, that is, dishonesty and the intention to permanently deprive. But this is irrelevant in respect of incitement. If D believed that the incitee would possess the *mens rea* for theft that is all that is required. As is pointed out in the commentary to the case (p 366), if the incitee had been charged with obtaining property by deception and Shaw as an accomplice, then there would have been no need to show that Shaw possessed the *mens rea* of the completed offence. On this basis, the *mens rea* for incitement is more difficult to establish than that of counselling the offence!

5.1.6   Impossibility

Later in this chapter, consideration is given to the liability for conspiracy and attempt in circumstances where the completed offence is impossible to achieve even though it is assumed by the defendant that it is perfectly possible to bring it about. The act to be committed by the incitee must amount to an offence, otherwise incitement of that event will not amount to a crime. D has made a mistake of law in that it is believed that the activity to be suggested to the incitee is a crime. In such circumstances, no harm will accrue as what has been done is perfectly lawful. But what if unknown to the inciter it is physically impossible for the incitee to achieve the ultimate goal? For example, D incites P to steal B's car. Unknown to D, P's car has been involved in a serious accident, consigned to the breakers yard and has been crushed. From D's point of view he believes that he is persuading P to commit a crime. If the car had been in existence the offence could have been committed. D has the necessary intent. Should he be absolved of responsibility because of a chance occurrence which unknown to him prevents the crime from taking place? One needs to examine the sections on impossibility in the context of attempt before analysing the law on inciting the impossible. Three possible situations may arise:

- at the time of the incitement, the act incited cannot be committed although D believes that it can, but subsequently it can. For example, the jewels to be stolen are lodged with the Bank of England, but later the owner removes them so that his wife may wear them at a Royal Garden Party;

- at the time of the incitement, the act incited can be committed, but at the time the completed offence is attempted it is impossible to achieve. For example, D incites P to steal a car which does exist at the time D speaks with P but is later involved in an accident before P can carry out the crime;

- at the time of the incitement, the act incited cannot be committed, nor can it ever be brought about, although the inciter believes that it is possible.

The statutory provisions which apply to impossibility in the context of attempt and conspiracy do not apply to incitement which is still determined by the common law. *McDonough* (1962) 47 Cr App R 37 determined, with regard to inciting butchers to receive stolen carcasses, that the fact that at the time of the incitement they may not even have existed, let alone have been stolen, was irrelevant. It was clear what he intended should happen and he had tried to persuade the butchers to accept stolen goods. The court regarded the absence of stolen carcasses as having no bearing on his liability. However, in the context of attempt and conspiracy, the House of Lords had two opportunities to examine and reassess the common law on impossibility in the cases *of Haughton v Smith* [1975] AC 476 and *DPP v Nock* [1978] 2 All ER 654. In the event, it was determined that in cases of physical or factual impossibility, an agreement to engage in a course of conduct which could not in any circumstances have resulted in the offence could not amount to a conspiracy. Similarly, an attempt to produce a consequence which was impossible, for example, stealing money from a pocket which is empty, would not lead to a conviction for attempt. These decisions were at odds with the law stated in *McDonough* with regard to incitement.

The matter was further complicated by Lord Scarman's attempts in *DPP v Nock* to distinguish between general and specific instances of criminality. If the agreement or attempt should relate to a specific thing or person, then, if the person had, unknown to the conspirators, died or the specific item, for example, a gold ring, had been melted down, they could not be guilty of the inchoate offence. However, if the agreement or attempt related to something general, for example, to steal from anyone with £50 in their pocket, such a person may not be found immediately but would undoubtedly be found if the participants continued with their efforts.

These cases were applied to incitement by the Court of Appeal in *Fitzmaurice* [1983] 1 All ER 189. The appellant had been asked by his father to find someone prepared to rob a woman on her way to a bank by snatching wages from her. He approached B and encouraged him to take part. In fact, the proposed robbery was a fiction thought up by the father in order, he hoped, to receive reward money from the police. The appellant genuinely believed the wages snatch was to take place. He was convicted of inciting B to commit robbery by robbing a woman near the bank.

The Court of Appeal held that the law relating to impossibility as stated by the House of Lords should equally apply to incitement. However, instead of quashing the appellant's conviction on the basis that no such robbery as planned would occur, the court adopted the 'general' and 'specific' distinction postulated by Lord Scarman in *Nock* and found these facts to fall into the 'general' category as undoubtedly they could, with patience, have found a woman carrying wages outside a bank in East London.

Neill J justified the conclusion in the following way:

> It is necessary in every case to decide on the evidence what was the course of conduct which was incited ... in some cases the evidence may establish that the persuasion by the inciter was in quite general terms whereas the subsequent agreement of the conspirators was directed to a specific crime and a specific target. In such cases where the committal of the specific offence is shown to be impossible, it may be quite logical for the inciter to be convicted even though the alleged conspirators (if not caught by s 5 of the CAtA 1981) may be acquitted [p 194(d)].

Note that, in *DPP v Armstrong*, the Divisional Court rejected the accused's argument based on impossibility, holding that the incitee (the undercover police officer) could have supplied pornographic material from police stores had he been so minded.

The present position is anomalous in that, since attempt and conspiracy are both statutory offences and parliament has addressed the issue of impossibility in the CAtA 1981, albeit without total clarity, the legal principles, with the exception of incitement, have been restated (see below, 5.7 and 5.12). The omission of incitement from the CAtA 1981 resulted from the recommendations of the Law Commission in its report on *Attempt and Impossibility in Relation to Attempt, Conspiracy and Incitement* (Law Com 102, 1980). The Law Commission accepted the view of the House of Lords in *DPP v Nock* and was prepared to distinguish the law relating to incitement from that of attempts.

5.2   DRAFT CRIMINAL CODE

The Law Commission now believes that, as far as possible, there should be consistency between the inchoate offences on the basis that they 'share a common rationale concerned with the prevention of substantive offences and they frequently overlap'. Sadly, no attempt has yet been made to put the code onto a statutory basis.

5.3   CONSPIRACY

It is not easy to find a totally convincing reason, other than perhaps historical precedent, why simply agreeing to commit a crime should be treated as an offence. By comparison with the law on attempts, the *actus reus* of the latter occurs only when one or more of the parties does something more than merely preparatory to the completed offence. In other words, mere preparation does not attract criminal liability. Therefore, discussing and agreeing to commit a crime would not become a criminal attempt until a preparatory action had occurred. The traditional view aired by the Law Commission in its report, *Criminal Law: Report on Conspiracy and Criminal*

Law Reform (Law Com 76, 1976) is that the reason that it allows the law to intervene at an early stage is to prevent the commission of an offence. But, as we shall see later when the law on attempts is considered in detail, actions taken on the way to committing an offence may still not be regarded as proximate enough to the completed crime to warrant liability for attempting to commit the offence. The case of *Campbell* (1990) 93 Cr App R 350 (see below, 5.10) is perhaps the most striking example. Why should a combination of people agreeing to commit a crime be more reprehensible than someone who actually begins the process of bringing about the crime but has not passed the merely preparatory stage?

A more convincing, albeit not necessarily acceptable, reason is that it helps to facilitate convictions on an *ex post facto* basis when prosecutors have insufficient evidence to substantiate, on an individual basis, criminal liability. The prosecution will use circumstantial evidence to establish that one or more individuals must beyond all reasonable doubt have been working in concert. It helps the fight against the modern scourge of terrorism as may be the case where a group of individuals across the globe are acting together to perpetrate a crime, such as the World Trade Center outrage of 2001.

Although it is not possible to go into great detail, it is advisable to give some thought to the common law as it related to conspiracy prior to the CLwA 1977. This Act introduced the offence of statutory conspiracy but crucially preserves elements of common law conspiracy: notably, conspiracy to defraud and to corrupt public morals. The common law recognised three other types of conspiracy: to effect a public mischief, to commit a tort and, of course, to commit a crime. A thorough review of the law was undertaken by the Law Commission in its 1976 report (Law Com 76), and it recommended that the vast scope of common law conspiracy should be limited with the focus of the offence of statutory conspiracy being an agreement to commit one or more criminal offences.

The concern of the Law Commission can be illustrated by examining the House of Lords' decision in *Shaw v DPP* [1962] AC 220. In this case, the defendant produced a contact magazine entitled *The Ladies Directory* in which prostitutes paid to advertise their services. He was convicted of three offences, one of which was conspiracy to corrupt public morals, despite one Law Lord seeming to accept that there may not be an exact precedent for such a conspiracy as this case reveals (*per* Viscount Simonds, p 462). There was much discussion amongst the Law Lords as to whether or not there was a substantive offence of corrupting public morals, the prevailing view appearing to be that there was not. Thus, if this is a separate head of conspiracy, one is entitled to ponder on the extent of the offence. Exactly what conduct is deemed to be capable of corrupting public morals? Lord Simonds had suggested that the House of Lords possessed the 'residual power' to 'enforce the supreme and fundamental purpose of the law, to conserve not only the safety and order but also the moral welfare of the State', although this was later denied by Lord Simon in *Knuller v DPP* [1972] AC 435. The real dilemma is how ordinary citizens are going to be aware in advance of whether any agreement which they propose to achieve will amount in law to a conspiracy although it is not a criminal offence. In other words, it appears to offend against a basic principle that the criminal law should be certain in its application (see above, 1.5, for further discussion of these cases).

The attempt at a full rationalisation failed because it was believed in 1977 that a comprehensive review of fraud offences and those offences relating to obscenity would be undertaken. The Law Commission has published its review of and recommendations for the law on conspiracy to defraud (*Criminal Law: Conspiracy to Defraud*, Law Com 228, 1994). However, thus far, there has been no attempt to put the recommendations onto a statutory footing and therefore we are faced with examining both statutory and common law conspiracy in order to appreciate the extent and significance of this area of law. The basic requirements are common to both offences. At the heart of a conspiracy is evidence of an agreement between two or more persons. This suggests consensus between the parties, although perhaps not to each and every minute detail, together with evidence that the parties have decided to put into effect the unlawful purpose at the centre of their discussions or negotiations. In *Walker* [1962] Crim LR 458, the accused and colleagues were planning to steal. However, it was held that because he withdrew before the plans were finalised, he was not guilty of conspiracy. Lord Parker posed the question whether what had occurred had gone past the sphere of negotiation and become a matter of agreement. Evidence of the agreement may be expressed or implied from the circumstances and it must be communicated to the other party or parties. It appears that there are two types of conspiracy which recognise that communication, not face to face meeting, is the crux of an agreement. In a 'chain' conspiracy, A may only meet with B, who then communicates with C, who likewise contacts D. All are parties to the same conspiracy even though A may not even know D. A similar agreement may be reached via a 'wheel' conspiracy where one person at the centre communicates with all other parties. That person is known to each, yet the others may not know each other. In *Phillips* (1987) 84 Cr App R 18, the accused, along with four named persons and others unknown, was charged with conspiracy to obtain by deception. The prosecution did not have to prove that everyone named was actually a party as long as it could be established that they each had conspired with at least one other person, whatever his identity. Richard Card ([1973] Crim LR 674) argues that:

> There are differing opinions on whether an agreement between two or more people to commit a crime should incur criminal liability. If, having reached the agreement, the parties put it into effect, at the point where they have gone beyond mere preparation the law of attempt will come into play. Few would argue against the principle that the function of the criminal law is to discourage individuals from attempting to commit crimes. But what of those who have not reached the stage at which the law on attempts kicks into play?
>
> ... if the further acts are insufficient to constitute an attempt, the punishment of the conspirators, both those who committed the overt acts and those who did no more than enter the agreement, can only be justified on the basis that it is the combination of persons which aggravates their conduct and produces liability [p 675].

He accepts that there is a compelling reason for retaining a law of conspiracy for those who have not fallen within the net of the law on attempts. If a large number of crimes have been committed at different times by different people, all acting pursuant to an agreement, it may be extremely difficult to obtain convictions for the substantive offences. However, it may be much easier to prove that they have been acting in concert and convict them of conspiracy.

Whatever the strength of the respective arguments, the fact is that a conspiracy is complete just as soon as the parties have reached agreement always assuming that they possess the intent required by the definition of the crime. (See also Dennis, 'The rationale of criminal conspiracy' (1977) 93 LQR 39.)

5.3.1   Limitations imposed by law

There are limitations imposed by the law as to with whom it may be possible to conspire (see s 2(2) of the CLwA 1977). For example, a person is not guilty of conspiracy if the only other party is his spouse or is a person under the age of criminal responsibility (10 years) or an intended victim of that offence or offences. In the first example, the parties must be married at the time the agreement is reached, that is, the *actus reus* completed. In *Chrastny (No 1)* [1992] 1 All ER 189, the Court of Appeal held that a defendant can be convicted of conspiracy when the only other person with whom he or she agrees is a spouse, providing it is known by the defendant that there are other conspirators, notwithstanding that he or she has no detailed knowledge of them nor has come to any positive agreement with them. It was alleged that she had knowingly played a part in concealing part of a consignment of cocaine and laundering some of the proceeds of sale of the drug. There was no evidence that she knew any member of the gang which had imported the drugs other than her husband.

One cannot conspire with the intended victim of the conspiracy. It has been suggested by the late Professors JC Smith and Brian Hogan (*Criminal Law*, 10th edn, 2002, London: Butterworths, p 323) that this can only apply where the offence exists for his or her protection. Thus, in circumstances such as those in *Brown and Others* [1993] Crim LR 961, where the appellants belonged to a group of sado-masochistic homosexuals who willingly participated in acts of violence against each other, a conspiracy charge would lie if the parties each agreed with one another to inflict violence. The fact that the 'victim' is consenting is, according to the decision, irrelevant and, in light of the view expounded by Smith and Hogan, the offence was certainly not one created for the victim's protection. The situation would, it is submitted, be different if D agreed to have intercourse with a girl under the age of 16. Here the law specifically seeks to prevent her exploitation and it can be maintained that the offence was therefore created for her protection. The situation is unlikely to arise often and most improbably at common law. In the case of a conspiracy to defraud, the 'victim' in the true sense of the words is unlikely ever to agree knowingly to be defrauded!

It has been established that any person may be convicted as an accessory to a crime even though he or she is incapable of being a principal offender. Likewise with conspiracy, there is authority to support the principle confirming guilt as a conspirator when the defendant is incapable of being prosecuted as a principal. In *Burns* (1984) 79 Cr App R 173, the father of a child was found guilty of conspiring with others to steal it from the mother, an offence contrary to s 56 of the Offences Against the Person Act 1861 (now repealed by the Child Abduction Act 1984). He could not be prosecuted for the full offence as he was the child's father. The Court of Appeal justified upholding his conviction on the basis that there was no authority which prevented the court from saying:

> ... that it is in any way wrong or unjust for a person who is exempt ... from prosecution for the substantive offence to be proceeded against for the crime of conspiracy. The dangers of permitting a father of children to collect a posse of men and suddenly launch a siege of the home of his estranged wife, to break in and then snatch away sleeping children is surely self-evident. The criminal law does not in our view permit that sort of conduct.

It is also possible for there to be an acquittal of the other party to a conspiracy and for the conviction of the remaining conspirator to be upheld. Care must be taken to distinguish between two situations. It may be that the parties (X and Y) charged with conspiracy are alleged to have conspired with a third party who has not been apprehended or may simply be unknown to the police. If the jury having considered all the evidence concludes that the case against one conspirator (X) is proved, yet the case against the other (Y) is not, then according to *Anthony* [1965] 1 All ER 440 there may still be a conviction against X. However, if X and Y are charged with conspiracy and there are no others involved, can a conviction against X be sustained if Y is acquitted? If yes, this would appear to offend against the principle that there should be two parties to a conspiracy. Section 5(8) of the CLwA 1977 provides:

> The fact that the person or persons who, so far as appears from the indictment on which any person has been convicted of conspiracy, were the only other parties to the agreement on which his conviction was based have been acquitted of conspiracy by reference to that agreement (whether after being tried with the person convicted or separately) shall not be a ground for quashing his conviction unless under all the circumstances of the case his conviction is inconsistent with the acquittal of the other person or persons in question.

There are various outcomes in such a situation which will primarily depend on the strength of the evidence in respect of each party. In *Longman and Cribben* (1980) 72 Cr App R 121, the former was the proprietor of a garage and car sales business. The latter worked for Longman as a car salesman. They were charged with conspiring to defraud an insurance company of £3,323 by making a false claim in respect of the theft of a car. The evidence adduced by the prosecution was almost all circumstantial but the case against Cribben was much stronger than that against Longman. The Lord Chief Justice outlined the various circumstances and outcomes in this type of situation.

The trial judge must tell the jury to consider the case against each defendant separately. If the evidence against each is markedly different, for example, because X has confessed and Y has not, the judge should go on to tell the jury they may convict one and acquit the other. Therefore, it is proved that X conspired with Y but not that Y conspired with X. This is logical providing that the cases are considered separately. Where the evidence is of equal weight or 'nearly so', there may be a real risk of inconsistent verdicts and the judge should rule that both are to be found guilty or not guilty. If the jury is unsure about the guilt of one defendant in these circumstances, then both should be found not guilty. The final situation deals with the position at the end of the prosecution case where the evidence against one is such that it would be unsafe to ask a jury to convict. In this situation there is nothing to prevent the case from proceeding against the other if the evidence is stronger. The court put the test to be employed in these terms:

> Is the evidence such that a verdict of guilty in respect of (X) and not guilty in respect of (Y) would be, to all intents and purposes, inexplicable and therefore inconsistent? If so, it would be an occasion for the 'both guilty or both not guilty' direction. If not, then the separate verdict direction is required.

5.4   STATUTORY CONSPIRACY

Section 1(1) of the CLwA 1977, as amended by s 5 of the CAtA 1981, provides:

(1) Subject to the following provisions of this Part of this Act, if a person agrees with any other person or persons that a course of conduct shall be pursued which, if the agreement is carried out in accordance with their intentions, either:

(a) will necessarily amount to or involve the commission of any offence or offences by one or more parties to the agreement; or

(b) would do so but for the existence of facts which render the commission of the offence or any offences impossible, he is guilty of conspiracy to commit the offence or offences in question.

It will be evident that it is difficult and unwise to seek to differentiate the *actus reus* and *mens rea* because an agreement invariably involves some form of consensus. We have already discussed the meaning of agreement, let us now focus on what the parties must agree, that is, to engage in a *course of conduct* which if carried out in accordance with their intentions will result in an offence being committed by one or more of the parties. The words 'course of conduct' must be taken to include reference to the intended consequences as far as result crimes are concerned. This is logical although the Act does not make it absolutely clear. In fact in the case of *DPP v Nock* a case of common law conspiracy the House of Lords, when using the words *course of conduct*, took the narrow view that it related only to the acts the parties intended to carry out and not the consequences of their intended actions. In this case the parties attempted to produce cocaine from a substance that did not contain the drug. It was held there was no conspiracy to produce a controlled drug because their actions would never have resulted in a controlled drug being produced. Section 5 of the CAtA 1981 sought to ensure this did not apply to statutory conspiracy by inserting a new s 1(1)(b) to the 1977 Act. If X and Y have agreed to kill Z and they decide the way to do it is to place a bomb under his car wired to the ignition, then that 'course of conduct' will not in itself lead to Z's death. He (or someone else) will need to start the car for the bomb to be detonated. It would be rather odd if X and Y were not to face a conspiracy (or attempt) to murder charge, simply because the words 'course of conduct' were taken to exclude reference to the intended consequences. It becomes crucial that one is clear as to what the particular intended consequences are.

It was accepted in *Siracusa and Others* (1990) Cr App R 340 that the *mens rea* sufficient to support the substantive offence will not necessarily suffice for a charge of conspiracy to commit the offence. For example, an intention to cause grievous bodily harm is sufficient to support a charge of murder but not a charge of conspiracy to murder. The appellants were convicted of conspiracy to be knowingly concerned in the fraudulent evasion of the prohibition on the importation of cannabis resin and a similar conspiracy to import heroin. O'Connor LJ stated the principle quite clearly:

... the prosecution must prove that the agreed course of conduct was the importation of heroin. This is because the essence of the crime of conspiracy is the agreement and in simple terms, you do not prove an agreement to import heroin by proving an agreement to import cannabis ... The *mens rea* sufficient to support the commission of a substantive offence will not necessarily be sufficient to support a charge of conspiracy to commit that offence.

Consideration should also be given to s 1(2) of the CLwA 1977 which refers to circumstances, as opposed to consequences, relating to the course of conduct. For there to be liability for conspiracy, at least two parties to the agreement must intend or know that that fact or circumstance shall or will exist at the time when the conduct constituting the offence is to take place; for example, on a conspiracy to rape charge that they intend that the woman will not be consenting, or on a conspiracy to handle charge that the goods will be stolen. In practice, parties at the time of making the agreement will not know whether a particular circumstance will exist nor is it correct to say one intends a consequence over which one may have no influence. It would have been far better if parliament had chosen to use the word 'believe'.

5.4.1   If the agreement is carried out in accordance with their intentions

The Law Commission, in its 1976 report (Law Com 76, para 7.2), was quite explicit on what it believed the requisite *mens rea* ought to be:

> Both must intend that any consequences specified in the definition of the offence will result and both must know of the existence of any state of affairs which it is necessary for them to know in order to be aware that the course of conduct agreed upon will amount to the offence.

The House of Lords in *Anderson* [1985] 2 All ER 961 faced the question of whether it was implicit in s 1(1) that the conspirators must intend the substantive offence to be committed. This is an important consideration, particularly for those who may enter an agreement for a myriad of reasons, none of which involve a commitment to take part in the course of conduct, let alone have any aspiration that the substantive offence should happen. Perhaps the person 'could not care less' or may even hope that, viewed from his own standpoint, the other parties to the agreement are all arrested before they can put their plan into action. In *Anderson,* the defendant met X in prison while on remand. The defendant expected to be released on bail and agreed with X to participate in a scheme effecting X's escape from prison, in which there were to be two other participants. He was to be paid £20,000 for his part in the scheme and actually received £2,000 on account on his release on bail. He was then injured in a road accident and took no further part in the scheme. He admitted that he had intended to acquire a diamond wire for cutting through metal bars and to give it to one of the other participants. He was charged with conspiracy to effect the escape of a prisoner lawfully detained at Her Majesty's Prison, Lewes, contrary to s 1(1) of the CLwA 1977. It was submitted for the defendant that he had never intended that the escape plan should be carried out, nor had he believed that it could succeed, and thus he lacked the *mens rea*. The judge rejected the submission and he changed his plea to guilty. His appeal against conviction was dismissed by the Court of Appeal and eventually by the House of Lords. The House of Lords stated that the *mens rea* for statutory conspiracy is established 'if and only if' it is proved that when one enters into an agreement the defendant intended to play some part in the agreed course of conduct involving the commission of the offence. It was also confirmed that a person could be guilty of conspiracy even though 'he secretly intended to participate in only part of the course of conduct involving the commission of our offence'.

As Lord Bridge makes clear, it may:

... be a matter of complete indifference to him whether (the crime) is in fact committed or not. Parliament cannot have intended that such parties should escape conviction of conspiracy on the basis that it cannot be proved against them that they intended that the relevant offence or offences should be committed [p 975(b)–(c)].

The difficulty, if indeed there is one, centres around the words 'if carried out in accordance with their intentions'. Clearly, a defendant such as Anderson could argue that it was never his intention that the substantive offence should be carried out. There is no 'collective' intention in such circumstances. However strong this argument, the House of Lords believed this would impose too onerous a burden on the prosecution if it had to be proved that all parties intended the substantive offence to be committed. It was also acknowledged that those such as law enforcement officers who infiltrate a criminal conspiracy in order to frustrate the enterprise will not have the necessary *mens rea*. This point needs clarification given the decision of the Privy Council in *Yip Chiu-cheung v R* [1994] 2 All ER 924. Lord Bridge said this in *Anderson*:

There may be many situations in which perfectly respectable citizens, more particularly those concerned with law enforcement, may enter into agreements that a course of conduct shall be pursued which will involve commission of a crime without the least intention of playing any part in furtherance of the ostensibly agreed criminal objective, but rather with the purpose of exposing and frustrating the criminal purpose of the other parties to the agreement. The *mens rea* implicit in the offence of statutory conspiracy must clearly be such as to recognise the innocence of such a person, notwithstanding that he will, in literal terms, be obliged to agree that a course of conduct be pursued involving the commission of an offence [p 965(d)].

Anderson was distinguished in *Yip*, where Lord Griffiths explained Lord Bridge's statement was meant to apply only to those situations where there was already a criminal conspiracy in existence. An undercover agent may be seeking to infiltrate an organisation in order to obtain information which will lead to the police being able to prevent a crime from taking place and to the arrest of the conspirators. In *Yip*, the defendant, a drugs dealer, met and agreed with N that they should together import drugs via Hong Kong into Australia. N was a drug enforcement officer from the US. The Hong Kong and Australian authorities were prepared to permit him to carry drugs in the hope of breaking up a drugs ring. The defendant argued that he could not be guilty of conspiracy because N did not possess the *mens rea* for the completed offence. This line of reasoning did not find favour with the Privy Council. Here was a situation where the 'respectable citizen' was involved from the outset and was therefore a party to the conspiracy. He intended to import drugs into Australia. The fact that this was being done with the tacit approval of the authorities was deemed to be irrelevant as it was held that the executive had no power to authorise a breach of the law and that it was no excuse for an offender to say he was acting under the orders of a superior officer. The fact that N intended to export the heroin to Australia was sufficient to ensure that he was to be regarded as a conspirator.

This is a potentially problematic decision. A law enforcement officer seeking to smash a drugs cartel is himself guilty of conspiracy. If the conspiracy is already in existence then according to the decision in *Anderson* he has nothing to fear, but if he becomes actively involved in the first instance and ostensibly 'creates' a conspiracy for the purpose of tracking the other party to the source of the drugs or to his receivers then he commits an offence. It could be argued that it is necessary to pursue this line in order to ensure the conviction of the other party for conspiracy if there is insufficient evidence to convict him of trafficking. However, if the parties put their agreement into effect, it potentially presents problems in jurisdictions such as Singapore or Malaysia that still have the death penalty for drug trafficking and where the offences are written in strict liability terms. Being found in possession of quantities in excess of the statutory minimum of, say, heroin, would on the face of it require executive action once the circumstances are known to avoid prosecution and the prospect of a day of destiny with the gallows. However, according to the Privy Council the executive in Hong Kong had no authority to sanction a breach of the law. Thankfully, neither Singapore nor Malaysia needs the Privy Council to rule on what the executive can or cannot do in such circumstances. This whole area of activity has strong public policy overtones and as such the law may at times appear to be irrational and uncertain.

Taken to its logical conclusion, if all parties to a conspiracy are indifferent to whether the course of conduct leads to a substantive offence, despite giving the impression to each other that they do want it to happen, then there really is no conspiracy at all, but according to Lord Bridge a conspiracy conviction could still ensue. It is suggested in situations such as the example cited by Lord Bridge of the proprietor of a car hire business who agrees for a substantial payment to make available a hire car to a gang for use in a robbery, that there is clear evidence of aiding and abetting the conspiracy of the robbers who obviously do intend that the substantive offence be carried out. Reference should be made to *Siracusa*, which sought to give meaning, if any be needed, to the clear words used by Lord Bridge in *Anderson*. He said, it will be recalled:

> ... beyond the mere fact of agreement, the necessary *mens rea* of the crime is established if, and only if, it is shown that the accused, when he entered into the agreement, intended to play some part in the agreed course of conduct in furtherance of the criminal purpose [p 965(h)].

O'Connor LJ said in *Siracusa*:

> We think it obvious that Lord Bridge cannot have been intending that the organiser of a crime who recruited others to carry it out would not himself be guilty of conspiracy unless it could be proved that he intended to play some active part himself, thereafter.

> ... participation in conspiracy is infinitely variable, it can be active or passive ... consent, that is the agreement or adherence to the agreement can be inferred if it is proved that he knew what was going on and intention to participate in the furtherance of the criminal purpose is also established by his failure to stop the unlawful activity.

One final point on *Anderson* is that, given that the whole *raison d'être* of conspiracy is the agreement made with the relevant *mens rea*, there appears to be no authority to support the contention that there must be an intention on the part of the accused to play some part in carrying out the agreed course of conduct.

5.4.2 The conditional intention argument

The courts have also had to deal with the so-called conditional intention argument, as demonstrated by the cases of *Jackson* [1985] Crim LR 442, *Reed* [1982] Crim LR 819 and *O'Hadhmaill* (1996) *The Times*, 13 February. In *Jackson*, the appellants were convicted of conspiracy to pervert the course of public justice. They were aware of a plan that would result in W being shot in the leg should he be convicted of burglary for which he was on trial. The avowed purpose of this attack on W was to provide him with mitigation should he have been convicted. In the event, he was found guilty and the shooting with his concurrence clearly took place. The appellants appealed against conviction on the ground that no offence had been committed since it depended on a contingency which might not have taken place – the conviction of W for burglary. The agreement, it was submitted, did not 'necessarily' involve the commission of an offence (see s 1(1)(a) of the CLwA 1977).

In dismissing their appeals, the court held that 'necessarily' in s 1 did not mean that there must inevitably be the carrying out of an offence. Rather, it meant that if the agreement were to be carried out in accordance with the plan, there must be the commission of the offence referred to in the conspiracy count. The rationale of this appears to be that there is a single agreement which is simply triggered by the occurrence of a particular event. The object of the agreement is a criminal offence, that is, to pervert the course of justice. See also the example cited in *Reed* where A and B agree to rob a bank, provided it is safe to do so, this being determined once they reach the bank. Without a doubt, there is an agreement to commit an offence, robbery, providing it is carried out in accordance with their intentions, that is, it is safe to do so.

But suppose the object of the agreement is a condition precedent to a further unlawful act. X and Y agree to rape Z and to kill anyone who might disturb them. Are they guilty of conspiracy to murder as well as a conspiracy to rape? This situation can be approached using the *Jackson* criteria or the two elements could be disaggregated into two separate conspiracies as there are after all two courses of conduct. If this is the case, then they could be guilty of conspiracy to murder on the basis they intend, subject to the condition precedent, to carry out a crime. The object of the agreement in each case is an offence. In *O'Hadhmaill*, the appellant was a lecturer at Central Lancashire University. He was found with explosive devices in his possession and it was the prosecution's case that he was to have played a controlling part in an IRA bombing campaign throughout the UK. The defence argued that there was no settled intention to carry out explosions. This was based upon the fact that in December 1993 there had been a joint declaration issued by the Prime Ministers of Great Britain and Ireland and in consequence it was highly unlikely that the IRA would wish to engage in a bombing campaign. He was convicted and sentenced to 25 years' imprisonment. His appeal was dismissed. The Court of Appeal accepted there was sufficient evidence for the *mens rea* of conspiracy to be proved. The joint declaration might have persuaded the IRA to refrain from planting bombs at that time but, as events have all too graphically illustrated, there would be no complete cessation of terrorist activity. In other words, there was clearly an intention to engage in a course of conduct that would ultimately result in criminal activity. The conditional intention argument is, therefore, unlikely to succeed where there is clear evidence that the parties' objective is to commit a crime, even though there is uncertainty as to when it might be achieved. There appears to be very little difference between this situation and the condition precedent case outlined above. There is an agreement to commit rape and an agreement to murder. They have clearly contemplated the act of killing and indicated that they are prepared to do it. There is a clear commitment to carry out the offence should they need to, a preparedness to act accordingly. Is this really so different in principle from the former case?

5.4.3 Strict liability

Certain crimes, as we know, can be proved without evidence of *mens rea* being adduced or by proving recklessness, in the absence of or as an alternative to intention. Section 1(2) of the CLwA 1977 states:

> Where liability for any offence may be incurred without knowledge on the part of the person committing it of any particular fact or circumstance necessary for the commission of the offence, a person shall nevertheless not be guilty of conspiracy to commit that offence by virtue of subsection (1) above unless he and at least one other party to the agreement intend or know that the fact or circumstance shall or will exist at the time when the conduct constituting the offence is to take place.

Thus, a charge of conspiracy to commit a strict liability offence or one that requires recklessness as to circumstances will not succeed unless the prosecution can prove intention or knowledge to all the elements of the *actus reus*. That of course includes particular circumstances, for example, consent, in relation to the offence of rape. As a result of the House of Lords decisions in *B (A Minor) v DPP* [2000] 1 All ER 833 and *K* [2001] 3 All ER 897 offences under s 1(1) of the Indecency with Children Act 1960 and s 14(1) of the SOA 1956 should no longer be viewed as requiring a 'strict' interpretation and therefore the limited number of 'serious' offences covered by this section is reduced. As Lord Nicholls said in the former case:

> Section 1(1) says nothing about the mental element. In particular, the section says nothing about what shall be the position if the person who commits or incites the act of gross indecency honestly but mistakenly believed that the child was 14 or over.

He concludes:

> Accordingly, I cannot find, either in the statutory context or otherwise, any indication of sufficient cogency to displace the application of the common law presumption (in favour of *mens rea*).

A similar conclusion was reached in the latter case which was not surprising given:

> It is at once obvious that if an absence of genuine belief as to the age of an underage victim must be proved against a defendant under s 1 of the 1960 Act but not against a defendant under s 14 of the 1956 Act, another glaring anomaly would be introduced into this legislation.

5.5 COMMON LAW CONSPIRACY

Considered in 1977 to be residual offences likely to be abolished once a review of fraud and obscenity laws had been undertaken, the offences are still with us and there are no signs of them being consigned into obscurity. The offences are conspiracy to corrupt public morals or outrage public decency and conspiracy to defraud. They will be considered separately.

5.5.1 Conspiracy to corrupt public morals or outrage public decency

Section 5(3) of the CLwA 1977 seemingly preserves the common law offence of conspiracy to corrupt public morals or outrage public decency. Section 5(3) is not clearly worded and begs the question whether there is a substantive offence of corrupting public morals (see the discussion in *Shaw v DPP* where the conclusion reached is that there is not). It would appear that if there were to be recognised at common law substantive offences covering this area, then a conspiracy to achieve these consequences would be classed as a statutory conspiracy. However, the better view is that agreement between two or more persons to corrupt public morals is a common law conspiracy although this means that if an individual were to engage in this type of conduct, apart from the conspiracy, he or she would not commit a substantive offence. It is the conspiracy element only which is made criminal. The uncertainty surrounding the whole concept of public morality and public decency had led the Law Commission (Law Com 76, 1976), to recommend abolition of common law conspiracy in this respect, but as we have seen, its views were ignored. There was conflict between the Court of Criminal Appeal and the House of Lords in *Shaw* over whether or not corrupting public morals was a substantive offence with the former holding it was and the latter concluding that it was not.

Further consideration was given in *Knuller v DPP*. The accused had agreed to publish advertisements in the *International Times* in an attempt to facilitate the commission of homosexual acts in private between consenting adults. The SOA 1967 had decriminalised this type of behaviour provided the acts were done in private, the parties consented and had attained the age of 21. Knuller faced two separate counts of conspiracy. First, to corrupt public morals based upon the advertisements seeking to:

> ... induce readers to meet other persons for the purpose of sexual practices and to encourage readers to indulge in such practices, with intent thereby to debauch and corrupt the morals of youth.

The second count charged conspiracy to outrage public decency through the publication of 'lewd, disgusting and offensive' advertisements. The appellants were convicted on both counts and they appealed to the House of Lords. On the conspiracy to corrupt public morals count, the conviction was upheld but the appeal was allowed on the public decency charge, although the majority held there is a common law offence of conspiracy to outrage public decency and significantly that there is a common law offence of outraging public decency. The House of Lords recognised three offences of 'general application' which involve indecency, indecent exposure of the person, keeping a disorderly house and exposure or exhibition in public of indecent things or acts. Lord Simon thought that outraging public decency 'goes considerably beyond offending the susceptibilities of, or even shocking, reasonable people'. He went on:

> Moreover, the offence is, in my view, concerned with recognising minimum standards of decency, which are likely to vary from time to time ... public decency must be viewed as a whole; and I think the jury should be invited, where appropriate, to remember that they live in a plural society, with a tradition of tolerance towards minorities, and that this atmosphere of toleration is itself part of public decency [p 936(f)].

(Remember that *Knuller* was decided before the CLwA 1977 created the offence of statutory conspiracy.) Consideration was given to the meaning of the word 'corrupt'. Lord Reid thought 'corrupt' a strong word and was of the opinion that the words 'deprave' and 'corrupt' are synonymous. Lord Simon also held the opinion that 'corrupt' was a 'strong word' and went on to state 'the words "corrupt public morals" suggest conduct which a jury might find to be destructive of the very fabric of society'. It should also be noted that the House of Lords distanced itself from the proposition in *Shaw* that there was a residual power to create new offences, but that is not to say that the courts should not seek to apply established offences to new circumstances.

5.5.2   Conspiracy to outrage public decency

As a result of *Knuller* and more recent authorities, one can state quite categorically that there is a common law offence of outraging public decency. The conclusion with regard to conspiracy to outrage public decency is that it ought now to be removed from the realms of common law conspiracy and be recognised as a statutory conspiracy, that is, an agreement to commit a recognised criminal offence. Whatever the logic in favour of treating conspiracy to corrupt public morals in the same way, one cannot point to a line of authority recognising the offence at common law and any conspiracy must therefore continue to be treated as a common law conspiracy. In *Rowley*, the appellant had left notes in public places, for example, public lavatories offering money and presents to boys who would make contact with him. It was alleged that the notes were designed to lure boys for immoral purposes, but there was nothing which would be classed as lewd or obscene in the notes. On appeal against conviction, the Court of Appeal recognised the common law offence of outraging public decency and determined that it consisted of the deliberate commission of an act which was in itself of a lewd, obscene or disgusting nature and outraging public decency. The crucial question for the jury to determine is whether a member of the public is outraged by the act. In *Gibson and Another* [1991] 1 All ER 439, the defendants exhibited, at a commercial art gallery to which the public had access, a model's head to which were attached earrings made out of freeze dried human foetuses. They were charged with outraging public decency contrary to the common law. The Court of Appeal made it clear that outraging public decency was distinct from and did not depend on proof of a tendency to corrupt public morals. Counsel for the appellant did not seek to argue that no such offence existed. It concluded, following Lord Simon in *Knuller*, that the authorities 'establish that it is an indictable offence to say or do or exhibit anything in public, which outrages public decency, whether or not it tends to corrupt or deprave those who see or hear it'.

In *Knuller*, the House of Lords allowed the appeal on the count of conspiracy to outrage public decency on the grounds that the jury had been misdirected on the meaning of the word outrage. It should, however, be noted that while the House of Lords recognised the substantive offence, it was by a simple majority and one is well advised to consider the speeches of Lords Diplock and Reid on this point.

5.5.3   Conspiracy to defraud

Conspiracy to defraud is an offence which has attracted judicial attention on many occasions in the last 30 years. It is perhaps best explained by emphasising that while many fraudulent activities will be criminal and a conspiracy to bring about these consequences will inevitably be charged as a statutory conspiracy, some activities of a fraudulent type may not attract criminal sanctions. The agreement to bring about these consequences may well result in a conviction for common law conspiracy to defraud. This begs the question, however, as to what type of behaviour is encompassed by the word 'defraud'.

As a preliminary to this, it may be instructive to consider the facts of *DPP v Withers and Others* [1974] 3 All ER 984. Care needs to be taken with this case as the charges relate not to conspiracy to defraud but to conspiracy to effect a public mischief, an offence which the House of Lords held was not one known to the law. It was, however, the opinion of the House of Lords that the facts were sufficient to have supported a charge of conspiracy to defraud. Withers and his partners ran an investigation agency and they used various ploys in order to obtain confidential information from financial institutions and governments when making reports on particular individuals for their clients. Deceit was practised on employees of the various organisations but this did not result in any substantive offence being committed. Lord Diplock said:

> It may be that the particulars of the offence which deals with deceiving officers charged with performing a public duty so as to induce them to act contrary to their duty would support a charge of conspiracy to defraud at common law [p 994(a)].

More recently, the Privy Council in *Wai Yu Tsang v R* [1991] 4 All ER 664 gave further consideration as to whether particular facts revealed a conspiracy to defraud. It was held that the matter would be determined by reference to what the parties had dishonestly agreed to do and 'in particular whether they have agreed to practise fraud on somebody'. What is clearly articulated is the principle that all that is required by way of proof is that 'the conspirators have dishonestly agreed to bring about a state of affairs which they realise will or may deceive the victim', that is, there is no need for anyone actually to be deceived. Nor is there any need to prove any actual loss had occurred as a result of the deception. It therefore appears that, as a result of this case, conspiracy to defraud is a crime which is not confined within narrow limits. Lord Goff said of 'intent to defraud' that it 'means simply an intention to practise a fraud on another, or an intention to act to the prejudice of another man's right'.

This view echoes Lord Denning's opinion in *Welham* [1961] AC 103 where he thought that fraudulent conduct would exist if '… anyone may be prejudiced *in any way* by the fraud …' (emphasis added).

In *Scott* [1974] 3 All ER 1032, the appellant had agreed with employees of cinema owners that they should temporarily remove copyrighted films from the various cinemas at which they were employed in order that they might be copied, and then the copies sold on a commercial basis. The master copy of the film would be returned to the cinema from whence it had been abstracted. The appellant's appeal against conviction was based upon the fact that the conspiracy did not involve any deceit being practised on the companies and persons who owned the copyright and the distribution rights to the films. If there was no deceit, it was argued there could be no conspiracy to defraud. The House of Lords held that conspiracy to defraud did not necessarily involve deceit by the defendant of the person whom it was intended to defraud. In this case, there was an agreement to inflict economic loss and, as this was to be achieved by dishonest means, then there had been a conspiracy to defraud. If the films were to be distributed on a commercial basis, then it is reasonable to expect that fewer people would go to see the films at the cinema, thus reducing the owners' potential profit. In addition, Scott would not have paid royalties to the copyright owners, thus denying them something to which they were legally entitled. The House of Lords relied upon a long line of authorities dating back over two centuries to *Orbell* (1703) 6 MOD 42. In the context of cases where the agreement is designed to lead to economic loss for the victim, Viscount Dilhorne defined the offence as follows:

> ... an agreement by two or more by dishonesty to deprive a person of something which is his or to which he is or would be or might be entitled and an agreement by two or more by dishonesty to injure some proprietary right [of the victim] [p 1039(f)].

As the Law Commission points out in its 1994 report (Law Com 228):

> The risk of possible injury to another's right is sufficient prejudice. Where deception is involved, a person is treated as defrauded if induced to take an economic risk that he would not otherwise have taken or even, it seems, if there is a risk that he may be so induced; it is immaterial that in the event he suffers no loss. A similar principle applies to cases involving no deception [para 2.5].

The reference to 'prejudice' harks back to Blackstone's time and the reference in the commentaries to '... the prejudice of another man's right'. Similarly, Lord Radcliffe in *Welham* refers to the '... criminal intent [which] is the prejudice of that person' (see further below).

One further point requires consideration. The cases mentioned make reference to the distinction between public officials and private individuals. We have seen that where the intended victim is a private individual, the purpose of the conspirators must be to cause the victim economic loss by depriving him of some property or right. The public official, however, is simply performing public duties and the conspiracy to defraud need intend only to cause him to act contrary to his duty. The Privy Council in *Wai Yu Tsang* regarded this distinction as otiose. The general principle is that conspiracies to defraud are not restricted to cases of intention to cause economic loss to the intended victim. The Board relied on a statement by Lord Denning in *Welham* [1960] 1 All ER 805:

> The important thing about this definition is that it is not limited to the idea of economic loss, nor to the idea of depriving someone of something of value. It extends generally to the purpose of fraud and deceit. Put shortly, 'with intent to defraud' means 'with intent to practise a fraud' on someone or other. It need not be anyone in particular. Someone in general will suffice. If anyone may be prejudiced in any way by the fraud, that is enough [p 815(H)].

The Privy Council accepted that cases concerned with people performing public duties should not be regarded as a special category, but rather as exemplifying the general principle that conspiracies to defraud are not limited to cases where it is intended that the victim should suffer economic loss.

5.5.4 *Mens rea* for conspiracy to defraud

The *mens rea* for conspiracy to defraud appears to require proof of an intention to defraud and evidence of dishonesty. But what do conspirators actually intend in such cases? Do they intend to cause loss to another or is it more accurate to say they are intent only on creating gain or profit for themselves? If, as is suggested in *Wai Yu Tsang*, the *mens rea* is present if it is the conspirators' purpose to cause prejudice to the victim by any fraudulent means, then what more is needed? However, the conspirators may not be at all concerned nor give any thought to the consequences of their agreement as it might affect the victim. They may be concerned only with the potential gain for themselves. In a complex fraud, they might not even comprehend how the victims may suffer loss. It is suggested by the authorities that an oblique intent may well be sufficient, that is, it is unnecessary to prove that the primary object of the conspiracy was to cause loss to another party. It is sufficient if the defendant has realised that loss would, nevertheless, be incurred. In *Cooke* [1986] 2 All ER 985, the defendant was employed by British Rail as a member of a buffet car crew. He took on board his own food and refreshment, along with other members of the crew with the intention, it was alleged, of selling them to passengers and keeping the proceeds. Did he intend to defraud the passengers or British Rail or both? The House of Lords was not convinced that had they known the truth the passengers would have refused to purchase the refreshments offered by Cooke and his colleagues. Cooke's conviction was upheld on the basis that there was an intent to defraud his employers, British Rail. To make a profit by selling to passengers would inevitably deprive British Rail of profit as the passengers would not be purchasing from the carrier, assuming of course that the British Rail food had not run out! It would be incorrect to assert that his primary intention was to cause loss to British Rail, although it was an inevitable consequence of his main intention to create profit for himself. This is in line with *Welham* which established that an intent to defraud could be proved by showing an intention to act to the prejudice of another person's rights. This view is supported in *Wai Yu Tsang*, where Lord Goff sought to distinguish a 'conspirator's intention' (or immediate purpose) from his motive (or underlying purpose). *Wai Yu Tsang* thus decides that it is sufficient to prove that the conspirators had dishonestly agreed to bring about a state of affairs which they realised would or might deceive the victim, thus causing him to suffer loss or act in a manner prejudicial to his public duty. This also means that the Court of Appeal's decision in *Attorney General's Reference (No 1 of 1982)* [1983] 1 QB 182 should no longer be treated as authoritative. Here, it was held that there was no conspiracy to defraud a company if it would sustain damage only as a 'side effect or incidental consequence' of the fraudulent scheme to label bottles of whiskey unlawfully and sell them purporting to be a well known brand. There would, said the court, be no conspiracy unless it was their 'true object' to inflict such economic loss. In practice, as both these cases show, we have entered into the realms of constructive intentions. It is unlikely in the *Cooke* case that the stewards gave a moment's thought to the consequences of their actions on their employer's profits. If the company's sandwiches had all been consumed and the employee's fare was only introduced at that point, there would be strong grounds for commending the initiative of the staff rather than seeking prosecution. However, the real point is that from those transactions *only*, the employees would gain monetarily, as it would be unlikely that they would have openly admitted to the managers what they had done. The fact still remains though that in such circumstances the employer could *not* have been prejudiced in any way as there was no more food to sell to prospective customers. One is left then to fall back on contract and argue that stewards have no lawful authority to sell their own food in such circumstances and arguably could have been contravening health and safety or food regulations in the production of the sandwiches.

In such cases the outcome may depend on the particular facts of the case and the sophistication and expert knowledge of the conspirators. Those who are familiar with the workings and obligations of businesses to their shareholders and clients, not to mention government bodies such as revenue services, are more likely to understand the wider implications and impact of their conduct and less likely to convince a jury of their innocence.

Dishonesty is also an ingredient of the offence and reference should be made to the decision in *Ghosh* [1982] 2 All ER 689, a case decided under the TA 1968. The courts have consistently held that the legal approach to the meaning of dishonesty should encompass both objective and subjective criteria and should be the same irrespective of whether the offence is statutory or common law. *Ghosh* decides that, in some cases, the judge should give the following direction to the jury: decide what is dishonest by applying the standards of ordinary reasonable people. If, by this test, the actions of the accused appear to be dishonest, then the jury must decide whether the defendant(s) realised that the actions contemplated were dishonest by those standards.

5.6   THIRD PARTIES

It would appear that common law conspiracy, unlike statutory conspiracy, may be committed when neither or none of the conspirators actually intends to perpetrate the offence. In *Hollinshead* [1985] 2 All ER 769, the respondents had agreed to make and sell to a third party 'black box' devices for altering electricity meters, to the advantage of the user. It was the expectation of the parties to the agreement that the third party would sell on the devices to others with the avowed purposes of defrauding electricity boards. In the event, the third party was a police officer and Hollinshead and his two colleagues were arrested. They were charged, *inter alia*, with conspiracy to defraud contrary to common law. The basis of their appeal against conviction was that the course of conduct upon which they had agreed, that is, selling the devices to the third party, was not unlawful even though, if carried through in accordance with their expectations, a fraud would, in all probability, be perpetrated upon the electricity boards. The Court of Appeal allowed their appeal and the Crown appealed to the House of Lords. The House of Lords reinstated the convictions on the basis that the agreement to manufacture and sell dishonest devices, the sole purpose of which was to cause loss, amounted to a common law conspiracy to defraud. The only use for these devices was a fraudulent one, that is, to alter electricity meters and it must be taken to mean that the House of Lords believed that in these circumstances the parties intended the fraud to take place albeit by parties unknown to them.

As always in such circumstances it is not inevitable that the consequence will occur. The third party may not pass them on; the electricity boards knowing of their existence may alter their meters to counteract the threat, thus making the devices obsolete. Once again, it is arguably the case that their real intention is profit from the sale and they may be completely indifferent towards the end consequence. Neither can they be certain that fraud will occur. At best, to borrow from Lord Hailsham in *Hyam* [1974] 2 All ER 41 and Lord Lane CJ in *Nedrick* [1986] 3 All ER 1 they can only be morally or virtually certain the consequence will occur.

The Law Commission, in reviewing the current law, acknowledged at the outset that there is no general offence of fraud in English law, but that 'conspiracy to defraud comes close to being such an offence since its scope is extremely wide'. It cannot, of course, be committed by one person acting alone. It will be recalled that, as a result of the review of the law on inchoate offences in the 1970s, the assumption was that conspiracy should be restricted to those agreeing to commit a substantive offence. The implication is that an agreement to commit something that was not a substantive offence should no longer attract criminal liability.

However, the Law Commission thought that to abolish conspiracy to defraud without having put new statutory offences in place would 'have left an unacceptable gap in the law. Abolition would be possible only when suitable offences had been devised'.

As a result, there was an immediate difficulty once the CLwA 1977 became law. Could a common law conspiracy be charged if the facts revealed a statutory conspiracy? This was most likely to occur with offences involving dishonesty, most notably theft. The House of Lords in *Ayres* [1984] 1 All ER 619 held that conspiracy to defraud should not be charged in such cases. Only where the dishonest conduct did not reveal a substantive offence would it be appropriate to charge conspiracy at common law. This, however, presented difficulties in cases of large scale fraud where the magnitude of what had been agreed encompassed conduct which both revealed substantive offences and fraudulent behaviour not amounting to an offence. The later House of Lords' decision in *Cooke* ameliorated the difficulty by permitting the use of conspiracy to defraud in such circumstances. Nevertheless, it was felt that the position needed statutory clarification and s 12 of the Criminal Justice Act 1982 reversed the *Ayres* decision. The section states:

(1) If a person agrees with any other person or persons that a course of conduct shall be pursued; and the course of conduct will necessarily amount to or involve the commission of any offence or offences by one or more of the parties to the agreement if the agreement is carried out in accordance with their intentions, the fact that it will do so shall not preclude a charge of conspiracy to defraud being brought against any of them in respect of the agreement.

The current position as a result of this section means that even though the facts would warrant a statutory conspiracy charge, this does not preclude a charge of conspiracy to defraud.

In November 1994, the Law Commission announced its intention to instigate a thorough review of the offences of dishonesty including those created by the TAs 1968 and 1978 and in consequence has concluded that conspiracy to defraud 'should remain intact pending our comprehensive review of the law. We have resolved that it would be inappropriate to make piecemeal recommendations for reform of other aspects of the law of dishonesty' (Law Com 228, 1994, para 1.20).

The report is therefore useful because the Law Commission reviews the working of the current law and identifies the major criticisms of conspiracy to defraud. Of particular interest is Pt IV which contains proposals as to which types of conduct would cease to be criminal if conspiracy to defraud were to be abolished. In consequence, the Law Commission is of the view that the following types of conduct should fall within the ambit of conspiracy to defraud, pending the outcome of the review of dishonesty offences:

- conduct which would amount to 'theft' if the property in question were capable of being stolen;
- some cases in which the owner of property is temporarily deprived of it;
- cases in which for the purposes of the TA 1968 there is no property belonging to another;
- secret profits made by employees and fiduciaries;
- the obtaining without deception of benefits other than property;
- the evasion of liability without intent to make permanent default;
- the dishonest failure to pay for goods and services;
- gambling swindles;
- corruption not involving consideration;
- 'prejudice' without financial loss;
- assisting in fraud by third parties;
- cases in which a party is ignorant of the details of the fraud;
- deception of computers and other machines.

5.7 IMPOSSIBILITY

Section 5 of the CAtA 1981 amended s 1 of the CLwA 1977 by inserting s 1(1)(b) which deals with the situation where the existence of certain facts renders the commission of the substantive offence impossible:

(1) ... if a person agrees with any other person or persons that a course of conduct shall be pursued which, if the agreement is carried out in accordance with their intentions, either:

(a) will necessarily amount to or involve the commission of any offence or offences by one or more parties to the agreement; or

(b) would do so but for the existence of facts which render the commission of the offence or any other offences impossible,

he is guilty of conspiracy to commit the offence or offences in question.

Crucially, everything would now seem to depend on the parties' intentions certainly as far as statutory conspiracy is concerned. Thus, if they agree to handle goods which they believe, wrongly, to be stolen, they may still be convicted of conspiracy to handle.

However, this provision relates only to statutory conspiracy and the common law would appear to be based upon the decision of the House of Lords in *Haughton v Smith* and *DPP v Nock*. Therefore, in the case of common law conspiracy, impossibility will be a defence unless the failure is occasioned through inadequate means to effect the crime.

The laws on conspiring to commit the 'impossible' and attempting to do so have been brought into line as a result of the CAtA 1981. In the case of both crimes, there has to be an intention to commit the offence that is in contemplation at the time that the *actus reus* of the inchoate offence is complete. The fact that it is physically impossible to complete the offence is irrelevant so long as the parties to the conspiracy believed that it was possible. This situation must be distinguished from the situation where the intended consequence is not criminal even though the parties believe it to be. In the latter situation neither inchoate offence is possible.

5.8   JURISDICTION

With the easing of restrictions on movement in the European Community and international travel so easily facilitated, it is likely that there will be an increase in the number of conspiracies which will have as their object a crime committed in another jurisdiction. Similarly, many agreements are likely to be concluded overseas with the crime taking place in England or Wales, or an agreement reached overseas for a crime to be effected in another overseas country but with some part of the plan being put into action in this jurisdiction (for example, an agreement in Kashmir to import heroin into England for onward transmission to the US).

5.8.1   Jurisdiction over conspiracies to commit offences outside the jurisdiction

Section 1(4) of the CLwA 1977 provides that, if parties make an agreement in England and Wales to commit an offence outside the jurisdiction, they will only be guilty of conspiracy if the completed offence would be triable in England and Wales. The most important example of such extraterritorial offences is murder (see further the speech of Lord Tucker in *Board of Trade v Owen* [1957] AC 602).

Three significant legislative initiatives have, however, massively increased the jurisdiction of courts in England and Wales in respect of conspiracies to commit offences abroad. The Sexual Offences (Conspiracy and Incitement) Act 1996, enacted in the light of concerns about 'sex tourism', makes it possible to be charged with the offence of conspiracy even though the course of conduct agreed upon is to be performed outside the jurisdiction, provided a number of conditions are met:

- the agreement was that the conduct would occur wholly outside the jurisdiction; and

- the conduct in question would be illegal where performed; and

- were the conduct agreed upon to be carried out within the jurisdiction, it would constitute one of the offences specified in the Act (rape, indecency with children, indecent assault, and so on); and

- some conduct occurred within the jurisdiction, performed either by a party to the agreement or an agent, this conduct either preliminary to or by the agreement being entered, or by action being taken in pursuance of the agreement within the jurisdiction.

Part 1 of the Criminal Justice Act (CJA) 1993, which came into effect on 1 June 1999, extended the jurisdiction of courts in England and Wales to deal with two groups of 'cross frontier' offences. Group A includes offences such as theft, handling stolen goods, blackmail, obtaining goods and services by deception, and avoiding a liability by deception. Group B includes offences of inciting, conspiring or attempting to commit any Group A offence. Courts in England and Wales have jurisdiction over Group A offences provided a 'relevant event' occurs within the jurisdiction. A 'relevant event' is any act or omission proof of which is required in order to establish the commission of the offence. An offence within Group B can be charged (for example, conspiracy to commit theft in France) even though no 'relevant event' is scheduled to occur within the jurisdiction, provided:

- a party to the conspiracy or his agent has done anything in England and Wales in relation to it before its formation; or

- a party became a party to it in England and Wales; or

- a party to it did or omitted anything in England and Wales in pursuance of the agreement.

It must also be shown that the act or omission agreed upon would have constituted an offence in the jurisdiction where it was intended to occur. The precise description of the offence under the 'foreign' law is not significant – what matters is that the conduct would be punishable as a criminal offence. A charge of conspiracy to defraud can also be maintained, provided these conditions are met. If the provisions of the 1993 Act are invoked, an accused will be charged with conspiracy contrary to s 1 of the CLwA 1977.

A more general jurisdiction to try conspiracies to commit offences abroad is given to courts in England and Wales by virtue of ss 5–8 of the Criminal Justice (Terrorism and Conspiracy) Act 1998. The Act, which came into force on 4 September 1998, provides that it is an offence to conspire to carry out a course of conduct that would result in the commission of an offence in another jurisdiction, provided:

- the conduct would also amount to an offence in England and Wales; and

- a party to the conspiracy or his agent does something in England or Wales in relation to it before its formation; or

- a party became a party to the conspiracy in England or Wales; or

- a party to the conspiracy did or omitted to do something in England or Wales in pursuance of the agreement.

An accused charged with conspiracy under the 1998 Act is charged contrary to s 1(A) of the CLwA 1977.

The provisions of the 1998 Act have been criticised on the grounds that they are obscurely worded, were hastily introduced in the wake of terrorist activity in Omagh, Dar es Salaam and Kenya, and go much further than is needed, effectively exporting the deficiencies and uncertainties of the domestic law of conspiracy to a wider world (see further the article by Colm Campbell 'Two steps backwards: the Criminal Justice (Terrorism and Conspiracy) Act 1998' [1999] Crim LR 941).

5.8.2 Agreement abroad to commit an offence within the jurisdiction

An agreement abroad to commit an offence within the jurisdiction was ruled by the common law and not s 1(4) of the CLwA 1977. In *DPP v Doot* [1973] 1 All ER 940, the respondents were American citizens who planned to import cannabis into that country by way of England. The cannabis was bought in Morocco, hidden in jars and brought to England. The respondents were charged with conspiracy to import dangerous drugs. It was contended that as the agreement had taken place outside England the court did not have jurisdiction to try the case. The House of Lords held that a conspiracy entered into abroad could be prosecuted in England if the parties acted in England in concert and in pursuance of the agreement.

As Viscount Dilhorne said:

> Proof of acts done by the accused in this country may suffice to prove there was at the time of those acts a conspiracy in existence in this country to which they were parties and if that is proved, then the charge of conspiracy is within the jurisdiction of the English courts, even though the initial agreement is made outside the jurisdiction [p 949(f)].

It is submitted that the House of Lords had to reach this conclusion to avoid the awful spectre of criminals taking a day trip to Calais in order to reach agreements to commit crimes in England and to escape liability for those agreements even though the object would be carried out within the jurisdiction.

Doot determines that some form of overt act is required within the jurisdiction but Lord Griffiths questioned this requirement in *Liangsiriprasert v US Government* [1990] 2 All ER 866:

> But why should an overt act be necessary to found jurisdiction? In the case of conspiracy in England, the crime is complete once the agreement is made and no further overt act needs to be proved as an ingredient of the crime. The only purpose of looking for an overt act in England in the case of a conspiracy entered into abroad can be to establish the link between the conspiracy and England or possibly to show the conspiracy is continuing. Their Lordships can find nothing in precedent, comity or good sense that should inhibit the common law from regarding as justiciable in England inchoate crimes committed abroad which are intended to result in the commission of criminal offences in England [p 878(d)].

This conclusion was also reached with regard to statutory conspiracy in the case of *Sansom and Others* [1991] 2 All ER 145. The defendants were arrested on board vessels which were stopped in the English Channel. It was alleged that a large amount of cannabis had been transported by ship from Morocco and was transferred to a second vessel in the Channel. It was submitted that as the agreement had been made outside the jurisdiction, no drugs had been imported into the jurisdiction, no unlawful act committed within the jurisdiction and no act in pursuance of the conspiracy had been carried out by the defendants in the jurisdiction, then the court did not have jurisdiction. The Court of Appeal held that, irrespective of whether the charge was statutory or common law conspiracy, it was triable in England even though no overt act had taken place within the jurisdiction. Taylor LJ justified the conclusion on three grounds:

- that it cannot have been parliament's intention when enacting the CLwA 1977 to alter the common law rules as to extraterritorial conspiracies without specific wording in the Act;

- that the rules would apply to conspiracy to defraud but not to other conspiracies which would be an 'absurdity';
- that the Privy Council in *Liangsiriprasert*, being aware that most conspiracies are statutory, would have specifically made clear that it was limiting its thinking to common law conspiracies if that indeed had been the case.

The CJA 1993 now confirms the position in respect of a conspiracy abroad to commit a Group A offence or a conspiracy to defraud in this country even though nothing occurs in this country. The crucial thing is to establish that a relevant event was planned to occur in this jurisdiction. A 'relevant event' in relation to any Group A offence is defined in s 2 of the CJA 1993 to mean: 'Any act or omission or other event (including any result of one or more acts or omissions) proof of which is required for the conviction of the offence.'

Thus, if X and Y agree in Germany that they will travel to England to receive a car stolen the previous day in Brighton and a few hours later they change their minds, the offence, assuming there is evidence of the agreement, would be complete and any subsequent change of mind irrelevant. Other offences not covered by the CJA 1993 will still be covered by the common law as outlined above.

One issue not decided by *Liangsiriprasert* is whether an agreement made wholly abroad by British citizens to commit a crime outside the jurisdiction is triable in England. In the case of an offence such as murder, that is triable in England and Wales irrespective of where the murder is carried out, there should be no jurisdictional problems to trying the conspirators in this country. In respect of other crimes, the decision in *Liangsiriprasert* and the legislation mentioned above, makes it more likely that the English courts may acquire jurisdiction even though the completed offence is one that would not normally be triable in England and Wales.

5.9   ATTEMPT

The law on attempts is to be found in the CAtA 1981, having until then been ruled by the common law. As an aid to appreciating some of the principles applicable to the modern law an understanding, in outline at least, of the difficulties encountered by the common law will be of value. This may be achieved by examining the Law Commission 1980 report (Law Com 102) or the article by Ian Dennis, 'The Criminal Attempts Act 1981' ([1982] Crim LR 5). For the avoidance of doubt, the common law relating to attempt was repealed by the Act (see s 6(1)).

The law on attempts primarily addresses the issue of failure, that is, the inability to make a success of the proposed criminal enterprise. It acknowledges that the accused has failed to bring about the *actus reus* of the particular crime he or she has in mind. The failure may take many forms. The poisoner who mistakenly uses a harmless substance or the hired assassin who misses his victim and thus fails in his attempt to kill certainly intends to bring about the *actus reus* of the crime in question. However, this is not meant to suggest that if the accused goes on to complete the offence its completion will provide a defence to a charge of attempt. Section 6(4) of the CLwA 1967 states:

... where a person is charged on an indictment with attempting to commit an offence or with any assault or other act preliminary to an offence, but not the completed offence, then – he may be convicted of the offence charged notwithstanding that he is shown to be guilty of the completed offence.

At common law, an attempt to commit a felony was a misdemeanour and according to the doctrine of 'merger' if the felony was completed, the misdemeanour disappeared having 'merged' with the completed offence. The CLwA 1967 abolished felonies and s 6(4) applies to indictable offences. But what of summary trials? In *Webley v Buxton* [1977] QB 481, the appellant was charged before justices with attempting to take away a motor cycle without the owner's consent. It was conceded by the prosecution that the full offence had in fact been committed. The defence contended that because of the doctrine of merger the defendant could not be guilty of an attempt. The court held that as a result of the abolition of the distinction between felonies and misdemeanours by s 1(2) of the CLwA 1967, the attempt did not merge with the completed offence and the justices were entitled to convict.

On this basis, it would appear possible to convict the defendant of both the attempt and completed offence at the same time, but in practice this is unlikely to happen.

While we should heave a collective sigh of relief when defendants fail to achieve their objectives, the one factor which should not be ignored is that a guilty mind is present and the moral culpability the same, irrespective of whether the desired consequence is achieved or even achievable! Schiemann J expressed the rationale underpinning the law on attempt in *Attorney General's Reference (No 3 of 1992)* [1994] 2 All ER 121:

One way of analysing the situation is to say that a defendant, in order to be guilty of attempt, must be in one of the states of mind required for the commission of the full offence, and did his best, as far as he could, to supply what was missing from the completion of the offence. It is the policy of the law that such people should be punished notwithstanding that in fact the intentions of such a defendant have not been fulfilled [p 126(c)].

Perhaps unsurprisingly, it is the mental element required for an attempt rather than the *actus reus* which has proved the more problematic. The following statement from Andrews SPJ in *Leavitt* [1985] 1 Qd R 343, p 345 sums up the importance of the mental element in attempt. Although this case emanates from the Court of Criminal Appeal in Queensland, Australia, it could easily have come from the English Court of Appeal:

The seeking to achieve a result involved in an attempt simply must involve an intention to achieve it. I can think of no practical use of the word which does not involve an intent. To inform a jury that it was necessary for them to find that the appellant had an intent to strike a police officer with one of the bullets is to ascribe a meaning to the word which it simply has not.

That parliament views an attempt to commit a crime as a serious action cannot be doubted and is reflected in the heavy sentences which may be imposed, for example, life imprisonment for attempted murder, and for indictable offences the same maximum penalty which may be imposed for the completed offence.

The offence is stated thus (s 1(1)):

If, with intent to commit an offence to which this section applies, a person does an act which is more than merely preparatory to the commission of the offence, he is guilty of attempting to commit the offence.

5.10   ACTUS REUS

The *actus reus* is clearly stated in the section as doing 'an act which is more than merely preparatory' to the completed offence. (For an appraisal of the Law Commission proposals which underpinned the CAtA 1981, see Dennis, 'The elements of attempt' [1980] Crim LR 758.) Dennis argued that the Law Commission tried to preserve a balance between the interests of the individual and the interests of society so that 'not all acts towards the commission of an offence should be punishable ...'.

This definition requires there to be an act and by implication it is impossible to be found guilty of an attempt in respect of an omission. The parents who, as in *Gibbins and Proctor* (1918) 13 Cr App R 134, deliberately starve their child with the intent to kill will be guilty of murder if the child dies. Should they be guilty of attempted murder if the child survives? Yet what is the act or series of acts they have carried out? The *Concise Oxford Dictionary* defines 'act' to mean 'something done' 'the process of doing something'. Could it not be maintained that they are doing something in letting their child die? Clearly, though, it would be difficult to imagine that a failure to act sits easily in the context of s 1 of the CAtA 1981.

One should clearly discern which *actus reus* and therefore which crime is being attempted; this may be achieved by not only considering the activities in which the defendant was engaged but any other evidence available to the jury, for example, a confession. Section 4(3) makes it clear that this is a matter of fact and, accordingly, is for the jury to determine. As may well be imagined, a substantial body of case law had evolved under the common law but this is now, at best, simply of illustrative value. Taylor LJ in *Kenneth Jones* [1990] 3 All ER 886, commenting on whether common law authority had any relevance, believed the approach of construing the s 1 words by reference to previous case law was 'misconceived' and went on to make the point that:

The 1981 Act is a codifying statute. It amends and sets out completely the law relating to attempts and conspiracies. In those circumstances the correct approach is to look first at the natural meaning of the statutory words, not to turn back to earlier case law and seek to fit some previous test to the words of the section.

The Law Commission (Law Com 102, 1980) in its report was clearly of the view that no one form of words would suit all types of behaviour from which one might conclude that an attempt to commit a crime has commenced. The prevailing view was that active consideration should be given to when *mere* preparation ended and actual preparation began. At that point the *actus reus* was complete. This will in practice depend very much on the circumstances of the case and of course liability should not ensue unless the intention to commit the offence is evident. Proof of intent alone without evidence that the preparatory stage has begun should result in an acquittal. This approach has been endorsed by the Court of Appeal in *Attorney General's Reference (No 1 of 1992)* [1993] 2 All ER 190:

In *R v Kenneth Jones*, and again in *R v Campbell* (1990), this court made it clear that the words of the Act were to be applied in their plain and natural meaning. The words are not to be interpreted so as to reintroduce either of the earlier common law tests. Indeed, one of the objects of the Act was to resolve the uncertainty those tests created [p 193(f)].

In *Kenneth Jones*, it fell to be determined whether, on a charge of attempted murder, the accused had done more than a merely preparatory act in pointing a sawn-off shotgun at his intended victim, when the safety catch was still in place and the victim was unable to confirm that the defendant's finger was on the trigger. The defendant, therefore, had three things to do before he could achieve his objective:

- take off the catch;
- put his finger on the trigger;
- pull the trigger.

It was held that the defendant's acts in obtaining a weapon, shortening the barrel and going to the place where he knew the victim would be, amounted only to mere preparation. However, to enter the victim's car, take out a loaded gun and point it at the victim were acts which were more than merely preparatory, even though there was more to do before the final act could be accomplished. Glanville Williams has argued that it is not 'an abuse of language to say that Kenneth Jones started his attempt as soon as he set out with his firearm, his disguise and his Spanish money, or even when he acquired his firearm and his disguise with the firm purpose of using it in the offence ...' (Williams, 'Wrong turnings in the law of attempt' [1991] Crim LR 417, p 419).

In the *Attorney General's Reference (No 1 of 1992)*, the Court of Appeal confirmed that a man could commit the *actus reus* of attempted rape even though he had not attempted to penetrate the victim's vagina, providing there was sufficient evidence available to show he had done acts which were more than merely preparatory to the completed offence. Lord Taylor CJ suggested that such evidence might be the woman's distress, the state of her clothing, the position in which she was seen, the man lowering his trousers and any interference with the woman's private parts.

Even this evidence may not prove conclusively that he was attempting to rape the woman. His intention might have been to indecently assault or commit actual bodily harm but that will be for the jury to determine in light of all the evidence presented by the prosecution. What is clear is that such evidence of her state of disarray is sufficient for a jury to conclude that the *actus reus* of attempted rape had been committed.

The two common law tests referred to by the Lord Chief Justice in *Attorney General's Reference (No 1 of 1992)* are the last act and the 'series of acts' tests. In the former, the defendant should have committed his intended last act before it could be said he was proximate (the former common law test) enough to the completed offence. The major authorities supporting this test were *Eagleton* (1855) Dears CC 376 and *DPP v Stonehouse* [1977] 2 All ER 909 in which in the latter case Lord Diplock asked whether the accused had 'crossed the Rubicon and burnt his boat', that is, passed the point of no return. In the latter, the process of turning preparation into attempt involves the defendant in a series of acts, some of which are merely preparatory, others illustrating his clear desire to bring about the completed offence and would if not interrupted have resulted in the actual commission of the offence (see *Stephen's Digest of the Criminal Law*, 9th edn, 1950).

The practical difficulty with the wording of the statute is that whilst all actions apart from the last act are 'preparatory', the use of the word 'merely' suggests that a distinction should be drawn between those acts of preparation which indicate the accused has embarked upon the crime, and those that do not send out this signal.

The dilemma is where the distinction is to be drawn and as this is a matter for the jury there is always going to be some uncertainty. The judge, of course, still has to rule on whether there is sufficient evidence to go to the jury. In *Campbell* (1990) 93 Cr App R 350, the Court of Appeal ruled that it was inevitable that matters had to be decided on a case-by-case basis. The defendant had been seen reconnoitring a post office and had in his possession an imitation gun, sunglasses and a threatening note. His appeal against conviction on a charge of attempted robbery was allowed. It was accepted that he might have still been of a mind to rob the post office, but many things remained to be done, including the crucial incident of entering the premises at which the alleged robbery was to take place.

On the face of it this is an amazing decision. Undoubtedly, it has logic to support it in the sense that the evidence conclusively proved the *mens rea* only. There was still much more to do before the individuals inside the post office would become aware that an attempt at a robbery was being instigated. But, suppose that an accomplice, whose role was to wait outside to facilitate Campbell's getaway, had driven Campbell to the post office. At the moment he emerged from the vehicle is it not a correct use of language to say that the robbery was underway? The course of action had commenced that would have directly led to Campbell making demands of the cashier inside the office. It is most unlikely he would have changed his mind between jumping out of the car and entering the office. If the police cannot intervene at that point because they are aware of the *Campbell* ruling, then surely they put at risk those inside the office who will witness the actual attempt to rob the post office. Whether he has an imitation gun or not would seem to be irrelevant to the innocent bystanders who would assume the weapon was capable of being fired. If in these circumstances a customer seeing and hearing what was taking place had a heart attack and died would his relatives be able to sue the police for negligence in not intervening to prevent the attempted robbery?

There are of course other crimes committed in these circumstances. Campbell was actually found guilty of carrying an imitation firearm. There may also be the s 25 of the TA 1968 offence of going equipped (in this case to steal).

Griffin [1993] Crim LR 515 makes it clear that the judge must decide if there is sufficient evidence to put to the jury but that it is for the jury to conclude whether or not the defendant's act falls within the provisions of s 1(1) of the CAtA 1981. In this case, the accused was charged with attempting to take her children, who were in the care of the local authority, out of the jurisdiction. To this end, she bought single tickets to the Republic of Ireland for herself and the children and made preparations for travel. She then sought permission to withdraw them from school on the pretext that she was to take them to the dentist. When challenged by the head teacher, she left the school without the children and was subsequently arrested. She was convicted and appealed on the basis that there was insufficient evidence of something more than merely preparatory to the completed offence, which would have occurred once the children were actually out of the jurisdiction. The Court of Appeal thought that the judge had been correct in putting the matter before the jury. It was accepted that most of her actions amounted only to mere preparation but once she approached the head teacher with the request to remove the children from school then attempted abduction was underway. It is worth comparing these facts with those in *Campbell* where, as we have seen, his actions did not in law constitute anything more than mere preparation, despite the fact that he was within a few feet of the post office which had been targeted for the 'crime'. It could hardly be said that the accused in *Griffin* came anywhere close to succeeding in her attempt to abduct the children and remove them from the jurisdiction.

The recent cases reflect an approach advocated by the Court of Appeal in *Gullefer* [1990] 3 All ER 882, a 1986 case. There the appellant had wagered £18 at a greyhound racing meeting and was facing the loss of his stake as the dogs rounded the final bend with his chosen greyhound nowhere in the running. He therefore jumped onto the track and waved his arms in an attempt to distract the dogs. If he had been successful in his endeavours, the race would have been declared void and his stake money returned to him. In the event he failed. He was charged with attempted theft. His appeal against conviction was allowed on the basis that his actions were merely preparatory to his attempt to steal. If the race had in fact been declared void, then that alone would not have indicated that theft was to be committed. Gullefer would still have had to go back to the bookmaker and then demand that his £18 be returned. Consider whether the acts of the defendant in *Rowley* were more than mere preparatory acts and thus whether he could be convicted of attempting to outrage public decency (see above, 5.5.2).

It might be worth considering whether some of the pre-1981 Act cases would still be decided in the same way under the legislation. For example, in *Robinson* [1915] 2 KB 342, a jeweller having insured his stock for £1,200 staged a burglary so that he might make a claim against the insurance company. He was convicted of attempting to obtain money by false pretences. His appeal against conviction was allowed on the basis that R's actions were only remotely connected with the commission of the full offence. Would the result be different today? By analogy with *Campbell* and *Gullefer*, the answer would be no. The staging of the fake burglary would in all probability amount to an act of mere preparation. Robinson would need to acquire the appropriate forms, complete and forward them to the insurance company before it could be said that he was attempting to obtain property by deception. This view is also supported by the decision in *Geddes* (1996) 160 JP 697. The appellant was seen by a teacher in the boys' lavatory block of a school. He had no right to be there. He had with him a rucksack which contained a large kitchen knife, some lengths of rope and a roll of masking tape. He was charged with attempted false imprisonment. His appeal against conviction was allowed. The Court of Appeal acknowledged that the demarcation line between acts which were merely preparatory and those which might amount to an attempt was not always clear or easy to recognise. It is legitimate to pose the question 'has he actually tried to commit the offence?'. Conversely, if an accused had only 'got ready or put himself in a position or equipped himself to do so', then this would not satisfy the statutory test. In this case, the appellant had not had contact with any pupils nor communicated with nor confronted anyone and therefore had not gone beyond mere preparation. This decision and that in *Campbell* gives rise to feelings of unease. The report indicates that the court in *Geddes* was 'filled with the greatest unease' and yet nevertheless felt bound to reach the decision it did. These are decisions which are difficult to explain to the general public, particularly when viewed in light of the tragedies involving firearms resulting in death and injury to members of the public which have occurred in the UK and elsewhere in the last decade. Also bear in mind that the s 25 of the TA 1968 offence will apply only where the accused was going equipped to carry out burglary, theft or to cheat. It should always be remembered that attempt is an offence in its own right. Everyone who successfully completes a crime has passed through the attempt stage and in doing so has committed the offence. However, in practice the defendant will not be charged with two offences. The attempt would appear to 'merge' with the completed offence and the prosecution would undoubtedly charge this in preference to the attempt. It therefore follows that once the perpetrator has gone beyond mere preparation, then any change of heart, voluntary or otherwise, will be ineffective in establishing a defence as the *actus reus* would already be complete.

5.11 MENS REA

There is only one state of mind acknowledged in the definition of the crime and that is intention. The accused must act with the 'intent to commit an offence'. This is one area where the pre-existing common law has seemingly influenced the post-1981 Act case law. In *Mohan* [1975] 2 All ER 193, the Court of Appeal had concluded that attempt was a crime of specific intent and had defined that to mean a:

> ... decision to bring about, in so far as it lies within the accused's power, the commission of the offence which it is alleged the accused attempted to commit, no matter whether the accused desired the consequences of his act or not [p 200(h)].

There does appear to be a contradiction in that it is difficult to imagine someone doing everything in his power to bring about a consequence and yet not desiring that consequence. In *Pearman* [1984] Crim LR 675, it was said that the court was trying to:

> ... deal with a case where the accused has, as a primary purpose, some other object, for example, a man who plants a bomb in an aeroplane, which he knows is going to take off, it being his primary intention that he should claim the insurance on the aeroplane when the freight goes down into the sea. The jury would not be put off from saying that he intended to murder the crew simply by saying that he did not want or desire to kill the crew, but that was something that he inevitably intended to do ...

A reckless state of mind will not suffice, nor will evidence which will establish that the accused knew or foresaw that the consequences of the act will 'be likely' to lead to the commission of the completed offence.

In the first post-Act case to consider the issue, the Court of Appeal could find 'no reason' why *Mohan* should not be binding. Therefore, a direction by the trial judge in *Pearman* to the effect that foresight of the probable consequences should be equated with intention was deemed to amount to a misdirection and the conviction for attempting to cause grievous bodily harm with intent was quashed.

It is incumbent upon those analysing this area of the law to be aware that whatever the *mens rea* for the completed offence only intention will suffice for a charge of attempt, as evidenced in *O'Toole* [1987] Crim LR 759, where reference in the indictment to recklessness on a charge of attempted criminal damage meant that the conviction had to be quashed. The accused must be doing everything in his power to bring about the completed offence and this is inconsistent with the concept of recklessness.

A relatively recent case raised the interesting point of how relevant, if at all, the *Moloney/Hancock/Nedrick* line of cases is with respect to the definition of intent. In *Walker and Hayles* [1990] Crim LR 443, the appellants had attacked the victim, saying they would kill him, and then threw him over the balcony of a third floor flat. He survived his ordeal. They were charged with attempted murder. Their appeals were based on the use, by the trial judge, of the concept of a high degree of probability in directing the jury on the issue of intent, that is, in throwing someone from a third floor balcony is death highly probable? The appeals were dismissed because the judge had at an early stage in his direction told the jury that they must be sure that the accused were 'trying to kill' and this was synonymous with 'purpose'. The problem with a charge of attempted murder as distinct from murder is that a person could intend serious injury to be occasioned by his action but not intend death. On a murder charge, the intent to cause serious injury would be enough to convict if death occurred, but not for an attempt where, according to *Mohan*, one must be doing everything in one's power to bring about the consequence. The court in *Walker and Hayles* confirms that a 'simple direction' indicating that the defendant must be trying to achieve death (the consequence) will almost always suffice. But what of the case where the jury believes the accused intended to cause serious harm but not to occasion death, but that death was a 'highly probable' consequence of the action deliberately performed by the accused? *Walker and Hayles* suggests that providing the jury is convinced that death was a 'virtually certain' consequence of the deliberate activity then it may convict of attempted murder, based upon the guidance given in *Nedrick*. The Court of Appeal preferred the use of 'virtual certainty' to 'high degree of probability' (see above, 3.3.2, for a full analysis of oblique intention).

The difficulties discussed in *Walker and Hayles* surfaced again in *Fallon* [1994] Crim LR 519. The defendant was charged with attempting to murder a police officer. The trial judge had directed the jury on the meaning of intent and at one stage had invited the jury to consider whether, if the officer had died, 'would his death as a matter of virtual certainty have been a natural consequence of the act ...?' There can be no doubt that his direction was influenced by the decision in *Moloney* [1985] AC 905. The Court of Appeal substituted a conviction on the alternative count of causing grievous bodily harm with intent and went on to observe that:

> ... the case was yet another example of the confusion that may be sown in the minds of a jury by unnecessary and elaborate analysis of the meaning of intent and by the failure to follow guidance given in *Hancock and Shankland* [p 519].

The preceding discussion has considered the mental element in respect of the consequence. The definitions of some crimes, of course, make reference to circumstances as well as consequences. If such a crime figures in an attempt charge, for example, rape, where reference needs to be made to the issue of consent, will it be a requirement of such a charge that intent is required for both consequences and circumstance? Thus, on a charge of attempted rape, is it necessary to prove both an intent to have unlawful sexual intercourse and an intent that the woman should not consent? The substantive offence demands either intent or recklessness in respect of the circumstance of consent. The issue was addressed in *Khan* [1990] 2 All ER 783, where the Court of Appeal concluded that it was enough if D intended to have intercourse and was reckless as to whether the woman was consenting. As Russell LJ put it:

... the intent of the defendant is precisely the same in rape and in attempted rape and the *mens rea* is identical, namely an intention to have intercourse plus knowledge or recklessness as to the woman's absence of consent. No question of attempting to achieve a reckless state of mind arises; the attempt relates to the physical activity; the mental state of the defendant is the same. A man does not recklessly have sexual intercourse, nor does he recklessly attempt it. Recklessness in rape and attempted rape arises not in relation to the physical act of the accused but only in his state of mind when engaged in the activity of having or attempting to have sexual intercourse [p 788(a)].

This view differs from that expressed by the Law Commission in its 1980 report (Law Com 102), which was in favour of requiring intent towards both consequences and circumstances. However, the 1989 proposed draft Criminal Code (Law Com 177, 1989, cl 49(2)) is in accord with the view expressed in *Khan*, so providing that, if recklessness as to circumstances is an essential element of the substantive offence, then it will suffice for the attempt to commit that offence.

The approach adopted in *Khan* was applied in *Attorney General's Reference (No 3 of 1992)*. The charge was one of attempted aggravated arson contrary to s 1(2) of the Criminal Damage Act (CDA) 1971. In the early hours of the morning, the appellants threw a petrol bomb from their vehicle in the direction of another car containing four people. There were two others standing on the pavement chatting to the occupants of the car. The bomb missed and smashed against a nearby wall. The respondents were arrested and inside their car was found a milk crate containing a number of petrol bombs.

Section 1(2) of the CDA 1971 requires either intent or recklessness in respect of whether life will be endangered as a result of the damage to property. The defendants were acquitted on the direction of the judge. She ruled there was no evidence to show that the defendants intended by the destruction of the car to endanger the lives of the occupants or the bystanders. Furthermore, acknowledging that intention towards damaging or destroying the property was a requirement for an attempt, she concluded that it was impossible to intend to be reckless as to whether the life of another would be endangered.

The Attorney General referred the matter to the Court of Appeal under s 36 of the CJA 1972. The court held that it was sufficient for the Crown to establish a specific intent to cause damage and that the defendant acted recklessly in respect of the threat to life. The court accepted that the mental state of a defendant in such circumstances 'contained everything which was required to render him guilty of the full offence'. There clearly was an intent to cause damage to property, that is, the car, and presumably, at least '*Caldwell* style' recklessness towards endangering life (see above, 3.4) The court noted:

... that at one time it was proposed that intention should be required as to all the elements for an offence, thus making it impossible to secure a conviction for attempt in circumstances such as the present. However, this proposal has not prevailed and has been overtaken by *R v Khan*, and the formulation of the Draft Code which does not incorporate the proposal [p 128(e)].

There are two major issues to consider as a result of this case. The first is that of recklessness. The draft Code would have the foresight of the accused in respect of the likelihood of endangering life assessed on a 'subjective' basis and not by reference to *Caldwell*. This decision means that a defendant must intend to damage or destroy property, that is, must realise the consequence of his action is virtually certain to result, yet at the same time need give no thought to the aggravated element of the offence, providing ordinary people in his situation would be inclined to do so. This would seem to be extremely favourable to the prosecution. Secondly, it is argued by Professor Smith ([1994] Crim LR 350) that, in respect of offences that do not require *mens rea* in respect of all elements of the *actus reus*, strict liability will be introduced into the law of attempts. If correct, this is a significant step, particularly as the offence is regarded as one of specific intent. Taking as his example the facts of *Prince* (1875) LR 2 CCR 154, Smith invites us to consider the case of a 25-year-old man who is intent upon having sexual intercourse with a girl who is in fact aged 15, but whom he reasonably believes to be aged 16. D attempts sexual intercourse but fails. He is charged with attempting to have intercourse with a girl under 16 contrary to s 6 of the SOA 1956. No *mens rea* needs to be proved in respect of the completed offence other than the intent to have intercourse which clearly he has. The girl is under 16 years of age. The man being over 24 has no defence based upon a reasonable belief that she is aged 16 or over. The conclusion is that strict liability is brought into the law on attempt. No intent needs to be established in respect of a circumstance, that is, her age.

There is, of course, no reason why the law should not follow this path but such a development should not result from one reference to the Court of Appeal, particularly, as Professor Smith says, 'one suspects that the issue was not fully appreciated or debated on the reference'.

5.12 IMPOSSIBILITY

The common law on impossibility as it applied to attempted crimes was thoroughly and controversially reviewed in *Haughton v Smith*. A brief look at this case should prove helpful in understanding the problems created by the decision of the House of Lords in *Anderton v Ryan* [1985] 2 All ER 355. In *Haughton v Smith*, the House of Lords concluded that where the substantive offence could not be achieved either because it was factually or legally impossible then no charge of attempt would lie. An example of factual impossibility is where the object of the crime is absent even though the accused believes otherwise, as in the case of someone seeking to steal a valuable ring from a locked drawer, when in fact the drawer is empty. An example of the latter is to be found in the facts of the actual case where Smith thought he was handling stolen goods which in fact did not possess that quality, having been returned to lawful custody prior to Smith receiving them (see s 24(3) of the TA 1968).

However, a person could be guilty of an attempt where the failure was occasioned by inadequacy as to the means employed to commit the substantive offence. One might be correct in assuming that it is possible to break into the Bank of England using a hairpin, although in practice one would believe it to be 'impossible'. If our locksmith was found with his hairpin inserted into the lock on the main door of the bank, one could quite logically conclude that he was attempting to steal, however remote in reality his chances might in fact be.

The decision was subject to intense debate and parliament purported to change the effect of *Haughton v Smith* in s 1(2) and (3) of the CAtA 1981 which reads:

(2) A person may be guilty of attempting to commit an offence to which this section applies even though the facts are such that the commission of the offence is impossible.

(3) In any case where:

    (a) apart from this sub-section a person's intention would not be regarded as having amounted to an intent to commit an offence; but

    (b) if the facts of the case had been as he believed them to be, his intention would be so regarded,

then, for the purposes of sub-s (1) above, he shall be regarded as having had an intent to commit that offence.

Section 1(2) seeks to ensure that liability will result even though the existence of certain facts makes it impossible to bring about the intended consequence. Section 1(3), which is strictly not needed as the state of the law is a 'fact' just as much as a non-existent ring is a 'fact', deals with legal impossibility and demands that attention is focused upon the accused's state of mind. Did Roger Smith intend to handle stolen goods? The answer to this is quite clearly yes. He believed them to be stolen and acted accordingly.

What appears to be a reasonably clear piece of drafting was called into question in *Anderton v Ryan* when the defendant's conviction for attempting to handle stolen goods was quashed on the basis that she had carried out an 'objectively innocent' act when purchasing a video recorder. She believed it to be stolen, and in all probability it was stolen, but the prosecution could not prove it. The decision would obviously be regarded as correct if *Haughton v Smith* still represented the law, as a case of legal impossibility, but s 1(2) and (3) had, according to the majority, not affected legal impossibility situations. You are advised to read the minority speech of Lord Edmund-Davies which is an accurate appraisal of what parliament actually intended to achieve. The law on this topic is now to be found in the decision of the House of Lords in *Shivpuri* [1986] 2 All ER 334, which overruled *Anderton v Ryan* and Lord Bridge's speech, in particular, is worth reading if only for its humility. Lord Bridge 'confessed' to reaching the wrong conclusion in *Anderton*, that it could not in any way be distinguished from the *Shivpuri* case and felt there was no other option available except to overrule the decision: 'If a serious error embodied in a decision of this House has distorted the law, the sooner it is corrected the better.'

Shivpuri had been caught in possession of a substance which he believed to be a prohibited drug. In fact the powder was snuff and it is not unlawful to possess or deal in the substance. He intended to deal in heroin or cannabis. His actions were on the face of it morally reprehensible and his conviction for attempting to be knowingly concerned in dealing with and harbouring a prohibited drug was upheld. He clearly had the requisite intent to satisfy s 1 of the CAtA 1981 and the *actus reus* was complete with regard to the intended offence.

The analysis of s 1(1) must, therefore, rely upon the assumption that what is required is proof of an act that is more than merely preparatory to the offence 'which the *defendant intended* to commit'. (*per* Lord Bridge, emphasis added). If something more were required then s 1(2) would render s 1(1) otiose because the two sub-sections would contradict each other.

One situation though is quite clear. If the object of the attempt is in fact not a crime, then logically one cannot be guilty of attempt to commit an offence however much the accused may think he is committing an offence. So in *Taaffe* [1984] 1 All ER 747, the accused thought he was importing currency into the UK *and*, wrongly, believed that was a crime. In fact he was in possession of cannabis. Clearly, he had the intention to commit what he thought was a crime but he did not and could not commit an *actus reus*. Lord Scarman quoted from Lord Lane CJ's judgment in the Court of Appeal:

> He is to be judged against the facts that he believed them to be? Had this indeed been currency and not cannabis, no offence would have been committed [p 749(e)].

Lord Scarman went on to endorse Lord Lane's approach with these words:

> ... I find the reasoning of Lord Lane CJ compelling ... the principle that a man must be judged on the facts as he believes them to be is an accepted principle of the criminal law when the state of a man's mind and his knowledge are ingredients of the offence with which he is charged [p 749(g)].

The point that runs through cases such as these is that the defendant has invariably made a mistake. In such circumstances, where it is believed by the defendant that he is embarking upon the commission of a crime, it is perhaps inappropriate to say that he has an 'honest', albeit mistaken, belief in the existence of a fact or series of facts from which he concludes he is about to commit a crime. But he certainly will be proved to have held a mistaken belief. Thus, if the failure is as a result of, say, the absence of the item he intends to steal or the drug he intends to import, he is guilty because he has committed the *actus reus* believing he is carrying out a criminal act which would be true if the facts had been as he believed them to be. Therefore, it follows that if he believes he is committing a crime but legally that activity is not proscribed then he cannot be said to be attempting to commit *a crime*.

Consider the following examples.

(a) Let us take the situation envisaged by Lord Lane CJ in *Ghosh*. The visitor to these shores who comes from a country where bus rides are free would not be guilty of attempting to obtain services by deception or attempting to steal if he boarded the bus without having money in his possession. He would be judged on the facts as he honestly believed them to be, albeit the activity is capable of amounting to a criminal offence, for example, when he alights from the bus without having paid.

(b) A man has intercourse with a 16-year-old girl knowing her to be 16 and believing that it is an offence to have sexual intercourse with girls under the age of 21. He may intend to break the law but he cannot be guilty of an attempt to commit a crime for the simple reason that the activity in which he is engaged is not criminal. This example assumes that the female is throughout consenting to the intercourse.

The provisions of the CJA 1993 (discussed above) in respect of jurisdictional issues affecting the law of conspiracy apply equally to the law of attempt, that is, attempting to commit a Group A offence. Therefore, the offence of attempt can be committed in England even though the completed offence is destined to take place abroad. The essential element is that the offence must be indictable in England. If so, then the attempt to commit that crime will also be indictable. Perhaps the clearest example is the offence of murder which is triable in England if committed anywhere in the world by a British citizen. Thus, to take a recent example, if D, a British citizen, posted a letter containing anthrax spores to P, who was resident in the US, with the intention that he dies, then he could be charged with attempted murder.

However, if he were to post a noxious substance with the intention that P consume it in order to cause actual bodily harm and not to kill, then there would be no legal basis for an attempt charge because the completed offence would not be triable here.

There are numerous exceptions to this rule as a result of statutory intervention in the 1990s. Particular attention should be paid to the Criminal Justice Act 1993 and the reference to Group A offences, a category which includes the key sections of the Theft Acts and the Forgery and Counterfeiting Act 1981.

In the reverse situation where the British citizen is abroad and intent upon committing an offence in England and Wales reference should be made to the important cases of *Stonehouse* and *Liangsiriprasert v US Government*. The former case decided that an act, such as Stonehouse's mysterious disappearance, carried out abroad intending to commit an offence here was indictable in this country. The accused had perpetrated a fraud on an insurance company based in the UK. The latter case was decided purely in relation to the offence of conspiracy concluding that even though nothing had been done in England, the conspiracy abroad was indictable here. The importance of the case in this context is the *obiter* statement that the reasoning applies equally to attempt and incitement.

A person can be guilty of an attempt to commit a Group A offence irrespective of whether the attempt was made in England and Wales or it had an effect in England and Wales (see s 3(3)).

The Law Commission in its draft Criminal Code proposed no change in respect of the law relating to impossibility other than to bring the law on incitement into line with that relating to attempt and conspiracy. Clause 50 treats the three preliminary offences together. Therefore, a person would be guilty of incitement, attempt or conspiracy although the commission of the completed offence is impossible: '... if it would be possible in the circumstances which he believes or hopes exist or will exist at the relevant time.'

SUMMARY OF CHAPTER 5

PRELIMINARY OR INCHOATE OFFENCES

This chapter has discussed the inchoate or preliminary offences of incitement, conspiracy and attempt. These offences give recognition to the fact that society seeks to discourage its members from contemplating as well as participating in criminal activity. Incitement unlike the other two crimes remains a common law offence and aims to deter those who seek to persuade or encourage others to commit crimes. The usual way to commit such an offence will be to make a direct approach, although as we have seen it is possible to influence a number of people, for example, by advertising in a newspaper inviting readers to commit a crime, such as murdering the Prime Minister.

INCITEMENT

Incitement may be either express or implied as seen in the *Invicta Plastics* case. A further important point is that the offence is only established once it has come to the other party's notice although the law does recognise an offence of attempting to incite when the communication fails. *Whitehouse* decides that, if the act to be done by the person incited would not amount to a crime, then there is no liability for incitement. The *mens rea* for the offence is intention that the offence incited be committed.

Care should be taken to remember that in 'impossibility' situations the common law still governs incitement, even though the CAtA 1981 has put the law onto a statutory basis in respect of conspiracy and attempt.

CONSPIRACY

Conspiracy is largely a statutory offence under s 1 of the CLwA 1977 but elements still remain part of the common law. Conspiracy to corrupt public morals and public decency and to defraud have not been incorporated into the statutory framework. The *actus reus* of conspiracy is proof of an agreement between two or more persons to commit an offence. So agreement is at the heart of the offence whether it be statutory or common law conspiracy. There are various limitations imposed by law as to who may be parties to a conspiracy. For example, a person is not guilty of conspiracy if the only other party is his spouse or is a person under the age of criminal responsibility. Nor can one conspire with the intended victim of the conspiracy. The strength of evidence against those accused of conspiracy may result in only one of a number of people charged being found guilty. Reference to the judgment of the Lord Chief Justice in *Longman and Cribben* is important. Close analysis of s 1 of the CLwA 1977 is crucial in respect of statutory conspiracy, the important elements being:

- agreement;
- course of conduct;

- in accordance with their intentions;
- will necessarily amount to or involve the commission of an offence.

It is worth recalling that a conditional intention is sufficient *mens rea* for conspiracy.

Common law conspiracy requires a study of two discrete areas of law. Important cases involving conspiracy to corrupt public morals are *Shaw* and *Knuller*, the latter recognising that there is a substantive offence at common law of outraging public decency. Conspiracy to defraud has attracted considerable judicial attention over the years as well as review by the Law Commission in 1994. The major rule appears to be that statutory conspiracy should be charged where the object of the conspiracy would amount to a substantive offence, for example, theft. Conspiracy to defraud will be available where the object of the agreement involves fraud, dishonesty or deceit but does not amount to a substantive offence. Good examples are *Scott* and *Cooke*. The *mens rea* for the offence is proof of an intention to defraud and evidence of dishonesty. Dishonesty is to be assessed using the *Ghosh* test.

If parties conspire to commit the impossible, then the outcome will be different depending on whether statutory or common law conspiracy is charged. In the former case, s 5 of the CAtA 1981 will apply but in the latter the common law as laid down in *Haughton v Smith* and *DPP v Nock* will apply.

There are jurisdictional issues which need to be assessed and attention should be paid to the provisions of the CJA 1993, the Criminal Justice (Terrorism and Conspiracy) Act 1998 as well as the important cases of *Doot*, *Sansom* and *Liangsiriprasert*.

ATTEMPTS

The law on attempt is to be found in s 1 of the CAtA 1981. The *actus reus* requires proof that the accused did an act which is more than merely preparatory to the completed offence. This is not easy to establish as numerous cases have illustrated, for example, *Gullefer*, *Griffin* and *Campbell*. There is no absolute test to determine when mere preparation becomes preparation. The *mens rea* required is an intention to commit the offence. The pre-Act law has influenced the post-Act case law and reference should be made to *Mohan* and *Pearman*. Also influencing this area of the law have been the decisions in *Hancock and Shankland*, *Moloney* and *Nedrick* and this has led to calls for the meaning of the word intention to be put onto a statutory basis. Intent is the only state of mind needed to establish an attempt, the *mens rea* for the full offence being irrelevant. Thus, for attempted murder only an intent to kill will suffice while for murder an intent to cause grievous bodily harm is enough to establish the *mens rea*. Note, however, the decision in *Khan* to the effect that recklessness to a circumstance may be sufficient providing there is intent towards the consequence. So, on a charge of attempted rape, an intent to have intercourse being reckless as to whether the woman is consenting is enough to ensure a conviction. Impossibility in attempt is covered by the statutory provisions and not the common law.

CHAPTER 6

HOMICIDE

There is no offence of homicide as such in English criminal law. It is a generic term encompassing various types of unlawful killing. Homicide encompasses murder, voluntary manslaughter, and various forms of involuntary manslaughter, together with the 'special' defences that may be available to a defendant charged with murder. Reference will also be made to offences against the unborn. Corporate liability for manslaughter is also considered, this topic attracting more attention in recent years as public opinion has hardened in favour of imposing more effective criminal sanctions on companies that cause death through their failures to ensure safety procedures are adhered to – consider the high profile transport disasters such as the sinking of the Zeebrugge ferry and the Paddington, Southall and Clapham rail crashes.

6.1   THE *ACTUS REUS* OF MURDER

Murder is a common law offence. The *actus reus* requires proof that D caused the death of the victim and the *mens rea* requires proof that D did so with intention to kill or intention to do grievous bodily harm. Coke defined the offence in these terms:

> Murder is when a man of sound memory, and the age of discretion, unlawfully killeth within any county of the realm any reasonable creature in *rerum natura* under the King's peace, with malice aforethought, either expressed by the party, or implied by law, so that the party wounded, or hurt, and die of the wound, or hurt, and within a year and a day after the same [Coke, 3 Co Inst 47].

Despite being regarded as the classic common law exposition upon the elements of murder, it is submitted that this definition has to be interpreted with care, as the explanation that follows will indicate.

6.1.1   Who can be killed? The concept of the 'reasonable creature'

Coke's definition requires a human being ('reasonable creature') as the victim of the crime of murder. It follows that a foetus cannot be the victim of a homicide (see further below, 6.7, for consideration of offences against the unborn). The issue of what constitutes a reasonable creature for the purposes of homicide was considered by Brooke LJ in *Re A (Children) (Conjoined Twins: Surgical Separation)* [2000] 4 All ER 961, as a result of the submission that a conjoined twin lacking essential organs of her own might not come within the scope of the definition, and therefore might not come within the scope of the offence of homicide. Rejecting such an argument he observed:

> I am satisfied that Mary's life [Mary being the conjoined twin lacking many of her own vital organs] ... is a human life that falls to be protected by the law of murder. Although she has for all practical purposes a useless brain, a useless heart and useless lungs, she is alive, and it would in my judgment be an act of murder if someone deliberately acted so as to extinguish that life unless a justification or excuse could be shown which English law is willing to recognise.

He added that recent editions of *Archbold* had suggested that the word 'reasonable' (in conjunction with 'creature') in Coke's definition of murder related to the appearance, rather than the mental capacity, of the victim and was, therefore, apt to exclude 'monstrous births'. He also approved a submission based on the following extract from *The Sanctity of Life and the Criminal Law* (London: Faber & Faber) written by Professor Glanville Williams in 1958:

> Advances in medical treatment of deformed neonates suggest that the criminal law's protection should be as wide as possible and a conclusion that a creature in being was not reasonable would be confined only to the most extreme cases, of which this is not an example. Whatever might have been thought of as 'monstrous' by Bracton, Coke, Blackstone, Locke and Hobbes, different considerations would clearly apply today. This proposition might be tested in this way: suppose an intruder broke into the hospital and stabbed twin M causing her death. Clearly it could not be said that his actions would be outside the ambit of the law of homicide.

Brooke LJ therefore rejected the argument that a deformed or disabled child was somehow to be regarded as sub-human and without the protection offered by the criminal law.

6.1.2   Act, omission and causation

As will have been seen from the consideration of causation in the context of *actus reus* (see above, 2.4), most of the major authorities that focus on the issue of causation relate to the offences of murder or manslaughter. Difficult ethical problems may arise as well as complex legal questions over the apparently simple question of who has caused the victim's death. Nicola Padfield, in her article, 'Clean water and muddy causation' ([1995] Crim LR 683), suggested that there are three elements which were vital when considering causation in homicide cases. The first is to establish that death would not have resulted 'but for' the accused's conduct. Secondly, the defendant's act must be more than a minimal cause of death and finally, there must be no *novus actus interveniens* that breaks the chain of causation. The terminally ill patient constantly in pain who begs a merciful and quick release from suffering will not absolve the doctor from legal responsibility for that death if the final injection is administered with the specific aim of bringing about the patient's demise. The doctor has accelerated death possibly by only a few hours or even minutes but it is clear in law who has caused the death. The potential ramifications for the medical practitioner who adopts this course of conduct, having taken the view that it is not only in the patient's best interests but also in accordance with the patient's (and possibly immediate family's) wishes, are enormous. In *Cox* (1992) *The Times*, 2 December, the doctor injected his patient with potassium chloride, death resulting very shortly afterwards. He had done so in accordance with the patient's wishes and with the full knowledge and concurrence of her immediate family. She was terminally ill and in great pain. He was convicted of attempted murder on the basis that his act was intended to bring about her death. The attempted killing was therefore unlawful. The impact on Dr Cox is powerfully spelt out by Hazel Biggs in her article, 'Euthanasia and death with dignity' ([1996] Crim LR 878):

> Here the doctor exercised absolute respect for his patient's autonomy by responding to her appeals that he curtail her suffering by killing her. He was then subjected to the indignity of a criminal trial, where he was convicted of attempted murder, and a professional disciplinary hearing which questioned his professional and moral

integrity. Cox received a suspended jail sentence and may now practise medicine only under the close supervision of other physicians. His dignity was jeopardised because he acceded to his patient's request for a dignified death [p 885].

6.1.3 The lapse in time between the cause and the result

At common law there was a rule to the effect that the death of the victim had to be shown to have occurred within a year and a day of the occurrence, which in law is deemed to have caused the death if murder or manslaughter was to be established. The rule can be traced back to the 13th century and, as the Law Commission stated in its consultation paper, *Criminal Law: The Year and a Day Rule in Homicide* (Law Com 136, 1994):

> The rule [was] a legacy of a time when medical science was so rudimentary that if there was a substantial lapse of time between injury and death, it was unsafe to pronounce on the question whether the defendant's conduct or some other event caused death.

Cases dealing with this issue were few and far between and the most usually cited example was *Dyson* [1908] 2 KB 454. This was a manslaughter case where the defendant had inflicted injuries upon his child in November 1906 and again in December 1907. The child died on 5 March 1908. The judge had left it to the jury to convict if they believed that death could have been caused by the injuries inflicted in 1906. The Court of Appeal accepted that this amounted to a misdirection and quashed the conviction.

The Law Commission favoured abolition and was clearly influenced by the fact that the rule did not command support in other jurisdictions. It was not part of the law in Scotland or South Africa, had been abolished in all Australian states except Queensland and law reform bodies in Canada and New Zealand had recommended abolition. The Model Penal Code in the US did not contain the rule. The reasons for advocating abolition are given in the 1994 consultation paper (Law Com 136, para 6.19). With advances in medical science, it is now much easier to ascertain the cause of death and the rule had prevented prosecutions where it was incontrovertible that the initial incident caused death, albeit more than a year and a day after the incident. It is also clear that the rule led to convictions for lesser crimes than were appropriate in the circumstances, merely because the victim lived for more than a year and a day.

Parliament accepted the Commission's favoured option and the rule was abolished as a result of the Law Reform (Year and a Day) Act 1996 which came into force in August 1996. If it is alleged that the cause of death occurred more than three years before the victim died, then the consent of the Attorney General is required before a prosecution can be brought. Otherwise, the normal rules of causation will apply. However, if the person to be prosecuted has been convicted of another offence referable to the death, then the Attorney General's consent will also be required.

6.1.4 What is death?

The guidelines laid down by the Royal Medical Colleges emphasise brain death as the major criterion for establishing death and although the Court of Appeal in *Malcherek and Steel* [1981] 2 All ER 422 drew back from endorsing them as the legal

test for death, it was plainly impressed with the approach. Lord Lane CJ put it this
way:

> There is, it seems, a body of opinion in the medical profession that there is only one
> true test of death and that is irreversible death of the brain stem, which controls the
> basic functions of the body such as breathing.

Thus, if this test represents the law, someone who is on a ventilator or a life support
machine, being brain dead, cannot be a murder victim, although a charge of attempt
may lie providing the necessary intent can be proved. In *Airedale NHS Trust v Bland*
[1993] 1 All ER 821, a young man had been crushed at the Hillsborough football
ground tragedy in 1989. He was in a 'persistent vegetative state' for some three and a
half years due to 'catastrophic and irreversible damage to the higher functions of the
brain'. It was accepted in law that he was still alive. Lord Goff said:

> It is true that his condition is such that it can be described as a living death; but he is
> nevertheless still alive. This is because, as a result of developments in modern medical
> technology, doctors no longer associate death exclusively with breathing and heart
> beat, and it has come to be accepted that death occurs when the brain, and in
> particular the brain stem, has been destroyed ... the evidence is that Anthony's brain
> stem is still alive and functioning and it follows that, in the present state of medical
> science, he is still alive and should be so regarded as a matter of law [p 865(g)].

6.2   THE *MENS REA* OF MURDER

Lord Browne-Wilkinson in *Airedale NHS Trust v Bland* describes the *mens rea* for
murder in one, apparently straightforward, sentence: 'Murder consists of causing the
death of another with intent to do so.' It is now well-established that either an
intention to kill or an intention to cause grievous bodily harm will satisfy the 'intent'
requirement. It is this 'intent' that differentiates murder from manslaughter; see
further the consideration of intent in Chapter 3 and its application in cases such as
Moloney [1985] AC 905, *Hancock and Shankland* [1986] AC 455, *Nedrick* [1986] 3 All ER
1 and *Woollin* [1998] 4 All ER 103. It will be recalled that these cases represent the
culmination of the protracted debate on whether or not an acceptable definition of
the word 'intention' could be formulated for trial judges to put to juries. The debacle
of *Hyam v DPP* [1974] 2 All ER 41 proved, if proof be needed, that a consensus was
almost impossible to achieve and this obviously influenced the approach approved
by Lord Bridge in *Moloney*. Judges should refrain from helping juries other than to
say that intention is a simple English word, invite juries to assess the evidence and
then reach a conclusion. However, as the late Professor John Smith pointed out in his
commentary to the case of *Scalley* [1995] Crim LR 504, 'intention is an ordinary word
of the English language [and] as an ordinary word, it usually implies that the result
is an aim or objective, a desired result, which is narrower than the legal meaning'
(p 506). In the light of the House of Lords' decision in *Woollin*, therefore, the model
direction to the jury in a murder case (where some direction on the meaning of intent
was required) would be to the effect that they are not entitled to find the necessary
intention unless they feel sure that death or serious bodily harm was a virtual
certainty (barring some unforeseen intervention) as a result of the defendant's
actions and that the defendant appreciated that such was the case. The jury would
also have to be reminded that the decision is one for them to reach on a
consideration of all the evidence.

The term 'malice aforethought' is best avoided when describing the *mens rea* for murder, even though Lord Goddard CJ in *Vickers* [1957] 2 All ER 741 described it as a 'term of art'. Notwithstanding the use of the phrase in s 1 of the Homicide Act (HA) 1957 (as to which see below) it is a phrase likely to mislead. The *mens rea* for murder does not require proof that the defendant acted with 'malice' towards the victim, or that the killing was in anyway premeditated.

6.2.1   Intention to cause grievous bodily harm

The development of the *mens rea* for murder has a rather inglorious history. Prior to the enactment of the HA 1957 a defendant could be convicted of murder if he killed with the intention to kill or do grievous bodily harm, or if he killed in the course of committing a felony, while seeking to evade lawful arrest, or while effecting or assisting an escape or rescue from legal custody. The principle whereby the defendant was treated as if he had the *mens rea* for murder even though he lacked the intent to kill or do grievous bodily harm was known as constructive malice. Section 1 of the HA 1957 effectively abolished the doctrine of constructive malice but, as Lord Goddard CJ explained in *Vickers*, the *mens rea* of murder has always been recognised as established by proof of intention to kill (express malice) or intention to do grievous bodily harm (implied malice). The justification for contending that implied malice had survived the enactment of the 1957 Act was the policy consideration that any defendant who intended to cause grievous bodily harm, which in fact resulted in the death of the victim, could not be heard to say that he should not be convicted of murder. How does a person, acting with intent to do grievous bodily harm, know for sure that the victim will not die?

Lord Edmund-Davies in *Cunningham* [1981] 2 All ER 412, whilst favouring the view that the *mens rea* of murder should be limited to an intention to kill, believed that any change to the law as expressed in *Vickers* would have to be brought about by parliamentary, not judicial, intervention:

> It is a task for none other than Parliament, as the constitutional organ best fitted to weigh the relevant and opposing factors. Its solution has already been attempted extra judicially on many occasions, but with no real success.

In the course of his speech in *Powell and Daniels; English* [1997] 4 All ER 545, Lord Steyn conceded that:

> In English law a defendant may be convicted of murder who is in no ordinary sense a murderer ... This rule [by which he meant the fact that intention to do grievous bodily harm would suffice for murder] turns murder into a constructive crime.

What then is the argument in favour of retaining this form of constructive liability enshrined in the current *mens rea* for murder? The conventional wisdom is based on a theory of 'just deserts' – an attacker bent on causing grievous bodily harm cannot guarantee that death will not follow, given the unpredictability, whether a serious injury will result in death. In effect, the law regards such a defendant as being willing to take the risk that the victim will die. The obvious riposte to this is that murder should be reserved for those who intend to kill. The offence of manslaughter exists to cater for those willing to risk the death of their victims, where the risk materialises. The shortcomings of the current law are, of course, compounded by the fact that the penalty for murder is a mandatory life sentence.

Clause 54 of the draft Criminal Code (*Criminal Law: A Criminal Code for England and Wales*, Law Com 177, 1989) declares that the *mens rea* for murder ought to require proof that the defendant acted:

(a) intending to cause death; or

(b) intending to cause serious personal harm and being aware that it may cause death.

This can usefully be read in conjunction with the proposals of the Law Commission contained in the draft Criminal Code Bill to be found in the Commission's report *Legislating the Criminal Code: Offences Against the Person and General Principles* (Law Com 218, 1993). The Law Commission proposes the new offence of intentional serious injury and 'intentionally' is defined this way:

1   For the purposes of this Part a person acts:

   (a) 'intentionally' with respect to a result when:

     (i) it is his purpose to cause it; or

     (ii) although it is not his purpose to cause it, he knows that it would occur in the ordinary course of events if he were to succeed in his purpose of causing some other result ...

If the law on non-fatal offences were to be reformed without any change to the law on murder, then it can be expected that this formula would form the basis for the definition of implied malice. However, if the draft Criminal Code formulation of the *mens rea* for murder were to become law, there would need to be at least an awareness on the part of the defendant that his conduct might result in death.

6.3   VOLUNTARY MANSLAUGHTER – PROVOCATION

Provocation is a common law defence available only as a defence to a murder charge – effectively a concession to human frailty. It is a recognition that, if subjected to sufficient provocation, even a reasonable person might be so provoked as to commit murder. The significance of the defence lies in the fact that, if made out, it reduces the defendant's liability to manslaughter, thus providing the trial judge with a wide discretion as to sentencing. The defence is available to both principal offenders and accomplices.

The classic definition of provocation was given by Devlin J in *Duffy* [1949] 1 All ER 932 were he stated that:

Provocation is some act, or series of acts, done (or words spoken) which would cause in any reasonable person, and actually causes in the accused, a sudden and temporary loss of self-control, rendering the accused so subject to passion as to make him or her for the moment not the master of his mind.

This statement must be read as having been modified by s 3 of the HA 1957, which states:

Where on a charge of murder there is evidence on which the jury can find that the person charged was provoked (whether by things done or by things said or by both together) to lose his self-control, the question whether the provocation was enough to make a reasonable man do as he did shall be left to be determined by the jury; and in determining that question the jury shall take into account everything both done and said according to the effect which, in their opinion, it would have on a reasonable man.

As will be seen from what follows, the essential issues raised by this defence are whether or not the defendant actually was provoked at the time of the killing and, if he was, whether or not his actions were reasonable. In crude terms a subjective/objective dichotomy, although such a description hardly does justice to the subtleties involved. The question of the extent to which the idiosyncrasies of the defendant are to be taken into account when assessing whether the degree of self-control displayed was reasonable has proved particularly troublesome.

Professor Andrew Ashworth, in his article 'The doctrine of provocation' ([1976] CLJ 292, pp 317–18), wrote that provocation:

> ... mitigates moral culpability to the extent that a person acted in a less-than-fully-controlled manner in circumstances in which there was reasonable justification for him to feel aggrieved at the conduct of another. The law's subjective condition operates to ensure that it was not a revenge killing, but rather a sudden and uncontrolled reaction to perceived injustice. The objective condition looks at the element of partial justification and, inevitably, to the conduct of the provoking party. It requires of the jury an assessment of the seriousness of the provocation, and a judgment as to whether the provocation was grave enough to warrant a reduction of the crime from murder to manslaughter. The question of sufficiency is one of degree, and the legal rules, although they can take the court so far, cannot determine this ultimate question. Of course there will be clear cases – as, for example, where the teenage son loses control and attacks his bullying father – and there will be doubtful cases – as, for example, where the husband kills his wife during a quarrel over infidelity, which the parties had more or less accepted for a considerable time. Each case is for the decision of the jury, properly directed as to the law.

This passage was cited with approval by the House of Lords in *Acott* (1996) 160 JP 655 as describing the 'core features of the modern law of provocation'.

6.3.1 Evidence that the defendant was provoked

A defendant seeking to rely on the defence of provocation bears no legal burden of proof in so doing. The burden of proof rests with the prosecution. As Lord Devlin said in *Lee Chun-Chuen* [1963] AC 220:

> It is not of course for the defence to make out a *prima facie* case of provocation. It is for the prosecution to prove that the killing was unprovoked. All that the defence need do is to point to material which could induce a reasonable doubt [p 229].

The role of the trial judge is to determine whether or not, as a matter of law, the evidence disclosed at the trial provides any basis for the issue of provocation being left to the jury for consideration. The matter was considered by the House of Lords in *Acott*. The appellant who lived with his mother had been charged with her murder after she was found dead from multiple injuries. He claimed that she had sustained the injuries as a result of a fall, although two pathologists called by the Crown testified that she had endured a sustained attack before she died. A pathologist called by the defence thought that there was a possibility that she could have died in the way described by her son.

Counsel for the prosecution had, throughout cross-examination, repeatedly put to the appellant the suggestion that he might have lost his self-control. This was, unsurprisingly, denied, as it would have been tantamount to admitting that his mother did not come by her injuries as a result of an accident. There was evidence that his mother used to berate him, treat him like a child and belittle him because he was financially dependent upon her. The defendant was aged 48. The trial judge did not put any issue of provocation to the jury and he was convicted of murder. His appeal to the Court of Appeal was on the basis that once the prosecution had raised the possibility of provocation, it should have been put to the jury. The appeal was dismissed both in the Court of Appeal and in the House of Lords on the ground that there had to be some evidence, either direct or inferential, of what was done or said in order to provoke the accused and that was absent in this case. The House of Lords ruled that there had to be some evidence of the nature of the provocation. If there was only the speculative possibility that there had been an act of provocation, it would be wrong for the judge to direct the jury to consider provocation.

The difficulty in such cases, of course, is that there is no triable issue of provocation. For counsel to raise the possibility, by way of cross-examination, without more direct evidence of provoking conduct, would in part detract from the real issues in the case under trial. It is virtually impossible for a jury to determine either the subjective and objective condition without some evidence as to the nature of the provocation.

Occasionally, the suggestion of provocation may arise as a result of a plea of some other defence which, if successful would result in acquittal for the accused, for example, self-defence. If such a defence were to fail, the accused may seek to appeal on the basis that provocation should have been considered by the jury. In the case of *Wellington* [1993] Crim LR 616, the trial judge had concluded there was no evidence of loss of self-control and as such refused to refer the issue of provocation to the jury. The Crown accepted that if there had been any evidence of the loss of self-control, then the judge was under a duty to leave the defence to the jury. However, no such foundation had been laid and this interpretation was supported by the Court of Appeal. The requirement to establish a proper foundation is not a particularly arduous one to fulfil, providing there is some evidence of specific provoking conduct. In this case, the appellant had not claimed that he had lost his self-control, although he maintained that he had been acting 'instinctively' when trying to fend off the victim, while he had a knife in his hand. The evidence of a pathologist might prove important if, for example, the injuries to the deceased showed a frenzied or savage attack had taken place, which might be consistent with the attacker having lost his self-control. In *Rossiter* [1994] 2 All ER 752, the Court of Appeal held that whenever there was evidence that supported the contention that the accused had lost his or her self-control, however tenuous it might be, then the judge should refer the issue of provocation to the jury. The Court of Appeal went further in *Cambridge* [1994] 2 All ER 760, holding that a trial judge is 'required' to leave provocation to the jury even though counsel had chosen not to rely on the defence. Lord Taylor CJ considered what type of evidence gave rise to the duty to pass the matter to the jury. It was not, he said, for the judge to 'conjure up a speculative possibility of a defence that is not relied on and is unrealistic' (p 765b). He was, however, of the opinion that the reference by Russell LJ in *Rossiter* to 'material capable of amounting to provocation, however tenuous it may be', described the provocative acts and words, 'and not the evidence of their existence'.

6.3.2   The nature of the provocation

As Lord Hoffmann explained, in the course of his speech in *Smith (Morgan)* [1998] 4 All ER 387, the defence of provocation has its origins in the world of Restoration gallantry where gentlemen:

> ... habitually carried lethal weapons, acted in accordance with a code of honour which required insult to be personally avenged by instant angry retaliation ... [t]o show anger 'in hot blood' for a proper reason by an appropriate response was not merely permissible but the badge of a man of honour.

Building upon this, the common law came to recognise that certain forms of provocation were generally sufficient to reduce murder to manslaughter. These included a quarrel that escalated from words to physical assault, the defendant finding another man committing adultery with his wife, and a defendant finding another man sodomising his (the defendant's) son.

The effect of s 3 of the HA 1957 has been to liberalise the defence so that anything can now be provocation, whether it takes the form of things said or done, regardless of whether or not the provocation comes from the deceased. Note, for example, that in *Doughty* (1986) 83 Cr App R 319, the Court of Appeal held that even the crying of an infant could be provocation. The key question related to the reasonableness of the defendant's reaction to that provocation.

In assessing the extent of the provocation the court must now be prepared to look at the history of the relationship between the parties. What appears to be a quite trivial act may be the 'straw that breaks the camel's back'. Lord Taylor CJ accepted in *Dryden* [1995] 4 All ER 987 that, in the context of the accused's obsession with his property and his long running dispute with the local planning authority, the threatened demolition of his bungalow by the authority could have been seen as the 'last straw' in the build-up of stress upon the accused. Similarly, in *Humphreys* [1995] 4 All ER 1008, Hirst LJ emphasised that, in considering the evidence of provocation, the jury should have been directed to consider the history of the 'tempestuous relationship' between the accused and the deceased, and the fact that the 'cumulative strands of potentially provocative conduct' could be seen as 'building up until the final encounter'.

There is no rule that excludes so-called self-induced provocation from the scope of the defence. D may taunt P, causing P to respond with highly provocative comments. In turn D loses his self-control and kills P. A trial judge would be in error if he or she were to withdraw the defence from the jury on the basis that D had 'started it' (see *Johnson* [1989] 2 All ER 839).

6.3.3   The immediacy of the response to the provocation

Devlin J's restatement of the defence of provocation in *Duffy* emphasised the need for evidence that the defendant relying on provocation had suffered a sudden and temporary loss of self-control. To the extent that these words seek to draw a distinction between the defendant who is genuinely provoked, and the defendant who is acting out of a desire for revenge, they represent an important limitation on the availability of the defence. The danger, however, is that they are read as requiring an immediate response by the defendant. This issue has caused concern in cases of domestic violence where women have been charged with murder, having been driven to kill their abusive partners. Whereas a man who is provoked might be quick to retaliate with his fists or feet, a woman provoked to attack a man might delay in order to seek a weapon, or might wait until the man is asleep or intoxicated so that she can counter his greater physical strength. Either course of action by a woman might lead a court to the view that her reaction was not 'sudden and temporary' (see *Thornton (No 2)* [1995] 2 All ER 1023).

In *Ahluwalia* [1992] 4 All ER 889, the appellant, an unwilling partner to an arranged marriage, had suffered many years of severe violence and abuse at the hands of her husband. There was evidence to show that on one occasion he had tried to run her down and on others had threatened to kill her. He also taunted his wife about affairs he had with other women. On the evening in question, the couple had argued and the husband threatened to beat up his wife the following morning. During the night, she entered his bedroom where he was sleeping, poured petrol on the floor and then, having retreated, set it alight. Her husband died as a result of the burns he received in the ensuing fire. The appellant was convicted of murder and sentenced to life imprisonment. She appealed contending, *inter alia*, that the violence and humiliation she suffered at the hands of her husband over a period of some 10 years amounted to provocation. The court confirmed that the longer the delay and 'the stronger the evidence of deliberation on the part of the defendant the more likely it would be that the prosecution would be able to negative provocation'. (The appellant's appeal was allowed in light of new medical evidence that raised the possibility that, at the time of the killing, she was suffering from diminished responsibility and a rehearing was ordered.) The response to the provocative behaviour, therefore, does not need to be immediate. The time lapse is something for the jury to take into account. The longer the time lapse between the last act and the response the more likely it is that the jury will reject the defence. If the severely abused wife says to herself, 'If he hits me again I will kill him' and in the event does so, then this is inconsistent with the requirement for a sudden and temporary loss of self-control. If, however, she responds to the last act of violence by picking up a knife and stabbing her husband, then the evidence ought to be put before the jury.

The safest course of action for the trial judge, once he has determined that there is evidence of provocation to put before the jury, is to leave the issue of immediacy to the jury as a question of fact. *Baillie* [1995] 2 Cr App R 31 would tend to suggest that a substantial delay between the acts relied upon as constituting provocation combined with a strong element of revenge underpinning the behaviour that led to the killing of the victim is not necessarily fatal to a plea of provocation. A father distraught at the fact that M had been pressurising one of his sons to purchase drugs from him had been informed by the son that M had threatened him. The defendant, B, who had been drinking heavily, armed himself with a sawn-off shotgun and a cut-throat razor and went looking for M. M received substantial injuries from the razor and as he fled, B fired the gun twice. M died as a result of being hit by flying particles from a wire fence, which had taken the brunt of the shotgun blasts. The judge did not direct the jury on the issue of provocation, as 'any sudden and temporary loss of self-control must have ceased by the time of the fatal act'. Nevertheless, the court allowed the appeal. While recognising the 'many and obvious difficulties' with the evidence, the court felt constrained by precedent and accepted that the jury should have had the opportunity to consider the evidence of provocation. If the words 'sudden and temporary loss of self-control' are meant to be synonymous with there being an absence of premeditation, it is difficult to see how a case such as *Baillie* can have been correctly decided. It is hard to avoid the conclusion that conscious control on the part of the accused during the build-up to the fatal event will not of itself lead to a plea of provocation being withdrawn from the jury.

6.3.4   The objective factor

The HA 1957 demands that, once the subjective element has been established, the objective factor must be considered. Would the reasonable man have lost his self-control? At common law, the reasonable man was not to be attributed with any of the characteristics of the accused. So, in *Bedder* [1954] 2 All ER 801, the House of Lords held that the jury should ignore the effects of taunts (about his impotency) on an impotent defendant and focus simply on what effect they would have on the reasonable man; see, further, *Mancini v DPP* [1941] AC 1 and *Holmes v DPP* [1946] AC 588. In *Camplin v DPP* [1978] AC 705, the House of Lords made it clear that, given the impact of s 3 of the HA on the common law, the objective test could not be applied fairly without taking into account certain characteristics of the accused. Camplin was a 15-year old who had been buggered by an older man. Camplin's response was to hit his assailant over the head with a large metal frying pan, killing him. He put forward a defence of provocation based upon the act of buggery, the fact that afterwards he was overwhelmed with shame and that he had lost his self-control when he heard the man laughing in response to his sexual triumph. Camplin was convicted of murder, the jury having been directed that they had to assess the response to the provocation by reference to a reasonable man of full age. The House of Lords, allowing Camplin's appeal, acknowledged that the degree of self-control to be expected of a boy of 15 was much less than that expected of an adult and, thus, the age and sex of the accused should have been attributed to the 'reasonable man' for the purposes of assessing the degree of self-control to be expected of the accused. As Lord Diplock explained, a trial judge would, in future, have to explain to the jury that:

> ... the reasonable man referred to is a person having the power of self-control to be expected of an ordinary person of the sex and age of the accused, but in other respects sharing such of the accused's characteristics as they think would affect the gravity of the provocation to him, and that the question is not merely whether such a person would in like circumstances be provoked to lose his self-control but also would react to the provocation as the accused did.

In the period between the decision in *Camplin*, in 1978, and what is now the leading authority on the objective element in the defence of provocation, the House of Lords' decision in *Smith (Morgan)*, the courts struggled with two linked questions. The first was whether or not characteristics other than the age and gender of the accused could be attributed to the reasonable person for the purposes of the objective test. If the answer to the first question was in the affirmative, the second question was whether these additional characteristics were relevant only to explain the gravity of the provocation, or whether they could be taken into account in assessing what degree of self-control it was reasonable to expect in the circumstances.

In *Camplin*, for example, we know that the House of Lords ruled that age and gender could be taken into account, so that the test (in that case) became one of how the reasonable 15-year-old boy would have reacted. It is clear, however, that the circumstance of having been sexually assaulted also had to be taken into account to explain the gravity of the provocation – it explains why the taunts were so provocative. The more difficult question was whether or not the fact that Camplin had been sexually assaulted could be taken into account in assessing the degree of self-control to be expected.

To understand the background to the debate, it is necessary to examine the two conflicting lines of authority that culminated in the House of Lords' ruling in *Smith (Morgan)*.

The Court of Appeal's view

In *Newell* [1980] Crim LR 576, the Court of Appeal, following *obiter* statements found in the New Zealand case of *McGregor* (1962) NZLR 1069, adopted the position that characteristics of the accused, including mental peculiarities, could be taken into account when assessing how the reasonable person would have responded to the provocation in question. Although not applied to the appellant's advantage in *Newell*, this argument was developed in later cases, such as *Thornton (No 2)*, where it was held that 'battered woman syndrome' could be important background information in relation to whatever had driven the accused to fatally stab her husband. It was the court's view that it could also have had an impact on the defendant's personality, thus making it a significant characteristic. The court effectively adopted the objective test, so that it became a question of whether or not the hypothetical reasonable woman would have reacted to the provocation in the same way as the defendant, given the personality disorder.

The problem was also considered at length in *Humphreys*. The appellant had, during her adolescence, turned to drugs and prostitution. At the age of 17, she commenced a relationship with a man aged 33. The relationship was described as 'tempestuous'. He was a jealous and possessive man who, on a number of occasions, had beaten the appellant. One night the appellant cut her wrists, fearing that on his return he would beat her and force her to have sex with him and possibly others against her will. The victim taunted her saying that she had not made a very good job of slashing her wrists. She responded by stabbing him with a kitchen knife. She raised provocation as a defence, citing the cumulative violent behaviour to which she had been subjected. Evidence was given which showed that she was of abnormal mentality, with 'immature, explosive and attention seeking traits'. The judge refused to allow the jury to consider these factors, reasoning that the reasonable young woman would not possess such characteristics. The Court of Appeal held that this amounted to a misdirection. The characteristics should have been taken into account, provided 'they were permanent characteristics which set the accused apart from the ordinary person in the community and were specifically relevant to the provocative words or actions relied on to constitute the defence'. The court thought that attention seeking behaviour could be regarded as a psychological illness or disorder that was not inconsistent with the concept of the reasonable person. The court followed the reasoning in *Dryden*, to the effect that juries were entitled to consider:

> ... those permanent characteristics or traits which served to distinguish the accused from the ordinary person in the community and were specifically relevant to the events relied on as constituting the provocation.

See also *Parker* [1997] Crim LR 760, where the Court of Appeal held that the defendant's chronic alcoholism, because it had caused damage to the left temporal lobe of his brain, ought to have been taken into account when assessing his defence of provocation.

The House of Lords and the Privy Council

Decisions such as *Camplin*, *Morhall* [1995] 3 All ER 659 and *Luc Thiet Thuan v R* [1996] 2 All ER 1033 all observed (to varying degrees) a dichotomy between characteristics of the accused (other than age and gender) that could be attributed to the reasonable person for the purposes of assessing the gravity of the provocation, and characteristics of the accused that could not be attributed to the reasonable person when assessing the degree of self-control to be expected, because such characteristics were seen as being inimical to the concept of reasonable self-control. At the heart of these decisions was a desire to preserve a clear distinction between the defences of diminished responsibility and provocation, and a desire to uphold an objective standard of reasonable behaviour in the face of provocation.

In *Camplin*, Lords Morris and Simon gave example 'characteristics' that might be influential in persuading a jury to accept the defence of provocation. Lord Simon drew attention to a statement such as: '"Your character is as crooked as your back." This would have a different connotation to a hunchback on the one hand and to a man with a back like a ramrod on the other.' In a similar vein, Lord Morris gave this example: 'If the accused is of a particular colour or particular ethnic origin and things are said to him which are grossly insulting, it would be utterly unreal if the jury had to consider whether the words would have provoked a man of different colour or ethnic origin, or to consider how such a man would have acted or reacted.' Their Lordships were quick to point out, however, that those who were exceptionally excitable, pugnacious, ill tempered or drunk would be denied the defence based upon these characteristics.

In *Morhall*, the House of Lords held that addiction to glue sniffing, although reprehensible and undesirable, was a characteristic that could be taken into account when assessing the gravity of the provocation, where that provocation consisted of taunts about the addiction. An addiction to glue sniffing, however, was not seen as a characteristic that could be invoked to argue for any relaxation of the objective test for self-control. The jury would have been expected to conjure with the rather surreal concept of the reasonable glue-sniffer, exhibiting the self-control to be expected from the reasonable person. On this basis, as indicated above, ethnic origin could be taken into account to explain the gravity of the provocation, where the provocation comprised racist taunts directed at the accused's ethnic origin. Belonging to a particular ethnic group would not, however, excuse a loss of self-control – the objective standard would be imposed.

In *Luc Thiet Thuan*, the Privy Council held that mental infirmity, which had the effect of reducing the appellant's self-control, was not to be attributed to the reasonable person for the purposes of the objective element of the test in provocation. There was evidence that, following a fall, the appellant was prone to 'hot flushes' which caused him to suffer explosive outbursts temporarily rendering him incapable of controlling his temper. The expert diagnosis was that he suffered from 'episodic dyscontrol condition'. Lord Goff refused to accept that this was a mental peculiarity that should be attributed to the reasonable person for the purposes of determining the objective self-control dimension of provocation. He dismissed decisions such as *Newell*, *Ahluwalia* and *Humphreys* as having exercised an 'unhappy influence' over the development of this branch of the law, adding that:

> [T]heir Lordships wish to add that they do not find it possible to segregate certain psychological illness or disorders as being 'in no way repugnant to or wholly inconsistent with the concept of the reasonable person' ... and so attributable to the reasonable person for the purposes of the objective test in provocation, notwithstanding that the effect of such an illness or disorder is to deprive the person so afflicted of the ordinary person's power of self-control.

Mental infirmity was, of course, seen as being relevant to the defence of diminished responsibility and, if successful, could lead to the same conclusion (as to which see below, 6.4).

The ruling in Smith (Morgan)

On the one hand, therefore, there was the Court of Appeal taking the view that characteristics of the accused, including those amounting to 'mental peculiarities', could be attributed to the reasonable person in assessing the degree of self-control to be expected of the accused. On the other hand, the House of Lords and Privy Council (albeit principally Lord Goff) insisted that, whilst virtually any characteristic would be taken into account, if it went to the gravity of the provocation, no characteristics beyond age and gender would be attributed to the reasonable person if they might be seen as undermining the objective nature of the self-control test.

A resolution of this conflict by the House of Lords was urgently required and was in due course supplied by the ruling in *Smith (Morgan)*. The accused had stabbed the victim to death and sought to rely on his severe depression as a characteristic to be taken into account in assessing how the reasonable person would have reacted to the provocation. The trial judge ruled that the characteristic could only be relevant in assessing the gravity of the provocation and the jury found the accused guilty of murder. Allowing the appeal, Potts J rejected the notion that the House of Lords' decision in *Camplin* necessitated any distinction between attributing such characteristics to the reasonable man in terms of their relevance to the gravity of the provocation, and their relevance to his reaction to it. He brushed aside the significance of *Morhall* on the basis that the House of Lords in that case had been:

> ... concerned with a different problem altogether – the characteristic supplying the sting of provocative conduct. There is nothing in Lord Goff's speech in that case inconsistent with Lord Taylor CJ's reasoning in *Thornton (No 2)* or of this court in the other decisions cited.

The Crown appealed to the House of Lords, where the following certified question was considered:

> Are characteristics other than age and sex, attributable to a reasonable man, for the purpose of s 3 of the Homicide Act 1957, relevant not only to the gravity of the provocation to him but also to the standard of control to be expected?

The House of Lords held (by a majority of 3:2, Lords Hobhouse and Millett dissenting) that, whilst the test for provocation still comprised a subjective element and an objective element, it was no longer appropriate to direct a jury to consider the objective stage by reference to how a reasonable person (with or without attributes of the defendant) would have reacted. Assuming the subjective element was satisfied, the correct approach was now to direct a jury to consider what degree of self-control it was fair and just to expect from a defendant. In effect, the distinction between characteristics having a bearing on the gravity of the provocation, and those having a bearing on the ability to exercise a reasonable degree of self-control has been swept aside. It is now simply a question of what it was reasonable to expect from the defendant, given his characteristics and circumstances. The decision vindicates the stance taken by the Court of Appeal.

Lord Slynn rejected the argument that Lord Diplock in *Camplin* had sought to lay down a purely objective test for self-control (age and gender notwithstanding). As he explained:

> ... it does not seem to me that Lord Diplock is saying that the question as to the reaction to provocation is wholly objective: on the contrary, he appears to me to be indicating that personal characteristics may be something the jury could take into account. He is certainly not limiting the characteristic which can be taken into account to age (or sex) ... in *Camplin* it was asked in effect what could reasonably be expected of a 15 year old boy. In my view the section requires that the jury should ask what could reasonably be expected of a person with the accused's characteristics. This does not mean that the objective standard of what 'everyone is entitled to expect that his fellow citizens will exercise in society as it is today' is eliminated. It does enable the jury to decide whether in all the circumstances people with his characteristics would reasonably be expected to exercise more self-control than he did or, put another way, that he did exercise the standard of self-control which such persons would have exercised. It is thus not enough for the accused to say 'I am a depressive, therefore I cannot be expected to exercise control'. The jury must ask whether he has exercised the degree of self-control to be expected of someone in his situation.

Lord Hoffmann considered the impact of s 3 of the HA 1957 and observed:

> ... in my opinion ... it would not be consistent with s 3 for the judge to tell the jury as a matter of law that they should ignore any factor or characteristic of the accused in deciding whether the objective element of provocation had been satisfied ... In a case in which the jury might consider that only by virtue of that characteristic was the act in question sufficiently provocative, the effect of such a direction would be to withdraw the issue of provocation altogether and this would be contrary to the terms of s 3 ... It meant, as I have said, that he could no longer tell them that they were obliged as a matter of law to exclude 'factors personal to the prisoner' from their consideration ... It seems to me clear, however, that Lord Diplock was framing a suitable direction for a case like *Camplin* ... and not a one-size-fits-all direction for every case of provocation ... The jury is entitled to act upon its own opinion of whether the objective element of provocation has been satisfied and the judge is not entitled to tell them that for this purpose the law requires them to exclude from consideration any of the circumstances or characteristics of the accused.

The effect of the decision is that, whilst the jury should be directed to the effect that the same standard of behaviour is to be expected from every person, regardless of what their individual psychological make-up might be, the jury should be left sufficient discretion to do justice. This might involve the jury in taking the view that there was some characteristic of the accused (temporary or permanent) that affected the degree of control that could reasonably be expected of him, and the characteristic was of such a nature that it would be unfair not to take it into account.

Lord Clyde adverted to the balancing act involved in the application of this more subjective and flexible approach. The challenge as he saw it was for the jury to arrive at a verdict that could be said to: '... fairly meet any peculiarities of the particular case consistently with the recognition of the importance of curbing temper and passion in the interest of civil order.' He saw the critical question as being that of the proportionality between the provocation and the response. As he put it: 'The gravity of the provocation, which prompts the loss of self-control, and the reasonableness of the response may both be aspects of the same question ...' He did not believe that the tension between the need to protect society from those unable to control their emotions and the desire of the law to show compassion to human frailty could be solved by recourse to the concept of the reasonable man. He concluded:

> When what is at issue is the scale of punishment which should be awarded for his conduct, it seems to me unjust that the determination should be governed not by the actual facts relating to the particular accused but by the blind application of an objective standard of good conduct.

If the test has become essentially one of 'what was it reasonable to expect from the accused?', the question inevitably arises as to whether there are conditions that are still nevertheless excluded when the jury comes to consider the reasonableness of the accused's reaction.

Lord Hoffmann, in the course of his speech, observed that an accused who flies into a rage and kills simply because he has been crossed or thwarted, or because he is unusually possessive or jealous, should not be allowed to rely on his anti-social propensities as the basis for the defence of provocation. He added that a direction that the jury should ignore characteristics such as jealousy and obsession 'was the best way to ensure that the defence was not brought into disrepute'. Further, in his speech, he sought to distinguish between characteristics and what he described as 'defects in character', such as a tendency to violent rages or childish tantrums. Lord Clyde similarly ruled out 'a quarrelsome or choleric temperament' or 'exceptional pugnacity or excitability' as characteristics that could render the accused's loss of self-control reasonable.

The accused's bad temper was always excluded as a characteristic as regards the objective test in provocation, for obvious reasons. There will doubtless be difficulties, however, in drawing the line between mental peculiarities that count as characteristics, and those that are merely seen as defects of character. Was the accused's obsession with his property in *Dryden* a characteristic or a character defect?

The difficulties that are likely to lie ahead in this post-'reasonable person' era were succinctly summarised by Lord Hobhouse in his dissenting speech, where he observed:

> It is not acceptable to leave the jury without definitive guidance as to the objective criterion to be applied. The function of the criminal law is to identify and define the relevant legal criteria. It is not proper to leave the decision to the essentially subjective judgment of the individual jurors who happen to be deciding the case. Such an approach is apt to lead to idiosyncratic and inconsistent decisions. The law must inform the accused, and the judge must direct the jury, what is the objective criterion which the jury are to apply in any exercise of judgment in deciding upon the guilt or innocence of the accused. Non-specific criteria also create difficulties for the conduct of criminal trials since they do not set the necessary parameters for the admission of evidence or the relevance of arguments.

6.3.5 Reform proposals

Clause 58 of the draft Criminal Code, restates the defence of provocation without any reference to the 'reasonable man'. It states:

A person who, but for this section, would be guilty of murder is not guilty of murder if:

(a) he acts when provoked (whether by things done or by things said or by both and whether by the deceased person or by another) to lose his self-control; and

(b) the provocation is, in all the circumstances (including any of his personal characteristics that affect its gravity), sufficient ground for the loss of self-control.

The commentary accompanying the draft code makes it clear that the defendant should be judged on the facts as he believed them to be. It is made absolutely clear that personal characteristics may be highly relevant to the success or failure of the defence (providing the provocation relates to those characteristics). So, as is pointed out at p 251 of the commentary, if the defendant were sexually impotent it would be irrelevant if the alleged provocation consisted in an assault with intent to rob. However, if it consisted of taunts as to the impotence, 'that personal characteristic would be highly relevant'. Compare this with the approach of the majority in *Smith (Morgan)*, where the House of Lords effectively abandons the distinction between characteristics that bear on the gravity of the provocation and those that bear on the degree of self-control to be expected of the defendant.

In January 2003 it was announced that the government was reviewing the defence of provocation. Options under consideration include scrapping the defence altogether, or limiting its availability by excluding issues such as sexual jealousy as a basis for the defence. This move has been motivated by Home Office research on homicides that found that women were far more likely to be attacked by a husband or lover whilst trying to extricate themselves from a relationship. Any future reform of provocation may be linked to a review of the defence of self-defence, so that women who kill abusive partners might be seen as having acted to protect themselves, rather than having to provide evidence that they were acting under provocation at the time of the defence.

6.4 VOLUNTARY MANSLAUGHTER – DIMINISHED RESPONSIBILITY

A defendant charged with murder has a range of general defences to choose from. Some, such as automatism might negate the *actus reus*. Others such as intoxication and insanity will effectively be a denial of *mens rea*. Others will act as excuses or justifications, as is the case with self-defence (see further Chapter 10).

For the mentally ill defendant charged with murder there was, before 1957, little to choose from by way of defences other than insanity. As will be seen (see below, 10.1) insanity is very limited in its scope, being available only to those who are unaware of their actions as a result of a disease of the mind, or those who, for the same reason, do not realise their actions are contrary to the criminal law. It is a hallmark of a mature and sophisticated criminal justice system that the rules of criminal liability enable a court to deal fairly with a defendant who is not in full control of his actions. Prior to 1957 a defendant who, though aware of his actions, killed because of some irresistible urge symptomatic of mental illness, would have had no obvious defence to a charge of murder. If the fact that the death penalty was still available as a punishment for murder is taken into account, the unsatisfactory nature of the law at that time becomes even more apparent.

In order to provide a partial defence to such defendants, parliament enacted s 2(1) of the HA 1957, which states:

> Where a person kills or is party to the killing of another, he shall not be convicted of murder if he was suffering from such abnormality of mind (whether arising from a condition of arrested or retarded development of mind or any inherent causes or induced by disease or injury) as substantially impaired his mental responsibility for his acts and omissions in doing or being a party to the killing.

The effect of this defence succeeding, as is the case with provocation, is that the defendant's liability is reduced from murder to manslaughter. The defence is only available where death actually occurs; hence, it is not a defence to a charge of attempted murder (see *Campbell* [1997] 1 Cr App R 1). As s 291 itself provides, it is available to a defendant charged with murder as a principal offender, or as an accessory.

In *Chambers* [1983] Crim LR 688, Leonard J outlined the sentencing options open to a judge in cases of diminished responsibility:

> His choice of the right course will depend on the state of the evidence and the material before him. If the psychiatric reports recommend and justify it, and there are no contrary indications, he will make a hospital order ... [if] the defendant constitutes a danger to the public for an unpredictable period of time, the right sentence will, in all probabilities, be one of life imprisonment ... In cases where the evidence indicates that the accused's responsibility for his acts was so grossly impaired that his degree of responsibility for them was minimal, then a lenient course will be open to the judge. Providing there is no danger of repetition of violence, it will usually be possible to make such order as will give the accused his freedom, possibly with some supervision ... There will however be cases in which there is no proper basis for a hospital order; but in which the accused's degree of responsibility is not minimal. In such cases the judge should pass a determinate sentence of imprisonment ...

Section 2(2) of the Homicide Act 1957 places the burden of proof upon the defence. *Dunbar* [1958] 1 QB 1 decides that the appropriate test is that of the balance of probabilities. At the centre of the defence is the concept of abnormality of mind, which was commented upon by Lord Parker CJ in *Byrne* [1960] 2 QB 396 in the following terms:

> [An abnormality of the mind is] a state of mind so different from that of ordinary human beings that the reasonable man would term it abnormal. It appears to be wide enough to cover the mind's activities in all its aspects, not only the perception of physical acts and matters, and the ability to form rational judgment as to whether an act is right or wrong, but also the ability to exercise will power to control physical acts in accordance with that rational judgment.

Lord Parker went on to point out that once the jury considers it more likely than not that the accused is suffering from an abnormality of mind, the crucial question is whether the abnormality was such as to substantially impair his mental responsibility for his acts. That is going to be a question of degree and for the jury to determine. Byrne was a sexual psychopath who had killed a young woman at the

YWCA in Birmingham and then mutilated her body. It was not disputed by the medical witnesses that he suffered from an abnormality of mind, the manifestation of which was that he suffered from violent perverted sexual desires that had proved impossible to control. The trial judge was held to have been wrong to withdraw the issue of diminished responsibility from the jury.

Without adequate direction, juries may be somewhat confused as to the distinction between an abnormality of mind and a disease of the mind, a vital ingredient in relation to the *M'Naghten* Rules and the defence of insanity. It must, however, be stressed that the defence of diminished responsibility has largely replaced the defence of insanity in cases of murder. The Court of Appeal held in *Brown* [1993] Crim LR 961 that it was 'generally desirable' for judges to supplement the statutory definition and refer to aspects of the 'mind' such as perception, understanding, judgment and will. It will be recalled that in *Sullivan* [1983] 2 All ER 673 the House of Lords ruled that the word 'mind' should be used in the 'ordinary' sense of 'reason, memory and understanding'. There would appear to be no reason why this 'definition' should not suffice for a plea of diminished responsibility. As with insanity, the final decision is not a medical but a legal one and there is no specific requirement that medical evidence needs to be adduced, as it does with the insanity defence. However, it is unlikely that juries would wish to agree that the accused is suffering from an abnormality of mind without some medical evidence to support their conclusions.

6.4.1   Intoxication and diminished responsibility

Section 2 of the HA 1957 requires that the diminished responsibility must result from one or more of the following:

* arrested or retarded development of mind;
* any inherent causes;
* disease or injury.

The Court of Appeal has considered the interrelationship between intoxication and the special defence in two cases, *Tandy* [1989] 1 All ER 267 and *Egan* [1992] 4 All ER 470. In *Tandy*, the appellant had killed her daughter. She was an alcoholic and the Court of Appeal confirmed that for drink to produce an abnormality of mind, the:

> ... alcoholism had to have reached such a level that the accused's brain was damaged so that there was gross impairment of his judgment and emotional responses or the craving had to be such as to render the accused's use of drink involuntary because he was no longer able to resist the impulse to drink.

If, as in this case, the accused had simply not resisted an impulse to drink she could not rely on the defence of diminished responsibility. The taking of her first drink was not an involuntary action. Three elements need to be established. First, that the accused must have been suffering from an abnormality of mind at the time of the act which resulted in death; secondly, that the abnormality was induced by disease, namely alcoholism; and, thirdly, that the abnormality of mind induced by the alcoholism was such as substantially impaired her mental responsibility for her act of strangling her daughter. The evidence had to prove that she was a chronic alcoholic if the second element was to be established. This means that there would need to be gross impairment of judgment and emotional responses and some evidence of brain damage. However, if brain damage could not be shown then providing that 'the appellant's drinking had become involuntary ... she was no longer able to resist the impulse to drink', then the defence would still be available to a defendant. It follows that, if the act of drinking is involuntary, then, in the absence of any other reason, the alcoholism must be the cause of the abnormality of mind. The evidence of the accused clearly indicated that she was capable of exercising some degree of control over her actions even after she had consumed her first drink.

In *Egan*, the defendant admitted that he had drunk 15 pints of beer and several gin and tonics before killing a 79-year-old widow. Medical evidence showed that he suffered from an abnormality of mind by reason of arrested or retarded development and intellectual impairment, with possibly a psychopathic disorder. His psychological problem was permanent, the intoxication relevant only to the night in question; he was not an alcoholic. The questions for the jury, ignoring the intoxication, were whether he would have killed as he did and whether he would have done so as a result of diminished responsibility. He was convicted of murder and his conviction was upheld by the Court of Appeal. The jury presumably decided that his diminished responsibility was not of such an extent that it substantially impaired his responsibility for the killing. 'Substantial' was to be approached in a 'broad common sense way' and 'substantial' meant more than:

> ... some trivial degree of impairment which does not make any appreciable difference to a person's ability to control himself, but it means less than total impairment.

These directions were taken from *Lloyd* [1966] 1 All ER 107 and were specifically approved by the Court of Appeal in *Egan*. The court referred to the 'troublesome' subject of diminished responsibility where drink was a factor. The cases of *Gittens* [1984] 3 All ER 252 and *Atkinson* [1985] Crim LR 314 were cited as 'high authority' on the subject. In *Gittens*, the appellant suffered from depression for which he received medical treatment. His wife 'preferred the company of another man to that of her husband' and no doubt this factor contributed to his depression. On the night in question, he drank to excess and also took some tablets that had been prescribed for him. In the early hours of the morning a violent argument ensued which resulted in him clubbing his wife to death. He then attacked, raped and strangled his stepdaughter. He was convicted of murder and appealed on the basis of a misdirection as to diminished responsibility. In allowing his appeal, the court referred to the fact that an abnormality of mind induced by alcohol or drugs is not generally speaking due to inherent causes and therefore does not fall to be considered within the terms of the section. The jury had been invited to consider whether the substantial cause of his behaviour was inherent causes or the alcohol or drugs. It was conceivable that if properly directed the jury would have reached the conclusion that drink, drugs and inherent causes all contributed to the abnormality of mind. In *Atkinson*, the court adopted Professor John Smith's analysis of *Gittens* contained in his commentary to the *Criminal Law Review* report ([1984] Crim LR 553) to the effect that, if a defendant had not taken drink:

- would he have killed as he in fact did?; and
- would he have been under diminished responsibility when he did so?

Egan also approved of this direction. Read together with *Tandy* this appears to suggest that if a defendant acted as he did because of drink then intoxication would be the appropriate defence to a murder charge. If the drink had been consumed involuntarily because the defendant is an alcoholic, then the jury is entitled to conclude that the defendant acted under diminished responsibility.

6.4.2 Provocation and diminished responsibility

It has long been recognised that an accused charged with murder might seek to raise the defences of provocation and diminished responsibility in tandem. Either defence, if made out, would have the effect of reducing the accused's liability to manslaughter. For many years, it was thought that the defences might, to some extent, be seen as mutually exclusive, in so much as diminished responsibility was based on a mental abnormality that resulted in an impairment of the accused's self-control, whereas in provocation, the question was whether a sane reasonable person would have been provoked to kill as the accused did.

In his seminal article, 'The doctrine of provocation' ([1976] CLJ 292), Professor Ashworth, observed that, although the conventional wisdom supported the 'mutually exclusive' view, it was nevertheless 'difficult to shed all one's misgivings about whether the law actually operates in this way'.

As outlined above, at 6.3.4, however, during the latter years of the 20th century, the Court of Appeal began to recognise that evidence of mental peculiarities could be relevant for both defences. Hence, in *Thornton (No 2)*, evidence that the accused had been suffering from battered woman syndrome at the time she killed was seen as a factor to be taken into account in assessing the reasonableness of her actions. In *Ahluwalia*, the appeal was allowed and a retrial ordered because diminished responsibility had not been raised at the defendant's trial despite medical evidence available at the time, which indicated that she suffered from endogenous depression when the act was committed. In *Hobson* [1998] 1 Cr App R 31, the Court of Appeal accepted that battered woman syndrome could provide a basis for the defence of diminished responsibility, not least because, since 1994, it had been included in the British classification of mental diseases recognised by the psychiatric profession.

Both *Humphreys* (accused suffering from 'abnormal mentality, with immature, explosive and attention seeking traits [such as] ... her tendency to slash her wrists') and *Dryden* ('eccentric and obsessional personality traits, a depressive illness and paranoid thinking') are cases where the evidence of mental abnormality could clearly have formed the basis of a plea of diminished responsibility, yet they are both cases where the Court of Appeal accepted that provocation could be put forward.

Lord Goff, in *Luc Thiet Thuan*, was fiercely critical of this development, observing that it cannot have been the intention of parliament, in creating a new defence of diminished responsibility in s 2 of the HA 1957, that there should be such an overlap between the statutory defence and provocation. As he argued:

> If diminished responsibility was held to form part of the law of provocation, the extraordinary result would follow that a defendant who failed to establish diminished responsibility on the burden of proof placed upon him by [s 2 of the HA] might nevertheless be able to succeed on the defence of provocation ... on the basis that, on precisely the same evidence, the prosecution had failed to negative, on the criminal burden, that he was suffering from a mental infirmity affecting his self-control which must be attributed to the reasonable man for the purposes of the objective test.

As has been seen from the subsequent House of Lords' decision in *Smith (Morgan)*, the reasonable man test has now effectively been abandoned, in favour of an inquiry into whether the accused displayed what was (for him) a reasonable degree of self-control. This is likely to have the effect of blurring still further the distinction between the two defences. Lord Hoffman appeared to admit as much when, in the course of his speech in *Smith (Morgan)*, he observed that:

> The boundary between the normal and abnormal is very often a matter of opinion. Some people are entirely normal in most respects and behave unusually in others. There are people (such as battered wives) who would reject any suggestion that they were 'different from ordinary human beings' but have undergone experiences which, without any fault or defect of character on their part, have affected their powers of self-control. In such cases the law now recognises that the emotions which may cause loss of self-control are not confined to anger but may include fear and despair ...

His view that, for example, abused wives should not have to plead that they are mentally abnormal in order to gain the protective shield of a defence in criminal law may be welcomed in many quarters, but it has to be asked whether, as Lord Millett put it in *Smith (Morgan)*, the objective element of provocation has been 'eroded and its moral basis subverted' in order to provide a defence of diminished responsibility wider than that intended by parliament. It is significant to note that the accused in *Smith (Morgan)* only sought to rely on provocation because the jury, having heard the evidence and having been properly directed upon the requirements under s 2 of the HA 1957, rejected the defence.

6.4.3   Reform of diminished responsibility

Consideration should also be given to the draft Criminal Code. Clause 56 covers diminished responsibility:

(1) A person who, but for this section, would be guilty of murder is not guilty of murder if, at the time of his act, he is suffering from such mental abnormality as is a substantial enough reason to reduce his offence to manslaughter.

(2) Mental abnormality means mental illness, arrested or incomplete development of mind, psychopathic disorder, and any other disorder or disability of mind, except intoxication.

(3) Where a person suffering from mental abnormality is also intoxicated, this section applies only where it would apply if he were not intoxicated.

The definition of mental abnormality proposed by the Law Commission follows word for word the definition of mental disorder to be found in s 1(2) of the Mental Health Act 1983. It will be noted that intoxication is excluded. The clause also makes it clear to a jury that the relevant time to consider diminished responsibility is at the time of the act and not the time of the trial.

6.5   OTHER FORMS OF VOLUNTARY MANSLAUGHTER

To complete the picture of voluntary manslaughter, it should be noted that there are two other defences that can be raised only by way of defence to a murder charge each of which, if successful, will reduce the defendant's liability to manslaughter. These defences are suicide pact and infanticide.

6.5.1 Suicide pact

Section 4(1) of the HA 1957 provides:

> It shall be manslaughter and shall not be murder for a person acting in pursuance of a suicide pact between him and another to kill the other or be party to the other being killed by a third person.

A suicide pact is defined by s 4(3) as a 'common agreement between two or more persons having for its object the death of all of them, whether or not each is to take his own life'.

It follows that for there to be an 'agreement' or 'pact' the parties must have a 'settled intention of dying in pursuance of the pact'. Section 4(2) places the onus on the defence to prove that the killing was carried out in pursuance of a suicide pact.

6.5.2 Infanticide

Section 1 of the Infanticide Act (IA) 1938 makes it an offence for a woman '... by any wilful act or omission (to cause) the death of her child being a child under the age of 12 months ...'.

The section goes on to indicate that, if, at the time of the act or omission, the balance of her mind was disturbed by reason of her not having fully recovered from the effect of giving birth or by reason of lactation consequent upon the birth, then what would appear at first sight to be murder will be treated as infanticide and, if convicted, she will be punished as though found guilty of manslaughter.

The limitations established by s 1 of the IA 1938 are:

- the benefit of the section is applicable only to the mother;
- it applies only if she causes the death of her child – if it is caused by anyone else then the charge will be murder or manslaughter depending on the intent although diminished responsibility might be an appropriate defence in such circumstances. The section is so phrased to suggest that it is the child to whom the mother has given birth that must be the victim.

  If she kills another child of her family then infanticide would appear not to be a defence;
- the child in question must be under 12 months old;
- the balance of the mother's mind must be disturbed by reason of the effect of giving birth or by reason of lactation consequent upon giving birth;
- if the balance of her mind is not disturbed and she kills, the charge will be murder;
- if the child is killed by someone other than the mother, the IA 1938 will not apply.

The Butler Committee on Mentally Abnormal Offenders recognised that, in 1938, the defence of diminished responsibility had not been created and expressed the view that this would now cover killing in such circumstances as described in s 1.

However, the Law Commission's draft Criminal Code recommends retention of the defence, albeit in a modified form. Clause 64(1) states:

> A woman who, but for this section, would be guilty of murder or manslaughter of her child is not guilty of murder or manslaughter, but is guilty of infanticide, if her act is done when the child is under the age of 12 months and when the balance of her mind is disturbed by reason of the effect of giving birth or of circumstances consequent upon birth.

The scope of the defence is thus broadened and can include circumstances, other than lactation, which caused the mother to kill. It has been suggested that social conditions, poverty or family pressures will be covered by the reference to circumstances but this may prove unacceptable to many people.

Support for this approach comes from RD Mackay in his research study, 'The consequences of killing very young children' ([1993] Crim LR 21). He concludes by stating:

> ... [the study] ... lends no support to the fact that diminished responsibility is either being widely used in cases which might otherwise be infanticide or that as it stands the Homicide Act 1957 would safely cover all the cases which presently fall within the IA 1938 ... if the lenient sentences which women receive when convicted under the IA 1938 are to be ensured then there appears to be a continued need for a separate offence of infanticide and cl 64 of the draft Criminal Code Bill seems an appropriate vehicle to secure this.

6.6 INVOLUNTARY MANSLAUGHTER

The term involuntary manslaughter is used to denote those unlawful killings where D has caused the death of the victim but did not have the *mens rea* for murder when doing so. For example, D might punch P in the face intending to do P actual bodily harm. If by some mischance P should suffer a brain haemorrhage and die as a result of this attack, D would be charged with manslaughter, as there is no evidence that he intended grievous bodily harm. It should not be assumed, however, that D has to be engaged in an unlawful activity in order for liability for manslaughter to arise. As will be seen below there are at least two formulations of involuntary manslaughter. Whilst the 'unlawful act' formulation requires proof that D committed a crime that caused the death of P, the alternative formulation, killing by gross negligence, simply requires proof that D performed an otherwise lawful activity so negligently (death resulting therefrom) that he deserves to be convicted of manslaughter.

6.6.1 Elements of unlawful act manslaughter

Unlawful act manslaughter has proved to be a very difficult offence to define – not least because of the variety of fact situations that can give rise to liability. The House of Lords struggled with this difficulty in *Newbury and Jones* [1976] 2 All ER 365, a case involving appellants who had stood on the parapet of a bridge which straddled a railway line and pushed a piece of paving stone over the parapet onto the front of the train. The ensuing impact with the train led to the death of the guard. Lord Salmon expressed the view that an accused was guilty of manslaughter if it was proved that he intentionally did an act, which was unlawful and dangerous, and that that act inadvertently caused death. It was, he said, unnecessary to prove that the accused knew that the act was unlawful or dangerous.

Liability for unlawful act manslaughter, as the name of the offence suggests, must be based on proof that D performed an act. An omission will not suffice. This much is confirmed by *Lowe* [1973] 2 WLR 481, where the accused had neglected his child and as a result caused death. He had clearly committed an offence under the Children and Young Persons Act (CYPA) 1933 but this was held not to be sufficient to establish a basis for a manslaughter conviction. Although *Sheppard* [1980] 3 All ER 899 overruled *Lowe*, which had treated the offence under the CYPA 1933 as one of strict liability, the wider principle appears to have survived unscathed. It is difficult to comprehend why a deliberate failure to act should be treated differently from an act of commission if the consequences are exactly the same. The failure to feed a child is clearly an unlawful act and if persisted in over a period of time can be every bit as devastating to the child as a positive course of conduct. However, if the conduct of a parent amounts to gross negligence, then a manslaughter charge will lie via that route rather than constructive manslaughter.

In *Khan (Rungzabe)* [1998] Crim LR 830, the Court of Appeal allowed an appeal against a conviction for manslaughter where the appellant had supplied heroin to a 15-year-old who subsequently died of an overdose. The court noted that it viewed the case as one of causing death by omission (effectively failing to supervise the deceased), and thus only liability for killing by gross negligence could arise. As the trial judge had not directed the jury on this issue the conviction could not stand (see further below, 6.6.3).

The act that causes death must be criminal. A tortious act alone will not suffice. The basis for this restriction can be traced back to 19th century cases such as *Franklin* (1883) 16 Cox CC 153, where it was held that criminal liability should not flow from the 'mere fact of a civil wrong'. In that case, the defendant was standing on West Pier at Brighton and threw a large box that he had removed from a refreshment stall over the side. It struck the victim who was swimming near the pier causing his death. The court regarded a civil wrong, trespass, against the stallholder as immaterial and the case was put to the jury on the broad ground of negligence.

In some cases, such as *Newbury and Jones*, it may not be immediately apparent what constituted the unlawful act. Workmen had left the paving stone on the parapet of a railway bridge. There can be no doubt that the defendants, who were aged 15, pushed it over the parapet, as a train was passing underneath. The case proceeded on the basis that they had committed an unlawful act but it is not obvious exactly what it was, unless it was the act of dropping the stone. But, if this act is viewed as a property offence, then one must question whether or not that should be sufficient foundation for the result. Criminal damage to the stone or the train is a more obvious candidate. Breach of various railway bye-laws might also have been a basis for liability.

A number of subsequent cases illustrate this difficulty. In *Cato* [1976] 1 All ER 260, death resulted from the appellant's act of injecting the deceased with a mixture of heroin and water, albeit with the deceased's approval. The jury convicted on two counts: manslaughter and under s 23 of the Offences Against the Person Act (OAPA) 1861, of 'unlawfully and maliciously administering a noxious thing so as to endanger the life of another person'. Lord Widgery CJ, in dealing with the issue of what conduct amounted to an unlawful act, thought that it was possible to 'rely on the charge under s 23 of the OAPA 1861'. Nevertheless he went on to comment that if one ignored s 23:

> ... we think there would have been an unlawful act here, and we think the unlawful act would be described as injecting the deceased Farmer with a mixture of heroin and water which at the time of the injection and for the purposes of the injection Cato had unlawfully taken into his possession.

This suggests that the possession of heroin supplies the necessary quality of unlawfulness whilst the administration of the heroin is the act. The combination of the two factors led to the conclusion that an unlawful act has been committed. It is submitted that the word 'unlawful' qualifies the act and that possession alone does not establish that the act was unlawful for the purposes of the crime of manslaughter.

In *Arobieke* [1988] Crim LR 314, the accused (A) had gone to a railway station looking for P. There had been animosity between A and P, and the latter, having seen A at the station, assumed that he was under potential threat of harm, left his train and was electrocuted trying to cross the tracks. There was no evidence that A had issued any threats or that, as a result of his demeanour, P could have naturally assumed that he was at risk. The court in allowing his appeal against conviction for manslaughter thought there was insufficient evidence for the jury to conclude that an assault had been committed. One might conclude that A's presence at the station, together with the knowledge that P was also present was only a preparatory act and, as such, insufficient conduct to establish the *actus reus* for an attempted assault or battery. Finally, in *Jennings* [1990] Crim LR 588, the victim tried to restrain his brother who was carrying a sheath knife and in so doing was stabbed. Jennings was charged with manslaughter by unlawful act. The Crown argued that the offence of carrying an offensive weapon contrary to s 1 of the Prevention of Crime Act 1953 was such an unlawful act. It was held that the knife was not an offensive weapon *per se*. Therefore, to walk down a street with a knife in hand was not a criminal offence unless he had the intention of using it to inflict injury. Therefore, there was nothing that could constitute an unlawful act for the purposes of manslaughter.

Even if it is established that a criminal act has caused the victim's death, liability for unlawful act manslaughter cannot arise unless it is proved that the act in question was 'dangerous'. Edmund-Davies J in *Church* [1966] 2 All ER 72 thought that it was not enough to tell a jury that whenever any unlawful act is committed that results in death a manslaughter verdict must inexorably follow. For such a verdict to result, the 'unlawful act must be such as all sober and reasonable people would inevitably recognise must subject the other person to, at least, the risk of some harm resulting therefrom, albeit not serious harm'.

The test is clearly based upon an objective assessment of the circumstances. For example, what conclusions might a reasonable person be expected to reach about the impact of a burglary, late at night, where the occupant of the property is not far short of his 90th birthday? If it is to be reasonably expected that he has a weak heart, or is in poor health, then the act of burglary immediately becomes a dangerous act. If, however, the reasonable person would not suspect that the householder might react in such a way as to put his life at risk, then a manslaughter conviction is unlikely to be secured, on the basis that the act is not a dangerous one. If one sets this against the *dictum* of Edmund-Davies J it would certainly be possible to sustain an argument that all burglaries are inherently dangerous in the sense that some harm, albeit not serious harm, could result to anyone who happens to be in the property at the time of the entry. Should the assessment include reference to the knowledge possessed by the accused before entering the property? If the house was thought to be empty and that was a reasonable conclusion to reach, then in such circumstances the act of burglary is not dangerous, as there is no risk of harm to the person.

Lord Salmon in *Newbury* had no doubt that the test remained objective: '... the test is not did the accused recognise that it was dangerous but would all sober and reasonable people recognise its danger.'

These issues were vividly illustrated in *Watson* [1989] 2 All ER 865 and *Dawson* (1985) 81 Cr App R 150. In the former case the 87-year-old occupier was confronted late at night by two men who had broken into his property by throwing a brick through a window. Unknown to the accused, the victim suffered from a serious heart condition and died some 90 minutes later from a heart attack. The Crown maintained this was a direct consequence of his property being invaded. The Court of Appeal treated the burglary as an ongoing event during which the accused were gathering knowledge and information about the victim. During the course of the burglary, they and therefore the reasonable person would have become aware of his frailty, albeit they may not have possessed such knowledge at the outset of the venture. In *Dawson*, the defendant and accomplices had attempted to rob the victim who was an attendant at a petrol filling station. He suffered from a diseased heart, a fact unknown to the men. They had pointed a replica gun at him, banged a pickaxe handle on the counter and demanded money. One man wore a balaclava. The victim died within an hour of the attempted robbery. The Court of Appeal allowed their appeals against conviction for manslaughter. All sober and reasonable people might realise that such an attack would cause some fear or apprehension, perhaps even terror, to be felt by the victim but would surely not foresee some harm being occasioned without knowledge of the victim's vulnerability. It is suggested, as a result of *Dawson*, that the reasonable person in such circumstances must foresee the risk that the shock or terror would result in physical injury before the act is classed as 'dangerous'. It is perhaps worth emphasising that the unlawful act must be a significant cause of death. In this case, one answer might be the fact that his medical condition was poor and that a heart attack might be brought on at any moment. Conversely, the victim might still be alive today if he had not been confronted by a gang of thugs intent upon robbery. There is an apparent clash with the causation principle that the defendant must take the victim as he finds him, but it should be borne in mind that the rule in *Blaue* [1975] 3 All ER 446 relates to whether or not the actions of the victim break the chain of causation, not whether or not the defendant's actions are dangerous.

The *mens rea* for unlawful act manslaughter is often referred to in terms suggesting that the defendant must have acted intentionally in committing the unlawful act that causes death (see *DPP v Newbury and Jones*). Whilst it is clear that, in order to have the necessary *mens rea*, the defendant does not need to have foreseen death at all, it begs the question as to whether or not he must have had the intention to commit the *actus reus* of the unlawful act in the *Woollin* sense (see Chapter 3 at 3.3.3.4). Alternatively, does he simply have to have had the *mens rea* for the unlawful act in question? The question is important because if the death of the victim results from criminal damage committed by the defendant, there is a huge difference between trying to prove that the defendant intended to commit criminal damage and proving that the defendant was *Caldwell* reckless in causing the criminal damage.

Lord Hope, in *Attorney General's Reference (No 3 of 1994)* [1997] 3 All ER 936, was also somewhat vague in expressing the view that in cases of unlawful act manslaughter the defendant:

> ... must be proved to have intended to do what he did, it is not necessary to prove that he knew that his act was unlawful or dangerous ... it is unnecessary to prove that he knew that his act was likely to injure the person who died as a result of it. All that need be proved is that he intentionally did what he did ...

It is submitted that the better approach is to require proof that the defendant had the *mens rea* required for the unlawful act. The decision in *Lamb* [1968] 2 All ER 1282 is illustrative here. Two young men were playing with a revolver. They knew there were two bullets in the chambers and that neither was opposite the barrel. As a joke Lamb pointed the gun at the other who also treated the incident as a joke. The gun detonated and the friend was killed. One could start by asking whether, on these facts, there was an unlawful and dangerous act. If the friend never feared any physical violence – believing that the gun would not fire – the *actus reus* of narrow assault was not made out. Where the victim was struck by the bullet a battery no doubt occurred, but the action in pulling the trigger would still have to be one that the reasonable sober person would regard as dangerous in the *Dawson* sense. If the defendant was ignorant as to the operation of the gun's revolver mechanism, perhaps the reasonable person at the scene would be deemed to be similarly ignorant? As to *mens rea*, since Lamb did not realise that the chamber would revolve when he pulled the trigger, thus enabling the gun to fire, he had no intention to commit a battery, hence no *mens rea* for the unlawful act. Lamb escaped liability on the basis that the *mens rea* was absent. Similarly, in *Scarlett* [1993] 4 All ER 629, the court, in allowing the appeal, stressed that a defendant should be guilty of an assault only if it is proved that he had acted with the mental element necessary to constitute his action as an assault, that is, 'that the defendant intentionally or recklessly applied force to the person of another'. On this basis juries ought perhaps to be directed that the prosecution must prove that the defendant acted with the *mens rea* required for the unlawful act alleged to have caused death.

6.6.2 Elements of killing by gross negligence

As indicated above, killing by gross negligence offers the prosecution an alternative basis for alleging involuntary manslaughter. Unlike unlawful act manslaughter, there is no need to show that D was engaged in a criminal act when he caused P's death. The rationale for liability is that D has performed a *per se* lawful act so negligently, his acts or omissions that lead to P's death deserve to be labelled criminal. This lawful activity might, for example, be the provision of medical treatment, the installation of a gas fire, the repair of a central heating boiler, the provision of a sponsored 'bungee-jumping' session, or the supervision of swimming lessons. Any such activity can, if done badly enough, result in death. Compensation for dependants can, of course, be obtained by pursuing a civil action for negligence. A criminal prosecution will be initiated where the prosecuting authorities take the view that it is in the public interest to do so. The public interest for these purposes is that the person who causes the death is 'labelled' as a criminal, and criminal sanctions can be imposed, both to punish the defendant and to serve as a warning to others. It is identifying the line that divides the 'merely tortious' from the 'truly criminal' that gives rise to many difficulties in this area.

Older cases such as *Bateman* [1925] 94 LJ ICB 791 show how this form of manslaughter was closely associated with incompetence on the part of medical practitioners. As Lord Hewart CJ observed:

> ... in order to establish criminal liability the facts must be such that, in the opinion of the jury, the negligence or incompetence of the accused went beyond a mere matter of compensation between subjects and showed such disregard for the life and safety of others as to amount to a crime against the State and conduct deserving punishment.

This statement, although open to criticism on the basis that it leaves matters of law to the jury, does emphasise that conduct sufficient only to establish negligence in civil law will never suffice in criminal law. Referring to the distinction between civil and criminal negligence, Lord Atkin in *Andrews v DPP* [1937] AC 576, commented that, for the purposes of the criminal law there are degrees of negligence, and a very high degree of negligence would be required before criminal liability could be established. The leading case is now the House of Lords' decision in *Adomako* [1994] 3 All ER 79. The appellant was the anaesthetist at an operation when he failed to notice that an endotracheal tube had become disconnected from the ventilator supplying oxygen to the patient. As a result, the patient suffered a cardiac arrest and subsequently died. The time between the disconnection occurring and the appellant noticing that this was the cause of the problem was some six minutes. He was charged with manslaughter and his appeal to the House of Lords was dismissed. Lord Mackay identified a number of key steps to establishing liability the prosecution had to prove:

- a duty of care owed by D to P;
- a breach of that duty of care in circumstances where D's act or omission created a risk of death;
- that the breach of duty caused the death of P; and
- negligence on the part of D that was culpable it warranted being labelled as criminal.

Note that, unlike unlawful act manslaughter, killing by gross negligence can be caused by the defendant's failure to act; consider *Stone and Dobinson* [1977] 2 All ER 341 as an example.

6.6.3 Establishing a duty of care

There has been some debate as to whether the tortious concept of duty of care can simply be transplanted to criminal law as a basis for liability in cases of alleged killing by gross negligence. *Adomako* itself is not helpful on this point as no one would seriously doubt that a medical practitioner owed a duty of care to a patient. In *Khan (Rungzabe)*, Swinton Thomas LJ left open the question of whether a supplier of heroin owed any duty of care to the 15-year-old recipient of the drug, not least because the matter had not been fully argued at first instance. Perhaps more encouraging was the approach taken by the Court of Appeal in *Singh* [1999]

Crim LR 582, where it was held that both the gas-fitter who had incompetently installed a gas fire, and the son of the landlord who had overseen the work, owed a duty of care to a tenant who subsequently died of carbon monoxide poisoning. Although the landlord's son had not personally installed the appliance, the court found that, as a result of his close involvement in the running of the properties owned by his father, he was aware of the need to ensure that gas fires were properly installed. On this basis, it was held that there was sufficient proximity for a duty of care to arise.

Sybil Sharpe, in her article 'Grossly negligent manslaughter after *Adomako*' ((1994) 158 JP 725), maintains that 'the tortious and criminal duty of care may not necessarily be coextensive'. This point was taken up by the Law Commission in its consultation paper, *Involuntary Manslaughter* (Law Com 135, 1994), where the point is made that 'negligence' in the manslaughter context means nothing more than 'carelessness'. The Law Commission report, *Legislating the Criminal Code: Involuntary Manslaughter* (Law Com 237, 1996, para 3.11), was of the view that 'it does not carry the technical meaning that it has in the law of tort, where it depends on the existence of a duty of care owed and a breach of that duty'. In the majority of situations, this should not create many problems because the conduct of the accused would be deemed to be 'bad' irrespective of which test was applied. However, the position in respect of omissions could be more problematic. In Chapter 2, it was stated that in criminal law there is no general rule that imposes upon any citizen a duty to act (see, for example, Ashworth, 'The scope of criminal liability for omissions' (1989) 105 LQR 424). Yet certain cases have outlined circumstances when it would appear there is a duty to act; the most controversial being that of *Stone and Dobinson*. If, having voluntarily assumed responsibility for the welfare of an elderly mentally incapacitated relative, the care provided is inadequate and as a result that person dies, a conviction for manslaughter is a distinct possibility. Examined from a tortious viewpoint, it is by no means certain that liability would ensue unless death had arisen through the carer's incompetence (see above, 2.5.1).

The question is: has the decision in *Adomako* changed the criminal law in respect of omissions and brought it into line with tortious principles? If the answer is yes, then it is possible that *Stone and Dobinson* no longer represents the law on manslaughter by omission. The Law Commission is clear in its conclusions:

> The law on this subject is so unclear that it is difficult to tell whether the effect of Lord Mackay's speech was indeed to change the law, and, if so, what the implications of this change might be. It is, however, clear that the terminology of 'negligence' and 'duty of care' is best avoided within the criminal law, because of the uncertainty and confusion that surround it [para 3.13].

In *R v Wacker* [2002] Crim LR 839, the defendant was convicted of killing by gross negligence after 58 illegal immigrants had died in the chilled storage compartment of his lorry. The victims had been concealed behind a consignment of tomatoes and in order not to arouse suspicion at border points the air vents had been shut. The victims died of asphyxiation. One of the points argued on behalf of the appellant at his appeal was that, since both he and the illegal immigrants had been involved in a joint unlawful enterprise, he had not owed them a duty of care. In civil law the doctrine of *ex turpi causa non oritur actio* provides that the law of negligence will not recognise the relationship between those involved in a criminal enterprise as giving rise to a duty of care. Rejecting this submission, Kay LJ explained that the criminal law did not necessarily follow the concepts developed in civil law. Hence, in civil law if D sold a harmless substance to P pretending it to be an unlawful dangerous drug, D could not be sued for breach of contract, whereas in criminal law D could be charged with obtaining property by deception. As he explained, the difference in approach reflects public policy preferences:

> The criminal law has as its function the protection of citizens and gives effect to the state's duty to try those who have deprived citizens of their rights of life, limb or property. It may very well step in at the precise moment when civil courts withdraw because of this very different function. The withdrawal of a civil remedy has nothing to do with whether as a matter of public policy the criminal law applies ... [f]urther the criminal law will not hesitate to act to prevent serious injury or death even when the persons subjected to such injury or death may have consented to or willingly accepted the risk of actual injury or death.

Kay LJ favours an approach that asks whether or not it is possible or appropriate to determine the extent of a duty of care. If it is, then normally the courts should recognise that duty. On the facts that gave rise to the appeal, for example, he was in no doubt that the appellant had voluntarily assumed a duty of care for the illegal immigrants hidden in his lorry. Certainly Kennedy LJ, in *Lewin v CPS* [2002] EWHC 1049, was happy to conclude that establishing the duty of care required for the imposition of liability for manslaughter by gross negligence should be undertaken by reference to the ordinary principles of the law of negligence. He spoke of a duty of care persisting in circumstances where a reasonable person would have foreseen that the appellant's actions or omission exposed the deceased to the risk, not merely of injury or even of serious injury, but of death.

6.6.4 When is negligence 'gross'?

The obvious weakness in Lord Mackay's formulation of gross negligence, and indeed one that he himself adverted to, is its circularity. Juries are to be directed to convict if they believe the defendant's conduct 'criminal'. It will be recalled that Lord Mackay used the following words:

> The jury will have to consider whether the extent to which the defendant's conduct *departed from the proper standard of care incumbent upon him involving as it must have done a risk of death to the patient, was such that it should be judged criminal* [emphasis added].

As juries do not give reasons for their decisions, it will be impossible to ascertain upon what criteria the conduct has been judged. It is suggested that this will lead to uncertainty in the law and thus go against a fundamental principle of the criminal law that it must be certain in its application.

Would it assist a jury to give a direction in terms of recklessness, or at least comparing gross negligence with recklessness? As Lord Atkin, in *Andrews v DPP* observed, of all the epithets that could be applied 'reckless' most nearly covered the sense of what gross negligence involved. However, he added that it was probably not all embracing, as 'reckless' suggests an indifference to risk, whereas the accused may have appreciated the risk (and intended to avoid it), yet shown in the means adopted to avoid the risk such a degree of negligence as would justify a conviction. Lane LJ in *Stone*, having cited the above passage from *Andrews*, said:

It is clear from that passage that indifference to an obvious risk and appreciation of such risk, coupled with a determination nevertheless to run it, are both examples of recklessness.

It is submitted that it is in fact unnecessary for the trial judge to direct the jury to consider the defendant's state of mind. Negligence is a term used to describe a person's actions, not their thoughts. Whether that negligence is gross or not is simply a matter of degree. One of the issues the Court of Appeal was asked to rule upon in *Attorney General's Reference (No 2 of 1999)* [2000] 3 All ER 182, was whether or not a defendant could be convicted of manslaughter by gross negligence in the absence of evidence as to that defendant's state of mind? Confirming that this was the case, the court noted that, although there might be cases where the defendant's state of mind would be relevant to the jury's determination of the degree of negligence involved, direct evidence of his state of mind is not a prerequisite to a conviction for manslaughter by gross negligence. Where a defendant was found by the jury to have been reckless in the sense in which that word was used in *Stone and Dobinson*, it might simply be easier for the jury to conclude that the gross negligence was criminal in its culpability. The danger in this approach is that juries do not embellish their verdicts. It would have to be left to the trial judge in passing sentence to decipher from the facts whether the case before the court was at the negligence end of the culpability scale, as opposed to being at the recklessness end. Presumably, cases involving evidence of advertent as opposed to inadvertent recklessness would attract the highest sentences for killing by gross negligence.

Bearing this last point in mind, it is submitted that, although there might still exist the technical possibility of a defendant being charged with a form of involuntary manslaughter that was referred to for a while as 'reckless manslaughter', the current state of the law makes such a charge unlikely (see further *Seymour* [1983] 2 All ER 1058 and *Kong Cheuk Kwan* (1985) 82 Cr App R 18).

It should also be noted that where D kills P whilst using a motor vehicle, the most likely charge (assuming there is no evidence of intention to kill or to do grievous bodily harm) will be one of causing death by reckless driving contrary to s 1 of the Road Traffic Act 1991. The offence does not require any *mens rea* in the conventional sense – the fault element lying simply in: (i) D driving or using a vehicle in a manner that, when looked at objectively, could be regarded as falling far below the standard to be expected of a competent and careful driver; and (ii) D doing so in circumstances where it would be obvious to the careful driver and competent driver that such driving would be dangerous. The offence carries the possibility of 10 years' imprisonment.

6.7 HOMICIDE AND THE UNBORN

As noted at the beginning of this chapter the offences of murder and manslaughter are concerned with situations where D causes the death of P, a live human being. Where D causes the death of a foetus *in utero*, the prosecution will rely upon offences of abortion (procuring a miscarriage) and/or child destruction.

6.7.1 Abortion offences

In English criminal law, the carrying out of an abortion is a criminal offence. This much is clear from the OAPA 1861. Section 58 makes it an offence to attempt to procure a miscarriage. Section 59 creates the offence of knowingly supplying the means for procuring a miscarriage. Liability arises regardless of whether or not the woman is pregnant, unless the defendant is a woman who has administered substances to herself, or used means upon herself, to procure the miscarriage.

There are two significant limitations on liability. The first is that the defendant procuring the miscarriage must act unlawfully. As *Bourne* [1939] 1 KB 687 makes it clear, a defendant acting in 'good faith' may escape liability. The defendant performed an operation terminating the pregnancy of a 14-year-old girl who had become pregnant as a result of a terrifying rape. The operation was performed with the consent of the child's parents, in a public hospital and no payment was made. Evidence was given by the doctor that he genuinely believed that the continuance of the pregnancy would probably cause serious injury to the girl and that he was acting to save the life of the mother. M'Naghten J took the view that the jury was entitled to conclude that the offence had not been committed, if the defendant believed 'that the probable consequence of the continuance of the pregnancy will be to make the woman a physical or mental wreck'. Ashworth J, in *Newton and Stungo* (1958) 1 BMJ 1242, also concluded that, when considering whether the act was done for the purpose of preserving the life of the mother, the impact on either physical or mental health or both could be taken into account. Preserving life has therefore been given a wider meaning than that of preserving the health, physical or mental, of the mother.

The second limitation is that the Abortion Act (AA) 1967 clearly provides doctors with a shield against prosecution under the 1861 Act, provided certain conditions are met, primarily that two or more doctors concur that the abortion can be justified in light of the threat that giving birth poses to the mother's mental or physical health.

Note that the offences created under the 1861 Act relate to causing the de-implantation of a fertilised ovum. No liability arises under that Act where steps are taken to prevent the fertilisation of an ovum or the implantation of a fertilised ovum. Hence inter-uterine methods of birth control and drugs such as the 'morning-after' pill fall outside the scope of the Act; see further *R (On the Application of Smeaton) v Secretary of State for Health* [2002] EWHC Admin 610.

6.7.2 Child destruction

A number of cases decided during the 19th century dealt with the question of whether or not murder or manslaughter had been committed where a baby was killed whilst the mother was in the process of giving birth. Clearly, if the child had become a human being a murder charge would have been appropriate. If the child was still to be regarded as a foetus a charge under s 58 of the 1861 Act would have been in order. In *Brain* (1834) 6 C & P 349, Park J thought that it was not essential (to support a murder charge) that the child should have taken its first breath prior to the act that caused its demise, reasoning that many children are born alive, 'yet do not breathe for some time after their birth'. *Senior* (1832) 1 Mood CC 346 would suggest that an attack on a child in the process of being born, even before it has breathed, will 'if the child is afterwards born alive, and dies thereof, and there is malice, be murder'.

Section 1(1) of the Infant Life (Preservation) Act (IL(P)A) 1929 creates the offence of child destruction and imposes criminal sanctions upon those who intentionally kill any child capable of being born alive. One aim of the legislation was to provide prosecutors with an offence that could be charged as an alternative to murder where a baby was killed in the course of being born. Note that the offence carries the possibility of life imprisonment. If the indictment contains two counts, one alleging murder and the other alleging child destruction, the issue of whether or not the victim was a human being at the time that death occurred becomes less crucial.

To the extent that the 1929 Act also provides a more serious form of the offence under s 58 of the 1861 Act (in that it deals with the destruction of what was a viable foetus), difficulties arise in determining at what point in the gestation process the law will accept that a child in the womb is capable of being born alive. This is a question of law for the judge, not an issue of fact for the jury. The Act creates a rebuttable presumption that a woman who has been pregnant for a minimum period of 28 weeks is carrying a child capable of being born alive. The 28-week criterion was imposed by parliament over 60 years ago and with advances in medical technology this requirement does not now accord with reality. The case of *C v S* [1987] 1 All ER 1230 addressed the issue in the context of a pregnancy of between 18 and 21 weeks. The mother wished to have an abortion and the father, who was not married to the mother, sought to prevent her by maintaining that a termination would breach the provisions of the 1929 Act. His contention was that a foetus of between 18 and 21 weeks was capable of being born alive because, to quote Sir John Donaldson's judgment:

> At that stage the cardiac muscle is contracting and a primitive circulation is developing. Thus the foetus could be said to demonstrate real and discernible signs of life.

The Court of Appeal concluded that a foetus at this stage of development 'would be incapable ever of breathing either naturally or with the aid of a ventilator', as the lungs would not be fully developed. Therefore, to abort at this stage would not amount to an offence under the IL(P)A 1929.

In *Rance v Mid Downs HA* [1991] 1 All ER 801, Brooke J was of the opinion:

> The anencephalic child (who lacks all or most of the cerebral hemispheres but is capable of using its lungs) and the spina bifida child ... is each born alive, if, after birth, it exists as a live child, that is to say breathing and living by reason of its breathing through its own lungs alone, without deriving any of its living or power of living by or through any connection with its mother. Once a foetus has reached that stage of development in the womb that it is capable, if born, of possessing those attributes, it is capable of being born alive within the meaning of the Infant Life (Preservation) Act 1929.

It was held that a child of 26–27 weeks' gestation, who could have breathed unaided for up to three hours, was, in law, capable of being born alive.

The AA 1967, as originally enacted, permitted abortion provided that the pregnancy had not extended beyond 24 weeks – the Act providing guidance as to when a pregnancy was deemed to have begun.

Although the AA 1967 expressly provides doctors with protection from prosecution under s 58 of the 1861 Act provided the conditions specified by the 1967 Act are met, it did not, as originally enacted, make clear that there would be any shield in respect of liability under the 1929 Act where a 'late' (that is post 28 weeks) abortion was carried out. The position has been clarified by amendments to the AA 1967 enacted by the Human Fertilisation and Embryology Act 1990. An offence under the 1929 Act will not be committed, providing the registered medical practitioner is terminating the pregnancy in accordance with the provisions of the AA 1967. Thus, if acting lawfully under the terms of that Act, a doctor causes the death of a child capable of being born alive, then the IL(P)A 1929 will not be breached. A jury may return a verdict of guilty of the offence under s 58 of the OAPA 1861 on an indictment for child destruction.

One further difficulty that should be considered here is that which arises where D attacks P, a pregnant woman, causing injuries to the foetus that cause the death of the child after P has given birth. Such was the legal problem considered by the House of Lords in *Attorney General's Reference (No 3 of 1994)*. The respondent had stabbed his girlfriend who, to his knowledge, was pregnant. As a direct consequence of the attack, the woman's uterus was penetrated, as was the abdomen of the foetus. The gestation period was estimated to be approximately 22–26 weeks. An operation was performed but the surgeon was of the opinion that the foetus had not sustained any injury and the pregnancy proceeded for some three weeks before the woman went into labour. The child was grossly premature and survived only four months. The defendant was charged with murder of the child. At his trial, the judge ruled there was sufficient evidence upon which the jury could conclude that the causal connection between the stabbing and death was established. However, as a matter of law, he ruled that there could in the circumstances be no conviction for either murder or manslaughter. The Attorney General, acting under powers conferred by s 36(1) of the Criminal Justice Act 1972, referred the following questions to the Court of Appeal and subsequently to the House of Lords:

- whether, subject to proof of requisite intent, the crimes of murder or manslaughter could be committed where unlawful injury was deliberately inflicted to a child *in utero* or to a mother carrying a child *in utero* where the child was subsequently born alive, existed independently of the mother and then died, the injuries *in utero* either having caused or made a substantial contribution to the death; and

- whether the fact that the child's death was caused solely as a consequence of injury to the mother rather than as a consequence of direct injury to the foetus could remove any liability for murder or manslaughter in those circumstances.

The House of Lords so confirmed that if there is evidence proving that after the birth the child enjoyed an existence independent of the mother, then the child may be a manslaughter victim, subject to the rules on causation and *mens rea*. In reaching its conclusion, the House of Lords stressed the importance to the prosecution of establishing that the child had an 'existence independent of its mother'. Lord Hope accepted that the fact that a child is not yet born did not prevent the requirements for the *actus reus* from being satisfied for both murder and manslaughter. This was because 'for the foetus life lay in the future. It could carry with it the effects of things done to it before birth which, after birth, might prove to be harmful'. Regarding the respondent's liability for manslaughter, the unlawful and dangerous act had been the stabbing of the mother. He had intended to attack the mother. The foetus/child came within the 'scope of the *mens rea* which the assailant had when he stabbed the mother' (*per* Lord Hope). All the necessary ingredients of the offence of manslaughter were present and, providing the assailant's conduct satisfied the principles of causation, the crime was complete.

Some questions remain unanswered, however. The ruling says nothing about the legal position of the neglectful mother. Let us assume that her foetus is born alive but dies a short time later as a direct result of the impact of the mother's behaviour over the period of her pregnancy. In our example, the mother may be a drug addict and in addition have a severe alcohol problem. Despite advice to the contrary, she persists in consuming large quantities of drink and drugs. The combination does irreparable damage to the internal organs of the foetus and the child succumbs to its injuries within minutes of its birth. If the mother has deliberately embarked upon this course of conduct intending that the foetus suffer serious injury, then there would appear to be a strong case against her for the murder of her child. What, however, if as a result of her addiction she fails to take reasonable care of herself with similar consequences ensuing? She may in her more lucid moments be aware of the likely consequences of her behaviour yet, nevertheless, fail to take remedial action. It follows from *Attorney General's Reference (No 3 of 1994)* that a manslaughter verdict ought to be possible based upon her grossly negligent behaviour. It is well established in civil law that there may be liability for post-natal damage caused by pre-natal acts. This proposition is not simply dependent upon the Congenital Disabilities (Civil Liability) Act 1976 for its authority but draws support from the Court of Appeal's decision in *Burton v Islington HA* [1992] 3 All ER 833. In that case, it was held that the health authority owed a duty of care to an unborn child and could be sued for medical negligence once the child had been born. There would appear to be little need to rely on the doctrine of transferred malice to establish liability in this type of case, which appears to fall neatly into the ambit of the current law on gross negligence manslaughter. So the current decision is limited to those cases where there is an attack, an act, against the mother and says nothing about omissions that may result in death. This may eventually be resolved when the Law Commission fulfils its stated intention to review the law on omissions.

Over the last decade, much has been written about various religious sects or cults whose beliefs often lead members to consider taking their own lives. Suppose that a pregnant member of such an organisation decided to take her own life by inflicting a serious stab wound to herself. This she does by plunging the knife into her lower abdomen causing serious injury to her child as well as herself. Luckily, she is able to receive immediate and sophisticated medical treatment. She survives and her baby is delivered by Caesarean section. Sadly, the child survives for only 15 minutes, death being attributed to the wounds perpetrated by the mother on herself. Section 1 of the Suicide Act 1961 abrogated the rule that it was a crime for a person to commit suicide. Does this mean that the mother's attack upon herself is not unlawful? If so, then she could not be convicted of homicide in respect of her child. It will be said that in such circumstances a compassionate rather than a legalistic approach ought to be adopted and perhaps rightly so, but it nevertheless remains uncertain whether or not there is sufficient *mens rea* to support a prosecution for causing death to the child. It could be argued that as the mother has failed to take her own life, then an attempted murder charge would be possible and thus provide the prosecution with the appropriate *mens rea* in respect of the child.

Nor does *Attorney General's Reference (No 3 of 1994)* decide whether *murder* is committed if there is a direct attack on the foetus intending to kill or cause it grievous bodily harm. Lord Hope's acknowledgement that an attack on the mother can satisfy the *actus reus* of both murder and manslaughter would seem to present no problems in that respect. But what of the *mens rea*? Is there an intent to kill or cause grievous bodily harm to a 'reasonable creature'? There would appear no reason in principle why the assailant should not face a murder charge if the child is born alive and then dies as a result of the attack. The defendant intended to kill the human being who has just passed away as a direct consequence of the attack incurred whilst in the womb. Unfortunately, the House of Lords declined to deal with this question on the basis that the issue did not arise from the facts before the court.

6.8   CORPORATE MANSLAUGHTER

Murder and manslaughter are, as has been explained above, common law offences developed to reflect the fact that, historically, the concern of the law has been with individuals who cause death. Corporate identity is a relatively new phenomenon in legal terms, hence the difficulties the courts have encountered in attempting to apply the principles of homicide (developed to deal with the thoughts and actions of real persons) to the actions of corporate bodies. Corporate criminal liability *per se* is not a novelty – there are many regulatory offences that can be committed by companies. Homicide is different of course, not only because it requires direct human intervention to cause a result, but also because it requires proof of a degree of fault. The *Herald of Free Enterprise* disaster in 1987 and, soon afterwards, the deaths of nearly 40 people in the King's Cross Underground fire brought questions relating to whether or not a company and members of its management ought to be able to face manslaughter charges into the mainstream. If a causal link could be established between inadequate management decision-taking and disasters in which there was loss of life, why should companies not suffer criminal sanctions?

For a consideration of both the direct and vicarious criminal liability of companies, see para 4.10. As regards liability for manslaughter, the court in *P & O European Ferries (Dover) Ltd* (1990) 93 Cr App R 72 (the *Herald of Free Enterprise* case) ruled that, as a matter of principle, a company could be found guilty of manslaughter. For this to occur, there had to be identified a person or persons who represented the company and who possessed the necessary *mens rea* for the crime of manslaughter. This is a relatively straightforward task if the company is small and the decision-makers are easily identified, as in the successful prosecution of Kite and OLL Ltd in 1994 (*Kite and OLL Ltd* (1994) *The Times*, 9 December). In that case, four schoolchildren lost their lives when taking canoeing lessons at a leisure activities centre run by the company. The managing director had on two occasions been made aware that safety at the centre was substandard and had failed to respond to the warnings given by qualified and experienced instructors. Both the managing director and the company were found guilty of the crime. If such circumstances were to occur again, then it would appear that either of the two major offences could apply. There is clearly a duty placed upon the company to take care of its customers and by failing to provide adequate supervision, there is a breach of that duty and a direct causal connection between the lack of supervision and the consequence. Similarly, given that the managing director was aware that there were serious safety deficiencies, yet nevertheless went ahead with the venture, there would seem to be little to prevent a finding of reckless killing.

In the *P & O* case, none of the defendants, ruled the judge, could on the evidence be found guilty of manslaughter in his own right and therefore the prosecution failed. It had been argued, without success, that the court should recognise the 'principle of aggregation' which would have permitted the individual faults, albeit minor, to be accumulated in order to reach the required degree of fault to underpin a manslaughter prosecution.

A similar argument in favour of aggregation of liability was also rejected in *Attorney General's Reference (No 2 of 1999)*, the prosecution arising from the Southall train crash in west London. The Court of Appeal held that, in the absence of any statutory intention to impose corporate liability on the basis of aggregation, the correct approach was still to identify the state of mind of the company with the state of mind of the person who could be regarded as the 'directing mind and will' of the company. Professor JC Smith, in his commentary on this decision ([2000] Crim LR 478), was deeply critical of the approach taken by the Court of Appeal on this point. Whilst accepting that the aggregation principle could not be used where an offence required proof of subjective fault, he argued that there was no objection to using it where, as the Court of Appeal had confirmed in the case, an offence such as killing by gross negligence involved proof that a specific standard of care had not been maintained. A finding of gross negligence was confirmation that the way in which an enterprise had operated fell way below acceptable minimum standards. Such a situation could arise where the combined effects of three separate, but factually related, failures by senior officers to maintain a safe system of working combined to produce a fatality.

How might the *P & O* case be dealt with in the context of the new offence of corporate killing? If one analyses the basic information, it will be seen that individual employees were found to be wanting in the way they carried out their duties. The ferry had sailed from Zeebrugge harbour and had capsized four minutes later. The ship had sailed with its inner and outer bow doors open. The doors should have been closed by an assistant bosun but he was asleep in his cabin at the moment the ferry set sail. The chief officer had responsibility to ensure that the bow doors were closed but the practice had emerged whereby he interpreted his duty as being to ensure that the assistant bosun was at the controls. The *Sheen Report (Department of Transport, Report of the Court No 8074*, 1987) into the disaster found the chief officer's failure to check on the doors to have been the immediate cause of the incident. Ultimate responsibility for the overall safety of the vessel lay with the master. He apparently simply followed the system approved by the senior master and there was no reference in the 'Ship's Standing Orders' to the fact that it should not sail with the bow doors open. The senior master had overall responsibility for co-ordination between all the masters and crews who worked on the *Herald of Free Enterprise*. The Sheen Report concluded that he should have introduced a 'fail safe system', designed to ensure that the ship and its passengers were not subjected to unnecessary dangers. It is worth quoting certain passages from the report in order to identify where the inquiry concluded the blame lay:

Full investigation into the circumstances of the disaster leads inexorably to the conclusion that the underlying or cardinal faults lay higher up in the Company. The board of directors did not appreciate their responsibility for the safe management of their ships. They did not apply their minds to the question: What orders should be given for the safety of our ships? The directors did not have any proper comprehension of what their duties were ... All concerned in the management, from the members of the board of directors down to junior superintendents, were guilty of fault in that all must be regarded as sharing responsibility for the failure of management. From the top to bottom the body corporate was infected with the disease of sloppiness. The failure on the part of the shore management to give proper and clear directions was a contributory cause of the disaster ... [para 14.1].

There is, of course, a fundamental question that needs to be addressed – that of causation. It is difficult to imagine that the accepted test of causation formulated nearly 40 years ago would be apposite in circumstances similar to those of the *P & O* case. The immediate cause of death was the failure of members of the crew to close the bow doors. This was also the operating cause and substantial cause of death. In circumstances where there has been a management failure, it would not be just to absolve the company from criminal responsibility simply because the immediate cause of death is the action of an employee of that company. Therefore, the Law Commission proposes that for purposes of any proposed new 'corporate manslaughter' offence (as to which, see below) a management failure may be regarded as the cause of death even though the immediate cause is the act or omission of an individual. (An individual is not to be subject to a prosecution for the corporate offence.)

6.9   REFORM OF MANSLAUGHTER

Dissatisfaction with the current state of the law relating to manslaughter is longstanding. The Criminal Law Revision Committee's 14th report, *Offences Against the Person* (Cmnd 7844, 1980), recommended abolition of the 'antiquated relic' of involuntary manslaughter based on the commission of an unlawful act and the adoption of a more rational and systematic approach to the offence of manslaughter.

In March 1996, the Law Commission published its long awaited report, *Legislating the Criminal Code: Involuntary Manslaughter* (Law Com 237), making clear the deficiencies of the current law. The first is the breadth of the offence. This is a reference to the different types of conduct that may be categorised as involuntary manslaughter. This creates problems for the sentencer, a point confirmed by Lord Lane CJ in *Walker* (1992) 13 Cr App R(S) 474, where he remarked: '... manslaughter ranges in its gravity from the borders of murder right down to those of accidental death.' In practice, this means that the same label is applied to vastly differing types of conduct and therefore degrees of culpability. The Law Commission believes that this 'devalues' the conduct of those seriously at fault by linking their act or omission within a crime that encompasses less heinous conduct.

A further major criticism is summed up by the Law Commission in this way:

Unlawful act manslaughter is therefore ... unprincipled because it requires only that a foreseeable risk of causing some harm should have been inherent in the accused's conduct, whereas he is convicted of actually causing death, and also to some extent punished for doing so [para 3.6].

The difficulties relating to gross negligence manslaughter and liability for omissions have been outlined above. Having highlighted the criticisms of the current law, the Law Commission went on to consider the moral basis of criminal liability for unintentionally causing death. It concludes that a person ought to be criminally liable only in the following circumstances:

- when the defendant unreasonably and inadvertently takes a risk of causing death or serious injury; or

- when the defendant unreasonably and inadvertently takes a risk of causing death or serious injury, fails to advert to the risk and is therefore culpable because:

(a) the risk was foreseeable; and

(b) the defendant has the capacity to advert to the risk.

The condemnation of the current offence because of the breadth of conduct encompassed within it led the Law Commission to recommend the creation of 'two offences of unintentional killing, based upon differing fault elements, rather than one single broad offence'. The first offence is that of reckless killing. Clause 1 of the draft Involuntary Homicide Bill defines the offence in this way:

A person who by his conduct causes the death of another is guilty of reckless killing if:

(a) he is aware of a risk that his conduct will cause death or serious injury; and

(b) it is unreasonable for him to take that risk having regard to the circumstances as he knows or believes them to be.

The second new offence is that of killing by gross carelessness. The Commission rejected an argument that there was little distinction between subjective recklessness and gross carelessness, favouring the view that there was a clear moral distinction between the two. A person who knowingly takes a risk is surely more culpable than one who carelessly fails to advert to a risk. The semantic argument is not in doubt; it remains to be seen how effectively the distinction is to be drawn in practice.

Clause 2 of the draft Bill defines the proposed offence in the following way:

2(1) A person who by his conduct causes the death of another is guilty of killing by gross carelessness if:

(a) a risk that his conduct will cause death or serious injury would be obvious to a reasonable person in his position;

(b) he is capable of appreciating that risk at the material time; and

(c) either:

(i) his conduct falls far below what can reasonably be expected of him in the circumstances; or

(ii) he intends by his conduct to cause some injury or is aware of, and unreasonably takes, the risk that it may do so.

(2) There shall be attributed to the person referred to in sub-s (1)(a) above:

(a) knowledge of any relevant facts which the accused is shown to have at the material time; and

(b) any skill or experience professed by him.

(3) In determining for the purposes of sub-s (1)(c)(i) above what can reasonably be expected of the accused regard shall be had to the circumstances of which he can be expected to be aware, to any circumstances shown to be within his knowledge and to any other matter relevant for assessing his conduct at the material time.

(4) Sub-section (1)(c)(ii) above applies only if the conduct causing, or intended to cause, the injury constitutes an offence.

The formulation of this offence suggests that there is a minimum standard of behaviour below which a person must not fall in order to avoid criminal liability. The Law Commission, however, suggests that a person will have to fall far below that standard for criminal liability inexorably to follow. Out go the terms 'negligence' and 'duty of care', thereby avoiding any unnecessary overlap with the civil law.

The risk of death or serious injury must be one that is obvious to the reasonable person in the accused's position. The Law Commission proposes that obvious should mean 'immediately apparent', 'striking' or 'glaring', making it absolutely clear that the failure to recognise a risk will not make the defendant culpable unless it would have been obvious to a reasonable person in his position. Attention is drawn to paras 5.36 and 5.37, which are examples of how it is proposed the new offence will operate.

The Law Commission, somewhat reluctantly, decided that there should be no change to the present law in respect of omissions. This aspect of the criminal law, the ambit of which is very uncertain, should, believes the Law Commission, be examined in respect of the whole of the criminal law and not just with reference to the law on manslaughter. When and in what circumstances the law should impose liability for an omission is described as a 'very controversial' issue and should at some future point form the basis for a discrete law reform project. The recommendation in respect of manslaughter by omission is that it should, for the time being, continue to be governed by the common law. Clause 3 states:

A person is not guilty of an offence under s 1 or s 2 (of the draft Involuntary Homicide Bill) by reason of omission unless the omission is in breach of a duty at common law.

The government subsequently confirmed its commitment to legislate in this area by publishing, in May 2000, its own consultation paper, *Reforming the Law on Involuntary Manslaughter: The Government's Proposals* (London: HMSO), largely building upon the work of the Law Commission. In one respect, the government's proposals go further than those of the Law Commission, in that they propose the introduction of a third form of involuntary manslaughter arising where the defendant kills intending to cause only a minor injury, but where death nevertheless results because of some unforeseeable event. This third head of involuntary manslaughter would carry a maximum penalty of between five and 10 years' imprisonment. An example of this type of liability might arise where the defendant blackmails his victim, causing his victim to die of a heart attack. The harm envisaged might be minor psychological distress, but the unforeseeable event causing death is the victim's pre-existing heart condition.

The Law Commission, in its 1996 report (Law Com 237), also took the opportunity to recommend the introduction of a new offence of corporate killing, designed no doubt to appease those who believed that companies, acting through their boards of directors, ought to face liability where it could be proved that a decision or decisions of the board resulted in death. For example, this could include the failure to commit the necessary finance in order to remedy known deficiencies in an aircraft or ferry.

Such a decision inevitably compromises safety, increases the likelihood of disaster and therefore puts passengers at risk of death. Of importance in this context is the extent of the knowledge possessed by the board as to the likely impact of a decision not to invest. If the board has commissioned a report from a safety expert that gives clear advice that the failure to invest will not compromise safety, then it is going to be extremely difficult for the prosecution to establish that the board was culpable in the circumstances.

The Law Commission looked closely at the issues and concluded that a new offence of corporate killing should be included in the draft Involuntary Homicide Bill. In essence, a corporation could become liable for the offence of corporate killing as defined by the Law Commission if:

• a management failure by the corporation is the cause or one of the causes of a person's death; and

• that failure constitutes conduct falling far below what can reasonably be expected of the corporation in the circumstances.

There is a management failure by a corporation if:

• the way in which its activities are managed or organised fails to ensure the health and safety of persons employed in or affected by those activities; and

• such a failure may be regarded as a cause of a person's death, notwithstanding that the immediate cause is the act or omission of an individual.

It should be noted that the existence of such an offence does not preclude a corporation being found guilty of either of the two major offences in the Bill, that is, reckless killing and gross carelessness (cl 4(5)).

The Law Commission expressed the view that if circumstances, such as those that arose in the *Herald of Free Enterprise* disaster, were to arise again and assuming the new offence of corporate killing was on the statute book, the company would be convicted of the new offence. The company had failed to ensure that a proper system operated to ensure the safety of its ferries and passengers. It is reasonable to expect that the board of a company operating ferries would never wish to compromise standards.

The Law Commission views the new offence as 'broadly corresponding' to the individual offence of killing by gross carelessness. Although the new offences of reckless killing and gross carelessness are referred to as 'individual' crimes, there is no reason in principle why a company should not face prosecution for either of these offences. It is suggested that this is likely to occur when it is possible to identify an individual as the 'controlling mind' of the company and the individual failure is synonymous with being a management failure (see *Kite* and *OLL Ltd*, above).

The government's own consultation paper (*Reforming the Law on Involuntary Manslaughter: The Government's Proposals*) endorses the Law Commission's proposals, but suggests that the new offence of corporate killing should apply to 'any trade or business undertakings not just incorporated organisations'. It also proposes that other organisations, such as the Health and Safety Executive and Civil Aviation Authority, should be empowered to investigate and prosecute the new offences. The Law Commission has rightly shied away from making recommendations in respect of the law relating to omissions purely in the context of manslaughter in favour of an overall review of the current position in criminal law. The law on omissions has evolved piecemeal over the last 100 years and would certainly benefit from a thorough reappraisal.

HOMICIDE

This chapter has discussed the law relating to the offences of murder, manslaughter, infanticide and child destruction. It has also drawn attention to the role of the special defences of provocation and diminished responsibility and makes passing reference to the legal position of those who fail to carry through the agreement at the centre of a suicide pact.

MURDER

Murder requires proof that the defendant caused the victim's death with intention to kill or the intention to cause grievous bodily harm. There is no longer any need to prove that death occurred within a year and a day of the incident relied upon as establishing the *actus reus*.

Note that, providing a child has been born alive and taken at least one breath independently from its mother, it is in law a human being and can, therefore, be the victim in respect of a homicide, even though the injuries that resulted in death were sustained while still in the womb.

VOLUNTARY MANSLAUGHTER

Voluntary manslaughter refers to the special defences in ss 2, 3 and 4 of the HA 1957, that is, diminished responsibility, provocation and suicide pacts. These defences apply only on a charge of murder and, if successful, reduce any conviction to one of manslaughter.

PROVOCATION

Provocation is currently a controversial defence and has come under scrutiny for two major reasons. The first is the requirement that provocation should require evidence of a sudden and temporary loss of self-control. The second is the requirement that the effect of the provocation should be assessed by reference to how reasonable the defendant's reaction was. The courts allow a number of characteristics of an accused to be taken into account, arguably making the assessment increasingly subjective. The relationship between provocation and diminished responsibility has recently come under scrutiny in the context of whether a defendant suffering from an abnormality of mind should rely on s 2 or s 3 of the HA 1957 for a defence. It is now clear that mental peculiarities can be taken into account in assessing whether or not the defendant pleading provocation exercised what was, for him, reasonable self-control in the circumstances.

DIMINISHED RESPONSIBILITY

Diminished responsibility should be considered along with other defences relating to the mind, that is, insanity and automatism. The abnormality of mind must have substantially impaired the defendant's responsibility for his actions. The burden of proof rests upon the defendant and he will have to have expert medical evidence to support his claim.

INVOLUNTARY MANSLAUGHTER

Involuntary manslaughter refers to unlawful act manslaughter and killing by gross negligence. The Law Commission report, *Legislating the Criminal Code: Involuntary Manslaughter* (Law Com 237, 1996), outlines the reasons why radical reform is needed and proposes new offences including one of corporate killing. In broad terms, this category of homicide will cover all those situations where death results but the accused does not possess the *mens rea* for murder (excluding, of course, pure accidents where there is no culpability).

INFANTICIDE AND CHILD DESTRUCTION

Infanticide and child destruction are statutory offences. The former offence is a recognition that society should seek to be compassionate when a mother kills her child within a year of birth while suffering from post-natal depression or some other form of illness which causes the balance of her mind to be disturbed. The latter seeks to protect foetuses capable of being born alive. Note the rebuttable presumption that a child is only capable of being born alive after the 28th week of gestation.

CHAPTER 7

NON-FATAL OFFENCES AGAINST THE PERSON

7.1   INTRODUCTION

In criminal law, the term 'non-fatal offences against the person' encompasses what might be called the 'mainstream' non-fatal offences against the person, such as causing grievous bodily harm, malicious wounding, actual bodily harm, assault and battery, ancillary offences such as poisoning, harassment and racially motivated offences, and sexual offences such as rape, indecent assault and various other forms of unlawful sexual conduct. It has long been acknowledged that this area of the criminal law is in need of urgent reform. The main statutory provision regarding assault-related offences is the Offences Against the Person Act (OAPA) 1861, which itself was largely a consolidating provision bringing together even earlier enactments in one piece of legislation. As will be seen there has been no shortage of law reform proposals, but for the moment it seems that only sexual offences are likely to be the subject of any significant statutory restatement in the near future (see below, 7.13).

7.2   COMMON ASSAULT AND BATTERY

Assault and battery existed as common law offences for centuries and, as will be seen, involve concepts that have been incorporated into more serious statutory offences such as assault occasioning actual bodily harm (s 47 of the OAPA 1861), assault upon a police officer (s 89 of the Police Act 1996) and indecent assault (ss 14 and 15 of the Sexual Offences Act (SOA) 1956).

7.2.1   *Actus reus* of common assault

The *actus reus* of assault, where the term assault is used in its narrow technical sense, merely requires proof that D has caused P to apprehend that immediate and unlawful violence is about to be inflicted upon him. Much confusion is caused by the fact that parliament, judges, lawyers and academics use the term assault in two senses. The narrow sense, as just described, but also in the broad sense to imply that there has also been some physical contact. Lord Lane CJ in *Mansfield Justices ex p Sharkey* [1985] 1 All ER 193 made it clear that an assault can occur without physical contact, where he observed that:

> [For the *actus reus* of assault to be made out] … there is no need for it to proceed to physical contact. If it does it is an assault and battery. Assault is a crime independent of battery and it is important to remember that fact.

The requirement that P should apprehend some immediate physical violence means that P cannot be assaulted, in the narrow sense, where he is asleep or where D approaches P from the rear. Such cases could be charged as attempted batteries, save for the fact that D cannot be charged with attempting to commit a summary-only offence.

The court should look at the effect on P of D's action. Even if D is a practical joker who merely intends to scare P 'for fun' the *actus reus* of assault will be made out if P nevertheless apprehends some immediate physical violence. In *Logdon v DPP* [1976] Crim LR 121, L pointed a toy gun at the victim indicating that he was going to shoot her. The victim was alarmed at this and L gave her the gun to indicate that it was not real. He had intended his actions as a joke, but the court held that an assault had been committed because the victim had genuinely feared immediate personal violence. As to the issue of immediacy, this will largely depend on the facts of the case. Typically, it will mean that the violence was capable of being carried out 'there and then', but the fact that D might have to enter a building or a train carriage in order carry out his attack will not be sufficient to prevent liability from arising. Suppose D stands outside the door of P's room and plunges his long bladed knife through the wood of the door so that the knife is visible by P from within the room. It would be wrong to suggest that P has not been assaulted at that point, simply because D has yet to complete the task of breaking the door down.

This contention is supported by *Smith v Superintendent of Woking Police Station* [1983] Crim LR 323, where D had entered private property and looked through the windows of a bed-sitting room where the occupier, P, saw him, was terrified and screamed, causing D to run away. His conviction was upheld on the basis that P had been frightened that personal violence could have resulted, although there was no immediate prospect that D could have entered the premises and inflicted harm on her. This decision has been criticised because it was obvious to P that D could not have entered the property and inflicted violence. Nevertheless, that does not take into account the fact that P may well be frightened of the unknown. She may know that all the doors and windows are locked, but what she may not know is what D intends to do next. D may have with him a large hammer which he intends to use to smash the window and gain entry. Shaking a fist at his intended victim may cause alarm but not fear of immediate harm, but shaking a fist containing a hammer would surely cause the victim to apprehend violence, even though she is locked in the house.

Despite the fact that threatening words, of themselves, can strike terror in the heart of the victim, until relatively recently, the criminal law has been reluctant to acknowledge that words alone can constitute an assault. Authority for the proposition that there could be no assault based only on what was said by D can be traced back to decisions such as *Meade and Belt* (1823) 1 Lew CC 184, when Holroyd J held that 'no words or singing could ever constitute an assault'. Against this, Goddard CJ in *Wilson* [1955] 1 All ER 744, thought that the defendant's words 'get out the knives' would amount to an assault. If words are accompanied by an appropriate gesture which indicates that what is said is likely to happen, then an assault would have taken place, based on the actions in the context of what was said.

In *Ireland* [1997] 4 All ER 225, the House of Lords had to decide whether or not silence could amount to an assault. The appellant had been convicted of assault occasioning actual bodily harm contrary to s 47 of the OAPA 1861. Over a four-month period, he had made numerous telephone calls to three women. One of the complainants received 14 telephone calls within an hour. The making of each call was followed by silence. The impact of this behaviour on each of the women was severe. All suffered significant psychological symptoms such as stress, inability to sleep, nervousness and anxiety. The appellant argued that his acts did not cause the victims to apprehend 'immediate and unlawful violence'.

The House of Lords expressly rejected the contention, based on *Meade and Belt*, that words alone could not constitute an assault. Lord Steyn, in particular, saw no reason why 'something said should be incapable of causing an apprehension of immediate personal violence'. The House of Lords also endorsed the ruling in *Chan-Fook* [1994] 2 All ER 552, to the effect that actual bodily harm, for the purposes of s 47 of the 1861 Act, could encompass psychiatric injury, supported by medical evidence, going beyond mere panic, distress and fear. The decision goes further, however, in recognising the possibility that silent telephone calls might actually cause the assault, provided the caller causes his victim to apprehend immediate personal violence, or the possibility of it.

Care must be taken not to fall into the trap of concluding that verbal abuse or threats will necessarily constitute an assault. Evidence will be required of the effect on the victim. The fact that the victim immediately feels threatened does not necessarily mean that the victim apprehends immediate physical violence. Much will depend on the circumstances of the case. Where D communicates his threats or warnings by means of some instantaneous form of communication, it is unlikely that an offence will be made out unless the victim and accused are in close proximity. If a secretary receives an email communication five minutes before she is about to close the office that tells her 'not to walk home alone tonight', she may be extremely concerned. If it is from the office practical joker, she may do nothing more than send a forthright response. If it is from someone within the organisation of whom she is unaware, then she may with some justification feel threatened. If the night is dark and she does indeed walk a fair distance to catch her train, she may then conclude that she is being watched. If she is aware that a serial rapist is at large in the vicinity, she may apprehend immediate and unlawful personal violence. Conversely, if the communication is by email from New Zealand, she may wonder what is going on but is unlikely to expect that she will suffer 'immediate and unlawful personal violence'.

The famous case of *Tuberville v Savage* (1669) 1 Mod R 3 illustrates the point that, far from amounting to an assault, the words used by the defendant might actually negative an assault. The defendant in that case uttered the words: 'If it were not Assize time I would not take such language from you.' D had spoken the words simultaneously with the action of putting his hand on the sword, the words thus giving P the impression that he was not at risk. If the action precedes the words, in all probability, it will be too late to rely upon any statement to negative an assault, as P will already have apprehended that a battery would occur. So, for example, in *Read v Coker* (1853) 13 CB 850, a group of men indicated quite forcefully to P that unless he left their premises they would break his neck. This was held to amount to an assault. They would have been entitled to use reasonable force to eject P on the basis that he was a trespasser and, therefore, such action would have been lawful. To amount to an assault, their actions would have needed to be regarded as excessive force.

7.2.2   *Mens rea* of common assault

The *mens rea* for assault requires proof that D either intended to cause P to apprehend immediate physical violence, or was reckless as to whether or not his actions would have this result. Recklessness in this context will be given its *Cunningham* [1957] 2 QB 396 rather than *Caldwell* (*Metropolitan Police Commissioner v*

Caldwell [1981] 1 All ER 961) meaning. *DPP v K* [1990] 1 All ER 331 applied *Caldwell* on a charge of assault occasioning actual bodily harm but this case was not followed by the Court of Appeal in *Spratt* [1991] 2 All ER 210, which applied *Cunningham*. *Parmenter* [1991] 2 All ER 225 followed *Spratt* and the House of Lords in the consolidated appeals in *Parmenter and Savage* [1991] 4 All ER 698 confirmed the applicability of the *Cunningham* approach to recklessness. The defendant must at least, therefore, be aware of the risk that P may apprehend immediate physical violence as a result of his actions. The practical joker, such as in *Logdon* (above), may not intend to frighten his victim, but he will incur liability for assault if he is aware that there is a risk that such might be the case.

7.2.3   *Actus reus* of battery

A battery is the actual infliction of unlawful personal violence. As indicated above, this may occur without P being aware that the *actus reus* has been committed. The *actus reus* may be complete as soon as D touches P, or may continue for as long as D continues to apply unlawful force upon the person of P (see *Fagan v Metropolitan Police Commissioner* [1968] All ER 442). There is no requirement that any force must be directly applied to the person; therefore, if, as in *DPP v K*, D places acid into an electric hand-dryer, thus causing the next user to be sprayed with the liquid, then that will be a battery, even though D did not spray the acid himself. In *Haystead v DPP* (2000) *The Times*, 2 June, the defendant punched W whilst she was holding her child. The force of the blow caused W to drop the child, the child falling to the floor sustaining an injury to his head. Upholding the conviction for the offence of assault against the child by beating, the Divisional Court held that the battery to the child could be caused by the defendant without his having used force directly to the child's person. The act of W, in dropping the child, could not be regarded as a 'fully voluntary' intervening act breaking the chain of causation. It appears that touching a person's clothing will be regarded as the equivalent of touching the person. In *Thomas* (1985) 81 Cr App R 331, the appellant was a school caretaker whose conviction for indecently assaulting two schoolgirls was quashed by the Court of Appeal. In one instance, he had touched and rubbed a girl's skirt. When she objected, he walked away. The court accepted that the touching of a person's clothing was the equivalent of touching the person who was wearing the clothes. The conviction was quashed on the basis that the circumstances were not inherently 'indecent'.

The reference to 'personal violence' is something of an overstatement because all that is required is the touching of another person without that person's consent and without lawful excuse. The touching need not necessarily be hostile or rude or aggressive; see further the comments of Lord Lane CJ in *Faulkner v Talbot* [1981] 3 All ER 469. To the extent that some of the *obiter* statements of the majority in *Brown* [1993] Crim LR 961 suggest otherwise, it is submitted that they should be treated with caution. Lord Jauncey in that case expressed the view that: 'If the appellant's activities ... were unlawful they were also hostile and a necessary ingredient of assault was present.' Lord Lowry was glad 'to adopt everything which has been said by my noble and learned friend Lord Jauncey' (on the issue of hostility). However, Lord Mustill, one of the minority, was not convinced. He observed:

> Hostility cannot, as it seems to me, be a crucial factor which in itself determines guilt or innocence, although its presence or absence may be relevant when the court has to decide as a matter of policy how to react to a new situation.

7.2.4   *Mens rea* for battery

In *Venna* [1975] 3 All ER 788, the appellant was involved in a struggle with police officers who were attempting to arrest him. He fell to the ground and lashed out with his feet and in so doing kicked the hand of one of the police officers, fracturing a bone. He was charged with assault occasioning actual bodily harm contrary to s 47 of the OAPA 1861 although this was a case of battery. The court held that either intention or recklessness (*Cunningham*) was sufficient to establish the *mens rea* for the offence. Therefore, an accused will have the requisite *mens rea* for battery if there is an intention to apply force to the body or there is recklessness whether force is applied.

It is worth noting that assault and battery are regarded as basic intent offences for the purposes of the law relating to intoxication, seemingly on the basis that either may be established by proof of recklessness.

7.2.5   How should assault and battery be charged?

As will have been seen from the above, assault and battery are two distinct concepts. A defendant ought to be charged with either assault or battery as the facts dictate. This much is underlined by s 39 of the Criminal Justice Act 1988, which provides that: 'Common assault and battery shall be summary offences ...' The Divisional Court in *DPP v Little* [1992] 1 All ER 299 held that the offences had, since the OAPA 1861, been separate statutory offences, on the basis that the 1861 Act had put pre-existing common law offences into statutory form. To allege battery on facts that do not provide evidence of any physical contact with the victim would be inept. In *DPP v Little* the court held that, since the two are separate offences, a count alleging assault and battery would be for duplicity (that is, would contravene the requirement that each count on an indictment should allege only one offence). The safe approach is for the prosecutor to opt for alternative charges, one alleging assault, and the other alleging battery. In respect of other offences incorporating assault, such as indecent assault, it is safe to assume that the courts will adopt the view that the term 'assault' is being used in its broad sense to include battery (see *Lynsey* [1995] 2 All ER 654). The term 'indecent battery' is hardly one in common usage.

7.3   ASSAULT OCCASIONING ACTUAL BODILY HARM: s 47 OF THE OFFENCES AGAINST THE PERSON ACT 1861

The offence of assault occasioning actual bodily harm enacted in s 47 of the 1861 Act carries with it the possibility of five years' imprisonment if the defendant is convicted following trial in the Crown Court.

7.3.1   *Actus reus* of s 47

The offence requires proof of an assault, but for these purposes this can be based on either an assault in the narrow sense, a battery as described above, or a combination of both. Actual bodily harm is not defined by the 1861 Act, but the courts have recognised that it encompasses any hurt or injury calculated to interfere with the health or comfort of the victim (see Lynskey J quoting with approval from *Archbold* in *Miller* [1954] 2 QB 282). Actual bodily harm would certainly include a graze, bruising, or inducing vomiting and nausea. Crown Prosecution charging standards indicate that s 47 should be charged where the harm done includes: the loss or breaking of a tooth or teeth; temporary loss of sensory functions; extensive or multiple bruising; a displaced broken nose; and minor fractures. Bear in mind that these injuries might technically give rise to more serious charges. The guidelines do not seek to define actual bodily harm, simply to indicate to prosecutors what might be appropriate charges if a conviction is to be secured.

In recent years the higher courts have been willing to accept that actual bodily harm could take the form of psychological harm as well as physical harm. In *Burstow; Ireland* [1998] AC 147, the victims in these appeals had developed neurotic disorders as a result of the appellants' actions. Lord Steyn observed that:

> Neuroses must be distinguished from simple states of fear, or problems in coping with every day life. Where the line is to be drawn must be a matter of psychiatric judgment. But for present purposes it is important to note that modern psychiatry treats neuroses as recognisable psychiatric illnesses ... it [is also] ... essential to bear in mind that neurotic illnesses affect the central nervous system of the body, because emotions such as fear and anxiety are brain functions.

He fully recognised that the draftsman of the 1861 Act would not have had psychiatric illness in mind when enacting s 47 but expressed the view that the subjective intention of the draftsman was 'immaterial', preferring to interpret the Act in the light of '... the best current scientific appreciation of the link between the body and psychiatric injury'. It is thus clear that psychiatric harm can be equated with actual bodily harm, provided the prosecution can adduce expert medical evidence to support this assertion.

Section 47 is clearly a 'result' crime, thus the prosecution will have to prove that D caused the actual bodily harm suffered by P, as denoted by the use of the word 'occasioning'. In most cases this will be a simple matter of applying the basic rules on causation in law (but for D's actions would P have suffered the harm?), and causation in law (the test for reasonable foreseeability). For a detailed consideration of the rules of causation refer to 2.4 of this book. It follows, therefore, that D will escape liability for the completed offence under s 47 if the chain of causation is broken by a *novus actus interveniens*. *Roberts* (1971) 56 Cr App R 95 provides that if P suffers actual bodily harm whilst attempting to escape from the threat posed by D, the escape itself will not amount to a *novus actus* provided it can be regarded as reasonably foreseeable in the circumstances. Where P is injured through attempting a 'daft escape', the chain of causation may be broken.

7.3.2   *Mens rea* of s 47

A defendant charged under s 47 must be proved to have intended the assault (broad or narrow) or to have been reckless as to whether an assault would occur. Recklessness here is again subjective – the defendant must be judged on the facts as he believed them to be. If he gave no thought to the risk that an assault would occur, or considered the risk only to dismiss it as less than negligible, he must be acquitted (see *Cunningham* and *Reid* [1992] 3 All ER 552). The Court of Appeal in *Roberts* proceeded on the basis that there was no need for the prosecution to establish any intention to cause actual bodily harm or recklessness as to whether such harm would be caused so long as it flowed naturally from the 'technical' assault or battery. In *Savage and Parmenter*, the House of Lords approved *Roberts* on this point, holding that there was no obligation on the Crown to prove either intention or recklessness on the part of the defendant towards the actual bodily harm. Critics would argue that this is a return to 'constructive' liability, that is imposing liability on D for the greater offence of actual bodily harm, simply because he has the *mens rea* for a lesser offence, assault.

7.4   MALICIOUSLY WOUNDING OR INFLICTING GRIEVOUS BODILY HARM: s 20 OF THE OFFENCES AGAINST THE PERSON ACT 1861

Section 20 of the 1861 Act provides that:

> Whosoever shall unlawfully and maliciously wound or inflict any grievous bodily harm upon any other person, either with or without any weapon or instrument, shall be guilty of a misdemeanour and shall be liable ... to imprisonment for not more than five years.

7.4.1   Wounding and grievous bodily harm

In law, a wounding requires proof that the continuity of the layers of the skin have be broken. In *JCC v Eisenhower* [1983] 3 All ER 230, the appellants had been charged under s 20 of the OAPA 1861 with wounding a young man by firing an air pistol, a pellet from which hit him in the eye. It was found as fact by the magistrates that the victim had bruising just below his eyebrow and internal rupturing of blood vessels in the eye. The Divisional Court quashed their convictions under s 20, on the basis there had not, in law, been a wounding. Goff LJ, after examining authorities as far back as 1831, concluded:

> There must be a break in the continuity of the skin. It must be a break in the continuity of the whole skin, but the skin may include not merely the outer skin of the body but the skin of an internal cavity ... where the skin of the cavity is continuous with the outer skin of the body.

There is authority which suggests that any wound must be a result of a battery having occurred. Glidewell LJ in *Savage* [1991] 2 All ER 220 stated: '... does the allegation of wounding import or include an allegation of assault? In our view, in the ordinary way, unless there are some quite extraordinary facts it inevitably does.' A battery, it will be recalled, is the actual infliction of unlawful personal violence, but it is not clear why, if D digs a pit and lines the bottom with broken glass, he should not be said to have caused a wound simply because he was not there to push P into it. D's actions have caused P's wound even though he was not around to apply force to P. *Wilson* [1983] 3 All ER 448 would suggest that providing the wound is directly inflicted there is no need to establish that a battery has been committed.

The offence under s 20 can be made out on two alternative bases – either D wounds P or D inflicts grievous bodily harm on P. It was decided in *DPP v Smith* [1961] AC 290 that grievous bodily harm means 'really serious harm'. It follows that there can be grievous bodily harm inflicted without any wounds being caused to the victim. The decision in *Ireland* (above) raises the possibility of really serious psychological injury amounting in law to grievous bodily harm, provided the expert evidence supports this. Whether or not harm amounts to grievous bodily harm is to be determined objectively. It is a misdirection to tell a jury that harm amounts to grievous bodily harm simply because they would regard the particular harm caused in the case before them to be 'grievous' (see *Brown and Stratton* [1998] Crim LR 485).

The Code for Crown Prosecutors suggests that, in practice, s 20 of the 1861 Act should be reserved for those wounds considered to be serious, that is on a par with grievous bodily harm. Injuries that should be equated with grievous bodily harm include: those resulting in permanent disability or loss of a sensory function; more than minor permanent visible disfigurement; broken or displaced limbs or bones; injuries causing substantial loss of blood (that is, necessitating a transfusion); and injury resulting in lengthy treatment or incapacitation.

7.4.2   *Actus reus* of s 20: 'inflicting'

The 1861 Act is perplexing in its inconsistencies and this is nowhere more obvious than in the wording of ss 47, 20 and 18. Whereas, actual bodily harm has to be 'occasioned' by the defendant under s 47, grievous bodily harm has to be 'inflicted' by the defendant under s 20, and 'caused' by the defendant under s 18. In any modern statute the use of three different words in three separate sections of an Act would be taken by the courts as an indication that parliament meant three different things. An examination of the history of the 1861 Act, however, reveals that there was no overall strategy behind the deviation in terminology. It is simply the haphazard outcome of pulling together disparate provisions under one consolidating Act. This is not to suggest, however, that the matter has not caused the courts considerable difficulty.

In *Clarence* (1888) 22 QBD 23, the defendant was charged under both s 20 and s 47 of the OAPA 1861. He was suffering from venereal disease, yet nevertheless engaged in sexual intercourse with his wife. She would not have consented to the intercourse had she known of his medical condition. He was convicted on both counts but his appeal was allowed by a majority of 9:4 on the basis that an assault was needed for both crimes. Contrast this with *Lewis* [1970] Crim LR 647 and *Martin* (1881) 8 QBD 54. In the latter case D, shortly before the end of a theatre performance, switched out the lights and placed an iron bar across a doorway. Panic ensued and numerous people were injured as a result of being unable to gain access to the exit stairs. The defendant was convicted of inflicting grievous bodily harm contrary to s 20. Similarly, in *Wilson*, Lord Roskill stated:

> I am content to accept, as did the full court, that there can be an infliction of grievous bodily harm contrary to s 20 without an assault being committed.

The House of Lords in *Wilson* relied upon the Australian decision of *Salisbury* (1976) VR 452. In this case, it was said that grievous bodily harm could be inflicted either by direct application or where the defendant's act resulted in force being applied violently to the body of the victim so that he suffers grievous bodily harm. In *Mandair* [1994] 2 All ER 715, Lord Mackay LC said:

> In my view, 'cause' in s 18 is certainly sufficiently wide to embrace any method by which grievous bodily harm could be inflicted under s 20 and since causing grievous

bodily harm in s 18 is an alternative to wounding I regard it as clear that the word 'cause' in s 18 is wide enough to include any action that could amount to inflicting grievous bodily harm under s 20 where the word 'inflicts' appears as an alternative to 'wound' ... the word 'cause' is wider or at least not narrower than the word 'inflict' [p 719f and h].

In *Burstow*, the House of Lords considered again the meaning of the two verbs. The appellant was convicted of inflicting grievous bodily harm contrary to s 20 of the OAPA 1861. He had become obsessed by a female colleague and had persecuted her by making nuisance telephone calls, damaging her car and breaking into her house. He served a term of imprisonment but on release continued with his behaviour. In consequence, the victim suffered psychological illness described as 'grievous harm of a psychiatric nature'. The prosecution accepted that grievous bodily harm included psychiatric injury. Counsel for the appellant submitted that 'inflict' in s 20 necessarily required the application of physical force directly or indirectly to the body of the victim and that that had not happened in this case.

Whilst accepting that the words 'inflict' and 'cause' were not entirely synonymous, the House of Lords' decision recognised that, for all practical purposes, the two expressions were largely interchangeable. As Lord Steyn observed, the problem is one of construction.

> What I am saying is that in the context of the Act of 1861 one can nowadays quite naturally speak of inflicting psychiatric injury. Moreover, there is internal contextual support in the statute for this view. It would be absurd to differentiate between ss 18 and 20 in the way argued on behalf of Burstow. As the Lord Chief Justice observed [in the Court of Appeal] this should be a very practical area of the law. The interpretation and approach should so far as possible be adopted which treats the ladder of offences as a coherent body of law.

The fact that *Burstow* was the third occasion that the House of Lords had considered ss 18 and 20 of the OAPA 1861 within the space of 10 years lent support to the view that new legislation is urgently needed to put this area of law onto a modern footing.

7.4.3   *Mens rea* of s 20: 'maliciously'

In *Cunningham* the Court of Appeal adopted the view that the word 'maliciously' meant more than simply 'wicked'. It required proof that the defendant had either intended to cause the harm specified by the section or had at least been reckless as to whether or not he would do so, in the sense that he was aware of the risk that he might cause such harm. Even allowing for the fact that *Cunningham* was a case involving liability for administering a noxious substance contrary to s 23 of the 1861 Act, one might be forgiven for expecting the word malicious to be given the same meaning in the context of s 20, but some caution is required here. In *Mowatt* (1968) 1 QBD 421, Diplock LJ said in respect of s 20: 'It is enough that [the defendant] should have foreseen that some physical harm to some person, albeit of a minor character, might occur.' The House of Lords in *Savage and Parmenter* confirmed that the defendant need not foresee the physical harm of the gravity caused but need only have foreseen some physical harm albeit of a minor character. A number of points should be noted here:

- the *mens rea* is subjective – D must be judged on the facts as he believes them to be;
- D need not foresee the harm actually suffered by P – it is sufficient that D foresees the risk of some harm. *DPP v A* [2001] Crim LR 140 confirms that it is sufficient that D foresees that some physical harm might occur, he does not have to foresee that it will occur;
- D must be shown to have foreseen the risk of some physical injury – hence foreseeing that P will be frightened will not suffice under s 20 unless the evidence shows that D foresaw P suffering some psychological harm having an effect on the body.

7.5   WOUNDING OR CAUSING GRIEVOUS BODILY HARM WITH INTENT TO DO SOME GRIEVOUS BODILY HARM: s 18 OF THE OFFENCES AGAINST THE PERSON ACT 1861

Section 18 of the OAPA 1861 states:

> Whosoever shall unlawfully and maliciously by any means whatsoever wound or cause any grievous bodily harm to any person with intent to do some grievous bodily harm to any person or with intent to resist or prevent the lawful apprehension or detainer of any person, shall be guilty of ... an offence.

The maximum penalty for this offence is life imprisonment. Many of the elements of this offence, such as causation, wounding, grievous bodily harm and maliciousness have already been considered above in the context of s 47 and s 20. The distinguishing feature is the need for the prosecution to prove that D acted with intent to cause grievous bodily harm. Note that it is not necessary to prove that D actually caused grievous bodily harm, provided he at least caused a wound with intent to do some grievous bodily harm. Where the charge is maliciously causing grievous bodily harm with intent to cause grievous bodily harm, the word malicious is somewhat superfluous, as D must have the intention to do some grievous bodily harm in any event. However, if the charge is one of malicious wounding with intent to cause grievous bodily harm, then it is perfectly feasible that D could act recklessly, in respect of the wounding, while intending to cause grievous bodily harm. Similarly, where the charge is wounding with intent to resist lawful arrest, the presence of an intent to resist arrest should not lead to the conclusion that the defendant foresaw the possibility of wounding resulting from his conduct. It is submitted that intention under s 18 bears the same meaning as that attributed to it by the House of Lords in *Woollin* [1998] 4 All ER 103. Although in that case the House of Lords was not purporting to determine the *mens rea* for the s 18 offence, it would be intolerable if the word intention had one meaning in the context of murder and another in the context of s 18, given that intention to do some grievous bodily harm is sufficient *mens rea* for murder.

7.6   THE POISONING OFFENCES

Sections 23 and 24 of the 1861 Act provide prosecutors with alternative offences where the ss 47, 20 or 18 offences cannot be established or are otherwise inappropriate. At one time it might have been argued that cases where D caused P to become seriously ill by lacing P's food with toxic substances might have posed problems for a prosecutor proceeding under s 20 because of the need to prove a direct assault upon P by D. Section 23 would have provided a convenient alternative because the *actus reus* merely requires 'administration' by D. *Burstow* makes clear that s 20 no longer necessarily requires proof of a direct assault, perhaps calling into question the need for s 23.

Section 23 of the OAPA 1861 provides that:

> Whosoever shall unlawfully and maliciously administer to or cause to be administered to or taken by any other person any poison or other destructive or noxious thing, so as thereby to endanger the life of such person, or so as thereby to inflict upon such person grievous bodily harm ... [shall be guilty of an offence ...]

The Act does not enlarge upon the meaning of poison or destructive things, but the Court of Appeal in *Cato* [1976] 1 All ER 260 assumed that the terminology was broad enough to encompass any substance likely to injure in common use. The best approach is to deal with each case on its facts, bearing in mind that whether or not a substance is noxious or destructive may depend on the quantity administered, the quality, strength or purity of the substance, and the vulnerability of the recipient (see further *Marcus* [1981] 1 WLR 774). Administration should be construed in wide terms to encompass any means by which D causes P to consume the toxic substance (see *Gillard* [1988] Crim LR 551). As indicated by reference to *Cunningham*, above, the *mens rea* requirement is met if D is shown to have been malicious, which in this context means he must at least have been aware of the risk that P might have suffered and the type of harm specified in s 23.

Section 24 is potentially more wide reaching in its ambit, given the broader terms in which it is couched. It provides that:

> Whosoever shall unlawfully and maliciously administer to or cause to be administered to or taken by any other person any poison or other destructive or noxious thing, with intent to injure, aggrieve, or annoy such person ... [shall be guilty of an offence ...]

It will be apparent that what sets this offence apart from the offence under s 23 is that D can commit the *actus reus* simply by administering the toxic substance – there is no need for the prosecution to prove any specific harm. The essence of the criminality lies in the *mens rea* that accompanies the administration, but even here the terminology is quaint if not odd. Intent to injure is readily understandable, albeit a little vague – is this actual bodily harm or grievous bodily harm? Intent to aggrieve or annoy is very open textured. Liability could possibly be imposed where D puts itching powder down the back of P's shirt, provided the itching power is regarded as a noxious substance. In *Weatherall* [1968] Crim LR 115, it was held that the necessary *mens rea* had not been established where D had given his wife sleeping tablets, so that he could look through her handbag for letters revealing details of her adultery whilst she was asleep. By contrast, in *Hill* (1986) 83 Cr App R 386, the House of Lords restored D's conviction under s 24 where he had given slimming tablets to teenage boys in the hope that they might lower the boys' inhibitions, possibly leading to some sexual contact. It was held that there was overwhelming evidence that D had intended the administration of the tablets to injure the metabolisms of the boys who took them. By contrast, the House of Lords felt that D might escape liability if he administered tablets to P because of a 'good' motive – the examples were given of keeping a pilot awake by plying him with stimulants so that he could safely land an aircraft, and keeping a child awake in order to greet the arrival of a relative late at night, or view a fireworks display. Motive is normally irrelevant in criminal law, hence it is not entirely easy to justify the distinctions upon which this ruling depends.

As part of the response to the perceived threat of terrorist attacks in the wake of the 11 September 2001 attacks in New York City, parliament has also enacted the Anti-Terrorism, Crime and Security Act 2001, s 113 of which introduces an offence of using a noxious substance to cause harm or intimidate. The offence carries the possibility of 14 years' imprisonment. The offence is made out where D uses a noxious substance or other noxious thing in a manner that is likely to:

(a) cause serious damage to real or personal property anywhere in the world;

(b) endanger human life or create a serious risk to the health or safety of the public or a section of the public; or

(c) induce in members of the public the fear that the action is likely to endanger their lives or create a serious risk to their health or safety.

Liability will depend on the prosecution being able to prove that D's actions were designed to influence the government (of the UK) or to intimidate the public or a section of the public (of any country). An inchoate form of the offence based on threatening to take such action is created by s 113(3).

7.7   THE PROBLEM OF CONSENT

Consent presents difficulties in the field of non-fatal offences as it raises questions as to the degree of autonomy the law should allow adult individuals. Clearly, the law does not currently recognise consent as defence to murder – the wishes of the victim are simply ignored on policy grounds. The problem is then identifying what lesser harm a victim should be allowed validly to consent to. Should the degree of harm to which an individual can validly consent vary according to the utility of the activity engaged in? Should the law distinguish between consent to inevitable harm and consent to the risk of harm?

In *Attorney General's Reference (No 6 of 1980)* [1981] 2 All ER 1057. Lord Lane CJ stated that:

> ... it can be taken as a starting point that it is an essential element of an assault that the act is done contrary to the will and without the consent of the victim ... Ordinarily, then, if the victim consents, the assailant is not guilty.

Whilst the defendant should provide evidence to substantiate his claim that the victim consented, it is up to the prosecution to negative consent beyond all reasonable doubt.

Donovan [1934] 2 KB 498 suggests that, as a very general rule, the common law will recognise P's consent as being a valid defence, provided the harm inflicted by D does not amount to actual bodily harm. The law recognises an implied consent in some circumstances where there is physical contact between people. If D jostles P as they stand together in a crowded underground train, then P is taken to have impliedly consented to the contact. In *Collins v Wilcock* [1984] 3 All ER 374, Goff LJ said:

> Generally speaking, consent is a defence to a battery; and most of the physical contacts of ordinary life are not actionable because they are impliedly consented to by all who move in society and so expose themselves to the risk of bodily contact. So nobody can complain of the jostling which is inevitable ... in ... an underground station or a busy street; nor can a person who attends a party complain if his hand is seized in friendship, or even if his back is (within reason) slapped.

He went on to say that these examples are regarded as instances of implied consent but suggests that it would be better to '... treat them as falling within a general exception embracing all physical contact which is generally acceptable in the ordinary conduct of daily life ...'. This is probably a better way to rationalise the situations, particularly as those who are very young or who have mental disabilities cannot give consent.

At the heart of the consent defence is the question: to what can P consent? The answer to this question involves giving consideration to what is deemed to be in the public interest. In *Attorney General's Reference (No 6 of 1980)*, it was acknowledged that the public interest will create exceptions to the general principle that, if the victim consents, then an assault or battery has not in law happened. In *Coney* (1882) 8 QBD 534, the consent of the prize-fighters was deemed irrelevant, as the fight was illegal. In *Donovan*, the defendant had caned a girl for the purpose of sexual gratification. His defence was that the girl had consented. The court deemed consent to be irrelevant if the act complained of was unlawful, which it would be if it involved the infliction of bodily harm. Swift J in *Donovan* defined 'bodily harm' to include:

> ... any hurt or injury calculated to interfere with health or comfort of the prosecutor. Such hurt or injury need not be permanent, but must, no doubt, be more than merely transient and trifling.

The court acknowledged that there were exceptions to this principle. The first relates to lawful sporting activity where the participants are bound by rules and regulations, for example, rugby, soccer, and boxing. This exception is justified on the ground that the law wishes to encourage 'manly diversions'. The consent, however, relates only to force that can be reasonably expected in the course of a game. If, as all too frequently happens, a rugby player hits an opponent in an 'off the ball' incident, then that clearly goes beyond the rules of the game and consent cannot be presumed. Boxing, of all these 'sports' presents the greatest difficulty. Here both fighters are intending to inflict harm on their opponent and there have been numerous instances where fighters have died as a result of the injuries received in the ring. Yet the activity was recognised as lawful by the House of Lords in *Brown*. The Law Commission in its consultation paper, *Criminal Law: Consent in the Criminal Law* (Law Com 139, 1995), takes the view that participating in an activity that is widely regarded as beneficial should not be regarded as being against a person's interests. The state though must be satisfied that the risks involved are properly controllable and ascertainable (para 13.19 and p 182, fn 23).

The second exception relates to surgery performed with the consent of the patient. If there is a benefit to the patient (and this might include psychological benefit as in the case of cosmetic surgery), then this would not normally amount to a criminal offence. Questions might still be raised, however, as regards outlandish and experimental surgery. Note that the practice of female circumcision is outlawed under the Female Circumcision Act 1985.

A third exception is illustrated by *Jones* [1987] Crim LR 123. Two schoolboys, aged 14 and 15, had been injured after being tossed into the air by the appellants. The appellants regarded the whole incident of horseplay as a joke and apparently this view was shared by the victims. The Court of Appeal held that 'consent to rough and undisciplined play where there is no intention to cause injury is a defence, in this case, to inflicting grievous bodily harm'. A similar line of reasoning was adopted in *Atkin and Others* [1992] 1 WLR 1006, where convictions contrary to s 20 of the OAPA 1861 were quashed on the basis that the victim had willingly taken part in horseplay or 'mess-games' being indulged in by RAF officers. The victim had white spirit poured over him and set alight, although he was wearing a fire resistant suit. The old adage 'boys will be boys' seems to be at the heart of these cases.

Sexual activity involving the deliberate infliction of harm is generally not seen as fulfilling any particularly useful public interest and has thus not been an area where the courts have been keen to extend the scope of the defence. In *Boyea* [1992] Crim LR 574, D placed his fist in P's vagina causing serious internal injuries. Although the court accepted that the degree of harm to which P could be said to have validly consented during heterosexual congress might now be greater than was the case when *Donovan* was decided, the harm caused to P exceeded the level of injury to which she could have consented. The leading case is the House of Lords' decision in *Brown*, where the six appellants had, over a 10-year period, willingly engaged in sado-masochistic acts for their own sexual gratification. The activities took place in private and all participants consented to the acts being committed upon them, including genital torture, branding and beatings with a cat-o'-nine tails. There were various charges of assault occasioning actual bodily harm (s 47 of the OAPA 1861) and unlawful wounding contrary to s 20 of the 1861 Act. It was held, by a 3:2 majority, that sado-masochistic acts which resulted in actual bodily harm or wounding were offences, irrespective of whether or not the victim gave consent. Of the majority, Lord Templeman thought:

> Society is entitled and bound to protect itself against a cult of violence. Pleasure derived from the infliction of pain is an evil thing ... such violence is injurious to the participants and unpredictably dangerous. I am not prepared to invent a defence of consent for sado-masochistic encounters which breed and glorify cruelty.

The majority further decided that, given the potential for serious physical injury, it was in the public interest to protect society from the danger of corrupting young people or seeking to influence them to participate.

Lord Mustill, dissenting, expressed the view that where consenting adults decided to inflict harm on each other in pursuit of their sexual predilections the law should not interfere. He added:

> ... these are questions ... of private morality ... the standards by which they fall to be judged are not those of the criminal law ... if those standards are to be upheld the individual must enforce them upon himself according to his own moral standards, or have them enforced against him by moral pressures exerted by whatever religious or other community to whose ethical ideals he responds. The point from which I invite your Lordships to depart is simply this, that the state should interfere with the rights of an individual to live his or her life as he or she may choose no more than is necessary to ensure a proper balance between the special interests of the individual and the general interests of the individuals who together comprise the populace at large.

Predictably, in *Emmett* (1999) *The Times*, 15 October, the Court of Appeal upheld the conviction of D who, as part of his 'sex games', was given to pouring lighter fuel on his wife's breast and lighting the fuel with a match.

What exactly does *Brown* decide? There seemed to be agreement that consent may be a defence to a common assault and indecent assault but not to either the s 47 or s 20 offences of the OAPA 1861. However, the House of Lords was prepared to recognise that there were certain lawful activities, where consent to engage in the activity knowing the risk of injury is present, provides a defence should bodily harm be caused. (Obvious examples are the sports of boxing and rugby.) The case also demonstrates the fundamentally different approach to the particular issue adopted by the majority and minority. The majority appeared to regard the problem as one of violence and cruelty, whereas the minority regarded it as an issue about private sexual relations and the response of the criminal law (see Lord Mustill's speech).

On the basis of the above, it can be stated that those who perpetrate actual bodily harm, or worse, will not be able to avail themselves of the defence of consent, unless the injury is caused during an activity falling within one of the public policy exceptions outlined above. The difficulty is in determining the contours of those public policy exceptions. This issue is usefully illustrated by the decision of the Court of Appeal in *Wilson* [1996] 3 WLR 125. The defendant, using a hot knife, branded his initials on his wife's buttocks. His wife had not made any complaint to the police and the marks were only discovered when she was being medically examined. He was charged with the offence of assault occasioning actual bodily harm under s 47 of the OAPA 1861. He admitted responsibility but claimed that the act was not only done with her consent but at her instigation. It had apparently been done as a tangible manifestation of their love for each other. The judge ruled that, in light of the decision in *Brown*, he was bound to rule that the wife's consent did not provide the defendant with a defence. The defendant was convicted. The Court of Appeal allowed his appeal, holding that '*Brown* was not authority for the proposition that consent was no defence to a charge under s 47 ... in all circumstances where actual bodily harm was deliberately inflicted'. The court thought there was no logical difference between this act of branding and that of tattooing, which is a lawful activity. It was also deemed not to be in the public interest that such consensual activity between husband and wife in the privacy of their own home 'should be visited by the sanctions of the criminal law where there was no aggressive intent ...' This decision is difficult to reconcile with the clear statement of Lord Jauncey in *Brown*:

> ... consent of the victim is no answer to anyone charged with the latter offence (s 47) or with contravention of s 20 unless the circumstances fall within one of the well-known exceptions such as organised sporting contests and games, parental chastisement or reasonable surgery. There is nothing in ss 20 and 47 of the Offences Against the Persons Act 1861 to suggest that consent is either an essential ingredient of the offence or a defence thereto [p 90h].

Is marital branding to be added to the list of 'well known' exceptions? Lord Templeman in *Brown* refers to one of the accused branding another on the thigh – the clear implication being that the first branding was consensual. Is there any real distinction between the two cases sufficient to justify the conclusion reached in *Wilson*? The evidence in *Wilson* indicates that the branding was at the wife's instigation. All the participants in *Brown* were willingly involved in the activities. In that sense, they were all instigators of what took place. In *Wilson*, the husband did not have any 'aggressive intent' towards his wife. There is no evidence in *Brown* that any of the individuals had aggressive intent against any of the others. In *Wilson* the incident was a single occurrence between a man and his wife in private. Does this mean that, if the parties had been long-term cohabitees, rather than husband and wife, the prosecution would have been successful?

Assume that, as a result of the publicity surrounding this case, Mr and Mrs Wilson are approached by some of their married friends asking if they will show them how the branding is done. The Wilsons invite three couples to their house, demonstrate the branding technique and then observe whilst the other couples engage in the activity. Are the three couples to be found guilty under s 47 of the 1861 Act on the basis that a group activity is unlawful, whereas a couple alone would not commit an offence? Common sense would say no. There is a clear need for basic principles to be developed. Otherwise, the case-by-case approach will only create further uncertainty. Certain activities are, from a public policy perspective, deemed lawful, but there appears to be no public policy dimension that will lead to the endorsement of sado-masochistic activities and, therefore, consent is irrelevant in these situations.

The current domestic law on the availability of consent as a defence to the infliction of harm, even amongst adults with a predilection for sado-masochistic activities, has been held to be consistent with the requirements of the European Convention on Human Rights (ECHR), as incorporated by the Human Rights Act 1998. The appellants in *Brown* took their case to the European Court of Human Rights (see *Laskey, Jaggard and Brown v United Kingdom* (1997) 24 EHRR 39) where it was unanimously held that the House of Lords' ruling was consistent with Art 8 of the Convention to the extent that the limitations on the defence of consent could be viewed as necessary in a democratic society for the preservation of health or morals.

7.7.1   Consent obtained by deception

The conventional wisdom is that, if D deceives P into consenting to his performing a particular act that would otherwise amount to an assault, battery, or indecent assault upon P, such consent is nullified where the deception relates to the identity of P or the nature of the act (see *Williams* [1987] 3 All ER 411, considered below, 7.11.1). The law is less clear where D exercises a deception as to his attributes. In *Richardson* (1998) *The Times*, 6 April, the defendant was a dentist who continued to treat patients, despite having been suspended from practice by the General Dental Council. She was convicted on six counts alleging offences contrary to s 47 of the OAPA 1861, the trial judge having ruled that the apparent consent of the patients to receiving treatment had been vitiated by the fraud (that is, that she was qualified to continue with the work). The Court of Appeal, allowing the appeal, held that what was in issue was the nature of the mistake made. As there had been no mistake on the part of the victim regarding the identity of the appellant or the nature of the act she was to perform, the consent was not vitiated by the appellant's silence as to her having been suspended.

Compare this with *Tabassum* (2000) *The Times*, 26 May, where the appellant was convicted of indecent assault as he had persuaded women to undergo breast examinations on the basis that they were participating in trials of software to be used by doctors. The Court of Appeal, confirming the conviction, held that there was clear evidence that the women concerned had only consented to being examined by the appellant because they believed he was medically qualified – which was not the case. Both *Clarence* and *Linekar* [1995] 3 All ER 69 were distinguished on the basis that, in both cases, the women concerned consented to sexual intercourse and sexual intercourse resulted, albeit with unforeseen consequences: in *Clarence*, the contraction of a venereal disease; in *Linekar*, the non-payment for sex. *Richardson* was distinguished as a case where the prosecution had (wrongly) proceeded on the basis that there had been a mistake as to identity. The court then concluded that the women examined by the appellant had consented to the nature of the acts performed (having their breasts examined) but not the quality of the act (a bogus medical examination) and therefore there had been no true consent. The decision seems questionable in the light of earlier cases. It suggests that deception as to the quality of the act can vitiate consent. It also suggests that there is a doctrine of informed consent in criminal law, a notion denied by the Court of Appeal in *Richardson*. Duress, that is, threats of death or serious physical violence will also negative consent providing the will has been overborne by the threats. Looked at from the defendant's point of view, if he genuinely and honestly believes the other person is consenting, then he is entitled to be found not guilty, even though his belief is a mistaken one (as determined by *DPP v Morgan* [1975] 2 All ER 347 and *Gladstone Williams* [1987] 3 All ER 411). There is no requirement that any belief in another's consent must be based upon reasonable grounds.

7.8   RACIALLY OR RELIGIOUSLY AGGRAVATED OFFENCES

The Labour Government elected in May 1997 specifically undertook to introduce legislation to deal with what were popularly referred to as 'race-hate' crimes. Rather than introduce a raft of new offences the government opted to created racially aggravated versions of existing crimes, including the most important statutory assaults. Under s 28 of the Crime and Disorder Act 1998, an assault is racially motivated if:

(a) at the time of committing the offence or immediately before or after doing so, the offender demonstrates towards the victim of the offence hostility based on the victim's membership (or presumed [by the offender] membership) of a racial or religious group; or

(b) the offence is motivated (wholly or partly) by hostility towards members of a racial or religious group based on their membership of that group. For the purposes of s 28 'racial group' means 'a group of persons defined by reference to race, colour, nationality (including citizenship) or ethnic or national origins'.

The fact that an assault is racially motivated is regarded under the Act as an aggravating factor, providing the court, following conviction, with the power to impose longer sentences than would otherwise be the case. The 1998 Act creates racially aggravated forms of common assault: ss 47 and 20 of the OAPA 1861; ss 2 and 4 of the Protection from Harassment Act 1997; criminal damage; and certain public order offences.

As a counterbalance to the increased powers given to the police and security services in the wake of the September 11 bombings in New York, the government proposed to introduce new offences of inciting religious hatred. In the light of opposition encountered outside and within parliament, however, the decision was taken to amend the racially aggravated offences outlined above, so as to make them 'racially or religiously aggravated' (see the Anti-Terrorism, Crime and Security Act 2001). For these purposes a religious group means '… a group of persons defined by reference to religious belief or lack of religious belief' (see s 28(4) of the 1998 Act, as amended).

7.9   HARASSMENT

The problems highlighted by the *Burstow* case have, to some extent, been addressed by the enactment of the Protection from Harassment Act (PHA) 1997. The Act creates two new criminal offences, as well as introducing civil remedies for those who suffer harassment. Section 1 of the PHA 1997 makes it an offence to pursue a course of conduct which:

- amounts to harassment of another; and
- which the defendant knows or ought to know amounts to harassment of the other.

Following *Colohan* (2001) *The Times*, 14 June, the court does not have to take into account any mental illness afflicting D when assessing what he ought to have known. As the court observed, the 1997 Act was aimed at the activities of persons who might be expected to suffer from some form of mental illness, 'stalking' being an example of an obsessive form of behaviour. To weaken the objective test would be to reduce the protection afforded by the Act.

A person is deemed to know that conduct will amount to harassment if 'a reasonable person in possession of the same information would think the course of conduct amounted to harassment of the other' (see s 1(2)). A person who commits an offence under s 1 is liable on summary conviction to imprisonment for a term not exceeding six months or a fine not exceeding level 5 on the standard scale, or both.

Section 4 of the PHA 1997 creates the more serious offence of 'putting people in fear of violence'. It states:

4(1) A person whose course of conduct causes another to fear, on at least two occasions, that violence will be used against him is guilty of an offence if he knows or ought to know that his course of conduct will cause the other so to fear on each of those occasions.

(2) For the purposes of this section, the person whose course of conduct is in question ought to know that it will cause another to fear that violence will be used against him on any occasion if a reasonable person in possession of the same information would think the course of conduct would cause the other so to fear on that occasion.

(3) It is a defence for a person charged with an offence under this section to show that:

– his course of conduct was pursued for the purpose of preventing or detecting crime;

– his course of conduct was pursued under any enactment or rule of law or to comply with any condition or requirement imposed by any person under any enactment; or

– the pursuit of his course of conduct was reasonable for the protection of himself or another or for the protection of his or another's property.

A person convicted on indictment is liable to a term of imprisonment not exceeding five years, a fine or both.

Henley [2000] Crim LR 582 is authority for the proposition that a threat of violence against a member of P's family could be regarded as a threat against P; but in *R v DPP* [2001] Crim LR 396, the Divisional Court held that words or conduct directed otherwise than at the complainant (in this case a threat to kill the complainant's dog) did not necessarily fall outside the scope of a course of conduct for the purposes of the 1997 Act. The proper approach was to look at the effect of D's actions on the complainant. It was held to be significant that the threats were directed at the dog in the presence of the complainant. These threats, coupled with the threats previously directed at the complainant, provided the evidence upon which a course of conduct could be based.

Although the 1997 Act was ostensibly introduced to deal with the problem of a defendant stalking a lone victim, it is clearly broad enough in its wording to encompass situations where D harasses more than one victim. In *DPP v Dunn* [2001] Crim LR 130, the Divisional Court held that, whilst the 1997 Act referred to victims in the singular, the Interpretation Act 1978 could be called into aid to support the argument that words such as 'another' and 'the other' could be taken to include the plural form. Members of a close-knit group could be subjected to the same course of harassing conduct even though they were, in fact, only ever exposed to it as separate individuals. *Caurti v DPP* [2002] Crim LR 131, emphasises, however, that where the more serious charge under s 4 is concerned, the provisions will be construed narrowly. D made threats to N that caused S to fear for N's safety, following which D made threats to S that caused N to fear for S's safety. D's conviction under s 4 was quashed. The offence was only made out if D caused a victim, on two or more occasions, to fear that violence would be used against himself. It was not enough that on the first occasion S feared for N's safety, and on the second occasion that N feared for S's safety.

Note that s 44 of the Criminal Justice and Police Act 2001 also amends s 7 of the PHA 1997 to make it clear that the sanctions that relate to a campaign of harassment by an individual also apply to a campaign of collective harassment by two or more people. Hence, conduct by one person shall be taken, at the time it occurs, also to be conduct by another if it is aided, abetted, counselled or procured by that other person.

A 'course of conduct' for the purposes of the 1997 Act can consist of just two incidents (see *Lau v DPP* [2000] Crim LR 580), but the further apart they are, the less likely the court is to find, as a matter of fact, that they constitute a course of conduct. In *Hills* [2001] Crim LR 318, D cohabited with P and was alleged to have assaulted her on at least two occasions. His appeal against conviction under s 2 was allowed not least because there was a gap of six months between the incidents, and because there was evidence that the incidents were separated by periods of marital harmony. On the other hand, a lengthy gap in time should not of itself be used as a basis for denying the existence of a course of conduct. The complainant might, for example, be subjected to abuse once a year on the occasion of a particular anniversary or religious celebration. There is no reason why the Act could not be invoked in such cases.

Further measures were introduced by way of the Criminal Justice and Police Act 2001 to counter the activities of campaigners who try to coerce or intimidate others into withdrawing from lawful activities, for example, anti-vivisectionists demonstrating outside the houses of those employed in animal testing laboratories, or outside the homes of those with shares in such companies. Section 42 of the Act, empowers a police officer to direct persons to leave the vicinity of the premises or to follow such other directions as the officer may give, in order to prevent harassment, alarm or distress to persons in the dwelling. This power is exercisable if persons are present in the vicinity of premises used as a dwelling, and there are reasonable grounds to believe that the person or persons are there for the purpose of persuading or making representations to any individual that they should do something which they are entitled not to do (or not do something they are entitled to do), and that the presence or behaviour of those persons is likely to cause harassment, alarm or distress to persons living at the premises. Failure to comply with a police officer's directions under this section becomes an offence.

7.10   REFORMING THE LAW RELATING TO NON-FATAL ASSAULTS

Decisions of the House of Lords and the Court of Appeal handed down during the last 10 years are replete with *obiter dicta* highlighting the need for a wholesale reform of the archaic laws relating to non-fatal, non-sexual offences against the person.

The Law Commission, in its report, *Legislating the Criminal Code: Offences Against the Person and General Principles* (Law Com 218, 1993), put forward a scheme for the rationalisation of the common law and statutory offences outlined above, and these proposals were adopted by the government as the basis for its consultation paper, *Violence: Reforming the Offences Against the Person Act 1861*, published in March 1998 (London: HMSO). The Home Office consultation paper included a draft Bill providing details of what the proposed new offences would look like.

Clause 1 seeks to replace s 18 of the 1861 Act with an offence of intentionally causing serious injury to another. As with the current offence, it would carry the possibility of life imprisonment. Clause 2 envisages an offence of recklessly causing serious injury to another. This would effectively replace s 20, at least as regards the infliction of grievous bodily harm. The maximum penalty envisaged following conviction on indictment is seven years. Section 47 of the 1861 Act would be replaced by the offence provided for in cl 3, which states that:

> A person is guilty of an offence if he intentionally or recklessly causes injury to another. The offence would carry the possibility of five years' imprisonment following conviction on indictment.

The offences of common assault and battery would be replaced by new offences set out in cl 4. They comprise the offence of intentionally or recklessly applying force to or causing an impact on the body of another, or intentionally or recklessly causing another to believe that any such force or impact is imminent. The offences would be summary only. The issue of the implied consent that is assumed to exist in respect of the physical contact with others that arises as a normal part of everyday life (for example, squeezing into an already crowded train carriage) is adverted to in cl 4(2), which provides that:

> ... no such offence is committed if the force or impact, not being intended or likely to cause injury, is in the circumstances such as is generally acceptable in the ordinary

conduct of daily life and the defendant does not know or believe that it is in fact unacceptable to the other person.

Injury for the purposes of the more serious assault offences is defined to encompass both physical and mental injury (cl 15) but, for the purposes of the offences proposed under cll 2 and 3, injury excludes harm that is caused by the transmission of disease. The aim here is that the deliberate transmission of the HIV virus could be an offence under cl 1, but there could be no liability for reckless transmission under cll 2 and 3.

The government's consultation paper outlines the rationale for adopting this position:

> The Law Commission's original proposal, which included illness and disease in the definition of injury, would have resulted in the intentional or reckless transmission of disease being open to prosecution. They argued that the width of their proposal would be balanced by the fact that prosecution would only be appropriate in the most serious cases. The Government has considered their views ... but is not persuaded that it would be right ... to criminalise the reckless transmission of normally minor illnesses such as measles or mumps, even though they could have potentially serious consequences for those vulnerable to infection ... [This is an issue of importance that] ... has ramifications beyond the criminal law, into the wider considerations of social and public health policy. The Government is particularly concerned that the law should not seem to discriminate against those who are HIV positive, have AIDS or viral hepatitis or who carry any kind of disease. Nor do we want to discourage people from coming forward for diagnostic tests and treatment, in the interests of their own health and that of others, because of an unfounded fear of criminal prosecution ... The Government therefore proposes that the criminal law should apply only to those whom it can be proved beyond reasonable doubt had deliberately transmitted a disease intending to cause a serious illness ... This proposal will clarify the present law which, because it is largely untested is unclear; by doing so the effect of the law will be confined to the most serious and culpable behaviour ... It is very difficult to prove both the causal linkage of the transmission and also to prove that it was done intentionally. To do so beyond reasonable doubt is even more difficult. The Government does not expect that the proposed offence will be used very often, but considers that it is important that it should exist to provide a safeguard against the worst behaviour [paras 3.12–3.19].

The draft Bill proposes the adoption of standard fault terms for the new offences. Clause 14 provides as follows:

14(1) A person acts intentionally with respect to a result if:

    (a) it is his purpose to cause it; or

    (b) although it is not his purpose to cause it, he knows that it would occur in the ordinary course of events if he were to succeed in his purpose of causing some other result.

(2) A person acts recklessly with respect to a result if he is aware of a risk that it will occur and it is unreasonable to take that risk having regard to the circumstances as he knows or believes them to be.

(3) A person intends an omission to have a result if:

    (a) it is his purpose that the result will occur; or

    (b) although it is not his purpose that the result will occur, he knows that it would occur in the ordinary course of events if he were to succeed in his purpose that some other result will occur.

(4)   A person is reckless whether an omission will have a result if he is aware of a risk that the result will occur and it is unreasonable to take that risk having regard to the circumstances as he knows or believes them to be.

(5)   Related expressions must be construed accordingly.

(6)   This section has effect for the purposes of this Act.

Some consideration has been given to reforming the law on the scope of the defence of consent to physical harm in the Law Commission's two consultation papers, Law Com 134 (1994) and Law Com 139 (1995). In summary, the Law Commission provisionally proposes that the intentional or reckless causing of seriously disabling injury to another person should continue to be criminal, even if the person injured consents. Consent should be available as a defence, however, in respect of the intentional causing of any lesser injury to another person. For these purposes a 'seriously disabling injury' would be one that involved serious distress and '... the loss of a bodily member or organ or permanent bodily injury or permanent functional impairment, or serious or permanent disfigurement, or severe and prolonged pain, or serious impairment of mental health, or prolonged unconsciousness ...' Consent for these purposes would involve '... a valid subsisting consent to an injury or to the risk of an injury of the type caused ...' either express or implied. Consent would be established if the victim consented to an act or omission that he knew was intended to cause injury to him of the type caused, or he consented to an act or omission that he knew to involve a risk of injury of the type caused.

7.11   SEXUAL OFFENCES – RAPE

Although the term 'sexual offences' suggests a discrete body of offences that should be seen as standing apart from other categories of crime, most sexual offences are, in fact, aggravated forms of assault. This is most obviously the case with offences such as indecent assault, but it is equally true in respect of more serious offences such as rape. Given its sub-text of sexual politics, the topic of sexual offences, perhaps more than other areas of criminal law, tends to be the subject of heated debate regarding issues such as relations between men and women, criminalisation and decriminalisation of homosexual activities, and the age at which young persons should be granted full bodily autonomy.

Certain offences, for example, rape, raise unique issues, such as the risk of pregnancy. Sexual offences involving penetrative intercourse carry with them the possibility of infection with serious, or even deadly consequences, such as the case where the victim becomes HIV positive following intercourse.

As a backdrop to all of these issues are the evidential problems peculiar to sexual offences. In many cases, there will be no third party witnesses to the event, given the very nature of the acts concerned. The result is a contest between the plausibility of the evidence given by the accused as against that given by the complainant. In rape cases, there is the additional factor of the 'lifestyle' of the complainant and its impact on the jury's view of whether or not he or she might have consented to the physical contact (that is, the sexual intercourse) – a debate that rarely if ever arises in cases of assault or wounding.

Section 1(1) of the SOA 1956 placed rape on a statutory basis by baldly stating that it was an offence for a man to rape a woman. Since then the common law has recognised that a husband can be guilty of raping his wife, and parliament has intervened to provide that a man can be the victim of rape as well as a woman. The current statutory definition of rape is to be found in the revised version of s 1(1) inserted into the 1956 Act by the Criminal Justice and Public Order Act (CJPOA) 1994. It provides as follows:

1(1)   It is an offence for a man to rape a woman or another man.

(2)   A man commits rape if:

(a)   he has sexual intercourse with a person (whether vaginal or anal) who at the time of the intercourse does not consent to it; and

(b)   at the time he knows that the person does not consent to the intercourse or is reckless as to whether that person consents to it.

7.11.1   The *actus reus* of rape

The *actus reus* of rape is complete if the following are satisfied:

- there is sexual intercourse by way of penile penetration, whether vaginal or anal; and

- there is an absence of consent.

Intercourse is deemed complete upon proof of penetration only (s 44 of the SOA 1956, as amended by the CJPOA 1994). If the man continues to penetrate the person after consent is withdrawn, then the *actus reus* of rape is complete even though the initial penetration was with consent. In *Kaitamaki* [1985] AC 147, the accused claimed that he became aware that she was not consenting after the initial penetration had taken place. He admitted that he did not desist from intercourse. He was convicted of rape. It follows, therefore, that in such circumstances rape becomes a crime of omission. Few people would view rape as a crime of omission and it would therefore be better if the definition of rape contained the words 'or continues to have sexual intercourse when he knows that consent has been withdrawn'. A defendant in the position of Kaitamaki would still be guilty of rape but at least his liability would be founded upon an 'act' rather than an 'omission' in the sense of a failure to withdraw.

Until comparatively recently the definition of rape included a requirement that the sexual intercourse should be 'unlawful', which was taken to mean that the intercourse had to be outside the bonds of matrimony (that is a man could not rape his wife). The House of Lords in *R* [1991] 4 All ER 481 dispensed with this requirement by holding that the word 'unlawful' was 'mere surplusage'. Lord Keith went on to say:

The fact is that it is clearly unlawful to have sexual intercourse with any woman without her consent, and that the use of the word in the sub-section adds nothing.

Prior to the passing of the SOA 1993, a boy under the age of 14 was to be conclusively presumed to be incapable of causing the *actus reus* of rape. That presumption was abolished by s 1 of the 1993 Act. It is now possible for a defendant as young as 10 to be charged with rape.

The most contentious aspect of the *actus reus* of rape is the need for the prosecution to prove the absence of consent on the part of the complainant. Consent will only be valid if it is freely given. Difficulties arise in cases where the complainant agrees to have sexual intercourse with D in the hope of securing some favour in return, or where the consent is induced by fear of what might happen if consent is not given. If D holds a knife to P's throat and threatens to kill her if she does not let him have sex with her, few would suggest that P has consented to any ensuing sexual intercourse with D. Yet it can be argued that P, in that situation, has made a choice. Be killed, or at least run the risk of being killed, or let D have sexual intercourse with her. The problem is one of degree. How much pressure and duress vitiates P's consent? Does anything turn upon the type of consequence that P fears if her consent is withheld? Suppose P consents to sexual intercourse with her tutor on the basis that he will enter her exam mark as a pass when in fact she has failed or P consents to sexual intercourse with D on the basis that he will not report the details of the crime he witnessed her committing. Suppose P consents to sexual intercourse with D because he has promised that if she does he will not sexually assault her young daughter.

There is no statutory definition of rape, but in difficult cases such as those suggested above the jury will require some guidance. The leading authority on this issue is the Court of Appeal's decision in *Olugboja* [1981] 3 All ER 433. The appellant had sexual intercourse with the complainant who claimed she had not been consenting. There was no evidence of the appellant physically overpowering the complainant, her explanation being that she was frightened of what the appellant might do to her if she did not comply with his demands. Dunn LJ directed the jury that consent should be given its ordinary meaning and that there was a difference between consent and submission. He stressed that whilst every consent involved a submission, it by no means followed that a mere submission necessarily involved consent. He added:

> In the less common type of case where intercourse takes place after threats not involving violence or the fear of it ... we think that an appropriate direction to a jury will have to be fuller. They should be directed to concentrate on the state of mind of the victim immediately before the act of sexual intercourse, having regard to all the relevant circumstances, and in particular, the events leading up to the act and her reaction to them showing their impact on her mind. Apparent acquiescence after penetration does not necessarily involve consent, which must have occurred before the act takes place. In addition to the general direction about consent which we have outlined, the jury will probably be helped in such cases by being reminded that in this context consent does comprehend the wide spectrum of states of mind to which we earlier referred, and that the dividing line in such circumstances between real consent on the one hand and mere submission on the other may not be easy to draw. Where it is to be drawn in a given case is for the jury to decide, applying their combined good sense, experience and knowledge of human nature and modern behaviour to all the relevant facts of that case ...

The difficulty with this approach is the amount of discretion it leaves to the jury. Inevitably, they will resort to their own preconceptions as to what is acceptable sexual behaviour and what is not. The complainant with a promiscuous lifestyle, or a complainant who works as a prostitute will have real problems in dispelling the notion that they are in some way less deserving of the protection of the law than others.

Consent may, as indicated above, be negated by duress or threats. Equally there are situations where it can be rendered void, or at least voidable, by the deception exercised by D. Section 1(3) of the SOA 1956 specifically provides that:

> A man also commits rape if he induces a married woman to have sexual intercourse with him by impersonating her husband.

In *Elbekkay* [1995] Crim LR 163, the complainant thought that the person who had entered her bed early in the morning was her boyfriend. She permitted intercourse to begin and then realised that something was not quite right. She opened her eyes and discovered that it was the appellant, a friend, who was staying with the couple. The Court of Appeal upheld the appellant's conviction for rape on the basis that the complainant had not been consenting to intercourse with the appellant. There had been a mistake as to identity and that was sufficient to negative the apparent consent to intercourse. It is submitted that this approach must be right (there being no basis in a modern society for the law to afford special protection to married women as compared to 'common law wives'), provided the situation is one where the identity of D is a matter of significance to P. Deception as to the nature of the act being performed should also be sufficient to render any apparent consent void. Hence, in *Williams*, a singing master had sexual intercourse with one of his pupils aged 16 by pretending that the act of intercourse was a method of training her voice. The girl showed no resistance as she believed what he said and was, apparently, unaware that he was having sexual intercourse with her. He was convicted of rape and his appeal was dismissed. The court approved the summing up of Branson J to the effect that:

> ... where she is persuaded that what is being done to her is not the ordinary act of sexual intercourse but is some medical or surgical operation in order to give her relief from some disability from which she is suffering, then it is rape although the actual thing that was done was done with her consent, because she never consented to the act of sexual intercourse. She was persuaded to consent to what he did because she thought it was not sexual intercourse and because she thought it was a surgical operation.

In this more enlightened age, it is difficult to comprehend that a 16-year-old girl would believe that she was engaging in a 'surgical operation'! Perhaps in 1920 it could have been conceivable but it was never actually proved that she was unaware of the facts of life, in which case she would not have consented to an operation but to the act of intercourse and Williams should have had his conviction quashed.

By contrast, mistake as to the quality of the act performed may simply render consent voidable. In *Linekar*, the complainant was a prostitute and agreed to have intercourse with the appellant for £25. After intercourse, he left without paying. The jury found that he had never had any intention of paying. The court held, allowing his appeal against conviction for rape, that the absence of consent, not the existence of fraud, was necessary to make the conduct rape. In this case, the prostitute had consented to sexual intercourse with the appellant. The reality of consent was not destroyed because she thought that he would pay her £25. The appropriate charge in such cases would appear to be one of procuring a woman, by false pretences or false representations, to have sexual intercourse in any part of the world, contrary to s 3 of the SOA 1956.

It would be foolish to suggest that a clear distinction can always be drawn as to mistake relating to the nature of the act performed and mistake as to the quality of the act performed. Suppose D lies to P when he tells her that he is not suffering from any sexually transmittable disease and they proceed to have sexual intercourse. On the one hand, P consented to sexual intercourse with D and that is what occurred. She was not deceived as to his identity or the nature of the act performed. On the other hand, she could argue that sexual intercourse without the risk of contracting a serious, even terminal, disease is something quite different to sexual intercourse with the certainty of contracting such a disease. Admittedly, other offences could be charged in such cases, such as causing or inflicting grievous bodily harm contrary to s 18 or 20 of the OAPA 1861 (perhaps even s 23 or 24 of that Act), but perhaps rape more accurately describes the nature of the offence committed.

What is tolerably clear is that if P lays down a precondition to sexual intercourse that D fails to comply with, the prosecution should be able to prove that there was no consent. In *Attorney General's Ref (No 28 of 1996)* [1997] 2 Cr App R(S) 206, the Court of Appeal confirmed that D would be guilty of rape if he forced P to have unprotected sex after she said she would only consent to sex if he wore a condom. Hence, in *Linekar*, if P had insisted on payment before allowing D to have sexual intercourse and D had ignored this demand and proceeded to have sexual intercourse regardless, D could have been guilty of raping P.

7.11.2   The *mens rea* of rape

To establish the *mens rea* for rape the prosecution must prove that the accused intended to have sexual intercourse with a person and that he knew that person was not consenting or was at least reckless as to whether that person was consenting. The House of Lords' decision in *Morgan* confirmed that the defendant is to be judged on the facts as he honestly believed them to be. In that case the defendants were encouraged to have sexual intercourse with P by her husband. He assured the defendants that his wife enjoyed sexual encounters with strangers and particularly enjoyed being forced to have sexual intercourse. The husband told the defendants not to be concerned if P struggled or told them to desist as this was all part of her role playing. In reality, P had no such desires. Her husband derived his sexual gratification from seeing her being raped. The defendants proceeded to have sexual intercourse with P who was not in fact consenting. She begged the defendants to stop and was visibly distressed during and after the sexual intercourse that took place. The defendants contended that they should not be convicted of rape, as they had honestly believed that P had been consenting. Although the House of Lords upheld the convictions in *Morgan* (the proviso being applied) the decision created a storm of protest and was denounced as a 'Rapist's Charter'. Taken at face value, the ruling of the House of Lords meant that any defendant charged with rape could escape liability if he honestly believed that the complainant had been consenting, regardless of the fact that a reasonable person would have been aware that the complainant was not consenting (for example, if a defendant honestly believed that when a woman said 'no' to sexual intercourse she actually meant 'yes' but was too coy to admit it). In an effort to assuage the criticisms aimed at the ruling in *Morgan* parliament enacted s 1(2) of the Sexual Offences (Amendment) Act 1976, which provides that:

It is hereby declared that if at a trial for a rape offence the jury has to consider whether a man believed that a woman was consenting to sexual intercourse, the presence or absence of reasonable grounds for such a belief is a matter to which the jury is to have regard, in conjunction with any other matters, in considering whether he so believed.

The sub-section really only states the obvious – the jury must look at all the relevant evidence. It does not alter the decision in *Morgan*. Note that even under s 1(2) the issue that the jury has to decide having considered all the relevant evidence is '... whether *he* so believed'. In other words, it still comes down to a question of what the defendant was thinking. The Home Office consultation paper *Setting the Boundaries: Reforming the Law on Sex Offences* (2000, London: HMSO) reviewed the arguments for and against a subjective test for *mens rea* in rape. On the one hand, a subjective test was seen as being desirable because:

(i)   The law should punish people not just for what they did but for what they intended to do. This underlies most modern law, and underpins for example the distinction between intentional killing being charged as murder whilst a death that results from poor driving, although deeply tragic, is not regarded as so blameworthy – because there was no specific intent, and in terms of the law is a less serious offence.

(ii)   A test of reasonableness is applying *external* standards. Should a person be found guilty of a very serious crime because they did not apply the same personal standards of reasonableness as those who determined the accused's guilt or innocence? Is it right to apply external standards when the accused did not think they were doing wrong, for whatever cultural or other factors? What if they did not have the capacity to realise there was no consent?

(iii)   How should a reasonableness test be applied? Does it have to be reasonable for a person of the same class, culture or level of intelligence? If so does this not risk accentuating and perpetuating stereotypes about behaviour?

(iv)   The nature of the belief and its reasonableness or lack of it are issues to be tested by evidence on the facts of the case. The testing of the nature of the belief by the prosecution is an essential part of the case [para 2.13.6].

Points against the continued adherence to a subjective approach were:

(i)   It implicitly authorises the assumption of consent, regardless of the views of the victim, or whatever they say or do.

(ii)   It encourages people to adhere to myths about sexual behaviour and in particular that all women like to be overborne by a dominant male, and that 'no' really means 'yes'. It undermines the fundamental concept of sexual autonomy.

(iii)   The mistaken belief arises in a situation where it is easy to seek consent and the cost to the victim of the forced penetration is very high. It is not unfair to any person to make them take care that their partner is consenting and be at risk of a prosecution if they do not do so.

(iv)   There is no justice in a situation whereby a woman (or a man) who has been raped in fact (because she or he did not consent) sees an assailant go free because of a belief system that society as a whole would find unreasonable – for example that he saw some or all women (or women of certain types) as sexual objects.

(v)   It is easy to raise the defence but hard to disprove it [para 2.13.7].

To maintain a sense of perspective in this debate, two points should be borne in mind. First, a key limiting factor will be the jury's common sense. Whilst a trial judge must emphasise to the jury that the test for *mens rea* is subjective, the more implausible the defendant's claim that he honestly believed the complainant to be consenting, the less likely the jury are to believe that he honestly held any such belief. Secondly, it is not necessary for the prosecution to prove that D knew P was not consenting. It will be enough to prove that D was reckless as to whether or not P was consenting. It is now clear that the recklessness involved is of the *Cunningham* not *Caldwell* variety. Bristow J observed in *S (Satnam) and S (Kewel)* (1983) 78 Cr App R 149 that:

> Any direction as to the definition of rape should therefore be based on s 1 of the Sexual Offences (Amendment) Act 1976 and upon *DPP v Morgan*, without regard to *R v Caldwell* ... which [was] concerned with recklessness in a different context and under a different statute ... In [criminal damage cases] the foreseeability, or possible foreseeability, is as to the consequences of the criminal act. In the case of rape the foreseeability is to the state of mind of the victim.

Further, it should not be assumed that a *Morgan* type direction is necessary in every rape case where knowledge of consent is in issue. *Adkins* [2000] 2 All ER 185 confirms that the need for such a direction will only arise where the evidence suggests the possibility of a genuine mistake by the defendant. As Roch LJ noted:

> The question of honest belief does not necessarily arise where reckless rape is in issue. The defendant may have failed to address his mind to the question whether or not there was consent, or be indifferent as to whether there was consent or not, in circumstances where, had he addressed his mind to the question, he could not genuinely have believed that there was consent.

The minimum *mens rea* for rape, therefore, is that the defendant was aware of the risk that the complainant was not consenting, but nevertheless went on to take that risk. It follows that a defendant who stops to consider whether or not there is a risk that the complainant might not be consenting, only wrongly to conclude that there is no such risk, must escape liability under the 'lacuna' formulation. Such a defendant *has* thought about the risk and has concluded that he is not taking a risk. See below, 7.13, for consideration of current reform proposals in respect of the *mens rea* for rape.

7.11.3 Other offences involving sexual intercourse

A person under the age of 16 cannot consent to sexual intercourse. In theory, therefore, any case involving a defendant having sexual intercourse with a person under the age of 16 could be charged as rape. There may be situations where proceeding with a rape charge is not the most appropriate or advantageous route for the prosecution to follow. Section 5 of the SOA 1956 makes it an offence, punishable with life imprisonment, for a man to have unlawful sexual intercourse with a girl under the age of 13. Charging a defendant under s 5, as opposed to charging rape, more accurately marks out the nature of the criminality. It is also significant that the prosecution does not have to establish any *mens rea* beyond, it is assumed, an intention to have sexual intercourse and knowledge that the victim is a girl.

Section 6 of the SOA 1956 creates the less serious offence of unlawful sexual intercourse with a girl under 16. Once again, very little in the way of *mens rea* is required. However, note that s 6(3) makes special provision for what is known as the 'young man's defence' whereby it will be a defence for a man under the age of 24, who has not been previously charged with a like offence, to show that he believed the girl to be over 16 and had reasonable cause for the belief. In *Kirk*

[2002] Crim LR 756, the Court of Appeal rejected a claim that s 6(3) was discriminatory and prevented a defendant from being able to have a fair trial as required by Art 6 of the ECHR. The court noted that a woman could not commit the offence under s 6(1) as a principal offender, although she could be charged as an accomplice, in which case she too would be able to rely on the s 6(3) defence if under the age of 24.

7.12   INDECENT ASSAULT

As the law currently stands, the offences of indecent assault upon a man (s 15 of the SOA 1956) and indecent assault upon a woman (s 14) have to be used to cover the whole range of sexual assaults that fall short of penile penetration of the anus or vagina. This means the matters that fall within the scope of these offences can range from the relatively trivial 'bottom pinching' episodes, to violent and degrading attacks that can be as traumatising as rape or even worse (such as those that involve violation of bodily orifices with weapons and other items). Victims under the age of 16 cannot in law give any consent that would prevent the act from being an assault.

Both ss 14 and 15 of the 1956 Act require evidence of a 'technical' assault or a battery. Assault in this context means that D puts P in fear of unlawful physical violence being inflicted. A battery requires actual contact with the victim. It follows that where the case proceeds on the basis of a 'technical' assault, D must have intended that it will be associated with circumstances of indecency. Hence, in *Sargeant* (1997) 161 JP 127, a conviction under s 15(1) was upheld where the appellant had grabbed the victim, aged 16, and forced him to masturbate into a condom. The boy had not been touched in a sexual manner but an assault had taken place when the appellant had grabbed him and the court had no doubt that this was done in circumstances of indecency. An indecent assault can occur even though there is no hostility towards the victim. As Lane CJ said in *Faulkner v Talbot* [1981] 3 All ER 469, an assault 'need not be hostile or rude or aggressive, as some of the earlier cases seem to indicate', but presumably P still needs to apprehend that force will be applied to him. An indecent assault can be committed by one female on another female, since s 14(1) of the 1956 Act makes it an offence for a person to commit an indecent assault on a woman. A woman may, of course, commit an indecent assault on a man or boy. In *Faulkner v Talbot*, the court held that it was not an offence for a woman to permit a 14-year-old boy to have intercourse with her. However, where the woman touched the boy in an indecent way as a preliminary to sexual intercourse, then she committed an indecent assault. This was held to be the case irrespective of whether the boy was consenting or not. This leads to the rather strange conclusion that it is an offence to do something on the way to intercourse but the act of intercourse is not. The conclusion though is justifiable on the basis of the wording of s 15(1) of the 1956 Act.

Lord Ackner in *Court* [1988] 2 All ER 221, stated that the indecency required under ss 14 and 15 could be established if the assault took place in circumstances capable of being considered as indecent by right-minded persons. If an assault could not be considered indecent by any reasonable person, the fact that D derives some furtive sexual gratification from the activity will not be enough to render it indecent. In *George*

[1956] Crim LR 52, the defendant tried to remove a shoe from his victim, an act from which he obtained some sort of sexual thrill. His conviction was quashed because, looked at objectively, the circumstances were not indecent. Therefore, if the circumstances do not include any perceived element of indecency, then, whatever the motive of the accused, this will not amount to an indecent assault. Right-minded individuals observing what was taking place would not conclude they were watching an indecent event unfolding before their eyes. At the other extreme are those situations that appear obviously to be indecent. Lord Ackner in *Court* gives the example of a man ripping off a woman's clothes against her wishes. Here, the assault will be presumed to be indecent unless the defendant can adduce evidence to rebut the presumption.

An intimate examination carried out by a doctor could, in one sense, be seen as obviously indecent. The fact that it is a *bone fide* medical examination provides the explanation, however, that negates the indecency. This leaves open the question of whether or not a male doctor, who obtains sexual satisfaction or gratification from a clinically necessary intimate examination of a female patient, nevertheless commits an indecent assault. Where the defendant's actions are ambiguous in the sense that they could be regarded as innocent or indecent, any admissible evidence of the defendant's state of mind can be relied upon to establish indecency. In *Court*, a 26-year-old man 'spanked' a 12-year-old girl against her wishes. He claimed he suffered from a 'buttock fetish' and could offer no further explanation for his conduct. The House of Lords held that this admission could be put before the jury to help them decide whether or not the defendant's assault had been indecent.

Lord Hobhouse, in *K* [2001] 3 All ER 897, expressed the view that proof of *actus reus* also involved the prosecution in establishing either the '… fact of the absence of consent or the fact of an age of less than sixteen years'. Where consent is raised as a defence, decisions such as *Donovan*, *Boyea* and *Brown* indicate that, subject to recognised exceptions, a victim cannot consent to an assault where actual bodily harm has been caused. Further consent can be vitiated by the defendant's deceit as to his identity or the nature of the act he proposes to perform. *Tabassum* is evidence of the difficulty in distinguishing between nature and quality and the law is in need of clarification on this point.

The *mens rea* of indecent assault requires proof that the defendant intentionally or recklessly assaulted the victim. Lord Ackner in *Court* asserted that in cases where the defendant's actions were capable of being seen as indecent or innocent, it was also necessary to prove that the defendant intended to commit such an indecent assault. It is submitted that this may not be correct, as indecent assault is surely an offence of basic intent. The *mens rea* should extend no further than the assault. Whether or not it is indecent is a matter of fact for the jury to determine. If a defendant can be guilty under s 47 of the OAPA 1861 without proof that he foresaw actual bodily harm, why should the offence of indecent assault require proof of any knowledge as regards indecency?

As indicated above, a child under the age of 16 cannot validly consent to an indecent assault. Even if a 15-year-old does consent, therefore, the *actus reus* will be made out as the apparent consent is of no consequence in law. If P, who is under the age of 16, is consenting to the indecent assault, and D honestly believes P to be over the age of 16, D should escape liability as (on the facts as he believes them to be) he is not committing a criminal offence. This much was confirmed by the House of Lords in *K*, where K, a 26-year-old man of previous good character was convicted of indecent assault on P, a girl aged 14. P had consented to the indecent physical contact and K gave evidence that he had honestly believed P to be over 16 years of age. Lord Bingham noted that the more serious offence of unlawful sexual intercourse contrary to s 6 of the 1956 Act actually allowed for a defence of mistake (the 'young man's defence'). On that basis he could see no reason why the (usually) less serious offence under s 14 or 15 of the 1956 Act should not be interpreted so as to allow the defendant to be judged on the facts as he honestly believed them to be. He added:

> Nothing in this opinion has any bearing on a case in which the victim does not in fact consent. While section 14(2) provides that a girl under the age of 16 cannot in law give any consent which would prevent an act being an assault, she may in fact (although not in law) consent. If it is shown that she did not consent, and that the defendant did not genuinely believe that she consented, any belief by the defendant concerning her age is irrelevant, since her age is relevant only to her capacity to consent ... While a defendant's belief need not be reasonable provided it is honest and genuine, the reasonableness or unreasonableness of the belief is by no means irrelevant. The more unreasonable the belief, the less likely it is to be accepted as genuine ... Nothing in this opinion should be taken to minimise the potential seriousness of the offence of indecent assault. While some instances of the offence may be relatively minor, others may be scarcely less serious than rape itself. This is reflected in the maximum penalty, now increased to 10 years.

7.12.1 Other offences involving young persons

The Indecency with Children Act 1960 (as amended by s 39 of the Criminal Justice and Court Services Act 2000) makes it an offence for any person to commit an act of gross indecency with or towards a child under the age of 16 (originally this was set at 14), or to incite a child under that age to such an act with him or another. The offence carries the possibility of 10 years' imprisonment. The offence has, in some respects, been interpreted broadly by the courts, with a view to maximising the protection than can be afforded to children in respect of the actions of sexual predators. In *Speck* [1977] 2 All ER 859, it was held that inactivity could amount to an 'act' for these purposes – the appellant had allowed a young girl to touch his penis and leave her hand there whilst he had an erection. It had been assumed that the offence was one of strict liability as regards the element of the *actus reus* relating to the age of the victim, but the House of Lords, in *B (A Minor) v DPP* [2000] 1 All ER 833, has held that a defendant can be acquitted if he honestly believes the child in question to be above the age of 14 (note that the relevant age would now be 16). The ruling is an emphatic statement of support for the subjectivist approach to criminal liability, the House of Lords noting that the offence in question was a serious one, carrying with it considerable social stigma in the event of a conviction. Their Lordships were also mindful of the breadth of the offence, covering as it did the activities of paedophiles preying on children at one extreme, and the activities of sexually precocious teenagers engaged in consensual sexual activity at the other. On that basis, it was felt that the imposition of strict liability could not be supported on the grounds of seeking to obtain a clear and focused statutory objective.

The Sexual Offences (Amendment) Act 2000 augmented the range of sexual offences that could be charged where young victims are involved by introducing a number of specific offences involving abuse of a position of trust. Essentially, the offences are committed if D is over the age of 18 and looks after persons under that age, such as where D is employed at an offender's institution, local authority home, or educational institution. The offence extends beyond sexual intercourse to encompass 'sexual activity' which is defined as any activity that a reasonable person would regard as sexual in all the circumstances, other than an activity that such a person would regard as sexual only with knowledge of the intentions, motives or feelings of the parties.

7.13   REFORM OF SEXUAL OFFENCES

The Home Office consultation paper published in July 2000 (*Setting the Boundaries: Reforming the Law on Sex Offences*) described the current law relating to sexual offences as a:

> ... patchwork quilt of provisions ancient and modern that works because people make it do so, not because there is a coherence and structure ... much [of it] is old, dating from nineteenth century laws that codified the common law of the time, and reflected the social attitudes and roles of men and women of the time. With the advent of a new century and the incorporation of the European Convention of Human Rights into our law, the time was right to take a fresh look at the law to see that it meets the need of the country today [para 02].

In January 2003 the government responded to these criticisms by introducing the Sexual Offences Bill, a measure that proposes a major and wide-ranging overhaul of sexual offences:

Clause 1 seeks to restate the offence of rape in these terms:

(1)   A person (A) commits an offence if –

  (a)   he intentionally penetrates the vagina, anus or mouth of another person (B) with his penis,

  (b)   B does not consent to the penetration, and

  (c)   subsection (2) or (3) applies.

For these purposes penetration is to be regarded as a continuing act from entry to withdrawal (cl 81(2)). References to parts of the body such as the vagina will be taken to include surgically constructed orifices (for example, through gender reassignment surgery).

The Bill makes elaborate provision for the issue of consent and, if enacted, will sweep away the effect of the House of Lords' decision in *DPP v Morgan* (considered above). Clause 77 provides generally that a person consents '... if he agrees by choice, and has the freedom and capacity to make that choice'.

Under what is proposed, D will have the *mens rea* for the offence of rape if the prosecution can prove that:

(a)   D did not believe that P was consenting; or

(b)   D gave no thought to whether P was consenting (that is, *Caldwell* recklessness); or

(c)   D thought about whether or not P was consenting but then deliberately put the matter out of his mind; or

(d)   a reasonable person would, in all the circumstances, have doubted whether P was consenting and D failed to act in a way that a reasonable person would have considered sufficient in all the circumstances to resolve such doubt.

Clause 78 then proceeds to establish a number of rebuttable and conclusive presumptions regarding whether or not the complainant consented and whether or not the defendant knew that the complainant was not consenting. If any of the circumstances described in cl 78(3) arise, there is a rebuttable presumption that P did not consent and that D did not believe that P was consenting. The circumstances described are that:

(a) any person was, at the time of the relevant act [that is, the penetration] or immediately before it began, using violence against the complainant or causing the complainant to fear that immediate violence would be used against him;

(b) any person was, at the time of the relevant act or immediately before it began, causing the complainant to fear that violence was being used, or that immediate violence would be used, against another person;

(c) the complainant was, and the defendant was not, unlawfully detained at the time of the relevant act;

(d) the complainant was asleep or otherwise unconscious at the time of the relevant act;

(e) because of the complainant's physical disability, the complainant would not have been able at the time of the relevant act to communicate to the defendant whether the complainant consented.

In any one of those circumstances, it will be presumed, for the purposes of establishing the *actus reus* of rape, that the complainant was not consenting. The evidential burden will then fall on the defendant to show that the complainant was in fact consenting. Similarly, it will be presumed that the defendant did not believe that the complainant consented. It will be open to the defendant to adduce evidence to the contrary but cl 78 places him under a legal burden of proof in this respect, that is, he must prove on the balance of probabilities that he did believe that the complainant was consenting. In proving this belief, the defendant will not be able to rely on anything said or done in the course of cross-examination of the complainant unless it amounts to an admission that the complainant consented.

This would appear to cover the situation that arose in *Olugboja* (considered above), where there was evidence that the complainant feared violence if she did not comply with the appellant's demands. Under these proposals the appellant would have faced a much heavier burden in establishing that the complainant was consenting and that he believed such to be the case.

Where (a) the defendant penetrates the vagina, anus or mouth of another person, (b) that person does not consent, and (c) the only evidence adduced of circumstances from which the defendant might have formed a belief that the complainant consented is evidence of anything said or done by a third party, or evidence of circumstances from which the defendant could not have formed such a belief except on the grounds that they were consistent with anything said or done by a third party, cl 78(6) provides that it is to be conclusively presumed:

(a) that a reasonable person would in all the circumstances have doubted whether the complainant consented, and (b) that the defendant did not act in a way that a reasonable person would consider sufficient in all the circumstances to resolve such doubt.

The combined effect of these provisions would be to counter the 'Rapist's Charter' criticisms made of the decision in *Morgan*. Were those facts to arise under the new proposals, the defendants would be convicted because it was proved that the complainant was not consenting and the defendants' belief that she was had been based on what a third party (her husband) had told them. Clause 78 would apply so as to give rise to a conclusive presumption that the defendants had not behaved reasonably, thus a conclusive presumption that the fault element stated in cl 1(3) had been made out.

Under cl 78(7), if it is proved that a defendant intentionally deceived the complainant as to the nature or purpose of the relevant act (for example, the penetration of the complainant's vagina, anus or mouth) or the defendant intentionally induced the complainant to consent to the relevant act by impersonating a person known personally to the complainant, it is to be conclusively presumed that:

> (a) the complainant did not consent to the relevant act, and (b) ... the defendant did not believe that the complainant consented to the relevant act.

This would clarify the law to the extent that deception as to nature of the act and deception as to identity of the sexual partner would vitiate any apparent consent and provide conclusive evidence of *mens rea*. Note that the clause extends to deception as to the nature and *purpose* of the defendant's act. It follows that D may incur liability if he inserts his finger into P's vagina or anus on the basis that such action is necessary for a medical examination, when in fact he is performing the act for his own sexual gratification. It does not clarify the issue of whether D commits an offence where the medical examination is necessary but he nevertheless derives sexual gratification from it.

Whilst cl 1 creates an offence based on penile penetration, cl 3 creates an offence of assault by penetration that can be committed by a man or a woman. The *actus reus* of the offence is made out if D penetrates the vagina or anus of P with a part of his body or anything else, the penetration is sexual (meaning that from its nature, a reasonable person would consider that it may be sexual because of its nature, its circumstances or the purpose of any person in relation to it), and P does not consent to the penetration. The *mens rea* would require proof that D intentionally penetrated P, as described, and D did not believe that P was consenting, nor gave any thought to whether P was consenting. Alternatively, as with the proposed rape offence, it would be sufficient for the prosecution to prove that a reasonable person would in all the circumstances doubt whether P was consenting and D does not act in a way that a reasonable person would consider sufficient in all the circumstances to resolve such doubt. Like rape the offence would carry the possibility of imprisonment for life.

The Bill envisages the offences of indecent assault under ss 14 and 15 of the 1956 Act being replaced by a single offence (as far as adult victims are concerned) of 'sexual assault' carrying the possibility of 10 years' imprisonment. The *actus reus* of the offence would involve the sexual touching of P by D to which P does not consent. As to the meaning of 'sexual' see above. For these purposes 'touching' comprises touching with any part of the body or with anything else, through anything, 'and in particular includes touching amounting to penetration' (see cl 81(6)).

As for *mens rea*, the touching must be intentional, and it must be proved that D did not believe that P consented, or that D gave no thought to whether P consented. As with other offences under this part of the Bill, the fault element could also be made out where a reasonable person would, in all the circumstances, doubt whether

P was consenting and D did not act in a way that a reasonable person would consider sufficient in all the circumstances to resolve such doubt. For those cases not involving an assault in the form of 'touching' cl 7 envisages an offence of 'causing a person to engage in sexual activity without consent'. The issue of consent would be dealt with in the same way as under the proposed offences considered above.

SUMMARY OF CHAPTER 7

NON-FATAL OFFENCES AGAINST THE PERSON

ASSAULT

Assault and battery are separate offences and are to be regarded as summary offences except when charged under s 47 of the OAPA 1861. Much confusion had resulted from the fact that judges used the word 'assault' to mean battery. Assault is causing another to apprehend immediate and unlawful violence will be inflicted upon him. Therefore, assault occurs without any physical contact. There is no need to prove that the victim was actually frightened. It is enough to show that he or she apprehended that some personal violence is likely to occur. It is not necessary for there to be any hostility or aggressive or rude behaviour. Words alone may amount to an assault and may of course negative an assault. The decision in *Ireland* holds that silence can amount to an assault but that will very much depend on the circumstances of the case. The House of Lords also held that the apprehension of psychological injury is sufficient but that may depend on a previous course of conduct having be established – as in *Burstow*.

The *mens rea* for assault is either intention or recklessness. Recklessness is to be given its *Cunningham* meaning.

BATTERY

Battery is the actual infliction of unlawful personal violence. Every battery does not include an assault as in the case of a victim who is asleep. There are many everyday situations were the law presumes consent to the application of 'force', as when people are crowded together at a football match or crammed into the carriage of an underground train. Force does not need to be directly applied as in the *Ireland* case. *Venna* establishes that the *mens rea* for the offence is either intention or recklessness.

Assault and battery are regarded as basic intent crimes for the purposes of the law relating to intoxication.

STATUTORY ASSAULTS CONTRARY TO THE OFFENCES AGAINST THE PERSONS ACT 1861

Section 47 requires proof that D caused P actual bodily harm (a term that encompasses psychological harm). The *mens rea* of s 47 requires intent or recklessness towards the assault or battery but no *mens rea* towards causing actual bodily harm.

Offences under ss 18 and 20 of the OAPA 1861 should be viewed together as there is considerable overlap between them. Section 18, a specific intent crime, requires an intent to wound or cause grievous bodily harm. Section 20 requires the defendant to have acted maliciously in wounding or inflicting grievous bodily harm. 'To wound' means that the continuity of the skin must be broken. *Burstow* suggests that there is little difference in the way one may cause or inflict grievous bodily harm. There is

House of Lord's authority in *Mandair*, which acknowledges that 'cause' is wide enough to cover anything subsumed under the word 'inflict'. The *mens rea* for s 18 is intent and, for s 20, malice, which is interpreted to mean acting intentionally or recklessly in the *Cunningham* sense.

Where D causes harm to another by administering a noxious substance, charges under ss 23 and 24 may be more appropriate.

CONSENT

Interest in the role of consent as a defence to a charge of battery was generated as a result of *Brown*. The Law Lords held by a 3:2 majority that consent could be no defence to a s 47 of the OAPA 1861 charge. Or at least that is what they appeared to decide. This ruling has now been called into question as a result of the decision in *Wilson*, which concluded that a wife's consent to having her buttocks 'branded' prevented an offence occurring under s 47. The court regarded the act as a private one between a married couple in the privacy of their own home and was the equivalent of tattooing which is lawful. The court also recognised certain activities as being lawful which otherwise would clearly amount to battery, for example, sporting occasions such as a boxing bout. What amounts to the public interest in this context is extremely hard to define. The House of Lords in *Brown* seemed to be saying that group sado-masochistic acts were contrary to the public interest.

SEXUAL OFFENCES

Statutory changes occurred to the law on rape in 1956, 1976 and 1994. Rape may only be committed by a man but, since the CJPOA 1994, a man may now commit rape against another man. The *actus reus* of rape is to have sexual intercourse with a man or woman without his or her consent. The *mens rea* is either an intention to have intercourse without consent or being reckless as to consent. Reckless is taken in its *Cunningham* sense to mean that the defendant was aware that there was a possibility that the woman was not consenting. Intercourse is deemed complete upon proof of penetration only. There is no longer a requirement that the sexual intercourse should be unlawful. The House of Lords in *R* held that the word was 'mere surplusage'. No special rules apply to the matrimonial relationship. A man can therefore rape his wife if all the requirements of the legislation are met.

The issue of consent has troubled the courts over a number of years. The key issue is whether or not the woman was consenting. So a woman who is sleeping at the time of penetration cannot be consenting. Consent may be 'manufactured' through fear, force or fraud and, although older cases hold that, when obtained in such circumstances, consent is vitiated, there is really only one question for the jury: was this victim consenting to intercourse with the accused? If there has been a mistake as to identity, then consent will be vitiated. *Collins* is a good example, where the woman's boyfriend was expected to pay her a nocturnal visit and she, believing

Collins to be her boyfriend, permitted intercourse to take place only discovering her mistake once the light was switched on.

It is an offence for a person to commit an indecent assault (ss 14 and 15 of the SOA 1956). Three things need to be established in order for the prosecution to succeed on a charge of indecent assault:

- the accused must intentionally assault the victim;
- the assault or circumstances accompanying it must be capable of being considered by right-minded people as indecent;
- that the accused intended to commit an assault in circumstances of indecency.

It will not always be obvious to right-minded people that an indecent event is unfolding before their eyes as in *George*, where the defendant tried to remove the victim's shoe as he obtained some sort of sexual thrill from this activity. Other cases will be more straightforward, as in *Court*, where the defendant slapped a young girl on the buttocks. A person charged with indecent assault may raise the defence of consent but case law decides that consent will be irrelevant where actual bodily harm has been caused.

An indecent assault can be committed by one female on another or a female on a male. There is no need for the indecent assault to be accompanied by any sort of hostility or aggressive behaviour.

Other offences involving sexual intercourse are to be found at ss 2, 3, 5, 6, 10 and 11 of the SOA 1956.

CHAPTER 8

OFFENCES AGAINST PROPERTY: THEFT

The next two chapters are concerned with offences against property which are detailed in the Theft Act (TA) 1968, Theft Act (TA) 1978 and the Theft (Amendment) Act 1996. There will also be an examination of the offence of criminal damage contrary to the Criminal Damage Act 1971.

8.1   INTRODUCTION

The TA 1968 is the result of the work of the Criminal Law Revision Committee (Eighth Report, *Theft and Related Offences*, Cmnd 2977, 1966). The Larceny Act 1916 had created innumerable problems of interpretation for the courts resulting in over-complexity because of the integration of many civil law concepts, particularly in respect of the crime of larceny. The TA 1968, therefore, set out to create a new order which it was hoped would be intelligible to the ordinary person. In many respects, the TA 1968 achieved this objective, but now, 35 years on, and many cases later, the ordinary person would have some real difficulty in understanding much of the law. As will be seen later, the House of Lords has hardly helped to create the certainty one expects from the criminal law.

The basic definition of theft is contained in s 1 of the TA 1968 and reads:

A person is guilty of theft if he dishonestly appropriates property belonging to another with the intention of permanently depriving the other of it; and 'thief' and 'steal' shall be construed accordingly.

The offence carries a maximum sentence of seven years' imprisonment. It will be immediately apparent that the *actus reus* and *mens rea* concepts can be easily distinguished. The *actus reus* is described by the words 'appropriates property belonging to another', and the *mens rea* requires proof of dishonesty and an intention permanently to deprive the other of the property.

Sections 2–6 of the TA 1968 give help and assistance as to how these key words are to be interpreted and therefore require careful consideration. Perhaps the starting point ought to be s 4 which deals with property because this determines what can actually be stolen.

8.2   PROPERTY

8.2.1   The basic definition – tangible property

Section 4(1) of the TA 1968 states that property includes 'money and all other property, real or personal, including things in action and other intangible property'. There are limitations imposed by other sub-sections but undoubtedly s 4(1) is a very wide provision. However, it is worth emphasising particular issues at this point. Section 4(1) draws an explicit distinction between 'real' and 'personal' property, and an implicit distinction between 'tangible' and 'intangible' property. For these purposes, 'real' property may be taken to mean land, both in terms of what we would normally think of as land, that is, soil, trees and so on, and also as buildings erected on the land. So, a house is real property, too. Personal property may be taken to mean all other kinds of property which are not land. The idea of 'tangible' property is easy enough to understand and it clearly extends to include both real and personal property. A house is land and is tangible property. When a house is being constructed and a pile of bricks is standing on the ground prior to being built into a wall, the bricks are personal property and, of course, tangible property. As will be explained below, however, though land is property, there are restrictions on the way in which it can be stolen (the same is true of wild animals).

8.2.2   Intangible property

'Intangible' property is a little more complex. Section 4(1) identifies a particular kind of intangible property, a *thing in action*, but also implies that there may be other kinds of intangible property. To date, nothing of much substance has emerged beyond the thing in action as an example of intangible property. One possibility that the courts could have identified is confidential information (by contrast with the medium in which the information is conveyed, such as on a piece of paper). However, it was held in *Oxford v Moss* [1979] Crim LR 199 that a student who had seen a proof copy of a university examination paper he was due to sit was not guilty of theft of the information because information was not 'property' and therefore was incapable of being stolen. Of course, if he had dishonestly appropriated the piece of paper on which the examination was printed, then he could have been found guilty of theft of the paper, providing there was evidence of an intention to permanently deprive the university of the paper. Strangely, he could also have been guilty of a conspiracy to defraud if he had agreed the plan with a fellow student since *Welham v DPP* [1961] AC 103 held that the term 'defraud' is not confined to causing or taking the risk of causing pecuniary loss to another. In the consultation paper on *Misuse of Trade Secrets* (Law Com 150, 1997), the Law Commission proposed that it should be an offence to use or disclose a trade secret belonging to another without the consent of the other. It invited views on whether the mere dishonest acquisition of a trade secret should also be an offence.

Consequently, things in action are the most important examples of intangible property for the purposes of theft. A 'thing in action' is a right which may be enforced against another person by an action in law. This right itself is property under the 1968 Act and so can be stolen. A simple example of a thing in action is a right possessed by one party to a contract against the other party to the contract. In the case of *Marshall and Others* [1998] 2 Cr App R 282, the defendants obtained unexpired London Underground tickets and travelcards from members of the public and then sold them to other travellers. The tickets were marked as not transferable and the convictions for theft of the tickets as *pieces of paper* were upheld. However, the Court of Appeal suggested that not only did a customer have a thing in action against London Underground (the right to travel) but also London Underground had a thing in action against the customer (the right to prevent transfer). Though not necessary to the decision, the Court then speculated that, by selling the tickets, the defendants might also have appropriated London Underground's right to prevent transfer. This is a very questionable conclusion since, even if the defendants assumed rights of ownership over that right when they re-sold the customer's ticket, they did not deprive, nor intend to deprive, London Underground of the right against its customer.

Perhaps the most important example of a thing in action in the context of theft is the right possessed by the holder of an account with a bank against the bank. Despite popular usage, the account holder does not have 'money in the bank', only the bank has money in the bank. Each account holder has a thing in action against the bank, the right to compel the bank to pay an amount of money equivalent to the credit in the account. Suppose the account holder has a credit of £5,000. That is £5,000's worth of right which, as property, can be stolen in whole or in part. It is important to be clear that it is not the money which is being stolen but the right to it (should a rogue subsequently get the money from the bank, he will steal the money itself from the bank). So, in *Kohn* (1979) 69 Cr App R 395, a company accountant authorised to draw cheques on the company's behalf drew cheques to meet his own debts and was convicted of theft of the company's thing in action against the bank. In that case, the account was sometimes in debit but within the limits of an agreed overdraft, and sometimes in debit outside those limits. An agreed overdraft also gives the account holder a thing in action which can be stolen (compare also the credit limit associated with credit cards, store cards and the like). If the account is in debit beyond any agreed overdraft, then the account holder has no thing in action against the bank and so nothing to steal. Consequently in *Kohn*, convictions against the accountant were upheld where they related to occasions when the account was in credit or within the agreed overdraft limits but quashed where they related to occasions when the account was in debit beyond the agreed overdraft limits.

8.2.3   Land

Though land is property within the definition in s 4(1) of the TA 1968, s 4(2) provides that land or things forming part of land and severed from it cannot be stolen except when:

- the defendant is a trustee or personal representative, or is authorised by power of attorney, or as liquidator of a company, or otherwise, to sell or dispose of land belonging to another, and he appropriates the land or anything forming part of it by dealing with it in breach of the confidence reposed in him; or

- the defendant is not in possession of the land and appropriates anything forming part of the land by severing it or causing it to be severed, or after it has been severed – for example, the defendant removes topsoil or turf, cuts branches from trees, but note the further limitation contained in s 4(3) and explained below, or takes slates from a roof; or

- being in possession of the land under a tenancy, the defendant appropriates the whole or part of any fixture or structure let to be used with the land – for example, the defendant removes a valuable fireplace from a room in a house of which he is the tenant.

In the case of a person who is not in possession of the land, there is a further limitation, for s 4(3) states:

> A person who picks mushrooms growing wild on any land, or who picks flowers, fruit or foliage from a plant growing wild on any land, does not (although not in possession

of the land) steal what he picks, unless he does it for reward or for sale or other commercial purpose.

So, even if a person who is not in possession of the land severs mushrooms, flowers, fruit or foliage, he will not be guilty of theft unless either he has not 'picked' it (for instance, he has uprooted a whole bush rather than picked fruit from the bush) or he has done it for reward or for sale or for some other commercial purpose. Thus, the provisions are designed to deter those who would ravage the countryside for commercial benefit. To remove flowers growing wild in order to enhance the appearance of one's office will not amount to an offence. To do so with intent to sell the flowers at the local market would bring one inside the ambit of the legislation.

8.2.4   Wild creatures

There are also limitations on the theft of wild creatures. Section 4(4) of the TA 1968 states:

> Wild creatures, tamed or untamed, shall be regarded as property; but a person cannot steal a wild creature not tamed nor ordinarily kept in captivity, or the carcass of any such creature, unless either it has been reduced into possession by or on behalf of another person and possession of it has not since been lost or abandoned, or another person is in course of reducing it into possession.

It will be seen that such creatures must have been reduced into someone's possession or be in the course of being so reduced before they can be stolen. To take animals from a zoo, whether tamed or untamed, would amount to theft providing there was the necessary *mens rea* of an intention permanently to deprive the zoo of the animals.

Conversely, if a fox were to come into a private garden on a regular basis in search of food one could hardly say that it had been reduced into the possession of the landowner and therefore if someone were to capture the fox that would not amount to theft.

8.3   APPROPRIATION

For theft to occur, the property has to be appropriated and this is a concept which has created many difficulties of interpretation over the last 30 years. The basic definition is contained in s 3 of the TA 1968:

(1) Any assumption by a person of the rights of an owner amounts to an appropriation, and this includes, where he has come by the property (innocently or not) without stealing it, any later assumption of a right to it by keeping or dealing with it as owner.

(2) Where property or a right or interest in property is or purports to be transferred for value to a person acting in good faith, no later assumption by him of rights which he believed himself to be acquiring shall, by reason of any defect in the transferor's title, amount to theft of the property.

8.3.1   Consent or authorisation by the owner

Section 3 of the TA 1968 makes no reference to the absence of consent as a vital ingredient in determining whether or not, in law, an appropriation has occurred.

Prior to the TA 1968 coming into force, the law was regulated by the Larceny Act 1916 and under this legislation it had been necessary to prove that the property alleged to have been stolen was taken 'without the consent of the owner'. However, there is strong evidence to suggest that when the Criminal Law Revision Committee chose 'appropriation' as the word to describe the conduct required for theft in the proposed new legislation, it assumed that it inevitably implied that it must be without the consent of the owner. Lord Lane CJ neatly summed up the perceived difficulty in the Court of Appeal in *Morris* [1983] 2 All ER 448 when he said:

> As to the meaning of the word 'appropriation' there are two schools of thought. The first contends that the word 'appropriate' has built into it a connotation that it is some action inconsistent with the owner's rights, something hostile to the interests of the owner or contrary to his wishes and intention or without his authority. The second school of thought contends that the word in this context means no more than to take possession of an article and that there is no requirement that the taking or appropriation should in any way be antagonistic to the rights of the owner [p 451].

Very early in the life of the 1968 Act, the House of Lords was presented with the opportunity to interpret the meaning of appropriation. In *Lawrence v Commissioner of Police for the Metropolis* [1972] AC 626, the appellant was a taxi driver who had collected a passenger from Victoria Station and transported him to Ladbroke Grove in London. The passenger was an Italian student who spoke little English and had his destination address written on a piece of paper. Lawrence tried to indicate that it was a long journey and therefore very expensive (which was untrue). The passenger offered him £1 from his wallet but the appellant, noticing the wallet was still open removed a further £6. The correct fare should have been just over 50p in today's currency. He was charged with theft and convicted of stealing £6. The House of Lords rejected the argument that there could not be theft if the owner of the property had authorised the acts which were done by the appellant. Viscount Dilhorne with whom the other Law Lords agreed said:

> I see no ground for concluding that the omission of the words 'without the consent of the owner' was inadvertent and not deliberate, and to read the sub-section as if they were included is, in my opinion, wholly unwarranted. Parliament by the omission of these words has relieved the prosecution of the burden of establishing that the taking was without the owner's consent. That is no longer an ingredient of the offence [pp 631–32].

This approach has since been confirmed in two further House of Lords' decisions, *Gomez* [1993] 1 All ER 1 and *Hinks* [2000] 4 All ER 833, though there were many earlier irreconcilable decisions at Court of Appeal level and the issue remains highly contentious. Before explaining the decisions in more detail, it may be worth emphasising that the effect of this approach is that appropriation is essentially a neutral term which, in itself, does not imply any unlawful conduct. Indeed, any person who acquires property from another, in whatever way, appropriates that property (a person who acquires it by paying for it appropriates it no less than a person who takes it for himself without permission). Thus, dishonesty becomes the crucial ingredient of theft. Moreover, save for some relatively unimportant exceptions, all cases of obtaining property by deception under s 15 of the 1968 Act will also be cases of theft.

Consent as inconsistent with appropriation

For a considerable period of time, the effect of the decision in *Lawrence* appeared to
be ignored, though courts which acknowledged it (such as the House of Lords in
Morris) were never able satisfactorily to explain why it did not determine the issue.
In *Skipp* [1975] Crim LR 114, the defendant had posed as a genuine haulage
contractor and had been given a job to deliver three loads of oranges and onions
from London to Leicester. The goods were duly loaded onto his lorry and he went on
his way. Before reaching Leicester, he drove off with the goods. The question arose as
to when he had appropriated the loads. The Court of Appeal held that Skipp was
guilty of theft of the loads only when he did an act inconsistent with his
authorisation, in other words, at the point where he departed from the chosen route
to Leicester. The original taking had been with consent. Similarly, in *Eddy v Niman*
(1981) 73 Cr App R 237, it was held that to take goods from a supermarket shelf and
put them in a trolley or basket was not yet an appropriation, and so not theft, even
though the defendant intended to steal when he did so. The defendant was simply
doing what all shoppers are permitted, if not encouraged to do, that is, place goods
in a trolley or basket and carry them around the shop prior to purchase. On the other
hand, the switching of price labels on goods in a supermarket is not an act to which
the owner consents and can in itself amount to an appropriation. This was the
decision in *Morris*, where Lord Roskill referred to appropriation as something which
has not been 'expressly or impliedly authorised by the owner'. It is interesting to
note that Lord Roskill also considered that an adverse interference with *any* right of
the owner was sufficient, there being no need for the prosecution to prove that *all* the
rights of the owner had been usurped – in switching the labels, the defendant
continued to acknowledge some rights in the supermarket. He was, after all,
prepared to pay *something* for the goods. Lord Roskill also suggested that there was
nothing inconsistent between his views and those of the House of Lords in *Lawrence*,
but he was singularly unable to explain this suggestion. A final example of this
approach appeared in *Fritschy* [1985] Crim LR 745, where the defendant was
convicted of the theft of a number of krugerrands. Fritschy was the agent of a Dutch
company which dealt in the coins and he was asked to come to England to collect a
consignment on behalf of a customer and to take them to Switzerland. He collected
them, went to Switzerland and then made off with them. His conviction for theft was
quashed on the basis that there was no evidence of any act within the jurisdiction
which was inconsistent with what he was expressly authorised to do.

The Gomez case – Lawrence confirmed

The first case to break the consensus that seemed to have developed that consent
prevented an appropriation from taking place was *Dobson v General Accident Fire and
Life Assurance Corpn* [1989] 3 All ER 927, a case heard by the Court of Appeal, Civil
Division. The claimant was insured by the defendants under a home insurance
policy which provided cover against all the usual contingencies including theft. The
claimant had advertised for sale a gold watch and diamond ring at a total price of
£5,950. He was telephoned by a man who claimed to be interested in purchasing the
items and a sale was agreed with payment to be by a building society cheque. The
transaction was completed but, a few days later, the claimant was informed that the
cheque had been stolen and was consequently worthless. Dobson then made a claim

on his insurance under the theft clause of his policy. The insurers denied liability on the basis that the watch and ring had not been stolen within the meaning of s 1 of the TA 1968. The county court in which he commenced the claim found for him and the insurers appealed on the basis, *inter alia*, that, as the owner consented to the taking, there could in law be no appropriation. The Court of Appeal preferred *Lawrence* to *Morris* and concluded there was sufficient authority in Viscount Dilhorne's speech in *Lawrence* to conclude that there would be an appropriation, even where there was evidence of consent to the taking. Parker LJ recognised the inconsistency between *Lawrence* and *Morris* and chose not to follow the latter of the two decisions of the House of Lords. Nor did he, perhaps wisely, attempt to reconcile the two cases. He put it this way:

> I am fully conscious of the fact that in so concluding I may be said not to be applying *R v Morris*. This may be so, but in the light of the difficulties inherent in the decision, the very clear decision in *Lawrence*'s case and the equally clear statement in *R v Morris* that the question whether a contract is void or only voidable is irrelevant, I have been unable to reach any other conclusion [p 935].

Bingham LJ while admitting it was difficult to find a basis upon which to reconcile *Lawrence* and *Morris* nevertheless suggested that, in the former case, the Italian student had simply permitted the taxi driver to take the money and this was not consistent with the concept of consent. Applying this to the case in point, the claimant had allowed or permitted the rogue to take the items, but because he lacked vital information had not consented to the taking.

Skipp was reconciled with *Lawrence* in *Dobson* on the basis that, as Parker LJ put it:

> ... there was much more than mere consent of the owner. There was express authority, indeed instruction to collect the goods. It could not therefore be said that the defendant was assuming any rights. Whatever his secret intentions he was, until he diverted the goods, exercising the owner's right on his instructions and on his behalf [p 934].

Parker LJ also treated *Fritschy* in the same way as *Skipp*, and pointed out the clear authority from his employers. This was completely different from *Lawrence* where there was evidence only that he allowed or permitted the act to take place.

The issues raised by the cases of *Lawrence* and *Morris* were considered by the House of Lords in *Gomez*. In this case, Gomez was employed as an assistant manager at an electrical goods shop. Along with two acquaintances, a plan was agreed whereby goods to the value of £17,200 would be supplied by the shop in return for two building society cheques, which the parties knew to be stolen. Gomez, as assistant manager, was to seek authorisation and therefore clearance for the goods to be supplied in return for the cheques. The manager, to whom the request was put, instructed Gomez to make enquiries of the bank in order to ascertain whether the cheques were acceptable. Gomez later dishonestly told the manager they were 'as good as cash'. The cheques were eventually returned with the order not to pay because they had been stolen. Gomez was charged with two counts of theft. The Court of Appeal was of the view that there was a voidable contract between the owners of the shop and the receiver of the electrical goods and therefore the transfer of goods was 'with the consent and express authority of the owner and that accordingly there was no lack of authorisation and no appropriation'. This approach by the Court of Appeal was based upon the *Morris* decision. The House of Lords by a 4:1 majority restored the conviction. Expressed in its narrow form, the *ratio* of the case is that an appropriation, for the purposes of s 1, is complete, even though it is expressly or impliedly authorised and was therefore with the owner's consent, if it was induced by fraud, deception or false representation. The House of Lords concluded that the fraud, deception or false representation practised on the owner made the appropriation dishonest. *Lawrence* together with the case of *Dobson v General Accident Fire and Life Assurance Corpn* was approved, the *dictum* of Lord Roskill in *Morris* disapproved and the decisions in *Skipp* and *Fritschy* were overruled.

In *Gomez* it was decided that consent or authorisation by the owner to the act in question is irrelevant in deciding if there has in law been an appropriation. On one reading of the decision in *Gomez* it can be maintained that the *ratio* applies only to cases where the consent has been induced by fraud, deception or false representation. If this were so, then the supermarket cases such as *Eddy v Niman* would probably still follow the *Morris* approach. The point of law of general public importance related only to where consent had been obtained by false representation. Therefore, anything considered by the Law Lords not involving false representations could be said to be *obiter dicta*. However, there is no indication that their Lordships intended the decision to be confined to consent obtained in that way. It will be noted that *Gomez* was a case where fraud was perpetrated on the manager through the false representation made by the appellant that he had checked with the bank and that the building society cheque was 'as good as cash'. The authorisation was then given for the transaction to proceed. The decision does not appear to differentiate between consent freely given and consent induced by a fraudulent representation. It will be apparent that Gomez could have been charged under s 15 of the TA 1968 with obtaining property belonging to another by deception and one may only speculate as to why this course of action was not adopted, as there would appear to be no obstacle to a conviction, given the clear deception practised on the manager.

Approval was given to Lord Roskill's statement in *Morris* that the assumption by the defendant of any of the rights of an owner was sufficient to satisfy s 3(1) of the TA 1968. Lord Keith's opinion was that any interference with any property belonging to another would amount to an appropriation, although whether or not it amounted to theft would depend on other factors, such as proof of dishonesty and an intention to deprive the other permanently of the item. Two examples were given by Lord Keith, using the supermarket context:

> It seems to me that the switching of price labels on the article is in itself an assumption of one of the rights of the owner, whether or not it is accompanied by some other act such as removing the article from the shelf and placing it in a basket or trolley. No one but the owner has the right to remove a price label from an article or to place a price label upon it. If anyone else does so, he does an act, as Lord Roskill put it, by way of adverse interference with or usurpation of that right.

He then dealt with the example of the practical joker mentioned by Lord Roskill in *Morris*:

> The practical joker (who has switched labels) ... is not guilty of theft because he has not acted dishonestly and does not intend to deprive the owner permanently of the article. So the label switching in itself constitutes an appropriation ...

One of the consequences of this approach is that an act which would probably not even amount to the *actus reus* of an *attempt* to obtain by deception is sufficient to amount to the *actus reus* of the full offence of theft.

The minority view was put forward by Lord Lowry. He acknowledged that 'any attempt to reconcile the statements of principle in *Lawrence* and *Morris* is a complete waste of time'. He advocated the simple approach of prosecuting under s 15 of the TA 1968 all offences involving obtaining by deception and prosecuting 'theft in general under s 1'. In that way, some thefts would come under s 15, but no 'false pretences will come under s 1'.

Subsequent interpretation of Gomez

The Court of Appeal experienced some difficulty in coming to terms with the full implications of the decision in *Gomez*. In *Gallasso* [1993] Crim LR 459, the appellant was a nurse in a home for severely mentally handicapped adults and part of her duties involved looking after the patients' finances. Each patient had a trust account at a building society and any monies were paid into these accounts. Gallasso was the sole signatory and regularly drew money out for the patients' day to day needs. J, a patient, received a cheque for £4,000 and Gallasso opened a second trust account for him into which she paid the cheque. Later, she transferred £3,000 into his first account and the remainder into her own account. A few months later, another cheque for £1,800 was received and she opened, on his behalf, a new cashcard account at the same building society branch. She faced three counts of theft relating to three transactions: count 1 relating to the opening of a second account; count 2, the payment of £1,000 into her own account; and count 3, the opening of the cashcard account. The judge rejected a submission of no case to answer on counts 1 and 3. Counsel had argued that, as the cheques had been properly paid in by Gallasso, there was no evidence of appropriation. The jury acquitted on count 1 and she did not challenge her conviction on count 2. She appealed against her conviction on count 3. In allowing her appeal, the court acknowledged that, since *Gomez*, it was 'now clear that a taking of property with the owner's consent could amount to appropriation'. The court thought that paying the cheque into the patient's account could not be regarded as an appropriation, since it was 'evidence of Gallasso affirming J's rights rather than assuming them for herself'. The court seems to have been swayed by the argument that there must be a taking even though it may be with consent and here the paying in 'was not a taking at all'. But *Gomez* did not say that there had to be a taking in order for there to be, in law, an appropriation. The label switching example given by Lord Roskill in *Morris* surely does not involve any taking but was held to be an appropriation and endorsed by the House of Lords in *Gomez*. It is difficult to see how *Gallasso* can stand as an authority on the meaning of appropriation given the clear statement of principle which emanated from *Gomez*. Lloyd LJ thought that: 'Lord Keith did not mean to say that every handling is an appropriation.' With respect, what Lord Keith may have meant to say is not important. That is what he did say but, of course, in practice, no criminal consequences will ensue without the other elements of the offence being present.

In *Mazo* [1996] Crim LR 435, it was difficult to identify any act of deception and the Court of Appeal had to decide whether to give effect to the decision in *Gomez*. M was a maid to Lady S and, claimed the prosecution, took dishonest advantage of S's mental incapacity by accepting cheques totalling £37,000 from S. S's bank was suspicious and the chief cashier telephoned S but was simply told to go ahead and cash the cheques. M claimed that the cheques were gifts from a grateful employer and the Crown accepted that if this were true then there could be no theft. Her appeal against conviction for theft was allowed. Clearly it is important to focus on the mental capacity of the donor and donee. If S had made the transfers having the mental capacity to make a valid gift, then it is difficult to see why, in the absence of fraud or undue influence, the donee should be guilty of theft. If, in applying civil law principles, there is a clear indefeasible transfer of ownership from the donor to the donee then it would be untenable for the criminal law to conclude that the recipient is guilty of theft. If one analyses the facts by reference to s 1 of the TA 1968 and applying *Gomez* it does appear that M should be guilty of theft. She has assumed all the rights of the owner over the £37,000. This money had been obtained with the approval of the former owner. Clearly, there is consent but as we have seen that is irrelevant as to whether or not there is an appropriation. There is little prospect of M returning the money to S and therefore there would appear to be an intention to deprive S permanently of her money and that leaves only the question of dishonesty. In circumstances such as these, it is not unusual for an elderly person to bestow gifts upon a devoted carer but not of this magnitude. That may be done by way of will but rarely before the death of the donor. If this is indeed the case, the jury, applying the *Ghosh* principles (see below, 8.5.2), would have to decide whether or not she was acting dishonestly in accepting such gifts. In *Mazo,* in returning a guilty verdict, the jury seems to have concluded that she was acting dishonestly. However, an application of civil law principles draws us to the conclusion that a valid gift has been made, given that S had the mental capacity required to make such a gift. In *Re Beaney (Decd)* [1978] 2 All ER 595, it was held that the degree of understanding required for the making of a valid *inter vivos* gift was relative to the transaction to be effected. If the subject matter and value of the gift were trivial in relation to the donor's other assets, a low degree of understanding was sufficient but:

> ... if the effect of the gift was to dispose of the owner's only asset of value and to pre-empt the devolution of his estate under his will or on his intestacy, the degree of understanding required is as high as that required for a will and the donor must understand the claims of all potential donees and the extent of the property to be disposed of [p 601].

If, therefore, the donee is legally entitled to keep the gift, it would be untenable for the criminal law to conclude that a case of theft had been made out.

This issue was revisited in *Kendrick and Hopkins* [1997] 2 Cr App R 524. H and K were convicted of conspiracy to steal. They ran a residential home and the Crown maintained that they had taken over the running of the affairs of a resident aged 99 who was virtually blind and incapable of managing her affairs. Over a period, they cashed her investments, obtained enduring power of attorney and effected a new will signed by her making them her beneficiaries. Their defence was that at all times they were acting with her authorisation and in her interests. The jury convicted and the Court of Appeal dismissed their appeal. The court distinguished *Mazo* on the basis that here the 'donor' did not have the mental capacity to understand the consequences of her actions. In such circumstances such dispositions are invalid and the property in law continues to belong to the 'donor'. Where the recipients are aware of the donor's incapacity, it is more likely than not that the jury will conclude that they were acting dishonestly in seeking to benefit from the donor's misfortune.

In *Kendrick and Hopkins*, the court expressed doubts about whether the concession had been properly made in *Mazo* that a valid indefeasible gift inevitably meant that no theft could be committed. By the time of the decision in *Hinks* (in 1998), these doubts had flowered into outright rejection of the proposition. *Hinks* was yet another case involving a barely competent and gullible victim being induced to part with large amounts of money in an exploitative relationship dominated by the defendant. Rejecting the defendant's attempt to rely on the argument that she could not be guilty of theft for receiving valid gifts, and upholding her conviction, the Court of Appeal asserted:

> In our judgment, in relation to theft, one of the ingredients for a jury to consider is not whether there has been a gift, valid or otherwise, but whether there has been appropriation. A gift may be clear evidence of appropriation. But a jury should not, in our view, be asked to consider whether a gift has been validly made because, first, that is not what s 1 of the Theft Act requires; secondly, such an approach is inconsistent with *Lawrence* and *Gomez*; and, thirdly, the state of mind of a donor is irrelevant to appropriation [p 9].

The court in *Mazo* did not specifically say why there can be no theft when there is a valid indefeasible gift. The argument advanced above is that it would be inconceivable that the civil law should acknowledge that the defendant has obtained rights of ownership over the property which cannot be taken away at the same time as the criminal law should declare the defendant to be a thief because of the very acquisition of the gift. The simple way of explaining this with regard to the elements of theft would be to say that there has been no appropriation but this explanation appears to be unavailable so long as the *Gomez* interpretation of appropriation prevails. This was the message of *Hinks*. Unless that interpretation was to be modified, those charged with theft in such circumstances would have to rely on absence of dishonesty or try to persuade the court that there is simply an overriding principle that the criminal law cannot be seen to be in conflict with the civil law in this area.

There are other areas of law in which conflicts between civil and criminal law occur, and Simon Gardner has argued that the two need not necessarily be congruent and that either criminal law should reflect moral perceptions which may not be applicable in the civil law or, more tentatively, that a conviction for theft where the civil law has bestowed an indefeasible title should render that title no longer indefeasible ('Property and theft' [1998] Crim LR 35). Not surprisingly, Gardner's interesting arguments provoked considerable opposition, most notably from Professor JC Smith, though the Court of Appeal in *Hinks* derived 'some comfort' from them and rejected Professor Smith's powerful arguments that the civil law of property is an essential foundation for the law of theft and that retrospective adjustment of property rights turning on a jury's perceptions of dishonesty is inconceivable ([1997] Crim LR 359; [1998] Crim LR 80).

It is also worth noting that the Court of Appeal in *Mazo*, albeit *obiter*, appeared to treat the *ratio* of *Gomez* as confined to consent obtained by fraud, deception or false representation. The decisions in *Kendrick and Hopkins* and, especially, *Hinks* gave no support to this view. An appeal from the decision in *Hinks* provided the House of Lords with yet another opportunity to reconsider the consent/appropriation issue, though this time the question was whether their Lordships were prepared not only to confirm the *Lawrence/Gomez* approach but to extend its ambit into the valid indefeasible transfer of property.

Hinks, the House of Lords and indefeasible transfers of property

The question certified for the House of Lords in *Hinks* [2000] 4 All ER 833 was:

> Whether the acquisition of an indefeasible title to property is capable of amounting to
> an appropriation of property belonging to another for the purposes of section 1(1) of
> the Theft Act 1968 [pp 841–42].

By a 4:1 majority (Lords Steyn, Jauncey, Slynn and Hutton, Lord Hobhouse
dissenting), their Lordships held that acquisition of an indefeasible title to property
is capable of amounting to an appropriation. By a 3:2 majority (Lords Hutton and
Hobhouse dissenting), their Lordships further decided that the defendant's
conviction should be upheld. Lord Hobhouse's dissent to the result followed from
his dissent on the answer to the certified question. Lord Hutton took the view that
the defendant could not have been dishonest in the circumstances (that is, that
there was a valid gift – this appears to say that a valid gift prevents theft not
because there is no appropriation but because there will be no dishonesty in its
acquisition). On the answer to the certified question, the speech for the majority
was given by Lord Steyn, who considered that there was no need to resort to the
1966 Criminal Law Revision Committee report (Cmnd 2977), and still less to the
opinion of any individual as to the intentions behind that Report, in interpreting
the statute. The correct approach was to start with the words of the statute and to
analyse their interpretation in the trilogy of House of Lords cases, *Lawrence, Morris,*
and *Gomez*. Though consistent in result, *Morris* was inconsistent with the other two
in terms of *obiter* views expressed on the issue of consent and appropriation.
Lawrence and, particularly, *Gomez* were absolutely clear on the answer to the
question:

> In *Gomez* ... the House was expressly invited to hold that 'there is no appropriation
> where the entire proprietary interest passes' ... That submission was rejected. The
> leading judgment in *Gomez* was therefore in terms which unambiguously rule out the
> submission that section 3(1) does not apply to a case of a gift duly carried out because
> in such a case the entire proprietary interest will have passed ... In other words it is
> immaterial whether the act was done with the owner's consent or authority. It is true
> of course that the certified question in *Gomez* referred to the situation where consent
> had been obtained by fraud. But the majority judgments do not differentiate between
> cases of consent induced by fraud and consent given in any other circumstances. The
> *ratio* involves a proposition of general application. *Gomez* therefore gives effect to
> section 3(1) of the Act by treating 'appropriation' as a neutral word comprehending
> 'any assumption by a person of the rights of an owner'. If the law is as held in *Gomez*,
> it destroys the argument advanced on the present appeal, namely that an indefeasible
> gift of property cannot amount to an appropriation [p 842].

Lord Steyn was prepared to concede that it was possible that the effect would be that
some cases which did not really appear to be cases of theft might be caught,
examples which 'may conceivably have justified a more restricted meaning of
section 3(1) than prevailed in *Lawrence* and *Gomez*'. But he considered that such cases
were unlikely to result in prosecution, or in success if a prosecution went ahead.
Conversely, not to adopt the interpretation here suggested but to adopt a narrower
definition would be 'likely to place beyond the reach of the criminal law dishonest
persons who should be found guilty of theft. The suggested revisions would
unwarrantably restrict the scope of the law of theft and complicate the fair and
effective prosecution of theft'. Additionally, in practice, 'the mental requirements of

theft are an adequate protection against injustice'. Lord Steyn also recognised that the interpretation created an undoubted tension between civil and criminal law, but denied that this was a factor which justified a departure from the law as stated in *Lawrence* and *Gomez*:

> The question whether the civil claim to title by a convicted thief, who committed no civil wrong, may be defeated by the principle that nobody may benefit from his own civil or criminal wrong does not arise for decision. Nevertheless there is a more general point, namely that the interaction between criminal law and civil law can cause problems: compare Beatson and Simester, 'Stealing One's Own Property' (1999) 115 LQR 372. The purposes of the civil law and the criminal law are somewhat different. In theory the two systems should be in perfect harmony. In a practical world there will sometimes be some disharmony between the two systems. In any event, it would be wrong to assume on *a priori* grounds that the criminal law rather than the civil law is defective. Given the jury's conclusions, one is entitled to observe that the appellant's conduct *should* constitute theft, the only available charge ... Moreover, these decisions of the House have a marked beneficial consequence. While in some contexts of the law of theft a judge cannot avoid explaining civil law concepts to a jury (eg in respect of section 2(1)(a)), the decisions of the House of Lords eliminate the need for such explanations in respect of appropriation. That is a great advantage in an overly complex corner of the law [p 843].

Since the issue of the true interpretation of the meaning of appropriation has taxed the courts for 35 years, it may perhaps be premature to conclude that it has now finally been resolved. Yet it is difficult to see where the proponents of the argument that consent prevents an appropriation go from here. It is even more alarming that their Lordships were so ready to take the argument to its logical conclusion and to deny that even a valid indefeasible transfer of property inevitably prevents theft from being committed. Their Lordships appear to be breathtakingly complacent about the competence of the authorities and the adequacy of other aspects of the elements of the offence of theft to do the job of distinguishing thieves from others. In particular, since dishonesty is a matter for a jury rather than a matter of law, there is inevitably a degree of unpredictability about the precise scope of the offence of theft. It is true to say that, in most of the consent/appropriation cases, the defendant has either committed a criminal offence or is in the process of trying to do so. In relation to the former, the argument is usually only about which offence the defendant has committed. Often, it seems that obtaining property by deception was the appropriate offence but the defendant was charged with theft (for example, *Gomez*). In relation to the latter, it may be that the defendant would have completed the offence (whether theft or deception) within a very short time (for example, *Skipp*). Even in a case such as *Eddy v Niman*, where the defendant changed his mind about going through with the theft, a conspiracy charge could have been brought. Inevitably, the defendant is unlikely to evoke much sympathy in such cases and protests about the effect of *Lawrence*, *Gomez* and *Hinks* depend upon a belief that it is important to convict for the correct offence and not to stretch the definition of offences artificially when perfectly suitable alternatives exist. Can this truly be said of the conduct which *Hinks* renders criminal? If the transfer was valid and indefeasible, then it was not tainted in any way which the civil law would recognise. It was not engineered by any deception, nor by any undue influence, nor did the transferor lack capacity to transfer. Yet the defendant could be guilty of theft on the basis of a decision by the jury that, somehow, his conduct was dishonest by the ordinary standards of decent people. Thus, he could be sent to prison for stealing property which, when he is released, he will be able to enjoy as undisputed owner. Is it conceivable that the civil and the criminal law could be in conflict in such a fundamental way? Is not Lord Steyn's response to this problem – 'in a practical world there will sometimes be some disharmony between the two systems. In any event, it would be wrong to assume on *a priori* grounds that the criminal law rather than the civil law is defective' – disingenuous in the extreme. If we are disturbed about the defendant's conduct in *Hinks* (and most of us would be) is that not either because we do not believe that her victim had capacity to transfer the property, or, if he did, that we believe that he was subjected to improper pressure or influence? Either would render the transactions void or defeasible. If there was nothing improper, then why should the defendant have been convicted? Of course, on the *Hinks* approach, how and why he came to transfer it is simply irrelevant. When the defendant got her hands on the property, she appropriated it. The rest is simply a matter of proof of dishonesty.

8.3.2   The 'company cases'

The *Gomez* decision also encompasses what were referred to as the 'company cases'. A company may own property and, as such, may be the victim of theft. The problem in this context is that of an owner or those in *de facto* control of the company who give consent to what is being done, for example, the removal of company property, thereby apparently preventing the act amounting in law to an appropriation. The decision in *Gomez* means that this is now a matter of academic interest as consent is irrelevant. Lord Browne-Wilkinson put it this way:

> Whether or not those controlling the company consented or purported to consent to the abstraction of the company's property by the accused, he will have appropriated the property of the company. The question will be whether the other necessary elements are present, viz was such appropriation dishonest and was it done with the intention of permanently depriving the company of such property?

Authorities such as *Roffel* (1985) VR 511 and *McHugh* (1988) 88 Cr App R 385 were not, in Lord Browne-Wilkinson's opinion, 'correct in law' and therefore should not be followed. In the latter case, the court had endorsed the proposition that an act which was done with the authority of a company cannot in general amount to an appropriation, although Mustill LJ was somewhat sceptical as to its correctness but acknowledged that the facts of the case did not require him to look at the issue more closely. In *Roffel*, the sole director and shareholder was not guilty of theft simply because the company had consented to his actions.

Specifically endorsed were the decisions of the Court of Appeal in *Attorney General's Reference (No 2 of 1982)* [1984] 2 All ER 216 and *Philippou* [1989] Crim LR 585. In the former case, the two defendants were the shareholders and directors of various companies engaged in property development and money lending. It was alleged that they had, with each other's consent, appropriated company funds for their own private use by drawing cheques on the companies' bank accounts. At their trial, the judge ruled that, as they were the only shareholders and directors of the companies, their consent to the appropriation had to be taken as the consent of the companies and, therefore, they had not acted dishonestly. It was accepted that there had been an appropriation within the meaning of s 3 of the TA 1968 and that the only issue was one of dishonesty.

In the latter case, the appellant and his colleague were directors of three companies and used the assets of one to buy property in Spain in the name of another company which they owned. Sums totalling £369,000 had been withdrawn from the account of one of their companies and the Court of Appeal held that this act amounted to an appropriation of company property. The act was clearly an adverse interference with the assets of the company as the company would receive no benefit from the transaction. The fact that the directors gave 'consent' was irrelevant to the matter of appropriation.

8.3.3 Appropriation where no possession or control is acquired

A thief will usually take possession or control of the property which he steals and so an appropriation will usually involve a taking of possession or control and some touching of the property. Yet it is clear that an assumption of the rights of an owner does not necessarily require that any of these things shall have taken place. In the case of intangible property, by definition no touching is possible. The consequence is that some acts which look like mere preparation (and so not even an attempt) may actually be sufficient for the full *actus reus* of theft.

In *Pitham and Hehl* (1977) 65 Cr App R 45, a man, knowing that his friend was in prison, took the two appellants to the friend's house and sold them some furniture. Crucial to deciding the question of whether they were guilty of handling was whether or not the goods had been stolen, that is, had the man appropriated his friend's property? Lawton LJ accepted that the man, one Millman, had assumed the rights of the owner. He had acted as the owner by showing them the property and inviting them to buy what they wanted. He was at that point assuming the rights of the owner. It is, of course, the owner's right to invite offers for his property and this right had been assumed by Millman. As the court put it: '... the moment he did that he appropriated McGregor's goods to himself. The appropriation was complete.' It might be unwise to assume that courts will feel bound to interpret all offers to sell property as amounting to an appropriation. The Court of Appeal was struggling to uphold the appellants' convictions for handling and may have been led into error in striving to do so.

As explained earlier, a thing in action is intangible property, an important form of which is the credit in a bank account. How can such a credit be appropriated? The simple answer might seem to be by any action which appears to result in the diminution of the balance. So, in *Kohn*, the defendant drew cheques which, when presented and acted upon by the paying bank, resulted in the company's account being debited. This might suggest that the appropriation takes place when the bank acts upon an instruction and records the debit to its customer's account. This was the approach taken in *Tomsett* [1985] Crim LR 369, in which a telex message sent by the defendant from London fraudulently diverted money from a New York bank to a bank in Geneva. It was held that the appropriation did not take place in London, but where the message was received and acted upon.

However, a contrary view was taken in the case of *Governor of Pentonville Prison ex p Osman* [1989] 3 All ER 701. Osman was chairman of a company, Bumiputra Malaysia Finance Ltd, a wholly owned subsidiary of a major Malaysian bank, Bank Bumiputra Malaysia Bhd. He had transmitted telex messages to a correspondent bank in New York with instructions to transfer funds from one account to another. It was clear that this had been done without authorisation. The only property capable of being stolen as a result of the transaction was the thing in action. The important question was, if there was an appropriation of the thing in action, within which jurisdiction had it occurred? Counsel for Osman argued that the moment of appropriation was when the account in the US was debited. Counsel for the respondents argued that there was an appropriation when the telex was sent and the appropriation therefore took place in Hong Kong from whence the telex originated. The Court of Appeal accepted the latter argument.

Lloyd LJ put it this way:

> ... we regard ourselves bound, or as good as bound, by the meaning attributed to the word 'appropriation' by the unanimous decision of the House of Lords in *R v Morris*. Applying that meaning to the facts, a defendant 'usurps' the customer's rights when he, without the customer's authority, dishonestly issues the cheque drawn upon the customer's account. If adverse interference adds anything to usurpation, then he also thereby adversely interferes with the customer's rights. The theft is complete in law, even though it may be said that it is not complete in fact until the account is debited [p 272].

Therefore, the Court of Appeal is confirming the fact that appropriation takes place at the moment the telex is sent and from wherever the telex is dispatched, in this case Hong Kong.

The issue was examined again in *Ngan* [1998] 1 Cr App R 331. The defendant had opened a bank account in England and was assigned an account number which had formerly been the account number of a debt collection agency. Consequently, in addition to modest credits from her work, her account was credited with sums totalling £77,767 which were intended for the agency. The defendant then signed blank cheques and sent them to her sister in Scotland, who knew of the circumstances. Two cheques were presented in Scotland and one in England for sums totalling £55,000 before the mistake was discovered by the bank. The Court of Appeal quashed the defendant's conviction for theft of the thing in action in respect of the two instances of presentation in Scotland, but upheld her conviction in respect of the presentation in England. (The credit balance to the amount of each cheque which properly belonged to the agency – of course, the credit balance in the account was a credit balance in the defendant's favour! The court held that it belonged to the agency by virtue of the operation of s 5(4) of the TA 1968, on which see below, 8.4.5.) The court applied the principle in *Osman* that the act of theft was the *presentation* of the cheque. So, the Scottish instances took place outside the jurisdiction, but the English one was within the jurisdiction. All the other acts done by the defendant, including the drawing of the cheque and the sending of it to her sister, were preparatory and did not amount to an assumption of the rights of the owner. Note that the court interpreted *Osman* as holding that the assumption takes place when a cheque is *presented*. In *Osman*, the argument was about whether the appropriation took place on the sending of a telex instruction or only when the bank acted on that instruction and made adjustments to the client's account. If presenting a cheque is equated with issuing a telex instruction, then, clearly, the point of presentation would *suffice*. However, what the court in *Osman* actually said was that the appropriation takes place when the defendant 'dishonestly *issues* the cheque'. Where the defendant herself presents the cheque for payment, this will be when she *issues* it. When she sends it to another to present (making that other person the payee), does she not issue it when she sends it, when she does the last act that she can do?

Note, however, that the defendant in *Ngan* did not identify any particular property over which she assumed rights of owner when she sent the cheques. The cheques were blank but for her signature.

Osman was distinguished by the court in *Governor of Brixton Prison ex p Levin* [1997] 1 Cr App R 335, in which the defendant operated a computer in Russia to gain access to the computer of a bank in the US and to effect transfers of money from that bank to accounts held at other banks. The court held that the defendant could not send any instructions until he had first gained access to the computer in the US. The appropriation of the account holder's right to give instructions took place in the computer, which was in the US. More realistically, it was argued, it took place in both places virtually simultaneously but, in the absence of a dual location theory, it made more sense to regard the appropriation as taking place in the US, because the defendant's physical location in Russia was of far less significance than the fact that he was looking at, and operating on, magnetic disks located in the US.

8.3.4 'Innocent' appropriation

The latter part of s 3(1) refers to someone who may have come by the property without stealing it. Any later assumption of a right by 'keeping or dealing with it as owner' will satisfy the section. In *Broom v Crowther* (1984) 148 JP 592, the accused offered to sell for £5 a stolen theodolite worth approximately £200. He thought it might be stolen but accepted assurances that it was not. Several months later, he was informed that the theodolite was indeed stolen. A few days later the police recovered the theodolite from his house. In the intervening period, he had been trying to make up his mind what, if anything, he should do. He was charged with handling and theft. The Divisional Court accepted his argument on the theft charge that appropriation needs conduct and that as there had been nothing positive once he had acquired the knowledge then there was no appropriation.

The TA 1968, however, is clear in that an appropriation can occur if there is 'any later assumption of a right to it by keeping' and surely this covers the situation in the *Broom v Crowther* case. Lord Roskill in *Morris* also refers to the possibility of appropriation by an act which need not necessarily be 'overt' but this does emphasise the requirement of an act as opposed to an omission or just doing nothing.

8.3.5 Continuing appropriation?

The Court of Appeal considered the question of whether property is capable of being appropriated more than once in *Atakpu and Abrahams* [1993] 4 All ER 215. The issue arose in connection with expensive motor vehicles hired by the defendants on the continent, brought into this country, and then sold on to unsuspecting buyers. Could these cars, stolen abroad, be stolen again and again within the jurisdiction each time a transaction occurred? Having reviewed the case law including *Hale* (1978) 68 Cr App R 415, the Court of Appeal concluded:

- theft can occur as a result of a simple appropriation but the transaction may not be complete until several appropriations later;
- 'theft is a finite act – it has a beginning and an end';

- there is no case law which suggests, let alone decides, that 'successive thefts of the same property' can amount to separate appropriations.

The court was content, *per* Ward LJ, to: '... see the logic that if there are appropriations each one can constitute a separate theft, [but] we flinch from reaching that conclusion.'

An analysis of s 3(1) provides the answer, so that if a person has come by property through stealing it (as in this case), any later dealing with it is, by implication, not included among the assumptions of the right of an owner which amount to an appropriation within the meaning of s 3(1):

> ... in our judgment if goods have once been stolen, even if stolen abroad, they cannot be stolen again by the same thief exercising the same or other rights of ownership over the property [p 223].

Gomez decides that any dishonest assumption of the rights of an owner made with the necessary intention is theft and this implies that there can be no such thing as a continuous appropriation. However, the court did not wish the law to become that rigid as it would lead to injustices occurring. It decided, therefore, that it should be left to the 'common sense' of the jury to decide that the appropriation can continue as long as the thief 'can sensibly be regarded as in the act of stealing', or is 'on the job'. Therefore, as the theft of the vehicles took place abroad, the defendants could not be charged with theft in England. Further consideration ought to be given to the facts of this case in trying to decide where the appropriation took place. The cars were obtained as a result of deception at the point of hiring. According to *Gomez*, the appropriation is complete at that point, that is, in Belgium or Germany. However, if the cars had been obtained as a result of a legitimate hiring agreement which confined the use of the vehicles to, say, Germany, as long as the driver was within that country, has he really appropriated the vehicle? He is simply doing what he is authorised to do and has in fact contracted and paid to do. Once he leaves Germany in order to bring the vehicle to the UK, then at that point he has clearly exceeded his authority and, but for *Gomez*, the appropriation would take place at that point. *Morris* required evidence of adverse interference with the rights of the owner and that does not occur until the German border is crossed, but of course the court in *Gomez* chose to follow *Lawrence* and not *Morris*. The situation in *Atakpu and Abrahams* was considered by Glanville Williams as long ago as 1978. In his article, 'Appropriation: a single or continuous act' ([1978] Crim LR 69), he concluded that any argument in favour of a continuous appropriation rule would turn on policy rather than authority. Taken to its logical conclusion, if there was in law a continuous appropriation rule then, as Williams says: 'This might enable handling, with all its complexities, to be abolished.'

8.3.6 Property belonging to the defendant

It is clear that, at the time an appropriation takes place, the property must belong to another within the meaning attributed to these words in s 5 of the TA 1968. In the overwhelming majority of cases, this will present no problems whatsoever, but occasionally property will actually belong to the defendant at the time of the alleged appropriation and, therefore, theft cannot be committed. *Greenberg* [1972] Crim LR 331 was a case in point, where the defendant, having filled his car with petrol, then decided not to pay and drove away from a self-service petrol station. It was decided that as the property in the petrol had passed to the defendant when it flowed from the pump into his tank, when he later decided not to pay for it, the petrol belonged to him, in that he had ownership, possession and control within the meaning in s 5. He had therefore not dishonestly appropriated property belonging to another and his conviction for theft was overturned. Similar reasoning underpins the decision in *Edwards v Ddin* [1976] 3 All ER 705. In this case, the defendant had driven into a petrol station and instructed the attendant to fill the tank with petrol. On completion of the refuelling, he drove away without paying. He was charged with theft. It was held that he had not appropriated property belonging to another, as, at the time of the alleged dishonest appropriation (driving away) the petrol was, for the purposes of s 5 of the TA 1968, deemed to belong to him. Of course, if the defendants in each case had, prior to initiating the transactions, determined not to pay, then a more appropriate charge would be under s 15 of the TA 1968 of dishonestly obtaining property by deception. Because of the decision in *Gomez*, a charge of theft could also be brought if the defendant was dishonest from the outset.

8.3.7 Conclusion

It will be apparent that *Gomez* and *Hinks* have failed to bring into this area of the criminal law the certainty which is demanded. The House of Lords in both cases chose to ignore the recommendations of the 1966 Criminal Law Revision Committee report (Cmnd 2977). Of course, in seeking the intention of parliament, a court is not bound to take such reports into account but, in this case, it was parliament's avowed intention to give effect to the Committee's recommendations. The Committee clearly intended that the word 'appropriates' should encompass the tort of 'conversion' and, therefore, the concept of usurpation of another's rights. An analysis of the report would, in all probability, lead the reader to conclude that the *Morris* decision more closely matches the intent of the Committee than does that in *Gomez*. Why was it not taken into account? Lord Keith offers the following reason:

> In my opinion, it serves no useful purpose at the present time to seek to construe the relevant provisions of the Theft Act by reference to the report which preceded it, namely the Eighth Report of the Criminal Law Revision Committee, *Theft and Related Offences* ... The decision in *Lawrence*'s case was a clear decision of this House upon the construction of the word 'appropriates' in s 1(1) of the TA 1968, which had stood for 12 years when doubt was thrown upon it by *obiter dicta* in *R v Morris. Lawrence*'s case must be regarded as authoritative and correct, and there is no question of it now being right to depart from it.

That decision by Lord Keith has not passed without critical comment. Professor Smith in commenting on the case ([1993] Crim LR 304, p 306) opines:

> The only reason for not doing so offered by Lord Keith was that the point of law was the subject of a decision in *Lawrence* while the flatly contradictory observations of the whole House in *Morris* were *obiter dicta*. If that was sufficient to settle the matter, the appeal was a waste of time and a great deal of public money. The decision shows scant respect for the five Law Lords in *Morris* who concurred in an opinion now held to be untenable and fails to have regard to the many doubts that have been expressed about the decision in *Lawrence*.

8.4   BELONGING TO ANOTHER

Section 5(1) of the TA 1968 provides the basic definition of when property belongs to another:

> Property shall be regarded as belonging to any person having possession or control of it, or having in it any proprietary right or interest (not being an equitable interest arising only from an agreement to transfer or grant an interest).

It will be obvious from this that property may belong to another for the purposes of theft even though that person has no proprietary interest in it, merely having possession and/or control.

This raises an interesting question of whether the owner of property can be guilty of stealing his own property. The typical example of theft involves a person who is not the owner of the property appropriating it from someone who is. However, the definition of 'belonging to another' encompasses lesser interests than ownership and it may be that the owner can steal his own property from a person who has one of those lesser interests. The sensible answer to this question might seem to be that the owner could only steal his own property from a person with a lesser interest if that person would be entitled to resist the owner's claim for the *immediate* return of the property – say, because there is a contractual hiring of the property or because there is a lien, a right to retain the property until money is paid (as in the case of an unpaid repairer of goods). This was not the view taken by the Court of Appeal in *Turner (No 2)* [1971] 1 WLR 901. In that case, the appellant had taken his car to a garage for repair. The repairs were completed and the car left outside the garage overnight awaiting collection by its owner. Unknown to the garage owner, Mr Brown, the appellant had a spare set of keys, one set having been handed to Mr Brown when the car was deposited with him. The appellant, without Mr Brown's consent, removed the car and omitted to pay for the repairs which had been carried out. The jury by a majority found Turner guilty of stealing his own car; this conclusion being possible as a result of the wording of s 5(1) of the TA 1968. The decision was upheld by the Court of Appeal on the grounds that, at the time when the defendant dishonestly took his car away, it belonged to the garage proprietor in the simple sense that he had possession and control of it. Of course, as an unpaid repairer he also had a lien over the car and so could have resisted the defendant's claim for its return, yet the court disregarded the lien and rested its decision purely on the fact of possession and control. The implication is that any owner of property who lends it to another could be guilty of theft if he were then dishonestly to take it back (say, secretly, in order to cause the other to fear that he had lost it) even though he could openly demand the return of the property and the other would have no claim to resist the demand. *Turner (No 2)* is to be compared with *Meredith* [1973] Crim LR 253, where the defendant removed his car from a police car pound, it having been placed there during the course of a soccer match at which he was a spectator, because it had been causing an obstruction. It was held that he could not be guilty of stealing his own property. The police had no legal right to retain the car as against the owner and, therefore, whatever his intent, he was not guilty of taking property belonging to another. If one disregards the lien in the *Turner* case, it is difficult to find a distinction between them. The car was undoubtedly in the possession and control of the police, it was on their property and had a police steering lock attached to it.

8.4.1   Control

The word 'control' was subject to judicial scrutiny in *Woodman* [1974] 2 All ER 955. The owners of a disused factory had agreed to sell all the scrap metal on the site. The purchasers entered the premises and removed the vast majority of the metal, apart from a small amount which proved too inaccessible to warrant removal. The metal remained there, unknown to the owners of the site, for a couple of years until removed by Woodman and an accomplice. His defence to a charge of theft of the metal was that the property did not belong to another because the owners of the land had sold their proprietary interest in the metal (to a person who had abandoned their rights in the residue) and, being unaware of its presence on their land, had neither possession nor control of the scrap metal. The Court of Appeal had no doubt that as the company controlled the site then they controlled the articles left on the site. As the company had erected fences around the property in order to exclude trespassers, there was sufficient evidence from which to conclude they controlled the site. Woodman had, therefore, appropriated property belonging to another. The court suggested that, if a third party had deposited explosives or drugs on the land, then the owner's lack of knowledge would 'produce a different result from that which arises under the general presumption to which we have referred'.

8.4.2   Abandoned property

Property may of course be abandoned, in which case it may not be the subject of a theft charge simply because it belongs to no one. However, the courts will be slow to conclude that property has been abandoned and, it is submitted, will require evidence that the owner could not care less what happened to the property. Discarding property in a council litter bin will not amount to abandonment, as the title to that property is being passed to the council. In *Hancock* [1990] 3 All ER 183, the defendant was charged with theft of gold and silver coins approximately 2,000 years old which he had discovered while using a metal detector on land near Guildford which had been the site of a Roman-Celtic temple. He claimed that, when he found the coins, they were not altogether in one place but scattered about. If this were untrue, it would have led to the inference that the coins had been hidden by someone who intended to return and recover them and could be viewed as treasure trove belonging to the Crown. Conversely, if they had been scattered over a wide area, the conclusion could be reached that they were dropped there at different times as sacrifices or votive offerings and there would be no intention that they should be recovered at a later stage. The legal position appears to be that the Crown has a prerogative right to all treasure trove, which was hidden by the owner with a view to later recovery. However, if the owner deliberately abandoned the property or it was accidentally lost it is not to be regarded as treasure trove. The Court of Appeal decided that it was for the jury to determine whether the coins were in fact treasure trove and therefore the property of the Crown. In doing so, they must apply the ordinary criminal burden and standard of proof. The jury had to be sure that the coins were deposited by someone intending to retrieve them at a later date before they could be regarded as belonging to the Crown. The Crown, therefore, has a proprietary interest not possession or control unless of course the treasure trove is discovered on Crown property. In *Waverley BC v Fletcher* [1995] 4 All ER 756, the defendant while using a metal detector in a public park discovered a valuable medieval gold brooch some nine inches below the surface. A coroner's inquisition subsequently determined that it was not treasure trove, that is, the Crown had no proprietary interest in the brooch. The local authority sought a declaration that the brooch was its property. The Court of Appeal agreed with the authority. It applied the principle that the owner or lawful possessor of land owned all that was in or attached to it. The court viewed the digging up and removal of property from the park as a trespass and was quite clear that the local authority had a better title to the brooch than the finder.

The Treasure Act 1996 abolishes the law on treasure trove. Treasure still vests in the Crown and therefore any appropriation of treasure will be from the Crown. In light of the *Waverley* decision and the new Act, it is possible that theft may be committed against both a landowner and the Crown, as each will have a proprietary interest in the property. The former because in owning the land he has a proprietary interest in anything buried on the land and the latter because of the terms of the Act.

8.4.3   Trust property

Section 5(2) of the TA 1968 deals with property held on trust and provides that:

> ... where property is subject to a trust, the persons to whom it belongs shall be regarded as including any person having a right to enforce the trust, and an intention to defeat the trust shall be regarded accordingly as an intention to deprive of the property any person having that right.

In the majority of cases, if a trustee steals from a trust, then the situation will be covered by applying s 5(1), because any beneficiaries of the trust will have an equitable interest, which amounts to a proprietary interest within the terms of s 5(1). The purpose of s 5(2) is to ensure that, where a trust does not have recognised beneficiaries, then any property appropriated by the trustee will still be regarded as belonging to another. An example of this would be a charitable trust.

8.4.4   Obligation to retain and deal

Section 5(3) of the TA 1968 states:

> ... where a person receives property from or on account of another, and is under an obligation to the other to retain and deal with that property or its proceeds in a particular way, the property or proceeds shall be regarded (as against him) as belonging to the other.

In some circumstances, property may be received by a person who is then expected to deal with it on behalf of the giver, but in circumstances where the legal title to the property passes to the recipient. If the property is then misappropriated, in the sense that the person acts in a way inconsistent with his obligation, a theft charge would, but for the existence of s 5(3), not lie against the wrongdoer simply because he owned the property, which was also in his possession and control. This is because the property would not belong to another. Let us assume that all members of the academic registrar's department of a university decide to operate a Christmas club, with each member contributing £2 each week throughout the year, to be collected by one of their number. The total each week is to be deposited in an interest bearing building society account and the total amount plus interest returned to the members of the syndicate to spend prior to the Christmas vacation. Each time a member gives £2 to the collector, he is in law making the collector the owner of the coins. That individual would, presumably, have no qualms if he saw the collector immediately use those coins in order to give change to another member who tendered a £5 note. However, although he has become the owner he is not free to deal with the money in any way he wishes. Each member expects him to place a sum equivalent to the total amount collected into a particular building society account. Were he to refrain from so doing, then, as a result of s 5(3), he could be found guilty of theft of the money. He has received property from another, he is under an obligation to the other to deal with the property in a particular way, and therefore the money is to be regarded as belonging to the other. The 1966 Criminal Law Revision Committee report (Cmnd 2977) cites a similar example:

> Sub-section (3) ... provides for the special case where property is transferred to a person to retain and deal with for a particular purpose and he misapplies it or its proceeds. An example would be the treasurer of a holiday fund. The person in question is in law the owner of the property; but the sub-section treats the property, as against him, as belonging to the persons to whom he owes the duty to retain and deal with the property as agreed. He will therefore be guilty of stealing from them if he misapplies the property or proceeds.

The starting point for the examination of this sub-section is the case of *Hall* [1973] QB 126. The defendant ran a travel agency and clients paid him money as deposits for holidays and flights. The tickets failed to materialise and many people lost their money. It transpired that, when he had received money, it was paid into the firm's general trading account and not into any specially created client or flight account. His defence was based on the assertion that he could not be convicted of theft simply because the business had not prospered. He was convicted of theft of the monies and appealed on the basis that the monies paid to him by clients belonged to him and he could not be said to have appropriated property belonging to another. The Court of Appeal allowed the appeal, despite criticising his 'scandalous conduct'. The court recognised that a contractual obligation was created between the clients and Hall, but that of itself did not prove that the clients expected him to retain and deal with that property or its proceeds in a particular way and, as such, no 'obligation' within the meaning of s 5(3) could be imposed upon him. As Edmund-Davies LJ said:

> ... what was not here established was that these clients expected them 'to retain and deal with that property or its proceeds in a particular way', and that an 'obligation' to do so was undertaken by the appellant ... each case turns on its own facts. Cases could, we suppose, conceivably arise where by some special arrangement (preferably evidenced by documents), the client could impose on the travel agent an 'obligation' falling within s 5(3). But no such special arrangement was made in any of the seven cases here being considered [p 130].

The Court of Appeal in *Rader* [1992] Crim LR 663 distinguished *Hall* in a case which involved Rader receiving sums totalling nearly £10,000 from the victim which he said 'would be put to good use' and returned to him on a fixed date with some sort of profit. None of the money was repaid, nor did any profit or interest accrue. It appeared that Rader had transferred the money to an acquaintance in the US who had failed to repay the funds. He was convicted of theft and his appeal dismissed. The Court of Appeal was left in no doubt that Rader had been under an obligation to invest the money in such a way (presumably non-speculative) as to produce a profit for the victim. Do note the overlap with s 15, as if it could have been proved that Rader had obtained the money by deception, for example, by telling the victim he would use it in one way when his intention was to the contrary, then he would have obtained the property by deception.

It will be apparent that business would grind to a halt if customers were to be allowed to insist that the actual money paid to travel agents or insurance agents were to be used in a particular way. *Lewis v Lethbridge* [1987] Crim LR 59 decided that the accused 'need not be under an obligation to retain particular monies. It is sufficient that he is under an obligation to keep in existence a fund equivalent to that which he has received'. Yet it is emphasised by the Divisional Court that there must be evidence of an obligation to do so. If the accused is permitted to do what he likes with the property, his only obligation being to account in due course for an equivalent sum, s 5(3) does not apply. The court cited with approval the summary by Professor Smith in *The Law of Theft* (5th edn, 1984, London: Butterworths) to the effect that 'the obligation is to deal with that property or its proceeds in a particular way'. The appellant had obtained sponsorship for a friend who was running in the London Marathon. He received £54 but did not hand it over to the relevant charity. The question was whether or not he was under an obligation to hand over the notes and coins he had been given or equivalent sum. The court allowed his appeal because the justices had wrongly concluded that the debt owed to the charity could be described as 'proceeds' of the money he had received. This decision would have surprised the many charities in this country and donors also would be wary of handing over sponsorship money if they were aware that the collector was under no obligation to deal with the money in a particular way. It would be different if money was placed directly into a collecting box provided by the charity, as the representative would not normally have access to the cash and would have an obligation to hand over the particular money in the box to the charity. If he destroyed the box in gaining access to the money then s 5(3) would be unnecessary as there would be sufficient evidence to show theft of the box which presumably belonged to the charity, and also of the contents. However, *Lethbridge* was disapproved in *Wain* [1995] Cr App R 660. The defendant had raised money for charity by organising various events. The money raised was paid into a special bank account. The money was to be distributed to various charities by another company and one of its representatives consented to Wain paying the money into his own account. He used the money for his own purposes. The Court of Appeal concluded that what he had done amounted to theft as he was under an obligation to retain the proceeds of the money collected and deal with them in a particular way. The approach in *Lewis v Lethbridge* was criticised as being too 'narrow'. In *Huskinson* [1988] Crim LR 620, the respondent was charged with theft of £279 from the Housing Services Department. He was a tenant who fell into arrears with his rent. He was sent a cheque for £479 but gave only £200 to his landlord, spending the rest on himself. It was held by the Divisional Court that the case could not be brought within s 5(3). Was he under an obligation to the Housing Services Department to deal with the cheque or its proceeds in a particular way? The relevant legislation and regulations did not impose an express obligation on a tenant to pay the sum received directly to the landlord and it was held to be impossible to imply such an obligation. The court suggested that, had the defendant been able to pay his landlord from other funds prior to receiving the cheque, he would have been quite entitled to use the cheque or its proceeds for his own purposes. This decision can be criticised on the basis that the money was paid to him to meet a specific need and, in such circumstances, surely he should be obliged to use it for that purpose? The obligation must be legal and not moral or social, according to the decision in *Gilks* [1972] 3 All ER 280. It would appear from *Mainwaring* (1981) 74 Cr App R 99 that a jury should be directed that whether or not there is an obligation is a matter of law. The Court of Appeal proposed that:

> What ... a judge ought to do is this: if the facts relied upon by the prosecution are in dispute he should direct the jury to make their findings on the facts, and then say to them: 'If you find the facts to be such and such, then I direct you as a matter of law that a legal obligation arose to which s 5(3) applies' [p 107].

This direction of Lawton LJ in *Mainwaring* was followed in *Dubar* [1995] 1 All ER 781. The appellant had received £1,800 from S with which to buy a car. In S's view, the money was given in the expectation that D would purchase a D-registration Ford Orion 1.4. D's version of events was that he was given the money in order to find a car of appropriate value whether it be a Ford, Vauxhall or any other make. He claimed that he had therefore not been placed under an obligation to deal with the money in a particular way as required by s 5(3). Needless to say, a car was never purchased and D used the cash in order to settle debts and on general spending.

The Courts Martial Appeal Court held that the correct approach was to invite the jury to reach a conclusion on the facts. In light of their conclusion, the judge would then direct them as to whether a legal obligation had or had not arisen. It was not for the jury to determine whether an obligation under s 5(3) had arisen. The judge had directed the jury in this way:

> If you are sure that S and D agreed and intended that D was to use the money for no other purpose than to buy a specific Ford Orion motor car for S or otherwise return the money to S ... if you are sure of those facts, then I tell you, as a matter of law, that D was under a legal obligation to deal with the money in a particular way [p 786].

That, said the Courts Martial Appeal Court, was a 'correct following of the classic division of function between judge and jury ...'. The appellant's appeal against conviction was allowed but on other grounds.

Clients investing money via a financial intermediary will also be pleased to discover that such agencies are not to be equated with travel agents for the purposes of establishing an obligation under s 5(3) of the TA 1968. This was stated by the Court of Appeal in *Hallam and Blackburn* [1995] Crim LR 323. Monies were received from clients for investment on their behalf or from insurance companies to be passed to clients, but instead paid into their own or their company accounts. Clients, it was said, retained an equitable interest in such monies and therefore in any cheques drawn and the proceeds resulting from the investment. The court was of the view that it was immaterial whether the property was regarded as belonging to the clients under s 5(1), (2) or (3). They had, therefore, appropriated property belonging to another.

Wills (1991) 92 Cr App R 297 determines that:

> ... whether a person is under an obligation to deal with property in a particular way can only be established by proving that he had knowledge of the obligation. Proof that property was not dealt with in conformity with the obligation is not sufficient in itself ... [p 301].

8.4.5   Mistake and obligation to make restoration

Section 5(4) of the TA 1968 deals with the situation where property is obtained as a result of another's mistake:

> Where a person gets property by another's mistake, and is under an obligation to make restoration (in whole or in part) of the property or its proceeds or of the value thereof, then to the extent of that obligation the property or proceeds shall be regarded (as against him) as belonging to the person entitled to restoration, and an intention not to make restoration shall be regarded accordingly as an intention to deprive that person of the property or proceeds.

A pre-Theft Act case will illustrate what the sub-section is attempting to cover. In *Moynes v Coopper* [1956] 1 QB 439, the defendant was paid his full entitlement to wages even though he had received an advance. His strict entitlement was to 3 s 9 d not the £7 3 s 4 d which had been paid. He was acquitted of stealing the excess, but it would appear that he would now be caught by the provisions in s 5(4), as he would be under a legal obligation to make restitution of the difference. There have been, as may be expected, a number of cases of overpayment in the context of employment.

In *Attorney General's Reference (No 1 of 1983)* [1984] 3 All ER 369, a woman police officer had by mistake received £74 for overtime and wages and this amount together with her salary was paid by giro into her bank account. She was not, initially, aware of the error but did at some later stage make the discovery and decided against making restitution to her employer, the Metropolitan Police. At her trial for theft, the judge stopped the case and directed the jury to acquit. The Attorney General referred the issue to the Court of Appeal, asking whether someone who receives overpayment of a debt due to him, for example, salary, may be guilty of theft if he intentionally fails to repay the amount of overpayment. In concluding that theft would be committed in such circumstances the court held that once the person's account had been credited, the bank owed him a debt, and, as we have seen, that is to be regarded as a thing in action and property within the meaning of s 4(1) of the TA 1968. There is clearly a mistake on the part of the employer and, applying the general principles of restitution, there is an obligation to repay the benefit received. Although the thing in action belonged to her, it was the value of the thing which she was obliged to restore to the Metropolitan Police. Accordingly, provided that the other elements of s 1 were present, there would be no obstacle to a conviction for theft.

In *Davis* [1988] Crim LR 762, a mistake by the London Borough of Richmond resulted in the defendant receiving housing benefit each week for some weeks by way of two identical cheques instead of just one. Even when he was no longer entitled to any benefit, one cheque each week continued to be sent. He endorsed the cheques to shopkeepers for cash or to his landlord to pay for his accommodation. He was charged with theft of the cash rather than of the cheques. Applying s 5(4), his convictions were upheld where he had obtained cash but were quashed where he had merely endorsed the cheques for accommodation. The cash represented the proceeds of the cheques and the defendant was under an obligation to make restoration.

However, s 5(4) may not be necessary to achieve a conviction in such cases. In *Chase Manhattan Bank NA v Israel-British Bank* [1979] 3 All ER 670, it was held that, where money is paid to another under a mistake of fact, the person who pays that money retains an equitable interest in it. In Theft Act terms, this could amount to a sufficient interest under s 5(1) for the property still to 'belong to' the original owner. Indeed, in *Shadrokh-Cigari* [1988] Crim LR 465, where the defendant had withdrawn money which he knew had been credited to a bank account by mistake, the Court of Appeal held that his conviction for theft could be supported by virtue of s 5(1) or 5(4).

Finally, in this section one ought to consider the decision of the Court of Appeal in *Gilks*. It establishes that the only obligation which will be recognised for s 5(4) is a legal one. Cairns LJ put it this way:

> In a criminal statute, where a person's criminal liability is made dependent on his having an obligation, it would be quite wrong to construe that word so as to cover a moral or social obligation as distinct from a legal one [p 283].

Gilks had placed a bet on the outcome of a horse race and, as a result of a mistake by the assistant manager of the betting shop, was given over £100 more than he was entitled to receive. He was, from the moment he was being paid, aware of the overpayment and afterwards refused to consider repayment on the basis that Ladbroke's (a well-known chain of bookmakers) could afford the loss! He was convicted of theft, but not, it should be noted, as a result of applying s 5(4). A gaming transaction is legally unenforceable and therefore there is no legal obligation to make restoration. The court managed to find other reasons to uphold the conviction. It held that ownership in the property had not passed to Gilks because of the mistake. When Gilks decided to keep the money, it still belonged to another, that is, the betting shop, the court relying on the old authority of *Middleton* (1873) LR 2 CCR 38, where the mistake had been as to the identity of the recipient. In this case, the assistant manager did not make any mistake as to identity nor as to the amount. He intended to, and did, give Gilks £117.25. *Gilks*, it is submitted, should be regarded as wrongly decided. Given the *ratio* in *Shadrokh-Cigari*, the betting shop retained an equitable interest in the money and a conviction would now be sustainable applying this principle. Of course, since the House of Lords decided in *Gomez* that the consent of the owner to the transfer of ownership has no bearing on whether or not the defendant appropriates the property, it would now be possible to convict Gilks simply on the grounds that he appropriated the money when the bookmaker paid it to him and he was dishonest in taking it. This is yet another reason why the scope of application of s 5(4) may be much narrower than originally intended.

The final point to note is that the property must belong to another at the time of the appropriation. It is important to determine at what point in a transaction ownership does actually pass. This issue was confronted in *Greenberg* where the court emphasised that the decision would depend on the intention of the parties. In this case (discussed above, 8.3.6) the court held that ownership of the petrol was transferred when the petrol flowed from the petrol pump into the car's petrol tank, and not when the customer tendered payment.

In *Dobson*, Parker LJ accepted Lord Roskill's view in *Morris* that it is:

> ... wrong to introduce into this branch of the criminal law questions whether particular contracts are void or voidable on the ground of mistake or fraud or whether any mistake is sufficiently fundamental to vitiate a contract [p 934].

Providing that the property belongs to someone other than the defendant at the time of the act of appropriation, then s 5 is satisfied and whether title passes under a voidable contract is unimportant.

8.5   *MENS REA*: DISHONESTY

The TA 1968 does not provide a definition of what amounts to dishonesty and, given that society's views of what is or is not dishonest are ever changing, it was probably wise for parliament not to attempt so to do. The Criminal Law Revision Committee (in its 1966 report, Cmnd 2977) preferred the word 'dishonestly' as opposed to 'fraudulently' on the basis that it would be easier for jurors to understand:

> 'Dishonesty' [is] something which laymen can easily recognise when they see it, whereas 'fraud' may seem to involve technicalities which have to be explained by a lawyer.

What, however, s 2(1) the TA 1968 does is to highlight some circumstances where a person's appropriation of property belonging to another is not to be regarded as dishonest. These are:

(a) if he appropriates the property in the belief that he has in law the right to deprive the other of it, on behalf of himself or of a third person; or

(b) if he appropriates the property in the belief that he would have the other's consent if the other knew of the appropriation and the circumstances of it; or

(c) (except where the property came to him as trustee or personal representative) if he appropriates the property in the belief that the person to whom the property belongs cannot be discovered by taking reasonable steps.

Section 2(2) confirms that 'a person's appropriation of property belonging to another may be dishonest notwithstanding that he is willing to pay for the property'.

8.5.1   The approach to the assessment of dishonesty

The assessment of dishonesty involves both judge and jury. The leading case is *Ghosh* [1982] 2 All ER 689. The charge was in fact under s 15(1) of the TA 1968, that of obtaining property by deception, a section which requires evidence of dishonesty before a conviction can be obtained. The test of dishonesty should be the same as for s 1 of the TA 1968, given the significant overlap between the two offences. The court rejected an assertion that the approach should be 'purely objective, however attractive from the practical point of view that solution may be'. The court showed extreme reluctance to adopt a purely subjectivist approach because that would be to abandon 'all standards but that of the accused himself, and to bring about a state of affairs in which Robin Hood would be no robber'. There had been instances where a court had prior to *Ghosh* proceeded on a subjective basis as in *Boggeln v Williams* [1978] 2 All ER 1061. Williams having had his electricity supply disconnected because of his failure to settle a debt owed to the East Midlands Electricity Board, he informed the Board that he proposed to reconnect the supply. He did not, however, bypass the meter and it was, therefore, possible for the Board to ascertain how much power had been consumed. He was charged with the offence of dishonestly using electricity without due authority, contrary to s 13 of the TA 1968. The Queen's Bench Divisional Court accepted that, in circumstances where a defendant genuinely believed he was not acting dishonestly and also genuinely and reasonably believed that he would have the ability to pay for the electricity consumed, then his state of mind could not be classed as dishonest. There are obvious disadvantages in leaving it to the jury to decide dishonesty by simply determining whether or not the accused held the belief that he was acting honestly or that he had no idea that his conduct could be viewed as dishonest by the majority of people in the jurisdiction. In an area of law where certainty and consistency of approach should be paramount in order that individuals can determine their behaviour patterns, the 'subjectivist' approach would appear to be undesirable.

8.5.2   The twofold test

Ghosh determines that the test for dishonesty should encompass objective and subjective strands. The first question to answer is the objective one of whether the jury would conclude by reference to the 'ordinary standards of reasonable and honest people', that the defendant's act is dishonest. If the answer is yes, then the jury must focus on whether the defendant himself 'must have realised that what he was doing was by those standards dishonest'. If the answer to the first question is no, then the defendant must be acquitted. Lord Lane CJ went on to add that:

> It is dishonest for a defendant to act in a way which he knows ordinary people consider to be dishonest, even if he asserts or genuinely believes that he is morally justified in acting as he did.

8.5.3   Criticisms of the twofold test

It will be apparent that this 'twofold' test does not eradicate the potential for inconsistency between juries, although the chances are much reduced because of the presence of the objective element. However, the first part of the test requires juries to apply the 'current standards of ordinary decent people' as Lawton LJ put it in *Feely* [1973] 1 QB 530, and views are bound to differ as to the appropriate standard. *Feely* is a case in point. The accused was the manager of a betting shop who along with other managers received a communication from his company that the practice of 'borrowing' from tills was prohibited. In spite of this warning he 'borrowed' £30 intending to repay the money at a later date. There was evidence to prove that he was owed more than double this amount by his employers and he also left an IOU once the shortfall had been discovered. Looked at objectively would a jury applying the current standards of ordinary decent people be at one in concluding his actions were dishonest? Members of the jury may well be those 'upright citizens as the ordinary run of British Rail passengers may be presumed to be', but Lord Bridge in *Cooke* [1986] 2 All ER 985 was 'not prepared to assume that they would necessarily refuse to take and pay for refreshments even if they knew perfectly well that the buffet staff were practising the kind of "fiddle" here involved'. Surely the type of conduct engaged in by *Cooke* or *Rashid* [1977] 2 All ER 237 (see Chapter 9) lays a fair claim to be considered as 'objectively' dishonest? The second part of the test also raises some queries. The jury has to assess whether the accused realised what he was doing was dishonest, but what of the person whom the jury accepts believed was acting honestly but who because of his lifestyle or beliefs does not subscribe to the standards of ordinary people? Lord Lane CJ in *Ghosh* gave the following example in order to illustrate the point:

> Robin Hood or those ardent anti-vivisectionists who remove animals from vivisection laboratories are acting dishonestly, even though they may consider themselves to be morally justified in doing what they do ... [p 696].

It is certainly arguable that an accused who did not realise that his conduct would not receive the assent of ordinary people should be entitled to be acquitted although it is likely that a jury which has found the conduct objectively dishonest will take a great deal of convincing that the accused did not so realise. Lord Lane CJ cites the example of a man who has come to this country from one where public transport is free. He alights from a bus without paying. The action would appear to be objectively dishonest but the defendant would, according to Lord Lane, be found not to be dishonest as a result of applying the second limb of the 'test'. Apart from the fact that one is unsure exactly which Theft Act offence Lord Lane CJ had in mind, this could be treated as a simple case of mistake. Based on this man's knowledge of the circumstances, he honestly believed that he was entitled to travel for free. (Presumably, he could face prosecution under s 3 of the TA 1978. He has certainly made off without paying, but a conviction would depend on whether or not he knew payment on the spot was required.)

However strong the criticisms levelled against *Ghosh*, there can be no doubt that the decision does represent the law on the matter. The direction was approved in *Lightfoot* [1993] Crim LR 137, where the Court of Appeal emphasised that there was a clear distinction between a person's knowledge of the law and his 'appreciation that he was doing something which, by ordinary standards of reasonable and honest people, was regarded as dishonest'. An individual may be unaware of the legal provisions which make his conduct an offence, but be well aware that his actions would be regarded as dishonest by his fellow citizens. It was pointed out in *Squire* [1990] Crim LR 343 that a *Ghosh* direction need not be given on each and every occasion where dishonesty is an issue. It was further stated in *Roberts* (1987) 84 Cr App R 117 and *Price* [1990] Crim LR 200 that it could be potentially misleading in some cases to give a *Ghosh* direction. In *Price*, it was said that the *Ghosh* direction was necessary only where the defendant might have believed that what he was alleged to have done 'was in accordance with the ordinary person's idea of honesty'.

8.5.4 Section 2(1)(a) of the Theft Act 1968

If the defendant believes that he has the legal right to deprive the other of his property then he is not to be regarded as dishonest. The sub-section appears to rule out any objective assessment as it is centred on the defendant's belief as to his right to deprive the other of the property. Thus, in *Small* (1988) 86 Cr App R 170, where the defendant claimed that he genuinely thought a car he was accused of stealing had been abandoned, a reference by the trial judge to whether or not he reasonably believed the car had been dumped or abandoned was held to be a misdirection.

8.5.5 Section 2(1)(b) of the Theft Act 1968

This sub-section deals with a defendant who believes he would have had consent if the other had known of the appropriation. Again, as with s 2(1)(a), the sub-section is written from a subjectivist viewpoint. The defendant, who by reference to past conduct, can establish that he believed the owner would have consented on this occasion if he had known of the actual appropriation will be entitled to benefit from the section and not be regarded as dishonest.

8.5.6   Section 2(1)(c) of the Theft Act 1968

This sub-section deals with property which has been lost and as such ownership rights remain with the loser, unlike the situation where property has been abandoned. The focus is, as with the other sub-sections, on the defendant's belief. What constitutes reasonable steps will vary with the circumstances. If a defendant finds a £5 note in the street, then it is reasonable to assume that the owner has not reported its loss to the police and a failure to hand it in would not be evidence of dishonesty. Conversely, if it is £5,000, then the opposite conclusion is likely to be reached.

8.5.7   Section 2(2) of the Theft Act 1968

A person may be willing to pay for property and even to pay over the odds, but, as a result of s 2(2) that would not prevent a finding of dishonesty if he were aware that the owner had no wish to dispose of his property. If, however, he has no reason to assume that the owner would not willingly accept a cash sum equivalent to the value of the article, then a jury may be inclined to the view that he is not dishonest. It is submitted that individuals should not receive encouragement to deal with other people's property as they would wish simply because they have the means to give value.

8.5.8   Conclusion

The *Ghosh* decision has been the subject of much critical comment. The decision was a compromise to avoid applying either a purely objective or subjective approach to the assessment of dishonesty. The difficulty, of course, as Andrew Halpin ('The test for dishonesty' [1996] Crim LR 283) maintains, 'is the absence of a moral consensus within modern society over dishonesty'. He argues that the *Ghosh* test should be abandoned in favour of one of two options. The first is a purely subjective approach to the issue of dishonesty, which allows the 'individual defendant to limit his criminal liability by his own moral standards'. The second is for parliament to create a legal definition of dishonesty. The first he rejects because the protection of a person's property is made dependent upon the 'the moral outlook of the person seeking to interfere with it'. The second option he believes should be given serious consideration. In his article, 'Dishonesty: objections to *Feely* and *Ghosh*' ([1985] Crim LR 341), Edward Griew argued that whether a defendant is dishonest is clearly for the jury to decide but they should be able 'to turn to the law for clear guidance'. In other words, what is dishonest should be a matter of law.

The current position is that *Ghosh* has 'technical authority' but there are quite clearly situations which the courts regard as being dishonest thus permitting 'objective standards to be imposed by the courts' (see Halpin, p 289).

8.6   INTENTION TO DEPRIVE PERMANENTLY

The TA 1968 requires that before theft can be committed there is evidence of the intention permanently to deprive the other of his or her property. There is no requirement that he or she should actually be deprived. The shoplifter who leaves the shop without paying will have some difficulty in refuting the allegation that he or she intended permanently to deprive the owner of the goods. The person who snatches a chocolate eclair from a confectionery stall and consumes it on the spot leaves no one in any doubt that he or she has not only the intention to, but actually did, permanently deprive the owner of his or her property. In discussing the *actus reus* of theft, above, reference was made to the fact that theft may be complete when a person takes items from a supermarket shelf and places them into his or her pocket rather than a basket. Or, in switching price labels, there is the assumption that having removed the goods from the shelf and switched the labels theft may be established. Yet the most difficult element for the prosecution is likely to be establishing proof of the intention permanently to deprive. In theory, if the customer changes his or her mind and replaces the goods on the shelf then it is too late, the theft is complete. Yet how strong is the evidence likely to be to prove that at the moment of appropriation the defendant had the intention permanently to deprive the store of the items, if a few minutes later the goods are returned to the shelf?

8.6.1   Section 6(1) of the Theft Act 1968

Section 6(1) provides:

> A person appropriating property belonging to another without meaning the other permanently to lose the thing itself is nevertheless to be regarded as having the intention of permanently depriving the other of it if his intention is to treat the thing as his own to dispose of regardless of the other's rights; and a borrowing or lending of it may amount to so treating it if, but only if, the borrowing or lending is for a period and in circumstances making it equivalent to an outright taking or disposal.

A particularly important word is 'dispose'. To intend simply to use someone else's property should not satisfy the section. The meaning of 'dispose of' in s 6(1) was considered in two cases. In *Cahill* [1993] Crim LR 141, the court found Professor Smith's comments in *The Law of Theft* (6th edn, 1989, London: Butterworths, p 73) 'helpful'. He stated:

> It is submitted, however, that an intention merely to use the thing as one's own is not enough and that 'dispose of' is not used in the sense in which a general might 'dispose of' his forces but rather in the meaning given by the *Shorter Oxford Dictionary*: 'To deal with definitely: to get rid of; to get done with, finish. To make over by way of sale or bargain, sell.'

However, the Divisional Court in *DPP v Lavender* [1994] Crim LR 297 thought the dictionary definition 'too narrow'. A disposal, it was said, could also include dealing with the property. To treat goods as one's own was also deemed to be within the definition of 'dispose of'. *Cahill* was not cited to the court and it is submitted that this latter interpretation unjustifiably extends the ambit of the offence and should not be relied upon. In *Lloyd* [1985] 2 All ER 661, it was held that in a case of 'borrowing or lending' the intention to permanently deprive would be proved only if the goods were returned in a fundamentally changed state, so that any utility value would have been lost. In this case, Lloyd had removed from the cinema, where he was employed, films which were intended to be shown commercially. They were copied by two accomplices and then returned to the cinema. His conviction for conspiracy to commit theft was questioned on the basis that:

... the goodness, the virtue, the practical value of the films to the owners has not gone out of the article. The film could still be projected to paying audiences, and ... audiences ... would have paid for their seats.

Thus, the borrowing was deemed not to be the equivalent of an outright taking or disposal.

Lord Lane CJ in *Lloyd* pointed out that s 6(1) covers the situation where a defendant takes something and then offers it back to the owner for him to purchase if so minded. The defendant could claim that he has no desire to hold onto the property for one second more than is necessary. The court felt that in such circumstances this would be the equivalent to an outright taking. The authority for the proposition is stated to be *Hall* (1848) 169 ER 291 and an example given by Lord Lane CJ is:

I have taken your valuable painting. You can have it back on payment to me of £X,000. If you are not prepared to make that payment, then you are not going to get your painting back.

It may be that in such 'ransom' cases the latter element is implicit in the former part of the statement. If the property which is appropriated is money, it is made clear by s 6(1) that even if the defendant has the intention to repay, there is still an outright taking because it is most unlikely that he will return the actual currency which he removed. This was illustrated in *Velumyl* [1989] Crim LR 299, where the appellant had taken over £1,000 from his company's safe in breach of his authority and company rules. He claimed to have given the money to a friend and expected to be able to return the equivalent amount two days later. The Court of Appeal had no doubt that Velumyl had the requisite intention to permanently deprive because he had no intention to return 'the objects which he had taken'.

If someone takes property belonging to another, intending to decide at a later stage whether he will retain the articles if they appear valuable or negotiable, is this to be regarded as a sufficient intention? The issue of 'conditional intention' was considered by the courts in the 1970s in cases such as *Easom* [1971] 2 All ER 945, *Husseyn* (1977) 67 Cr App R 131 and *Walkington* [1979] 2 All ER 716, culminating in the decision of the Court of Appeal in *Attorney General's References (Nos 1 and 2 of 1979)* [1980] QB 180. It was held in this case that a person charged with burglary and who had entered a building intending to steal anything of value, that is, conditional upon there being anything of value in the building, did have the necessary intent under s 9(1)(a) of the TA 1968 because it is not necessary to prove that he intended to steal any specific item (see, more generally, below, 9.2). Similarly, if one takes a handbag intending to steal and upon examination discovers it to be empty, there is nothing to prevent a charge of attempted theft being preferred. In the case of the full offence of theft, however, the prosecution has to be able to prove that the defendant intended permanent deprivation in relation to a specific item of property. So, if the defendant has not made up his mind whether he wishes to keep a particular item of property and rejects it after inspection, he has not demonstrated any such intention in relation to that item and cannot be guilty of stealing it. In essence, these were the facts of *Easom* in which the defendant fell into a trap set for him by the police who were trying to catch a thief operating in a cinema. Posing as an ordinary member of the public, a police woman put her bag on the floor by her seat in the cinema. The defendant sat close to her, picked up her bag and looked through it. However, he did not find anything worth taking and he returned the bag and all its contents. His conviction for theft of the handbag and its contents was quashed. Note that he could not have been convicted of attempted theft of the handbag and its contents either, but that he could have been convicted of attempted theft more generally (as indicated above, 5.12, impossibility – the absence of anything worth taking – is no barrier to a conviction for attempt).

8.6.2 Section 6(2) of the Theft Act 1968

Section 6(2) states:

> Without prejudice to the generality of sub-section (1) above, where a person, having possession or control (lawfully or not) of property belonging to another, parts with the property under a condition as to its return which he may not be able to perform, this (if done for purposes of his own and without the other's authority) amounts to treating the property as his own to dispose of regardless of the other's rights.

This sub-section covers the situations where a defendant who may have come by the property lawfully, for example, as a bailee, or unlawfully, pledges the property, intending to fulfil the necessary conditions in order to redeem the pledge at a later date and then return it to the owner. The sub-section emphasises that if the condition imposed is one which he may not be able to perform then the action may be treated as the equivalent of an intention permanently to deprive, that is, treating the property as his own to dispose of, regardless of the other's rights.

8.7 THEFT AND THE EUROPEAN CONVENTION ON HUMAN RIGHTS

As explained earlier, the determination of the House of Lords in *Lawrence, Gomez* and *Hinks* to maintain the approach that consent does not prevent an appropriation from taking place has effectively rendered 'appropriation' a neutral term and has thrown the burden of the illegality in theft onto the concept of dishonesty. It will be recalled that, in *Hinks*, Lord Steyn was content to argue that one of the reasons why he was satisfied that the decision would not result in inappropriate convictions was that 'the mental requirements of theft are an adequate protection against injustice'. Yet there is a serious problem in placing so much faith in dishonesty in this way. The issue of dishonesty is one for the jury to determine, albeit that under the *Ghosh* test the jury must apply the ordinary standards of reasonable and honest people. This must inevitably introduce a degree of uncertainty into the definition of theft, since the views of a jury cannot be predicted with any great confidence, especially in those very areas where opinions may differ.

This question of uncertainty has become much more significant since the Human Rights Act 1998 came fully into force in 2000. As far as criminal courts are concerned, they are obliged by the 1998 Act to apply relevant provisions of the European Convention on Human Rights. Article 7 of the Convention provides that:

> No one shall be held guilty of any criminal offence on account of any act or omission which did not constitute a criminal offence under national or international law at the time when it was committed.

It is arguable that this provision is infringed by any offence the elements of which are defined with insufficient certainty. More generally, *prima facie* infringements of other Articles of the Convention may only be justified on grounds specified in those Articles and when 'prescribed by law'. Under the Convention, this term also requires the law to be sufficiently certain. So, in *Hashman and Harrup v United Kingdom* [2000] Crim LR 185, being bound over for conduct *contra bonos mores* (against the public good) was an infringement of the right to freedom of expression (Art 10.1) which could not be justified under Art 10.2 because the definition of the conduct lacked the precision which would give the applicants sufficiently clear guidance as to how they should behave in the future (in other words, it was not adequately 'prescribed by law'). Though the argument has been forcefully made, it would perhaps be surprising if the law of theft were to be held to infringe these requirements, and, to date, no case has yet accepted it. In *Pattni and Others* [2001] Crim LR 570, a case involving offences of cheating the Inland Revenue, the Crown Court judge rejected the argument, which was taken to be about dishonesty across all the offences, and not just in relation to the cheating offences.

OFFENCES AGAINST PROPERTY: THEFT

The starting point of any consideration of the law relating to theft should be the Criminal Law Revision Committee's Eighth Report on *Theft and Related Offences* (Cmnd 2977, 1966). The TA 1968 was based upon the Committee's recommendations and although we have seen that there has been a reluctance on the part of the House of Lords to use the report as an aid to construction it does provide the foundation knowledge needed for a study of this branch of the criminal law. We have seen that, over the past three and half decades, the law has become increasingly complex and, in some cases, fraught with uncertainty (see the whole issue of appropriation and consent), which has led judges such as Beldam LJ to call for urgent reform.

It has to be noted that the prosecution must prove all elements of the offence, that is, that there has been a dishonest appropriation of property belonging to another with the intention to permanently deprive the other of it. If the defence can establish that one of the five elements is absent then the accused is entitled to be acquitted.

ACTUS REUS

The *actus reus* of theft is proved by showing beyond all reasonable doubt that there has been an appropriation of property belonging to another. The *mens rea* requires proof that the appropriation was done dishonestly and with the intention to permanently deprive the other of that property.

It has been seen that whether or not an appropriation has occurred may be difficult to establish. As a result of *Gomez* and *Hinks*, it is possible to maintain that any action may in law amount to an appropriation however innocent it may appear. Taking my elderly neighbour's pension book to the post office to collect her pension would appear to be an appropriation. I am exercising one of her rights in that I am using the book and therefore denying her the right to do the same. My actions though would not amount to theft because I am doing so with her permission and for her benefit and therefore I do not act dishonestly. If *Morris* were to represent the law, then, in such circumstances, there would be no appropriation because there would be no adverse interference with her property. At the heart of appropriation is whether or not there is an assumption of any of the rights of the owner.

The property must belong to another and s 5 aids the prosecution by deeming that property shall for the purposes of theft belong to anyone having ownership, possession or control. Therefore, if A lends her portable colour television to B who takes it home, B has possession and control but A still retains ownership. If D were to steal the set from B's house he would commit theft against both A and B.

Property may belong to someone for the purposes of the TA 1968 even though that person is unaware of its existence as, for example, where a person owns land but is unaware of all the items on the land.

Section 5(3) and (4) deem that, in certain circumstances, property which in civil law will belong to the defendant may be regarded as belonging to another. It will be recalled that there is some uncertainty over s 5(3) when a person has been put under an obligation to deal with property or proceeds in a particular way. Remember also that s 5(4) may be redundant if it is accepted by the court that the person who transfers property under a mistake retains an equitable interest in the property. More generally, the decision in *Gomez* has significantly increased the scope of the offence of theft and may also have reduced the need for use of s 5(4).

MENS REA

The *mens rea* word of dishonesty is proved by applying a twofold test based upon a jury's assessment of both objective and subjective criteria. Would ordinary people conclude that the act done by the accused is dishonest? If the answer is yes, the jury must then proceed to listen to the accused's version of events and may conclude that in the circumstances he should not be regarded as dishonest. Having reached a conclusion that the act is objectively dishonest, it is more than likely that the jury will then go on to reject the individual's explanation although this is not inevitable.

The accused must also be shown to have intended to permanently deprive the other of the property within the meaning of s 6. It will be recalled that a borrowing can be the equivalent of an outright taking.

Finally, remember that there is a significant overlap between ss 1 and 15 of the TA 1968. Where fraud or deception are used in order to obtain property belonging to another, then s 15 will be the most appropriate charge. On the face of it, *Gomez* was a straightforward obtaining by deception rather than a s 1 offence.

CHAPTER 9

OFFENCES AGAINST PROPERTY: OTHER OFFENCES UNDER THE THEFT ACTS 1968 AND 1978 AND CRIMINAL DAMAGE

9.1   ROBBERY (s 8 OF THE THEFT ACT 1968)

It will be apparent that theft is at the heart of the offence of robbery. The purpose of engaging in a robbery is to steal and it is differentiated from the primary offence by the additional, aggravating element of force. Section 8(1) of the Theft Act (TA) 1968 provides:

> A person is guilty of robbery if he steals, and immediately before or at the time of doing so, and in order to do so, he uses force on any person or puts or seeks to put any person in fear of being then and there subjected to force.

Section 8(2) states:

> A person guilty of robbery, or of an assault with intent to rob, shall on conviction on indictment be liable to life imprisonment.

As the first part of this definition emphasises, to be guilty of robbery one must first steal, and all elements of s 1 of the TA 1968 will have to be established. So, even though force may be used, if the accused is not acting dishonestly or the intention to permanently deprive is lacking then a robbery charge will be inappropriate. In *Robinson* [1977] Crim LR 173, the appellant's conviction for robbery was quashed on the basis that he honestly believed he was entitled to the money which was owed by the victim to him. If force was used to enforce such an obligation, then an assault charge or a more serious offence might lie depending on the nature of the physical attack. If the theft has been completed with the necessary force being applied then robbery is established as soon as the theft is complete. In *Corcoran v Anderton* (1980) 71 Cr App R 104, the defendants wrestled with the owner for possession of her handbag and the theft was complete as soon as she lost possession, although in the event one of the assailants dropped it as they ran off, without having succeeded in their objective of permanently depriving her of the bag.

9.1.1   Force

The TA 1968 requires proof of either the use or the threat of force against the person. It appears that it is to be left to the jury to determine whether or not force has been used or threatened. The Act does not provide a definition. In *Clouden* [1987] Crim LR 56, the Court of Appeal, following *Dawson and James* (1976) 64 Cr App R 170, confirmed that the old distinction between force on the person and force on property had not survived the Act. The matter should be left to the jury. Clouden had followed a woman who was carrying a shopping basket. He approached her from behind and wrenched the basket from her grasp and ran away. He was charged with robbery and theft and convicted of the former offence. In his appeal against conviction, he argued that as there had been little resistance to his actions, in law it could not be established that he had used 'force'. The court rejected the submission, holding that it was for the jury to decide, taking into account all the circumstances.

The Criminal Law Revision Committee (Eighth Report, *Theft and Related Offences*, Cmnd 2977, 1966, para 65) had doubts as to whether or not this type of situation should amount to anything more than theft. It stated:

> We should not regard mere snatching of property such as a handbag, from an unresisting owner, as using force for the purpose of the definition, though it might be so if the owner resisted.

The use or threat of force may be against any person, and it is clear from the wording that the threat of the application of force at some stage in the future is not covered by s 8 ('then and there subjected to force').

In the overwhelming majority of cases, the force will be applied against the victim who is in possession and control of the property. However the section refers to force on 'any person' so long as it is used or threatened in order to steal. Therefore, to threaten or use force on a security guard, in order to facilitate access to a strongroom containing gold bars, would be enough, even though he had no proprietary interest whatsoever in the property.

9.1.2   Immediately before or at the time of stealing

A literal interpretation of these words would have a limiting effect on the scope of the section and draw attention to those aspects of the conduct which are closely related in time to the act of appropriation. It would, for example, rule out the gang who hold a bank manager captive in his house overnight before escaping with his keys which they use hours later to gain access to his bank. It is submitted that all the circumstances should be considered and, if the force used has a direct bearing on facilitating the theft, then one should view it as part of the same transaction. The force in the above example has been used with one purpose in mind: to commit theft. Similarly, the use of or threat of force seconds after the appropriation has taken place would seem to rule out a robbery conviction. However, the Court of Appeal in *Hale* (1979) 68 Cr App R 415 held that the act of appropriation was a continuing act and that it should be left to the jury to decide when it has finished. In this case, Hale and his accomplice entered the victim's house and Hale put his hand over her mouth to stop her from screaming, while the other went upstairs and took her jewellery box. They then tied her up and made their escape. The jury could have convicted of robbery on the basis of the force used against the victim in order to prevent her from raising the alarm, but the court also considered whether a robbery conviction could be sustained on the basis that the tying up was the act of 'force', an act which apparently took place when the jewellery box was already in their possession. Eveleigh LJ said:

> We also think that they were also entitled to rely upon the act of tying her up provided they were satisfied (and it is difficult to see how they could not be satisfied) that the force so used was to enable them to steal. If they were still engaged in the act of stealing the force was clearly used to enable them to continue to assume the rights of the owner and permanently to deprive Mrs Carrett of her box, which is what they began to do when they first seized it [p 418].

This approach was confirmed by the Court of Appeal in *Lockley* [1995] Crim LR 656. The appellant and two others took cans of beer from an off licence and, when challenged by the shopkeeper, used violence against him. It was submitted on their behalf that the theft was complete before any force was used and, therefore, the robbery issue should not have been left to the jury. In confirming that *Hale* was still good law, the court held that an appropriation was an act that continued until the transaction was complete and, thus, force was used in order to steal.

9.1.3   *Mens rea*

Clearly, there must be evidence of an intent to steal and the defendant must be shown to have acted dishonestly and with intent to permanently deprive. It is suggested that there should also be proved an intent in respect of the force used. If the accused intends to steal, yet has no intention to subject the victim to the use of force or cause that person to apprehend that force may be used against him, the crime should amount to theft but not to robbery.

9.2   BURGLARY (s 9 OF THE THEFT ACT 1968)

Section 9 of the TA 1968 creates two offences, one where a person enters a building as a trespasser with intent to commit one or more of a range of ulterior offences and a second where a person has entered as a trespasser and then commits one or more of a more limited range of offences:

(1) A person is guilty of burglary if:

    (a) he enters any building or part of a building as a trespasser and with intent to commit any such offence as is mentioned in sub-s (2) below; or

    (b) having entered into any building or part of a building as a trespasser he steals or attempts to steal anything in the building or that part of a building or inflicts or attempts to inflict on any person therein any grievous bodily harm.

(2) The offences referred to in sub-s (1)(a) above are offences of stealing anything in the building or part of a building in question, of inflicting on any person therein any grievous bodily harm or raping any person therein, and of doing unlawful damage to the building or anything therein.

(3) A person guilty of burglary shall on conviction on indictment be liable to imprisonment for a term not exceeding –

    (a) where the offence was committed in respect of a building or part of a building which was a dwelling, fourteen years

    (b) in any other case, 10 years.

(4) References in subsections (1) and (2) above to a building, and the reference in sub-s (3) above to a building which is a dwelling, shall apply also to an inhabited vehicle or vessel, and shall apply to any such vehicle or vessel at times when the person having a habitation in it is not there as well as at times when he is.

There are numerous elements of these offences to which consideration must be given. The *actus reus* of the crimes centre on the entry into any building or part of a building as a trespasser.

9.2.1   Building

Sub-section (4) makes it clear that the word 'building' includes an 'inhabited vehicle or vessel, and shall apply to any such vehicle or vessel at times when the person having a habitation in it is not there as well as at times when he is'. Nevertheless, despite this limited guidance, there is no all embracing definition included in the TA 1968. In the old case of *Stevens v Gourley* (1859) 7 CBNS 99, Byles J considered that a building comprised 'a structure of considerable size and intended to be permanent or at least to endure for a considerable time'. In *Norfolk Constabulary v Seekings and Gould* [1986] Crim LR 166, the appellants had tried to gain entry to two articulated lorry trailers being used by a supermarket as temporary storage space while building redevelopment was taking place. Each was supported by its own wheels and struts and an electricity cable ran from the supermarket to supply the lighting. Access was gained via steps which had been placed against each trailer. It was held that the character of the structure had not changed from that of a vehicle and therefore it was not a building for the purposes of an attempted burglary charge. This case is distinguishable from *B and S v Leathley* [1979] Crim LR 314, where a freezer container was classed as a building because it did not have any wheels and was immobile.

Given its literal meaning, the word 'building' covers structures which house many smaller units, for example, a large block of flats or suites of offices belonging to or leased by different companies. This means that an entry into the building with intent to steal from any of the smaller units would amount to burglary even though the defendant is arrested before reaching the particular unit from which he proposes to steal. If, indeed, the culprit is apprehended at the moment entry is effected into a block of flats and it is clear that the proposed theft is to occur from the penthouse flat, the TA 1968 would allow a conviction for burglary to follow. If not, the charge would have to be attempted burglary or theft and whether or not the accused is convicted is likely to depend on whether or not a jury would regard the acts as being more than merely preparatory. In practice, the judge will have to decide that there is sufficient evidence from which to conclude that a building within the meaning of the TA 1968 is in existence.

Walkington [1979] 2 All ER 716 considered the meaning of the words 'part of a building'. The appellant had entered an Oxford Street store as, he claimed, a *bona fide* customer. He had noticed a cash register behind a three-sided movable counter with the drawer partially open. He placed himself behind the counter, opened the drawer and, on realising it was empty, slammed it shut. He was arrested and charged with burglary. The Court of Appeal held that, as the store's management had 'impliedly prohibited customers' from entering that area, there was 'ample evidence' from which it could be concluded by the jury that the counter area amounted to 'part of a building' for the purposes of s 9(1)(a). The court also confirmed that, if the accused entered that part of the building as a trespasser with the intent to steal, it was 'immaterial' that there was nothing worth stealing or nothing to steal. On the assumption that he entered the store lawfully, the trespass occurred only in relation to the part of the building to which he was not entitled to go.

In *Laing* [1995] Crim LR 395, the defendant was found in a department store some time after it had closed for the day. He was apprehended in a stock area not open to the public. Surprisingly, the prosecution did not suggest that he might be guilty of burglary having entered the store lawfully and then moved to a part of the building to which the public were denied access at which point he would have become a trespasser. The judge directed the jury to consider whether he was a trespasser when found.

In allowing the appeal, the court confirmed that there was no evidence to prove that he was a trespasser when he entered the store and it was not suggested that he became a trespasser by moving from one part of the building to another. There is only one question to be answered, whether the charge is under s 9(1)(a) or (b). Did the defendant enter the building or part of the building as a trespasser?

Note that burglary in respect of a building which is a 'dwelling' attracts a higher penalty. Under the former common law of burglary, and burglary under the Larceny Acts, the concept of the 'dwelling house' was of a building in which someone lived as his home, whether or not he was currently there. A place where a person stays temporarily, such as a hotel bedroom, may not be a dwelling because it is not the person's home. On the other hand, a flat or bedsit in which a person is living until something better is available will probably be a dwelling, and it may be that a hotel bedroom occupied in such circumstances would also be a dwelling. It is unlikely that anything other than the building in which people actually live will be the 'dwelling', thus excluding outhouses and the like.

9.2.2   Entry

The section requires that the defendant 'enters' or 'entered' as a trespasser. Prior to the TA 1968 the common law regarded the insertion of any part of the body into the building as sufficient to constitute an entry. After a serious flirtation with a different approach, the courts seemed to have settled upon an interpretation of the requirements of the 1968 Act as to entry which is indistinguishable from the original common law approach. An apparent decision to begin afresh was initially signalled in the leading case of *Collins* [1972] 2 All ER 1105, which was described by Edmund-Davies LJ as:

> ... about as extraordinary a case as my brethren and I have ever heard either on the Bench or while at the Bar – were [the facts] put into a novel or portrayed on the stage, they would be regarded as being so improbable as to be unworthy of serious consideration and as verging at times on farce [p 1107].

Collins was charged with burglary with intent to commit rape. Naked, apart from his socks, he was balancing on the window sill of the victim's bedroom when she, mistaking him for her boyfriend, invited him into her bed and full sexual intercourse took place. It was only later that she suspected things were not quite right, switched on the bedside light and discovered that her visitor was not the person she believed she had been inviting into her bed. Collins's defence was that he had not entered the building before she gave her consent and therefore had not entered the building as a trespasser. The Court of Appeal considered that it was imperative that an 'effective and substantial entry' must have taken place before consent was given in order for an entry to be complete.

This ruling was reassessed in *Brown* [1985] Crim LR 212. The appellant had been seen by a witness with the top half of his body inside a shattered shop window and he appeared to be rummaging about inside the window. His feet were on the ground outside. He appealed against his conviction for burglary on the ground that he had not entered the building, since his body was not entirely within it. The court held that it was not required for the whole of a person's body to be inside the building. The crucial word of the Edmund-Davies test in *Collins* was 'effective' and '"substantially" did not materially assist in the matter'. It was hardly surprising that the court upheld the conviction as it was obvious that he could give effect to his purpose with only half his body inside the shop. In this case, there was an effective entry because Brown was able to reach the articles he wished to steal. But this is not always going to be the case, even if the whole body is in the building. If Collins had entered the house through the front door without any consent having been given, he would be guilty of burglary, given that his physical condition and state of undress indicated his purpose in being there. Yet it could hardly be claimed that his entry was 'effective', if this word is meant to refer to the ulterior offence, as he may have been apprehended straightaway, or the girl's bedroom door may have been bolted so that he would be unable to gain entry or she may not have been in the house. The better view is that 'effective' must refer to the entry and the crucial question is whether or not the defendant is better able to carry out the ulterior offence.

The importance of *Collins* as an authority has undoubtedly diminished and this was confirmed by the Court of Appeal in *Ryan* (1996) 160 JP 610. At approximately 2.30 am, an elderly householder found Ryan stuck in a downstairs window of his house. His neck and right arm were inside the window, the rest of his body was outside. He claimed that he was trying to reach a baseball bat that a friend had put through the window. He was convicted of burglary. His appeal was based on the proposition that in law there had been no entry as, given his predicament, he was unable to steal anything from the premises. The court dismissed his appeal holding that it was totally irrelevant whether a defendant was or was not capable of stealing anything from the premises. This decision appears to suggest that for there to be an entry in law there does not need to be either an 'effective' or 'substantial' entry. It would appear that we are back to the common law position stated above.

It is possible for the defendant to be regarded as entering a building even without physically putting any part of his body inside the building. Thus, he may use an innocent agent (such as a child or a well trained animal) or an instrument to make the entry. If an instrument is inserted into a building only in order to *facilitate* an entry, then the common law view was that this did not in law constitute an entry on the part of the person using the instrument. However, if the instrument was used in order to bring about the ulterior offence then this was an entry. Thus, if a fishing rod is pushed through an open window in order to 'hook' jewellery lying on a bedside cabinet, this would be sufficient to constitute an entry on the part of the person manipulating the rod. There is no authority which challenges the view that the common law has survived the TA 1968.

9.2.3 Trespasser

A person must enter a building as a trespasser before the *actus reus* of burglary is complete. The civil law recognises that a person is a trespasser if without permission or any legal right he enters a building intentionally, recklessly or negligently. The requirements of the civil law need to be satisfied before a person can be convicted of burglary. The criminal law requirements were stated by Edmund-Davies LJ in *Collins* as follows:

> ... there cannot be a conviction for entering premises 'as a trespasser', unless the person entering does so knowing that he is a trespasser and nevertheless deliberately enters, or, at the very least, is reckless whether or not he is entering the premises of another without the other party's consent [p 1110].

A question raised in *Collins* was whether he had entered the building as a trespasser before the young lady purported to give authorisation. There can be no doubt that, from the outset, he was intent upon entering the property as a trespasser. If permission to enter was granted before there had been an effective and substantial entry, then he could not be guilty of burglary as he would not have entered as a trespasser. Conversely, if he was inside the room before she invited him into her bed, then the offence would already be complete.

Attention should be paid to the position or status of the person who purports to give authority to enter a building. In *Collins*, it was argued that the girl's mother was the occupier and, therefore, the daughter did not have the authority to give consent to his entry. This was dismissed by Edmund-Davies LJ with these words: 'Whatever be the position in the law of tort, to regard such a proposition as acceptable in the criminal law would be unthinkable.'

In a case such as *Collins*, much will depend upon the knowledge of the defendant prior to or at the time of entry. If he knew that the girl's mother had specifically instructed her not to allow anyone into the house, then he would be a trespasser. Conversely, if he had no such knowledge nor reason to believe such a prohibition existed, then his entry with 'permission' would appear lawful. If he is given apparent authority to enter by a mature young lady who, from his point of view, could be the occupier, or he has no reason to suspect anyone else may be the occupier, again he ought to be found not to be a trespasser. Parents may impliedly give consent to their children to invite their friends into the house but one suspects that implied authority will be subject in many cases to the proviso that it is for a purpose which they would endorse, and intercourse with their daughter at 3 am is unlikely to feature on an 'approved' list of activities!

The Court of Appeal has given consideration as to whether or not a person is a trespasser if he enters intending to exceed the permission granted or to act in a way which is inconsistent with that permission. In *Jones and Smith* [1977] Crim LR 123, the appellants had been charged under s 9(1)(b) of the TA 1968 as they entered a house belonging to Smith's father and stole two television sets. Smith's defence was that his father had given him a 'general licence' to go into his house whenever he wanted to, and consequently his entry together with Jones into the house was lawful. It was argued on Smith's behalf that in these circumstances the fact that Smith had already made up his mind to take the television sets before entering the property would not make him a trespasser.

James LJ, citing *Collins* and *Hillen and Pettigrew v ICI (Alkali) Ltd* [1936] AC 65, held that a person is a trespasser for the purposes of s 9(1)(b) if:

> ... he enters premises of another knowing that he is entering in excess of the permission that has been given to him, or being reckless whether he is entering in excess of the permission that has been given to him to enter, providing the facts are known to the accused which enable him to realise that he is acting in excess of the permission given or that he is acting recklessly as to whether he exceeds that permission ... [p 123].

In *Jones and Smith*, the Court of Appeal dismissed their appeal on the basis that they had entered the premises with knowledge that they were exceeding the permission granted by Smith's father. In *Collins*, the court allowed the appeal because of the uncertainty over whether or not he had entered the bedroom before the permission was granted.

General permission to enter premises implies that someone entering can never be classed as a trespasser whatever the purpose. This idea was, however, rejected by the court in *Jones and Smith*, where James LJ applied the reasoning of Lord Atkin in *Hillen and Pettigrew v ICI (Alkali) Ltd* that the general permission to an invitee:

> ... only extends so long as and so far as the invitee is making what can reasonably be contemplated as an ordinary and reasonable use of the premises (he is not invited to use any part of the premises for purposes which he knows are wrongfully dangerous and constitute an improper use) [p 69].

9.2.4 *Mens rea* in relation to the entry of a building as a trespasser

Though the statute does not mention *mens rea* in relation to these three *actus reus* elements, *mens rea* is required in accordance with the general common law presumption. In s 9(1)(a), the *actus reus* is complete as soon as the entry occurs. Therefore, the *mens rea* must be present at the point of entry. In s 9(1)(b), the *actus reus* is not complete until the defendant goes on to steal or attempt to steal, or inflict or attempt to inflict grievous bodily harm. The general principle is that, in a crime with a continuing *actus reus*, it is sufficient if *mens rea* is present at some time during the continuation, it does not have to be present from the outset (*Fagan v MPC* [1968] All ER 442). Therefore, in s 9(1)(b) burglary, the defendant need not have *mens rea* as to his trespassory entry at the time of that entry. It is sufficient that he knows or is aware of the risk before he completes the *actus reus* by stealing, or inflicting grievous bodily harm and so on. Suppose, for example, that the defendant is very drunk and forces his way into a house which he believes to belong to his friend, who has invited him to look after it in his absence. The next day, the defendant wakes up to discover that he was mistaken and that it is not his friend's house. He then helps himself to breakfast. The defendant entered as a trespasser but was initially unaware of it. However, by the time he came to eat the breakfast (which involves theft of the breakfast ingredients), he knew that he was a trespasser. Consequently, all the elements of s 9(1)(b) burglary were present.

In this context, knowledge or awareness of risk does not require proof that the defendant knew that, in law, his conduct constituted an entry, that the structure was a (part of a) building, or that he was a trespasser. Few people would be aware of the technical definitions. It is sufficient that the defendant knows the facts or is aware of the risk of their existence. For example, if he knows that he is putting his hand through a window opening to reach for some item inside a house, then he knows that he is entering, even though he does not know that, technically, this constitutes an entry. Conversely, if he thinks he is entering a caravan which is not currently in use as a caravan, even though it turns out that it is, then he does not know the facts (and is not aware of the risk of their existence) which make the caravan a building. This is so whether or not he appreciates the significance of the caravan's being an 'inhabited vehicle'. In the case of 'dwellings', it may be that it is necessary to show that the defendant knew, or was aware of the risk, of the existence of facts which made the building a dwelling, for example, that he knew that the building was someone's residence. Otherwise, the offence might have to be regarded as burglary in a non-dwelling.

9.2.5   The ulterior offences

Under s 9(1)(a) of the TA 1968, four offences are specified – theft, rape, grievous bodily harm and criminal damage – and it must be established that the defendant had the necessary intent at the time of entry to the building or part of a building. A conditional intention to steal will be sufficient to prove intent for these purposes. It was held in *Attorney General's References (Nos 1 and 2 of 1979)* [1979] 3 All ER 143 that, providing the indictment does not aver specifically to a specific item to be stolen, all that is required is proof that the accused intended to steal. It may be that the intent is simply to steal 'anything of value' found on the premises but, in law, it does not matter that those premises may not contain anything of value.

Under s 9(1)(b), only two offences are specified: those of theft and inflicting grievous bodily harm, or the attempt to do either. The major point of contention centres around the meaning of the words 'inflicting upon any person therein any grievous bodily harm'. The decision in *Jenkins* [1983] 1 All ER 1000 means that the infliction of grievous bodily harm need not amount to an offence. Section 9(1)(a) requires an 'offence' to be committed but that word is absent from s 9(1)(b). Purchas LJ gave the following example:

> An intruder gains access to the house without breaking in (where there is an open window, for instance). He is on the premises as a trespasser, and his intrusion is observed by someone in the house of whom he may not even be aware, and as a result that person suffers severe shock, with a resulting stroke. In such a case it would be difficult to see how an assault could be alleged; but nevertheless his presence would have been a direct cause of the stroke, which must amount to grievous bodily harm. Should such an event fall outside the provisions of s 9, when causing some damage to the property falls fairly within it [p 1004]?

The problem with this example is that the trespasser does not appear to possess the intent to cause grievous bodily harm and, if the section is read as a whole, then it would appear that, for a conviction to result under s 9(1)(b), the infliction of grievous bodily harm must amount to an offence. The draft Criminal Code (*Criminal Law: A Criminal Code for England and Wales*, Law Com 177, 1989, cl 147) seeks to remedy this apparent deficiency of the TA 1968:

> This clause takes the opportunity to correct a plain and unintended error in s 9 of the Theft Act 1968. Taken literally, burglary (contrary to s 9(1)(b)) could be committed accidentally by someone in a building as a trespasser.

It reads:

> (b) having entered a building or part of a building as a trespasser he commits in the building or part of a building in question an offence of theft or attempted theft; or causing, or attempting to cause, serious personal harm.

9.3   AGGRAVATED BURGLARY (s 10 OF THE THEFT ACT 1968)

This is a serious offence punishable by a maximum of life imprisonment. The 'aggravated' element of the offence relates to the possession of firearms, imitation firearms, offensive weapons or explosives at the time the burglary is committed.

Section 10(1) of the TA 1968 makes it an offence for:

> A person ... [to commit] any burglary and at the time has with him any firearm or imitation firearm, any weapon of offence, or any explosive; and for this purpose –

(a) 'firearm' includes an airgun or air pistol and 'imitation firearm' means anything which has the appearance of being a firearm, whether capable of being discharged or not; and

(b) 'weapon of offence' means any article made or adapted for use for causing injury to or incapacitating a person, or intended by the person having it with him for such use; and

(c) 'explosive' means any article manufactured for the purpose of producing a practical effect by explosion, or intended by the person having it with him for that purpose.

'Weapon of offence' is to be given a wider meaning than 'offensive weapon' in s 1(4) of the Prevention of Crime Act 1953. First, the definition goes beyond that of 'offensive weapon' by including not only any article made or adapted for use for or carried with an intention of causing *injury* to a person but also of *incapacitating* a person. Secondly, a weapon is not an offensive weapon merely by virtue of its use as such. So, if a person is lawfully carrying an article without any intention of using it for causing injury but he uses it spontaneously to do so, he does not thereby commit the offence under the Prevention of Crime Act 1953. Nor does he do so by spontaneously seizing some article and using it. However, the courts have taken the view that use is sufficient for aggravated burglary. So, in *Kelly* [1993] Crim LR 763 the defendant was held to have been properly convicted of aggravated burglary when he used a screwdriver (which he had with him to gain entry) to prod the victim in the stomach.

The article must be with him at the time of committing the burglary. In *Francis* [1982] Crim LR 363, the defendants armed with sticks demanded entry to a house by kicking and banging on the door. They were allowed to enter. It was unclear whether they discarded their sticks just before or just after entering and then going on to steal items from the house. They were charged with aggravated burglary. Their convictions for the offence were quashed because the judge's direction to the jury had not made it clear that either the defendants had to have committed burglary under s 9(1)(a) whilst having the weapons with them or burglary under s 9(1)(b) whilst having the weapons with them. The judge had stated that the prosecution were required to prove only that the defendants were armed when they entered the house as trespassers. However, they might not have committed burglary under s 9(1)(a) (which would inevitably rule out aggravated burglary), because they might have entered with the sticks, but without intending any further offence. Conversely, though they had committed burglary under s 9(1)(b), they might not have committed aggravated burglary because they might already have discarded the sticks before they committed theft in the house. By contrast, the conviction in *O'Leary* (1986) 82 Cr App R 341 was easy to affirm. The defendant had entered a house as a trespasser and had then picked up a kitchen knife before going upstairs, where he used it to threaten the victim into handing over property. Here, he had armed himself with the knife before committing burglary under s 9(1)(b) and so had the knife with him at the time of committing burglary. It is possible that, where two or more are engaged in committing burglary, the one who enters the building will enter without any weapon and will leave accomplices outside who do have weapons. This is not sufficient to convert the burglary into aggravated burglary. A burglar must have the weapon with him in the building. In *Klass* [1998] 1 Cr App R 453, the defendant and two others went to a caravan, wrenched open the door and demanded money from the victim. When he said that he had none, one of the other men hit him with a pole and pursued him as he ran away, hitting him repeatedly. There was evidence that the defendant had entered the caravan and he was convicted of aggravated burglary. His conviction was quashed and one for burglary was substituted. Aggravated burglary could only be committed if the burglar (or one of them, if there were two or more) had the weapon with him in the building.

To comply with the requirement that a person 'has with him' an article included in s 10 it has been held that the accused must know that he has the article, that is, that he was aware that the article had the qualities listed in s 10(a), (b) or (c). It was no defence to the accused in *Stones* [1989] 1 WLR 156 to claim that he carried a knife only as a defensive measure in case of attack. He knew he had the weapon, was aware that it would cause injury or incapacitate a person, and could resort to using it in the course of a burglary should the circumstances demand it.

9.4   TAKING A MOTOR VEHICLE OR OTHER CONVEYANCE WITHOUT AUTHORITY (s 12 OF THE THEFT ACT 1968)

The taking of a conveyance without authority does not require proof of an intention to permanently deprive in order to obtain a conviction. It is this element which differentiates the offence from that under s 1 of the TA 1968 of theft of a conveyance. The basic offence is contained in s 12(1) of the TA 1968:

> Subject to sub-ss (5) and (6) below, a person shall be guilty of an offence if, without having the consent of the owner or other lawful authority, he takes any conveyance for his own or another's use or, knowing that any conveyance has been taken without such authority, drives it or allows himself to be carried in or on it.

The sub-sections referred to, that is, (5) and (6), make it clear that sub-s (1) does not apply to pedal cycles (but these are subject to proceedings for a less important summary offence) and that a person does not commit an offence (s 12(6)):

> ... by anything done in the belief that he has lawful authority to do it or that he would have the owner's consent if the owner knew of his doing it and the circumstances of it.

A conveyance is defined as 'any conveyance constructed or adapted for the carriage of a person or persons whether by land, water or air, except that it does not include a conveyance constructed or adapted for use only under the control of a person not carried in or on it, and "drive" shall be construed accordingly'. *Bogacki* [1973] 2 All ER 864 decided that the words 'use' and 'take' were not synonymous and that, before a person can be convicted of the offence, it must:

> ... be shown that he took the vehicle, that is to say, that there was an unauthorised taking possession or control of the vehicle by him adverse to the rights of the true owner or person otherwise entitled to such possession or control, coupled with some movement, however small ... of that vehicle following such unauthorised taking [*per* Roskill LJ, p 837].

In this case, Bogacki had boarded a bus in a depot and attempted to start the engine. He failed to get it to move before he was apprehended. His conviction was quashed on appeal.

The taking must be for his own or another's use and this means that it must be used as a conveyance. Any taking which involves using the conveyance as a conveyance will inevitably qualify – most obviously, driving away a vehicle or sailing off in a boat – but it is also possible to commit the offence by taking the conveyance for later use as a conveyance. For example, taking away a boat on a trailer with the intention of subsequently sailing in it, as happened in *Pearce* [1973] Crim LR 321.

In *Bow* (1976) 64 Cr App R 4, the defendant together with his brother and father had driven to a country estate. They had with them air rifles and the assumption was that they were on a poaching expedition. The men, when challenged by a gamekeeper, refused to identify themselves and the police were summoned. The gamekeeper blocked their exit from the estate with his Land Rover. Bow got into the vehicle, released the handbrake and allowed it to coast for some 200 yards so that their own car, driven by his brother could proceed from the estate. He was charged and convicted of the s 12 offence. His appeal was dismissed. The court accepted he was using the vehicle as a conveyance. Presumably, if he had released the handbrake and pushed the vehicle in order to increase momentum that would not amount to an offence under s 12. But to sit in it and be transported led to the conclusion that it was being used as a conveyance. It is submitted that the defendant must intend to use the conveyance as a means of transport and not for some other purpose. So, in *Dunn and Derby* [1984] Crim LR 367, following *Pearce*, the court accepted a submission of no case to answer when the prosecution could not prove that the defendants had intended to use the motorbike as opposed to simply admire it. The two men had admitted pushing the motorcycle some 40 yards in order, they claimed, to look at it by a porch light. There can be no doubt that they had unauthorised possession of the cycle but it had not been used as a means of transport nor could it be established that it was their intention to use it as a conveyance. If what they claimed was the truth, then they were clearly not guilty. However, if they took it to the spot in order to discover how to start it, intending to drive away, then they should be guilty. If they were walking away with the cycle, intending to sell it to the first person who would offer them £1,000, then once again the offence would not be established. A charge under s 1 of the TA 1968 would be appropriate in such circumstances as they clearly intended to permanently deprive the owner of the property.

If the conveyance is already lawfully in the defendant's possession, he may still commit the offence if his use of the vehicle does not comply with the terms of the authorisation. In *McGill* (1970) 54 Cr App R 300, the defendant borrowed the vehicle under strict instruction to return it once he had driven a friend to a railway station. He retained the vehicle and continued to use it for his own purposes for a few more days. His claim that as long as the original taking was with consent it did not matter that he did not fulfil the conditions was rejected by the Court of Appeal. The car had been borrowed for a particular purpose and once that purpose had been achieved it was clear that he had taken the car for his own use.

The taking of the conveyance must be without the 'consent of the owner or other lawful authority'. In a case such as *McGill*, where the authorisation was given in very specific terms, there are few problems, but what is the position if the consent is obtained as a result of deception and without the owner being in full possession of all the facts including the use to which the defendant intended to put the conveyance, information which, of course, is likely to influence his judgment? In

Peart [1970] 2 All ER 823, P had induced B to lend him his car, falsely stating that he intended to drive to Alnwick, when in fact he wished to drive to Burnley. It was agreed that the car should be returned by 7.30 pm and P was still in possession of the vehicle at 9 pm. He had known that B would not have consented if he had revealed the true destination. His conviction was quashed on the basis that the misrepresentation did not vitiate consent. The taking had been with consent, the mistake had been towards the purpose for which the car was to be used. In *Whittaker v Campbell* [1983] 3 All ER 582, where the appellant had used a driving licence which he had found to hire a van, the conviction was quashed on the basis that fraud did not vitiate consent. The fraud related only to the acquisition of the vehicle and not to the purpose for which it was to be used. Contrasting the decision in *McGill*, with that in *Peart*, one can easily identify the similarities in each case. In *McGill*, the consent was exceeded once he retained the vehicle after delivering his friend to the station. In *Peart*, one may argue that the consent was exceeded once he was still in possession of the vehicle beyond 7.30 pm, irrespective of whether he was in Alnwick or Burnley or any point between the two towns. Further evidence to sustain an argument to the effect that *Peart* should be regarded as being equated with *McGill* relates to the moment Peart departed from the route to Alnwick in order to take the road to Burnley. At that point, he was exceeding his authority and there was no consent for that particular journey.

9.4.1   *Mens rea*

Section 12(6) of the TA 1968 provides that, if the accused can show he believed that he had lawful authority or would have had the owner's consent if the owner knew of his doing it and the circumstances of it, the prosecution will not be able to establish the *mens rea*.

It was held by the Court of Appeal in *Clotworthy* [1981] Crim LR 501 that a subjective assessment of belief was appropriate. It was irrelevant whether or not Clotworthy actually had authority or would have had consent, it is simply a matter of proving to a jury's satisfaction that he honestly held that belief. In line with the law on mistake, the more unreasonable the belief the more likely it is that the prosecution case will succeed.

It was decided by the Divisional Court, in *DPP v Spriggs* [1993] Crim LR 622, that, once a vehicle which has been unlawfully taken is abandoned, any further taking without authority by someone other than the original offender amounts to a new offence. There would appear to be no reason in principle why the original offender who has returned the vehicle or abandoned it and who subsequently decides to retake it should not also be convicted of the offence. *MacPherson* [1973] RTR 157 is authority for the proposition that s 12 is a basic intent crime and therefore intoxication will be irrelevant in deciding whether or not the accused had the requisite *mens rea* for the offence.

9.5   AGGRAVATED VEHICLE-TAKING

The Aggravated Vehicle-Taking Act (AVTA) 1992 came into force on 1 April 1992 and inserted a new s 12A into the TA 1968. As a result, a person commits the offence of aggravated vehicle-taking in relation to a mechanically propelled vehicle (note that this is a narrower category than 'conveyance') when he commits an offence under s 12(1) of the TA 1968, referred to as the basic offence, and (s 12A):

(1)(b) it is proved that, at any time after the vehicle was unlawfully taken (whether by him or another) and before it was recovered, the vehicle was driven, or injury or damage caused, in one or more of the circumstances set out in paragraphs (a) to (d) of sub-s (2) [they being]:

(2)(a) that the vehicle was driven dangerously on a road or other public place;

(b) that, owing to the driving of the vehicle, an accident occurred by which injury was caused to any person;

(c) that, owing to the driving of the vehicle, an accident occurred by which damage was caused to any property, other than the vehicle;

(d) that damage was caused to the vehicle.

It is a defence under s 12A(3)(a) for the defendant to show that the driving, accident or damage occurred before the person charged committed the basic offence. It is a defence under s 12A(3)(b) for the defendant to show that he was 'neither in nor on nor in the immediate vicinity of the vehicle' when that driving, accident or damage occurred.

This Act is parliament's response to the increasing and justified concern over the number of vehicles being taken and used for 'joyriding' and other dangerous activities. The AVTA 1992 seeks to impose punishment in circumstances where, if other Road Traffic Act offences were charged, it would be difficult to secure the proof of who caused the damage. For example, where four or five people are in the vehicle, their stories may be at variance, one with another, or where the vehicle is stripped of its saleable components and then left abandoned, there could be difficulty in proving that those who took the car actually caused the criminal damage without the provisions of this Act.

It would appear that, as regards s 12A(2)(b), (c) and (d), no fault element needs to be established. In *Marsh* (1996) 160 JP 721, the appellant was charged with aggravated vehicle-taking, the aggravating circumstance being that under sub-s (2)(b), that is, owing to the driving of the vehicle, an accident occurred by which injury was caused to any person. In this case, the car had been unlawfully taken but was not being driven in a negligent or careless manner. A woman had run into the road and was knocked down by the car. She was not seriously injured. Nevertheless, the Court of Appeal upheld the conviction despite the lack of any culpability on the part of the appellant. The only question said the court, given the wording of the Act, was whether the driving of the vehicle was the cause of the accident. On this very strict interpretation, the mere fact that the basic s 12 offence has taken place followed by a non-culpable accident will be enough to convert the offence into one of aggravated vehicle-taking. The child who is knocked down having rushed into the road in pursuit of her ball without paying any attention to the road conditions will unwittingly establish the offence if the car she runs into has been unlawfully taken from its owner. If the car, which is being driven well within the speed limit and with the driver taking all due precaution is owned by the driver, then there would appear to be no offence nor would the facts establish civil liability for negligence. It would be difficult to conclude in either situation that the driving of the vehicle was the 'cause of the accident'. Nevertheless, as a result of this case, the provision is to be subject to a strict interpretation and 'simply by being there' the defendant will in all probability be convicted. The court justified its decision on the basis that heavier sentences should be imposed on those who take vehicles and then cause an accident, irrespective of any fault in the driving. In other words, there would have been no risk to the person crossing the road if the defendant had not acted unlawfully in removing the vehicle.

Whatever the merits of this offence as an attempt to deal with the problems of 'joyriding', it is evident that the provisions of s 12A(2)(b)–(d) are highly unusual in not requiring any fault at all on the part of the defendant beyond his initial fault in taking the vehicle. Nor can the defendant easily determine what he must do to divest himself of responsibility, for the section refers in the vaguest terms imaginable to proof that he was not 'in nor on nor *in the immediate vicinity* of the vehicle' when the incident occurred. For the person who has committed the basic offence by 'allowing himself to be carried in or on' the vehicle, the liability is potentially even harsher, since he will not be able to escape responsibility even by protesting to the driver and urging him to stop. It will be interesting to see whether anyone seeks to challenge the offence of aggravated vehicle-taking in its present form by way of the Human Rights Act 1998.

9.6   BLACKMAIL (s 21 OF THE THEFT ACT 1968)

The *Compact Oxford English Dictionary* gives the following information about the origins of the word blackmail:

> A tribute formerly exacted from farmers and small owners in the border counties of England and Scotland and along the Highland Border, by freebooting chiefs, in return for protection or immunity from plunder.

The word is defined in these terms:

> Any payment extorted by intimidation or pressure, or levied by unprincipled officials, critics, journalists etc upon those whom they have it in their power to help or injure. Now usually a payment extorted by threats or pressure, especially by threatening to reveal a discreditable secret; the action of extorting such a payment.

Section 21(1) of the TA 1968 expresses it this way:

> (1) A person is guilty of blackmail if, with a view to gain for himself or another or with intent to cause loss to another, he makes any unwarranted demand with menaces ...

9.6.1   The demand

The *actus reus* of the offence is to make a demand with menaces. Section 21(2) of the TA 1968 refers to acts or omissions and the demand may take either of these forms in addition to a spoken demand. It is not necessary for the demand to be explicit as seen in *Collister and Warhurst* (1955) 39 Cr App R 100. The defendant heard two police officers discussing the chances of them dropping a charge against him in return for payment. It was their intention that the defendant should overhear this conversation and a direct demand was never actually made to him. Nor does the section imply that the demand must actually be received by the victim. If the victim is actually outside the jurisdiction the offence may be committed provided the demand is issued within the jurisdiction. In *Treacy v DPP* [1971] AC 537, a letter containing the unwarranted demand with menaces was posted in this country, the intended recipient residing in Germany. The House of Lords held that the offence had been committed. Lord Diplock considered that if the letter had been posted in Germany to a victim in this country it would still amount to an offence on the basis that the demand continues as the letter continues its journey and it is not straining the wording of the Act to say the demand is 'made' in this country. The demand must be made 'with a view to gain for himself or another or with intent to cause loss to another'. Section 34(2) of the TA 1968 indicates that '"gain" and "loss" are to be construed as extending only to gain or loss in money or other property'.

In *Bevans* [1988] Crim LR 236, the appellant, who was crippled with osteoarthritis, pointed a handgun at his doctor and demanded a morphine injection to ease his pain, threatening to shoot the doctor if he failed to comply with his demand. He was charged with blackmail and his conviction was upheld by the Court of Appeal. The court had no doubt that the substance injected into him was 'property' and the demand involved gain to Bevans. The reasons why he wanted the drug were deemed irrelevant. Property had been given to him as a result of the demand. The limitation imposed by the TA 1968 means that someone who obtains services as distinct from money or other property will not be guilty of blackmail even if those services have resulted from an unwarranted demand with menaces, unless these services can be viewed as having a monetary value.

9.6.2 Menaces

Lord Wright in *Thorne v Motor Trade Association* [1937] AC 797 offered the following opinion on the meaning of the word menaces:

> I think the word 'menace' is to be liberally construed and not as limited to threats of violence but as including threats of any action detrimental to or unpleasant to the person addressed. It may also include a warning that in certain events such action is intended [p 817].

And Cairns LJ in *Lawrence* [1971] 2 All ER 1253 thought that 'menaces' was an ordinary English word which needed no elaboration from trial judges. This was confirmed by the Court of Appeal in *Garwood* [1987] 1 All ER 1032. The use of the word 'menace' as opposed to 'threat' results in greater flexibility and for a more common sense approach to be adopted if required. An example is *Harry* [1974] Crim LR 32, where the accused, the treasurer of a college rag committee, was charged with blackmail after having sent letters to 115 shopkeepers inviting them to contribute to rag funds and thus avoid 'any rag activity which could in any way cause you inconvenience'. The judge ruled, applying the test in *Clear* [1968] 1 All ER 74, that there were no menaces. *Clear* required that 'the mind of an ordinary person of normal stability and courage might be influenced or made apprehensive so as to accede unwillingly to the demand'; and the shopkeepers who had received letters were as a group unconcerned about the 'threat'. The Court of Appeal in *Garwood* concluded that there were two occasions when a further direction on the meaning of menaces might be required.

The first is: 'Where the threats might have affected the mind of an ordinary person of normal stability but did not affect the person actually addressed.' The court thought that in such circumstances there would be sufficient menace. The second situation is where the threats 'in fact affected the mind of the victim, although they would not have affected the mind of a person of normal stability'. In this case, the menaces are again proved, always assuming that the accused is 'aware of the likely effect of his actions on the victim'.

The *mens rea* for the offence is determined by proof that the defendant's demand must be with a view to gain for himself or another, or with intent to cause loss to another, and s 34(2)(a) makes it clear that it is irrelevant whether or not any such gain or loss is temporary or permanent. The 'gain' and 'loss' elements are expressed disjunctively although in practice a demand upon the victim will usually cause him loss and as a consequence the blackmailer will gain. A further aspect of *mens rea* is contained within the requirement that the demand with menaces must be 'unwarranted'.

9.6.3   Unwarranted

Whether or not the demand is unwarranted should be determined by reference to the defendant's belief:

- in whether he has reasonable grounds for making the demand; and
- that the use of menaces is a proper means of reinforcing the demand.

The approach is subjective. In the first case, the crucial issue is whether the defendant believed there were reasonable grounds for making the demand, not whether reasonable grounds existed. It was put this way by Bingham J in *Harvey* (1981) 72 Cr App R 139:

> It matters not what the reasonable man, or any man other than the defendant, would believe save in so far as that may throw light on what the defendant in fact believed. Thus the factual question of the defendant's belief should be left to the jury ... [p 141].

The second limb requires that the defendant believes that his use of menaces is a 'proper' means of reinforcing the demand. Bingham J thought it to be a word of:

> ... wide meaning, certainly wider than (for example) 'lawful'. The test is not what he regards as justified, but what he believes to be proper. And where the threats were to do acts which any sane man knows to be against the laws of every civilised country no jury would hesitate long before dismissing the contention that the defendant genuinely believed the threats to be a proper means of reinforcing even a legitimate demand [p 142].

Harvey also makes it clear that the matter is not to be resolved by reference to the defendant's own moral beliefs:

> ... no assistance is given to any defendant, even a fanatic or a deranged idealist, who knows or suspects that his threat, or the act threatened, is criminal, but believes it to be justified by his end or peculiar circumstances [p 142].

9.7   HANDLING STOLEN GOODS (s 22 OF THE THEFT ACT 1968)

Handling is a crime which attracts a substantially higher maximum sentence than theft, on the basis that without those who are prepared to deal in stolen property there would be fewer thefts. Deter the handlers, reduce the amount of theft seems to be the message! The maximum sentence for theft is seven years while the maximum for handling is 14 years.

Section 22(1) of the TA 1968 provides:

> A person handles stolen goods if (otherwise than in the course of stealing) knowing or believing them to be stolen goods he dishonestly receives the goods, or dishonestly undertakes or assists in their retention, removal, disposal or realisation by or for the benefit of another person, or if he arranges to do so.

9.7.1   Stolen goods

Section 34(2)(b) of the TA 1968 informs us that 'goods' includes money and every other description of property except land, and includes things severed from the land by stealing.

Section 24(4) of the TA 1968 provides that:

> goods obtained in England or Wales or elsewhere either by blackmail or in the circumstances described in s 15(1) of this Act shall be regarded as stolen; and 'steal', 'theft', and 'thief' shall be construed accordingly.

This definition is extended by s 24A(8) to include money derived from a wrongful credit made to an account. This means that the proceeds of a money transfer obtained by deception under s 15A of the TA 1968, when withdrawn, are stolen goods for the purposes of handling (for a discussion of s 15A, see below, 9.8.6).

Section 24(2) of the TA 1968 provides:

> For the purposes of these provisions references to stolen goods shall include, in addition to the goods originally stolen and parts of them (whether in their original state or not):
>
> (a) any other goods which directly or indirectly represent or have at any time represented the stolen goods in the hands of the thief as being the proceeds of any disposal or realisation of the whole or part of the goods stolen or of goods so representing the stolen goods; and
>
> (b) any other goods which directly or indirectly represent or have at any time represented the stolen goods in the hands of a handler of the stolen goods or any part of them as being the proceeds of any disposal or realisation of the whole or part of the stolen goods handled by him or of goods so representing them.

For example, if the original stolen goods are sold for cash, either by the thief or the initial handler, then the proceeds will also be regarded as 'stolen' and may be the subject of a charge of handling. Similarly, if the stolen goods are exchanged for other property, this will be regarded as stolen for the purposes of s 22 of the TA 1968. Therefore, if A steals a Roman coin from the British Museum and sells it for £15,000 to B, an antiques dealer, who knows of its origins, the sum represents the original stolen goods, being the proceeds of the disposal or realisation.

If A then gave £5,000 to his wife in order for her to go on holiday, assuming she is aware of its origins, then she would be guilty of handling. If A was to bank the £10,000 and subsequently write cheques against that account, anyone receiving a cheque knowing of the origins of the account would also be guilty of handling. The thing in action 'represents' the original stolen goods. The Court of Appeal in *Attorney General's Reference (No 4 of 1979)* [1981] 1 All ER 1193 accepted that:

> ... a balance in a bank account, being a debt, is itself a thing in action which falls within the definition of goods and may therefore be goods which directly or indirectly represent stolen goods for the purposes of s 24(2)(a) [p 1198].

The court added:

> ... where ... a person obtains cheques by deception and pays them into her bank account, the balance in that account may, to the value of the tainted cheque, be goods which 'directly ... represent ... the stolen goods in the hands of the thief as being the proceeds of any disposal or realisation of the ... goods stolen ...' within the meaning of s 24(2)(a) [p 1198].

Reference should also be made to s 24(3) of the TA 1968, a little known provision which played a significant role in helping to shape the common law on attempted crime in the case of *Haughton v Smith* [1973] 3 All ER 1109. In that case, the police had stopped a lorry containing stolen corned beef and had eventually allowed it to proceed to its destination in the hope of apprehending those waiting to receive and distribute the stolen goods. A charge of handling stolen goods was not proceeded with against Smith, who had received the goods, because s 24(3) provides that goods cease to be regarded as possessing the quality of being stolen if they have been 'restored to the person from whom they were stolen or to other lawful possession or custody'. In this case, they were in the possession and custody of the police, although Lords Hailsham and Dilhorne doubted whether this point should have been conceded by the prosecution, as the goods were not in the physical custody of the police once the lorry was allowed to proceed.

Whether or not goods are in the possession of the police or 'other lawful possession or custody' will depend to a large extent on the intention of the person seeking to take possession. In *Attorney General's Reference (No 1 of 1974)* [1974] 2 All ER 899, a constable came across an unattended vehicle in which he saw packages of new clothes. He suspected that they were stolen, so he immobilised the vehicle by removing the rotor arm and kept watch. A few minutes later the accused appeared and was arrested and charged with handling. The question arose as to whether the goods had been restored to lawful possession or custody before the accused appeared and endeavoured to start the car.

The Court of Appeal held that in the circumstances everything would depend upon the constable's intention. It should be left to the jury to decide whether a decision had been reached to take possession of the items so that they could not be removed. If the jury concluded that the officer had not yet made up his mind, then the goods would not have been reduced into lawful possession and the s 24(3) 'defence' would not be applicable, that is, the goods would possess the characteristic of being stolen.

9.7.2   Otherwise than in the course of stealing

Handling can only occur once the 'course of stealing' (that is, the stealing by which the goods become stolen in the first place) is over, and this to a certain degree differentiates the activity of theft from that of handling. A thief can become a handler once the course of stealing is over, for example, by assisting in the retention of the property by or for the benefit of another person. Conversely, the handler of stolen property will also himself steal it by dishonestly appropriating it. This theft is a different theft from that by which the property became stolen in the first place.

The crucial question therefore is when exactly does stealing finish, thus allowing handling to occur? If two accomplices, X and Y, break into A's warehouse, one (X) going inside, while the other (Y) remains outside, placing goods into their van which have been passed to him by his friend, does this make Y a handler or is he to be more appropriately considered a joint principal to theft?

In *Pitham and Hehl* (1977) 65 Cr App R 45, the Court of Appeal favoured the view that an appropriation is an instantaneous act. Therefore, when the defendants handled the furniture offered to them, the theft was already complete and they were guilty of handling stolen goods. If it is correct that theft is an instantaneous act, then there would appear to be no need for parliament to use the words, 'otherwise than in the course of stealing' in s 22 of the TA 1968. *Hale* supports this contention by holding that an appropriation may be a continuing act. This view is also endorsed in *Atakpu and Abrahams* [1993] 4 All ER 215, where Ward J, giving the judgment of the court, said:

> We would prefer to leave it for the common sense of the jury to decide that the appropriation can continue for so long as the thief can sensibly be regarded as in the act of stealing ... so long as he is 'on the job' [p 224].

The conclusion must be that *Pitham and Hehl* is of doubtful authority on this point.

9.7.3   The forms of handling

The section is quite specific on the ways in which handling can occur. There are four different types of activity:

(a) receiving stolen goods;

(b) undertaking the retention, removal, disposal or realisation of the goods by or for the benefit of another person;

(c) assisting in the activities mentioned in (b);

(d) arranging to do any activities in (a), (b) or (c).

9.7.4   Receiving

This mode of handling, together with arranging to receive, does not require that it should be carried out for the benefit of another person. The TA 1968 offers no guidance on the meaning of 'receiving' and therefore recourse should be had to the existing authorities, even though many predate the Act. In the majority of instances, the person receiving the stolen goods will gain immediate possession or control of the property. This will mean that the thief divests himself of possession or control. The thief who retains total control of the stolen goods prevents handling by receiving from occurring. The old case of *Miller* (1854) 6 Cox CC 353 determines that the goods do not need to be in the physical possession of the handler. It will be sufficient to establish receiving if the defendant has authorised a friend or colleague to take possession on his behalf. Possession or control must be distinguished from inspection as the latter activity will not result in handling until such time as a decision has been reached on whether the defendant will retain the goods or take possession or control. If that occurs at a date different to that of the inspection, then handling by receiving will occur once the goods are taken into his possession or control. However, a person may be guilty of arranging to receive once the agreement has been struck.

The crucial point is that whatever the actual circumstances the prosecution will have to show that the defendant had possession or exercised control over the stolen property albeit that it may only be for a limited period.

One may only arrange to receive goods which are actually stolen. The argument advanced on behalf of the prosecution in *Park* [1988] Crim LR 238, to the effect that one could arrange to handle goods which were yet to be stolen, was decisively rejected by the Court of Appeal. Any arrangement with a person who is aware of the nature of the goods is additionally likely to amount to a conspiracy to handle, that is, a statutory conspiracy contrary to s 1 of the Criminal Law Act 1977.

9.7.5   Undertaking or assisting

These two activities must be directly connected to the retention, realisation, removal or disposal of the stolen goods. In *Sanders* (1982) 75 Cr App R 84, it was held that mere use of stolen goods with the knowledge that they were stolen did not amount to assisting in their retention. In that case, the defendant's conviction for handling was quashed where it was proved only that he had *used* a stolen battery charger and heater in his father's garage. Adopting this view, Cantley J in the Court of Appeal in *Kanwar* [1982] 2 All ER 528 stated:

> ... something must be done by the offender, and done intentionally and dishonestly, for the purpose of enabling the goods to be retained. Examples of such conduct are concealing or helping to conceal the goods, or doing something to make them more difficult to find or identify.

He went on to stress that physical acts were not essential and that verbal representations, oral or written, would suffice if designed to conceal the identity of the stolen goods. In this case, the defendant had told lies to the police when they executed a search warrant for stolen goods at her house. She knew that her husband had brought the stolen goods to the house, but tried to persuade the police that she had bought the goods. Though the judge misdirected the jury by suggesting that it was enough that she was willing to have the goods in the house and to use them, her conviction for handling was upheld because of the clear evidence that she had tried to mislead the police.

In *Coleman* [1986] Crim LR 56, the appellant had been convicted of handling by assisting in the disposal of money stolen by his wife. Large sums had been siphoned off from her employers and some £650 had been used to pay solicitors' fees relating to a property purchase which was in their joint names. A direction by the trial judge that 'assisting' was proved by the prosecution establishing that he had benefited from the property purchase was held to be wrong. The *actus reus* is assisting in the disposal and obtaining a benefit was not evidence that he had assisted in the disposal. If he had taken an active part in advising his wife on which property to choose, that would lead to a different conclusion. To do nothing other than receive a benefit from another's disposal of money does not amount to handling.

In *Pitchley* (1972) 57 Cr App R 309, the word 'retention' was held to mean 'keep possession of, not lose, continue to have'. In this case, the appellant was given £150 by his son and requested to take care of it for him. He placed it into his post office savings account. The money had been stolen but the appellant only became aware of this two days later and then left it in his account. He was questioned by police four days later. He was convicted of handling on the basis that permitting the money to remain under his control was sufficient to amount to a retention on behalf of another person.

'Removal' is defined as the 'act of conveying or shifting to another place; the fact of being so transferred' (*Compact Oxford English Dictionary*). Therefore, if D takes stolen goods from A's abode to an agreed hiding place, this would be enough, even though D may be getting absolutely no benefit from the transaction and it may even cost him money if he were to use his own vehicle and petrol. 'Realisation' relates to the selling of stolen property or if the goods are exchanged for something else whether that has value or not. 'Disposal' is defined as 'putting away, getting rid of, settling or definitely dealing with' (*Compact Oxford English Dictionary*).

These activities must be carried out *by or for the benefit of another person*. In *Bloxham* [1982] 1 All ER 582, the appellant had purchased a car which unknown to him had been stolen. He later suspected that the car had been stolen and sold it on to a third party. He was charged with handling by undertaking in its disposal for the benefit of another person. He submitted that he had disposed of the car for his own benefit, not that of the purchaser and therefore the purchaser was not 'another person' within the meaning of the term. The House of Lords held that he had been wrongly convicted. It was the purchase not the sale, that is, disposal which was for the purchaser's benefit, and by no stretch of the imagination could a purchase be described as a disposal or realisation of the goods 'by' the purchaser.

9.7.6   *Mens rea*

There are two elements to the *mens rea* for handling. First, proof of dishonesty, which will be judged by reference to the test in *Ghosh* [1982] 2 All ER 689 and the approach adopted with respect to theft. Secondly, the section requires knowledge or belief that the goods are indeed stolen. Prior to the TA 1968, the law required proof of actual knowledge that the goods were stolen. The Criminal Law Revision Committee recognised that this could present real difficulties for the prosecution:

> Often the prosecution cannot prove [actual knowledge]. In many cases guilty knowledge does not exist, although the circumstances of the transaction are such that the receiver ought to be guilty of an offence. The man who buys goods at a ridiculously low price from an unknown seller whom he meets in a public house may not know that the goods are stolen, and he may take the precaution of asking no questions. Yet it may be clear on the evidence that he believes that the goods were stolen [Cmnd 2977, 1966, para 64].

Lawton LJ in *Harris* (1987) 84 Cr App R 75 thought the words 'knowledge or belief' to be 'words of ordinary usage' and that trial judges should not in the majority of cases attempt any elaboration. In *Grainge* [1974] 1 All ER 928, Eveleigh J held that suspicion alone was insufficient to establish either knowledge or belief. However, if a defendant was suspicious and then intentionally closed his eyes to the consequences, a jury might conclude that he held the requisite belief although it is improbable that jurors would conclude that he knew the goods to be stolen.

The test is a subjective one: did this defendant know or believe the goods to be stolen? In *Atwal v Massey* [1971] 3 All ER 881, magistrates had found that the accused ought to have known from the circumstances that the goods were stolen. The Court of Appeal, in allowing his appeal against conviction, held that the test was: did this defendant realise the theft has occurred, or did he suspect the goods to be stolen and deliberately shut his eyes? *Brook* [1993] Crim LR 455 confirms this subjective approach. A direction by the trial judge that the jury could be assisted in determining the accused's belief by deciding 'if there could be no other reasonable conclusion but that the goods were stolen' was flawed and led to the appeal being allowed. As the court put it, 'what was relevant was B's state of mind at the time of receipt, not an independent view as to whether there could be any other reasonable conclusion than that the goods were stolen'. The court approved of the test laid down in *Hall* (1985) 81 Cr App R 260 that belief was something short of knowledge:

> It might be said to be the state of mind of a person who said to himself, 'I cannot say I know for certain that those goods are stolen', but there can be no other reasonable conclusion in the light of all the circumstances, in the light of all that I have heard and seen [p 264].

The court also considered that a person would be said to know goods to be stolen if told by someone with first-hand knowledge, such as the thief or burglar. However, it is evident that the Court of Appeal has not yet settled on a way of interpreting the 'belief' aspect which can be properly and confidently explained to a jury by the trial judge. In *Forsyth* [1997] 2 Cr App R 299, the trial judge had based his direction on *Hall*, but the conviction was quashed because that direction was considered to be potentially confusing. The problem is that 'suspicion', whether weak or strong, is neither knowledge nor belief but the *Hall* approach comes close to accepting that strong suspicion is enough. In these circumstances, it may be that the judge simply has to leave the jury to determine the issue for themselves because, whatever he says, there is a good chance that it will be considered to be incorrect!

Occasionally, the prosecution may wish to prove knowledge or belief by reference to the common law doctrine of 'recent possession' or by using s 27(3) of the TA 1968 (which deals with the admission of evidence, either that the defendant had engaged in similar activities within the past 12 months or that he had been convicted of theft or handling within the last five years). The 'recent possession' doctrine applies in circumstances where the defendant is found in possession of stolen property and declines to offer any explanation. The judge may direct the jury that they may infer knowledge or belief. The doctrine also applies where the defendant offers an explanation but the jury is satisfied beyond all reasonable doubt that it is false.

9.8   DECEPTION OFFENCES

Deception offences are to be found in the TA 1968 and the TA 1978, as amended. There are various offences of dishonestly obtaining 'something' by deception. Deception offences relate to:

- property;
- money transfers;
- pecuniary advantage;
- services;
- evasion of liability.

Deception is defined in s 15(4) of the TA 1968 and means:

> ... any deception (whether deliberate or reckless) by words or conduct as to fact or as to law, including a deception as to the present intentions of the person using the deception or any other person.

Section 5(1) of the TA 1978 incorporates this definition into the offences under ss 1 and 2 of the 1978 Act. The s 15(4) definition refers to 'any deception (whether deliberate or reckless)'. Therefore, if the defendant has knowingly made a false statement or representation, then he will be liable to conviction, as he will if he believes it may not be true. In *Goldman* [1997] Crim LR 894, the Court of Appeal held that the recklessness required in the offence of obtaining property by deception is subjective since an objective interpretation would be inconsistent with the requirement for dishonesty. The same must be true for all the deception offences.

The deception may result from words or conduct, and be either express or implied. If the defendant expressly represents to P a shopkeeper that he is a famous film actor and produces documentary evidence which purports to support his claim, thereby obtaining goods from the shop as a direct consequence of the representation, he will be guilty of the s 15 of the TA 1968 offence. In *Gilmartin* [1983] 1 All ER 829, the Court of Appeal held that a person who issues a post-dated cheque is impliedly representing that at the due date the cheque would be met. Goff LJ stated the general presumption in these terms:

> For the sake of clarity, we consider that in the generality of cases under ss 15 and 16 of the 1968 Act the courts should proceed on the basis that by the simple giving of a cheque, whether post-dated or not, the drawer impliedly represents that the state of facts existing at the date of delivery of the cheque is such that in the ordinary course the cheque will on presentation for payment on or after the date specified in the cheque, be met [p 835].

The implied representation here is that, when a person issues the cheque, he knows of no reason why there will not be sufficient funds in his account when the cheque is presented for payment. An implied representation is something that 'goes without saying'. The customer in a restaurant or the driver pulling into a petrol station are impliedly representing that they are honest customers who will pay for what they receive at the end of the transaction. In *Hamilton* [1990] Crim LR 806, the defendant had forged the authorising signature on stolen company cheques, paid them into his own account and then withdrawn cash. It was held that, in presenting a withdrawal slip, he was representing that the credit balance in the account was genuine and that he was legally entitled to demand the money:

> By identifying the account, he represented that he was the person to whom the bank was indebted in respect of the account, and by demanding withdrawal of a stated sum he necessarily represented that the bank owed him that amount [p 806].

If, at the time of making the representation, the defendant genuinely believes there are sufficient funds in his account or believes there will be prior to the post-dated cheque being presented, then the question is simply whether or not the jury accepts that the defendant acted dishonestly. If so, the defendant will be convicted, if not, acquitted. However, the person to whom the statement is made will still be deceived, that is, a deception has been practised albeit that the defendant genuinely believed that he had sufficient credit in his account to meet his liabilities. However, if he does not have the 'present intention' which is referred to in s 15(4) of the TA 1968, the representation will be false. Comparison between these cases and *Greenstein* [1976] 1 All ER 1 is instructive because the appellants believed there would be sufficient funds in the account when cheques sent to a company in order to purchase shares were presented for payment. The convictions were upheld, seemingly on the basis that they had given assurances there would be funds in the account when the cheques were first presented but were reckless in the sense that they could not be sure in the circumstances that sufficient funds would be available.

Statements of a price at which a job can be done or a service can be provided ('quotations' or 'estimates') raise an interesting issue. Such statements usually imply only that the maker intends to perform the service for that sum (subject to any reasonably understood margins of error) which, clearly, will involve some profit to himself. If the recipient believes that the estimate does not represent good value, he is free to look elsewhere. If he chooses to engage a workman at a price far higher than he could have negotiated, he usually can blame no one but himself. But, in limited circumstances where a relationship of *trust and confidence* exists between the maker and the recipient, it may further imply that the price is reasonable by reference to what would usually be charged. This relationship of trust and confidence was established and a conviction upheld in *Silverman* (1988) 86 Cr App R 213, where a tradesman fitted central heating for an excessively high price for two old ladies, for whom he had previously done satisfactory, reasonably priced work.

9.8.1   Implied representations

A person who enters a restaurant and consumes a meal or a motorist filling up his car with petrol imply that they have the ability to pay for the service or property. They are 'honest' customers in the eyes of those delivering the goods or services although in practice the waiter in the restaurant or the petrol pump attendant probably gives no thought at all to the honesty or creditworthiness of the person in front of them. It follows though that they would not wish to deal with the potential customer if they were aware that the person was impecunious. In *DPP v Ray* [1973] 3 All ER 131, the defendant had ordered a meal and at that stage intended to pay for it. Having then consumed the meal he decided not to pay. The customer is making an implied representation throughout the meal that he intends to pay. At the moment as he changes his mind, yet nevertheless continues to act as an honest customer, the deception is perpetrated. The consequence is that the law recognises that deception can occur as a result of silence.

In *Rai* [2000] Crim LR 192, the defendant applied to the local council for a grant towards providing a downstairs bathroom for his elderly and infirm mother. Two days after a grant of £9,500 had been approved, his mother died. He did not inform the local council and the work on the bathroom went ahead. He was subsequently charged with obtaining services by deception. The prosecution sought to argue that his silence in failing to notify the council of his mother's death itself constituted conduct within s 15(4) of the 1968 Act. He accepted that he had remained silent, and had not told the council of his mother's death at any time until after the building works were completed, but the contention on his behalf was that he had no legal or contractual duty to inform the council and that mere silence or inactivity could not constitute the required conduct. Thus, there had been no deception. The judge ruled that there was evidence that the defendant had committed a deception, basing his decision principally on an analogy with *DPP v Ray*. The Court of Appeal dismissed the appeal against conviction, holding that:

> ... on a common sense and purposive construction of the word 'conduct', it does, in our judgment, cover positive acquiescence in knowingly letting this work proceed as the appellant did in the present case [p 192].

In essence, this was a simple case in which silence amounted to a deception because the defendant made a statement which was initially true but later became untrue before acted upon (even though approval of the grant preceded the death of his mother) and he did not correct it. It certainly did not require the rather artificial search for a deception in which the court in *DPP v Ray* was forced to engage.

In the case of *Firth* (1990) 91 Cr App R 217, the failure by a consultant obstetrician to comply with his duty to declare whether patients referred by him to an NHS hospital were private patients was held to be a deception, as a result of which he avoided charges which would otherwise have been levied against him. The Court of Appeal thought 'it mattered not whether it was an act of commission or omission'. The *Compact Oxford English Dictionary* would support this, offering two definitions of the word 'deception' viz:

(a) the action of deceiving or cheating;

(b) that which deceives; a piece of trickery; a cheat; sham.

The words or conduct must relate to 'fact or as to law or present intentions', although in practice the overwhelming majority of deceptions will be of fact.

9.8.2   Guarantee and credit cards

Problems have arisen in circumstances where a cheque is supported with a bank guarantee card and where credit cards are used. The effect of using a guarantee card is that the cheque must be honoured by the bank providing certain conditions as to the use of the card are fulfilled. This is the case even if there are insufficient monies in the account or an overdraft facility has not been arranged. The issue was examined by the House of Lords in the case of *Metropolitan Police Commissioner v Charles* [1976] 3 All ER 112. Having opened a current account, Charles's bank manager granted an overdraft facility of £100 and issued him with a cheque card. This allowed Charles to write cheques of up to £30 in the knowledge that they would be honoured by the bank. He proceeded to use 25 cheques, each for £30, backed by the cheque card to fund his gambling activities. He did not have enough money in his account to cover the cheques when presented at his bank and had quite clearly exceeded his overdraft limit. The bank was obliged to pay the total of £750 as the cheques were backed by a guarantee card. Charles was charged under s 16(1) of the TA 1968 with obtaining a pecuniary advantage by deception. It will be evident that there is no misrepresentation regarding the honouring of the cheques. The conditions of use were complied with and the defendant therefore knew the cheques would be honoured. However, the House of Lords held that there was a false representation in the sense that he was holding himself out as having the bank's authority to use the card, when he knew that conditions as to the use of cheques had been imposed. His bank manager had told him that he should not cash more than one cheque a day for £30.

Where the giving of a cheque is supported by a guarantee card the representee need not be concerned about the 'ordinary' representations. The correct use of the card will result in payment being made by the bank.

In *Lambie* [1981] 2 All ER 776, the House of Lords applied similar reasoning in concluding that a person who pays by the use of a credit card represents that she has the authority of the bank (the credit card company) to bind the bank to the transaction. So, the defendant was guilty of obtaining a pecuniary advantage from a store by deception when she obtained goods by using her credit card despite knowing that she had exceeded her credit limit and that she was no longer permitted to use the card. Note that the particular form of pecuniary advantage in question was contained in a provision since repealed by the TA 1978 (and replaced by s 2 of that Act) but that the principle in relation to the deception remains valid. Contrast this case with *Nabina* [2000] Crim LR 481, where the defendant had dishonestly obtained credit cards from various companies by giving false information about his personal details. The cards would not have been issued to him had the companies known the truth, but his authority to use them had not been revoked. He then used the cards to obtain goods from stores and was convicted under s 15 of the 1968 Act of obtaining those goods by deceiving the stores as to his authority to use the cards. Here, the convictions were quashed because there was no evidence from any of the issuers of the cards that any of the transactions had not been, or would not be, honoured, nor that, in the circumstances, they regarded the defendant as acting outside the authority which they had respectively conferred on him. Note that the difficulties about proving a deception might have been circumvented here by charging the defendant with theft. After *Gomez* [1993] 1 All ER 1, the fact that the owners of the goods willingly handed them over to him is irrelevant when the question of appropriation is being examined. The defendant appropriated all the goods when he obtained them. The only stumbling block is dishonesty. If it could be proved that because of his fraud in *acquiring the cards* he was dishonest when he *used the cards to obtain the goods*, then all the elements of theft were present. Would a jury conclude that he was dishonest? The jury in *Nabina* itself obviously did. The argument for theft in the *Lambie* kind of case, where the defendant's dishonesty at the time of the transaction was undeniable, is all the stronger.

9.8.3   Deception must cause the obtaining

It is the deception which must be the cause of the obtaining. Therefore, if the intended victim does not believe the representation which has been made or cannot understand what is being said, then it cannot be proved that the deception is the cause of the obtaining. In *Laverty* [1970] 3 All ER 432, the defendant had practised a deception regarding the age of a motor vehicle but the purchaser gave evidence that he had not relied on the false information as an inducement to buy. The Court of Appeal quashed his conviction for obtaining property, that is, the price of the vehicle, by deception, as this had not resulted in him obtaining the money.

The Court of Appeal in *King* [1987] 1 All ER 547 held that it was a matter of fact to be decided by the jury whether or not the deception was 'an operative cause of the obtaining of property'. In *Miller* (1992) 95 Cr App R 421, the applicant was convicted of three counts of obtaining property by deception. He had operated from time to time as an unlicensed taxi driver working between Heathrow and Gatwick airports.

The amount charged to those foreign visitors enticed into travelling with him was some 10 times in excess of the normal fare. The accused sought leave to appeal against his convictions on the grounds that at the time the money changed hands the victims realised to some extent that he had been lying. In other words, they did not hand over the money because they believed he was entitled to that amount as representing the correct fare, but because they felt under some pressure or obligation to do so. The court refused leave to appeal. This case has been criticised (see Smith [1992] Crim LR 745) on the basis that it was not the deception which caused the passengers to part with their money. They did so because they felt intimidated. In such a situation, the appropriate charge would appear to be theft and not the s 15 offence. As Professor Smith says:

> If D gains entry to P's house by pretending to be the rent collector and then demands 10 times the rent from P, who now knows that D is not the rent collector but pays because she is frightened, this is surely not obtaining by deception [p 745].

In *Coady* [1996] Crim LR 518, the accused was convicted on two counts of obtaining petrol by deception. He had informed the garage attendant that he should charge the amount to the company account of a former employer. His convictions were quashed on the basis that the prosecution had not established that the representations were made before the petrol flowed into his tank. It is clear that the representation must have been made prior to the obtaining and must have operated on the mind of the other. The court was sceptical about the wider representation for which the prosecution also contended, namely, that, when the accused drove onto the forecourt, he represented an intention to pay which he did not in fact possess. It is arguable that, if the defendant intends to pay by a method which he knows he should not use but which he also knows will secure payment (for example, unauthorised use of a credit card), then he intends to pay. Can the same truly be said of a person who uses a method which he knows will not secure payment? Presumably, in *Coady*, it was impossible for the defendant to bind his former employer to the transaction. Why then should he not have been guilty of obtaining the petrol by the deception that he intended to pay unless there was genuine doubt about when he decided that he would not pay himself but, instead, would 'pay' by charging it to his former employer's account? In any case, if he was acting dishonestly at the time when he put the petrol into his tank, he must have stolen it.

It was held in *Rozeik* [1996] 1 WLR 159 that, if a deception is practised on a company, the deception must be upon a person in the company who is responsible for the transaction in question unless he was a party to the fraud.

It is worth examining these cases and asking exactly what amounted to the causal connection between the deception and the obtaining. For example, in the cheque and credit card cases (*Charles* and *Lambie*), it was evident that the casino and the shop were guaranteed to receive the money, providing they complied with certain procedures which were not connected to the question of authorisation to use the cheques or the creditworthiness of the person tendering the credit card. The cases proceed on the basis that if the parties had known the truth regarding lack of authorisation they would not have conducted business with the accused, but, as they did transact with him, there was an operative deception. It was pointed out by Lord Ackner in *Kassim* [1991] 3 All ER 713 that:

> ... the whole object of the card (cheque guarantee) is to relieve the tradesman from concerning himself with the relationship between the customer and his own bank, the

tradesman may well not care whether or not the customer was exceeding authority accorded to him by his own bank. All he will be concerned with is that the conditions on the card are satisfied. Such cases obviously give rise to the difficulty of establishing an operative deception [p 721].

In *Lambie*, the shop assistant gave evidence to the effect that neither she nor her shop were in the least bit concerned about the relationship between the customer and her bank. Providing the conditions were met, then the credit card would be honoured irrespective of whether the bank had authorised their customer to use the card. It is therefore difficult to see how the assistant was deceived into accepting the card *as a result of the false representation*. Nevertheless, that is what the House of Lords concluded.

In *DPP v Ray*, the House of Lords held that the waiter had been deceived by Ray into leaving the room, so enabling him to attempt to leave the restaurant without having first settled the bill. Applying the same reasoning as above, if the waiter had known of Ray's change of mind, then it is extremely unlikely that he would have left him alone, and the House of Lords was prepared to accept that this was evidence of an operative deception. Whether the deception would have worked on the mind of the representee is not always easy to determine. It is worth revisiting the discussion in *Cooke* [1986] 2 All ER 985, where Lord Bridge ponders the likely response of the British Rail passenger faced with the prospect of deciding whether or not to purchase the sandwich prepared by the steward as opposed to the variety provided by the company. The approach appears to be to leave the matter to the jury as to whether the evidence will support the conclusion that the deception, express or implied, is the effective cause of the obtaining. In *Doukas* [1978] 1 All ER 1061, it was necessary to decide whether a waiter could have been guilty of obtaining money by deception from customers of the hotel in which he worked. His plan had been to substitute his own wine for carafe wine ordered by the customers and to keep the payment for himself. The Court of Appeal accepted that the judge had been correct in leaving the issue of deception to the jury because customers must be considered to be honest and not willing to participate in a fraud on the hotel, so that they would have rejected the wine had they known the truth. The court also suggested that a customer would reject the waiter's wine because, whether or not it was inferior to the hotel's carafe wine, he would not know exactly what he was getting or be able easily to take action if something was wrong with it.

9.8.4 Dishonesty

Dishonesty is a common factor in all five offences. *Ghosh* was a s 15 case and its approach to the assessment of dishonesty should apply to all offences. In *Woolven* [1983] Crim LR 623, it was held on a charge of attempting to obtain property by deception that a direction based on *Ghosh* seemed likely to cover all occasions. It must be made clear that, even though the deception may be dishonest, it does not automatically follow that the obtaining will be dishonest, for example, where the defendant believes he has a legal right to claim the property in question. In other words, the issue of dishonesty is a separate issue from the other *mens rea* requirement, whether or not the deception was either deliberate or reckless. Consequently, in *Clarke* [1996] Crim LR 824, the defendant's conviction for obtaining a pecuniary advantage by deception had to be quashed because he had changed his plea to guilty when the judge indicated that he considered that the defendant had committed the offence if he made the representations alleged, they were false and that the victim had engaged him as a result of those representations. This wrongly implied that it was necessarily dishonest to tell lies to obtain employment, no matter what the defendant's explanation for the lies or more general explanation for his conduct. In *Buzalek and Schiffer* [1991] Crim LR 130, the Court of Appeal accepted that, in the majority of cases, a *Ghosh* direction was unnecessary and should only be given where the defendant was saying 'I thought that what I was doing was honest but other people, and the majority of people, might think it not ...' (following *Price* [1990] Crim LR 200).

9.8.5 Obtaining property by deception

Section 15(1) of the TA 1968 provides:

A person who by any deception dishonestly obtains property belonging to another, with the intention of permanently depriving the other of it, shall ... be liable ...

For these purposes, 'property' has the same meaning as in s 4(1) but the limitations specified in s 4(2)–(4) on what property can be stolen do not apply to the deception offence. For instance, land can be obtained by a deception, such as moving boundary markers where theft could only be committed if it was first severed.

It follows that a thing in action can be obtained by deception just as much as any tangible item of property. However, a particular problem has arisen in connection with the thing in action associated with a bank account. It will be recalled from the discussion of theft that the credit balance in a bank account can be appropriated by some act which amounts to an assumption of rights over that credit, such as presenting a forged cheque designed to result in the payment of cash or the transfer of the credit. It is sufficient for theft that the defendant assumes the rights over the credit balance. He does not have to acquire the thing in action itself. By contrast, the offence of obtaining property by deception requires proof that the property which the defendant obtains is the very property which the victim owned or possessed. This is unproblematic with most kinds of property. The defendant purports to buy a car for cash but the notes are forgeries. The property which he obtains, the car, is the very property which the victim both owned and possessed. But, if the defendant induces the victim to transfer a credit from the victim's bank account to the defendant's bank account, even though the debit to the victim's account exactly matches the credit to the defendant's account, does the defendant now own the property which belonged to the victim? It took the courts a very long time to heed the warnings of commentators and to declare that there are two different things in action, so that the defendant does not obtain property *belonging to another*. The pronouncement was finally made by the House of Lords in *Preddy* [1996] 3 All ER 481.

The accused had been charged under s 15(1) of the TA 1968 with obtaining property by deception. The appellants had applied to building societies or other lending institutions for advances which were to be secured by mortgages on properties to be purchased by the applicant. The mortgage documentation or other accompanying documentation contained one or more false statements. The appellants accepted that the applications were supported by false representations, but claimed that at the time the advances were to be repaid there would be sufficient funds because the houses could be resold at a higher price than the purchase price. The basis of the decision by the House of Lords to allow the appeal was that the borrowers, the alleged mortgage fraudsters, had not obtained property belonging to another as required by s 15. In crediting the bank accounts of the appellants, there was no property belonging to the lending institutions. The lending institution's credit balance was a chose in action which as a result of the transfer was extinguished. The asset, that is, the debt owed to the appellant by his bank, was an:

> ... asset created for him and had therefore never belonged to anybody else. Thus, the prosecution could not show that the borrower defendant had obtained property belonging to another ... [Law Commission, *Offences of Dishonesty: Money Transfers*, Law Com 243, 1996, para 1.5].

This decision caused considerable consternation and provoked a number of appeals. Parliament acted very rapidly to plug the gap now at last revealed and passed the Theft (Amendment) Act (T(A)A) 1996. This inserted s 15A into the 1968 Act, creating a new offence of obtaining a money transfer by deception (see below, 9.8.6).

To obtain ownership without possession or control of the property will be sufficient to satisfy s 15. In *Wheeler* (1990) 92 Cr App R 279, it was agreed that Wheeler, a market stall holder, would sell a medal to a customer for £150, possession being retained by Wheeler until the customer returned with the payment. The contract was therefore concluded and the customer became the owner even though he did not take possession. Wheeler, subsequent to the customer's return, discovered the medal was stolen, but when at a later stage the customer returned and enquired about the status of the medal, Wheeler said that he was the owner. He was charged with obtaining property by deception, that is, the £150. His conviction was quashed because, at the time of the deception as to ownership, the medal already belonged to the customer. Wheeler therefore could not give any assurances or representations that he was the owner because the customer knew that he, not Wheeler, was the owner. (Title passed from Wheeler to the customer as, under a rule now abolished, this was a sale in 'market overt', whereby a person without title could give good title to the purchaser.)

Earlier discussion has made it clear that the decision in *Gomez* means that almost all cases of obtaining property by deception will also be cases of theft. However, proving the former will often be more difficult than proving the latter. Consequently, the prosecution may well be able to avoid the complications of the deception offence by opting instead to prosecute for theft. A good example of this proposition is *Talbott* [1995] Crim LR 396. The defendant was charged with six counts of obtaining property by deception. She was in receipt of income support and made an application for housing benefit in which she made certain untrue statements. It was not contended that she was not entitled to the benefit. What was at issue was whether the payment officer at the local authority would have made payment if it had been known that the statements were untrue. The local authority gave evidence to say they would not and had therefore been deceived by the representations made on the application form. She was convicted and her appeal dismissed.

However, it is arguable that theft would have been a more appropriate charge. Since the decision in *Gomez*, it cannot be maintained that an appropriation has not taken place simply because cheques were received with the consent of, in this case, the local authority. The defendant appropriated property belonging to the local authority with the intention to permanently deprive each time she paid a cheque into her bank account. The issue of dishonesty is the same whether or not the charge is under s 15 or s 1 of the TA 1968.

A person obtains property if he obtains 'ownership, possession or control ... and "obtain" means obtaining for another or enabling another to obtain or to retain' (s 15(2)).

The mental element, in addition to dishonesty, is the intention to permanently deprive the other of the property. Section 15(3) states that s 6 shall apply for the purposes of s 15 with, of course, the reference to 'appropriating' changed to that of 'obtaining'.

9.8.6   Obtaining a money transfer

Section 15A of the 1968 Act provides:

(1) A person is guilty of an offence if by any deception he dishonestly obtains a money transfer for himself or another.

(2) A money transfer occurs when –

(a) a debit is made to one account,

(b) a credit is made to another, and

(c) the credit results from the debit or the debit results from the credit.

(3) References to a credit and to a debit are to a credit of an amount of money and to a debit of an amount of money.

(4) It is immaterial (in particular) –

(a) whether the amount credited is the same as the amount debited;

(b) whether the money transfer is effected on presentment of a cheque or by another method;

(c) whether any delay occurs in the process by which the money transfer is effected;

(d) whether any intermediate credits or debits are made in the course of the money transfer;

(e) whether either of the accounts is overdrawn before or after the money transfer is effected.

'Deception' is to carry the same meaning as contained in s 15 of the TA 1968.

Section 15A(1) and (2) makes it an offence to act as did *Preddy* and his colleagues. It is important to note that sub-s (3) limits the offence to 'money'. If D induces P to give him a cheque, D will be guilty of the new offence when he presents the cheque at his bank and it is honoured. It is not strictly true to say that the deception has induced the transfer of the money, but s 15A(4)(b) would imply that this is the case. If, having received a cheque, D decides not to cash it, then he will in all probability not be guilty of an attempt to commit the offence, as he has not done something which is more than merely preparatory. On presenting the cheque, he will be guilty of an attempt and when it is honoured the full offence will be committed.

9.8.7   Obtaining a pecuniary advantage by deception

By s 16(2) of the TA 1968, pecuniary advantage is obtained in cases where a person:

(b) ... is allowed to borrow by way of overdraft, or to take out any policy of insurance or annuity contract, or obtains an improvement of the terms on which he is allowed to do so; or

(c) he is given the opportunity to earn remuneration or greater remuneration in an office or employment, or to win money by betting.

Section 16(1) provides that:

A person who by any deception dishonestly obtains for himself or another any pecuniary advantage shall ... be liable to imprisonment for a term not exceeding five years.

Under s 16(2)(b) it had been held that a pecuniary advantage is gained when an overdraft facility is obtained and there is no need to prove the facility was used (*Watkins* [1976] 1 All ER 578). Emphasis was placed on the words 'allowed to borrow', which of course do not suggest that the defendant actually borrowed money. If the cheque card cases are considered, it will be apparent that, in a case such as *Metropolitan Police Commissioner v Charles*, the writing of cheques to the total of £750 increased his indebtedness to the bank, that is, increased his overdraft beyond the limit which the bank imposed. At first sight, this appears to amount to a s 16(2)(b) offence, but on further consideration it is difficult to accept that the bank has allowed him to borrow by way of overdraft by deception. The bank is in full possession of the relevant information and agrees to honour the cheques, it is hardly deceived into this 'act of will' as it was described in *Bevan* [1987] Crim LR 129. Yet, whatever the weakness in the reasoning, the authorities support the view that 'a bank card transaction is a borrowing by way of overdraft'. Professor Smith in his commentary on *Bevan* makes the point that:

The notion that [an] appellant was allowed to borrow money on overdraft when his bank reimbursed the paying bank is, with respect, a curious one [p 130].

The court in *Bevan* had cited Professor Smith's own commentary to the case of *Waites* [1982] Crim LR 369 where it was said in considering the words 'allowed to borrow by way of overdraft':

The effect of the decision is this: if the bank, on issuing a card, tells the customer, 'You may use this card to back your cheque but in no circumstances may you overdraw your account', and the customer does overdraw, the bank has allowed him to borrow by way of overdraft. Views differ as to the ordinary meaning of the words: but to say that the bank has allowed conduct which it has expressly forbidden seems hard to justify [p 370].

Section 16(2)(c) covers those who as a result of making false claims as to their qualifications or experience gain the opportunity to earn remuneration or greater remuneration in an 'office or employment', or win money by betting. *Callander* [1992] 3 All ER 351 will serve as an illustration of some of the key elements. The appellant had falsely represented that he was a member of the Chartered Institute of Management Accountants and that he also held qualifications from the Institute of Marketing. He was as a result employed by two businessman to prepare accounts and submit tax returns. He collected fees but did not do the work. He was charged under s 16(1) on the basis that he had dishonestly obtained the opportunity to earn remuneration in an office or employment by the deception that he possessed the necessary qualifications to do the job. He appealed against conviction on the grounds that he offered to provide services as an independent contractor and thus he had not gained remuneration 'in an office or employment'. The Court of Appeal held that despite being an independent contractor he had been 'employed' by the businessmen.

The *Shorter Oxford English Dictionary* defines 'employ' as 'to find work or occupation for', and 'employment' as 'that on which [one] is employed; business; occupation; a commission'. The court accepted that the word 'employment' was wide enough to describe this particular relationship.

However, in *McNiff* [1986] Crim LR 57, the appellant was granted the tenancy of a public house after having made false statements regarding previous convictions, his date of birth and his forenames. He was granted a tenancy to take effect once the appropriate justices' licence had been obtained. He appealed, claiming that a tenancy was not an 'office' or 'employment' within s 16(2)(c). The court allowed his appeal against conviction, seeing what he had done as gaining the opportunity to apply for an office in which remuneration would be earned as distinct from the opportunity to earn remuneration.

9.8.8   Obtaining services by deception

Section 1 of the TA 1978 provides:

   (1) A person who by any deception dishonestly obtains services from another shall be guilty of an offence.

   (2) It is an obtaining of services where the other is induced to confer a benefit by doing some act, or causing or permitting some act to be done, on the understanding that the benefit has been or will be paid for.

Though the original intention was that the offence should be based on deceptions as to the intention to pay for the services, it seems that, as actually expressed, any deception will suffice. Thus, a person may be guilty, even though he intends to pay, if he tells lies which enable him to get services that he would not otherwise have got.

'Services' as defined in s 1(2) include any case where:

(a) the victim is *induced to do an act* – this is the most obviously recognisable kind of service in everyday terms. For example, V repairs D's car, cuts D's hair, or cleans D's house;

(b) the victim *causes an act to be done* – for example, D contracts with V for the repair of his car but V does not do the work himself, rather he instructs his employees to do it;

(c) the victim *permits an act to be done* – for example, D goes to the swimming baths and is allowed to swim there on payment of money, or D enters a petrol filling station where he is allowed to put petrol into the petrol tank of his car.

The obtaining of the services must confer a benefit. It is probable that *benefit* is interpreted liberally, so that it does not necessarily have to appear as such to others as long as it appears so to the defendant. At any rate, anything which would be regarded as *consideration* in contract will surely be regarded as a benefit for these purposes.

There must be an *understanding that the benefit has been or will be paid for*. It follows that a service performed without expectation of payment will not fall within the offence even if only performed because of the deception. If D induces V, her neighbour, to look after her baby by telling V that she needs to attend hospital when in reality she wants to go out for a drink, the offence will not be committed because there was never any expectation that the service would be paid for. On the other hand, there seems to be no requirement for a contractually enforceable obligation. Thus, where D obtains services from, say, a prostitute with no intention of paying, he commits the offence even though the prostitute could not enforce payment in civil law because it would be an illegal contract. It is possible that 'paid for' can extend beyond cash or its equivalent to encompass, say, reciprocal services (in a way that would constitute consideration in contract). If V repairs D's plumbing on the understanding that D will repair one of V's windows, that may be sufficient but the point remains open for argument. Finally, the understanding does not necessarily require a belief that that specific service has been or will be paid for. D may mislead V into believing that he is entitled to services of that nature by virtue, for instance, of his membership of a club or similar organisation. Thus, D will be guilty of the offence where he uses his friend's membership card to obtain roadside repairs to his car from a vehicle breakdown and recovery organisation.

In *Halai* [1983] Crim LR 624, the defendant (who had only £28 in the bank) was convicted of obtaining services by deception from C, the agent of a building society, when he induced C to instruct a surveyor to prepare a report on a house by paying with a post-dated cheque for £40 which was dishonoured. However, it was held that he was not guilty of obtaining services from the building society either in being allowed to open a savings account on the basis that he could pay in a valid cheque for £500 or in getting a mortgage advance on the (false) basis that he had been in a particular job for 18 months. In the first case, it was suggested there was no understanding about payment (this would surely depend on whether any charges would be made); in the second case, it was said that a mortgage is not a service but, rather, 'a lending of money for the purchase of property' (the two do not seem to be mutually exclusive!). By contrast, in *Widdowson* (1985) 82 Cr App R 314, the Court of Appeal asserted that the defendant could be guilty of this offence where, by deception, he managed to enter into a hire purchase agreement for the purchase of a car. This, too, seems to be 'a lending of money for the purchase of property' but the Court of Appeal said: 'The finance company confers a benefit by delivering possession of the vehicle to the hirer, or by causing or permitting the garage to do so, on the understanding that the hirer has paid, or will pay, a deposit and subsequent instalments.'

The decision in *Halai*, that obtaining a loan by way of a mortgage does not amount to a service, was persistently criticised and was eventually overturned by s 4 of the T(A)A 1996. This section inserts a new s 1(3) into the TA 1978. The new sub-section reads:

> ... it is an obtaining of services where the other is induced to make a loan, or to cause or permit a loan to be made, on the understanding that any payment (whether by way of interest or otherwise) will be or has been made in respect of the loan.

The decision in *Halai* was in any case revisited in two Court of Appeal cases in 1997. In *Graham* [1997] Crim LR 340, the court purported to overrule *Halai* on the mortgage point but uncertainty persisted because this was not part of the *ratio decidendi*. Subsequently, the court in *Cooke*, as part of the *ratio decidendi* of the decision, held that *Graham* was correct. Consequently, the *Halai* approach is no longer valid law. The main, and temporary, significance of the subsequent overruling of the case by

Cooke is that its effect is completely retrospective. By contrast, s 1(3) of the TA 1978 took effect only from December 1996.

9.8.9   Evasion of liability by deception

Section 2 of the TA 1978 replaced s 16(2)(a) of the TA 1968 which had proved unworkable, having been described by Edmund-Davies LJ in *Royle* [1971] 3 All ER 1359 as a 'judicial nightmare'. The new offence is stated in these terms:

... where a person by any deception –

(a) dishonestly secures the remission of the whole or part of any existing liability to make payments, whether his own liability or another's; or

(b) with intent to make permanent default in whole or in part on any existing liability to make a payment, or with intent to let another do so, dishonestly induces the creditor or any person claiming payment on behalf of the creditor to wait for payment (whether or not the due date for repayment is deferred) or to forgo payment; or

(c) dishonestly obtains any exemption from or abatement of liability to make a payment;

he shall be guilty of an offence.

The liability referred to must be an existing one with the exception of s 2(1)(c) which simply refers to 'liability'. However, the liability which must exist for the purposes of s 2(1)(a) and (b) is one which may have been created only moments before the evasion takes place. For example, if the defendant takes goods to a cashier and then pays by credit card, the liability to pay will have come into existence shortly before the card is used. Section 2(2) makes it clear that liability means 'legally' enforceable liability; gaming debts, for example, would not be covered.

'Remission' means release from a payment or debt (*Compact Oxford English Dictionary*). It follows from this that the creditor must be aware of the debt and respond to the deception by reducing the amount or cancelling it altogether. So, in *Jackson* [1983] Crim LR 617, a stolen credit card had been presented to pay for petrol and other goods. The Court of Appeal upheld the conviction on the basis that the garage would have received full payment from the credit card company and the appellant had therefore secured full remission of the debt.

Inducing a creditor to wait for or forgo payment is an offence, providing it is done with the intent to make permanent default. Assume X owes Y £1,000, the payment of which is due at the end of the month. If X spins Y a hard luck story designed to get Y to agree to the date for payment being put back, and in which period X knows he will leave the jurisdiction, then, assuming X never intends to pay, the offence will be committed. However, if X is simply stalling for time and does intend to pay at a later stage, an offence is not committed.

A creditor may be induced to forgo payment where the deception simply causes him to stop expecting or seeking payment even though he does not give up the right to the payment. A creditor may also forgo payment where the deception results in the creditor believing that he has already been paid, for example, where D tells P, falsely, that he has already settled the debt with P's wife or agent. Section 2(1)(b) also covers deceit on behalf of a third party which results in payment being delayed, providing the third party intends to make permanent default. *Attewell-Hughes* [1991]

4 All ER 810 is authority for the proposition that s 2(1)(b) envisages an offence being committed in two ways: first, where a defendant wishes to make permanent default in respect of his own liability; and, secondly, where a defendant 'intends to make permanent default in whole or in part on behalf of another' (*per* Bingham LJ). It is, of course, important to recognise in the latter case that the third party must be the one who makes permanent default of his own liability. The liability does not attach to the person uttering the deception.

Section 2(1)(c) does not refer specifically to existing liability and the Criminal Law Revision Committee's example (13th Report, *Section 16 of the Theft Act 1968*, Cmnd 6733, 1977, para 15) quite clearly illustrates this. It envisaged a ratepayer (now, council tax payer) making a false statement in order to obtain a rebate to which he is not entitled. He acquires an abatement of his liability to pay. In *Firth*, the consultant obtained an exemption from his liability to pay NHS charges by not declaring that his referrals were private and not NHS patients. In consequence, the hospital was unaware that charges should have been levied.

9.9   MAKING OFF WITHOUT PAYMENT (s 3 OF THE THEFT ACT 1978)

Section 3(1) of the TA 1978 provides:

> ... a person who, knowing that payment on the spot for any goods supplied or service done is required or expected of him, dishonestly makes off without having paid as required or expected and with intent to avoid payment of the amount due shall be guilty of an offence.

This offence 'fills the gap' created by decisions such as *Greenberg* [1972] Crim LR 331. Greenberg, it will be recalled, made off from a self-service petrol station after having filled up his car with petrol. He was not guilty of theft because at the moment of appropriating the petrol it belonged to him and he was not charged with obtaining property by deception because he had entered the garage as an honest customer, only making up his mind not to pay once he had the petrol in his tank. Greenberg would now be found guilty of this offence. He would know that payment on the spot was required; in fact, many garages post notices on the petrol pumps informing customers of this expectation and possible liability under s 3 if they should fail to pay. Goods, that is, petrol, have been supplied and he has no good reason for making off without payment. There is clearly an intent to avoid payment.

As a result of this section the prosecution is spared the task of trying to prove theft or obtaining property by deception.

9.9.1   *Actus reus*

The *actus reus* centres on the supply of goods or service provided. Consider *Troughton v Metropolitan Police* [1987] Crim LR 138 in which a taxi driver was in breach of contract for failing to take the defendant to his destination. Under s 3(3), the offence is not made out if the supply of goods or the doing of the service is contrary to law, or where the service done is such that payment is not legally enforceable. The driver could not therefore lawfully demand the fare and the appellant was 'never in a situation in which he was bound to pay or even tender money for the journey'. As a result, he had not made off without payment.

There is no liability where payment on the spot is not required or expected and this requirement or expectation may well be affected by a prior arrangement made between the parties. So, in *Vincent* [2001] 2 Cr App R 150, though the defendant would normally have been expected to settle his hotel bill when his stay at the hotel ended, his conviction for making off without payment was quashed when it appeared that he had discussed with the proprietors when payment would be made, had told them he was waiting for money due to him, and believed that they had reached an arrangement to defer payment. In the court's view, either the agreement defeated the expectation or there was no 'making off', 'giving that expression its ordinary meaning which may suggest a surreptitious departure'. The court further suggested that, in taxi or restaurant cases, it would be more difficult for a customer to establish an agreement which defeated the expectation. The argument that any such agreement would itself be invalidated by deception was also rejected. In the court's view, the wording and purpose of s 3 did not contemplate what could be a complex investigation of alleged fraud underlying the agreement. If the expectation was defeated by an agreement, it could not be said to exist. The fact that the agreement was obtained dishonestly did not reinstate the expectation.

For the offence to be complete, the defendant must have made off! In *McDavitt* [1981] Crim LR 843, it was said that in restaurant cases the defendant must have left the premises, although a literal interpretation of the section would suggest this is unnecessary. This reasoning is akin to that under s 6 of the TA 1968, which *prima facie* indicates an intention to permanently deprive if the alleged thief has left a supermarket or bookshop without making payment. In this case, if the defendant has left the premises, that is, the spot where payment is required to be made, then it is difficult to refute the allegation that he has made off. Where there is more than one spot for making payment, then it would be for the judge to rule where exactly payment was required and then up to the jury to decide on the evidence if the defendant has made off. The Court of Appeal in *Brooks and Brooks* [1983] Crim LR 188 considered that the words 'dishonestly makes off' were easily understandable by any jury. In *Aziz* [1993] Crim LR 708, the defendant and a friend had requested a taxi in order to take them to a club some 13 miles away. They refused to pay the fare, whereupon the driver started to take them back to their hotel. He then decided to take them to a police station, whereupon the defendant's colleague damaged the vehicle and they both ran away. The defendant was caught and charged with the s 3 offence. It was argued in his defence that he had not made off from the spot where payment was required, that is, the end of the journey. The Court of Appeal held that the TA 1968 did not require that payment should be made at any particular spot. Payment in this case could have been made at any number of places and the obligation to pay certainly continued even when the driver was taking the man back to the hotel. According to the Court of Appeal, one normally 'makes off' when departing from the place where payment would normally be made.

9.9.2 Consent

The issue of consent is relevant to this offence. Can it be said that D has made off if he has consent to go? Or suppose the consent is induced by deception as where D tells P he cannot pay for his meal but he will leave his name and address and will return later in order to pay? If this is false information, then the departure by D in such circumstances will undoubtedly amount to making off. In *Hammond* [1982] Crim LR 611, the trial judge ruled that tendering a worthless cheque and thereby leaving with 'consent' meant the offence was not committed. Section 3(1) expects 'payment on the spot ... [as] required or expected' and certainly the passing of a worthless cheque is neither 'required or expected'. *Hammond* may have been wrongly decided.

The position is not so clear where D gives P his correct name and address and is allowed to leave. Unknown to P, D does not intend to pay. This form of departure does not sit easily with the term 'makes off' which seems to imply without consent. In the final analysis, everything may depend on the honesty or otherwise of the person departing. Dishonesty is required and this will be assessed using the *Ghosh* direction in the light of whether the defendant knew that payment on the spot was expected or required. If he had an honest belief that it was not, then he should be acquitted. The House of Lords in *Allen* [1985] 2 All ER 641 held that the words 'intent to avoid payment' meant the defendant intended to avoid payment *permanently*. Therefore, if the defendant's intention was simply to avoid or put off payment for a few hours or days, then the offence would not be complete. In this case, the defendant had left a hotel where he had been staying without settling his account which amounted to £1,286. His defence was that he genuinely expected to be able to pay the bill, expecting to receive sufficient funds from which to pay the account at some point in the near future. The House of Lords held that an intention to defer or delay payment did not suffice to establish the offence. It could be argued that, if parliament had intended this outcome, then the word 'permanently' could have been included in the offence. The decision encourages those who make off to run bogus defences based upon the argument that they expected to return to pay at a later stage. However, the point has never seriously been challenged since the decision in *Allen* and, therefore, for all practical purposes, the point was concluded by the House of Lords' ruling.

9.10   GOING EQUIPPED TO BURGLE, STEAL OR CHEAT (s 25 OF THE THEFT ACT 1968)

This offence is aimed at deterring those who, being away from their place of abode, carry with them articles which may be used in connection with burglary, theft or cheating.

Section 25(1) of the TA 1968 states:

A person shall be guilty of an offence if, when not at his place of abode, he has with him any article for use in the course of or in connection with any burglary, theft or cheat.

'Theft' includes the offence of taking and driving away a conveyance contrary to s 12 of the TA 1968 and cheating is defined by reference to s 15 of the TA 1968 (see above, 9.8, on deception offences).

9.10.1 Away from his place of abode

In order to be guilty of the offence, a defendant must be away from his place of abode. An unusual argument was advanced by the defendant in *Bundy* [1977] 2 All ER 382 that his car was his place of abode as he was at the relevant time 'sleeping rough'. It was held that, while it was not disputed that a car might constitute a 'place of abode' in the circumstances, it was being used as a vehicle and the point where he was arrested was not the site where the vehicle was being used as a place of abode. Lawton LJ thought there were two elements in the meaning of the phrase 'place of abode':

> ... the element of site and the element of intention. When the appellant took the motor car to a site with the intention of abiding there, then his motor car on that site could be said to be his 'place of abode', but when he took it from that site to move it to another site where he intended to abide, the motor car could not be said to be his 'place of abode' during transit [p 384].

9.10.2 Any article

Being away from his place of abode the defendant must be proved to have with him or her any article for use in the course of or in connection with burglary, theft or cheating. The use of the words 'any article' means that literally anything could come within the scope of the Act. In *Rashid* [1977] 2 All ER 237, bread and tomatoes which were to be used by a British Rail steward in order to make sandwiches to sell to travellers came within the words 'any article'. The Court of Appeal in *Doukas* had no difficulty concluding that the defendant had 'articles' when he was arrested carrying two bottles of cheap wine which he intended to sell to diners at the hotel where he was a wine waiter. In *Corboz* [1984] Crim LR 629, a small quantity of coffee was the subject matter of the s 25 charge in circumstances reminiscent of those in *Rashid*.

In the matter of *McAngus* [1994] Crim LR 602, the defendant sought to sell counterfeit clothing and had taken potential purchasers to a warehouse to show them what appeared to be branded goods. It was held that he had with him items to be used in connection with cheating, even though it was not his intention to sell the items directly to the public. Indeed, it may have been of no concern to him at all what the purchasers told their clients.

9.10.3 Has with him

The fact that the article must be 'with him' does not mean it has necessarily to be on his or her person. Notions of possession and control spring to mind so that if the articles are in the defendant's car, which is parked a short distance away from the scene of the burglary or theft, then that will be sufficient if the defendant drove the car with the articles to the scene of the crime.

The decision in *Minor v DPP* [1988] Crim LR 55 would, however, suggest that, providing the 'theft was to follow the acquisition of possession of the articles', then it would not matter if they had been found only minutes before the theft was attempted. In this case, the articles were two petrol cans and a siphoning tube and the appellant was seen with another man preparing to siphon petrol from the tanks of two cars. There was no evidence before the court to suggest that they had taken the articles with them to the cars, although there was no other reasonable explanation of how the cans and tubing came to be where they were.

It would seem to follow from this decision that, if one is walking late at night down the local high street and notices a piece of wood in the gutter which is then used to smash a shop window in order to steal a range of designer clothes displayed in the window, a s 25 offence is committed. The section is aimed at those who go equipped and this type of conduct ought not to be covered by it. There are many other offences with which this person could be charged, particularly criminal damage and theft. However, if, on taking the piece of wood into his or her possession, he or she places it in his or her car and drives around with it for a few days while seeking to locate appropriate premises to burgle, s 25 would be the appropriate offence.

9.10.4 Cheating

The crime of cheating within s 25 of the TA 1968 has caused difficulty for the courts. (See, for example, the discussion in *Cooke*). In *Doukas*, the court had no doubts that the hypothetical customer should be viewed as reasonably honest and reasonably intelligent and, if aware that wine not supplied by the hotel was being offered to him, would have refused to participate in the transaction. The House of Lords in *Cooke* and the Court of Appeal in *Rashid* declined to adopt the same reasoning in respect of British Rail passengers:

> The immediate reaction of all three members of this court was that in the ordinary case it would be a matter of complete indifference to a railway passenger whether the materials used in making a sandwich were materials belonging to British Rail or materials belonging to the steward employed by British Rail, so long as the sandwich was palatably fresh and sold at a reasonable price. Who knows but that the steward's sandwiches might have been fresher than British Rail's? Why should the passenger concern himself with the source of the materials [*per* Bridge LJ, p 239(d)]?

'Cheat' is defined by s 25(5) of the TA 1968 to mean an offence under s 15 of the Act, obtaining property by deception. It is, therefore, important to consider the response of the hypothetical railway passenger in order to determine whether if offered such items the response would be an outright and possibly indignant refusal or acceptance without question. Under s 15, the deception must be the cause of the obtaining of the property, that is, money and, therefore, if the passenger knowing the truth would have handed over his money then that could not have been obtained as a result of the deception.

It would appear that the issue is one for the jury taking account of all the circumstances. In *Whitehouse and Antoniou* [1989] Crim LR 436, the appellants were charged with going equipped to cheat in that they had with them counterfeit cassette tapes which they were seeking to sell to passers-by outside an underground station. However, they stated they never claimed the tapes were genuine, and if asked told potential customers that they were good quality copies. The Court of Appeal thought that it was open to the jury to conclude from the evidence that 'any purchaser was relying upon a representation that they were genuine', even though they were sold for much less than the retail selling price. Did the defendants intend to deceive? If the tapes were 'genuine', in the sense that they contained all the music on the original recording, then they would not appear to intend to deceive the purchasers as to content. Quality is another matter, but, if they were convinced there was no difference between the copies and the masters, in what way do they intend to deceive the potential customers? Would the buyers have been deceived? Would they have refused to buy if they had known the truth? One suspects not, if the price was acceptable to them.

9.10.5 Knowledge

For a conviction to be obtained, the prosecution must prove knowledge on the part of the defendant that he has with him the relevant articles. If the articles have, unknown to him, been placed into his car or suitcase by a third party then he should be found not guilty, because he is unaware he has the articles and cannot intend to use them to carry out one of the listed offences. *Ellames* [1974] 3 All ER 130 decided that there is no need for the defendant to have a specific crime in mind, any theft or burglary will be sufficient. This reasoning was taken one step further in *Hargreaves* [1985] Crim LR 243 where the Court of Appeal held that if a defendant had the intention to use an article in order to steal, given a suitable opportunity, that would be sufficient to establish the *mens rea*. It would not, however, reach the same conclusion where a defendant had yet to decide whether he should use an article should the opportunity arise. Section 25(3) places the evidential burden on the accused. It states:

> Where a person is charged with an offence under this section, proof that he had with him any article made or adapted for use in committing a burglary, theft or cheat shall be evidence that he had it with him for such use.

This puts pressure on the accused to give evidence as to why he had such equipment in his possession. If he does not do so, the jury may be invited to conclude that he had the necessary intent.

9.11   CRIMINAL DAMAGE

Section 1(1) of the Criminal Damage Act (CDA) 1971 provides:

> A person who without lawful excuse destroys or damages any property belonging to another intending to destroy or damage any such property or being reckless as to whether any such property would be destroyed or damaged shall be guilty of an offence.

If the criminal damage is caused by fire then the offence is charged as arson, with the maximum punishment being life imprisonment as opposed to the 10 year maximum for the s 1(1) of the CDA 1971 offence.

9.11.1   Destroys or damages

One fundamental feature of the offence is that it may be committed without the property being destroyed. The *actus reus* requirement is for property belonging to another to be either damaged or destroyed. It is difficult to give precise meaning to these two words, but case law would indicate that factors to be taken into account include whether the value or usefulness of the property has been affected, whether there has been any physical harm of a permanent or temporary nature, the nature of the property and whether there has been any expenditure incurred to remedy the damage. In *Cox v Riley* [1986] Crim LR 460, the erasure by the defendant of the programmes on a plastic circuit card was held to amount to damage as the card required reprogramming in order to reinstate its utility value. The machine, a computerised saw, depended on the card being programmed in order to be operable and, as a consequence of the defendant's actions, its usefulness was impaired and cost was incurred in order to restore it to its former state. In *Hardman and Others v Chief Constable of Avon and Somerset Constabulary* [1986] Crim LR 330, members of CND had used water soluble 'paint' to paint human silhouettes on a pavement to mark the 40th anniversary of the Hiroshima bombing. Their expectation was that rainwater and pedestrian traffic use would result in the paintings being erased. However, before this occurred, the local authority employed a group of people to clean the pavements. It was held that there had been damage because the local authority had been put to expense and inconvenience. The court approved the approach of Walters J in *Samuels v Stubbs* (1972) 4 SASR 200 to the effect that:

> ... it is difficult to lay down any very general and, at the same time, precise and absolute rule as to what constitutes 'damage'. One must be guided in a great degree by the circumstances of each case, the nature of the article, and the mode in which it is affected or treated. Moreover, the meaning of the word 'damage' must be controlled by its context.

In *Blake v DPP* [1993] Crim LR 586, the use of a marker pen to write a biblical quotation on a concrete pillar amounted to criminal damage (see below, 9.11.5). However, in *A (A Juvenile) v R* [1978] Crim LR 689, a young football supporter who had spat on a policeman's coat was found not to have committed criminal damage because the coat did not require to be dry cleaned nor was the officer put to any expense. In *Morphitis v Salmon* [1990] Crim LR 48, a scaffold bar had been scratched but its value or usefulness was not impaired in any way and therefore Morphitis's conviction for criminal damage was quashed. Placing a clamp on a car which is unlawfully parked will not amount to damage according to the Queen's Bench Divisional Court in *Lloyd* [1992] 1 All ER 982.

In *Whiteley* [1991] Crim LR 436, a computer 'hacker' was convicted of criminal damage having gained unauthorised entry to JANET, the Joint Academic Network, and altered passwords and changed and deleted files. His appeal against conviction was based upon the submission that it was only intangible information on the computer disks and not the disks which had been damaged and, as criminal damage was limited to acts against tangible property (see s 10(1) of the CDA 1971), then he had been wrongly convicted. Lord Lane CJ thought that argument flawed. There was no need to show that any damage was tangible, only that tangible property had been damaged. The authorities (such as those quoted above) indicated that, if the usefulness of the disks had been impaired, then that amounted to damage for these purposes. However, the Computer Misuse Act (CMA) 1990 now deals with the types of occurrences found in *Whiteley* and *Cox v Riley* which should now be charged under s 3 of the CMA 1990 and not the CDA 1971. But similar types of activity not involving computers could still attract liability under the CDA 1971, for example, activity involving audio cassette tapes or compact discs.

It is obviously difficult to establish a general rule as to what amounts to damage and much will depend on all the circumstances of the case. It appears unnecessary for there to be damage in the conventional sense that the property is harmed or its appearance changed. To remove the rotor arm from a car causes damage in the sense that the vehicle cannot be used but this does not necessarily involve damage to any of the car's components or bodywork. If property cannot be used for its normal purpose, then that should be sufficient evidence to prove that the property has been damaged.

9.11.2   Definition of property

Property is defined in s 10(1) of the CDA 1971 and in many ways is similar to the s 4 provision in the TA 1968. It deals only with tangible property, whether real or personal including money and:

(a) including wild creatures which have been tamed or are ordinarily kept in captivity, and any other wild creatures or their carcasses if, but only if, they have been reduced into possession which has not been lost or abandoned or are in the course of being reduced into possession; but

(b) not including mushrooms growing wild on any land or flowers, fruit or foliage of a plant growing wild on any land.

For the purpose of this sub-section, 'mushroom' includes any fungus and 'plant' includes any shrub or tree.

9.11.3   The damaged property must belong to another

The property damaged or destroyed must belong to another, that is:

• any person having the custody or control of it;

• any person having in it any proprietary right or interest (not being an equitable interest arising only from an agreement to transfer or grant an interest); or

• any person having a charge on it;

• where property is subject to a trust, the person to whom it belongs shall be treated as including any person having a right to enforce the trust;

• property of a corporation sole shall be treated as belonging to the corporation notwithstanding a vacancy in the corporation.

Strangely, in s 10(2) of the CDA 1971, the words 'custody or control' are used rather than the more familiar 'possession or control' found in s 5 of the TA 1968. The concept of possession has caused difficulties particularly with regard to drug offences, but it has caused few problems for the courts in interpreting the TA 1968 and, therefore, would have been unlikely to produce problems if it had been included in this Act.

9.11.4   Intention or recklessness as to destroying or damaging

The defendant must be shown to have caused the destruction or damage intentionally or recklessly and without lawful excuse. It has to be proved that the defendant intentionally destroyed or damaged property belonging to another or was reckless as to whether it would be. Thus, he cannot be guilty of the offence if he honestly believes that the property he is damaging or destroying is his own.

This was confirmed by the Court of Appeal in *Smith (David Raymond)* [1974] 1 All ER 632. Providing the belief of law or fact is honestly held, then there will be no offence. In this case, the appellant, a tenant, had damaged floorboards in order to remove wiring attached to his stereo equipment. He had actually laid the floorboards months earlier with permission from the landlord. He believed the floorboards were his and that he was entitled to damage them, when, as a matter of law, they had become part of the landlord's property. His conviction was quashed. Recklessness was defined in *Metropolitan Police Commissioner v Caldwell* [1981] 1 All ER 961, which was, it will be recalled, a criminal damage case (see Chapter 3). If the prosecution charges the defendant with either intentionally or recklessly causing damage, then intoxication can be excluded as a defence in the latter case, as criminal damage would not be viewed as a specific intent crime (see the discussion of *Merrick* [1995] Crim LR 802, above, 3.4.1).

The role of transferred malice in criminal damage cases needs to be explored. If D, intending to damage or destroy P's property, fails but causes damage to X's house, then there is no reason why his *mens rea* against P's property should not be transferred to X's property. However, there may be no need to rely on the doctrine of transferred malice providing it can be shown that D in carrying out his plan was reckless as to whether X's property would be damaged. For example, it may be quite foreseeable that there was a real risk that X's property would suffer in consequence of the attack against P's property. This helps to resolve the problem highlighted in *Pembliton* (1874) LR 2 CCR 119, where the *mens rea* is directed against the person but in the event property is damaged. D throws a brick at P who is standing in front of a shop window. His purpose is to harm P. If the brick misses and shatters the window, then liability for criminal damage is likely to follow on the basis of D's recklessness in respect of the property.

9.11.5 Lawful excuse

What does or does not amount to a lawful excuse has generated much discussion. Section 5 of the CDA 1971 provides that a person will have a lawful excuse:

(2)(a) if at the time of the act or acts alleged to constitute the offence he believed that the person or persons whom he believed to be entitled to consent to the destruction of or damage to the property in question had so consented, or would have so consented to it if he or they had known of the destruction or damage and its circumstances; or

   (b) if he destroyed or damaged or threatened to destroy or damage the property in question or, in the case of a charge of an offence under s 3 above, intended to use or cause or permit the use of something to destroy or damage it, in order to protect property belonging to himself or another or a right or interest in property which was or which he believed to be vested in himself or another, and at the time of the act or acts alleged to constitute the offence he believed –

     (i) that the property, right or interest was in immediate need of protection; and

     (ii) that the means of protection adopted or proposed to be adopted were or would be reasonable having regard to all the circumstances.

(3)   For the purposes of this section it is immaterial whether a belief is justified or not if it is honestly held.

The section is additional to any defences recognised by law as a defence to criminal charges.

Section 5 was considered in *Blake v DPP*. Blake, a vicar, was convicted of criminal damage. He had been one of a group of people protesting against the military action against Iraq in the Gulf War. He had used a marker pen with which to write a biblical quotation on a concrete pillar close to the Houses of Parliament. He claimed to be simply carrying out God's instructions and as he believed God to be the person entitled to consent to the damage of property he had a defence within s 5(2)(a). He also sought to invoke s 5(2)(b) in that he damaged the pillar in order to protect the property of others, that is, those likely to be affected by military action.

The Divisional Court dismissed his appeal against conviction. While accepting that he genuinely and honestly believed he had the consent of God, the court could find no legal authority which would recognise this as a lawful excuse under English law. Was his action taken to protect or was it capable of protecting property? The court made an objective assessment of the facts and found the act incapable of offering any protection to property in the Gulf states. Nor could he rely upon duress of circumstances or necessity as there was no immediate danger to himself or others who were with him at the demonstration.

One difficulty with this reference to objectivity is that s 5(2)(b) is written in subjective terms. *Hunt* (1977) 66 Cr App R 10 and *Ashford and Smith* [1988] Crim LR 682 had concluded that an objective assessment had to be made of whether an act had been done 'in order to protect property'. *Hall* [1989] Crim LR 228, a decision of the Court of Appeal, holds that the first step is to establish the accused's purpose in acting as he did. This depends on the accused's own view and employs a subjective test. Once the accused's purpose has been established, the second step is to determine whether he acted in order to protect property. Here, an *objective* test is used, even though this seems to be plainly contrary to the words of s 5(2)(b). Thus, in *Hall* itself, it was held that cutting the perimeter fence of RAF bases as part of a protest designed to get the bases closed down so that they would no longer be targets for a Soviet nuclear strike and thus, ultimately, to protect surrounding houses, was not within the defence of lawful excuse. The possibility of protecting property by this method was far too remote from the damage. A further ground for the decision in *Hall* was that there was no evidence that the accused believed that the property was in *immediate* need of protection. Compare *Johnson v DPP* [1994] Crim LR 601, where the accused was a squatter who had changed locks on the doors of the house. The court did not accept that he had genuinely believed that he was doing so to protect his property, but held that, even if he had, there was no evidence that he believed that it was in any immediate need of protection rather than that there was some vague, unspecified future danger. Once again, the application of an objective approach is evident.

Section 5(2)(a) was subject to judicial scrutiny in *Denton* [1982] 1 All ER 65. An employee acting on his employer's instructions had set fire to some machinery at a cotton mill, causing damage in the amount of £40,000. The fire had been started in the hope of collecting insurance monies in order to prop up what was a faltering business enterprise. The trial judge had ruled that there could be no lawful consent given by the owner to Denton when the whole venture had been undertaken for fraudulent purposes. This meant that the defendant could not rely on s 5(2)(a). He appealed against conviction. In allowing the appeal the court acknowledged that the owner had a right to destroy his own property and could therefore authorise someone else to do it on his behalf. To this extent, the defendant perhaps had no need to rely on s 5(2)(a) for a defence because s 1 requires the act to be done without lawful excuse and in these circumstances there was a lawful excuse. It is clear the defendant honestly believed he had his employer's consent and therefore the judge's ruling was incorrect.

An honest belief, including one which results from an excessive consumption of alcohol, even though it might not be held if the person was sober, is what is required, as illustrated by *Jaggard v Dickinson* [1980] 3 All ER 716. In this case, the appellant went to a house late one night. She was drunk and mistakenly thought the house to belong to her friend who she believed would not be averse to her breaking in. She appealed against her conviction on the ground of lawful excuse, despite having reached her conclusions while intoxicated. The court allowed her appeal.

9.11.6 Destroying or damaging property with intent to endanger life

Section 1(2) of the CDA 1971 states:

A person who without lawful excuse destroys or damages any property, whether belonging to himself or another:

(a) intending to destroy or damage any property or being reckless as to whether any property would be destroyed or damaged; and

(b) intending by the destruction or damage to endanger the life of another or being reckless as to whether the life of another would be thereby endangered;

shall be guilty of an offence.

The section does not require that life actually be endangered, only that the accused intended to endanger life or was reckless as to whether life would be endangered.

In *Dudley* [1989] Crim LR 57, the defendant threw a firebomb at a house. The fire was extinguished, having caused only minor damage, and the occupants were not harmed or their lives actually endangered. He was convicted of the s 1(2) offence even though there was no evidence that life was endangered, or was likely to be so. The Court of Appeal, in dismissing his appeal, held that the words 'destruction or damage' referred to that which was intended or as to which there was recklessness.

In *Sangha* [1988] 2 All ER 385, the appellant had set fire to furniture which resulted in the premises in question being burnt out. When he started the fire, there was no one else in the flat and apparently there was little or no danger of the fire spreading to nearby properties. He submitted that there was no case to answer under s 1(2)(b) as his act did not create a danger to the life of another and consequently he could not be reckless in that respect. It was held by the Court of Appeal, applying the *Caldwell* test of recklessness, that:

... the question was whether the ordinary prudent bystander would have perceived an obvious risk that property would be damaged and that life would thereby be endangered? ... The time at which his perception is material is the time when the fire is started [*per* Tucker J, p 390].

The appeal was dismissed. Section 1(2)(a) does not provide that the property to be destroyed or damaged must belong to another, so to damage one's own property with the intent to endanger the life of another would be sufficient.

The House of Lords has held that with regard to endangering life a defendant's mental element must go beyond the initial damage to the consequence of that damage.

In *Steer* [1987] 2 All ER 833, the defendant had fired shots with an automatic rifle at the house of a former business partner. Windows were shattered but the occupants of the house were unhurt. There was no evidence to show that the shots had been aimed at the occupants. He was convicted of causing criminal damage, being reckless as to whether life would be endangered. He appealed on the basis that the only danger to his former partner and his wife had come from the firing of the gun, and not from the damage, that is, shattered windows, caused by firing the gun. The House of Lords upheld this submission, finding that the damage to life must result from the damage to or destruction of property. Therefore, a defendant must intend the damage to endanger life or be reckless as to whether it does. Thus, if a defendant severs the brake pipes on his wife's car, intending that her life should be endangered as soon as she drives the vehicle, he would be guilty of the offence if the car failed to respond to the brake pedal being depressed. The ordinary prudent bystander would presumably conclude that this type of activity has really only one purpose and on that basis the offence would be complete even if she did not drive the vehicle. Another and possibly more appropriate charge would be attempted murder. In *Webster and Warwick* [1995] 2 All ER 168, each case had concerned acts which damaged property and caused individuals to be showered with glass and roofing material. In neither case did anyone receive any injuries. The appellants submitted that the actual damage created had to endanger life not the means by which the damage had been caused. It was held, applying *Steer*, that the prosecution had to prove that the danger to life resulted from the destruction of or damage to property and it was not sufficient for the prosecution to prove that the danger to life resulted from the defendant's acts which caused the destruction or damage. The words 'destruction or damage' in s 1(2)(b) referred to the consequence of what the defendant intended to cause or to the risk of which he was reckless, not that which in fact occurred. The key questions were whether there was an obvious risk of life being endangered (reckless), and how the defendant intended that life should be endangered. If the intended consequence and the actual consequence resulting from the damage are the same, there is absolutely no problem. However, if the intended consequence or the consequence to the risk of which he was reckless and the actual consequence are different, then the Court of Appeal is firmly of the view that it is the intended consequence which is important in determining whether there was intention or recklessness as to endangering life.

It should be noted that s 5 of the CDA 1971, which deals with lawful excuse, does not apply to s 1(2) of the CDA 1971. However, s 1(2) of the CDA 1971 does refer to lawful excuse and this is to be read in conjunction with any excuse which is recognised by law, for example, where D causes criminal damage while acting in self-defence to save the life of someone receiving a vicious beating. If D damages property and as a result puts the assailant's life at risk, then he would not commit the offence under s 1(2) of the CDA 1971.

9.11.7 Other sections

Section 2 of the CDA 1971 provides:

> A person who without lawful excuse makes to another a threat, intending that that other would fear it would be carried out –
>
> (a) to destroy or damage any property belonging to that other or a third person; or
>
> (b) to destroy or damage his own property in a way which he knows is likely to endanger the life of that other or a third person;
>
> shall be guilty of an offence.

Section 3 of the CDA 1971 provides:

> A person who has anything in his custody or under his control intending without lawful excuse to use it or cause or permit another to use it –
>
> (a) to destroy or damage any property belonging to some other person; or
>
> (b) to destroy or damage his own or the user's property in a way which he knows is likely to endanger the life of some other person;
>
> shall be guilty of an offence.

9.12 REFORM OF THEFT ACT OFFENCES

The discussion of theft and related offences in this and the previous chapter has revealed that, though the Theft Act 1968 significantly clarified and improved the law, deficiencies have continued to emerge in the 35 years since its enactment. Some of these deficiencies have been met by amendments to the 1968 Act and the creation of new offences (as, for example, in the TA 1978) but there is a case for a more broad ranging review of the property offences. The discussion of conspiracy to defraud in Chapter 5 has explained that the aspiration to complete a general review of fraud in criminal law sometimes impeded the enactment of a comprehensive and coherent set of offences in certain areas. However, there are now signs that the Law Commission has tried to grasp the nettle of extensive review of fraud offences, and this has brought with it proposals about various offences currently found in the TAs 1968 and 1978.

This initiative began with the publication of a consultation paper, *Legislating the Criminal Code: Fraud and Deception* (Law Com 155, 1999) in which the Law Commission considered and rejected arguments for a general fraud offence based either on dishonesty or on deception. Their objections to the first possibility were that far too much would rest on the uncertain characterisation of conduct as criminal by fact finders (most obviously, juries) and that the consequent uncertainty in the definition of the offence might result in a serious conflict with the requirements of the European Convention on Human Rights. Their objections to the second were that such an offence would extend the law too far, and in such an indeterminate way that it could not be justifiable in principle. They considered that any gaps in the current law could be closed by extensions to existing offences. For example, they proposed that:

- the offence of obtaining property by deception (s 15 of the TA 1968) should be amended to provide simply that the owner of the property be deprived of it, irrespective of whether anyone else obtains it (dealing with the *Preddy* problem);

- the requirement in the s 15 offence for an intention permanently to deprive should be abolished;

- the offence of obtaining services by deception (s 1 of the TA 1978) should encompass a service for which no payment was expected, provided that, but for the deception, payment would have been expected;

- in view of the fact that the use of a deception is generally wrongful and that an additional dishonesty requirement in the deception offences unduly favours those who should be found guilty, the dishonesty requirement should be abandoned. This would be subject to a defence that the defendant genuinely believed him or herself to be legally entitled to the property, service, and so on;

- a new offence involving misuse of payment cards (credit, debit and cheque cards and the like) should be created so that the current law of deception need no longer be used. This offence would involve causing a legal liability to pay money to be imposed on another without the other's consent.

However, in the final report, *Fraud* (Law Com 276, 2002), the Law Commission has abandoned this approach in favour of the enactment of a new general fraud offence which could be committed in three ways and which would enable the common law offence of conspiracy to defraud to be abolished, along with all the existing deception offences (though an offence of obtaining services dishonestly would need to be enacted). The three different ways of committing the fraud offence would be by false representation, by wrongfully failing to disclose information, and by abuse of position. The first way would amount to a radical change from the kind of offences currently characterised as deception offences. It would require of the defendant only the dishonest making of the false representation and an intention to make a gain for himself or another or an intention to cause loss to another or to expose another to a risk of loss. It would not depend upon the making of the gain or the causing of the loss, or indeed upon whether the representation was believed. The other two ways are intended to deal with fraudulent conduct which does not involve any kind of deception or misrepresentation, conduct which the Law Commission describes as 'secrecy'. Both would require the intention to make a gain or cause a loss previously described in relation to the first way of committing the offence. The wrongful failure to disclose information form of the offence would be committed where the defendant was under a legal duty to disclose or where the defendant was aware that the other person trusted him to disclose. The third form, abuse of position, would involve relationships of trust where the defendant was expected to safeguard, or not to act against, the financial interests of another person. Such relationships would include, though not be confined to, trustee and beneficiary, professional person and client, employer and employee, agent and principal, and the like. As the Law Commission describes it, the offence of fraud would be an inchoate offence. This would inevitably rule out the existence of an offence of attempt or, at least, require a re-think of what might amount to an attempt to commit the offence. The fraud offence would be supplemented by an offence of obtaining services dishonestly, which would not require any deception and would extend, for example, to obtaining services through the medium of a machine or where the service provider is unaware that the defendant is taking advantage of the service (say, where a spectator watches a sporting event after surreptitiously gaining entry to a stadium without paying). The offence would require some kind of dishonest act and an intention not to pay the full amount expected (or anything at all). Though not entirely free from difficulty, these provisions, if enacted, would certainly enable the law to circumvent many of the problems that have arisen in the interpretation of the current deception offences, whilst at the same time achieving the aim of confining the offence of conspiracy to agreements to engage in conduct which would amount to a criminal offence if carried out by one person.

SUMMARY OF CHAPTER 9

OFFENCES AGAINST PROPERTY: OTHER OFFENCES UNDER THE THEFT ACTS 1968 AND 1978 AND CRIMINAL DAMAGE

ROBBERY

Robbery is an offence under s 8 of the TA 1968. In essence, it requires the use of force in order to commit theft. The force or threat of force must be used 'immediately before or at the time of' the stealing and 'in order to' steal.

BURGLARY

Burglary is a fairly complex offence that requires a defendant to enter a building or part of a building as a trespasser with the intent to commit one or more of a range of ulterior offences. Difficulties centre around the concept of trespass, particularly at what point a person is deemed to have entered a building as a trespasser. The aggravated element relates to the possession of weapons or imitation firearms at the time the burglary is committed.

TAKING A CONVEYANCE/AGGRAVATED VEHICLE-TAKING

Taking a conveyance and aggravated vehicle-taking are the 'old' and 'new' together in one offence. The key element for a basic offence is absence of authority or consent for the taking.

BLACKMAIL

The *actus reus* of the offence of blackmail is to make an unwarranted demand with menaces. Section 21 of the TA 1968 specifies when a demand is warranted.

HANDLING

The offence of handling has the potential for complexity, particularly over the *mens rea* requirements of knowledge or belief. Handling can result from a wide range of conduct. A thief can be a handler in certain circumstances, just as a handler can be a thief.

DECEPTION OFFENCES

These offences are found in the TA 1968 and TA 1978, as amended. The TA 1968 deals with obtaining property by deception and the TA 1978 obtaining services by deception. To obtain a pecuniary advantage by deception is covered by s 16 of the TA 1968; the evasion of liability by s 2 of the TA 1978. Section 15A of the TA 1968 makes it an offence to obtain a money transfer by deception.

GOING EQUIPPED

To be away from one's place of abode having articles which may be used for the theft, burglary or cheating will mean that the offence of going equipped under s 25 of the TA 1968 is likely to have been committed. 'Articles' is given a wide construction by the courts.

CRIMINAL DAMAGE

Destroying or damaging property belonging to another without lawful excuse either intending or being reckless to the consequence amounts to criminal damage.

CHAPTER 10

GENERAL DEFENCES

In Chapter 6, certain special defences only available to a defendant charged with murder such as provocation and diminished responsibility were examined. In this chapter attention is focused on the defences that do not relate to specific crimes, such as homicide, but have a relevance to crimes in general. Most academic commentators and the Law Commission's draft Criminal Code (*Criminal Law: A Criminal Code for England and Wales*, Law Com 177, 1989) emphasise the twin themes of justification and excuse as a basis for the existence of most defences. In the former case, it is argued that although the accused possessed the *mens rea* for the offence and caused the *actus reus* there is a justification that should preclude a conviction. A good illustration is where the accused pleads self-defence. Imagine the case of a defendant, D, who, returning home after an enjoyable evening at the theatre, finds himself confronted with a gang of would-be robbers who have entered his property and are holding his wife hostage. He is threatened that unless he reveals the whereabouts of the key to his safe his wife will have her throat cut. He refuses and one of the men moves menacingly towards his wife and, as he does so, pulls a knife from his pocket. D picks up a poker from the hearth and hits one of the robbers over the head killing him instantly. The second robber seeks to escape but is pursued and caught. It transpires that both men were carrying knives. Is it really accurate to say that D has engaged in wrongful conduct? Would ordinary people regard with abhorrence the action that D took upon himself? Should he not be applauded for seeking to protect his wife from a potentially murderous attack? His conduct should not be regarded as unlawful. He was justified in taking the action he did.

Where excuse is pleaded by way of defence, the accused does not deny causing either the *actus reus* or possessing the requisite *mens rea*. Instead, he seeks to deny culpability and thus be excused from the consequences, because, for example, he was intoxicated at the time of the act. The consequence of raising a successful defence, upon whichever basis, is an acquittal. This may lead one to conclude that it is unnecessary to perpetuate the distinction between excuse and justification if the outcome is the same. However, there are reasons why the distinction should be preserved. One key issue centres on the crime of aiding and abetting. Assume in our example above that D and a friend, A, had returned from the theatre and found D's wife held hostage. D attacks the robbers and calls upon his friend to assist. Providing D's actions were deemed appropriate in the circumstances, the friend would not become liable for aiding and abetting the killing. D's action is lawful and it is not a crime to abet a lawful activity! Let us now assume that A visits D's house and discovers D attacking his wife. D calls on A to assist him. A, who has never liked D's wife, does so and she is severely injured. It transpires that D is, unknown to A, suffering from a mental disorder and successfully pleads the defence of insanity. There is no reason why A should not be convicted of aiding and abetting or, for that matter, convicted in his own right of causing grievous bodily harm, subject to the rules of causation (see Chapter 4 and the decision in *Cogan and Leak* [1975] 2 All ER 1059).

10.1   INSANITY

In a very small number of criminal trials, a defendant might contend that he is not guilty because his mind was not controlling his actions. Where this arises from some external cause that is not the fault of the defendant, the defence of automatism may be available (see further Chapter 2). Where, however, the defendant's inability to appreciate the nature of his actions arises from some inherent defect that manifests itself in violence, and which is likely to recur, his condition is much more likely to be regarded as falling within the scope of insanity, or insane automatism as it is sometimes called. By pleading insanity, the defendant is seeking to deny responsibility for the crime by reference to his mental condition at the time of committing the *actus reus*. It should be appreciated, however, that the issue of insanity can arise at the time of the trial leading to a finding that the defendant is unfit to plead.

10.1.1 Prior to the trial

As indicated above, insanity may be an issue at the outset of the trial, in that the accused may seek to establish that he is unfit to plead to the charge. The relevant law is to be found in s 4 of the Criminal Procedure (Insanity) Act (CP(I)A) 1964, as substituted by s 2 of the Criminal Procedure (Insanity and Unfitness to Plead) Act (CP(IUP)A) 1991. The question of fitness to be tried is determined by the jury. If the trial proceeds, that is, the jury finds that the accused is fit to plead and stand trial, then another jury has to be empanelled. Section 4(2) makes it clear that the judge may defer a decision on the mental disability of the accused 'until any time up to the opening of the case for the defence'. The issue of fitness to be tried must be determined as soon as it arises. The jury is not entitled to make a determination, except on the written or oral evidence of two or more registered medical practitioners and at least one must have been approved by the Secretary of State as having special expertise in the field of mental disorders.

In *Podola* [1960] 1 QB 325, the accused had been indicted for murder. He claimed that he was unfit to plead owing to loss of memory of events prior to and at the time of the alleged homicide. The jury found that his memory loss was not genuine and he was eventually found guilty of murder. The Home Secretary referred the issue of fitness to plead to the Court of Criminal Appeal. It will be apparent that this case was judged not by reference to the CP(I)A 1964 but its predecessor, s 2 of the Criminal Lunatics Act (CLA) 1800. The relevant words were:

> ... if any person indicted for any offence shall be insane, and shall upon arraignment be found so to be by a jury lawfully empanelled for that purpose, so that such person cannot be tried upon such indictment ...

The appellant was perfectly capable of pleading to the charge, was able to follow the evidence and could exercise his right to challenge jurors. The crux of the matter was 'where there was the partial obliteration of memory ... a prisoner could not make a proper defence and could not "comprehend" the details of the evidence ...'. The court held that the appeal should be dismissed. The accused's amnesia in respect of the period when the alleged offence took place would not necessarily prevent the accused receiving a fair trial, providing he was thereafter of normal mental capacity. The CLA 1800 was superseded by the CP(I)A 1964 which does not refer to the word 'insane' but the decision in *Podola* would appear to remain good law.

Even if an accused is found unfit to plead, the court must determine whether or not he has actually committed the *actus reus* of the offence charged. To do otherwise would run the risk of incarcerating a defendant who was wholly innocent of the charge alleged. Any doubt as to the correctness of this approach was dispelled by the House of Lords in *Antoine* [2001] 1 AC 340. The accused had been found unfit to plead in respect of charges of murder and manslaughter and a second jury was empanelled, under the terms of s 4 of the CP(I)A 1964, as amended by the CP(IUP)A 1991, to assess whether or not the accused had committed the acts alleged. The question arose as to whether or not, in the course of this hearing, he could put forward the defence of diminished responsibility. Confirming that this was not possible, the decision of the House of Lords stresses that such a hearing is concerned with whether or not the prohibited act has been caused by the accused. Diminished responsibility, relating as it does to *mens rea*, is therefore not in issue. To the extent that it appeared to suggest a contrary conclusion, the earlier decision of the Court of Appeal in *Egan,* was to be disregarded. As Lord Hutton explained:

> The purpose of section 4A, in my opinion, is to strike a fair balance between the need to protect a defendant who has, in fact, done nothing wrong and is unfit to plead at his trial and the need to protect the public from a defendant who has committed an injurious act which would constitute a crime if done with the requisite *mens rea*. The need to protect the public is particularly important where the act done has been one which caused death or physical injury to another person and there is a risk that the defendant may carry out a similar act in the future. I consider that the section strikes this balance by distinguishing between a person who has not carried out the *actus reus* of the crime charged against him and a person who has carried out an act (or made an omission) which would constitute a crime if done (or made) with the requisite *mens rea* [pp 375–76].

Similarly, in *Grant (Heather)* (2001) *The Times*, 10 December, the Court of Appeal held that the issue of provocation was not relevant to proceedings under s 4 of the CP(I)A 1964, on the basis that it clearly fell on the '*mens rea*' side of the line. The extent to which the s 4 procedure is compatible with the European Convention on Human Rights (ECHR) was raised before the House of Lords in *H* (2003) unreported, 30 January. The basis of the appeal was that, as s 4 involved the determination of a criminal charge and thereby attracted the safeguards supplied by Art 6, the procedure failed to meet the requirements of that article because, if the accused had been found unfit to plead, he could not conduct his defence properly. Rejecting this assertion Lord Bingham explained that the s 4 procedure did not resolve the issue of criminal liability, as it could not result in a conviction. Even if the accused was found to have committed the act, he would be detained and would not face trial unless it was decided at a later date that he was fit to do so. Only then would his criminal liability be determined in a manner that created the risk of a conviction.

Similar issues will arise where the accused, although fit to plead, claims that he was suffering from insanity at the time of the offence. The Court of Appeal's ruling in *Attorney General's Reference (No 3 of 1998)* [1999] 3 All ER 40, expressly affirmed by the House of Lords in *Antoine*, was to the effect that a special verdict could be returned, provided there was evidence that D had committed the *actus reus* of the offence charged (see the Trial of Lunatics Act 1883).

If the accused is found unfit to plead and the jury concludes that the accused did the act or omission which forms the basis of the charge, then the court may deal with the accused by making an admission order to a suitable hospital, a guardianship order under the Mental Health Act (MHA) 1983, a supervision or treatment order or an absolute discharge.

10.1.2 At the trial

An examination of some of the case law cited in Chapter 2 indicates that defendants often go to great lengths to avoid pleading insanity and risking committal to a special hospital. The consequence of the trial judge's ruling in *Quick and Padisson* [1973] QB 90 that insanity not automatism was the appropriate defence, was a change of plea from not guilty to guilty in order to avoid the stigma or consequences of being found not guilty by reason of insanity. The CP(IUP)A 1991, now gives the court a wider range of powers of disposal except where the penalty is fixed by law, as in murder, when a hospital order must be made. However, the insanity plea is not widely used, as RD Mackay pointed out in his article, 'Fact and fiction about the insanity defence' ([1990] Crim LR 247). If the insanity defence proves successful, a special verdict is returned that the accused is not guilty by reason of insanity. The court possesses the following powers:

- to order that the accused be admitted to a hospital;
- to make a guardianship order within the meaning of the MHA 1983;
- to make a supervision and treatment order within the meaning of Sched 2 to the CP(IUP)A 1991;
- to order an absolute discharge.

10.1.3 *M'Naghten* Rules

The legal rules relating to an insanity plea are to be found in the *M'Naghten* Rules of 1843. Daniel M'Naghten was in that year acquitted because of his mental condition at the time he shot Sir Robert Peel's secretary. This generated extensive debate in the legislative chamber of the House of Lords, culminating in the House of Lords inviting judges of the common law courts to answer five questions on the topic of insanity as a defence to a criminal charge. The result was the *M'Naghten* Rules:

> ... the jurors ought to be told in all cases that every man is presumed to be sane, and to possess a sufficient degree of reason to be responsible for his crimes, until the contrary be proved to their satisfaction; and that to establish a defence on the ground of insanity, it must be clearly proved that, at the time of the committing of the act, the party was labouring under a defect of reason, from disease of the mind, as not to know the nature and quality of the act he was doing; or, if he did know it, that he did not know he was doing what was wrong.

The advent of the special defence of diminished responsibility which is available only to those charged with murder (see Chapter 6) and the abolition of the death penalty has resulted in little use being made of the Rules but this does not mean to suggest that they are redundant.

Despite their antiquity, the Rules received endorsement from Lord Diplock in *Sullivan* [1983] 2 All ER 673 when he said: 'The *M'Naghten* Rules have been used as a comprehensive definition for this purpose by the courts for the last 140 years.'

Sullivan is a significant case which highlighted once again the dilemma faced by a defendant whose attempt to establish a defence of automatism fails. Sullivan suffered from epilepsy. There had been a period in his life when he was subject to major seizures but medication had lessened their intensity and at the time of the relevant conduct he was proved to suffer minor seizures, known as *petit mal*, perhaps once or twice each week. On the day in question, he was chatting to elderly neighbours when he was suddenly overcome by a seizure. One of the neighbours, a Mr Payne, aged 80, was kicked by the appellant and required hospital treatment. The prosecution accepted that the defendant had no recollection of the events but the trial judge ruled that his defence was one of insanity and not automatism. As a consequence of that ruling, the defendant pleaded guilty to assault occasioning actual bodily harm. He appealed against the judge's ruling. Lord Diplock, in giving the decision of the House of Lords, considered that the word 'mind' in the Rules 'is used in the ordinary sense of the mental faculties of reason, memory and understanding'. Therefore:

> If the effect of a disease is to impair these faculties so severely as to have either of the consequences referred to in the latter part of the Rules, it matters not whether the aetiology of the impairment is organic, as in epilepsy, or functional, or where the impairment itself is permanent or transient and intermittent, provided that it subsisted at the time of the commission of the act.

Lord Diplock ended his speech by saying: 'Sympathise though I do with the appellant, I see no other course open to your Lordships than to dismiss this appeal.'

10.1.4 The nature and quality of the act

The second part of the *M'Naghten* Rules refers to the nature and quality of the act. In *Codere* (1916) 12 Cr App R 21, it was held that these words refer to the physical, as opposed to the moral or legal quality of the act. The remaining element applies in circumstances where the defendant knows the nature and quality of his act, but does not know that it is wrong to act in such a manner. In *Codere*, it was suggested that the test should be based upon the 'ordinary standard adopted by a reasonable man', in circumstances where he was unaware that his act was contrary to the law of the land. In *Windle* [1952] 2 QB 826, the accused had killed his wife by giving her a fatal dose of aspirin tablets. The report indicates that his wife was some 18 years older than her husband and that she was probably certifiably insane and constantly talked about committing suicide. Her husband endured a miserable existence until he decided to kill her. After the event he apparently told police that 'he supposed he would be hanged for it'. This statement indicated that he knew his actions were contrary to law. He had raised insanity as a defence but Devlin J at Birmingham Assizes had withdrawn it from the jury. The Court of Criminal Appeal held that he was correct to do so. Lord Goddard CJ put it this way:

> The question ... in all cases is one of responsibility. A man may be suffering from a defect of reason, but, if he knows that what he is doing is wrong – and by 'wrong' I mean contrary to law – he is responsible.

He went on to reject the notion that 'wrong' had some qualified meaning such as 'morally' wrong.

The case for a review of the defence, given that it is now over 150 years since the questions posed to the judges were answered, is strong albeit few defendants resort to using it. The Butler Committee on Mentally Abnormal Offenders (*Report of the Committee on Mentally Abnormal Offenders*, Cmnd 6244, 1975) suggested that the word 'insanity' should be dropped in favour of 'mental disorder'. It recommended that a verdict of 'not guilty by reason of mental disorder' should be introduced, first, where the mental disorder prevented the defendant from forming the requisite *mens rea* for the offence, and, secondly, where the defendant was aware of what he was doing but it was medically proved he was suffering from a mental disorder.

10.1.5 Draft Criminal Code

The draft Criminal Code (Law Com 177, 1989) pursues the idea of the defence being based upon proof of a mental disorder. Clause 34 defines 'mental disorder' in these terms:

(a) severe mental illness; or

(b) a state of arrested or incomplete development of mind; or

(c) a state of automatism (not resulting only from intoxication) which is a feature of a disorder whether organic or functional and whether continuing or recurring, that may cause a similar state on another occasion.

Clause 35 establishes the basis of the proposed defence:

(1) A mental disorder verdict shall be returned if the defendant is proved to have committed an offence but it is proved on the balance of probabilities (whether by the prosecution or by the defendant) that he was at the time suffering from severe mental illness or severe mental handicap ...

(2) Sub-section (1) does not apply if the court or jury is satisfied beyond reasonable doubt that the offence was not attributable to the severe mental illness or severe mental handicap.

(3) A court or jury shall not, for the purposes of the verdict under sub-s (1) find that the defendant was suffering from severe mental illness or severe mental handicap unless two medical practitioners approved for the purposes of s 12 of the MHA 1983 as having special experience in the diagnosis or treatment of mental disorder have given evidence that he was so suffering.

Severe mental illness is defined in cl 34 as including one or more of the following:

(a) lasting impairment of intellectual functions shown by failure of memory, orientation, comprehension and learning capacity;

(b) lasting alteration of mood of such degree as to give rise to delusional appraisal of the defendant's situation, his past or his future or that of others, or lack of any approval;

(c) delusional beliefs, persecutory, jealous or grandiose;

(d) abnormal perceptions associated with delusional misinterpretation of events;

(e) thinking so disordered as to prevent reasonable appraisal of the defendant's situation or reasonable communication with others.

'Severe mental handicap' means a state of arrested or incomplete development of mind which includes severe impairment of intelligence and social functioning.

Clause 35 is designed to cover the second limb of the *M'Naghten* Rules, that is, the defendant who knows the nature and quality of his act but does not know that it is wrong. Clause 36 covers the nature and quality 'limb'. This clause makes it clear that it is the fault element which is lacking and if this is proved on the balance of probabilities to be a result of the defendant suffering from mental disorder at the time of the act, then he would be entitled to the 'special' verdict.

10.1.6 The burden of proof in respect of insanity

The burden of proof is upon the accused based upon the balance of probabilities. Normally, it is for the prosecution to prove its case beyond all reasonable doubt but the *M'Naghten* Rules state that in the case of insanity the burden of proof is on the defence. As Viscount Kilmuir LC said in *Bratty v Attorney General for Northern Ireland* [1963] AC 386:

> To establish the defence of insanity within the *M'Naghten* Rules the accused must prove on the preponderance of probabilities first a defect of reason from a disease of the mind, and, secondly, as a consequence of such a defect, ignorance of the nature and quality (or the wrongfulness) of the acts [p 402].

In respect of the first limb of the Rules, it is a moot point whether the common law presumption placing the burden of proof on the defence is strictly necessary. The burden of proof in criminal cases is on the prosecution. If it fails to establish beyond all reasonable doubt that the accused had the requisite *mens rea* for the crime, then the case fails. It would appear unnecessary for the defence to have to disprove a fact which clearly falls, in the overwhelming majority of cases, within the ambit of the prosecution.

Yet, if one considers the second limb of the Rules, there is a clear case for placing the obligation on the defence to establish that the accused did not know the nature and quality of the act or that it was wrong. This is because it is not part of the prosecution's role in criminal law to prove that the accused knew, for example, that the act was wrong. The obligation is to prove that the accused intended or was reckless to the consequence or circumstance as defined by the requirements of the offence. It is also open to either the judge or the prosecution to raise the defence of insanity. On the evidence, the prosecution may wish to allege that the accused is insane as an alternative to the accused raising the defence of automatism. In this situation, both defences may be left to the jury and the burden of proof in respect of insanity falls upon the prosecution.

It is worth adding that insanity will not be a defence unless a guilty intent is an essential element of the offence. If the offence, for example, driving with excess alcohol, is one of strict liability, there being no requirement for *mens rea*, then insanity is not available as a defence. In *DPP v H* (1997) *The Times*, 2 May, the defendant suffered from manic depressive psychosis, an illness which involved symptoms of distorted judgment and impaired sense of time and morals. On the day of the offence, the accused had been behaving irrationally. The court held that he was not entitled to plead insanity as the offence under s 59(1)(a) of the Road Traffic Act (RTA) 1988 was one of strict liability.

10.2 INFANCY

Harper J, in *R (A Child) v Whitty* (1993) 66 A Crim R 462, began his judgment with these words:

> 'No civilised society,' says Professor Colin Howard 'regards children as accountable for their actions to the same extent as adults'. The wisdom of protecting young children against the full rigour of the criminal law is beyond argument. The difficulty lies in determining when and under what circumstances that protection should be removed.

Do children have the capacity to appreciate fully the consequences of their actions and that they may lead to the committing of a criminal offence? Age is a relevant factor in other areas of law, for example, a person under the age of 16 does not have the legal capacity to contract a valid marriage. The answer to the question is obviously yes, depending one suspects, on the age of the child. The levels of understanding of seven and 17-year-olds differ enormously and the criminal law seeks to reflect this in its approach to criminal responsibility and fault for those who have not reached the age of majority.

10.2.1 Terminology and trial

The various statutes which make provision for young people use different terminology, for example, 'juvenile', 'young person', 'child', 'young offender'. In the criminal law context, the great majority of juveniles are now tried in youth courts, formerly known as juvenile courts (s 70 of the Criminal Justice Act (CJA) 1991). These are courts of summary jurisdiction. However, if the juvenile is charged with a serious offence, the magistrates may decline jurisdiction and the case will be remitted to the Crown Court for trial. The limited circumstances where a juvenile may be tried on indictment are to be found in s 24 of the Magistrates' Courts Act 1980 (as amended by the Criminal Justice and Public Order Act 1994):

(1) Where a person under the age of 18 appears or is brought before a magistrates' court on an information charging him with an indictable offence other than homicide, he shall be tried summarily unless:

   (a) he has attained the age of 14 and the offence is such as is mentioned in sub-s (2) of s 53 of the Children and Young Persons Act 1933 (under which young persons convicted on indictment of certain grave crimes may be sentenced to be detained for long periods) and the court considers that if he is found guilty of the offence it ought to be possible to sentence him in pursuance of that sub-section; or

   (b) he is jointly charged with a person who has attained the age of 18 and the court considers it necessary in the interests of justice to commit them both for trial; and accordingly in a case falling within para (a) or (b) of this sub-section the court shall commit the accused for trial if either it is of the opinion that there is sufficient evidence to put him on trial or it has power under s 6(2) above so to commit him without consideration of the evidence.

(2) Where, in a case falling within sub-s (1)(b) above, a magistrates' court commits a person under the age of 18 for trial for an offence with which he is charged jointly with a person who has attained that age, the court may also commit him for trial for any other indictable offence with which he is charged at the same time (whether jointly with the person who has attained that age or not) if the charges for both offences could be joined in the same indictment.

In *T v UK; V v UK* (1999) *The Times*, 17 December, the European Court of Human Rights held that the practice of trying juveniles in adult courts could involve, and had done so in these particular cases, violations of the defendants' rights under the ECHR, notably, the right to a fair trial guaranteed by Art 6. The Court found that the defendants had not been able to communicate effectively with their legal advisers due to the trauma of the proceedings and the fact that some measures taken to help the defendants, such as providing a raised dock area, simply exacerbated their sense of being on show to the public. The response to this ruling has taken the form of a

Practice Direction (*Practice Direction* (Criminal: Consolidated) [2002] 1 WLR 2870, para 39, Trial of Children and Young Persons). This provides that all efforts should be made to ensure that attendance at such trials is strictly limited; that a timetable is agreed to ensure that young defendants can concentrate on events at the trial and follow what is happening; and that the trial should be conducted with the minimum level of formality consistent with a fair procedure. Whether these measure satisfy the requirement of the ECHR in practice remains to be seen.

10.2.2 Under 10 years of age

A child under the age of 10 is irrebuttably presumed incapable of criminal fault, irrespective of whether or not the *actus reus* was committed with the relevant *mens rea*. The child is said to be *doli incapax*. A child under 10 will be absolved of all criminal responsibility for his actions but civil proceedings may be commenced by the local authority under s 31 of the Children Act (CA) 1989 if, as a result of his behaviour, the relevant sections of the CA 1989 are satisfied. It should, however, be noted that simply because a child has committed a 'crime' does not mean the child will automatically be taken into care. The CA 1989 makes the welfare of the child the paramount consideration and it will have to be shown that the child is suffering, or is likely to suffer, significant harm and the harm or likelihood of harm is attributable to lack of parental care or control. Evidence, therefore, that a child is engaged in criminal activities may be used to establish that harm is being suffered through the inattention or indifference of the parents.

The minimum age for attracting criminal responsibility was fixed at seven, eight and 10 during the 20th century and it may be that, in light of well publicised cases involving young children, the age of responsibility should be reviewed again. It must be emphasised that, whatever the consequences, however serious they may be, in law no crime has occurred if the actions were carried out by someone who, at the time of the act, was under 10 years of age.

This is in stark contrast to the law in Scotland. Normal criminal responsibility operates from the age of eight and in the opinion of Lord Jauncey of Tullichettle, 'I do not understand that injustice is considered to have resulted from this situation' (*C v DPP* [1995] 2 All ER 43, p 45j).

In *Walters v Lunt* [1951] 2 All ER 645, a seven-year-old boy passed on to his parents a tricycle which he had 'stolen'. They were aware of this fact. They were found not guilty of handling stolen goods as the goods could not in law be regarded as being stolen. It would, of course, have been different if they had persuaded or forced their son to take the tricycle. In those circumstances, they would have been acting through an innocent agent and would have become principals to the act of theft.

10.2.3 Over 10 years of age

Following the enactment of s 34 of the Crime and Disorder Act 1998, the law in England and Wales imposes criminal liability (in the sense of culpability) on children aged 10 and above in the same way as it imposes liability on adults. This major change was achieved with the following words: 'The rebuttable presumption of criminal law that a child aged 10 or over is incapable of committing an offence is hereby abolished.'

As the provision hints, prior to the enactment of s 34, special rules applied to juvenile defendants between the ages of 10 and 14. In essence, no defendant falling within that age range could be convicted of an offence, unless the prosecution had been able to prove, in addition to establishing whatever *mens rea* was required by the definition of the offence, that the defendant had acted with what was known as 'mischievous discretion'. According to *Corrie* (1919) unreported, this involved proof that the defendant had known that what he was doing was gravely or seriously wrong.

The change to the law brought about by s 34 was heralded by *Criminal Law: Codification of the Criminal Law: A Report to the Law Commission* (Law Com 143, 1985), which stated:

> The law at present is that such a child [over 10 but under 14] can be guilty of an offence but only if, in addition to doing the prohibited act with such fault as is required in the case of an adult, he knows that what he is doing is 'seriously wrong'. It is presumed at his trial that he did not have such knowledge, and the prosecution must rebut this presumption by proof beyond reasonable doubt. The presumption, it has been said, 'reflects an outworn mode of thought' and 'is steeped in absurdity'; and it has long been recognised as operating capriciously. Its abolition was proposed in 1960 by the Ingleby Committee on Children and Young Persons. We believe there is no case for its survival in the Code.

Indeed, the move towards the criminalisation of younger defendants can also be found in earlier provisions, such as s 1 of the CJA 1993, which abolished the longstanding presumption that a boy under 14 years of age could not be convicted of the serious offence of rape. There have been a number of convictions since the law was changed.

The House of Lords was presented with the opportunity to alter the law in the way that the 1998 Act now has, in *C v DPP*. It declined to so on the grounds that such a radical change in the law should result not from judicial decision-making, but rather from parliamentary intervention, should it be accepted that such a change of policy was desirable.

Notwithstanding that the special provision for defendants between the ages of 10 and 14 has now been removed by the 1998 Act, debate continues as to whether it is fair and appropriate to impose criminal liability at such a young age. Laws J, when *C v DPP* was before the Divisional Court, cited the following reasons for abolishing the doctrine of 'mischievous discretion':

- children grow up more quickly now than at any time in our history;
- the presumption was out of step with the general law;
- the phrase 'seriously wrong' was conceptually obscure;
- the rule is illogical because the rule can be rebutted by proof that the child was of normal mental capacity for his age;
- the need for the prosecutor to rebut the presumption may give rise to injustice where the rebuttal involves proving previous convictions.

Blackstone (4 Bl Corn, 22nd edn, pp 23–24) said 'the capacity of doing ill, or contracting guilt, is not so much measured by years and days, as by the strength of the delinquent's understanding and judgment'. It may, therefore, be worthwhile giving consideration to the points raised by B Lloyd-Morris and H Mahendra in their article, 'Doli incapax and mental age' ((1996) 146 NLJ 1622). They argue that in 'normal' children 'mental development keeps pace with physical growth and the passing of years'. They go on:

> However, in children with what are now called learning difficulties or disabilities ... there may be substantial discrepancies between such mental functions as intellectual aptitude or educational attainment and physical attributes as chronological age.

They conclude that mental age is a more reliable index of a child's understanding than chronological age. Whilst the law still regards chronological age as the foundation of the *doli incapax* rule, perhaps it is time for more research to be undertaken on this particular issue.

It is perhaps worth noting that, in *T v UK; V v UK*, the applicants sought, *inter alia*, to argue that the imposition of liability for murder on defendants as young as 10 or 11 years of age amounted to a violation of Art 3 of the ECHR. In rejecting the argument, the Court noted the absence of any common standard amongst other signatory states. In effect, the rule in England and Wales was regarded as being within the margin of appreciation afforded to each signatory state.

It should be borne in mind that s 34 of the 1998 Act places juvenile defendants in the same position as adults, only as regards establishing fault. Special procedures and safeguards apply as regards the trial process and the giving of evidence.

10.3   INTOXICATION

The issue of intoxication may be relevant when seeking to determine the question of whether the accused possessed the *mens rea* necessary for the crime with which he is charged. Evidence of intoxication either from drink or drugs may show quite clearly that the defendant was incapable of forming the *mens rea* or, even though capable, because of intoxication, did not. Intoxication may also lead a person to engage in conduct which he believes, because of his condition, to be lawful, when in fact it is not. The inebriated student staggering home from the Union and coming across a group of fellow revellers may believe they are about to attack him. He therefore 'gets in his retaliation first' and assaults one of them believing he is acting in self-defence. Should he be exonerated?

The Court of Appeal in *Bowden* [1993] Crim LR 380 made it clear that the fundamental question was whether or not the accused possessed the necessary intent for the specific intent crime in question. Hence, in *McKnight* (2000) *The Times*, 5 May, the fact that the accused had consumed large quantities of alcohol so that he could not remember what he had been doing at the time of the alleged offence was held not to be conclusive proof that he had been 'intoxicated' in the sense that the word is used to denote the defence at common law at the time. The degree of intoxication was the key issue. There had to be evidence that he had been prevented from having the required degree of foresight in respect of his actions – in particular, that he had been prevented by the intoxication from foreseeing or knowing what he would have foreseen or known had he been sober.

The fact that an accused has been, without his knowledge, supplied with intoxicants that subsequently lower his inhibitions and lead him to perform criminal acts that he might not have performed had he been sober is again no defence, if there is evidence that the accused nevertheless acted with sufficient *mens rea*. The House of Lords in *Kingston* [1994] 3 All ER 353 expressly rejected any suggestions (accepted by the Court of Appeal) that the law should recognise a new defence of 'disinhibition', even though the accused was able to argue plausibly that it was not his 'fault' that he had had the *mens rea*.

Intoxication may also form part of the *actus reus* of an offence, for example, s 3A of the RTA 1988 of causing death by careless driving when under the influence of drink or drugs.

The Law Commission in its consultation paper, *Intoxication and Criminal Liability* (Law Com 127, 1993), puts it this way:

> The person who commits criminal acts while he is intoxicated, at least when he is voluntarily so intoxicated, does not therefore appeal to excuse; but rather raises the prior question of whether, because of his intoxicated state, he can be proved to have been in the (subjective) state of mind necessary for liability. Issues of intoxication are, thus, intimately bound up with the prosecution's task of proving primary guilt of the defendant: that he did indeed do the act prohibited by the definition of the offence with the relevant state of mind [para 1.12].

The law has developed, albeit on a piecemeal basis, around two concepts, each of which is difficult to define. The first is specific intent and the second basic intent. As a result, all crimes have to be allocated to one or other of these categories for the purposes of the law on intoxication. The outcome is that defendants relying on voluntary intoxication as a defence to a basic intent crime may be convicted 'notwithstanding that the prosecution has not proved any intention or foresight, or indeed any voluntary act' (Criminal Law Revision Committee, 14th Report, *Offences Against the Person*, Cmnd 7844, 1980, para 257).

The Law Commission in its report, *Legislating the Criminal Code: Offences Against the Person and General Defences* (Law Com 218, 1993), recognised the difficulty:

> There is, however, no agreement as to the criteria by which offences are divided between crimes of basic and of specific intent; and that fact alone makes it impossible to formulate this approach as a general legislative test [para 44.3].

10.3.1 Specific and basic intent crimes

In *DPP v Morgan* [1975] 2 All ER 347, Lord Simon gave the following definition of basic intent crimes:

> By 'crimes of basic intent' I mean those crimes whose definition expresses (or more often, implies) a *mens rea* which does not go beyond the *actus reus* ... I take assault as an example of a basic intent crime where the consequence is very closely connected to the act.

Unfortunately, there is no clear principle which applies to specific intent crimes. Lord Simon in *DPP v Morgan* referred to ulterior intent crimes where the *mens rea* goes beyond the *actus reus* and gave s 18 of the Offences Against the Persons Act (OAPA) 1861 as an example, that is, wounding with intent to cause grievous bodily harm. The *actus reus* is wounding and there must be *mens rea* towards this, but the prosecution must also prove a mental element going beyond the wounding. As Lord Simon puts it, 'it must show that the accused foresaw that serious physical injury would probably be a consequence of his act'. Burglary, contrary to s 9 of the Theft

Act 1968, is another example of an ulterior intent crime. The difficulty occurs because, certainly as far as the law on intoxication is concerned, certain crimes which do not accord with this definition have been designated as specific intent crimes. The most obvious example is murder where the *mens rea* does not go beyond the *actus reus*, in which case, on Lord Simon's definition, it should be categorised as a basic intent crime.

In *Metropolitan Police Commissioner v Caldwell* [1981] 1 All ER 961, the House of Lords had to decide whether criminal damage was a crime of basic intent and therefore whether or not drunkenness was available as a defence. The majority decided that if the charge was worded so as to indicate clearly that the prosecution sought to prove the defendant intended to destroy or damage property belonging to another, evidence of self-induced intoxication was admissible in his defence. Conversely, if the charge was so framed as to include reference to reckless behaviour, then it would be classed as a basic intent crime and evidence of self-induced intoxication would be inadmissible.

Thus, the law appears to have developed on the strength of that decision although that is to pay little heed to the dissenting voice of Lord Edmund-Davies in *Caldwell*. He referred to Professor Glanville Williams's conclusion in his *Textbook of Criminal Law* (1978, London: Stevens, p 431) to the effect that all crimes of recklessness, however serious, will be held to be crimes of basic intent. He concludes, 'It is a very long time since we had so harsh a law in this country' (p 972j). Crimes which include recklessness as part of the definition will be considered to be basic intent crimes and those requiring proof of intent, specific intent crimes. It is suggested that one simply examines the case law on intoxication and attempts to categorise on that basis, instead of seeking some overarching principle which differentiates the two types of crime.

The so-called specific intent rule emanates from the decision of the House of Lords in *DPP v Beard* [1920] AC 479. Lord Birkenhead LC, after considering the case law, concluded:

> ... that where a specific intent is an essential element in the offence, evidence of a state of drunkenness rendering the accused incapable of forming such an intent should be taken into consideration in order to determine whether he had in fact formed the intent necessary to constitute the particular crime. If he was so drunk that he was incapable of forming the intent required, he could not be convicted of a crime which was committed only if the intent was proved ...

Lord Birkenhead described the proposition as 'plain beyond question' and, since the unanimous decision of seven Law Lords in *DPP v Majewski* [1976] 2 All ER 142, the specific intent rule is part of our law until parliament decrees otherwise. However, as Lord Elwyn-Jones LC pointed out in *Majewski*, the position 'becomes less plain in the later passage of his speech'. Lord Birkenhead concluded that what he had previously stated was:

> ... only in accordance with the ordinary law applicable to crime, for, speaking generally (and apart from certain special offences), a person cannot be convicted of a crime unless there was *mens rea*. Drunkenness, rendering a person incapable of the intent, would be an answer, as it is for example in a charge of attempted suicide.

The current position, as a result of *Majewski*, is not in doubt, but the above passage indicates the shaky foundation upon which the specific intent rule is based. *Caldwell* determined that, subject to how the charge is laid, criminal damage may be viewed as a basic or specific intent crime and *Majewski* confirms that assault is a basic intent crime for the purposes of the defence of intoxication.

In *Majewski*, the defendant had attacked the landlord of a public house and after the arrival of a number of police officers at the property had also assaulted some of them. Later at the police station he had struck two other officers. The following morning he attacked a police inspector who had gone into his cell. He was charged with a total of seven counts of assault. At his trial he testified that over the 48 hours culminating in the attack on the publican, he had consumed a considerable quantity of drugs and alcohol and that at the time of the attacks he had no idea what he was doing. He claimed to have no recollection of the incidents that had occurred. The trial judge directed the jury to ignore the fact that the defendant had been intoxicated at the time of the disturbances. He was convicted on all seven counts.

Clearly, the defendant had been incapable of forming the *mens rea* for assault which is a crime requiring either intention or recklessness in respect of the *actus reus*. On the basis of the definition offered by Lord Simon in *Morgan* (above), assault is to be regarded as a basic intent crime. He appealed on the basis that, in informing the jury to disregard his intoxicated state, the trial judge had contravened s 8 of the CJA 1967. It will be recalled that s 8 states that a court or jury in determining whether a person has committed an offence:

(a) shall not be bound in law to infer that he intended or foresaw a result of his actions by reason only of its being a natural and probable consequence of those actions; but

(b) shall decide whether he did intend or foresee that result by reference to all the evidence, drawing such inferences from the evidence as appears proper in the circumstances.

The appellant's contention was that his state of intoxication was part of 'all the evidence' and should, therefore, have been taken into account. However, as the law stood prior to *Majewski*, assault not being a specific intention crime, it had to be regarded as one of basic intent. Recklessness is part of the *mens rea* of the crime. Thus, to become intoxicated to such a degree should be regarded as evidence of recklessness which should help to convict, rather than exonerate him from the consequences of his actions.

The House of Lords held that s 8 was irrelevant as it dealt only with matters of evidence and the specific and basic intent rules were matters of the substantive law. All seven Law Lords agreed that the specific intent rule should be confirmed and that in crimes of basic intent of which assault was one, the intoxication 'supplies the evidence of *mens rea*' (*per* Lord Elwyn Jones LC). He posed the vital question in these terms:

> If a man consciously and deliberately takes alcohol and drugs not on medical prescription, but in order to escape from reality, to go 'on a trip', to become hallucinated, whatever the description may be, and thereby disables himself from taking the care he might otherwise take and as a result by his subsequent actions causes injury to another – does our criminal law enable him to say that because he did not know what he was doing he lacked both intention and recklessness and accordingly is entitled to an acquittal?

Lord Elwyn-Jones having reviewed the major authorities (*Beard; Attorney General for Northern Ireland v Gallagher* [1963] AC 349; *Bratty*) concluded that intoxication was relevant only to specific intent crimes. He cited Lord Denning's statement in *Bratty*:

If the drunken man is so drunk that he does not know what he is doing, he has a defence to any charge, such as murder or wounding with intent, in which a specific intent is essential, but he is still liable to be convicted of manslaughter or unlawful wounding for which no specific intent is necessary ...

... I do not for my part regard that general principle as either unethical or contrary to the principles of natural justice. If a man of his own volition takes a substance which causes him to cast off the restraints of reason and conscience, no wrong is done to him by holding him answerable criminally for any injury he may do while in that condition. His course of conduct in reducing himself by drugs and drink to that condition in my view supplies the evidence of *mens rea*, of guilty mind certainly sufficient for crimes of basic intent. It is a reckless course of conduct and recklessness is enough to constitute the necessary *mens rea* in assault cases: see *Venna* (1975) *per* James LJ. The drunkenness is itself an intrinsic, an integral part of the crime, the other part being the evidence of the unlawful use of force against the victim. Together they add up to criminal recklessness.

Support for this view was found in the US Model Penal Code:

When recklessness establishes an element of the offence, if the actor, due to self-induced intoxication, is unaware of a risk of which he would have been aware had he been sober, such unawareness is immaterial.

The outcome as Lord Salmon said in *Majewski* may 'not comply with strict logic' (because after all these are *mens rea* crimes) but 'this rule accords with justice, ethics and common sense, and I would leave it alone' (p 159c).

Further support for this distinction in approach to specific and basic intent crimes comes from Lord Mustill in *Kingston*:

As to proof of intent, it appears that at least in some instances self-induced intoxication can be taken into account as part of the evidence from which the jury draws its conclusions; but that in others it cannot. I express the matter in this guarded way because it has not yet been decisively established whether for this purpose there is a line to be drawn between offences of 'specific' intent. That in at least some cases a defendant cannot say that he was so drunk that he could not form the required intent is however clear enough. Why is this so? The answer must, I believe, be the same as that given in other common law jurisdictions; namely that such evidence is excluded as a matter of policy [p 364c].

There would appear to be two reasons underpinning this policy. The first is to regard intentional drunkenness as a substitute for the mental element ordinarily required by the offence. The second supports the view that a person should not be able to rely on the absence of a mental element when that has occurred as a result of his own voluntary actions.

The impact of this rule is that the voluntary consumption of alcohol or dangerous drugs to an excessive degree will be presumed to be reckless behaviour and as a result relieve from the prosecution the burden of proving recklessness. As we have seen, the law recognises two types of recklessness, *Caldwell* and *Cunningham.* In the former, a person can be deemed to have been reckless as a result of failing to consider the risk or risks associated with the particular course of conduct. Intoxication in such circumstances is totally irrelevant. There is little point trying to establish lack of foresight when none needs to be proved. However, what if the accused does give thought to the element of risk but because of his intoxicated state concludes wrongly there is nothing which ought to prevent him from proceeding?

The answer would appear to be that he would have no defence. *Majewski* is absolutely clear on the point. Under consideration is a basic intent crime and evidence of intoxication is irrelevant to the issue of *mens rea*.

What should be borne in mind, however, is the proposition that (assuming an offence requires proof of *Cunningham* recklessness) D should not be convicted of a basic intent crime, even where his intoxication is voluntary, if there is evidence that he would not have been aware of the risk in question even if he had been sober. This proposition was cited with approval by the Court of Appeal in *Richardson and Irwin* [1999] 1 Cr App R 392, and is recited in cl 22 of the draft Criminal Code Bill (see below, 10.3.6) and the US Model Penal Code (see above).

10.3.2 Dangerous and non-dangerous drugs

As a consequence of two decisions in the early 1980s it is necessary to consider drugs as falling into two categories: those which are 'dangerous' and those which are not, that is, do not lead to aggressive or unpredictable behavioural patterns. In *Hardie* [1984] 3 All ER 848, the accused was in a distressed state because his domestic arrangements had broken down and he had been asked by the woman with whom he had cohabited for nearly a decade to leave their home. He admitted taking a limited number of valium tablets which had been prescribed for his former partner. He expected that the tablets would have calmed him down. In fact it resulted in him displaying signs of intoxication and eventually setting fire to a wardrobe at their flat. He claimed to have no memory of the event. He was charged with criminal damage. The trial judge had ruled that because the defendant had voluntarily taken the drug, then he could not use intoxication as a defence. He was convicted. The Court of Appeal took a different view. It confirmed that the 'basic intent rule would apply in circumstances where the intoxication resulted from the introduction into the body of alcohol or dangerous drugs'. However, the court recognised that 'intoxication or similar symptoms may arise in other circumstances' from those which would conclusively indicate reckless behaviour on the part of the accused. It was suggested that the taking of a sedative or soporific drug would therefore not automatically rule out the availability of a defence in the case of basic intent crimes, because their consumption alone would not indicate a defendant was reckless. The court was adamant, however, that the consumption of any drugs prior to driving would never be a defence to a charge of reckless driving (now, of course, dangerous driving).

In *Bailey* [1983] 2 All ER 503, a diabetic had failed to take sufficient food after his normal dose of insulin and had struck his victim over the head with an iron bar. He was charged with offences contrary to ss 18 and 20 of the OAPA 1861. The trial judge ruled that his defence of automatism, based upon hypoglycaemia, was not available on either count because it was self-induced. This was clearly incorrect in respect of the s 18 offence which is regarded as a specific intent crime. The accused had failed to take food after drinking a mixture of sugar and water. In respect of the s 20 offence (a crime of basic intent), the Court of Appeal also found for the appellant. Self-induced automatism could be a defence in circumstances where the condition had arisen other than from intoxication due to alcohol or drugs. To consume alcohol or dangerous drugs would be regarded as reckless conduct, whereas in this case it could not be presumed to be reckless conduct to fail to take food after a dose of insulin. As Griffiths LJ put it:

> The question in each case will be whether the prosecution has proved the necessary element of recklessness. If the accused knows that his actions or inaction are likely to make him aggressive, unpredictable or uncontrolled with the result that he may cause some injury to the others and he persists in the action or takes no remedial action when he knows it is required, it will be open to the jury to find that he was reckless.

In essence, what is being said is that the defendant became involuntarily intoxicated and therefore the vital evidence of culpability is absent. It should not matter whether this involuntary intoxication results from another's actions or where the defendant, as in *Hardie*, makes an 'innocent' (or non-reckless?) mistake as to the consequences of his actions. One might query whether *Hardie* should not be regarded as *Caldwell* reckless, as that case was one of criminal damage. Was it not the case that he failed to give thought to the consequences of taking drugs prescribed for someone else? If so, then he was *Caldwell* reckless if ordinary people in a similar position would have given thought to the possible outcome of taking the drugs. Conversely, it could be regarded as a lacuna case, where he addressed the issue and concluded that, given the nature of the drugs, they would not have any adverse effect on him.

The law on involuntary intoxication was reviewed by the House of Lords in *Kingston*. It was not prepared to recognise a defence of exculpatory excuse since the absence of moral fault was not sufficient to negative the *mens rea* of an offence. In circumstances where a person unwittingly became intoxicated as a result of another's actions, the only question was whether at the time of committing the offence the defendant possessed the necessary *mens rea*. The reasons for getting into that condition would be for mitigation not liability. So, involuntary intoxication is not a defence to a criminal charge where there is evidence of *mens rea*. Conversely, if, as a result of the involuntary intoxication, the defendant was incapable of forming the necessary intent and therefore did not possess the *mens rea*, then the offence could not be made out. Arguably, this should apply to both basic and specific intent crimes. In the former case, the recklessness required for the offence is established as a result of the voluntary intoxication of the accused. That provides the necessary fault and is, according to Lord Mustill, 'substituted' for actual evidence of recklessness. However, if the defendant is completely unaware that his lemonade, for example, has been 'spiked' and as a result becomes intoxicated, there is no element of fault present and he deserves to have his defence of lack of *mens rea* recognised as a defence to a basic intent crime. It would be anomalous to do otherwise, particularly as *Hardie* permits a jury to consider the behaviour of the defendant in cases of voluntary consumption of non-dangerous drugs. In the latter case, the specific intent rule will apply and the only question will be did the accused possess the *mens rea* for the offence?

10.3.3 Application of the law

The basic strategy is to attempt to negative the *mens rea* required for specific intent crimes. As we have seen (above) and, as was pointed out in *Cole* [1993] Crim LR 300, the true question for the jury is whether the accused actually formed the intent, not whether he or she was capable of forming the intent. Proof that a defendant was capable of forming the *mens rea* does not mean that he or she actually did form the required intent.

The decision when to consume alcohol or to take drugs is also a relevant consideration in respect of the defence of intoxication. Therefore, if there is evidence that the intent was formed prior to the consumption of alcohol or dangerous drugs, then there are *dicta* to suggest that the defendant cannot rely on his drunken state in order to establish a defence. In *Attorney General for Northern Ireland v Gallagher*, Lord Denning referred to what has become known as the 'Dutch courage situation'. The accused had made up his mind to kill his wife. He bought a knife and a bottle of whisky – either to give himself Dutch courage to do the deed or to drown his conscience after it or perhaps both! He did in fact carry out his intention: '... the wickedness of his mind before he got drunk is enough to condemn him, coupled with the act which he intended to do and did do.'

He went on:

> I think the law on this point should take a clear stand. If a man, whilst sane and sober, forms an intention to kill and makes preparation for it knowing it is a wrong thing to do, and then gets himself drunk so as to give himself Dutch courage to do the killing, and whilst drunk carries out his intention, he cannot rely on self-induced drunkenness as a defence to a charge of murder, nor even as reducing it to manslaughter. He cannot say he got himself into such a stupid state that he was incapable of an intent to kill [p 382].

The difficulty with this view is that it does not appear to recognise that the *mens rea* needs to coincide with the *actus reus* and that the basic principle for the defence of intoxication is whether or not the accused actually did have the intent when the *actus reus* was committed. It requires one to accept the principle of the *actus reus* commencing at the time the intent was formed, that is, buying the alcohol and getting drunk is all part of the *actus reus* of the killing. It is part of a premeditated plan which ultimately will result in the death of a human being.

It will be recalled that s 8 of the CJA 1967 establishes that a court or jury in determining whether a person has committed an offence 'shall decide whether he did intend or foresee that result by reference to all the evidence'.

The House of Lords in *Majewski* responded by confirming that s 8 was inapplicable in this context because the section was evidential only, whereas the intoxication rule was one of substantive law.

For an application of this principle, however illogical it may appear in the context of a *mens rea* crime, one ought to examine the decision in *Lipman* [1969] 3 All ER 410. Lipman, after taking the hallucinatory drug LSD, had killed his girlfriend. She was found by her landlord having suffered two blows to the head and with some eight inches of sheeting crammed into her mouth. He claimed that he had been on an 'LSD trip' and believed that he was fighting serpents at the centre of the earth. He had awoken to find his companion dead. He was found guilty of manslaughter, a basic intent crime, even though it was not seriously disputed that he had no knowledge of what he was doing. In light of subsequent decisions, one could argue that he was reckless in putting himself in the position whereby he lost control of his actions. Conversely, he could maintain that he had no prior knowledge or reason to believe that such a consequence would occur and a jury, properly directed, might well be disposed to believe him. In light of the *Hardie* decision, if a court were to find

LSD not to be a dangerous drug, however unlikely that may be, for the purposes of the intoxication defence, then the jury would be entitled to consider whether he was reckless in taking the drug.

This case and the House of Lords' decisions remind us that public policy considerations are likely to underpin the legal principles in this area of law. As Lord Denning acknowledged in *Attorney General for Northern Ireland v Gallagher*: '... the general principle of English law (is) that, subject to very limited exceptions, drunkenness is no defence to a criminal charge.'

10.3.4 Intoxication and mistake

The law at present distinguishes between different kinds of mistake made by someone who is voluntarily drunk. If the offence is one of specific intent, then the drunken mistake is a relevant consideration for the jury. If the drunken mistake is to self-defence, or the amount of force needed for self-defence, then it is not a relevant mistake, irrespective of whether the accused is charged with a basic or specific intent crime. As will be seen below, at 10.10.2, a mistake as to circumstances may provide a defence provided that belief is honestly held. The *Gladstone Williams* [1987] 3 All ER 411 case establishes that belief does not need to be reasonable. What, then, is the situation if that mistaken belief is engendered because of intoxication? If the offence is one of specific intent, then intoxication is a factor in considering whether or not the accused had the necessary intent as where the defendant is charged with murder but claims he acted in self-defence.

The interrelationship between intoxication and mistake has been explored in a number of cases. In *O'Grady* [1987] 3 All ER 420, the Court of Appeal held that a defendant was precluded from relying on self-defence if, as a result of voluntary intoxication, he had used excessive force when defending himself. This would apply, irrespective of whether the charge was one relating to a basic or specific intent crime. The reason for this finding is to be found in a statement of McCullough J, who gave the defendant leave to appeal to the Court of Appeal, which was cited by Lord Lane CJ:

> Given that a man who mistakenly believes he is under attack is entitled to use reasonable force to defend himself, it would seem to follow that, if he is under attack and mistakenly believes the attack to be more serious that it is, he is entitled to use reasonable force to defend himself against an attack of the severity he believed it to have. If one allows a mistaken belief induced by drink to bring this principle into operation, an act of gross negligence (viewed objectively) may become lawful even though it results in the death of the innocent victim. The drunken man would be guilty of neither murder nor manslaughter.

This decision has been supported by *O'Connor* [1991] Crim LR 135, where the defendant who had been drinking heavily had killed another man, but maintained that he believed himself to be under attack and was therefore acting in self-defence. The Court of Appeal held that *O'Grady* was binding upon it and therefore the fact that the trial judge had failed to direct the jury on the issue of drunkenness and self-defence was irrelevant. *O'Grady* has been savagely criticised because it can lead to illogical results and at best must be seen as a policy decision. The Law Commission has found it impossible to support the decision. From a self-defence viewpoint, the jury is not entitled to recognise the defendant's intoxication in deciding whether or not he intended to act in self-defence. However, when considering whether he had sufficient intent to kill or cause grievous bodily harm, it is entitled to consider intoxication, via the specific intent rule.

The common law rule as regards self-defence would therefore appear to be that, where a mistake arises as a result of voluntary intoxication, the defendant cannot rely on his mistake. The problem with the *O'Grady* decision is that it divorces the issue of proof of intent from that of mistake. *Richardson and Irwin*, on the other hand, suggests that voluntary intoxication should be taken into account if it leads D to believe mistakenly that P is consenting to harm (in this case, rough horseplay) in circumstances where P's consent could afford a defence. How this is to be reconciled with earlier cases, such as *Woods* (1981) 74 Cr App R 312, where D's drunken mistake as to P's consent was held to provide no defence to a charge of rape, is not at all clear. Logic and policy decisions do not sit easily together in this area of law!

10.3.5 Statutory as opposed to a common law defence

The issue has also arisen with respect to a statutory as opposed to a common law defence. *Jaggard v Dickinson* [1980] 3 All ER 716 concerned a charge of criminal damage arising from an attempt by the defendant to gain entry into what she believed was a friend's property but which in fact belonged to a neighbour, although it was identical in appearance. She broke two windows and damaged a curtain. It transpired that she was drunk. Criminal damage was treated as a basic intent crime; therefore, voluntary consumption of alcohol is to be regarded as a reckless act and intoxication would not succeed as a defence. However, s 5(2) and (3) of the Criminal Damage Act 1971 allows a defendant to plead an honest belief that there is a lawful excuse why one should be permitted to damage or destroy another's property. The court accepted that an honest belief induced by intoxication was a factor which would be taken into account in determining whether a defence within the terms of s 5 had been set up. She claimed that, as she knew the occupant of the house she wished to break into and thought that he would consent if he had known the circumstances, she should be allowed the benefit of s 5(3). The Divisional Court allowed her appeal.

This decision further illustrates the inconsistency and illogicality of this area of law. In this statutory context, a mistaken belief induced by drink can be taken into account in deciding whether a defendant actually held that belief, but in respect of the common law of self-defence, drunkenness, which makes the defendant mistakenly believe he is under attack, cannot help to justify his response.

10.3.6 The Law Commission

Clause 22 of the draft Criminal Code Bill deals with intoxication. If the fault element of the crime requires recklessness to be proved it is proposed that someone who is voluntarily intoxicated shall be treated:

(a) as having been aware of any risk of which he would have been aware had he been sober;

(b) as not having believed in the existence of an exempting circumstance (where the existence of such a belief is in issue) if he would not have so believed had he been sober.

Intoxicant is defined to mean 'alcohol or any other thing which, when taken into the body, may impair awareness or control'.

Voluntary intoxication means 'the intoxication of a person by an intoxicant which he takes, other than properly for a medical purpose, knowing that it is or may be an intoxicant'.

The Law Commission was extremely active in this area of the law in the 1990s and considered the role of intoxication in the criminal law on no less than three occasions. In 1993, it published its consultation paper (Law Com 127) and, later in the same year, its report (Law Com 218) makes reference to the effect of intoxication. In 1995, its report, *Legislating the Criminal Code: Intoxication and Criminal Liability* (Law Com 229), was published. It is worthwhile looking at both the consultation paper and the final report, as the Law Commission's views demonstrate an amazing *volte face*. The 1993 paper contained two major proposals: first, that the *Majewski* rule be abolished; and, secondly, that a new offence of criminal intoxication be created. The Law Commission had no doubt that what was required was a 'thorough going replacement of the common law rule, rather than any attempt at marginal reform' (para 4.19).

In its report it expresses the view that 'the *Majewski* approach operates fairly, on the whole, and without undue difficulty, but it is both desirable and necessary to set out the relevant principles clearly in codified form' (para 1.32). Apparently, the Law Commission accepted the views of the senior judiciary that the public would find abolition of the *Majewski* rule objectionable. The Law Commission, therefore, proposes that the bulk of the present law should be put onto a statutory footing. This means that, when addressing primary considerations, such as intention, knowledge, purpose, belief, fraud or dishonesty, intoxication should be a factor to take into account. However, in respect of other aspects of *mens rea*, most notably recklessness, a defendant will be treated as having been aware of anything which he would have been aware of, if not for his intoxication. The focus will be upon the actual *mens rea* for each offence and the terminology of basic and specific intent will disappear. In effect, this will introduce a rebuttable presumption in respect of recklessness, allowing the court to take into account factors that might have affected an awareness of risk. This might include the physical and mental problems of the accused.

The Law Commission seeks to reverse the effect of the decisions in *O'Grady* and *O'Connor* although the wording employed to describe this change is tortuous in the extreme. In essence, it is proposed that, if the accused is charged with a specific intent offence, his 'intoxicated' mistake may be taken into account to determine liability, but not in cases of basic intent. (It should be noted that these terms will become redundant if the recommendations are implemented.)

Someone taking drugs in circumstances such as those in *Hardie* will be able to benefit from the law only if the drugs were consumed for medicinal purposes, in which case it will be treated as a case of involuntary intoxication. Other 'involuntary' situations are where the intoxication resulted from duress or the intoxicant was taken without knowledge or awareness on the part of the accused.

A person is to be regarded as intoxicated if 'awareness, understanding or control is impaired'. 'Intoxicants' are alcohol, drugs and any other substance which once in the body has the capacity to impair awareness, understanding or control.

In February 1998, the Home Office published its White Paper, *Violence: Reforming the Offences Against the Person Act 1861*, accompanied by a draft Bill. Clause 19 of that Bill proposes reforms to the law relating to intoxication in so far as that defence relates to non-fatal offences against the person. In essence, the Home Office proposals endorse the approach taken by the Law Commission in its 1993 report (Law Com 218) (and, indeed, the draft Criminal Code Bill, cited above). Under this formulation, a defendant who becomes intoxicated of his own volition would be treated as having been aware of any risk of which he would have been aware had he not been intoxicated, and as having known or believed in any circumstances which he would have known or believed in had he not been intoxicated.

10.4   MISTAKE

Although mistake is commonly referred to as a defence in criminal law, in reality it will normally involve a denial of *mens rea*. As such it is not a 'true' defence, more a denial of one of the elements of the criminal offence. Hence, a defendant may allege that he did not possess the *mens rea* for the crime with which he is charged because he was labouring under a mistake of fact and thus did not intend or was not reckless to the particular consequences or he was not aware of the circumstances required by the definition of the crime. The leading cases of *DPP v Morgan* and *B (A Minor) v DPP* [2000] 1 All ER 833 make it clear that, where such a mistake prevents the accused from possessing the requisite mental element, he should be acquitted. This holds true even if the defendant's mistaken belief is so unlikely that a reasonable person would not have made such a mistake. Lord Nicholls, in the course of his speech in *B (A Minor) v DPP*, indicated that the requirement of reasonable belief should be abandoned altogether save where expressly required by statute. As he observed, when *mens rea* is ousted by a mistaken belief, it is ousted. It matters not that the belief is an unreasonable belief. He added:

> Considered as a matter of principle, the honest belief approach must be preferable. By definition, the mental element in a crime is concerned with a subjective state of mind, such as intent or belief.

Where an overriding objective limit, such as a requirement that a belief had to be held on reasonable grounds, is imposed by statute it has the effect of displacing the subjective element, so that a conviction can follow a failure to achieve an objective standard, even though the defendant lacks a particular culpable state of mind.

The issues raised in *DPP v Morgan* are considered in Chapter 7 (7.11.2). Where the defendant is charged with a strict liability offence involving no *mens rea*, any mistake of fact he may have made will be irrelevant. Often, however, where offences are silent as to *mens rea* the courts will 'read in' a *mens rea* requirement, in which case mistake of fact may become relevant (see further the consideration of *B (A Minor) v DPP* in Chapter 3).

Mistake of law is generally thought not to provide a defence to a criminal charge. This is often expressed in terms that an individual is always presumed to know the law. In reality, it means that no individual can be excused liability for his criminal act on the basis of his ignorance of the law. As with all such truisms there are exceptions. A defendant may be found to be criminally insane because he does not realise that his actions are unlawful (see further above, 10.1.4). Further, a defendant might escape criminal liability because he makes a mistake of *civil* law – typically in the areas of theft or criminal damage, where the defendant honestly believed that the property he appropriated or damaged was actually his own. Beyond such exceptions, however, the courts are understandably reluctant to recognise errors of law as providing any form of defence to a criminal charge. In *Lee* (2000) NLJ 1491, the defendant was convicted of assault with intent to resist lawful apprehension contrary to s 38 of the OAPA 1861. He appealed on the basis that the trial judge should have directed the jury that they should acquit if the defendant had honestly, albeit mistakenly, believed that there were no lawful grounds for his arrest. The Court of Appeal refused to imply any requirement into s 38 to the effect that the prosecution had to prove the defendant knew or believed the apprehension to be lawful. The result was that a defendant could rely on a mistake of fact (that is, was the arrest by a police constable) but could not rely on a mistake of law (that is, was the apprehension lawful). In practical terms it cannot be left to each person to determine for himself or herself whether or not an arrest is lawful, especially where the lawfulness of an arrest may depend on the state of mind of the arresting officer.

10.5   DURESS BY THREATS

The common law has, for centuries, recognised a defence of duress (specifically duress *per minas*) that arises where X forces D to commit a particular crime by threatening to kill D or cause grievous bodily harm if D refuses. Duress is regarded as a 'true defence' in the sense that it is not a denial of *actus reus* or *mens rea*. Lord Morris in *Lynch v DPP* [1975] 1 All ER 914 posed the question:

> If someone acts under duress – does he intend what he does? Does he lack what in our criminal law is called *mens rea*? If what he does amounts to a criminal offence ought he to be convicted but allowed in mercy and in mitigation to be absolved or relieved from some or all of the possible consequences.

He later rejected the view that duress could act only to mitigate the consequences of a conviction or absolve from punishment. The accepted approach was put by Lord Wilberforce in *Lynch* to the effect that 'the element of duress prevents the law from treating what was done as a crime'. In other words, the victim of the duress commits the *actus reus* and may have *mens rea*, but, if proved, duress will prevent the law from treating the enterprise as criminal. Lord Morris was clear as to why duress should be allowed as a defence:

> If then someone is really threatened with death or serious injury unless he does what he is told to do is the law to pay no heed to the miserable, agonising plight of such a person? For the law to understand not only how the timid but also the stalwart may in a moment of crisis behave is not to make the law weak but to make it just. In the calm of the courtroom measures of fortitude or of heroic behaviour are surely not to be demanded when they could not in moments for decision reasonably have been expected even of the resolute and the well disposed.

The defence of duress *per minas* can only arise where D is ordered to commit a specific offence by the third party. In *Cole* [1994] Crim LR 582, C claimed that he had 'no choice' as to whether he robbed two building societies. He owed cash to moneylenders whom he claimed had threatened him, hit him with a baseball bat and threatened his girlfriend and child because of his inability to repay. The judge ruled that duress was only available where the threats were directed to the commission of the particular offence charged. In his case the threat related to his inability or unwillingness to repay the loan. He was not threatened with the unpleasant consequences if he failed to rob a building society. There had to be a direct link between the threat and the offence. The decision would appear to limit the scope of the defence to those situations where the duressor is very specific in terms of what he or she requires the defendant to do. If A says to D, 'You owe me £1,000 and if you don't rob the Pontypridd Building Society I'll seriously injure you and your child' that would appear to be adequate to comply with the test. However, if D is told 'You owe me £1,000 and if I don't have it by Friday I'll seriously injure you and your child and – oh! – by the way all building society offices in Pontypridd lack proper security' that may not be enough. Or suppose he simply says 'Get the £1,000 to me by Friday or else … I don't care what you do but I want my money'. Only in the first of these examples had the duressor nominated the crime. In terms of impact on the defendant, are the other examples really so different in character as to deny him the opportunity to have his plea considered by the jury?

10.5.1 The test for duress

The test for duress has been developed by the common law over many years. An individual's response to the threat must be judged against the likely reaction of the ordinary person in a similar situation. In *Graham* [1982] 1 All ER 801, it was stated that as a matter of public policy it was essential 'to limit the defence of duress by means of an objective criterion formulated in terms of reasonableness'.

Lord Lane CJ drew parallels between provocation and duress. With provocation the court looks at the reasonableness, or otherwise, of the defendant's loss of self-control. He concluded that it would be rational, therefore, for the courts, when considering the defence of duress, to require a defendant to display reasonable fortitude when faced with threats. The test for duress thus contains both subjective and objective elements. In *Graham*, Lord Lane CJ suggested the following formulation:

(1) was the defendant, or may he have been impelled to act as he did because, as a result of what he reasonably believed [the person making the threat] had said or done, he had good cause to fear that if he did not so act [the person] would kill him or cause him serious physical injury?

(2) if so, have the prosecution made the jury sure that a sober person of reasonable firmness, sharing the characteristics of the defendant, would not have responded to whatever he reasonably believed [the person] said or did by taking part in the killing. The fact that a defendant's will to resist has been eroded by the voluntary consumption of drink or drugs or both is not relevant to this test.

Note that under this formulation a defendant was not allowed to rely on the defence unless his belief in the facts giving rise to the duress was reasonable. Subsequently, in *Martin* [2000] Crim LR 615, the Court of Appeal recognised the unfairness and inconsistency in this restriction and confirmed that a defendant raising the defence of duress should be judged on the circumstances as he honestly believed them to be, taking into account the evidence of any psychiatric condition that might affect the defendant's ability to perceive and evaluate the threats made by a third party.

Introducing an element of subjectivity into the second limb of the *Graham* test has been more troublesome, given that the rationale for the second limb is that a defendant is expected to have the steadfastness reasonably to be expected of the ordinary citizen.

In *Bowen* (1996) 146 NLJ 442, the defendant had an IQ of 68. At his trial on a charge of obtaining services by deception contrary to s 1 of the Theft Act 1978, the defendant raised the issue of duress. He claimed that his actions in obtaining electrical equipment on credit, failing to make any payments and then selling them was motivated by his desire to avoid having his house petrol-bombed. Two men, he said, had threatened to carry out the attack if he did not obtain the goods for them. The Court of Appeal referred to the 'classic statement' of the law in *Graham*, which alludes in the second limb to a sober person of reasonable firmness, 'sharing the characteristics of the defendant'.

The court has to consider which characteristics of the accused were relevant to the second objective test. In the earlier case of *Hegarty* [1994] Crim LR 353, the court had acknowledged that age, sex and physical health were all characteristics that could be taken into account but doubted whether a personality disorder of the type possessed by the accused was relevant. Medical evidence could be assessed in connection with the subjective part of the equation and this would include mental abnormality but would only be relevant in the objective part of the test if connected to the ability to resist the threats.

In *Horne* [1994] Crim LR 584, the Court of Appeal held that 'characteristics' should be interpreted narrowly in respect of the objective test, otherwise that element of the two-limb test would be completely undermined, that is, if virtually all of the characteristics of the accused were to be taken into account then the test would in effect be wholly subjective. The appellant had sought to adduce psychiatric evidence to the effect that he was unusually pliable and vulnerable to pressure. The judge refused to admit the evidence, saying that mental characteristics, such as inherent weakness, vulnerability and susceptibility to threats, were inconsistent with the requirements of the objective test. The Court of Appeal affirmed this view.

The court in *Bowen* agreed that age, sex and physical health or disability may be relevant characteristics but: '... beyond that it is not altogether easy to determine from the authorities what others may be relevant.' The court considered that the following principles were to be derived from the authorities:

- if the accused is more 'pliable, vulnerable, timid or susceptible to threats than the normal person ... these are not characteristics with which the reasonable/ordinary man is to be invested';

- the defendant may be in a category of persons that the jury would recognise as being less able to resist pressure, for example, as a result of pregnancy or serious physical disability;

- some characteristics relevant to provocation may not be relevant to duress, for example, a person's homosexuality may be the subject of taunts and therefore going to the heart of provocation, but homosexuality could not be relevant to duress. There is no reason to assume that a homosexual is any less or more robust in resisting the type of threats relevant to duress;

- characteristics due to self-induced abuse, for example, alcohol or glue-sniffing cannot be relevant;

- psychiatric evidence is admissible to show the accused is suffering from some recognised mental illness or psychiatric condition providing persons suffering from such conditions may be more susceptible to pressure or threats. This may help the jury to decide whether a reasonable person suffering from such an illness might have been impelled to act as the accused did.

Having reviewed the principles, the court concluded that a low IQ short of mental impairment was not a characteristic that made an individual less courageous or less able to withstand threats and pressure. The effect of these decisions has been to erode the force of the objective test in duress, moving the law on the test for duress closer to that proposed by the Law Commission, that is, 'the threat is one which in all the circumstances (including any of [the defendant's] characteristics that affect its gravity) he cannot reasonably be expected to resist'.'

What type of threat?

The threats giving rise to a defence of duress *per minas* must be of death or serious bodily harm. Murnagham J, in *Attorney General v Whelan* [1934] IR 518, in a passage approved by the House of Lords in *Lynch* commented:

> It seems to us that threats of immediate death or serious person violence so great as to overbear the ordinary power of human resistance should be accepted as justification for acts which would otherwise be criminal.

A similar comment can also be found in *Hudson and Taylor* [1971] 2 All ER 244. The law will not place threats to property on a par with threats of death or serious physical injury. Lord Simon's 'working definition', as expounded in *Lynch*, was put in these terms:

> ... such [well grounded] fear, produced by threats, of death or grievous bodily harm [or unjustified imprisonment] if a certain act is not done, as overbears the actor's wish not to perform the act, and is effective, at the time of the act, in constraining him to perform it.

Where so little is clear, this at least seems to be established:

> ... that the type of threat which affords a defence must be one of human physical harm (including, possibly, imprisonment), so that threat of injury to property is not enough.

Lord Simon does go on to acknowledge that a threat in certain circumstances, 'may be as potent in overbearing the actor's wish not to perform the prohibited act as a threat of physical harm' but 'the law must draw a line somewhere; and as a result of experience and human valuation, the law draws it between threats to property and threats to the person'. The threat of physical harm or death cannot be from D himself (that is, D escapes from prison to stop himself committing suicide) (see *Roger* (1997) *The Times*, 30 July).

The threat of death or serious harm may not be the only factor influencing the defendant to act as he did. In *Valderrama-Vega* [1985] Crim LR 220, the defendant had received death threats from a Colombian Mafia-style organisation and had as a result tried to import cocaine into England. He was also in financial difficulty and additionally feared that the organisation would disclose his homosexual inclinations to his family. Duress was available, said the trial judge, if the defendant had acted solely on the basis of the death threats. This was potentially misleading because the jury might have believed the defence should have been rejected if other factors affected his decision. The correct approach was to ask whether he would have acted differently but for the death threats.

The imminence of the threat

It was stated in *Hudson and Taylor* that the threats must be effective on the mind of the accused at the time the *actus reus* is perpetrated. Two girls, aged 19 and 17, were charged with perjury but claimed that when they gave false evidence they had done so only because of threats which had been made against them. They had actually seen one of those who had threatened them sitting in the public gallery, as they were about to give evidence. The defence failed, presumably, on the basis that the girls had failed to seek protection when it was readily available to them. The Court of Appeal, in allowing the appeal against conviction, thought the threat no less effective, simply because it would not be carried out at the time the crime was committed; it was certainly a possibility that the threats could have been carried out later that night 'in the streets of Salford'. Of course, a threat of future violence may be so remote as to have little impact on the will of the defendant, but that was not the position in this case.

In *Abdul-Hussain and Others* [1999] Crim LR 570, the defendants sought to raise the defence of duress in respect of charges of hijacking a plane. They feared that, as Shiite Muslims from southern Iraq, if they were deported to Iraq, they would be tortured and or killed by the authorities there. The trial judge had refused to leave the defence of duress to the jury, on the basis that the threat of death or grievous bodily harm had been insufficiently imminent at the time of the hijacking. Allowing their appeals, the Court of Appeal accepted the contention that the threat of death or grievous bodily harm need not actually be immediate. What mattered was that the defendant's will to resist the threats was overborne by the prospect of imminent peril of death or grievous bodily harm. The court usefully illustrated this point by giving the example of Anne Frank not having to wait for the Gestapo to knock on her door before being able to rely on the defence of necessity in relation to fleeing in a stolen car.

Self-induced duress

The defence of duress is likely to be denied if the accused has voluntarily joined a criminal organisation, because he has put himself into a position where he may expect others to use force to exert their will over him, particularly if he should try to resile from their operations. The leading case is *Sharp* [1987] 3 All ER 103, where Lord Lane CJ stated the principle thus:

> Where a person has voluntarily, and with knowledge of its nature, joined a criminal organisation or gang which he knew might bring pressure on him to commit an offence and was an active member when he was put under such pressure, he cannot avail himself of the defence of duress.

In *Ali* [1995] Crim LR 303, the Court of Appeal applied *Sharp* and stated the rule thus:

> The crux of the matter was knowledge in the defendant of either a violent nature to the gang or the enterprise which he had joined, or a violent disposition in the person

or persons involved with him in the criminal activity he voluntarily joined. If a defendant voluntarily participated in criminal offences with a man 'X' whom he knows to be of violent disposition and likely to require him to perform other criminal acts, he could not rely on duress if 'X' does so.

These cases may usefully be contrasted with *Shepherd* (1987) 86 Cr App R 47. The appellant was convicted of five counts of burglary. A number of men would enter a shop, some would distract the shopkeeper while the others took the goods. S claimed that after the first expedition he wanted to withdraw but was threatened by other gang members with violence to him and his family and so he felt compelled to carry on. The trial judge ruled that duress was not available. The appeal was allowed and the convictions quashed. This case can be distinguished from the others on the basis that the defendant was not at the outset joining a gang with a known propensity for violence and who could anticipate what might happen if his nerve failed. This might apply, for example, to those joining paramilitary groups or gangs of armed robbers. In this case, there would be no immediate assumption that, should he wish to withdraw, then he might be faced with serious violence. As the court said:

> ... there are certain kinds of criminal enterprises the joining of which, in the absence of any knowledge of propensity to violence on the part of one member, would not lead another to suspect that a decision to think better of the whole affair might lead him into serious trouble. In such cases, if trouble materialises unexpectedly and puts the defendant into a dilemma in which a reasonable man might have chosen to act as he did, the concession of human frailty is available to the defendant.

The defence of duress may also be denied to a defendant who can be regarded as having brought about the situation whereby he is subjected to threats forcing him to commit offences. In *Heath* (1999) *The Times*, 15 October, D had incurred debts with a drugs dealer and relied upon this as the explanation as to why the dealer had forced him into committing offences in order to 'repay' the debt. The court thought it a sufficient basis for denying the availability of duress that D had placed himself in a situation where he was aware of the risk that he might be compelled to commit offences. This was endorsed in *Harmer* [2002] Crim LR 401, where the Court of Appeal held that the defence of duress would not be available where D voluntarily became involved with others and he could foresee that they might threaten him with unlawful violence. There was no need for the prosecution to show that D had foreseen that he would be forced to commit particular crimes.

10.6   DURESS OF CIRCUMSTANCES

A defendant may claim that he was compelled to commit a criminal offence, not because he was ordered to do so by another under pain of death or grievous bodily harm, but simply because the circumstance in which he found himself gave him no option. For example, take the prisoner who is in lawful custody during an earthquake. Should he remain in his cell and risk certain death, or should he escape from the prison to avoid harm? If he escapes he commits an offence. His defence will be that he had to break the law to save his life. Similarly, the defendant who drives the wrong way up a one-way street to escape from an unruly mob of football fans because he fears they will attack him. The mob is not ordering the defendant to commit a traffic offence, but he feels that, in the circumstances, it is the only sensible option. Whilst these scenarios can be distinguished from duress *per minas*, in that the duressor does not nominate a crime to be committed by D (indeed there may be no human threat), duress of circumstances may overlap to a certain extent with necessity and self-defence, considered below.

The leading decision is now the Court of Appeal's ruling in *Martin* [1989] 1 All ER 652. The defendant claimed that his wife had suicidal tendencies and on a number of occasions had attempted to take her own life. Her son (the appellant's stepson), had on the day in question overslept and risked losing his job if he arrived late for work. His mother apparently distraught, urged the appellant to drive the son to his place of employment. She threatened to commit suicide if he did not accede to her requests. The appellant had been disqualified from driving and was naturally reluctant to take his car onto the highway. Eventually, he relented because he said 'he genuinely and ... reasonably believed that his wife would carry out her threat unless he did as she demanded'. He was apprehended by the police. Simon Brown J, delivering the judgment of the Court of Appeal, summarised the principles applicable to what was in effect a plea of necessity (the defence had adduced medical evidence to the effect that in her mental condition Mrs Martin would have attempted suicide if her husband had not done what she demanded):

(1) English law does, in extreme circumstances, recognise a defence of necessity. Most commonly this defence arises as duress, that is pressure on the accused's will from the wrongful threats of violence of another. Equally however, it can arise from objective dangers threatening the accused or others. Arising thus it is conveniently called 'duress of circumstances'.

(2) ... the defence is available only if, from an objective standpoint, the accused can be said to be acting reasonably and proportionately in order to avoid a threat of death or serious injury.

The judge should invite the jury to consider two questions when duress of circumstances is raised as a defence: first, whether or not the accused acted as he did because he had reason to fear that death or serious injury would result; and, secondly, whether 'a sober person of reasonable firmness, sharing the characteristics of the accused' would have responded by acting in the same way as the accused. If a positive answer is given to both these questions, the defence of duress of circumstances is established and the accused must be acquitted.

10.7   NECESSITY

The Law Commission (Law Com 218, 1993, paras 35.4 and 35.5) draws a distinction between duress and necessity:

By contrast with the defence of duress ... there appear to be some cases, more properly called cases of 'necessity' where the actor does not rely on any allegation that circumstances placed an irresistible pressure on him. Rather he claims that his conduct, although falling within the definition of an offence, was not harmful because it was, in the circumstances, justified.

The basis for a defence of necessity distinct from the defences of duress is, therefore, that a defendant pleading necessity might not have been acting to protect himself, and may not have acted under an overwhelming compulsion. He may simply have acted to prevent harm to others by opting for the lesser of two evils.

Perhaps predictably, much of the case law in this area arises out of decisions taken by medical practitioners. Typical is the case of *Bourne* [1938] 3 All ER 615, where a surgeon performed an abortion on a 14-year-old girl who had been raped. He was charged under s 58 of the OAPA 1861 with unlawfully using an instrument with intent to procure a miscarriage. In his direction to the jury, the judge asked them to consider whether the surgeon had acted in good faith. If they concluded that he had they were to find that he had not acted unlawfully. To save the life of the mother, it was necessary to destroy the foetus, thus the jury's acquittal of Bourne was a clear signal that they viewed the act as justified, that is, necessary. Note, however, that this is not an authority supporting the existence of necessity as a defence. It merely illustrates how the issue of necessity enabled the jury to conclude that the doctor's actions were not unlawful. Similar considerations explain decisions such as *Gillick v West Norfolk and Wisbech AHA* [1985] 3 All ER 402, where the House of Lords held that it would not be unlawful for a doctor to prescribe contraceptive pills to a girl under the age of 16, knowing that she was going to engage in sexual intercourse. The doctor in such a case believes it is necessary for the patient's well being that she should be protected against an unwanted pregnancy. He thus escapes liability for aiding and abetting unlawful sexual intercourse. In *Re F (Mental Patient: Sterilisation)* [1989] 2 All ER 545, the House of Lords recognised that a 36-year-old woman with a mental capacity of a four or five-year-old could be sterilised, even though she had no comprehension of what was happening and could not give her consent. Despite her mental age, the woman either was or was likely to become sexually active or vulnerable to sexual activity, hence the intervention of the authorities. Lord Goff viewed the situation as one of necessity, observing:

> That there exists in the common law a principle of necessity which may justify action which would otherwise be unlawful is not in doubt. But historically the principle has been seen to be restricted to two groups of cases, which have been called cases of public necessity and cases of private necessity.

As an example of the former, he cites destroying another man's property in order to prevent a catastrophic fire – as in the Great Fire of London in 1666. In the latter case, the unlawful act is done by an individual in order that his own person or property might be saved from imminent danger. He then goes on to recognise a third group of cases:

> ... which is also properly described as founded on the principle of necessity. These cases are concerned with action taken as a matter of necessity to assist another person without his consent. To give a simple example, a man who seizes another and forcibly drags him from the path of an oncoming vehicle, thereby saving him from injury or even death, commits no wrong.

The third group of cases to which Lord Goff alludes are brought within the doctrine of necessity only if two requirements are satisfied:

(1) it is not practicable to communicate with the assisted person; and

(2) the action taken must be such as a reasonable person would in all the circumstances take, acting in the best interests of the assisted person.

These principles are of course expounded in the context of a civil case and do not go so far as to establish a 'wide ranging' doctrine of necessity within the confines of the criminal law. More explicit support for the existence of such a defence in criminal law can be found in the Court of Appeal's ruling in *Re A (Children) (Conjoined Twins: Surgical Separation)* [2000] 4 All ER 961. Conjoined twins M and J were both bound to die if not surgically separated. Because M was being kept alive only because she was being supplied with blood whilst attached to J, any operation to separate the two would result in the immediate and inevitable death of M. One of the questions for the Court of Appeal (Civil Division) was as to whether doctors performing such a separation would be able to avail themselves of any compulsion based defence. Brooke LJ observed that a defence of necessity could arise, even though there was no emergency, nor any threat amounting to unjust aggression. The necessary preconditions were that:

(i)   the act is needed to avoid inevitable and irreparable evil;

(ii) no more should be done than is reasonably necessary for the purpose to be achieved;

(iii) the evil inflicted must not be disproportionate to the evil avoided.

Ward LJ accepted that by separating the twins and helping to ensure the survival of one, as opposed to the certain death of both, doctors should be allowed a defence based on the choosing of the lesser of the two evils. Robert Walker LJ, also saw the case as one where the principles of necessity should apply so as to absolve the surgeons performing the operation from liability.

10.8   DURESS, NECESSITY AND MURDER

The compulsion defences of duress *per minas*, duress of circumstances and necessity are rightly regarded as general defences, but that does not mean that they can be raised as defences to all crimes. The particular moral difficulty that arises is the question of whether or not a defendant charged with murder should be able to raise a defence of duress or necessity so as to escape liability for the killing.

To understand the nature of the debate on this issue in English criminal law it is necessary to go back to 1884 and the trial of Tom Dudley and Edwin Stephens at Exeter Assizes. Cast adrift in an open boat, they had killed a young member of their crew, who admittedly was near to death, in order that they might feast on his flesh. A few days later, they were rescued and, following that, amid intense publicity, stood their trial for murder. They claimed that it was necessary for them to act as they did in order to stay alive. Baron Huddleston, the trial judge, told the jury:

> There was no more necessity that they should kill the boy than that they should kill one of themselves. All they required was something to eat: but the necessity of something to eat does not create the necessity of taking and excuse the taking of the boy.

The common law has steadfastly taken the view that a defendant should not be entitled to save his own life at the cost of another innocent life. *Dudley and Stephens* is, strictly speaking, authority for the proposition that duress of circumstances is not available as a defence to murder, but the principle has been extended more generally to duress *per minas*. Lord Griffiths in *Howe* [1987] 1 All ER 771 saw the defence of duress *per minas* as a 'merciful concession to human frailty', but the House of Lords confirmed in that case that the defence was not available to a defendant charged with murder, either as the principal offender or as an accomplice. In *Gotts* [1992] 1 All ER 832, the House of Lords extended this prohibition to a defendant charged with attempted murder. The appellant, who at the time of the offence was aged 16, seriously injured his mother with a knife. He was charged with attempted murder and pleaded not guilty. At his trial, he raised the defence of duress, stating that his father had threatened to shoot him unless he killed his mother. The trial judge ruled that such evidence was inadmissible since duress was not, as a matter of law, a defence to a charge of attempted murder. He changed his plea to guilty and appealed against the judge's ruling. On a 3:2 majority, it was decided that, as a matter of public policy, the defence was unavailable to someone charged with attempted murder. This would appear to be a logical conclusion, given that duress is not a defence to a charge of murder. Attempted murder requires an intent to kill, yet the *mens rea* for murder can be satisfied by proving an intent to cause serious bodily harm. There is often no certainty that, in carrying out the act, the accused will achieve his purpose in bringing about death. If he should be successful, duress is not available as a defence. If, by sheer good fortune, the victim survives the attack and the charge is one of attempted murder, he would, in the absence of the decision in *Gotts,* be able to introduce duress.

As a result of this decision, there is one anomaly still to be resolved. It would appear that duress may be a defence to a charge of causing grievous bodily harm with intent (s 18 of the OAPA 1861). Thus, if a person causes death, having an intent to kill, duress is not available. However, if he has the intent to cause grievous bodily harm, which is after all part of the *mens rea* for murder, and again through good fortune the person survives, then duress is available.

Although a decision of the civil courts *Re A (Children) (Conjoined Twins: Surgical Separation)*, is a very persuasive authority for the proposition that necessity should be available as a defence to murder where the evidence is that the defendant did not act to save his own life, provided the preconditions adverted to by Brooke LJ are met.

10.9   REFORM OF DURESS AND NECESSITY

Why should the common law refuse to recognise duress as a defence to murder? The reason generally given is that the law cannot be seen to place a greater value on the life of one person as opposed to another. Is it forgivable to save one's own life at the expense of another person or group of people? Equally, is the person who kills 40 people by planting a bomb in a busy shopping centre in order to save the life of his wife and daughter to be regarded as a hero? One suspects not, at least by the relatives and friends of those killed. Yet is it reasonable to expect a person to sacrifice his own life and that of his family in order to save the lives of those engaged upon a shopping expedition? One suspects most people would plant the bomb in the hope that it might be discovered and life not placed in jeopardy, particularly if he or his family faced certain death for disobeying. In many of the cases in which duress has been considered, the judges have made reference to the threat of terrorism and the potential exploitation of the defence by those who force others to commit atrocities on their behalf (see, for example, Lord Hailsham LC in *Howe*) as a reason for not extending the defence to one charged with murder as a principal offender.

The Law Commission, in its 1993 report (Law Com 218), recommends that duress of threats should be a complete defence to all crimes and, to reduce concern at this extension of the law in respect of murder and attempted murder, the Law

Commission proposes that the burden of proof would move to the defence. At the moment, the obligation of disproving duress rests upon the Crown. Therefore, the accused would have to prove that he knew or believed:

- that a threat has been made to cause death or serious injury to himself or another if the act is not done; and

- that the threat will be carried out immediately if he does not do the act or, if not immediately, before he or that other can obtain effective official protection; and

- that there is no other way of preventing the threat being carried out; and

- the threat is one which in all the circumstances (including any of his personal characteristics that affect its gravity) he cannot reasonably be expected to resist (cl 25 of the draft Criminal Law Bill).

As regards the defence of duress of circumstances the Law Commission has proposed the following in cl 26:

(1) No act of a person constitutes an offence if the act is done under duress of circumstances.

(2) A person does an act under duress of circumstances if:

(a) he does it because he knows or believes that it is immediately necessary to avoid death or serious injury to himself or another; and

(b) the danger that he knows or believes to exist is such that in all the circumstances (including any of his personal characteristics that affect its gravity) he cannot reasonably be expected to act otherwise.

It is for the defendant to show that the reason for his act was such knowledge or belief as is mentioned in para (a).

Note that the defence would not apply to a person who has knowingly and without reasonable excuse exposed himself to the danger known or believed to exist.

The Law Commission also endorses the retention of a defence of necessity, observing:

We therefore consider that, as part of the policy of retaining common law defences ... this specific defence of necessity should be kept open as something potentially separate from duress. That is provided for by cl 36(2) of the Criminal Law Bill, which expressly saves 'any distinct defence of necessity' when abrogating the common law defences of duress by threats and of circumstances [para 35.7].

10.10 SELF-DEFENCE AND PREVENTION OF CRIME

Self-defence (or private defence as it is sometimes referred to) has long been part of the common law and allows an individual to use reasonable force in one of three situations: defence of his own person; defence of others; defence of his property. Note that the defence will be available even if the defendant kills in order to achieve any one of these three objectives, provided the force in question was reasonable. As the Court of Appeal observed in *Oatridge* [1992] Crim LR 759, the questions to be asked when self-defence is raised by the defendant are:

- Was the defendant under actual or threatened attack by the victim?

- If yes, did the defendant act to defend himself against this attack?

- If yes, was his response commensurate with the degree of danger created by the attack?

In addition to the common law defence it should be noted that a statutory defence is also provided by s 3(1) of the Criminal Law Act 1967, which provides:

> A person may use such force as is reasonable in the circumstances in the prevention of crime, or in effecting or assisting in the lawful arrest of offenders or suspected offenders or of persons unlawfully at large.

The statutory defence overlaps to a very large extent with the common law defence but there are areas where only the statutory or common law defence will be available. Hence, if D uses reasonable force to protect himself from an attack by P, P being eight years old, D cannot rely on the statutory defence, as P is incapable of committing an offence. Conversely, if D sees P trying to smash the window of a shop owned by X and uses reasonable force to restrain P, D cannot rely on the common law defence as he is not acting to protect his own property; but he can rely on the statutory defence as he is acting to prevent the commission of an offence.

Where it is made out self-defence operates as a complete defence, the defendant's actions are seen as justified, hence they are not unlawful. If a defendant's actions go slightly beyond what the jury regards as reasonable force the defence fails entirely. Hence, where D is charged with murder, he is either acquitted because the defence is made out or receives a sentence of life imprisonment because it fails. Attempts to persuade the House of Lords in *Clegg* [1995] 1 All ER 334, that there might be a compromise position whereby the use of excessive force, albeit by way of self-defence, could mitigate murder to manslaughter were unsuccessful. Whether there should be a change in the law will be a matter for parliament to consider, as it is bound up with the issue of whether there should be a mandatory life sentence for murder. If a judge had a discretion in sentencing, the issue raised in *Clegg* would not be so acute. At worst, Clegg (a soldier on active duty in Northern Ireland at the time) shot intending to kill or seriously injure an occupant of a vehicle knowing that he was not under any threat: a clear case of murder. At best, he was responding instinctively to a potential terrorist attack. He had little time to assess all the relevant factors before making a decision. In other words, this was a misjudgment on his part that was understandable, given the prevailing environment in Belfast at the time.

10.10.1 What is reasonable force?

What amounts to reasonable force will depend upon the facts and circumstances of each particular case. In *Whyte* [1987] 3 All ER 416, for example, the defendant had used a lock-knife with a six-inch blade, which he had already opened against an unarmed man whom it appeared had not made any sort of threatening gesture towards him. His conviction for wounding with intent contrary to s 18 of the OAPA 1861 was upheld, the court noting that what is reasonable will depend on the nature of the attack, the defendant's response must not be out of all proportion to the demands of the situation, and that if someone is in imminent danger, it may be necessary to take instant action in order to avert that danger.

In *Palmer* [1971] 1 All ER 1077, Lord Morris of Borth-y-Gest thought that, in some situations, it would be possible to take 'simple avoiding action'. Yet some attacks may be very serious and certainly dangerous:

If there is some relatively minor attack, it would not be common sense to permit some action of retaliation which is wholly out of proportion to the necessities of the situation. If an attack is serious so that it puts someone in immediate peril then immediate defensive action may be necessary. If the moment is one of crisis for someone in imminent danger, he may have to avert the danger by some instant reaction. If the attack is all over and no sort of peril remains then the employment of force may be by way of revenge or punishment or by way of paying off an old score or may be pure aggression. There may no longer be any link with a necessity of defence.

Lord Morris accepted that a person under attack cannot weigh to a nicety the exact measure of his necessary defensive action. If a jury thought that, in a moment of unexpected anguish, a person attacked had only done what he honestly and instinctively thought was necessary, that would be the 'most potent evidence that only reasonable defensive action had been taken'.

On the basis of *Martin* (2001) *The Times*, 1 November, a court could also have regard to the physical characteristic of a defendant in determining what was reasonable force. Hence, if D, who is confined to a wheelchair, is faced with an imminent attack by P wielding a knife, it might be reasonable for D to open fire with a shotgun, as there is little he can do physically to prevent P from causing harm. Attention would then switch to how the shotgun was used, how many times it was fired, and where D aimed the gun.

In order not to appear to be the aggressor in such circumstances, it is obviously going to support the defendant's case for self-defence if it can be shown that he retreated from the attacker before seeking to defend himself. It must be emphasised that there is no rule of law to the effect that one must retreat, before the defence can be set up. *Bird* [1985] 2 All ER 513 decided that the jury should weigh up all the evidence. A failure to indicate clearly an unwillingness to get involved is one factor to be taken into account. As Lord Lane CJ said:

> Evidence that the defendant tried to retreat or tried to call off the fight may be a cast-iron method of casting doubt on the suggestion that he was the attacker or retaliator or the person trying to revenge himself. But it is not by any means the only method of doing that.

Edmund-Davies LJ in *McInnes* [1971] 3 All ER 295 reflected on a defendant's willingness to 'disengage and temporise' to be seen to be acting as the peacemaker rather than aggressor.

10.10.2 Mistake and self-defence

Where D mistakenly believes that he is under attack he can still rely on self-defence as he will be judged on the facts as he honestly believed them to be (see *Gladstone Williams, Oatridge* and *Beckford* [1987] 3 All ER 425). In *Scarlett* [1993] 4 All ER 629, Beldam LJ said:

> [The jury] ought not to convict him unless they are satisfied that the degree of force used was plainly more than was called for by the circumstances as he believed them to be and, provided he believed the circumstances called for the degree of force used, he is not to be convicted even if his belief is unreasonable.

There are actually two possible mistakes here. The first is that D may mistakenly believe himself to be under attack. The rule is that he must be judged on the facts as he believes them to be – hence it becomes a situation where he can use reasonable force even though there is in reality no ground for doing so. The second type of mistake relates to the degree of force necessary to prevent the harm. Suppose X, aged 11, tries to rob D, a 30-year-old man, using a toy gun. It is a self-defence situation in the sense that D is entitled to use reasonable force to protect his property. The amount of force that is reasonably required should relate to the threat posed by X. In fact, the threat is fairly slight given that the weapon is not real. D should not have to use too much force to stop X. D believes, however, that the gun is real. Fearing that X might deliberately or accidentally pull the trigger, D pulls out a knife and stabs X in the neck, killing him. Logically the rule that D should be judged on the facts as he believes them to be should be extended to cover this type of mistake. Hence, if D honestly believes the weapon to be a loaded gun, the reasonableness of the force he used should be looked at as if he had been faced with a loaded gun. The Privy Council has considered this issue in *Shaw (Norman) v R* [2002] Crim LR 140, concluding that, in such cases, a proper direction to the jury on self-defence would be: (a) did D honestly believe that it was necessary to defend himself?; if so, (b) on the basis of the facts and the danger perceived by D, was the force used reasonable. The decision is significant because it suggests that D's characteristics would be relevant in determining the degree of danger he perceived. The Court of Appeal does not appear to be willing to go quite this far at present (see *Martin* (above)).

10.10.3 The Human Rights Act 1998 and self-defence

Article 2(2) of the ECHR, as incorporated by the Human Rights Act 1998, provides that:

> Deprivation of life shall not be regarded as inflicted in contravention of this Article when it results from the use of force which is no more than absolutely necessary ...
>
> (a) in defence of any person from unlawful violence ...

In *McCann v United Kingdom* (1996) 21 ECRR 97, the European Court of Human Rights held that, where agents of the state use force in reliance on one of the exceptions listed in Art 2(2), and it transpires that the action was based on a mistake of fact (that is, a *Gladstone Williams* scenario), there will be no violation of Art 2, provided the honest belief of those acting in self-defence is based on good reasons. This creates the possibility that the law relating to mistakenly acting in self-defence in England and Wales may be in contravention of the requirements of the Convention, as the former simply requires evidence that D honestly believed it was necessary to act in self-defence, even where lethal force is used. There is no need for D additionally to establish that his belief was based on 'good reason'. See further *Andronicou v Cyprus* (1998) 25 EHRR 491, and Andrew Ashworth's commentary on the case at [1998] Crim LR 823.

10.10.4 Reform of self-defence

The Law Commission in its 1993 report (Law Com 218) recommends that an offence will not be committed if there is justifiable use of force:

> 27(1) The use of force by a person for any of the following purposes, if only such as is reasonable in the circumstances as he believes them to be, does not constitute an offence:

(a) to protect himself or another from injury, assault or detention caused by a criminal act;

(b) to protect himself or (with the authority of that other) another from trespass to the person;

(c) to protect his property from appropriation, destruction or damage caused by a criminal act or from trespass or infringement;

(d) to protect property belonging to another from appropriation, destruction or damage caused by a criminal act or (with the authority of the other) from trespass or infringement; or

(e) to prevent crime or a breach of the peace.

The above relates to the protection of person, property or the prevention of crime. A further clause, cl 28, deals with the justifiable use of force in effecting or assisting an arrest and states:

(1) The use of force by a person in effecting or assisting in a lawful arrest, if only such as is reasonable in the circumstances as he believes them to be, does not constitute an offence.

A person is to be taken as using force when applying force to or causing impact on the body of another. Additionally, if he threatens to use force or detains another without using force, he shall still be treated as using force (see cl 29).

SUMMARY OF CHAPTER 10

GENERAL DEFENCES

This chapter covers a range of defences recognised by the law which if successful will result in the acquittal of the defendant or in the case of insanity possible hospitalisation. Justification and excuse are the bedrocks upon which the defences are built.

INSANITY

Insanity may be relevant before the trial or at the time of the trial. Is the defendant fit to plead? Is he mentally capable of understanding the charges laid against him? The relevant law is to be found in the CP(I)A 1964, as amended by the CP(IUP)A 1991. If the defence of insanity is raised at the trial, then it is covered by the *M'Naghten* Rules. These presume every person to be sane unless proved otherwise. The defence is likely to succeed if it can be shown that at the time of the act the accused was suffering from a defect of reason caused by a disease of the mind so as not to know the nature and quality of the act or if he did that he did not know it was wrong. The burden of proof is on the defence on the balance of probabilities.

INFANCY

Children under the age of 10 incur no criminal liability. Children over the age of 10 are treated as adults for the purposes of establishing *mens rea*. Section 34 of the Crime and Disorder Act 1998 has abolished the concept of mischievous discretion as that applied to defendants between the ages of 10 and 14.

INTOXICATION

If D is intoxicated when he commits a crime he may seek to maintain they he had no *mens rea* for the crime. That may be true but it will not necessarily lead to an acquittal. A defendant may be intoxicated as a result of drink or drug consumption or both. The result may be that D was intoxicated, in that he did not form the specific intent required for the offence. He may still be regarded as having the basic intent, if that is all that an offence requires. The basic intent is satisfied by proof of recklessness. Recklessness can be inferred from D's voluntarily becoming intoxicated. Intoxication may therefore be admitted in evidence as a defence to specific intent crimes (see *Majewski*). Basic intent crimes require recklessness, and the excessive consumption of alcohol or drugs is likely to be deemed a reckless act. A distinction also needs to be drawn between dangerous and non-dangerous drugs. It will not be automatically presumed to be reckless to consume non-dangerous drugs (see *Hardie*). Where a defendant is mistaken as a result of intoxication and acts in light of that mistake, he will not be allowed to rely on mistake as a defence.

MISTAKE

A person may allege that he did not possess the *mens rea* for the offence because of labouring under a mistake of fact. Where an offence involves proof of *mens rea*, mistake will provide a defence providing the belief was honestly held. The reasonableness of the grounds for holding that belief will undoubtedly influence a jury in deciding whether the defendant honestly held the belief.

DURESS

Evidence of duress prevents the law from treating what was done as a crime. It has been said that the defence is a 'merciful concession to human frailty'. It does not, however, apply to murder, attempted murder or treason. There has to be evidence of a threat to kill or cause serious injury to the defendant or a near relative. The test for duress contains both subjective and objective factors as outlined by Lord Lane CJ in *Graham*. A defendant is expected to have the steadfastness to be expected of the ordinary citizen. The characteristics of the defendant will be pertinent in assessing whether a person's will has been overborne. Those who voluntarily join criminal or terrorist organisations are unlikely to be able to rely on duress if 'forced' to commit crimes. The last decade has seen the emergence of the defence of duress of circumstances. The defence appears to work where the defendant acts to avoid an imminent danger of death or serious injury to himself or another, if in the circumstances he could not reasonably be expected to act otherwise.

NECESSITY

There is growing evidence that such a defence exists at common law, although it has been strictly limited to a number of specialised situations. The essence of the defence is that, faced with a choice of two evils, the defendant is justified in adopting a course of action that breaches the criminal law. For example, breaking the speed limit in order to deliver someone in need of emergency medical treatment to hospital. Examine Lord Goff's examples of necessity in *Re F*.

SELF-DEFENCE

Long part of the common law, this defence allows persons to use reasonable force in order to defend themselves. What amounts to reasonable force will depend on all the circumstances. If excessive force is used, then the defence is lost.

FURTHER READING

Chapter 1: An Introduction to the Study of Criminal Law

Ashworth, A and Blake, M, 'The presumption of innocence in English criminal law' [1996] Crim LR 306

Brooke, Sir H, 'The Law Commission and criminal law reform' [1995] Crim LR 911

Buxton, R, 'The Human Rights Act and the substantive criminal law' [2000] Crim LR 331

Devlin, P, *The Enforcement of Morals*, 1967, Oxford: OUP

Farmer, L, 'The obsession with definition: the nature of crime and critical legal theory' (1996) 5 SLS 57

Hart, HLA, *Law, Liberty and Morality*, 1972, Oxford: OUP

James, A, Taylor, N and Walker, C, 'Criminal Cases Review Commission: economy, effectiveness and justice' [2000] Crim LR 140

Lacey, N, 'Contingency and criminalisation', in Loveland, I (ed), *Frontiers of Criminality*, 1995, London: Sweet & Maxwell

Lacey, N *et al*, *Reconstructing Criminal Law*, 1990, London: Weidenfeld & Nicolson

Law Commission, *Legislating the Criminal Code: Offences Against the Person and General Principles*, Law Com 218, 1993, London: HMSO

Law Commission, *Criminal Law: A Criminal Code for England and Wales*, Law Com 177, 1989, London: HMSO, Vols I and II

Norrie, A, 'After *Woollin*' [1999] Crim LR 532

Roberts, P, 'Taking the burden of proof seriously' [1995] Crim LR 783

Smith, ATH, 'Judicial law making in the criminal law' (1984) 100 LQR 46

Smith, ATH, '*Legislating the Criminal Code*: the Law Commission proposals' [1992] Crim LR 396

Spencer, JR, 'The case for a code of criminal procedure' [2000] Crim LR 519

Williams, G, 'The definition of crime' [1955] CLP 107

Wolfenden Committee, *Report of the Committee on Homosexual Offences and Prostitution*, Cmnd 247, 1957, London: HMSO

Chapter 2: *Actus Reus*

Ashworth, A, 'The scope of criminal liability for omissions' (1989) 105 LQR 424

Butler Committee on Mentally Abnormal Offenders, *Report of the Committee on Mentally Abnormal Offenders*, Cmnd 6244, 1975, London: HMSO

Hart, HLA and Honoré, T, *Causation in the Law*, 2nd edn, 1985, Oxford: OUP

Hogan, B, 'Omissions and a duty myth', in Smith, P (ed), *Criminal Law: Essays in Honour of JC Smith*, 1987, London: Butterworths

Hogan, B, 'The *Dadson* principle' [1989] Crim LR 684

Norrie, A, 'A critique of criminal causation' (1991) 54 MLR 685

Padfield, N, 'Casenote on *Hennessy*' [1989] CLJ 354

Padfield, N, 'Clean water and muddy causation' [1995] Crim LR 683

Smith, JC, 'Casenote on *Cheshire*' [1991] Crim LR 709

Williams, G, 'Criminal omissions – the conventional view' (1991) 107 LQR 86

Williams, G, '*Finus* for *novus actus*' [1989] CLJ 391

Chapter 3: The Mental Element – *Mens Rea*

Lacey, N, 'A clear concept of intention: elusive or illusory' (1993) 56 MLR 621

Leigh, LH, *Strict and Vicarious Liability*, 1982, London: Sweet & Maxwell

Norrie, A, 'After *Woollin*' [1999] Crim LR 532

Norrie, A, *Crime, Reason and History*, 2001, London: Butterworths

Norrie, A, 'Subjectivism, objectivism and the limits of criminal recklessness' (1992) 12 OJLS 45

Richardson, G, 'Regulatory crime: the empirical research' [1987] Crim LR 295

Rowan-Robinson, J, 'Crime and regulation' [1988] Crim LR 211

Smith, JC, 'A note on intention' [1990] Crim LR 85

Smith, JC, 'Casenote on *Reid*' [1992] Crim LR 821

Williams, G, 'Unresolved problems of recklessness' (1988) 8 LS 74

Wilson, W, 'Doctrinal rationality after *Woollin*' (1999) 62 MLR 448

Wootton, B, *Crime and the Criminal Law*, 2nd edn, 1981, London: Stevens

Chapter 4: Participation in Crime

Beynon, H 'Causation, omissions and complicity' [1987] Crim LR 539

Gobert, J, 'Corporate criminality: new crimes for the times' [1994] Crim LR 722

Lanham, D, 'Accomplices and withdrawal' (1981) 97 LQR 575

Law Commission, *Assisting and Encouraging Crime*, Law Com 131, 1993, London: HMSO

Smith, JC, 'Secondary participation in crime can we do without it?' (1994) 144 NLJ 679

Smith, KJM, 'Complicity and causation' [1986] Crim LR 663

Smith, KJM, 'The Law Commission consultation paper on complicity' [1994] Crim LR 239

Smith, KJM, 'Withdrawal in complicity: a restatement of principles' [2001] Crim LR 769

Sullivan, GR, 'Intent, purpose and complicity' [1988] Crim LR 641

Williams, G, 'Letting offences happen' [1990] Crim LR 780

Chapter 5: Preliminary or Inchoate Offences

Aldridge, P, 'The Sexual Offences (Conspiracy and Incitement) Act 1996' [1997] Crim LR 30

Orchard, GL, 'Agreement in criminal conspiracy' [1974] Crim LR 297

Silber, S, 'The Law Commission, *Conspiracy to Defraud* and the dishonesty project' [1995] Crim LR 461

Smith, JC, 'Conspiracy under the Criminal Law Act 1977' [1977] 598

Smith, JC, 'Some thoughts on the Law Commission's report: *Conspiracy to Defraud*' [1995] Crim LR 209

Smith, KJM, 'Proximity in attempt: Lord Lane's midway course' [1991] Crim LR 576

Williams, G, 'The Lords and impossible attempts' [1986] CLJ 33

Williams, G, 'Wrong turnings in the law of attempt' [1991] Crim LR 417

Chapter 6: Homicide

Ashworth, A, 'Reforming the law of murder' [1990] Crim LR 75

Biggs, H, 'Euthanasia and death with dignity: still poised on the fulcrum of homicide' [1996] Crim LR 878

Gardner, J, 'Compassion without respect: nine fallacies in *R v Smith*' [2001] Crim LR 623

Keating, H, 'Law Commission report on involuntary manslaughter: the restoration of a serious crime' [1996] Crim LR 535

Mackay, RD, 'The consequences of killing very young children' [1993] Crim LR 21

Nicolson, D and Sanghvi, R, 'Battered women and provocation: the implication of *R v Ahluwalia*' [1993] Crim LR 728

Padfield, N, 'Clean water and muddy causation: is causation a question of law or fact, or just a way of allocating blame?' [1995] Crim LR 683

Wells, C, 'Law Commission report on involuntary manslaughter: the corporate manslaughter proposals: pragmatism, paradox and peninsularity' [1996] Crim LR 545

Williams, G, '*Mens rea* for murder: leave it alone' (1989) 105 LQR 387

Chapter 7: Non-Fatal Offences Against the Person

Burney, E, 'Using the law on racially aggravated offences' [2003] Crim LR 28

Criminal Law Revision Committee, 15th Report, *Sexual Offences*, Cmnd 9213, 1984, London: HMSO

Criminal Law Revision Committee, 14th Report, *Offences Against the Person*, Cmnd 7844, 1980, London: HMSO

Finch, E, 'Stalking the perfect stalking law: an evaluation of the efficacy of the Protection from Harassment Act 1997' [2002] Crim LR 703

Gunn, M and Ormerod, D, 'The legality of boxing' (1995) 15 LS 181

Lacey, N, 'Beset by boundaries: the Home Office review of sex offences' [2001] Crim LR 3

Law Commission, *Criminal Law: Consent in the Criminal Law*, Law Com 139, 1995, London: HMSO

Leigh, LH, 'Sado-masochism, consent and the reform of the criminal law' (1976) 39 MLR 130

Reed, A, '*Contra bonos mores*: fraud affecting consent in rape' (1995) 145 NLJ 174

Rogers, J, 'Necessity, private defence and the killing of Mary' [2001] Crim LR 515

Tyler, L, 'Towards a redefinition of rape' (1994) 144 NLJ 860

Wells, C, 'Stalking: the criminal law response' [1997] Crim LR 463

Williams, G, 'Force, injury and serious injury' (1990) 140 NLJ 1227

Chapter 8: Offences Against Property: Theft

Beatson, A and Simester, A, 'Stealing one's own property' (1999) 115 LQR 372

Elliott, DW, 'Directors' thefts and dishonesty' [1991] Crim LR 732

Gardner, S, 'Property and theft' [1998] Crim LR 35

Griew, E, 'Dishonesty: the objections to *Feely* and *Ghosh*' [1985] Crim LR 341

Halpin, A, 'The test for dishonesty' [1996] Crim LR 283

Heaton, R, 'Decieving without thieving?' [2001] Crim LR 712

Shute, S, 'Appropriation and the law of theft' [2002] Crim LR 445

Smith, JC, 'Stealing tickets' [1998] Crim LR 723

Spencer, JR, 'The metamorphosis of section 6 of the Theft Act' [1977] Crim LR 653

Sullivan, GR and Warbrick, C, 'Territoriality, theft and *Atakpu*' [1994] Crim LR 650

Williams, G, 'Appropriation: a single or continuous act?' [1978] Crim LR 69

Williams, G, 'Temporary appropriation should be theft' [1981] Crim LR 129

Williams, G, 'Theft and voidable title' [1981] Crim LR 666

Chapter 9: Offences Against Property: Other Offences under the Theft Acts 1968 and 1978 and Criminal Damage

Ashworth, A, 'Robbery reassessed' [2002] Crim LR 851

Law Commission, *Offences of Dishonesty: Money Transfers*, Law Com 243, 1996, London: HMSO

Smith, JC, 'Obtaining cheques by deception or fraud' [1997] Crim LR 397

Spencer, JR, 'Handling, theft and the *mala fide* purchaser' [1985] Crim LR 92

Spencer, JR, 'The mishandling of handling' [1981] Crim LR 682

Chapter 10: General Defences

Glazebrook, P, 'The necessity plea in English criminal law' [1972] CLJ 87

Leverick, F, 'Is English self-defence law incompatible with Article 2 of the ECHR?' [2002] Crim LR 347

Leverick, F, 'The use of force in public or private defence and Article 2: a reply to Professor Sir John Smith' [2002] Crim LR 963

Lynch, ACE, 'The scope of intoxication' [1982] Crim LR 139

Orchard, G, 'Surviving without *Majewski* – a view from down under' [1993] Crim LR 426

Parish, S, 'Self defence: the wrong direction?' [1997] Crim LR 201

Paton, E, 'Reformulating the intoxication rules: the Law Commission's report' [1995] Crim LR 382

Smith, JC and Hogan, B, *Criminal Law*, 10th edn, 2002, London: Butterworths

Smith, JC, 'The use of force in public or private defence and Article 2' [2002] Crim LR 958

Williams, G, 'The theory of excuses' [1982] Crim LR 732

INDEX